The Complete History of

Ancient
Greece

The Complete History of

Ancient Greece

Don Nardo, *Book Editor*

David L. Bender, *Publisher*
Bruno Leone, *Executive Editor*
Bonnie Szumski, *Editorial Director*
Stuart B. Miller, *Managing Editor*

Greenhaven Press, Inc., San Diego, California

Dedication

The editor respectfully dedicates this volume to American classicist
Victor Davis Hanson
for his important contributions to
the understanding and preservation
of the Greek legacy.

Library of Congress Cataloging-in-Publication Data

Ancient Greece / Don Nardo, editor.
     p.   cm. — (Complete history of)
  Includes bibliographical references and index.
  ISBN 0-7377-0425-X (lib. bdg. : alk. paper)
  1. Greece—Civilization—To 146 B.C. 2. Civilization, Ancient, in literature. I. Nardo, Don, 1947–   II. Series.

  DF77 .A586 2001
  938—dc21
                                            00-086966
                                                CIP

Contents

sumed control and rapidly transformed the alliance into its own lucrative empire.

The critical turning point in the Spartan domination of Greece came at Leuctra (in Boeotia) in 371 B.C., when the Theban army, led by the brilliant military innovator Epaminondas, defeated the supposedly invincible Spartan phalanx.

In 200 B.C., following their decisive defeat of Carthage, the Romans marched into Greece and in the years that followed the Greek states began to fall, one by one, to the force of Roman steel.

CHAPTER 7: DEMOCRACY, CITIZENSHIP, AND JUSTICE

In addition to epic poetry, early Greek poets turned out a wide variety of shorter works, including wedding songs, funerary laments, drinking songs, hymns, love poems, odes honoring athletes, and others.

Introduction

Modern visitors to Greece almost always rush to view its many ruins. Invariably topping the list of "must-see" sites are the remains of the magnificent Parthenon and other temples atop Athens's central hill, the Acropolis; the vast theater at Epidaurus, so well preserved that plays are still produced there; the atmospheric sanctuary and Temple of Apollo at Delphi, where the famous oracle once foretold future events; and the sprawling, brooding Bronze Age palace-centers at Mycenae (on the southern Greek mainland) and Knossus (on the large island of Crete).

These and numerous other ancient sites attest that Greece, which is today a small nation of modest means and influence, was once the home of one of the most culturally splendid and influential civilizations in world history. Indeed, the ancient Greeks, who called their land Hellas and themselves Hellenes, left behind a remarkable and momentous cultural heritage. Their art, architecture, sculpture, political ideas, social and military customs, literature, philosophic and scientific ideas, and language helped in profound ways to shape the cultures and ideas of all later Western (European-based) lands and peoples.

Some of these Greek influences are obvious. For example, thousands of modern banks, government buildings, and other structures employ the familiar columns and triangular gables of classical Greek temple architecture. And every four years, most of the earth's nations, Western and non-Western alike, take part in the Olympic Games, inspired by and still featuring many of the same events of the original Greek version. On the other hand, thousands of other aspects of Greek culture are so subtly interwoven into the very fabric of modern life that we are scarcely aware of their origins. Each time we attend the theater; or work out in a public gym; or compete on or watch a wrestling, boxing, or track and field team; or listen to a political speech; or go to the polls to vote; or formulate a political bill; or sue someone in court; or read a novel, essay, biography, or literary critique; or study or discuss philosophy; or contemplate atoms, the universe, or other scientific concepts; or attempt to solve problems using logic, we are doing things the Greeks invented over two millennia ago.

One of the simplest, yet also one of the noblest and most profound ideas the Greeks developed and passed on to future generations, is the belief that the individual human being possesses innate dignity and worth. As noted historian C.M. Bowra puts it in *Classical Greece*:

> At the center of the Greek outlook lay an unshakable belief in the worth of the individual man. In centuries when large parts of the earth were dominated by the absolute monarchies of the East, the Greeks were evolving their belief that a man must be respected not as an instrument of an omnipotent overlord, but for his own sake. . . . Nature nursed the Greeks in a hard school, but this made them conscious of themselves and their worth. Without this self-awareness, they would never have made their most important contribution to human experience: the belief that a man must be honored for his individual worth and treated with respect just because he is himself. . . . This feeling among the Greeks may have started as something vague, but it was deeply felt, and it matured into reasoned philosophy which long after shaped, and still shapes, our own.

The Greeks did not invent the basic foundations of Western culture overnight, of course.

19

Their brilliant legacy was forged bit by bit over many centuries on nature's cruel anvil of trial and error, struggle and perseverance, and triumph and defeat. The colorful panorama of their history is alive with stories that continue to capture our imaginations, or horrify us, or inspire us. And these alone justify and amply reward learning about the gripping Greek historical saga. But most of all we study the Greeks because what they did and thought long ago still affects what people do and think today. Their society was far from perfect. But their lives, deeds, and special spirit have shaped the social, political, and intellectual course of Western civilization more than those of any other single people in history. And for that, we and our descendents must stand forever in their debt.

The Complete History of

An Overview

Chapter 1

A Brief History of Ancient Greece

Don Nardo

The thrilling story of the ancient Greeks and how they laid the foundations of Western society and thought begins in the distant past in what modern scholars call the Bronze Age (ca. 3000–ca. 1100 B.C.). This was the era in which the inhabitants of Greece (including the nearby islands of the Aegean Sea) used tools and weapons made of bronze, an alloy of copper and tin. Experts find it difficult to determine exactly when Greek-speaking people arrived in mainland Greece. "At what point in time," asks Holy Cross scholar Thomas Martin,

> does it make sense to use the term *Greeks* to refer to the inhabitants of the region called Greece? No simple answer will do. The process by which Greeks became Greeks does not lend itself to easy categorization because the concept of identity encompasses not just basic social and material conditions but also ethnic, cultural, and linguistic traditions.[1]

Archaeological evidence shows that people speaking an early form of Greek inhabited mainland Greece in the mid-second millennium B.C. They are referred to as Mycenaeans, after their chief fortress-town of Mycenae (in the northeastern part of the Peloponnesus, the large peninsula that makes up the southern third of Greece). Scholarly debates continue, but the best guess is that they entered Greece in two or more waves, beginning about 2000 B.C.[2] The Mycenaeans, says noted historian C.M. Bowra, "were spectacular builders. Their palaces were built within formidable citadels with walls 10 feet thick, and some of their royal tombs were enormous beehive structures made of stones weighing, sometimes, as much as 120 tons."[3]

For a long time the Mycenaeans came under the cultural influence, and perhaps also to some degree the military domination, of the Minoans, a highly civilized non-Greek-speaking people inhabiting Crete and other Aegean islands. This situation may be the basis for the well-known myth of Theseus, in which Cretan overlords periodically demanded and got supplies of sacrificial victims from the mainland city of Athens.[4] Whatever their relationship with the mainland, the Minoans built huge, splendid palaces of their own (featuring highly advanced facilities, such as flush toilets and hot and cold running water) and carried on a prosperous trade with Egyptian and Near Eastern cities.

The Trojan War and Homeric Epics

For reasons that are still unclear, by about 1400 B.C. Minoan power had declined enough to allow Mycenaean warlords to take over the Cretan sphere.[5] For the next two centuries, the Mycenaeans prospered. They apparently frequently raided the coasts of Asia Minor (or Anatolia, what is now Turkey); and one of these expeditions turned out to be the most important event in their history (at least as it relates to later Greek history). Circa 1250–1200 B.C., they attacked and burned Troy, an independent trading city on Asia Minor's northwestern coast.

The memory of the Trojan War was later preserved in oral traditions and became the basis for the *Iliad* and *Odyssey,* epic poems attributed to the legendary eighth-century B.C. bard Homer. The importance of these epics to the later Greeks, especially in the Classic Age, cannot be overstated. Their leading characters, including the larger-than-life heroes Achilles, Hector, and Odysseus, interacted with the Gods in what was seen as a glorious past age. In fact, the later Greeks referred to that legendary era, what we call the late Bronze Age, as the "Age of Heroes." Most of the important Greek myths originated in that era and a good many of them revolved around Mycenaean cities and culture. (The later Greeks called the Mycenaeans the Achaeans.) More significantly, as scholar Michael Grant explains, the Homeric poems

> supplied the Greeks with their greatest civilizing influence, and formed the foundation of their literary, artistic, moral, social, educational, and political attitudes. . . . They attracted universal esteem and reverence, too, as sources of general and practical wisdom, as arguments for heroic yet human nobility and dignity, as incentives to vigorous . . . manly action, and as mines of endless quotations and commentaries: the common property of Greeks everywhere.[6]

Sudden Decline and the Dark Age

Not long after Troy's fall—perhaps about 1200 B.C. or shortly thereafter—the Aegean sphere, as well as many parts of the Near East, underwent a period of unexpected and unprecedented upheaval. Most of the major Mycenaean strongholds were sacked and burned, never to be rebuilt. Civil conflicts, economic collapse, invasion by tribal peoples migrating from the north and east, and other theories have been advanced to explain the demise of Mycenaean civilization.[7] Regardless of whether one or a combination of these factors caused the catastrophe, apparently the only mainland city that survived intact was Athens. But in time even there, as in the rest of Greece, writing, record-keeping, large-scale political organization, and other aspects of advanced civilization all but vanished. Greece slipped into what is now referred to as its Dark Age (ca. 1100–ca. 800 B.C.), a period about which scholars know very little.

In the Dark Age, the Minoan-Mycenaean world steadily passed into legend and the surviving Greeks (including any invaders who had recently settled the area) more or less forgot their heritage. Poverty was widespread and most people probably made a meager living from whatever fish they could catch, animals they could raise, or crops they could grow.[8] Small groups of people began identifying themselves only with the particular isolated valley or island where they lived. (As time went on, these areas would become the nuclei for new political-social units commonly described as city-states.)

Society in the Dark Age was likely similar to that portrayed in Homer's epics. As Hunter College scholar Sarah B. Pomeroy and her colleagues state, although the stories of these works

> take place in the glory days of the Mycenaean period, the poems do not describe the society revealed by the material remains. . . . The social background of the Homeric narratives fits instead the archaeological picture of the late Dark Age. The question of where in the period . . . to place "Homeric" society is far from

settled, but there is a growing belief that it largely reflects the actual society of the late ninth and early eighth century B.C.[9]

For the most part, people in this society lived in wooden or stone houses clustered in small villages, each dominated by a local chieftain (*basileus*). Apparently, there were also a few more powerful chiefs who had limited authority over groups of villages or small regions. (Autocratic kings with massive palaces and splendid courts like those Homer describes were memories of Bronze Age rulers, whom his epics transplanted into the more primitive Dark Age society.)

Farmers and Fighters in the Archaic Age

As time went on, some villages grew into large towns, each of which came, both militarily and culturally, to dominate the affairs of a valley, island, or other local region. This marked the rise of city-states in what historians call the Archaic Age (ca. 800–ca. 500 B.C.). The Greeks called the city-state the polis (poleis in the plural). A typical polis consisted of the central town (or urban center), surrounded by its supporting small villages and farmland; and the town itself was often built around a hill or cliff called an acropolis, which means "the city's high place" in Greek, and which the inhabitants fortified to defend against attackers. But though the majority of city-states had such physical similarities, they evolved differing local governments and traditions and came to think of themselves as tiny separate nations. (Still, all Greeks felt linked by their common language, religious beliefs and rituals, and heritage of myths from the Age of Heroes.)

During Archaic times, as many cities grew increasingly prosperous, Greece steadily and rapidly rose from its backward state. Trade and commerce revived; reading and writing reappeared (this time using an alphabet borrowed from the Phoenicians, a Near Eastern trading people) and literature (beginning with the Homeric epics) emerged; philosophy and scientific inquiry about nature and the universe emerged as well; monumental architecture, best exempli-

fied by stately religious temples, developed; Panhellenic (all-Greek) shrines, oracles (dispensers of divine prophecy), and athletic games (including the Olympics) arose; and local populations expanded, prompting several cities to establish colonies along the shores of the Aegean, Black, and Mediterranean seas.

There was also much political experimentation. Power was originally in the hands of aristocrats (from the Greek word *aristoi*, meaning "best people"). But beginning in the mid-600s B.C., ambitious individuals in several leading cities exploited the common people's anti-aristocratic feelings to place themselves in power. The Greeks came to call these men, who were essentially petty dictators, tyrants. The negative definition of the term tyrant, an "oppressive leader," developed later, for a number of tyrants, at least at first, upheld most local laws, supported the arts, and enjoyed wide popular support. But as a form of government tyranny was unstable and short-lived in Greece. This is because a tyrant needed to maintain popular support, especially that of his community's soldiers, to stay in power. The citizen bodies of many city-states, which included the soldiers, increasingly came to eliminate the tyrants and to assume governing authority themselves.

This trend toward democratic ideals and government was part of an ongoing revolution in agriculture and warfare that had begun sometime in the Dark Age. Noted classical scholar Victor D. Hanson calls it "an enormous transformation . . . nothing less than the creation of an entire class, which through sheer preponderance of numbers overwhelmed" the aristocratic rulers.[10] This class, one unlike any the world had yet seen, was made up of tough, independent farmers who neither needed nor wanted control by aristocratic or other ruling elites. (By contrast, the Mycenaeans had practiced a collective form of agriculture, in which farmers were poor peasants controlled and exploited by the state.) Expressions of human freedom and individualism in Greek poetry and philosophy in Archaic times, says Hanson, were "manifestations of an ongoing and radically new private approach to rural life, and farming in particular."[11]

This class of independent farmers became not only the economic backbone of the typical polis, but also the source of its military strength. The practice of individual farmers, and later small communities of farmers, taking up arms to protect their lands, private property, and heritage against aggressors (most often other farmers) steadily led to the development of citizen militias. By the seventh century B.C., well-organized military units and tactics had developed. These were built around heavily-armored infantry soldiers called hoplites (perhaps after the word *hopla,* meaning "heavy equipment"), who wielded thrusting spears and short swords. They fought in a special formation known as a phalanx, most often composed of eight ranks (rows) of soldiers. When standing in close order, their uplifted shields created a formidable unbroken protective barrier. As the formation marched toward an enemy, the men in the front rank jabbed their spears at their opponents, while the hoplites in the rear ranks pushed at their comrades' backs, giving the whole unit a tremendous and lethal forward momentum. The members of local phalanxes, full-time farmers and part-time but highly effective fighters, Hanson states, "helped to establish agrarian control of the political life of their respective city-states."[12]

Athens Ascendant

Thus, it was only a matter of time before agrarian ideals of freedom and independence translated into political ones. The slow but steady movement toward democracy in Greece reached its first and greatest expression in Athens in the late sixth and early fifth centuries B.C., the dawn of the Classic Age. Building on the earlier and significant legal, social, and political reforms of the statesman Solon (in the 590s B.C.), in about 508 a popular leader named Cleisthenes spearheaded the creation of complete citizen control of government. In the years that followed, other reformers, most notably the statesmen Ephialtes (died 461) and Pericles (died 429), expanded the Athenian democracy; and many other poleis followed Athens's lead and instituted their own versions of democratic government.

During these same years, Athens acquired great power and prestige and came to dominate international affairs in the Greek sphere. This was partly because it was the largest, most populous, and wealthiest polis in Greece.[13] Another important factor in its ascendancy was the leading role it played in the back-to-back Persian invasions of the early fifth century. The Persian Empire, centered in the Near East in what is now Iran, had been established in the 550s B.C. by Cyrus II, "the Great." The sudden rise of the Persian realm, which quickly grew into the world's largest empire up to that time, was, historian Alessandro Bausani writes,

one of those astonishing but not infrequent phenomena in the history of Asia past or present. It shows how a tiny state can, for no apparent reason, trigger off an explosion, like that of a new star, widely extending its boundaries to include many peoples of various races.[14]

One of the peoples the Persians wanted to absorb into their realm were the Greeks. In the 540s B.C., Cyrus gained dominance over the cities of Ionia, the largely Greek region encompassing the coasts and islands of western Asia Minor. This marked the beginning of a two-century-long period in which the histories and destinies of Greece and Persia were constantly and intimately intertwined, often with bloody consequences.

The first major bloodshed came in 499 B.C., when the Ionian cities rebelled against their Persian overlords. Athens aided the rebels; and after crushing the insurrection, in 490 Persia's king, Darius I, sent an army to punish the "insolent" Athenians. However, the confident Persian forces that landed at Marathon, northeast of Athens, soon found themselves humbled when a much smaller force of Athenian hoplites decisively defeated them. The stunning victory gained Athens the image among a majority of Greeks as their savior; so it is not surprising that when Darius's son, Xerxes, launched another assault on Greece a decade later, Athens once more took the lead. Indeed, its skilled politician and admiral, Themistocles, became the chief architect of a tremendous naval victory over the invaders at Salamis (southwest of Athens).

After the complete expulsion of the Persians in 479 B.C., Athens headed an alliance of over a hundred city-states, the original purpose of which was to protect Greece from further Persian incursions. Over time, however, the Athenians transformed the alliance into their own very lucrative maritime empire. Under the direction of Pericles, the dominant Greek political figure of the mid-fifth century B.C., much of the wealth that flowed from that empire into Athens's coffers went into public construction projects designed to beautify the city and make it the wonder and envy of Greece. This goal was achieved with the creation of a magnificent temple complex (begun in the 440s) atop the Athenian Acropolis, crowned by the famous Parthenon (temple of Athena, Athens's patron goddess). These monuments became a wonder not only to the Greeks of that time, but to all succeeding generations. Over five centuries later, they inspired the following remarks by the Greek biographer and moralist Plutarch:

> It is this, above all, which makes Pericles' works an object of wonder to us—the fact that they were created in so short a span, and yet for all time. Each one possessed a beauty which seemed venerable [impressive in old age] the moment it was born, and at the same time a youthful vigor which makes them appear to this day as if they were newly built. A bloom of eternal freshness hovers over these works of his and preserves them from the touch of time.[15]

Incessant Warfare Leads to Decline

But the ambitious and energetic Athenians were unable to maintain the incredible momentum that had propelled them to the heights of power and glory. In large part this was the result of a longstanding rivalry with Sparta, a city-state located in the southern Peloponnesus. While Athens had Greece's strongest navy, Sparta, with a highly regimented social and political life built around military training, possessed its most

formidable land army. Each of the two states was convinced that it alone should enjoy supremacy in Greece; and after many decades of mutual distrust and small-scale fighting, each finally reached a point where it was willing to wage a major war to gain that supremacy.

The result of this rivalry was the Peloponnesian War (so named because Sparta and its major allies resided in the Peloponnesus), which erupted in 431 B.C. In the words of Thucydides, the contemporary Greek historian who chronicled the war:

> If both sides nourished the boldest hopes and put forth their utmost strength for the war, this was only natural. Zeal is always at its height at the commencement of an undertaking; and on this particular occasion the Peloponnesus and Athens were both full of young men whose inexperience made them eager to take up arms, while the rest of Greece stood straining with excitement at the conflict of its leading cities.[16]

The "rest of Greece" ended up doing more than watching from the sidelines, however, for the conflict inevitably drew in most of the city-states, who aligned themselves in two blocs, one led by Athens, the other by Sparta. And the eagerness to fight that so many had expressed at first eventually turned to regret and lament. In a scenario no one expected, the war dragged on for twenty-seven grueling years and ultimately proved ruinous for all involved. Athens went down to defeat in 404 B.C., ending its golden age and hegemony (dominance) of Greece, and for a short time even lost its cherished democracy.

Following the great war, the Greek city-states entered a period of political and military decline. Not only had the conflict caused widespread death and destruction, but its combatants had failed to learn from it the lesson that continued disunity and rivalry was futile and dangerous. At first, because of its victory over Athens, Sparta dominated Greek affairs. But the Spartans failed to maintain their hegemony of Greece, partly because they were not able administrators. Also, they were insensitive and heavy-handed in their dealings with other states. In 382 B.C., for example, Spartan troops sent to stop a civil conflict in Thebes seized that city's acropolis and initiated a blatant military occupation that most Greeks heartily condemned. Athens responded to this and other Spartan aggressions by beginning to build up another bloc of its own allies; and soon the two sides were at each other's throats again.

But it was not Athens that was fated to humble the Spartan bully. Led by two talented and popular statesmen-generals, Pelopidas and Epaminondas, Thebes (northwest of Athens) overhauled its military and surprised everyone by crushing Sparta's phalanx in a pivotal battle in 371 B.C. Soon afterward, Epaminondas invaded the Peloponnesus, where the political climate underwent a sudden and drastic change. Supported by Thebes, most of the Peloponnesian cities, which had long followed Sparta out of fear, overthrew their Spartan-backed regimes and instituted new governments (usually some form of democracy). This ended the Spartan hegemony and initiated a Theban one.

Thebes did not enjoy its position of power and influence for long, however. Less than a decade after gaining it, the Thebans fought a major battle against an unlikely, and decidedly temporary, coalition led by Athens and Sparta. Afterwards, according to the Athenian historian Xenophon (ZEN-uh-phon), "There was even more uncertainty and confusion in Greece . . . than there had been previously."[17]

Philip and Alexander

Decades of bickering, war, destruction, and shifting political alliances had left the major mainland city-states exhausted, weakened, and vulnerable to outside attack. This time, however, the threat did not come from Asia, as it had in the previous century, but from Macedonia, a kingdom in extreme northern Greece. Its tribes had themselves long been disunited and militarily weak. The city-state Greeks had generally viewed them contemptuously as backwoods types living outside the mainstream of the civilized world and for the most part had ignored them, which turned out to be a grave mistake. In the mid-fourth century B.C., just as Theban power was on the decline and exhaustion and confusion reigned in southern Greece, a brilliant and capable young man ascended the Macedonian throne. He was Philip II, who in an amazingly short time united the Macedonian tribes, forming a strong nation with a powerful army.

Eventually, Philip set his sights on making himself master of all the Greeks. Over the course of several years, he employed a highly effective combination of diplomacy, deceit, and naked aggression to seize large tracts of territory in northern and central Greece. In the summer of 338 B.C., accompanied by his eighteen-year-old son, Alexander (who would later be called "the Great"), he marched his army to Chaeronea, northwest of Thebes. There, the Macedonian forces clashed with those of a hastily organized coalition led by Athens and Thebes. In the face of Philip's superior strategy and tactics (some of them borrowed from Epaminondas), most of the allies eventually broke ranks and fled. Philip's victory was complete and the Greek city-states now faced the dawn of a new political order.

In the wake of Chaeronea, Philip attempted to create a confederacy of Greek states, in effect to unite them at last into a single political organization (although it was intended to be an alliance of small nations rather than a single large nation). In September 338, Philip presided over an assembly attended by delegates from many mainland and island city-states (the principal absentee being Sparta, which remained stubbornly aloof). In effect, he forced them to make a common peace and to form a federal "Hellenic League," with himself in the pivotal role of hegemon (supreme leader).

The city-states also found themselves swept along in the tide of Philip's grandiose plans for invading Persia (supposedly to avenge the Persian invasions of Greece in the previous century, but more likely to further his own goals). In a twist of fate, however, he was assassinated (in 336) and his son ended up leading this fateful expedition. In 334, Alexander crossed the Hellespont (the narrow strait separating northern Greece from Asia Minor) at the head of a small but, as it turned out, very formidable army. In the next few years he twice defeated the Persian king, Darius III; besieged and captured the island city of Tyre; liberated Egypt (which had been under Persian rule for two centuries) and there established a new city in the Nile Delta, naming it Alexandria after himself; occupied the three Persian capitals—Babylon, Susa, and Persepolis; and continued eastward, eventually reaching India. He may have gone on to further conquests. However, his exhausted troops, many of whom had not seen home and family in many years, mutinied and demanded that he turn back. This proved to be the end of the road for Alexander, for shortly after returning to Persia, he died, at the age of thirty-three, in Babylon on June 10, 323.

The Successors and the "Inhabited World"

In just ten years, Alexander had conquered the vast Persian domain, in the process spreading Greek language, political administration, and culture to many parts of the Near East. But the huge kingdom he had created was immediately torn asunder as his leading generals and governors faced off and came to death grips. For the next forty-odd years, these men, who came to be called the "Successors" (*Diadochoi*), waged almost unrelenting war. During the many, complex, and often confusing rounds of rivalry and warfare among them, they frequently made, broke, and shifted alliances. And all the while

This detail from the "Alexander Mosaic," discovered in the House of the Faun in the Roman town of Pompeii, shows the young conqueror Alexander charging the Persian king at the battle of Issus.

they and their armies spread fear, chaos, and destruction throughout the eastern Mediterranean–Near Eastern sphere.

Finally, by about 280 B.C., three major new Greek kingdoms had emerged in that sphere. These so-called successor-states included the Ptolemaic Kingdom, founded by Ptolemy, consisting mainly of Egypt and parts of nearby Palestine; the Seleucid Kingdom, established by Seleucus, encompassing the lands north and west of the Persian Gulf—the heart of the old Persian Empire—and parts of Asia Minor; and the Macedonian Kingdom, created by Antigonus Gonatas (grandson of Alexander's general Antigonus the One-Eyed), made up mostly of Macedonia and portions of the Greek mainland. Among the smaller but still influential states of the day were the kingdoms of Pergamum (in western Asia Minor) and Epirus (in northwestern Greece); the Aetolian League (in western Greece) and Achaean League (in the Peloponnesus), federations of cities that had banded together for mutual protection; and some powerful independent city-states, notably the island of Rhodes (off the coast of Asia Minor) and Byzantium (on the Propontis, the waterway on the far side of the Hellespont).

Historians refer to these realms as Hellenistic, meaning "Greek-like," since their societies often consisted of various Eastern languages, customs, and ideas overlaid by a veneer of Greek ones. Likewise, the period lasting from Alexander's death in 323 B.C. to the death of the last Hellenistic ruler, Cleopatra VII, in 30 B.C., is called the Hellenistic Age. Historically speaking, this era, the last period of major Greek political independence in antiquity, was the hinge, so to speak, between the Greek Mediterranean domination of the past and the Roman domination of the future. Yet as Michael Grant points out, the age

> must emphatically not be seen as just the forerunner of the Roman epoch [era], any more than it must be seen as a sort of appendix of classical Greece. For the epoch was rich and fertile in versatile creations which, despite all debts to the past, were very much its own.[18]

Indeed, it is perhaps ironic that, though Greek autonomy ended in Hellenistic times, it was an era of widespread experimentation, new horizons, and notable achievement in the arts, sciences, and numerous social institutions. Greek scientists, for example, especially those working in Alexandria, which had become the known world's foremost commercial and intellectual center, made significant strides in anatomy, astronomy, and other fields. One of these men, Eratosthenes, correctly measured the earth's circumference to within one percent of the value accepted by modern science.[19] This spirit of searching for the underlying truth of things found further expression in the arts, as poets, sculptors, and painters achieved levels of vividness and realism unknown in prior ages. The new spirit also generated, in Grant's words,

> a greatly enhanced interest in the individual human being and his mind and emotions, an interest given vigorous expression by biographers and portrait artists. And this concern for the individual was extended not only to men but to women, whose position in society, literature and art underwent an unprecedented transformation that was one of the most remarkable evolutionary changes of the age.[20]

Perhaps more remarkable still was the transformation of society itself. There emerged in the eastern Mediterranean and Near East a vast cultural sphere—the *oikoumene* (ee-koo-MEH-nee), or "inhabited world"—in which almost all realms, large or small, bore common political, economic, and cultural institutions. So a traveler might feel more or less at home anywhere he or she went in the Hellenistic sphere, assuming that his destination was not at war with his own homeland.

Repeating the Same Mistakes

Indeed, the political reality of the day, as it had been in the Classic Age, was that sharing a common culture did not guarantee peace and harmony. Sadly, the Hellenistic Greeks proceeded to repeat the same fatal mistake the city-states and Successors had; in short, they constantly argued and fought among themselves. History seemed perversely to repeat itself as their disunity led to weakness and vulnerability to still another outside power.

This time, that power would prove to be the most formidable the Greeks had ever faced. In the mid-third century B.C., as the Hellenistic realms squabbled, far to the west Rome, master of the Italian peninsula, was engaged in its first war against the maritime empire of Carthage (centered in Tunisia, in northern Africa). Shortly before, one of the Hellenistic rulers, Pyrrhus of Epirus, had briefly fought the Romans. He had answered a plea for aid from the most prosperous and important of the Greek cities that had for several centuries dotted southern Italy.[21] Taras (Tarentum in Latin), located in the "instep" of the Italian boot, was at odds with the Romans and was therefore delighted when Pyrrhus landed his army in Italy in the spring of 280 B.C.

However, though Pyrrhus several times fought the Roman legions to a standstill, he was unable to defeat them decisively, and his own losses were extremely heavy. So he decided to cut those losses and return to Epirus. The failure of his Italian adventure had extremely ominous overtones; the fact that he, one of the greatest Greek generals of that or any day, could not stop the Romans did not bode well for either Carthage's or Greece's future.

Indeed, just eleven years after Pyrrhus had vacated Italy, Rome engaged and defeated Carthage in the First Punic War (264–241 B.C.), the most destructive conflict the world had yet seen. The Second Punic War (218–201) soon followed. In this truly stupendous conflict, Macedonia's king, Philip V, made the mistake of allying himself with the ultimate loser—Carthage. (The Romans later referred to their involvement with him as the First Macedonian War, a sub-conflict of the greater war with Carthage.) And just two years after their victory, the Romans were ready to punish Philip for his interference in their affairs. In this way, Rome, which had recently become master of the western Mediterranean sphere, now turned its attention to the Greek states in the sea's eastern sphere.

Largely because these states remained disunited, their fates were virtually sealed. In 197 B.C., at the climax of the Second Macedonian War, a Roman army demolished Philip's phalanx at Cynoscephalae ("Dogs' Heads", in Thessaly). And the results of the Greco-Roman battles and wars of the ensuing decades were hauntingly similar. In 189 B.C., the Romans soundly defeated the ruler of the Seleucid Kingdom, Antiochus III, at Magnesia (in Asia Minor); the Third Macedonian War (171–168), against Philip's son, Perseus, ended with the abolition of the Macedonian Kingdom (Rome annexed the area as a new province in 148); and in 146, after a courageous but futile military resistance by the Achaean League, the Romans brutally destroyed the once-great city of Corinth as an object lesson to other Greeks who might dare to rebel.

Dreams of Empire Dashed

Meanwhile, the rulers of the Ptolemaic kingdom wisely submitted to Roman domination without a fight. For the next century, Egypt remained independent, but was in reality no more than a Roman client state (or vassal), allowed to pursue its own local affairs as long as it did Rome's bidding in the international scene. The Ptolemies of the first century B.C., who were weak, pale shadows of the formidable Greek general who had founded their dynasty, did their best to appease Rome and maintain their autonomy. But Egypt, with its vast stores of grain and royal treasure, increasingly became a prize coveted by the ambitious leading Romans of the day, who were vying for mastery of Rome's domains. Cleopatra VII, sister of the young and inept Ptolemy XIII, boldly allied herself with two of these men—Julius Caesar (who was assassinated in 44 B.C.) and Marcus Antonius (Mark Antony).

For a while, Antony and Cleopatra seemed on the verge of consolidating the whole East, including large portions of Alexander's former empire and the now defunct Hellenistic monarchies. Had they succeeded, the course of Western history would undoubtedly have been quite different. As it was, however, a third powerful Roman, Octavian (later Augustus Caesar, the first Roman emperor), decisively defeated them at Actium (in western Greece) in 31 B.C. With her ally/lover dead and her dreams of empire dashed, the famous queen, last of the Ptolemies, as well as the last Hellenistic ruler, committed suicide shortly afterward.

Back in 213 B.C., when the Romans were fighting Carthage and positioning themselves for Mediterranean mastery, a Greek orator, Agelaus of Aetolia, had recognized the potential danger and warned:

> It would be best of all if the Greeks never went to war with one another, if they could regard it as the greatest gift of the gods for them to speak with one voice, and could join hands like men who are crossing a river; in this way they could unite to repulse the incursions of the barbarians and to preserve themselves and their cities.[22]

At the time, the Hellenistic world's great powers could have and certainly should have joined forces, as Agelaus urged, and presented a united front against the Roman threat. But his warning went unheeded.

It was the Romans, therefore, and not the Greeks who subsequently went on to unite the whole Mediterranean world into a vast commonwealth administered by one central government. The Romans were mightily impressed and influenced by Greek culture; and by absorbing much of it they ensured that the Greek cultural legacy would survive. But over nineteen centuries would pass before the Greeks knew self-rule again. Pericles, Alexander, and the other towering figures who had shaped Greece's glorious past now settled quietly into the long sleep of eternal fame. The epic two-thousand-year-long journey of the Greeks at the forefront of Western civilization had finally reached its end.

Notes

1. Thomas R. Martin, *Ancient Greece: From Prehistoric to Hellenistic Times.* New Haven: Yale University Press, 1996, p. 16.

2. For analyses of the various theories, see Robert Drews, *The Coming of the Greeks: Indo-European Conquests in the Aegean and Near East.* Princeton: Princeton University Press, 1988. A useful overview of Mycenaean civilization is William Taylor's *The Mycenaeans.* London: Thames and Hudson, 1983.

3. C.M. Bowra, *Classical Greece.* New York: Time-Life Books, 1965, p. 31.

4. In the story, the young Athenians were sacrificed to the Minotaur, a creature half-man and half-bull. Theseus slew the beast and released the prisoners. The Minotaur was likely a garbled memory of Minoan priests, who, some evidence suggests, wore bull masks when performing sacrifices.

5. The theory that the catastrophic eruption of the volcano on the small island of Thera, just north of Crete, caused the demise of Minoan civilization is still not proven. The most recent calculations date the eruption to ca. 1600 B.C., too early to account for the damage done to Minoan palaces ca. 1400. However, the evidence is quite convincing that the eruption and its destruction of the thriving Minoan community on Thera gave rise to the legend of the lost city of Atlantis. See Charles Pellegrino, *Unearthing Atlantis: An Archaeological Odyssey,* New York: Random House, 1991; and Rodney Castleden, *Atlantis Destroyed,* New York: Routledge, 1998.

6. Michael Grant, *The Rise of the Greeks.* New York: Macmillan, 1987, p. 147.

7. For an overview of these theories, see Robert Drews, *The End of the Bronze Age: Changes in Warfare and the Catastrophe of ca. 1200 B.C.* Princeton: Princeton University Press, 1993. Drews himself contends that military innovations among the peoples living on the periphery of the Mediterranean world allowed them to defeat the chariot corps of the Bronze Age kingdoms.

8. There were apparently some exceptions to this rule. Recent archaeological evidence shows that a settlement at Lefkandi, on the western shore of Euboea (the large island lying along the eastern coast of the Greek mainland) enjoyed considerable prosperity in this period. Such sites remain unusual however, and perhaps represent rare and relatively short-lived surviving pockets of Mycenaean culture.

9. Sarah B. Pomeroy et al., *Ancient Greece: A Political, Social, and Cultural History.* New York: Oxford University Press, 1999, p. 42.

10. Victor D. Hanson, *The Other Greeks: The Family Farm and the Agrarian Roots of Western Civiliza-*

tion. New York: Simon and Schuster, 1995, p. 114.

11. Hanson, *The Other Greeks,* p. 31.

12. Hanson, *The Other Greeks,* p. 222.

13. At first, Athens's wealth derived partly from trade and partly from the large quantities of silver that flowed from its mines at Laurium, in southern Attica. Later, the Athenians gained and exploited for their own purposes huge amounts of revenue in the form of tribute (payment acknowledging submission) from the member states of its maritime empire.

14. Alessandro Bausani, *The Persians: From the Earliest Days to the Twentieth Century.* Trans. J.B. Donne. London: Elek Books, 1971, pp. 15–16.

15. Plutarch, *Life of Pericles,* in *The Rise and Fall of Athens: Nine Greek Lives by Plutarch.* Trans. Ian Scott-Kilvert. New York: Penguin, 1960, p. 179.

16. Thucydides, *The Peloponnesian War,* published as *The Landmark Thucydides: A Comprehensive Guide to the Peloponnesian War.* Trans. Richard Crawley, ed. Robert B. Strassler. New York: Simon and Schuster, 1996, p. 93.

17. Xenophon, *Hellenica,* published as *A History of My Times.* Trans. Rex Warner. New York: Penguin Books, 1979, p. 403.

18. Michael Grant, *From Alexander to Cleopatra: The Hellenistic World.* New York: Charles Scribner's Sons, 1982, p. xiii.

19. Eratosthenes of Cyrene (ca. 276–194 B.C.) served for many years as the chief librarian of Alexandria's famous university, the Museum. For an account of how he measured the earth, as well as other achievements of Hellenistic scientists, see Don Nardo, *Greek and Roman Science.* San Diego: Lucent Books, 1997.

20. Grant, *From Alexander to Cleopatra,* p. xiii.

21. These cities, including Sybaris, Croton, Rhegium, and Tarentum, among many others, had been established in an intensive burst of Greek colonization spanning the period ca. 750–550 B.C. In Pyrrhus's day, some were larger, and all were more cultured, than Rome.

22. Quoted in Polybius, *Histories,* published as *Polybius: The Rise of the Roman Empire.* Trans. Ian Scott-Kilvert. New York: Penguin Books, 1979, pp. 299–300.

Greek History— The Bronze Age

Chapter 2

Introduction

The Bronze Age is so named because those who lived in these times primarily used tools and weapons made of bronze, an alloy of copper and tin. For the sake of convenience, modern scholars break down the long span of the Greek Bronze Age into various shorter periods. The most commonly used periods for sites on the Greek mainland are referred to as "Helladic": Early Helladic (ca. 3000–ca. 2100 B.C.), Middle Helladic (ca. 2100–ca. 1550), and Late Helladic (ca. 1550–ca. 1100). Each of these breaks down into three sub-periods, denoted I, II, and III. For sites on Crete, the periods are labeled "Minoan": Early Minoan (ca. 3000–ca. 2200 B.C.), Middle Minoan (ca. 2200–ca. 1600), and Late Minoan (ca. 1600–ca. 1100), each broken down into sub-periods I, II, and III. Scholars also divide Cretan culture into the First Palace Period (ca. 2200–ca. 1700 B.C.), Second Palace Period (ca. 1700–ca. 1500), and Third Palace Period (ca. 1500–ca. 1200). (There is also a dating system for the southern Aegean islands, the Cyclades, consisting of periods labeled Early, Middle, and Late Cycladic). It is important to note that most of these dates are not rigid and often vary, according to individual scholarly opinion, by fifty to one hundred or more years.

The need for these separate dating systems underscores the reality that separate and distinct pre- or proto-Greek civilizations grew up and flourished on Crete and the Greek mainland. The Minoans (named by modern scholars after the legendary Cretan king, Minos) built splendid, multistoried palaces on Crete, the largest and most famous at Knossus (or Cnossus), near the northern coast. This is often referred to as the Knossus Labyrinth because it is thought to be the model for the maze-like Labyrinth from the Greek legend of Theseus. The site was excavated largely between 1900 and 1932 by English archaeologist Sir Arthur Evans.

Minoan palaces also rose at other Cretan sites, including Phaistos (near the southern coast), Mallia (on the northern coast, east of Knossus), and Zakros (or Zakro, near the eastern coast); and Minoan colonies or outposts were constructed in some of the Cyclades, notably at Thera (about eighty miles north of Crete). In the 1960s, a Bronze Age Minoan town that had been buried in a catastrophic eruption of the island's volcano was discovered at Akrotiri on Thera. This eruption, dated variously from 1620 to 1475 B.C., may have contributed to the Minoans' decline. The Minoans used a syllabic writing script that modern scholars call Linear A, which remains largely undeciphered.

Although definitive evidence is lacking, the Minoans may have for a time dominated the mainland Mycenaeans (named by modern scholars after Mycenae, one of their chief fortress-towns). The Cretans certainly exerted a cultural influence over the mainlanders, who built settlements and eventually imposing palace-citadels at Mycenae and Tiryns (in the northeastern Peloponnesus, a region that came to be called Argolis), Athens (on Attica, the triangular peninsula lying northeast of the Peloponnesus), Sparta (in Laconia, the region making up the southeastern Peloponnesus), and Pylos (near the southwestern coast of the Peloponnesus). The Mycenaeans, who used a script called Linear B (which turned out to be an early form of Greek), eventually came to exert political dominance over Crete and the islands.

Mycenae was first excavated between 1876 and 1878 by German excavator Heinrich Schliemann, who pioneered Greek Bronze Age archaeology. A few years earlier, Schliemann had stunned the scholarly world by showing that Troy, the legendary city sacked by the Greeks (now identified as the Mycenaeans) in Homer's epic poem, the *Iliad,* was a real place. He uncovered a series of cities, built on top of one another, at a site in northwestern Asia Minor (or Anatolia); and evidence shows that the city labeled Troy VIIa underwent siege circa 1220 B.C., in the approximate period the later classical Greeks believed the Trojan War took place. It remains unproven, however, that the war remembered by Homer (if there actually was such an event) took place at this time. The destruction of Troy VIIa may be related to the widespread upheavals that wracked the eastern Mediterranean sphere circa 1200 to 1100 B.C., laying low Mycenaean civilization and bringing Greece's Bronze Age to a close.

The physical evidence available to scholars for the Bronze Age is on the whole scattered and meager, although ongoing excavations reveal new clues and information each year. No contemporary literature of the period (if any such ever existed) has survived. So historians must study remains of the palaces and other structures, jars and other kinds of pottery, painted murals, sculptures, tools and weapons, and Linear B inventory lists preserved on clay tablets. Scholars also study ancient myths, especially Homer's telling of the Trojan War, recognizing that, though highly romanticized and partly fabricated, they often contain kernels of historical truth.

Selection 1

The Early Bronze Age and Arrival of the First Greeks

Sarah B. Pomeroy, Stanley M. Burstein, Walter Donlan, and Jennifer T. Roberts

The first Greek-speaking people arrived on the Greek mainland sometime between the end of the Early Helladic period (ca. 2100 B.C.) and the end of the Middle Helladic period (ca. 1600 B.C.). Linguistic and other evidence shows that they were part of a large "Indo-European" folk migration originating somewhere in western Asia. This excerpt from Ancient Greece: A Political, Social and Cultural History *is written by Sarah B. Pomeroy (Hunter College), Stanley M. Burstein (California State University, Los Angeles), Walter Donlan (University of California, Irvine), and Jennifer T. Roberts (City University of New York Graduate Center).*

Excerpted from *Ancient Greece: Political, Social, and Cultural History*, by Sarah Pomeroy et al. Copyright © 1998 by Sarah Pomeroy, Stanley Burstein, Walter Donlan, and Jennifer T. Roberts. Used by permission of Oxford University Press, Inc.

*T*he technology of smelting and casting copper appears to have originated independently in both western Asia and southeastern Europe before 6000 BC. The crucial next step, of adding 10 percent of tin to the copper to produce bronze, a much harder metal, was taken in the Near East during the fourth millennium. The technique came to Greece around

3000 BC; by about 2500, the use of bronze as well as other metals such as lead, silver, and gold became widespread throughout Greece and the Aegean.

The introduction of metallurgy was a major technological advance, for tools and weapons of bronze were considerably more efficient than those made of stone, bone, or copper. The impact was not just utilitarian, however; the movement into the Bronze Age marked a turning point in Greek social and economic relations, just as it had in the East. It was the high-ranked individuals and families, those with greater surpluses of wealth, who had the most access to bronze and scarce metal products. Possession of these and other prestige items set them further apart from the mass of the population. Their increasing demand for metal goods gave rise to local specialists and workshops and accelerated trade for copper and tin and other metals, not only with the East, but also with the peoples of central and western Europe. Early Bronze Age Greece was edging its way into the wider economy and culture of the Mediterranean world. And as the economy expanded and the settlements grew larger, so did the wealth, power, and authority of their leaders, now established as hereditary chiefs who ruled for life and were accorded exceptional honors and privileges.

A major Early Bronze Age settlement was the town of Lerna in Argolis, where the remains of strong stone fortifications and some monumental buildings have been found, the largest of which may have been the house of the ruling chief. The sophistication of the architecture and the quality of the artifacts betoken a fairly complex political and economic system, though far less advanced than those of the Near East and Egypt. Lerna flourished from about 3000 to about 2100, when it was destroyed along with a number of other towns and villages in Argolis, Attica, and Laconia. Similar devastation of settlements occurred throughout much of Europe at this time.

After the destructions, Greece entered what appears to have been a period of cultural stagnation. During the next five hundred years the ar-

chaeological record is both sparse and generally unimpressive. Most historians connect both the destructions of the sites and the ensuing cultural lag to the incursion of a new people into the central and southern mainland of Greece. The arrival of these newcomers, who spoke a very early form of Greek, marked a decisive turning point in the history and culture of Greece and the Aegean.

As is usual with events that occurred so early in prehistory, there is uncertainty about when the speakers of proto-Greek entered Greece. It may have been as early as 2100 BC, or two centuries later, when there is evidence of a new type of pottery and other possibly new cultural features. On the basis of such material, archaeologists have labeled this intermediate cultural stage the "Middle Helladic" period (c. 1900–1580). The picture is confused by a third theory, which places the arrival of the Greek-speakers at the end of the Middle Helladic period, around 1600 BC. Despite the ongoing controversy about when they entered, however, it is unanimously agreed that the newcomers were part of a huge wave of migrating groups from the north and east known collectively as the Indo-Europeans. This knowledge was the result of modern linguistic discoveries.

In the eighteenth century AD, scholars began to recognize that ancient Greek bore many similarities to other dead languages, such as Latin, Old Persian, and Sanskrit (the language of ancient India), as well as to entire families of spoken languages, such as the Germanic and Slavic. They observed, for example, a striking similarity in words such as "mother": Sanskrit *mātar*, Greek *mētēr*, Latin *mater*, Anglo-Saxon *mōdor*, Old Irish *mathir*, Lithuanian *mote*, Russian *mat'*. The close likenesses in vocabulary and grammatical structure among ancient languages and their descendants soon led to the insight that they had all sprung from a common linguistic ancestor, which was termed "Proto-Indo-European." It was reasoned that there had once been a single Indo-European homeland, located perhaps in the vast steppes north of the Black and Caspian seas (one of several suggested homelands), and that the separate languages developed in the course of emigrations from the homeland into distant places. The speakers of proto-Greek were thus a part of a great and lengthy ancient exodus of peoples, which gradually over the centuries spread the Indo-European languages across Europe and Asia, from Ireland to Chinese Turkestan.

The First Greek-Speakers

Eventually, the language of the Greek-speaking newcomers replaced the non-Indo-European "Aegean" languages, which survived in Greek primarily in place names (e.g., *Korinthos*) and in names for indigenous animals and plants, such as *hyakinthos* ("hyacinth"). This would seem to indicate that the Greek-speakers were the dominant group within the society, but one language may displace another for reasons other than conquest and dominance. At any rate, the process of displacement was probably a long one, with both Greek and indigenous languages existing side by side for centuries.

During the nineteenth and early twentieth centuries, there was considerable conjecture about the nature of the social organization and culture of these earliest Greek-speakers. It was assumed that the Indo-Europeans were a superior race of northern horse-riding "Aryan" warriors, who swept down into southern Europe and violently imposed their languages and customs on the weaker, unwarlike, agrarian natives. Such suppositions were the products of a racially biased Eurocentrism. No scholar today accepts any part of this "Aryan myth," which was the pretext for so many crimes against humanity in the nineteenth and twentieth centuries, culminating in the horrors perpetrated by the Nazis and Fascists in the 1930s and '40s.

The most we can safely say about these incoming Indo-European Greek-speakers is that for subsistence they practiced herding and agriculture, and they knew metallurgy and other crafts, such as pottery and cloth-making. Of their society, we can surmise only that they were organized in families and larger groups (clans and tribes) that were patriarchal (the father was the supreme authority figure) and patrilineal (descent was reckoned in the male line). Their primary divinity was Zeus, a powerful male god; and they were a warlike people with a hierarchical leadership system. The once common notion that the pre-Indo-European societies of Greece around 2000 BC were polar opposites—peaceful, nonhierarchical, and matriarchal (where descent, inheritance, and authority came down through the mother)—is now discredited. In most respects, except for language, religion, and some relatively minor features (such as architecture and pottery), the two peoples were probably very similar.

The drop in the cultural level during the archaeological Middle Helladic period (c. 1900–1580 BC) is best explained as a long stage of adjustment, during which the native people and the newcomers gradually merged into a single people through generations of intermarriage, and their two cultures fused into a single Greek-speaking culture that contained elements of both. Nor in fact was the Middle Bronze (Middle Helladic) period totally static. Population increased, new settlements grew up, there were advances in metallurgy, and contacts with the civilizations of Crete and the Near East began. These would lead, toward the end of the period, to a sudden cultural quickening that ushered in the high civilization of the Late Bronze (Late Helladic) period.

Selection 2

The Minoan Culture Flourishes on Crete

Rodney Castleden

This overview of Minoan history, pieced together from archaeological and other evidence since the Minoans left no written history, is by Rodney Castleden, a noted scholar of early European cultures. He traces the ebb and flow of Minoan power through the Old Temple Period (roughly corresponding to the Middle Helladic period), and Second Palace Period (ca. 1700–ca. 1470 B.C.), pointing out that Minoans probably influenced the Greek-speaking mainlanders. Castleden also discusses the eruption of the volcano on the tiny island of Thera (located just north of central Crete), believed to have been the most destructive natural disaster in recorded history. The most recent evidence dates the catastrophe to circa 1600 B.C. or shortly before. However, the matter is far from settled; and Castleden's dating of 1500–1470 B.C., as well as his general scenario of Minoan decline, is still plausible, especially the suggestion that the Mycenaeans were able to take control of Crete as a result of that decline.

inoan society grew out of a long period of indigenous cultural development. The neolithic [late stone age]

levels under the Knossos Labyrinth are among the deepest in Europe, and contain the remains of many successive settlements. Those layers represent something approaching a 3,000-year-long neolithic preamble to the Minoan civilization. Then, shortly after 3000 BC, there was a rapid surge forwards into the bronze age. Traditionally, this is explained as a result of immigration—large numbers of new people arriving with new ideas—but now there is a tendency to explain change in terms of local native developments. There may have been small numbers of incomers to Crete at this time, as seems likely at all stages in Cretan prehistory, because of the island's situation, but new ideas could have been introduced by social and cultural contact alone.

Ideas and goods arrived from the Cyclades and the practice of burying people in domed round tombs seems to have been imported from Anatolia [Asia Minor]. [The noted scholar of bronze-age Greece] Sinclair Hood likens Early Minoan Crete to America: with its fermenting mixture of ideas and traditions it was a prehistoric New World. Some of the Early Minoan II pottery (2600–2300 BC) is reminiscent of Syrian ware and the first Minoan seals, produced at this time, are also reminiscent of seals from Syria. . . . The Pre-Temple Period of Minoan Crete gives us little evidence of its social and political life, but it is likely that society revolved mainly round the clan.

The Old and New Temple Periods

In 1930 BC, the Old Temple Period began with the building of the first huge labyrinth at Knossos. This was so distinctive a development that it is tempting to attribute it to invaders or migrants bringing in an exotic architectural idea from abroad. But there is no need to postulate invaders from Greece or Anatolia. The maze-like, multi-chambered temples—the so-called 'palaces'—had their native Cretan precursors. There was a cellular multi-room building, albeit much smaller, on the site of the Knossos Labyrinth itself, and a recognizable L-shaped predecessor for the temple plan, complete with central courtyard, was built at Vasiliki in 2600 BC. The big Minoan temples should be seen as resulting from a long period of indigenous development, increasing prosperity and increasingly centralized organiza-tion, in religion and in the economy.

The evidence of social and political develop-ment in the Old Temple Period (1930–1700 BC) is fragmentary, though it looks as if social class-es based on rural or urban roles and divisions based on occupational specialization led to the development of a more stratified society than before. The bonds of the old clan system were beginning to loosen. The growth of towns at this time probably had much to do with the process, and we should see Minoan society developing towards something like the much later city-state system, although in Crete it looks as if the towns lived in relative harmony with each other.

Widespread physical damage brought the Old Temple Period to an end in 1700 BC. Both tem-ple and city at Knossos suffered extensive dam-age, perhaps more than once. The temple at Phaistos was apparently damaged at the same time by an earthquake, then repaired, only to be

The ruins at Knossos, a small section of which are pictured here, cover several acres. In its heyday, the palace rose as high as four or five stories in some places.

destroyed by a catastrophic fire. The destruction at Phaistos was complete; the ruins of the old temple were levelled, the site was filled in and a new temple built on top of the rubble with a different plan. At Monastiraki, a small 'palace' or temple was destroyed by fire at the same time as Knossos and Phaistos. The destructions may not have occurred simultaneously all over Crete, and they may have been due to different causes: nevertheless, the Phaistos evidence apart, the effects of a large-scale earthquake seem sufficient to explain events.

Sinclair Hood believes that foreign settlers arrived in Crete in 1700 BC in the wake of the temple destructions. He rejects mainland Greeks in favour of Luvians from south-west Anatolia, a people with a language related to that of the Hittites further east. . . . Arguing against this idea is the fact that the New Temples were very similar in concept and design to the Old Temples. . . . But arguing in support of a Luvian influx is the appearance of one of the Minoans' distinctive forms of writing, the script known as Linear A. The later Linear B script has been interpreted as a primitive form of Greek. Linear A, which contributed some of its signs to Linear B, was nevertheless not Greek but some other language yet to be identified. [Historian] Leonard Palmer noticed a link between Linear A and the Luvian language, a link which may prove to be very significant. . . . This certainly reinforces the general idea of significant cultural contact between the Minoans and . . . south-west Anatolia during the Second Temple Period, though it does not necessarily mean that there was any large-scale immigration from Anatolia into Crete. . . .

The New Temple Period (1700–1470 BC) was to be the most exuberant phase of Minoan civilization, producing the most elaborate architecture, the finest frescoes and the most sophisticated and beautiful works of art. The population grew to a point where the island may actually have become overpopulated. The remedy then, as in later times, was to found overseas colonies. These colonies were established across the southern Aegean and some may even have been on the Greek mainland, which seems to have become strongly 'Minoanized' at this time. There is every possibility that this process of Minoanization was mainly the result of consumer demand, because the Minoans were producing goods that were extremely attractive and of the highest quality. The legend of Theseus, the tribute-children and the Minotaur may suggest that there was a time, before the classical period, when Greek cities like Athens and Mycenae were tributary to Crete, but the legend may conceal a rather different folk-memory. It may have been a sore point with the classical Greeks that once there had been a time when they were culturally inferior to their neighbours on Crete; the Minoans' cultural and therefore trading superiority may, to a proud race, have *felt* like political subjugation. It may have been this subjective and exaggerated view which found its way into the folklore.

There is more evidence of the Minoan social structure from the New Temple Period. Women emerged as dominant figures in ceremonial contexts, and society as a whole had become much more strongly stratified. Social classes were now more important than the clans as the towns came to dominate the organization of rural areas. The government may have been more or less theocratic, with priestesses and other religious officials occupying positions of importance. One peculiarity of Minoan society, even at this zenith stage, is that it shows no sign whatever of personal ambition. There are, in the archaeological record, no signs at all of boastful, self-aggrandizing rulers or viziers, which is a striking contrast to the situation that prevailed in contemporary Egypt or Anatolia.

Destruction and Decline

The New Temple Period came to an abrupt end with the catastrophic Thera eruption of 1470 BC. The precise date is still a matter of controversy, but the most likely scenario is a long series of premonitory earthquakes and minor eruptions beginning in about 1500 BC and culminating in a caldera eruption of enormous violence in 1470 BC. Thera is 120 kilometres north of Crete, but major earthquakes with their epicentres on

Thera would have caused significant damage to Knossos and other Minoan sites on Crete. The final eruption would have been experienced as a multiple disaster at the Minoan sites. The initial damage to walls and foundations by blast and earthquake was followed by a towering tsunami, or 'tidal' wave, which would have washed across the northern coastal lowlands, destroying the principal Minoan harbour towns of Katsamba, Amnisos, Agii Theodhori and possibly quays at Kytaiton, Kydonia and Mallia too. A link between the Thera eruption and events in Crete is very plausible; in AD 1650, volcanic activity on Thera was responsible for earthquakes and tsunamis in Crete, though on a much smaller scale than envisaged in the prehistoric eruption.

After the waters of the 1470 tsunami receded, a great cloud of white ash blown south-eastwards by the wind covered the whole of central and eastern Crete, blotting out the sun and then settling over the landscape; on the sea-bed 120 kilometres south-east of Thera it is still 78 centimetres thick. Knossos and Mallia were not directly downwind at the time of the eruption, but the ashfall there must have been 20–30 centimetres thick, and half that amount would have been enough to put the farmland out of production for several years and paralyse the Minoan economy.

The archaeological evidence is patchy, but the town of Palaikastro at the eastern end of Crete was apparently destroyed in about 1470 BC. Some houses were repaired, but others were so badly damaged that the new houses built on their ruined foundations had a completely different alignment. There is evidence of disaster at Zakro, Mochlos and Pseira, which were never rebuilt. Knossos was extensively damaged by earthquake in 1470 BC and also somewhat earlier, presumably in the long premonitory series of earthquakes.

The Thera eruption must have been an appalling experience for the Minoans. The massive earthquake, the blasting bull-roar of Thera exploding, the darkening skies, the tsunamis and the silent rain of white ash must have reduced them to terror and despair. The interruption to food production created an economic crisis. The

unparalleled unleashing of the cosmic forces may have precipitated a religious crisis. The reduced importance of the peak sanctuaries in the period following the Thera eruption may reflect a loss of faith in the god Poseidon or in the ritual procedures designed to propitiate him. . . .

After Thera, the Minoan economy was reconstructed, but it was not the same as before. Many sites were too badly damaged to rebuild. The Phaistos temple was reoccupied and a new residential building (sometimes called a Mycenean megaron) was raised at Agia Triadha. The Knossos Labyrinth was systematically repaired and redecorated and became the principal religious focus of Minoan Crete. The severe damage and the economic, political, and social crisis that followed directly from it accentuated a tendency towards centralization. Thera led directly to a focus on Knossos as a capital city, an administrative centre for the greater part of Crete, and a major cult centre. . . .

It was at this time that people from mainland Greece, often called 'Myceneans' for convenience, invaded a weakened and disoriented Crete, and succeeded in conquering it. It would have been relatively easy for them to do so at this time; we can imagine that a great many ships of the Minoan fleet, whether merchantmen or war galleys, were sunk either at sea or at anchor in the many harbours along the north coast; we can imagine also that the normal efficiency of Minoan bureaucracy and communications had broken down. Physically weakened by food shortages as well, the Minoans would have been easy prey to an envious neighbour who had been waiting for his opportunity to strike. Alternatively, Myceneans may have taken over peacefully at Knossos, perhaps as a result of a dynastic marriage between Cretan and mainland royal houses. . . .

The period which followed, the Late Temple Period (1470–1380 BC), was one of partial recovery, but to a rather formal, highly centralized and bureaucratic system with Knossos as the leading city of Crete. . . . In the Late Temple Period, many of the artistic influences seem to be Mycenean, and the implication is that the mainland culture had become the dominant one, even though it was still Cretan artists who executed much of the finest artwork and metalwork, on mainland sites as well as on Crete. The adoption of Linear B Greek as the scribal language has been taken by many as proof that the Greeks controlled Crete, but it may be that this reflects a preference for Greek as the Aegean *lingua franca*, the language of officialdom, administration and trade: it does not prove that Greeks ruled at Knossos.

1380 BC was a major turning-point for Minoan civilization. It was the date when the Knossos Labyrinth was devastated by fire and abandoned, never to be rebuilt, never to be repaired, never to be fully reoccupied. The fire may have been the result of an accident—perhaps an overturned hearth or lamp—but if so the temple would surely have been rebuilt, as it was after the 1700 and 1470 destructions. The 1380 fire seems to have been a deliberate act of arson. In fact *this* may have been the time when the Myceneans invaded. The so-called Palace of Kadmos at Thebes was sacked at the same time as the Knossos Labyrinth; we may see both as part of a process of expansion and domination by which thirteenth-century Mycenae appears to have become the capital of an empire extending across most of the Aegean.

Selection 3

Mainland Mycenaean Traders and Builders

M.I. Finley

This discussion of the Mycenaeans, who occupied the Greek mainland beginning in the mid-Bronze Age, is authored by the widely respected former Cambridge University scholar M.I. Finley. Eventually, he says, the mainlanders expanded their power and influence southward and westward into the Aegean sphere and took control of the Minoan centers on Crete and other islands, including Cnossus (or Knossos). Finley cautions, however, that the exact nature of the political and other connections between the Mycenaeans and Minoans, before and after the advent of Mycenaean dominance, are still unclear.

Excerpted from *Early Greece: The Bronze and Archaic Ages*, by M.I. Finley. Copyright © 1981, 1970 by M.I. Finley. Reprinted by permission of W.W. Norton & Company, Inc., and Chatto & Windus Ltd.

*a*t a date which falls within the great Cretan palace-period, that is, . . . about 1600 B.C., something happened on the Greek mainland which gave a radically new turn to developments there, and to the history of the Aegean generally. Precisely what happened remains mysterious, the subject of continuing speculation and controversy without agreement, but the visible consequences are clear enough. Mycenae suddenly became a centre of wealth and power, and of a warrior civilization, without an equal in this region. Soon other important centres arose in central and southern Greece, and influences then radiated to the Aegean islands and the coasts of Asia Minor and Syria in the east, and to Sicily and southern Italy in the west. The next four hundred years or so, both on the mainland and in many of the islands, reveal such uniformity in the archaeological record that, by an unfortunate convention, the label 'Mycenaean' has come to be applied to the whole civilization (though it was never used in antiquity). There is no harm done if the label is retained in an abstract sense, comparable to 'Islamic', but the danger must be avoided of sliding over to an implication of centralized political authority, of a territorially extensive society ruled from Mycenae, as the Assyrian Empire, for example, was ruled from Assur. There is, as we shall see, no justification for such a political implication.

The remarkable prelude to this civilization is fully attested only at Mycenae. It amounts to no more than two grave circles, an older one the pivotal date of which is 1600 B.C., excavated by Greek archaeologists late in 1951, now known as Circle B, and another perhaps a century later (Circle A), which Heinrich Schliemann found in 1876 (six years after his discovery of Troy) to make the fundamental breakthrough in modern study of the Greek Bronze Age. Both circles were part of a large cemetery, presumably outside the settlement proper. Three features are noteworthy: first, the circles were deliberately marked out and were intended to be significant; second, the grave goods were numerous, luxurious and in part warlike; and third, the idea of memorializing power and authority was wholly concentrated in these tombs, for no trace of the settlement has been found, which must mean that there were neither walls nor fortifications nor palaces built of stone. The actual burials were scattered irregularly within the circles, in ordinary graves or cists or deep burial shafts—some twenty-four in Circle B, only six in Circle A, all the latter of the deep shaft type.

The interments themselves were no radical departure from older practices, nor was the unceremonious pushing aside of earlier bones and grave-goods to make room for later corpses. But everything else was new. The graves were marked on the surface by upright stone slabs, many of them inscribed with figured decorations or animals or military and hunting scenes (but never with a name or a proper portrait or other immediate link with a particular personality, thus remaining strictly within the Bronze Age tradition of the anonymity of power). The circle must have had some sacral significance, which survived a long time. In the great building programme on the citadel after 1300 B.C., when the 1000-yard circuit wall was constructed, Circle A was brought within the precinct and retained as 'hallowed' ground, marked off by an elaborate double ring of limestone stabs. Whatever the builders of that period may have known or believed about the grave circle, the impulse behind their beliefs was a powerful one, since by that time the original surface was well underground and they would have given themselves far less trouble had they ignored it. . . .

Whoever the men and women were who were buried in these specially prepared graves, they were at the top of a power structure within the community different from any Greece had known before. It is tempting to link their emergence with the arrival of the battle chariot and the long sword, though the first graves in Circle B seem a bit early for that. In any event, chariots figure prominently on the slabs marking the later shaft-graves, as in the still later Linear B inventories from Cnossus and Pylos. The chariot was an import—the idea, that is, not the actual vehicles themselves—but that is no argument that the people who took advantage of this new military weapon were themselves migrants. Nor is the abundant gold, which might represent the fruits of mercenary service, for example in Egypt as some scholars believe, or of successful raiding, or of trade, or of all three in combination. For the present we must confess that the causes of the sudden upsurge in power and the possession of treasure are unknown.

The shaft-graves and their contents reveal a steady increase in technical and artistic skills and in concentration of power. Similar growth occurred in many parts of central Greece and the Peloponnese during Late Helladic I and II [circa the 1500s and 1400s B.C.] but outside Mycenae (and eventually in Mycenae too) the visible symbol was a very different kind of burial-chamber, the spectacular *tholos*- or beehive-tomb. These were circular chambers cut into a hillside, with a special runway (*dromos*) leading to them, roofed over by the careful building up of a dome-like frame of stones in ever-decreasing rings, ending with a capstone above the natural height of the hill. The whole structure was sealed and covered with earth, leaving an imposing mound in view. Some idea of the scale can be had from the dimensions of the greatest and one of the latest of them all, the popularly but inaccurately named 'Treasury of Atreus' at Mycenae: 48 feet in diameter, 43 feet in height (both inside measurements), a *dromos* 118 feet in length, and a lintel over the entrance-door weighing perhaps 100 tons.

Nothing prepares us for such tombs. There is no architectural forerunner, either in Greece or anywhere else. But any doubt that they indicate not just power but more or less unique status in the hierarchy, kingship in effect, is removed by the co-existence with the *tholos*-tombs of many chamber-tombs containing rich grave-goods, the resting-places of families well up the hierarchical scale but not at the top. The spread and location of the new dynasties in central and southern Greece can be plotted on a map by following the erection of *tholos*-tombs, the largest number of which were constructed in the fifteenth century (Late Helladic II). . . .

The *tholos*-tomb period is also the age when mainland activity becomes clearly visible abroad, in the form of extensive pottery finds, at first primarily in the west (Sicily and southern Italy), but by the end of Late Helladic II also in quantity in the other direction, in Rhodes, in Cyprus, in Miletus in Asia Minor, and elsewhere, an activity which mounted to a crescendo in the final phase of the Bronze Age. . . . It is at this point that the limitations of the Linear B tablets are particularly exasperating. They have been found in considerable numbers in Mycenae and Pylos (and a few in Thebes), and thus far nowhere else on the mainland. They are comparable in language and content to those from Cnossus, equally lacking in the dimension of time because they, too, date from a moment of destruction and conflagration. If the commonly accepted date of 1400 for the fall of Cnossus is right, then Greek speakers took control there at the height of the *tholos*-tomb period. . . .

The question of the relations between the mainland centres and those sites in which pottery finds are particularly concentrated is therefore a most troublesome one. That there was extensive trade (and that even before 1400 the mainland was beginning to push Crete out) can be taken as certain. Some materials, such as amber and ivory, could not have been brought to Greece otherwise, nor, in all probability, could most of the gold, tin and copper. Scattered Mycenaean objects and motifs reached central Europe and as far as southern England (including Stonehenge), from about 1500 B.C., and their presence is to be explained by the Mycenaean search for metals. Amber is common in Greece from the shaft-graves to the end of the Mycenaean age, though rare in Minoan Crete and post-Mycenaean Greece, and much of it is Baltic in origin.

But who were the traders and under what conditions did they operate? The Linear B tablets from the mainland are as silent on these questions as are those from Cnossus. Very likely the concentration of Mycenaean pottery at Scoglio del Tonno in the Taranto region of southern Italy reveals the presence of a 'Mycenaean' trading post, linked with the movement of goods from central and western Europe. It is not so easy, however, to find satisfactory criteria for assessing the view of some writers that Rhodes and Miletus were Mycenaean colonies. That the material remains in those two places (unlike Cyprus) look 'Mycenaean' is true, but that proves nothing about their *political* connexions with the mainland, one way or the other. . . .

It is not certain whether the takeover of Cnossus by Greek speakers was followed by actual allegiance or subjection to a mainland power. Trade, migration, conquest and colonialism do not always interact in a neat package.

Political Relations Unclear

Nor are the political relations clear on the mainland itself. The notable fact has already been mentioned that the *tholos*-tombs are earlier than large-scale domestic architecture, that, in other words, the kings and nobles lavished their wealth and expressed their power, architecturally, in their burial-chambers before they turned their attention to their palaces and houses. The excavators at Pylos have found evidence of an extensive settlement of the lower town earlier than the construction of the great palace, but they cannot trace its history back very far, and that is the picture in Greece generally. We know that the population had grown considerably and that they were clustered in villages, usually on hillsides overlooking the farmland. (Some 400 Mycenaean settlements on the mainland have already been located.) And we know that society had become hierarchically stratified, ruled by a warrior class under chieftains or kings. Then, after 1400 (and in most places not until about 1300) there came the dramatic shift from concentration on impressive burial-chambers to the erection of a number of palace-fortresses. Such places as Tiryns and Mycenae in the western Peloponnese, the Acropolis in Athens, Thebes and Gla in Boeotia, Iolkos in Thessaly, now looked more like medieval fortress-towns than like the open, agglutinative [formed from many smaller pieces coming together] Cretan complexes. There was still cell-like growth, but the nucleus was the so-called *megaron* type of house, consisting of a columned fore-porch or vestibule, a long main room and usually a store-room behind.

This stress on fortification and the warlike cannot have been merely a matter of taste. Something in the social situation required it, as presumably it was not needed, at least not on anything like such a scale, in Crete. The mainland Linear B tablets record the same activities and the same kinds of inventories as at Cnossus, the same pattern of palace control and administration over the community and over the surrounding region (but not at any considerable distance beyond). However, the tablets give no clues about the warlike factor, for which we must try to draw implications from the distribution and fate of the fortresses themselves. In simplified form, the key question may be posed like this. Why were the Argolid and the region around Corinth relatively thick with fortresses, whereas in Messenia to the west, Pylos was only lightly fortified and twelve miles to the north there were large *tholos*-tombs and a heavily fortified hilltop site at Peristeria, the ancient name for which is unknown? There was a considerable settlement at Argos in the Middle Helladic period, and then again continuously from Late Helladic II on, but there was no palace, no fortification, not a single *tholos*-tomb, no arms in the graves. Apparently Argos was subject to Mycenae six miles to the north, or to the slightly less distant Tiryns in the south, and had no warrior aristocracy of its own. On the other hand, it is hard to imagine that Mycenae and Tiryns were on a par, dividing the Argive plain between them (or that Thebes and Gla were equal powers in Boeotia). In the generations following the early *tholos*-tombs, persistent raids and wars presumably raised a few successful dynasts to positions of superpower and suzerainty, with the lesser or defeated chieftains destroyed in some instances, and in others allowed to survive in some form of subordinate status. There are signs at several places, for example, Mycenae, Tiryns and Thebes, of heavy destruction and burning in this period, followed by changes in the building-complex and the fortifications. That suggests war damage. No doubt there were also inter-dynastic marriages to complicate the succession to the throne and the inter-state relations, as they always do.

The picture that emerges from such an analysis of the tablets and the archaeology combined is one of a division of Mycenaean Greece into a number of petty bureaucratic states, with a warrior aristocracy, a high level of craftsmanship, extensive foreign trade in necessities (metals) and luxuries, and a permanent condition of armed neutrality at best in their relations with each other, and perhaps at times with their subjects. . . .

Apart from some battle scenes, Mycenaean palace art fails to reflect in any direct way the warrior-society. That art is, indeed, astonishingly derivative (except in pottery), with the same love of abstract and floral decoration, the same monotonous processionals, the same conventionality and static quality as its Cretan prototypes. There is the same impersonality, too. Almost never, for example, is a 'foreigner' portrayed, distinguishable in features, dress, hair or beard. . . .

Although the Linear B tablets abound with names of gods and goddesses, and with lists of what appear to be personnel in their service or of offerings to them, Mycenaean religion is archeologically still less noticeable than Minoan. There are altars and there are representations of divinities and rituals on gems and seal-stones, most of them Cretan in origin without any distinguishing features to mark them off as Mycenaean, but, until the summer of 1968, no clearly identifiable shrine or special room for ritual purposes had been found within the palace-complexes. That summer the excavators at Mycenae came upon a small scaled 'storeroom' (about six feet square) in which were stacked, among other things, some sixteen hollow nude figures in clay, up to two feet in height, made on a potter's wheel, with short upraised or extended arms (but no legs), notional breasts (most were females), hair and facial features added afterwards, as was done with handles and spouts on vases. The room also contained six coiled clay snakes, realistically modelled. The latter are rather splendid objects, but the statuettes are extremely 'primitive' and ugly, save for a single exceptional small one, which is clothed and painted and carries a design that points to a date not later than 1300 B.C. Nearby was another curious room . . . in which there were platforms so arranged as to suggest the possibility of cult activity. . . .

No other such 'storeroom' has been found. All of which serves as a warning that most general statements about Mycenaean culture are tentative in the nature of the case. One is almost reluctant to record the fact that, at present, only at Eleusis, Ceos and Delos have reasonably certain traces been discovered of a 'temple' in the Mycenaean era; or to comment that it is perhaps not accidental that none of these places was a centre of secular power.

Selection 4

The Discovery That the Mycenaeans Spoke Greek

J. Lesley Fitton

The decipherment of the Bronze-Age script known as Linear B in 1952 by Michael Ventris was one of the most important historical discoveries of the twentieth century. Ventris showed that Linear B is an early form of

Greek, which proved once and for all that the Mycenaean mainlanders were not "pre-Greek" inhabitants of the region, as had long been supposed, but actual early Greeks. Instrumental in his work were the so-called "Pylos tablets," a large cache of Linear B–bearing tablets found on the southern mainland in 1939, as explained here by J. Lesley Fitton, curator of the Department of Greek and Roman Antiquities in the British Museum. (In addition to Ventris and Arthur Evans, who excavated the Minoan palace at Knossos, Fitton mentions Greek archaeologist Christos Tsountas, American archaeologist Carl Blegen, and Blegen's colleague, linguist J.B. Haley.)

The debates about relations between Minoan Crete and Mycenaean Greece, and indeed between the Bronze Age and the Classical period, were completely changed in the post-war years by the decipherment of Linear B, and its identification as an early form of Greek.

In retrospect, it seems strange that the possibility of Greek being the language of the Linear B tablets was not more immediately apparent. As early as 1893 Tsountas had suggested that the Bronze Age inhabitants of Mycenae spoke Greek. Blegen and Haley had then established a correspondence between traces of a pre-Greek language and the sites inhabited in the Early Helladic period, and had therefore suggested that the next cultural break after this—at the transition from Early to Middle Helladic—was probably the horizon that saw the arrival of Greek-speakers in what we now know as Greek lands. This was accepted by many scholars . . . who had argued against Evans increasingly firmly in support of the independence of Mycenaean culture. Evans allowed that a Mycenaean 'underclass' may have spoken Greek, but thought the dominant stratum of mainland society was Minoan speaking the Minoan language.

Consideration of the language of the tablets was, however, very much conditioned by the fact that until the discovery of the Pylos tablets in 1939, Linear B had been found only in Crete. Moreover, it had on the island a clear predecessor in Linear A, so that both could reasonably be assumed to have been used to write the Minoan language. Even when the Pylos tablets were uncovered, it was still possible to believe that they were written in Minoan. . . .

Enter Michael Ventris

In 1936 the British School at Athens held an exhibition in Burlington House in London to celebrate its fiftieth anniversary. Sir Arthur Evans arranged a special section to illustrate his discoveries in Crete, and on 16 October gave a lecture entitled 'The Minoan World'. In the audience was a fourteen-year-old boy from Stowe School called Michael Ventris.

Fascinated by Evans' account of the clay tablets from Knossos that no one could read, some of which were included in the exhibition, Ventris decided that he would try to decipher them. He never forgot this early resolve. Though he trained and practised as an architect he spent much spare time in his adult life pursuing the decipherment. He was a talented linguist and cryptographer, and the story had a fairy-tale ending in Ventris' eventual success. In June 1952 he made his famous BBC radio broadcast in which he said, 'During the last few weeks, I have come to the conclusion that the Knossos and Pylos tablets must, after all, be written in Greek—a difficult and archaic Greek, seeing that it is five hundred years older than Homer, and written in a rather abbreviated form, but Greek nevertheless.'

He had been tentative at first, because he himself had not expected this outcome. . . . It was only when he had recognised the possibility of a Greek identification on what one might call cryptographic grounds that he rationalised the possibility in a way essentially still accepted today, pointing out that Linear A might have been used to write the Minoan language, and Linear B adapted from it to write Greek. Linear B was, after all, the script of the mainland palace at Pylos, but was found at Knossos only at a late stage of the palace's history, when Evans had noticed other signs of foreign influence. The idea of foreign—Mycenaean—domination of Knossos in the Late Minoan II period . . . was thus powerfully supported.

Tragedy was to strike with the untimely death of Michael Ventris in a car accident at the age of thirty-four. By then he had a collaborator, John Chadwick, a Cambridge philologist who had written and congratulated him on his decipherment as soon as it had been made public. Their epoch-making *Documents in Mycenaean Greek* was published in 1956, just weeks after Ventris' death.

The decipherment built on earlier work was achieved partly by Arthur Evans himself and partly by the American scholar Alice Kober. It was a source of great frustration to Evans that, having found in Crete the evidence for early writing that he had predicted before he even visited the island, the scripts proved so intractable. . . .

In spite of this, Evans himself did make some progress that would later be seen as useful, not only in the classification of the scripts and the workings of the systems of numbering that they incorporated, but also in his recognition that the signs in Linear A and B were likely to represent syllables and, moreover, that Linear B seemed to represent an inflected language (that is, a language where the nouns have different endings in different cases). He was helped towards these conclusions by the work of the philologist A.E. Cowley, who based them partly on comparisons with the later syllabary of Cyprus, a writing system that was related to Linear B. Evans observed that if the values for the Cypriot syllabary were borrowed and applied on one of his Knossos tablets the word 'po-lo' would appear next to an ideogram of a horse, instantly bringing to mind the Greek word 'polos', meaning 'foal'. Evans pointed this out only to dismiss it as coincidence: he was never to know how prophetic his remark had been.

In articles published between 1943 and 1950 Alice Kober argued that the language of the Linear B tablets was probably different from that of Linear A, and made further progress towards the establishment of plausible case-endings for certain sign groups on the tablets. Her conclusions proved to have been entirely correct, though she worked in the abstract and never allocated phonetic values to the Linear B signs. The amount of progress she could make was, though, limited by the fact that so few tablets were published. This situation was to be immeasurably improved with the appearance in 1951 of the preliminary publication . . . of the Pylos tablets. . . .

Ventris had, from the beginning, circulated to a small group of interested scholars a series of 'Work-Notes' charting the progress of his research and soliciting responses at each stage. The first of these was dated 28 January 1951; it was the twentieth, dated 1 June 1952, which was tentatively entitled 'Are the Knossos and Pylos Tablets Written in Greek?' Much careful and complex thought is represented by these 'Work-Notes', to which no summary can do justice. . . .

The Kinds of Information Revealed

The first formal publication of the decipherment came in 1953, when Ventris and Chadwick published in the *Journal of Hellenic Studies* their article 'Evidence for Greek Dialect in the Mycenaean Archives'. By this stage the decipherment was substantially complete, its results thenceforth usable by other scholars working on other tablets. Some linguistic problems did still remain—in particular, the loose spelling rules of Linear B meant that many alternative readings could be given for certain sign groups. Moreover, the very early stage of the Greek language had unfamiliar features. Some tablets remain incomprehensible to this day. Scepticism about the correctness of the decipherment was, however, largely allayed by the discovery of new tablets from the reopened excavations at Pylos, where Blegen began work again in 1952. Here tablets came to light that worked well according to the rules Ventris and Chadwick proposed, though they had not been discovered at the time the rules were formulated.

The exciting work of interpretation could begin, and the process has been continuous from that time. Although the tablets are simply lists and inventories of goods and personnel controlled by the palaces, careful study can extract from them much information about the Mycenaean world. They throw light, to a greater or lesser degree, on such diverse matters as political geography and the organisation of the Mycenaean kingdoms, social structures, palatial economy, religion and so on. Naturally the information is limited by the sorts of records the tablets represent; it is sad that no literary or other, longer texts are preserved. It is arguable that none such ever existed: the Mycenaean world may have known only limited literacy with writing being used only for this somewhat prosaic record-keeping.

This is the view of John Chadwick, though others have argued that the forms of the Linear B signs seem designed for some more flowing medium than a stick on wet clay and surmise that pens and other writing surfaces must have existed. The existence of signs painted on vases may support this view, but the evidence is otherwise almost entirely lacking. Nonetheless, the decipherment of Linear B unlocked a whole new field of information about the Greek Bronze Age. For this reason it must be ranked with the great excavations of Greek Bronze Age sites as a major and important discovery.

Selection 5

The Age of Heroes and the Trojan War

Michael Grant

As pointed out here by classical scholar Michael Grant, author of numerous books about ancient Greek history and culture, a large number of Greek myths originated in the late Bronze Age. The later classical Greeks remembered this distant time as the "Age of Heroes," in which larger-than-life heroes interacted regularly with gods and monsters. For the Greeks, the most important of these stories concerned the Greek siege of Troy, an event described in Homer's Iliad. *It now appears that at least one and maybe several of the ancient cities found by modern excavators on the site of Troy underwent attack and burning in the late Bronze Age. This shows that, although the exact events of Homer's Trojan War may be exaggerated or even largely fabricated, the war itself is probably based to some degree on the memory of a real siege from that era.*

On the Greek mainland, people speaking a language somewhat resembling Greek, and perhaps originating from the South Russian steppes, began to arrive during the first centuries of the second millennium BC. Intermingling with other racial strains, they developed a culture partly indebted to Crete—and revealing common ground with the Hittites of inland Asia Minor—but partly novel. This reached its climax in the royal fortresses of southern Greece, such as Mycenae, Tiryns and Pylos. The monarchs of those places, whose luxury caused a sensation when the German archaeologist [Heinrich] Schliemann disclosed the royal Mycenaean graves in 1876, possessed powerful new armaments—bronze rapiers, shields and chariots. By 1500 BC the Mycenaeans were influencing Cretan civilization in their turn, and ruled the whole island for about fifty years. Thousands of clay writing tablets found at Cnossus, dating apparently (though this is contested) from *c.* 1400 BC—and others of *c.* 1200, still strangely similar, at the mainland centres—are written in a script known as "Linear B," which has been shown to be an early form of the Greek language.

Mycenaean Cnossus seems to have fallen in *c.* 1400, but during the next two hundred years the cities of the mainland, and especially Mycenae, were at their height as powerful land empires and Mediterranean trading centres. The thirteenth

century was a time of great upheavals throughout the near east; Mycenaean exports to Egypt and the Levant ceased abruptly, and in about 1250 BC, as archaeology confirms, invaders (of whom there were many at this time, in Asia Minor and in Egypt) besieged and burnt the key-city of Troy near the Hellespont (Dardanelles). . . .

Almost all the principal Greek myths are connected with centres of this Mycenaean civilization, which provided many a subject and hero. However mythical their exploits, the names of the *Iliad*'s great warriors are likely enough to be the real names of men who lived in Mycenaean Greece—and fought the Trojans; another "Hector" appears on a Linear B tablet. Moreover, the catalogue of contingents in the *Iliad* seems to go back to an historically true Order of Battle of that period. There may well be some historical truth (though coloured by his own time) in the picture the poet [Homer] gives of the Greek besiegers as a loose confederacy, under their overlord Agamemnon, of proud, recalcitrant, meat-fed chiefs, jealous of their reputations. Possibly, too, the invading army already believed in the Olympian gods as a similar loose confederacy under Zeus—who may conceivably appear with his scales of destiny upon a Mycenaean amphora. At any rate, Homer's knowledge of Mycenaean objects came from a poetic tradition going back to those days. The huge shield of Ajax like a tower, Hector's bronze helmet, the cup of Nestor, the silver-studded swords, and the only reference to writing, are traceable to the Mycenaean age.

A Siege Based on Historical Fact

One of its last and culminating efforts must have been the siege of the horse-rearing, textile-fabricating city of Troy, in its strategic position on the Hellespont. That city, where there had been at least six earlier successive settlements, was already at this epoch, as archaeologists have shown, somewhat beyond its prime ("Troy VIIa"); Homer's tales of its grandeur rather fit the immediately preceding fourteenth century BC ("Troy VI"), in which there had been a great

This image of the poet Homer, based on an old statue, is fanciful. His actual appearance is unknown.

rise in the importance of the town. Excavators have also proved that "Troy VIIa" fell to a violent fire, probably by human agency. There was nothing new about sieges in the ancient world, nor were they new to near eastern storytellers. From the Hittites, for example, who had ruled until the thirteenth century on the Anatolian plateau and display resemblances to the peoples across the Aegean, we have a tolerably preserved account of the siege of Urshu (somewhere in northern Syria) by their army; while the epics of Ugarit, in the same area, tell of a siege of Udum.

"And so," says the geographer Strabo (himself from Asia Minor) in the days of Augustus [late first-century BC], "Homer took the Trojan War, an historical fact, and decked it out with his fanciful stories." According to one convenient definition of terms, this makes his story a legend (that is to say a story based, however remotely, on historical fact), as opposed to a myth which has no basis of fact at all. At any rate the Greeks, who felt their lack of ancient records such as those of Egypt and Asia, took the whole thing as history, and based a great part of their entire cultural tradition upon this acceptance. The heroes and their doings were believed to have been authentic—a supposition which Homer had encouraged by the careful orderliness with which he circumscribes them all within two or three generations. Some of the leading figures, it has been suggested, may really have been personifications of warring tribes, whose varying fortunes during the migrations are reflected in the victories or deaths of this or that hero. Be that as it may, the poem, though its subject is the Wrath of Achilles and not the war as a whole—of which we do not see the end—is made to look like a chronicle.

Since people like having remote ancestors to venerate, the stories were perpetuated and elaborated as each family or city attached a glorious pedigree to itself. Down to Roman times, there were tombs and relics attributed to the heroes to be seen everywhere in Greece, and they were accorded a specific kind of worship of their own. Similar remains are also found in Homer's native country, western Asia Minor. Myths and legends of Greece had been transplanted there when the country was colonized (amid raids and migrations such as those which had earlier given birth to epics) at the end of the first millennium BC; and so we find "tombs" of Achilles, Idomeneus and Calchas on those coasts. The island of Lesbos retained stronger links: for across the gulf of time which separated the Trojan War from the Greek city-states, the royal house and the constitution survived and remained the same. At Cyme in Aeolis, too, there was a king Agamemnon who claimed descent from the Homeric hero.

Selection 6

The Greek Forces Assemble Before Troy

Homer

The so-called "Catalogue of Ships" from Homer's Iliad, *excerpted below, describes the Achaean forces assembled from all over Greece to fight the Trojans. Since Homer was describing events of the Age of Heroes (i.e., the late Bronze Age), we know now that these warriors were Mycenaean Greeks. But were the places listed in the catalogue actual Mycenaean settlements? Most scholars agree with the late expert on the Homeric legends, T.B.L. Webster, who pointed out that the entries on the list follow a set formula: "All that dwelt in Y, Z, etc., them led A, and with him followed* n *ships." This closely resembles the formulae of military lists found on actual Mycenaean tablets. "It is difficult to deny," said Webster, "that the Catalogue of Ships may go back to an actual operation order, which was absorbed into Mycenaean poetry." Moreover, "the muster [of the ships] took place at Aulis [in eastern Greece], where a Mycenaean cemetery has . . . been discovered, and the first town mentioned [in the Catalogue], Hyria, has yielded a Mycenaean stele decorated with ships." (From* Mycenae to Homer, *pp. 99, 122.) Thus, the Catalogue may well describe the main popu-lated regions of Greece in late Mycenaean times; if so, it lends credibility to a large-scale Mycenaean expedition like the one Homer describes.*

*T*he armies massing . . . crowding
    thick-and-fast
    as the swarms of flies seething
    over the shepherds' stalls
in the first spring days when the buckets flood
    with milk—
so many long-haired Achaeans swarmed across
    the plain
to confront the Trojans, fired to smash their lines.

The armies grouping now—as seasoned
    goatherds
split their wide-ranging flocks into packs with
    ease
when herds have mixed together down the
    pasture:
so the captains formed their tight platoons,
detaching right and left, moving up for action—
and there in the midst strode powerful
    Agamemnon,
eyes and head like Zeus who loves the lightning,
great in the girth like Ares, god of battles,
broad through the chest like sea lord Poseidon. . . .

Sing to me now, you Muses who hold the halls of
    Olympus!
You are goddesses, you are everywhere, you

know all things—
all we hear is the distant ring of glory, we know
      nothing—
who were the captains of Achaea? Who were the
      kings?
The mass of troops I could never tally, never
      name,
not even if I had ten tongues and ten mouths,
a tireless voice and the heart inside me bronze,
never unless you Muses of Olympus, daughters of
      Zeus
whose shield is rolling thunder, sing, sing in
      memory
all who gathered under Troy. Now I can only tell
the lords of the ships, the ships in all their
      numbers!

First came the Boeotian units [from Boeotia, the
      region just north of Athens] led by Leitus and
      Peneleos:
Arcesilaus and Prothoënor and Clonius shared
      command
of the armed men who lived in Hyria, rocky Aulis,
Schoenus, Scolus and Eteonus spurred with hills,
Thespia and Graea, the dancing rings of
      Mycalessus . . .
fighters from Coronea, Haliartus deep in
      meadows,
and the men who held Plataea and lived in Glisas,
men who held the rough-hewn gates of Lower
      Thebes. . . .
Fifty ships came freighted with these contingents,
one hundred and twenty young Boeotians
      manning each. . . .

Then Schedius and Epistrophus led the men of
      Phocis [the region west of Boeotia]—
two sons of Iphitus, that great heart, Naubolus'
      son—
the men who held Cyparissus and Pytho's high
      crags,
the hallowed earth of Crisa, Daulis and Panopeus,
men who dwelled round Anemoria, round
      Hyampolis,
men who lived along the Cephisus' glinting
      waters,
men who held Lilaea close to the river's

wellsprings.
Laden with all their ranks came forty long black
      ships
and Phocian captains ranged them column by
      column,
manning stations along the Boeotians' left
      flank. . . .

And the men who held Euboea [the large island
      lying along the mainland's eastern coast],
      Abantes breathing fury,
Chalcis and Eretria, Histiaea covered with
      vineyards,
Cerinthus along the shore and Dion's hilltop
      streets,
the men who held Carystus and men who settled
      Styra.
Elephenor, comrade of Ares, led the whole
      contingent,
Chalcodon's son, a lord of the fierce Abantes. . . .
In Elephenor's command sailed forty long black
      ships.

Next the men who held the strong-built city of
      Athens,
realm of high-hearted Erechtheus. Zeus's
      daughter Athena
tended him once the grain-giving fields had borne
      him,
long ago, and then she settled the king in Athens,
in her own rich shrine, where sons of Athens
      worship him
with bulls and goats as the years wheel round in
      season.
Athenians all, and Peteos' son Menestheus led
      them on,
and no one born on the earth could match that
      man
in arraying teams of horse and shielded fighters—
Nestor his only rival, thanks to Nestor's age.
And in his command sailed fifty long black ships.

Out of Salamis [an island off the coast south-west
      of Athens] Great Telanionian Ajax led twelve
      ships
drawn up where Athenian forces formed their line
      of battle.

Then men of Argos and Tiryns [two cities in the
    northeastern Peloponnesus] with her
    tremendous walls and Hermione and Asine
    commanding the deep wide gulf,
Troezen, Eionae and Epidaurus green with vines
and Achaea's warrior sons who held Aegina and
    Mases—
Diomedes lord of the war cry led their crack
    contingents
flanked by Sthenelus, far-famed Capaneus'
    favorite son.
Third in the vanguard marched Euryalus strong as
    a god,
son of King Mecisteus son of Talaus, but over
    them all,
with cries to marshal men Diomedes led the
    whole force
and his Argives sailed in eighty long black ships.

Next the men who held Mycenae's huge walled
    citadel [north of Argos], Corinth in all her
    wealth and sturdy, strong Cleonae,
men of Orniae, lovely Araethyrea and Sicyon. . . .
They came in a hundred ships and Agamemnon
    led them on,
Atreus' royal son, and marching in his companies
came the most and bravest fighting men by far.
And there in the midst, armed in gleaming
    bronze,
in all his glory, he towered high over all his
    fighters—
he was the greatest warlord, he led by far the
    largest army.

Next those who held Lacedaemon's hollows deep
    with gorges,
Pharis, Sparta and Messe [all in the southern
    Peloponnesus], crowded haunt of the wild
    doves. . . .
Agamemnon's brother, Menelaus lord of the war
    cry
led their sixty ships, armed them apart,
    downshore,
and amidst their ranks he marched, ablaze with
    valor,
priming men for attack. And his own heart blazed
    the most

to avenge the groans and shocks of war they'd
    borne for Helen.

Next the men who lived in Pylos [on the
    southwestern coast of the Peloponnesus] and
    handsome Arene,
Thryon, the Alpheus ford and finely-masoned
    Aepy,
men who lived in Cyparisseis and Amphigenia,
Pteleos, Helos and Dorion. . . .
Nestor the noble old horseman led those troops
in ninety sweeping ships lined up along the shore.

And those who held Arcadia [the region of the
    central Peloponnesus]
under Cyllene's peak,
near Aepytus' ancient tomb where men fight
    hand-to-hand,
men who lived in Pheneos and Orchomenos rife
    with sheep,
Stratia, Rhipe and Enispe whipped by the sudden
    winds,
men who settled Tegea, Mantinea's inviting
    country,
men who held Stymphalus, men who ruled
    Parrhasia—
the son of Ancaeus led them, powerful Agapenor
with sixty ships in all, and aboard each vessel
crowded full Arcadian companies skilled in war.
Agamemnon himself, the lord of men had given
    them
those well-benched ships to plow the wine-dark
    sea,
since works of the sea meant nothing to those
    landsmen. . . .

Next Odysseus led his Cephallenian companies,
gallant-hearted fighters, the island men of Ithaca
    [an island off Greece's western coast],
of Mount Neriton's leafy ridges shimmering in
    the wind,
and men who lived in Crocylia and rugged
    Aegilips,
men who held Zacynthus and men who dwelled
    near Samos
and mainland men who grazed their flocks across
    the channel.

That mastermind like Zeus, Odysseus led those fighters on.
In his command sailed twelve ships, prows flashing crimson.

And Thoas son of Andraemon led Aetolia's units [from Aetolia, the region west of Phocis]. . . .
In Thoas' command sailed forty long black ships.

And the great spearman Idomeneus led his Cretans,
the men who held Cnossos and Gortyn ringed in walls,
Lyctos, Miletus, Lycastus' bright chalk bluffs,
Phaestos and Rhytion, cities a joy to live in—
the men who peopled Crete [the large Aegean island that had earlier been ruled by the Minoans], a hundred cities strong.
The renowned spearman Idomeneus led them all in force
with Meriones who butchered men like the god of war himself.
And in their command sailed eighty long black ships.

And Heracles' son Tlepolemus tall and staunch
led nine ships of the proud Rhodians out of Rhodes [a large island off the south-western coast of Asia Minor],
the men who lived on Rhodes in three island divisions,
Lindos and Ialysus and Camirus' white escarpment,
armies led by the famous spearman Tlepolemus

whom Astyochea bore to Heracles filled with power. . . .

And now, Muse,
sing all those fighting men who lived in Pelasgian Argos,
the big contingents out of Alus and Alope and Trachis,
men of Phthia and Hellas where the women are a wonder,
all the fighters called Achaeans, Hellenes and Myrmidons
ranked in fifty ships, and Achilles was their leader. . . .

Then men who lived in Methone [just south of Pylos] and Thaumacia,
men who held Meliboea and rugged ridged Olizon:
Philoctetes the master archer had led them on
in seven ships with fifty oarsmen aboard each,
superbly skilled with the bow in lethal combat. . . .

And Prothous son of Tenthredon led the Magnesians [from Magnesia, the coastal region of the eastern Greek mainland],
men who lived around the Peneus, up along Mount Pelion
sloped in wind-whipped leaves. Racing Prothous led them on
and in his command sailed forty long black ships.

These, these were the captains of Achaea and the kings.

Selection 7

The End of the Bronze Age

Thomas R. Martin

For much of the twentieth century, historians thought that the violent upheavals attending the collapse of Mycenaean civilization, circa 1200–1100 B.C., were the result of invasions by the Dorians. These more primitive Greek-speakers supposedly swept down from the north and laid waste to the Bronze-Age palaces. As explained here by Holy Cross professor Thomas R. Martin, most scholars now believe that the Dorians took advantage of, rather than caused, the destruction of the Mycenaean kingdoms. Interkingdom warfare, innovations in military tactics, and/or other factors, says Martin, caused upheavals that affected not only the inhabitants of Greece, but also the Hittites in Anatolia (Asia Minor), the Egyptians, and other eastern Mediterranean peoples.

The Bronze Age development of extensive sea travel for trading and raiding had put the cultures of the Aegean and the Near East in closer contact than ever before. The wealth that could be won by traders and entrepreneurs, especially those seeking metals, encouraged contacts between the older civilizations at the eastern end of the Mediterranean and the younger ones to the west. The civilizations of Mesopotamia and Anatolia particularly overshadowed those of Crete and Greece in the size of their cities and the development of extensive written legal codes. Egypt remained an especially favored destination of Mycenaean voyagers throughout the late Bronze Age because they valued the exchange of goods and ideas with the prosperous and complex civilization of that land. By around 1200 B.C., however, the Mediterranean network of firmly established powers and trading partners was coming undone. The New Kingdom in Egypt was falling apart; foreign invaders destroyed the powerful Hittite kingdom in Anatolia; Mesopotamia underwent a period of political turmoil; and the rich palace societies of the Aegean all but disintegrated. The causes of the disruption are poorly documented, but the most likely reasons are internal strife between local centers of power and overexploitation of natural resources in overspecialized and centralized economies. These troubles, whose duration we cannot accurately gauge, apparently caused numerous groups of people to leave their homes, seeking new places to live or at least victims to plunder. These movements of peoples throughout the eastern Mediterranean and the Near East further damaged or even destroyed the political stability, economic prosperity, and international contacts of the civilizations of most of these lands, including that of the Mycenaeans. This period of disruption certainly lasted for decades; in some regions it may have gone on much longer. As a rough generalization, it seems accurate to say that the period from roughly 1200 to 1000 B.C. saw numerous catastrophes for Mediterranean civilizations. The consequences for the Mycenaeans were disastrous.

Excerpted from *Ancient Greece: From Prehistoric to Hellenistic Times*, by Thomas R. Martin. Copyright © 1996 by Yale University. Reprinted by permission of Yale University Press.

Invasions of the Sea Peoples

The most informative records of this period are Egyptian and Hittite. They speak of foreign invasions, some from the sea. According to his own account, the pharaoh Ramesses III around 1182 B.C. defeated a fearsome coalition of seaborne invaders from the north who had fought their way to the edge of Egypt: "All at once the peoples were on the move, dispersed in war. . . . No land could repulse their attacks. . . . They extended their grasp over territories as far as the circuit of the earth, their spirits brimming with confidence and believing: 'Our plans will succeed!'. . . . The ones who came as far as my border, their seed is no more, their heart and their soul are done for forever and ever. . . . They were dragged in, surrounded, and laid prostrate on the shore, killed, and thrown into piles from tail to head" (J.B. Pritchard, *Ancient Near Eastern Texts Relating to the Old Testament*. Princeton: Princeton University Press, 1969, pp. 262–263).

The Egyptian records indicate that many different groups made up these sea peoples, as they are called today. We can surmise that sea peoples originated from Mycenaean Greece, the Aegean islands, Anatolia, Cyprus, and various points in the Near East. They did not constitute a united population in any sense; rather, they should be thought of as independent bands displaced by the various political and economic troubles of their homelands. Some had previously been mercenary soldiers in the armies of once-powerful rulers, whom they eventually turned against in a grab for power and booty. Some came from far away to conduct raids in foreign lands. it may be that one important origin of these catastrophes, which ended the power of Mycenaean civilization, was a relatively sudden reconceptualization of military tactics. That is, previously the preponderance of military might had lain with the chariots carrying archers that the kingdoms of the Bronze Age Mediterranean customarily mustered. These chariot forces had been supplemented by infantrymen, mostly foreign mercenaries. At some point around 1200, the argument goes, these hired foot soldiers realized that they could use their long swords and javelins to defeat the chariot forces in direct battle by swarming in a mass against their vehicle-mounted overlords. Emboldened by this realization of their power and motivated by a lust for booty, the motley bands of mercenaries attacked their erstwhile employers and plundered their wealth. They also conducted raids on other rich targets, which were no longer able to defend themselves with their old tactics dependent on chariots. With no firm organization among themselves, the rebels fatally weakened the civilizations they betrayed and raided but were incapable of or uninterested in putting any new political systems into place to fill the void created by their destruction of the existing ones.

Whether this explanation for the end of the Bronze Age will win widespread assent remains to be seen, if only because one might ask why it took the mercenary infantrymen so long to grasp their advantage over chariots, if such it was, and to put it into play. But one important assumption of this scenario does ring true: what evidence we have for the history of the sea peoples points not to one group spreading destruction across the eastern Mediterranean in a single tidal wave of violence but rather to many disparate bands and conflicts. A chain reaction of attacks and flights in a recurring and expanding cycle put even more bands of raiders on the move.

Some bands of sea peoples were perhaps made up exclusively of men conducting raids, who then expected to return to their homeland. Other groups of warriors and their families may have been looking for a new place to settle, where they could live a more prosperous and secure life than in the disturbed area from which they had voluntarily departed or been driven by other raiders. Any such people in flight could not expect a friendly welcome on foreign shores, and they had to be prepared to fight for new homes. The material damage such marauding bands of raiders would have wreaked would have been made worse by the social disruption their arrival in a new area would also have caused to the societies already in place. However common such migrations may have been—that they were widespread has been both affirmed and denied in modern scholarship–destruction and disruption were ubiquitous in this era. In the end, all this fighting and motion redrew the political map of the Mediterranean, and perhaps its population map as well, although it is unclear how many groups actually resettled permanently at great distances from their original sites in this period. The reasons for all this violent commotion must still be regarded as mysterious in our present state of knowledge, but its dire consequences for Near Eastern and Greek civilization are clear.

The once mighty Hittite kingdom in Anatolia fell about 1200 B.C., when invaders penetrated its borders and its supply lines of raw materials were cut by incessant raids. The capital city, Hattusas, was burned to the ground and never reinhabited, although smaller Neo-Hittite principalities survived for another five hundred years before falling to the armies of the Neo-Assyrian kingdom. The appearance of the sea peoples weakened Egypt's New Kingdom by requiring a great military effort to repel them and by ruining Egypt's international trade in the Mediterranean. Struggles for power between the pharaoh and the priests undermined the centralized authority of the monarchy as well, and by the middle of the eleventh century B.C., Egypt had shrunk to its old territorial core along the banks of the Nile. Egypt's credit was ruined along with its international stature. When an eleventh-century Theban temple official named Wen-Amon traveled to Byblos in Phoenicia to buy cedar for a ceremonial boat, the city's ruler insultingly demanded cash in advance. The Egyptian monarchy continued for centuries after the New Kingdom, but internal struggles for power between pharaohs and priests, combined with frequent attacks from abroad, prevented the reestablishment of centralized authority. Egypt never again assumed the role of an active and aggressive international power that it had enjoyed during much of the Old and New Kingdoms.

The calamities of this time also affected the copper-rich island of Cyprus and the flourishing cities along the eastern coast of the Mediterranean. The Greeks later called these coastal peoples the Phoenicians, apparently from the much sought after reddish-purple dye that they extracted from shellfish. The inhabitants of cities such as Ugarit on the coast of Syria thrived on international maritime commerce and enjoyed a lively polyglot culture. A catastrophic attack of the sea peoples overwhelmed Ugarit. . . .

Mycenaean Civilization Disintegrates

The Mycenaeans in mainland Greece had reached their pinnacle of prosperity after 1400 B.C., the period during which the enormous domed tomb at Mycenae called the Treasury of Atreus was constructed. Its elaborately decorated façade and soaring roof testify to the confidence of Mycenae's warrior princes. The last phase of the extensive palace at Pylos on the west coast of the Peloponnese also dates to this

The Lion Gate at Mycenae, pictured here, leads to the ruins of a once imposing stone citadel and palace.

time. It was outfitted with everything that wealthy people of the Greek Bronze Age required for comfortable living, including elaborate and colorful wall paintings, storerooms crammed with food, and even a royal bathroom fitted with a built-in tub and intricate plumbing.

Their wealth failed to protect the Mycenaeans from the spreading violence of the late Bronze Age. Ominous signs of the dangers of this period occur in Linear B tablets from Pylos, which record the disposition of troops to guard this unwalled site around 1200 B.C. The palace inhabitants of eastern Greece, such as those at Mycenae and nearby Tiryns, now constructed such massive stone walls for defense that later Greeks thought they must have been built by giants. These fortifications could have served to protect these palaces near the coast against raiders from the sea, who may have been either seafaring Greeks or outsiders. The wall surrounding the palace at Gla in central Greece, however, a settlement located far enough from the coast that foreign pirates presented no threat, confirms that above all the Mycenaeans had to defend themselves against other Mycenaeans or rebellious mercenaries. Never united in one state, the fractious "princes" of Mycenaean Greece by the late thirteenth century B.C. were fighting each other at least as much as they did foreigners. On Crete, inhabitants at the eastern end of the island constructed small, remote settlements in the mountains to serve as refuges from the violence of the era.

Internal conflict among the rulers of Mycenaean Greece, not foreign invasion, offers the most plausible explanation of the destruction of the palaces of the mainland in the period after about 1200 B.C. The destructive consequences of this conflict were probably augmented by major earthquakes in this seismically active region. Near-constant warfare placed great stress on the elaborate economic balance of the redistributive economies of the palaces and hindered recovery from earthquake damage. The eventual failure of the palace economies had a devastating effect on the large part of the Mycenaean population that was now dependent on this system for its subsistence. Peasant farmers, who knew how to grow their own food, could support themselves even when the redistribution of goods and foodstuffs broke down, but the palaces fell into ruins. Warriors left unattached to their old rulers by the fall of the palaces set off to find new places to live or at least plunder, forming roving bands of the kind remembered by the Egyptians as sea peoples. The later Greeks remembered an invasion of Dorians (speakers of the form of Greek characteristic of the northwest mainland) as the reason for the disaster that befell Bronze Age Greece, but the Dorians who did move into southern Greece most likely came in groups too small to cause such damage by themselves. Indeed, small-scale movements of people, not grand invasions, characterized this era, as bands of warriors with no prospects at home emigrated from lands all around the eastern Mediterranean to become pirates for themselves or mercenaries for foreign potentates.

The damage done by the dissolution of the redistributive economies of Mycenaean Greece after 1200 B.C. took centuries to repair fully. Only Athens seems to have escaped wholesale disaster. In fact, the Athenians of the fifth century B.C. prided themselves on their unique status among the peoples of Classical Greece: "sprung from the soil" of their homeland, as they called themselves, they had not been forced to emigrate in the turmoil that engulfed the rest of Greece in the twelfth and eleventh centuries B.C. The nature of the Athenians' boast gives some indication of the sorry fate of many other Greeks in the period c. 1200–1000 B.C. Uprooted from their homes, they wandered abroad in search of new territory to settle. The Ionian Greeks, who in later times inhabited the central coast of western Anatolia, dated their emigration from the mainland to the end of this period. Luxuries of Mycenaean civilization like fine jewelry, knives inlaid with gold, and built-in bathtubs disappeared. To an outside observer, Greek society at the end of the Mycenaean Age might have seemed destined for irreversible economic and social decline, even oblivion. As it happened, however, great changes were in the making that would create the civilization we today think of as Classical Greece.

Greek History– The Dark Age and the Archaic Age

Chapter 3

Introduction

Historians date Greece's so-called Dark Age variously, placing its beginning as early as ca. 1150 B.C. or as late as ca. 1050, and its end from ca. 800 to ca. 750. The Archaic Age is usually dated from ca. 800 or ca. 750 B.C. to ca. 500 or, occasionally, to 490 or 479 B.C., the years marking the beginning and end of the Greco-Persian Wars, respectively. (Historians and archaeologists frequently make reference to the Geometric Period, lasting from ca. 900 to ca. 700 B.C.; however, the term *Geometric* mainly describes styles of art and is based on types of pottery, which developed markedly new shapes and decorative styles in the period).

The Dark Age is so labeled partly because material evidence for the period is scarce and therefore researchers know very little for certain about it. It also appears to have been, for the most part, characterized by the loss of literacy, major decreases in population (for at least the first century or so), widespread poverty, and an overall decline in both the standard of living and cultural standards. The main causal event for this period of recession was the collapse, between ca. 1200 and ca. 1100 B.C., of the Bronze Age Mycenaean political and administrative apparatus (which had long maintained record-keeping, collective agriculture, and architectural and artistic skills). "It seems clear," writes University of Missouri scholar William R. Biers in his work *The Archaeology of Greece*, "that the mainland palaces represented the heart of the Mycenaean system, and when that system ceased to exist, society changed. When the palaces fell, their bureaucracy disappeared, and with them the need for and eventually the knowledge of writing. The same thing happened to large-scale architecture and representational art."

Nevertheless, Greece was neither primitive nor stagnant during the Dark Age. As early as the mid-to-late eleventh century B.C., new ideas and skills were filtering in from the outside. The most obvious example is the introduction of iron-smelting (from the Near East, where it had long been known; probably via Cyprus, the large island lying south of Asia Minor), which spread across Greece between ca. 1050 and ca. 950. This was a major advance, since tools and weapons made of iron are tougher and keep their edges better than those made of bronze.

The early Dark Age was also a time of large population movements. The reasons for these migrations are not completely clear, but many mainland Greeks appear to have been displaced by other migrants who were *entering* Greece, including the tribal Dorians from the Balkan region south of the Danube River. Most of those who were displaced crossed the Aegean and settled on the coasts of western Asia Minor, which later came to be called Ionia. Other mainlanders may have migrated in search of better farmland and other opportunities for a fresh start.

Social and political life during the Dark Age was centered on individual villages (as opposed to the city-palace centers of Mycenaean times). The local leader was the *basileus,* about which Sarah Pomeroy and her colleagues write in *Ancient Greece:*

> The Greek word *basileus* is usually translated as "king" wherever it appears in literature, including [Homer's] *Iliad* and *Odyssey.* It would be misleading, however, to call the Dark Age leaders "kings," a title that conjures up in the modern mind visions of monarchs with autocratic powers. A more appropriate name for the Dark Age *basileus* is the . . . term "chief," which suggests a man with far less

power than a king. The *basileus,* nevertheless, was a man of great stature and importance in the community. . . . The construction and renovations of the chieftains' homes required the time and labor of a substantial number of persons, unlike the ordinary houses, which could be built by the occupants themselves. The chiefs' houses may also have had some communal functions.

The political or governing institutions for villages and groups of villages described in Homer's epic poems, which scholars believe roughly reflect those that existed in the late Dark Age, were fairly simple. A group of local chiefs, headed by an overall chief, met in a council (*boule*) to decide policy for the whole community or people (*demos*). To achieve a consensus in the community, the chiefs presented their ideas and decisions to an assembly of the fighting men, who gave their approval. The overall chief probably also led public sacrifices to the gods and conducted "diplomatic" relations with chiefs from neighboring regions. As portrayed in Homer's works, society was male-dominated and generally characterized by a competitive spirit, the desire to be recognized as "best" (*aristos*) and thereby to acquire honor and respect (*time*). As would prevail in later ages in Greece, women had no political voice and remained under the strict control of their fathers, husbands, and other male relatives.

Eventually, Greece's population began to increase once again. During the late Dark Age and early Archaic Age, this helped to spur important agricultural developments, including more intensive cultivation of olives and vines and a corresponding reduction in the prevalence of pastoralism (the raising and herding of livestock), which had been the main means of food production in Mycenaean times and the early Dark Age. These agricultural changes promoted the spread of small independent farmers, who became the backbone of the citizenry and military militias of the emerging city-states.

The development of the city-state (which the Greeks called the polis; plural, poleis) was one of several important developments and trends of the Archaic Age, in which Greece rapidly recovered from its long recession. Once characterized as a mere prelude to the "glorious" Classic Age, the Archaic Age is now recognized as the crucial formative period of the political and cultural institutions that would prove so productive in the fifth and fourth centuries B.C. In addition to the rise of poleis, which saw themselves as tiny separate nations, Archaic times witnessed: a long burst of overseas colonization, which established Greek settlements along the shores of the Mediterranean and Black Seas and brought the Greeks into contact with new peoples (including the Etruscans of north-central Italy, who themselves subsequently exerted a profound influence over the small emerging state of Rome); vastly increased trade; the adoption of a new alphabet, the rediscovery of writing, and the emergence of literature; the expression of new, more rational (what might be termed scientific) views about the universe; the development of monumental architecture, especially in religious temples (at first of wood, but by the end of the age of stone); a growth in panhellenism, the concept that all Greeks were culturally united (if not politically so), exemplified by shrines, oracles, and athletic games attended by all Greeks (including the shrine and oracle at Delphi, in central Greece, which dispensed divine prophecies, and the Olympic Games, initiated, according to tradition, in 776 B.C.); the development of a new mode of warfare built around heavily armored infantry soldiers (hoplites) who assembled to form a rigid and formidable battlefield formation (the phalanx); and widespread political experimentation, in which the Greek states tried various forms of oligarchy (rule by a council of the "best" men) and tyranny (rule by a single "strongman"), and increasingly instituted law codes and social reforms (most notably in Athens) that shifted more power to the common people and thereby laid the foundations for democracy.

As for the sources available to historians for the Archaic Age, the main surviving literature consists of the epic poems of Homer, who probably lived in the early eighth century B.C., and the works (*Theogony* and *Works and Days*) of the Boeotian poet Hesiod, who likely flourished ca. 700 B.C. The only other written evidence that has survived from the period are assorted pieces of lyric poetry (describing various aspects of personal and daily life) and fragments of a few philosophical treatises. Literary works by writers from later periods provide some information, but are less reliable because they incorporate a good deal of fable and legend. The rest of the evidence consists of inscriptions carved in stone, coins (first minted in late Archaic times), and the remains of buildings, tombs and graves, statues, pottery, jewelry, weapons, and other artifacts.

Selection 1

Independent Farmers Transform the Land and Community

Victor D. Hanson

The reasons for the rise of small independent farmers in Greece (the first such in the Western world) are summarized here by Victor D. Hanson, a professor of Greek at California State University, Fresno. In time, he says, these individuals would become the Greek community's backbone of citizen-soldiers. Drawing on the writings of the fifth-century B.C. Greek historian Thucydides and other sources, Hanson traces a series of crucial developments that occurred after the collective form of agriculture practiced by the Mycenaeans disappeared in the Dark Age. These included a significant rise in population (creating the need for a more efficient food-production system), an increase in the use of marginal lands, and more intensive cultivation of olives and vines, thereby reducing the importance of pastoralism (the raising and herding of livestock).

Reprinted with permission from The Free Press, a division of Simon & Schuster, from *The Other Greeks: The Family Farm and the Agrarian Roots of Western Civilization*, by Victor D. Hanson. Copyright © 1995 by Victor Davis Hanson.

*T*he breakdown of the Mycenean agricultural hierarchy and the indifference to farming shown by succeeding clans in the Dark Ages created an environment that might allow for family-owned and independent small farms. However, another catalyst was needed to ensure the spread of revolutionary privately held, intensively worked farms. A critical factor was the slow but steady rise in population in Greece at the end of the Dark Ages. It began in the early eighth century B.C., when demographic increases at certain brief periods may have approached two to three percent per annum.

This development was not always a year-by-year steady population increase, but more likely cyclical: a few years of dramatic spurts in fertility, marked by decades of retrenchment, always varying from one Greek-speaking locale to another. Nevertheless, the overall picture in Greece from (say) the ninth century to the end of the eighth is clear enough: a far more densely populated Greece, and more important, a fairly consistent pattern of varying but sustained population increase throughout the life of the later *polis*. . . .

But the critical question inevitably remains *why* population in Greece increased at all at this time, even if sporadically and cyclically at first. Did greater economic opportunity afforded by improved agricultural practices lead to bigger families? Or did *preexisting* trends for greater fertility *require* agricultural transformation?

In the case of Greece, like many other non-industrial societies, population growth may have come first: it often initiates, drives, and maintains agricultural intensification. Growing numbers of people at the end of the Dark Ages simply needed to eat, and they found existing methods of food production completely inadequate. This demographic pressure forced radical changes in the way the Greeks farmed and had previously organized themselves in the countryside. After centuries of strict agronomic control, followed by the other extreme of relative agrarian neglect, agriculture in Greece was finally becoming the property of numerous individual and autonomous families.

Two Sorts of Colonization

But *why* did the number of people in Greece begin to multiply during the latter Dark Ages, nearly four centuries after the fall of the palace economies? If greater fertility first forced agricultural change, what initially forced greater fertility? Some have recently suggested that Dark Age demography must be studied in relationship to "age-class" systems, or the regulations the elite clans of the Dark Ages used to discourage early marriage and procreation. . . . Before having children, men first sought to accumulate a military reputation, wealth, and prestige in nonagricultural spheres. Marriage occurred rela-

tively late. Women delayed childbearing. Thus family size was small. Such an age-class culture, inherently part of a warrior society, unnecessarily prolonged a dramatic rebound from the chaos and collapse of the Mycenean centers.

At the end of the Dark Ages, the gradual modification and erosion of such an intrinsically regimented (and hence fragile) "system" may have led to social experimentation. Greeks no longer waited for the appropriate and agreed-on moment to marry, to raise and to limit families. Instead they sought power and influence through other mechanisms (the *size* of their own households, the ability to raise private raiding parties, the chance to travel)—all activities outside the traditional purview of local strongmen. Fertility was seen as socially advantageous, not a drawback. Military regimentation gave way to other pursuits like agriculture. Land in Greece usually used for stock or extensive agricultural practices was unable to support growing populations, threatening not only the system of pastoralism, but the military hierarchy that sponsored inefficient land use.

Population pressure can be handled in a variety of ways. In the absence of an improvement in food supply or the widespread use of contraceptive practices, famine and disease can simply eliminate the population surplus. People then die, usually the very old and young. Yet surprisingly we hear of little fatal hunger on any mass scale in early Greece. Nor was there much wholesale conquest of foreign territory or mass importation of foodstuffs from abroad.

Thucydides and other sources remind us that another option was colonization, the mass migration of landless Greek peoples to virgin territories, usually across the Mediterranean and Aegean. Although these large scale emigrations indicate population problems at home, not *all* colonization was undertaken by the very poor in search of new farmland, the destitute who chafed at existing land tenure practices. At least some settlers were relatively prosperous traders and merchants, or social opportunists and outcasts who desired a completely new economic and political environment. . . .

Population pressure can also trigger a different and potentially more volatile sort of colonization. I do not refer to the conquest and annexation of neighboring territory in mass . . . but rather a more gradual *internal* colonization of land previously unwanted and underdeveloped. This incorporation of new farmland was an earlier response to demographic pressure, one far more serious to the existing social order, since changes in economic and social practice took place at home and thus were bound to have immediate local repercussions. The seeds of local Greek agrarian transformation surely *antedated* overseas colonization.

Often in the eighth century many Greeks must have also turned to alternative types of land use in response to the growing numbers of farm laborers who were ill-served by past methods of utilization. As many more Greeks sought to feed their own households, the first option would have been to look for vacant lands—either communal or unowned—in their immediate vicinity. These plots were usually on somewhat "marginal" lands. Given the nature of the Greek terrain and low density of the Hellenic population, new farmlands were thus to be found almost everywhere.

In the old Dark-Age social and economic sense, that meant less accessibility to manorial centers, and less fertility for native grazing, less suitability for easy ploughing of cereals, but not unsuitability for crops such as vines and trees. "Marginal" land (*eschatia*) is ubiquitous in many parts of Greece, an ideal, relatively safe springboard for anyone brave enough to embark on a new sort of agricultural strategy of outright private ownership and intensive working of permanent crops. Once private ownership by adventurous farmers was the rule, each Greek rural household sought its own parcel, to improve and pass on. Previously unused and unowned land was thus developed by men on their own, marking the real beginning in the West of individual property holding on any wide scale.

But this expansive process of Greek intensive agriculture did not cease at the mere incorporation of newer farm ground and novel concepts of land tenure. It assumed other equally dynamic forms as well. The other option of internal colonization, besides the cultivation and improvement of unfarmed ground, was simply to "colonize" someone else's land, to apply new strategies of intensive agriculture to previously farmed but *underused* land. That was, in practical terms, to engage in some sort of lease agreement with a wealthier Greek landowner, who initially had neither the desire nor expertise to farm the ground productively himself, but saw advantages in drawing off surpluses from the successful work of others. Whether Greek farmers (*geôrgoi*) first sought out marginal land, and then in the wake of success turned their attention to prized baronial estates, is unknown, but it seems a likely course of progression. For those Greeks who lacked capital or were unable to find underdeveloped land, and so entered into *unfavorable* rental agreements or other forms of early repressive tenancy, agricultural success was questionable from the start and was left unresolved for generations.

Slow and sporadic, rather than uniformly gradual, rises in Greek population then created pressures on Dark-Age society and revealed the inefficiency of traditional land use. Because there was not a sophisticated central political organization, a majority of *geôrgoi* gradually drifted away from past protocols, becoming relatively "liberated." They could now see that pastoralism was *not* a solution to the problem of feeding additional mouths. Crops alone, not animals, could feed the greater population. Because the aristocratic landholders may have been uninterested at first in agricultural innovation, the young, disaffected elite—and perhaps later the more ambitious on the lower end of the Dark-Age social scale—were prone to deviate from the traditional social patterns and military castes. One result was encroachment on marginal ground without fear of reprisal. For many aspiring farmers this must have been a preferable alternative to moving in mass across the sea.

Population increase, however, alone did not end the Dark Ages. The neglect of farming by the old elite and the presence of unused open ground cannot entirely explain the Greek agrarian renaissance of the eighth century and later. There was no guarantee that the population might not regress into past cycles of decline, as local food production failed to match population growth. Thus one or more of the following must also have taken place: (1) a quiet revolution in agricultural technique and rural social organization in general, (2) an incorporation of new technologies and crop species, (3) an intensification of labor, or (4)—perhaps most likely—*all three* factors, which could coalesce to increase food production, and hence provide the prosperity needed to ensure that a new economic class, the independent small farmer, would be a permanent, rather than transitory, fixture on the Greek landscape.

A Lasting Alternative to Pastoralism

In characteristically Greek fashion, there was a critical adoption of foreign knowledge in a uniquely ingenious manner. Improved species of olives, grains, and cereals, along with completely novel crops, were borrowed from Asia Minor which had a rich and old tradition of intensive viticulture and arboriculture. In the different environment of Greece, these species were farmed in new, more productive ways. Permanent crops and diverse types of cereals can increase production remarkably under intensive cultivation—labor, both free and increasingly slave, at this juncture must have been plentiful for the first time in Greek history—and they could be uniquely integrated to fit available soil and manpower conditions.

Olives and vines are fertile even on rocky hillsides, where cultivation with the plough is impossible or difficult. Neither requires the moisture or fertility of bottom land to produce adequate crops; the richer ground, like the more accessible and better terraced parcels, can be reserved for barley and wheat. The triad—cereals, vines, olives—intensively farmed can provide an entire diet and produce storable crops for times of scarcity. At the beginning of the eighth century the Greeks discovered how to cultivate the domesticated olive on a wide scale, along with other trees and vines, and mastered the techniques of easy propagation such as grafting. That knowledge allowed for a lasting alternative to pastoralism.

Any farmer who plants trees and vines, unlike the pastoralist or even the grain grower, invests his labor and capital in a particular locale *for the duration of his life*. In this interdependent relationship, the cultivator's presence and commitment to a stationary residence ensure that the young orchard and vineyard will be cared for and become permanent fixtures on the landscape. People who choose this form of agriculture have confidence that they can and will stay put, that they can and will keep the countryside populated, prosperous, and peaceful. They are not just a different sort of farmer, but a different sort of person as well. The Greeks understood this. No wonder Thucydides associated the pre-*polis* Greeks' inability to settle in one place with their reluctance to plant trees and vines, all characteristic of unsettled times when there were no "large cities or any other form of greatness." No wonder later during the *polis*, Greek cultural historians themselves envisioned a clear sequence of their early Hellenic state development: primitive and random food-gathering, followed by herding, and culminating in a dynamic agriculture of "the plough, the grafting of trees, and the extension of land under cultivation."

At the beginning of the *polis*-period [ca. 750–650 B.C.] increasing tension grew between livestock men and the less affluent. Sheep and goats gradually lost pasturage to cultivated land. More and more people homesteaded small plots. Intensive agriculture also meant a loss of political control and social prestige for the old Dark-Age clique and a greater dispersion of wealth among the populace. The process enriched the rural culture of Greece as a whole.

The end of the Greek Dark Ages was a rare time in history. A period of fluidity in, and opportunity for, land ownership, it was an era where competence and work, not mere inherited wealth and birth, might now become criteria for economic success. . . .

In a military sense . . . there is little doubt that the superiority of Greek citizen infantry, the "planters of trees," in wars both foreign and domestic derived from the resoluteness, conservatism, independence, and physical courage prerequisite to the intensive farming of trees and vines, the need to protect and to honor the *visible* inherited vineyards and orchards of past generations. Aristotle saw a vast difference between such men and hired mercenaries: "Professional infantry turn out to be cowards whenever the danger proves too much and whenever they are at a disadvantage in their numbers and equipment. They are, then, the first to run away, while the militias of the *polis* stand their ground and die. . . ." (*Nichomachean Ethics*).

A variety of conditions—increasing population, lackadaisical political authority, available land and labor (both servile and free), new crops and rural strategies—were operating in Greece during the latter centuries of the Dark Ages. They were all conducive to fundamental changes in agriculture. An increase in population created pressures on land use. This peopling of Greece brought into question the wisdom of livestock raising on a wide scale. The challenged aristocratic elite who controlled the "economy" at first would have been unenthusiastic about experimenting in intensive agriculture. Wealthy barons had a long cultural tradition that stressed cattle, pigs, sheep, goats, and horses, and so they would have exhibited disdain (but also fear) for the toiler in the fields. Much land with productive potential was simply underused or even unowned in Greece, the population heretofore seeing little need or value in developing it agriculturally.

Now began the *slow* spread of improved and novel domesticated plant species that could be grown in a variety of climates, bringing in an entirely new approach to farming, whose unique properties could ensure the farmer independence and survival. Once the new agrarianism caught on, the control of farming was gradually dispersed into too many hands ever to revert back to either the agricultural fragility of palace bureaucracies or the subsequent neglect of Dark-Age manorial clans.

In that sense, all of Greek history in the *polis* period follows from the successful creation of a new agriculture and the efforts of the many to protect a novel agrarian way of life. The rural system of the *geôrgoi* created the surplus, capital, and leisure that lay behind the entire Greek cultural renaissance. It was an agrarianism that was highly flexible and decentralized economically, socially egalitarian, and politically keen to avoid the accumulation of power by a nonagricultural elite. No surprise that the later *polis* Greeks envisioned the rise of agrarianism—which had created their city-state—primarily in moral terms. . . .

The story of the farmers' slow emergence from the centuries of the Dark Ages . . . can provide a glimpse of how men set themselves against nature in a heroic effort to create an entirely new society in their own image.

Selection 2

A New Alphabet and the Rediscovery of Writing

Anthony M. Snodgrass

Most modern scholars agree that the art of writing (Mycenaean Linear B, probably understood and used mainly by palace scribes and/or other elite groups) disappeared in the opening years of the Dark Age. This essay, by Anthony Snodgrass, an archaeologist and noted scholar of Greece's Dark and Archaic Ages, describes how the Greeks acquired a new alphabet sometime in the eighth century B.C. As he points out, this single development paved the way for dozens of other cultural advances in the succeeding few centuries.

*O*f all the achievements of this time, there is perhaps none that impresses the Western world today so much as the recovery of the art of writing—particularly as it took the form of the adoption of an alphabet from which our own is still derived. It is the material evidence on which we mainly base not only our attempts to date this achievement but also our belief in a preceding age of illiteracy. There may still be a need today to justify this latter belief: that a formerly literate society should lose the gift of writing for several hundred years is a notion so foreign to our experience that it is not easily accepted. There is in this case another cat-

egory of evidence which may help: that of the Homeric poems, whose method of composition has been widely accepted . . . as being of a kind peculiar to illiterate societies. But if this conclusion is like almost every other one reached about Homer, then it is unlikely to stand unchallenged for ever. We should thus be unwise to depend entirely on the epic [i.e., Homer's epic poetry] as decisive proof of the disappearance of literacy in Greece.

Linear B Versus Alphabetic Greek

Let us revert to the physical evidence. What it tells us is that the syllabic script known as Linear B was in use (but apparently restricted use) down to the destruction of most of the Mycenaean palaces in the years round 1200 BC; that a fully-formed alphabetic system, modelled on the Phoenician, was adopted no later than about 750 BC; but that the intervening years offer virtually no evidence for the knowledge of either system. The difference between the two forms of writing, and the absence of any influence of the older one on the newer, are so absolute and complete that we should in any event be surprised to find that they were in consecutive use, without any intervening break. After all, even when making the change from a syllabic script, where each single sign is used for an open syllable of the form *-ba-*, to an alphabetic script with a separate letter for *b* and *a*, there are opportunities for assimilation: Linear B, for example, had to have signs for the simple vowels, mainly for use in the initial position. The Greek alphabet entirely ignores these pre-existing symbols, and derives its vowels from Phoenician signs, such as glottal stops, aspirates and the consonantal *y*, for which Greek had no use in their received form.

Then there are the differences in the range of literacy under the two systems. Linear B was essentially an administrative script, used by palace scribes for official documentation, and occasionally by craftsmen for what appears to be communication within a very restricted group: thus one- to three-word painted inscriptions (mostly apparently place-names) were sometimes applied to a pot before it was fired; but these do not seem to have been of general circulation. But graffiti hardly appear, and public inscriptions not at all. We infer that very few people could read the script, and perhaps fewer still write it. If it was the almost exclusive preserve of the palace bureaucracies, as seems likely, then their disappearance will have removed its *raison d'être* [reason for existing]. The early alphabetic inscriptions show a sharp contrast. Pottery is again favoured as a writing-surface, but now most of the inscriptions are not painted by the makers, but scratched later by the users. They refer to private matters—ownership, entertainment, personal comments; a striking proportion of them are in verse. Some time later, makers' signatures also begin to appear on pottery; the actual learning process is illustrated by a few abecedaria [alphabets]; and permanent inscriptions on stone follow. Already before 700 BC alphabetic inscriptions are known from a dozen sites—more than have produced Linear B inscriptions from the whole of its life of 200 years or more. It is clear that the conditions of literacy have changed, and that the simplicity of the alphabet was making it accessible to almost everyone. A completely fresh start had been necessary; and there is no sign, now or later, that anyone in Greece had more than a faint notion that an earlier script had even existed. Homer, too, was able to present his heroes as living in an essentially illiterate society and later Greeks were not disturbed by this. True to form, they nevertheless credited the Heroic Age, in the person of Kadmos [or Cadmus, the legendary founder of the city of Thebes], with having brought writing to Greece from Phoenicia; but the legend almost certainly refers to the alphabetic script, not the syllabic. It thus reflects a geographical truth, but perpetrates a major anachronism. Those few scholars who believe in continuity of literacy through the dark age would probably prefer to bridge the gap by extending the use of the alphabet backwards in time, rather than that of Linear B forwards; but even they must concede that it was not the script of the Mycenaean age. When one adds to these arguments the weight of negative evidence, the case seems well established: for 450 years, not so much as a letter of Greek alphabetic writing is known. About the only apparent survival of Linear B in Greece proper is on the stones of a building, probably of eleventh century date, at Iolkos in Thessaly, where a single symbol which resembles a sign of that script is used as a mason's mark; but such practices have a history in Greece which goes back well before the first writing-system was known there, and in no sense imply real literacy.

For Commerce or Epic Poetry?

Present evidence thus suggests that the alphabet was introduced to an illiterate Greek world, probably not very long before 750 BC. The common features between the various local Greek alphabets—all of which from the very start add four or more vowels, with other letters, to the vowel-less Phoenician alphabet—further suggests that the innovation was originally diffused through a single Greek source. There is room for some disagreement as to the geographical setting of this event, between the Levant [the region of the Near East bordering the Mediterranean Sea] on one hand and some part of the Aegean on the other; and as to the identity of the first Greeks involved—Euboians perhaps or Athenians, with Cretans a less likely possibility. But nevertheless the transmission of the alphabet to Greece is relatively well understood, in comparison with another and ultimately more significant problem: the motives for its adoption. The evidence here is perplexing. Since the alphabet unquestionably came from Phoenicia, and since Greek relations with the Phoenicians appear to have been largely commercial in nature, it is only natural to infer that the *initial* impetus for the adoption of this writing-system was in some way connected with commerce: that Greek traders, for example, saw the commercial advantages which their Phoenician counterparts were deriving from recording and even transacting business in writing. This may be true of the very first steps in the process; and the likelihood increases if (according to the currently prevailing view) these steps were taken somewhere on the Levantine coast, since the Greek settlers known to us at this time were largely traders. . . . On the other hand, it must be observed, first, that none of the early surviving Greek inscriptions has anything to do with commerce, and second, that the commercial explanation does not satisfactorily account for the distinctive feature of the Greek alphabet—one which in the view of some purists makes it the first *truly* alphabetic system: the addition of the vowels. The Phoenicians and other Semitic peoples had long conducted their activities, including commercial and religious transactions, with a consonantal script, and continued to do so. . . . What gave the Greeks the urge to develop, before the date of the earliest surviving alphabetic inscription, a complete set of six vowel-signs (including both a long and a short *e*) and to retain and even add to this range in later years?

The answer should lie in some peculiar feature of Greek society at this time. . . . If one looks around for a unique feature . . . there is no doubt as to which is the first to offer itself: the epic. To many, the suggestion that the peculiar features of the Greek alphabet were designed as a notation for epic poetry appeared far-fetched, when it was first voiced . . . in 1952. The best arguments in its favour might seem to be the frequency of verse-inscriptions in early Greek writing, and the fact that vowel-notation does indeed serve the purpose of poetic communication—as will be apparent to anyone who compares a critical edition or translation of the *Iliad* with one of, say, the Psalms of David. It seems to me just possible that this was the decisive factor in the Greek modification of the alphabet, but only after commercial motives had inspired the original desire to use alphabetic writing at all. If so, it offers an illustration of the central place in eighth-century life that epic poetry had now assumed and, indirectly, of the pervasive concern with the Heroic Age. This explanation of the rise of the Greek alphabet (and for that matter most others) presupposes a vastly more extensive use of writing, both in length of texts and in range of writing-material, than is reflected by our tiny sample of early incised sherds and stones. But since a literary purpose was best served by writing on perishable materials, especially papyrus, the theory seems more plausible than, for instance, those which would posit an extensive use of stone for public inscriptions, none of which happens to have survived.

What is much clearer is that the alphabet, once adopted, proved an enormous asset to the progress of Greek society. By making the art of reading and writing widely available, it enabled organizations to communicate beyond the close circle of those actually operating them, and individuals beyond their immediate acquaintances. Governments could write down procedures and law-codes, cult-associations could record forms of rituals and names of officials, sanctuaries could list their property and record information of wider interest, as the priests of Apollo may have done at Delphi. At the same time, merchants could record payments, craftsmen sign their products, property-owners publish their claims against potential usurpers, poets set down their compositions. But permanency did not necessarily mean immutability: on the contrary, once a thing is set down in writing, it becomes inherently more open to analysis and criticism than when it is secreted in the memories of a specialist group. In this way alphabetic writing, despite the fact that in our view it was adopted with no such intention, must have made a considerable contribution to the speed of development in the institutions of Archaic Greece.

It provides a final illustration of the way in which a discovery in one field can precipitate advances in quite another.

Selection 3

The Rise of City-States

Chester G. Starr

The development of the city-state, which the Greeks called the polis (plural, poleis), was one of the fundamental and most far-reaching developments of the Archaic Age. The following informative discussion of the advent, qualities, and problems of the polis, including new military developments and early warfare among the poleis, is by the late Chester G. Starr, former professor of history at the University of Michigan.

The century following 750 B.C. was one of the most fruitful in all Greek history. . . . Politically, the period witnessed the rise of the Greek city-state, a form of government which expressed a noble set of political values still fundamental today. On the one hand the political and military strengths inherent in this organization permitted the Greeks to expand abroad widely; but on the other hand local patriotism and mutual suspicion divided the homeland into a host of tiny, absolutely sovereign units. While these states were bound together by a common culture and could occasionally cooperate against an outside enemy, their continuing rivalry eventually was to destroy Greek freedom. . . .

Much later, in the fourth century B.C., the great political theorists Plato and Aristotle discussed the nature of an ideal political unit. Both of them took it for granted that all truly civilized men would prefer the *polis* or city-state. Aristotle, indeed, went so far as to assert, "Man is by nature an animal intended to live in a *polis*" [*Politics*]. Yet even at this date not all Greeks were so organized, and in the dark ages there had been no city-states at all, as we understand the term in Greek history. The *polis* evolved out of the tribal kingdom in the late eighth century and continued to consolidate its institutions over the next 300 years. Basically it was the unit of conscious political history in Greece and of the great Greek colonization.

The city-state, in simplest terms, was a small but sovereign political unit, in which all important activity was conducted at one spot and in which communal bonds—expressed in terms of law—were more basic than personal ties. In all these respects the *polis* grew out of the political organization of the dark ages.

Geographically, thus, Greek peoples had often met together from wide areas at religious shrines, and some religious leagues, such as the Amphictyony of Delphi, long continued to play an important role. But on the whole Greeks had been accustomed to act politically and religiously in tiny units, and these were to jell into the separate city-states of historic times. Athens, which was the largest unified city-state of mainland Greece, covered only 1000 square miles; the ordinary *polis* was far smaller and numbered its adult male citizens as a few thousands at the most. The historic Greek world consisted of some 200-odd absolutely independent states.

In the earlier tribal kingdoms two mutually antagonistic political principles had existed. One was that of personal leadership; the other, that of collective unity and basic equality of the tribesmen. A modern observer might expect that, as the Greeks came together in tighter political unity, they would have done so under the direction of the kings. This was the course which the evolving national states of western Europe followed in the Middle Ages. If Greece did not follow the same path, the reasons were several. The tribal kings were weak financially; new military techniques made the kings less important as war chiefs; the isolation of the Aegean limited serious foreign threats; and, above all, the enduring simplicity of Greek life (materially speaking) permitted a survival of the principle that all tribesmen had rights.

During the age of revolution, in consequence, kings virtually disappeared in most Greek states, though they lingered on in Sparta, Argos, and a few other areas. Instead the Greeks improved their political and military machinery for collective action and underwrote this unity by guarantees of common justice and by patriotic symbols especially in the field of religion. This more perfected, more conscious union was the *polis*.

Physical, Political, and Moral Qualities of Poleis

The average Greek *polis* was no larger than a small American county. Its frontiers were usually natural boundaries such as the sea or ranges of hills, but a state like Athens comprised several plains and valleys while the open country of Boeotia was divided into several states. As a result of its smallness, the citizens of a *polis* could assemble fairly easily at a central point for major political and religious activities.

This central point usually was a grouping of villages, far enough inland to be safe from sudden seaborne raids. At times there was a hill, like the Acropolis at Athens, which could serve as a refuge and on which a temple could be erected to the patron divinity of the *polis* (Athena at Athens). Below it lay an *agora*, an open place where the citizens met in political assembly and also engaged in trade. The upper classes perhaps more commonly lived here, though they had also relatively large rural estates; more surely, the artisans and traders would dwell at the focal point. But the modern equivalent of *polis*, "city-state," is somewhat misleading, for only as trade and industry grew after 700 did true city clusters begin to appear in the Greek world. Most of the citizens in an ordinary state always dwelt in farming villages over the countryside, where they carried on their basic economic, social, and even minor political activity.

The citizens of a *polis* assembled periodically to vote on major issues and to elect officials. The role of the assembly tended to grow as the city-states coalesced, and a mark of this growth was the creation of a steering committee or council to prepare its business. Such councils had appeared by about 600 B.C. at Sparta and Athens. Elsewhere, however, the council represented the developing aristocracy and really ran the government; in these cases its members were chosen in one way or another virtually for life. Even in those states where the assembly had genuine powers, membership was limited in early days to landholders or was otherwise restricted.

Generally the single office of king was replaced by a number of officials. One such officer might still be called "king" so as to conduct the ancestral religious rites which the gods expected from kings; another would be the general (*polemarch* at Athens); another, the civil head (*archon* at Athens); others directed the judicial machinery and supervised state cults. Since the problems of these small states were simple, so too was their machinery; but over the next several centuries the Greeks were to meet and face, in a host of interesting solutions, some of the basic political problems which rise in any devel-

*In this view of ancient Sparta, the Eurotas River flows through
the foreground and the Mt. Taygetos range rises in the distance.*

oped community. Both by subdividing the executive power and by commonly electing officials
for only one year the Greeks seriously weakened
the principle of personal leadership in favor of
forms of collective action; but at the same time
they took other steps which increased the power
of the state as a whole as against local social and
religious groups.

In its earliest stages the Greek *polis* was not a
democracy, but spiritually it rested upon political
ideals of great significance. "A state," observed
Aristotle, "aims at being, as far as it can, a society composed of equals and peers" [*Politics*];
and we can understand neither the origins nor
the long endurance of the *polis* unless we keep in
mind its moral and ideal qualities. The Greek
city-state originated in a very simple world,
where rich and poor were not too sharply distinguished and where both upper and lower classes
felt themselves bound together in a communal

unity. The lower classes were willing to see the
kings disappear and to permit the upper classes
to take over the day-to-day direction of activities
so long as they felt they were justly treated. . . .

Theoretically, thus, all citizens were equal
members of the *polis* in the sense that they were
protected in the possession of fundamental private rights. Slaves continued to exist, elements
of the farming population might be serfs (as in
Sparta, Crete, and Thessaly), women were considered politically incompetent; but the citizen
body proper had its rights as well as its duties.
Ultimately the *polis* was based on the principle
of justice, and this in turn rested upon the mastery of law over arbitrary action. . . . By the middle of the seventh century Greek city-states were
beginning to set down law codes as summations
of ancestral customs, so that all might see their
rights on public display.

The *polis* incarnated the principles of basic

equality, even-handed justice, participation in public activities (by all citizens who met certain requirements), and government by law. Two other qualities were also implicit in the new system. One was local patriotism, which was marked in the religious field by the growing worship of state heroes and the veneration of one great god or goddess as patron of the community; in the mythological field old tales were reworked to celebrate the glories of this or that city. . . .

Military Developments and Wars Among City-States

The growing political unity was especially visible in the military field. Whereas the Homeric heroes fought individual duels, by about 700 B.C. Greek citizens were beginning to troop out for battle in a tight block of infantry called the phalanx. The members of a phalanx were heavily armored with bronze helmet, breast plate, greaves, and round shield, and carried a long spear as well as a short sword. In battle these *hoplites* stood several men deep so as to give greater weight and moral support when one phalanx pushed at another on level ground. The role of the general now was to determine when his troops were ready to give battle. Before the fray he encouraged his soldiers by proper religious rites and exhortation, but in the action maneuvers were almost impossible. Since each man provided his own armor, the men of property, both aristocrats and the middling farmers, formed the major defense of the state. They were aided by a few light-armed troops on the flanks, and the richer nobles were proud of their horses; but cavalry remained very weak in the absence of good forage. In coastal communities simple warships appeared and were rowed by the lower classes.

Initially both the style of armor and the pattern of fighting were adaptations of military development in the Near East, but the spiritual cohesiveness of a Greek *polis* as well as the intellectual ferment of its civilization gave its warriors a strength far beyond their numbers. "It is not stones nor timber nor the craft of crafts-men, but wherever there are men knowing how to defend themselves, there are walls and a city [Alcaeus, *fragment 426*]."

During the dark ages there had been no political history as such. Not only do we lack any written records for the era, but also conscious political organization was absent. At the most, legends give some hints as to the migrations of the era 1100–750. Dorian-speaking peoples, for example, were said to have moved into Sparta, into Epidaurus, and into Megara later than into Argos and Corinth.

Once the *polis* had emerged, its firmer political and military organization permitted more deliberate political action, and the growth of population made states more contentious over prize bits of farmland on the frontiers. The first great war of which we know was fought just before 700 by Chalcis and Eretria to determine possession of the small but rich Lelantine plain [on Euboea, the large island lying along the eastern coast of the Greek mainland]. Many states far afield from Euboea, such as Samos and Miletus in the eastern Aegean and Corinth and Megara on the Saronic gulf, were drawn into this clash by their commercial rivalries and local antipathies; in the end Chalcis was successful.

In other wars Megara vied now with Corinth, now with Athens; Sparta conquered its western neighbor, Messenia; and Argos, under its greatest king, Pheidon, held temporary power over much of the Peloponnesus. These events, however, cannot be woven into a continuous pattern of international relations in the seventh century.

Down past 500, fortunately, the Greek states did not press severely and continuously upon one another. Internally, at least, the rise of the *polis* brought order and security, though piracy on the seas and brigandage in the mountains remained enduring problems; and the states of Hellas rarely pushed their wars, in view of the difficulty of sieges, to the total destruction of a defeated foe. In times of emergency, such as the Persian wars, some of the major states—but not all—were able to group themselves in a common bond for the moment of peril. In the long run, however, the division of Greece into many sovereign units, each jealously patriotic, was a terrific burden to which its fall was partly attributable. To understand Greek history it must be remembered that "Greece" was a geographical expression, not a united country. All the Hellenes worshiped the same gods, shared the same basic culture, and met periodically in great international festivals and games; but this cultural unity meant no more politically than has the common cultural outlook of the western European states in modern times.

Consecutive internal development also began slowly to be evident, once the *polis* had emerged and the writing of laws and other documents became customary. The *polis* incarnated noble ideals, but each state was inhabited by men who were moved by passions and were divided into classes. The richer farmers, who controlled the political machinery, did not always treat their weaker neighbors justly; in the tremendous economic and intellectual expansion of the era, tensions and explosions were inevitable.

Selection 4

The Greeks Establish Colonies Far and Wide

Hermann Bengtson

This synopsis of Greek colonization in the Archaic Age is taken from noted German scholar Hermann Bengtson's massive and widely acclaimed history of Greece. He begins with the reasons that many poleis founded colonies (apoikiai) and describes some of the individuals who participated, including the seventh-century B.C. poet Archilochus, who hailed from the Cycladic island of Paros and helped to settle the northern Aegean island of Thasos. Bengtson covers both the colonies in the western Mediterranean (which were so numerous in southern Italy that the area became known as Magna Graecia, "Greater Greece") and in the north, i.e., along the shores of the Propon-
tis (now called the Sea of Marmara) and Pontus (southern Black Sea region).

Excerpted from *History of Greece: From the Beginnings to the Byzantine Era*, by Hermann Bengtson, translated and updated by Edmund F. Bloedow. Copyright © 1988 University of Ottawa Press. Reprinted by permission of University of Ottawa Press.

The second period of Greek expansion in the Mediterranean began about the middle of the eighth century, almost half a millennium after the end of the Achaean [Mycenaen] colonisation. It was carried out by members of all classes of the Greek people, from the nobility to the landless peasants. In its origin and course it is ultimately a phenomenon which defies all historical explanation. Whatever the causes, it is above all the expression of a fundamentally new outlook on life, for which the frontiers of the homeland had become too constricted. It is therefore no accident that the man who first appears before us in his individuality, Archilochus of Paros, was an active participant and sufferer in this movement. In contrast to the

Achaean expansion, its dimensions in terms of area and demo-political considerations extended almost infinitely. When the colonisation gradually abated about the middle of the sixth century after a period of two hundred years, flourishing Hellenic colonies extended over almost the entire basin of the Mediterranean. Only in the East did the great empires of Western Asia prevent the Greeks from settling on the coast of Syria. The expansion is the more amazing in view of the fact that in planning and execution it was undertaken by individual Greek communities and individual Greek personalities, without any central supervision. The initiative came from the Greek communities, the poleis, or from certain groups within the population. Of far-reaching consequence for the history of the Western world was this transplanting abroad of Greek political institutions, especially the community state, the polis. In a foreign environment it most demonstrated its vitality. Through the great colonisation the Greeks for the first time became a leading people in the ancient world and the destiny of the Greek people was henceforth inseparably interwoven with that of East and West.

The leadership of this great mass movement was undertaken by the Greek nobility. From their numbers came the founders, the *oikistai*, of the new colonial towns. The multitudes of emigrants assembled in the harbour cities of the motherland, in Chalcis, Eretria, Megara and Corinth. In Asia the prime coloniser was Miletus, which actually attained a monopolising position in the seventh century. The community which provided the ships in general also sent out the *oikistos*, and after his death the colonists ascribed heroic honours to him. The close ties between the mother-city and the colony are first and foremost documented in the religious sphere. Tribe-divisions, the names of magistrates, the calendar system, the cult of the city gods—all migrated from the metropolis into the new homeland, where the bonds with the mother-city were piously cultivated. Of cardinal importance was the fact that the majority of *apoikia*—colonies—were autonomous communities independent of the *polis* which sent them out. . . .

The causes for emigrating are to be found in the internal conditions of the Greek motherland. In the first place there is the (relative) overpopulation of Hellas, a periodically recurring phe-

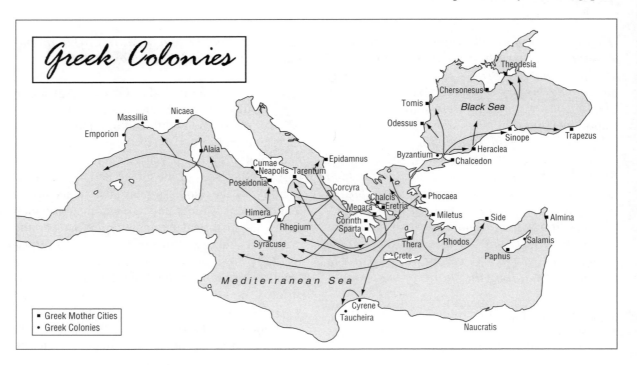

nomenon in Greek history. For the archaic period it is attested by various documents. Hesiod, for instance (*Works and Days* 376), counselled that the family be restricted to a single child! It is moreover known that the exposure [leaving outside to die] of new-born infants was generally practised in Greece. Places such as Thessaly, Boeotia and Attica—even at first—probably participated in the emigration. They too must have channelled their surplus population abroad through the great harbours. In addition to overpopulation, serious social conflicts, like the internal struggles in cities like Megara, Corinth, Athens and Mytilene must also have prompted many thousands to leave their homelands. Opposition to the tyrants too by a certain sector of the citizenry repeatedly drove people of all classes from their country.

Trade and a search for new arable land were from the very outset connected. To date, reliable evidence for the important extension of Greek navigation and Greek trade in the period immediately preceding the colonisation exists only for the West. In no less than thirty different places in the area from Apulia to Marseilles, archaeological finds have brought to light evidence for Greek imports in the eighth and seventh centuries, above all in the form of Greek vases. The vases came from almost the entire Greek world—from Crete, from the Cyclades, from Boeotia and Corinth. Certain features suggest the idea that even in the first half of the ninth century Greek artists found themselves in Etruria, in Falerii and Tarquinii [regions of Italy]. . . .

The considerations governing the choice of location for founding settlements were as varied as the reasons which motivated the Greeks to leave their homes. One may have been moved abroad by the urge into distant unknown places, another by dire affliction or the hope of acquiring fabulous treasures and riches from commercial enterprises. The new cities were sited for the economic importance of the hinterland, the quality of the soil for agriculture, the attitude of the native population to foreigners, the protected character of a given place, the communications with traffic routes, and various other factors which are in part imponderable.

The fact that the direction of the Greek colonial expansion was primarily towards the west and north of the Mediterranean is explained by the international situation. In the East, in Western Asia, the [Assyrian] empire under Tiglath-pilesar III was then continuously expanding. . . . Assyria had placed a barrier to the Greeks in the East. In Syria only very sporadic commercial colonies are to be found at the mouth of the Orontes and perhaps also at Tell Sukas. They served to expedite immediate exchange between Hellas and Western Asia while avoiding the land route through Anatolia.

In contrast to this the conditions for a colonial expansion in the West were all the more favourable. Here there was no political power such as the Assyrian empire. The Italic tribes, in themselves discordant, and the Etruscans, who originated from the east, were particularly open to Greek trade and Greek civilisation. An important general condition for colonisation was provided by the great progress in nautical skill, the gradual increase in the size and cargo capacity of ships and finally by the geographical information about the western world which had been obtained by Greek voyagers since the end of the Mycenaean period.

Colonies in the West

Sailing through the straits of Messina the Chalcidians were the first to reach Campania [on the western Italian coast], a district that was fertile and favoured by nature. In a region similar to the motherland in climate and vegetation they founded the city of Cyme (Cumae), about the middle of the eighth century at the latest. Before this they had in all probability established a base on the off-shore island of Ischia. No other Hellenic colony in the West was destined to such far-reaching cultural significance as Cyme, the first Chalcidian settlement. It probably furnished the Etruscans, and through them the Romans, with the alphabet of Chalcis. If today we regard the letter X as "ks" and do not read it with the Greeks as "k," we are following Chalcidian practice. Cyme no doubt also introduced the Greek gods to the Italics, who then received them into their pantheon [group or family of gods]. Colonists from Cyme (Cumae) were responsible for founding Neapolis (c. 600 B.C.), which later far outstripped the mother-city.

The east coast of Sicily was also a goal of the Chalcidian voyagers. At the foot of Mount Aetna the settlement of Naxos emerged (founded according to tradition in 735 B.C.). In the fertile hill-country, sloping as far as the Symaethus River, Chalcidians founded the colony of Catana. Greek settlers from Chalcis also established themselves on the small island of Ortygia, the germ cell of Syracuse, later founded by Corinth. . . . Syracuse . . . became the most powerful city in Sicily. In general the great commercial metropolis of Corinth, supported by her possession of the island of Corcyra, succeeded in creating for herself a superior position in the west in the seventh century. . . .

At first, however, the Chalcidians still continued to set the pace in the West. They gained a strong foothold on both sides of the straits—Zancle on Sicily and Rhegium at the southern tip of Italy were Chalcidian settlements. With the stronghold of Mylae and the colony of Himera, founded by Zancle, the Chalcidians established strong bases for themselves on the northern coast of Sicily. . . . Of the eastern Greeks the Rhodians alone took part in the Sicilian colonisation and were responsible for Gela, founded approximately 688 B.C., and Acragas, a colony of Gela, about 580 B.C. . . . The interior of Sicily, however, was beyond the energies of the Hellenes. Here the native population asserted itself—in the east the Siculi, in the west the Sicani. Both soon entered into ardent cultural and economic exchange with the Greeks. The western tip of the island remained Punic [Carthaginian]. The Carthaginians maintained their bases in Motye, Panormus (Palermo) and Solus. . . .

The Greek colonisation in southern Italy presents an essentially different picture. Here commercial considerations were not the determining factor. Rather the need for land forced thousands of emigrants out of the north of the Peloponnesus and Locris to the fertile plains of southern Italy. Thus many settlements appeared in the Gulf of Tarentum, where even the smallest coastal plain was exploited, and when there was no more land on the east coast the Greeks pushed directly across Italy to the western sea. Here on the west coast, from Rhegium (Reggio di Calabria) to Poseidonia (Paestum), was a string of flourishing Hellenic colonial towns. Croton, Sybaris and Metapontum were settlements of Achaean colonists, whereas Locri Epizephyrii by its name indicates that the settlers originated from Locris. Tarentum, founded by the legendary Parthenians (c. 700 B.C.), was the only colony Sparta ever founded. Of the settlements in southern Italy Croton and Sybaris conquered an extensive territory. In the end Sybaris allegedly ruled over four Italic peoples and twenty-five cities, but the 300,000 armed troops which she could allegedly throw into the field is definitely a considerable exaggeration. Today the great Doric temples on the coast at Poseidonia (Paestum), a colonial town of Sybaris, with their stark beauty still bear witness to the power and the determination of the Hellenes in southern Italy. . . .

In addition to the Ionians it is above all the Hellenes of southern Italy, and among them the Achaean element from the Peloponnesus, who emerge as the political and cultural leaders among sixth century Greeks. . . . It is here that Greek culture and Greek intellectual life shed the rays of their influence on the world around, which in turn readily accepted the gifts of a higher civilisation, especially that of the Greek language. Up to the present day in certain [southern Italian] localities . . . the Greek dialect has preserved undeniable elements of "Dorian" (that is, pre-Byzantine) Graecisms, which are to be traced back to the one-time Greek population of the country! In the sixth century the term "Magna Graecia" came into use for southern Italy. It is possible that it was intended to designate the contrast between the expansive territory encompassed by the colonial region in southern Italy and the much more constricted conditions in the motherland. It was also in southern Italy that the name *Graeci* was coined for the Hellenes. . . .

Probably in the middle or towards the end of

the seventh century a Greek ship, that of Colaeus of Samos, after sailing beyond the "Pillars of Hercules" (Straits of Gibraltar), for the first time reached the open ocean and ancient Tartessus, a colony of the Iberi and the centre of the active tin trade maintained with the British Isles. The Phocaeans [from Phocaea, a Greek city located northwest of Smyrna in Ionia] above all took advantage of the connections with the distant West. In the vicinity of the estuary of the Rhône they established the colony of Massalia (c. 600 B.C.). Its favourable location at the terminus of the great trade artery leading up the Rhône soon made it the largest and wealthiest Greek city of the western Mediterranean. Its cultural influence penetrated deep into the hinterland; the Helvetii in the time of Caesar used the Greek alphabet because of the influence of the Massaliots. Traces of ancient Phocaean Graecisms also appear to be preserved in a number of dialects of southern France. Along the coast of southern France as far as the Pyrenees there emerged a great many factories, established by Massalia as bases for trade with Spain. . . .

Colonies in the North and South

Greeks of almost all tribes took part in the colonisation of the West, whereas the settling of the Black Sea coasts was, according to tradition, the work of a single city, Miletus, which allegedly founded more than ninety colonial towns on the Pontus and Propontis. . . . The actual colonisation of the Pontus by Milesian *apoikiai* began in the course of the seventh century. Considerations of trade policy combined with the search for agricultural land. The main object was to open up the rich hinterland of southern Russia, with its trade routes connecting it equally with the Baltic amber district and with central Asia, and to establish communications with metal-rich Iberia at the Caucasus and with the region of Lake Van. The estuary branches of the large rivers in southern Russia were, like the Propontis (Sea of Marmara), famous for their wealth in fish. The inland regions provided grain as well as flax and wool in abundance, and Scythian slaves were no less eagerly sought, finding their

way to Ionia on Milesian ships. The Scythians, a people of Iranian origin, inhabiting the steppes of southern Russia, were friendly towards the Greeks. The distinguished Scythian nobles in particular gladly welcomed Greek art objects. Milesian vases and splendid articles of goldsmith work have been found in many tumuli [grave sites] of southern Russia. The Greek settlers for their part were impressed by the Scythian way of life, by their dress and manner of fighting, so that in many places a Graeco-Scythian civilisation was beginning to emerge. One of the oldest Milesian colonies was situated on the island of Berezan at the mouth of the Dnieper (Borysthenes). Here excavations have disclosed a large number of articles; the settlement had to be abandoned by the Greeks on account of floods. It was Olbia, however, at the mouth of the Bug (Hypanis), founded at the end of the seventh century, that developed into the most important city in southern Russia. . . . There were numerous Hellenic settlements in the Crimea. . . . The Greek settlers were particularly attracted by the mild climate and the fertile soil, which in sheltered places made even viticulture possible. . . . Across the straits on the Taman peninsula Tean settlers founded Phanagoreia about 540 B.C. At the mouth of the Don, Tanaïs sprang up as the most northerly and easterly Greek city, at the ancient frontier between Europe and Asia.

The west coast of the Pontus also became fringed with flourishing colonies: Istrus, Tomis (Constantsa), Odessus and Apollonia were cities planted by Miletus. The Milesians were, however, forced to share the possession of the Propontic coasts and the straits with the Dorian Megarians, who had arrived here before them and had founded Chalcedon and Byzantium, the former as early as the first half of the seventh century, the latter later. . . .

Even the inhospitable south coast of Thrace, inhabited by war-like tribes, became the goal of colonial endeavours in the seventh and sixth centuries. The Parians landed on the densely forested island of Thasos and penetrated its hinterland (c. 680 B.C.). One thousand colonists are said to have taken part in the expedition. Archilochus participated in the later battles with the natives, and trenchantly calls the colonists "the woe of all Greece." Subsequently a closer relationship continued to exist between Paros and Thasos, a circumstance to be assumed as usual between a mother-city and an *apoikia*. Like many another settlement the colony of Abdera, founded by Clazomenae about 650 B.C., fell victim to attacks by Thracian tribes. Teans who had abandoned their homeland on account of the Persians resettled in the place and within a very short time it began to flourish and actively participated in the cultural life of the Greek people. Settlers from Chalcis on Euboea gave Chalcidice [the three-fingered peninsula in the northwest Aegean] its name. . . .

In North Africa the most important Greek settlements were Cyrene in Libya and Naucratis on the Canopitic branch of the Nile. After reaching the small island of Platea, colonists from Thera (c. 630 B.C.) penetrated into the interior of Libya, and in a region rich in resources they laid the foundations for the city of Cyrene. In contrast to the colonies founded almost exclusively under the leadership of the Greek aristocracy, in Cyrene the monarchy, taken over from the mother-city of Thera, was continued. Its close connection with the sanctuary of Libyan Ammon in the Oasis of Siwah, its wealth in horses and sheep, its export of curative silphium plants, its daughter-cities founded in the sixth century on the plateau of Barca and on the nearby coast (Barce, Taucheira, Euhesperides)—all these enabled Cyrene to develop into an imposing power in Libya, one which even could assert itself against Egypt.

The second colonisation marks a crucial turning point in the political and cultural life of the Greek people. By giving to their settlements the form of "community state" wherever they established a new homeland, the Greeks carried the idea of the autonomous, self-sufficient polis abroad into distant lands and continents. In this period the polis first superseded the tribal state and for the first time became the prevailing and characteristic political form throughout the Greek world. Overcoming the constricted conditions of the motherland and constant association with foreign cultures and peoples—Scythians and inhabitants of Asia Minor, Thracians and Illyrians, Sicels and Italics, Ligurians and Iberians, Libyans and Egyptians—whetted the sensitivity of the Greeks to their own and to things foreign. It taught them to regard themselves as a single great community in language and culture, customs and religion, in the face of which tribal differences receded more and more into the background. Greek culture and Greek religion migrated to foreign lands and the Greeks repeatedly recognised in foreign deities attributes with which they were familiar in their own gods. As high as the Greeks in many places towered over the natives, whom they called "*Barbaroi*" ["Barbarians"] for their non-Greek language, they none the less established many lasting ties with the native aristocracies through intermarriage, as in Scythia and Libya. A thousand bonds, however, united the colonists with their homeland. It was the particular pride of the overseas communities to send their youth to the great Olympian festival in the motherland. Cyrene and the Sicilian communities in particular were able to boast of an imposing number of Olympian victors. The world had now become larger for the Greeks than in earlier times.

Selection 5

Rule by Tyrants

Robert B. Kebric

In this excerpt from his fascinating book, Greek People, *University of Louisville scholar Robert B. Kebric ably summarizes the short-lived political phenomenon of tyranny in many Greek cities during Archaic times. He concludes by focusing on the personality and deeds of one of the most famous tyrants—Polycrates of Samos.*

In an attempt to relieve the many pressures facing their small city-states, the Greeks began sending out colonies to other parts of Greece and the Mediterranean. . . . The establishment of colonies, however, could not eliminate the many problems facing the Greeks. They were half-measures at best, providing only short-term relief. In time, a new governmental institution—tyranny—would grow out of the social, economic, and political difficulties of the day.

Today, the word *tyrant* carries with it many negative connotations that were not implied in the original Greek usage, at least not before the fourth century B.C. To the Greeks, a tyrant was simply one who had seized or been given power in an irregular fashion, contrary to any constitutional process. "Tyrant" was never either a formal title or an official position. . . . In many ways, tyranny represented a revival of monarchy, but "dictator" or "strongman" is probably the more accurate rendering.

Tyrants usually, but not always, held their position by force. They took over when the existing aristocratic governments could not cope successfully with society's problems—to provide a more effective rule. However, balancing public necessity with personal ambition was not always a major concern, and many tyrants became oppressive. They could be cruel or kind, competent or incompetent. They came in all shapes and sizes. The only aspect they all shared was that they had aristocratic backgrounds.

Tyrants took advantage of the factionalism within some of the city-states to establish their power. There must have been a connection between their rise and the rise of hoplite warfare, because the two are essentially contemporary and tyrants often had hoplite support. Tyrants mostly represented a revolution against the aristocracy, although conceivably, they could find their support anywhere—even among their fellows, who often needed leadership in fighting nonaristocratic challengers. The latter group also might place their hopes in one man. Sometimes, the various quarreling factions might even agree to confer power on an acceptable individual, who, during a specified period, was to settle a city-state's problems. Most tyrants, however, received their support from the masses, and for this reason—although it may seem a contradiction in terms—the institution of tyranny must be viewed ultimately as a step toward popular government in Greece.

The Age of Tyrants did not last long, most tyrannies having disappeared by 500 B.C. Tyrannies were largely family affairs, and seldom did they extend past the tyrant's son, grandson, or other male relative, although the city of Sicyon [in the northeastern Peloponnesus] experienced such rule for a century. One person's lifetime could encompass much of most cities' experience with the institution, as evidenced by this tomb inscription of a member of a family of tyrants, Archedice of Athens:

> This dust hides Archedice, daughter of Hippias, the most important man in Greece in his day; but though her father, husband, brothers, and children were tyrants, her mind was never carried away into arrogance.

(Thucydides, *Peloponnesian War* 6.59)

One obvious reason for the rapid demise of tyranny was that tyrants were easy targets for assassins: A government could be overthrown by killing one person. However, the main explanation for the rise and fall of the institution in such a short period of time was the simple fact that the circumstances in society which produced tyranny soon passed. Tyrants filled a gap between the time when the old order was breaking down and a new order had not yet been established.

There would be another Age of Tyrants in the Greek West, which, because of its later foundation through colonization, lagged behind developments in the East; but ultimately, both East and West would advance to more sophisticated and stable forms of government—among them, democracy.

Polycrates of Samos

Of the many tyrants who ruled during the seventh and sixth centuries B.C., the greatest was probably Polycrates of Samos. During his reign (c. 532–522 B.C.), he established Samos, a large and wealthy Ionian island, as a major commercial center and one of Greece's first great naval powers, extending its influence over neighboring islands, the coast of Asia Minor, and elsewhere. He also supported artists and poets and made the island an important cultural center. . . .

Polycrates came from a prominent family, and his father, Aeaces, was a man of some influence. The general circumstances that led to his rise as tyrant are not clear, but Samos' fortunes had probably been declining recently because of Persian pressures. About 532 B.C., the story goes, he seized control with the aid of only fifteen hoplites and appears to have ruled with his two brothers until he executed one and exiled the other.

As sole ruler, Polycrates' power expanded rapidly, and few could challenge his fleet of 100 Samian warships and 1,000 archers. Although some critics styled him a pirate, Polycrates' actions reveal him to be much more than a random raider. The wars he waged and his interference with shipping, friend and foe, in the area were chiefly designed to keep Samos atop the commercial world. Naturally, his enemies, particularly the nearby mainland city of Miletus, with whom Samos was usually at war, would squawk. On one occasion, he defeated a fleet from Lesbos that had come to the aid of Miletus and put the prisoners to work digging a moat around his city wall.

Polycrates' greatest enemy was the nearby Persian Empire, and in his dealings with it, as in his other actions, he predictably chose to pursue the dangerous course. Unwilling to become a Persian dependent, he determined, instead, to be the champion of Persian resistance. Although the Persians may have felt that Samos lay within their sphere of influence, Polycrates' fleet was too formidable for them to challenge, and they had to leave him alone, a fact that was said to have caused embarrassment to Oroites, the Persian governor of the area nearest the island. At the same time, Polycrates was never foolish enough to push the Persians too far, and he even cooperated with them when it was to his benefit.

Polycrates' desire to expand trade and his general anti-Persian attitude led him into an association with Amasis, king of Egypt, who had his own doubts about Persian intentions. The friendship apparently was at the root of a popular story told about Polycrates by Herodotus.

Generally regarded as the first historian, Herodotus was no fan of Polycrates. Although born at Halicarnassus, he had fled tyranny there and moved to nearby Samos, where he lived for a time. Consequently, he was very familiar with the island's history. The combination of his dislike for tyrants and a sympathy with whatever anti-Polycrates tradition that remained in the first half of the fifth century B.C. resulted in his portraying an end for Polycrates that resembles a Sophoclean tragedy.

Herodotus still believed that the gods would punish human beings for their "hubris," or overweening pride. In his minitragedy about Polycrates, he has the tyrant progress through the same steps that similarly doomed tragic figures on the stage would go through. According to Herodotus, Amasis became alarmed at the unceasing good fortune of Polycrates and cautioned him that the gods would notice his success. Amasis told Polycrates that before he offended the gods and earned their wrath, he should demonstrate his humility by throwing away his most prized possession. Polycrates proceeded to toss an emerald and gold ring into the sea—but it was already too late.

A few days later, a fish was caught, its size and markings so striking that it was brought before the tyrant as a special gift. Polycrates was delighted, but his initial joy soon turned to dismay when he cut open the fish and found his ring in its belly. His offering had not been accepted, and the gods were already moving to bring about his ruin. Amasis, knowing that his friend was doomed, renounced his dangerous friendship with him.

The story, although entertaining, has its shortcomings—and pro-Samian overtones. It was Polycrates, *not* Amasis, who broke the friendship. In fact, Amasis did not outlive the wily tyrant, who, at about the time of his former friend's death, had found it opportune to aid the Persians when they invaded and conquered Egypt in 525 B.C.

Polycrates' "betrayal" of Egypt did not, however, end in the expected benefits. The contingent of forty ships he had sent was manned by political enemies, whom he expected would not return from the expedition. Return they did—with the intention of overthrowing the tyrant—and they rallied the Spartans and Corinthians, who had gripes against Polycrates. Polycrates was hard-pressed but survived a forty-day siege and successfully defended the city.

Ultimately, the tyrant's phenomenal luck ran out. He supposedly was tricked into a secret meeting with the Persian governor, Oroites, who apparently whetted Polycrates' appetite with promises of treasure in return for his assistance, and was unceremoniously crucified about 522 B.C.

Selection 6

Lawgivers and Political Experimentation

M.I. Finley

The distinguished classical scholar M.I. Finley, a former fellow at Jesus College and author of the groundbreaking book The World of Odysseus, *here presents an overview of the major kinds of political experimentation that highlighted the Archaic Age. A number of different scenarios transpired, he explains, depending on the local social and political conditions and needs of the various Greek states. Some, like Corinth, retained their oligarchic councils for a long time; others passed through the stage of tyranny; and a few, like Athens (which had its tyrants, too), laid the legal and social foundations for the democracies that would appear in Greece in the Classic Age.*

Some cities escaped tyranny altogether, the most famous instance being Sparta. She was in a unique position: having conquered and permanently subjugated the people of Laconia very early (no doubt in the Dark Age), she then subjected Messenia [the region west of Sparta] to the same treatment. Possessing very extensive and fertile lands and a large servile labour force (called "helots") in consequence, the Spartans created a military-political organization without parallel, and they were long immune from both the economic and the political troubles characteristic of most archaic Greek states. Traditionally this system was the work of a single "lawgiver," Lycurgus. Modern scholars are not even agreed on whether such a man existed at all, let alone on his date or what he actually did. Much of the tradition about him cannot be right, and it seems corrupted beyond rescue. It is a fact, but one which proves nothing one way or the other about Lycurgus, that the lawgiver was not a rare figure in archaic Greece—one thinks especially of Solon in early sixth-century Athens, but also of lesser names such as Zaleucus and Charondas among the western Greeks. The laws, constitutional, civil, sacral and criminal, had to be fixed and codified if the community was to emerge from its embryonic state in which a handful of families controlled all the resources and all the sanctions. . . . There were no precedents to fallback on either, giving room for free invention as men tried to think up ways by which a state could be administered, power distributed, laws passed and enforced.

Political Changes in Athens

The lack of precedent can hardly be overstated; in whatever field the archaic Greeks made new moves, no matter what the motive, they rarely had models to imitate or improve upon. This situation of compulsory originality, so to speak, is visible in many aspects of their life: in the individualism of their lyric poetry; in their new public architecture; . . . in the speculative philosophers who began to inquire, again on their own authority and supported only by their own mental faculties, into the nature of the universe; and in politics, where the originality is more easily overlooked. In the instance of the lawgiver about whom we know most, Solon, it was present in the very action which brought him to that position. The Athenian class struggle had reached an impasse and in 594 Solon was *chosen*, by agreement, and charged with the task of reforming the state. That is the point: he was chosen by the Athenians themselves, on their own initiative and their own authority, because he was respected for his wisdom and righteousness. He was not "called" and he had no vocation. Nor did he seize power as a tyrant.

Solon, like the other lawgivers, agreed that justice came from the gods, of course, but he made no claim to a divine mission or even, in any significant sense, to divine guidance. "I gave the common people such privilege as is sufficient," he wrote in one of his poems. As to those in power, "I saw to it that they should suffer no injustice. I stood covering both parties with a strong shield, permitting neither to triumph unjustly." Superficially, there may seem to be a resemblance with Hammurabi's preamble to his famous code a thousand years earlier; the Babylonian monarch also said that his aim was "to make justice to appear in the land, to destroy the evil and the wicked that the strong might not

Excerpted from *The Ancient Greeks*, by M.I. Finley. Copyright © 1963 by M.I. Finley. Copyright renewed © 1991 by Paul O'Higgens and Charles Richard Watten. Used by permission of Viking Penguin, a division of Penguin Putnam Inc.

oppress the weak." But the distinctions are far more important and consequential. In the first place, there is the secular [non-religious] quality of the Greek codification, whereas Hammurabi acted in the name of the gods. And then there is the decisive fact that the Eastern king legislated for subjects; the Greek lawgiver laid down rules by which the community should govern itself. Having completed his work, in fact, Solon left Athens for ten years so that the community could test his programme without prejudice; his own great prestige, he feared, might otherwise weight the balance of judgment unfairly.

In one sense Solon failed. He did not solve the economic difficulties lying behind the civil strife and after a generation tyranny, which he sought to stave off, came to Athens. Yet Solon remained in the memory of later Athenians, regardless of party, as the man who finally set them on the path to greatness. When Aristotle summed up Solon's achievements in his brief account of the Athenian constitution, he chose the following three as the most crucial: abolition of enslavement for debt, creation of the right of a third party to seek justice in court on behalf of an aggrieved person and the introduction of appeals to a popular tribunal. All three had one thing in common: they were steps designed to advance the community idea (and reality) by protecting the weaker majority from the excessive and, so to speak, extra-legal power of the nobility. Or, stated differently, they stopped up loopholes in the rule of law, an idea which was coming to be the Greek definition of civilized political organization; more than that, they were steps towards equality before the law, which Athenians in the classical period considered the central feature of democracy.

The role of the great Athenian tyrant Peisistratus in this development was paradoxical. By his very existence as tyrant he breached the idea of rule by law. On the other hand, later writers generally praised him, much as they condemned tyranny as an institution, because, in actual practice, "he wished to govern according to the laws without giving himself any prerogatives" (Aristotle, *Constitution of Athens* XVI 8). This cannot be accepted as literally true, but it is not simply untrue either. Using different techniques, and no doubt acting from altogether different motives, Peisistratus nevertheless carried Athens a very long way along the road Solon had sketched out. Himself a member of the nobility (he traced his ancestry to Nestor, the Homeric king of Pylos), he refused to play their game against the peasantry and the dispossessed. Indeed, being a tyrant, he could accomplish what Solon could not, and it was in his reign that the peasantry finally obtained a reasonably secure and independent position on the land, with financial assistance when required, that the civil strife was abated, and that the political monopoly of the aristocratic families was broken once and for all. Nobles continued to hold the leading civil and military offices—as they did well into the next century under the democracy, too—but the circumstances and the psychology were radically altered. They were now, increasingly, servants of the state, instruments of the law, and not arbitrary wielders of power; just as the common people were now genuinely free men, no longer threatened with debt bondage or with wholly partisan justice. The two factions were far from equals, but at least the differences between them had been reduced to a workable scale and proportion.

Peisistratus was in power from 545 (after one or two brief spells before that) until his death in 527, succeeded by his elder son Hippias, who was expelled in 510. For thirty years this was a peaceful rule, a time when Athens advanced rapidly in power and wealth, and when there were many new visible signs of this growth and of the spirit of community—one might almost say "nationalism"—which accompanied it: in public works and in great religious festivals particularly. But in 514 Hippias's younger brother Hipparchus was assassinated by an embittered rival in a love affair with a young boy, and the tyranny quickly turned into a cruel despotism and was overthrown. In one way or another this story was repeated in many Greek cities from the latter part of the seventh century to the end of the sixth. Tyranny never sat so securely that it was not easily brutalized, because of some incident, or for no reason at all, and then the tyrant was usually thrown out. The institution therefore tended to be ephemeral (with the notable exception of Sicily). But its historical significance cannot be judged by its duration, for tyranny was often the decisive feature in the transitional stage from the personal, familial rule of the nobility to the classical city-state.

None of this was a matter of intention or design. No tyrant, not even Peisistratus, saw himself as the bearer of the historic destiny of the Greeks, as the forerunner of Athenian democracy or of anything else (nor did Solon, for that matter). They wanted power and success, and if they were intelligent and disciplined, like Peisistratus, they gained it by advancing their communities. Solon may have thought that he "stood covering both parties with a strong shield," but it was Peisistratus and Hippias who in fact had the necessary strength. Solon was followed by a renewal of the old civil war; Hippias, after a very short struggle lasting less than two years, by a wholly new, democratic state.

The New Freedom

That was in Athens. The development in other cities took other lines: the unevenness of development already noticed was to remain a feature of Greek history at all times. The most backward regions, such as Aetolia or Acarnania, were scarcely affected by this whole trend, but they,

by and large, counted for little anyway (except as so much manpower available for war and piracy). Sparta went its own way, the Sicilian cities theirs, each because of special circumstances—the presence of a subjugated servile population or the constant threat of an external power such as Carthage. Sometimes, as in Corinth, the nobility remained strong enough to impose an oligarchy for a very long time. And in much of Greece the struggle between "the few" and "the many" (in their own phrasing) was never permanently stilled. Nevertheless, the generalization can be made that by the end of the archaic period, and in particular wherever there had been a phase of tyranny, the form of government, whether more democratic or more oligarchical, was on a different level of political sophistication from anything that had come before. This was the period in which some among the Greeks achieved a workable compromise between the competing and, historically speaking, often irreconcilable demands of social obligation and personal freedom; in which, indeed, they may be said to have discovered the idea of freedom, as distinct from the personal, fundamentally asocial power of the Homeric chieftains, the privilege of the aristocratic families, or the anarchy of the freebooters. The imperfections and the mistakes, both on the way and in the final product, cannot diminish the achievement.

Selection 7

Solon Reforms Athens's Social and Legal Systems

Plutarch

This excerpt from Plutarch's Life of Solon *picks up the story of Solon's famous reforms just after he has rejected his countrymen's offer to make him tyrant (so as better to facilitate his difficult task of reorganizing the state). First, Solon forgives all debts, ends the practice of debt-bondage (whereby a creditor could force a destitute borrower into slavery to recoup his investment), and allows those debtors already sold into foreign slavery to return home. Then he repeals the harsh laws formulated earlier by a legal reformer named Draco (except for those relating to homicide). In addition, Solon creates a new social ranking based on wealth, which provides political opportunities and rights to many who before had had few or none. Although a majority of those in the highest class remain aristocrats, any number of commoners can now join them, since wealth, rather than birth, has become the criterion for entry.*

hough he refused the government, he was not too mild in the affair; he did not show himself mean and submissive to the powerful, nor make his laws to pleasure those that chose him. For where it was well before, he applied no remedy, nor altered anything, for fear lest—

> "Overthrowing altogether and disordering the state,"

he should be too weak to new-model and recompose it to a tolerable condition; but what he thought he could effect by persuasion upon the pliable, and by force upon the stubborn, this he did, as he himself says—

> "With force and justice working both in one."

And therefore, when he was afterwards asked if he had left the Athenians the best laws that could be given, he replied, "The best they could receive." The way which, the moderns say, the Athenians have of softening the badness of a thing, by ingeniously giving it some pretty and innocent appellation, calling harlots, for example, mistresses, tributes customs, a garrison a guard, and the jail the chamber, seem originally to have been Solon's contrivance, who called cancelling debts Seisacthea, a relief, or disencumbrance. For the first thing which he settled was, that what debts remained should be forgiven, and no man, for the future, should engage the body of his debtor for security. Though some . . . affirm that the debts were not cancelled, but the interest only lessened, which sufficiently

Excerpted from "The Life of Solon," in *The Lives of the Noble Grecians and Romans*, by Plutarch, translated by John Dryden (New York: Modern Library, 1932).

pleased the people; so that they named this benefit the Seisacthea, together with the enlarging their measures, and raising the value of their money; for he made a pound, which before passed for seventy-three drachmas, go for a hundred; so that, though the number of pieces in the payment was equal, the value was less; which proved a considerable benefit to those that were to discharge great debts, and no loss to the creditors. But most agree that it was the taking off the debts that was called Seisacthea, which is confirmed by some places in his poem, where he takes honour to himself, that—

"The mortgage-stones that covered her, by me
Removed,—the land that was a slave is free;"

that some who had been seized for their debts he had brought back from other countries, where—

"—so far their lot to roam,
They had forgot the language of their home;"

and some he had set at liberty—

"Who here in shameful servitude were held.". . .

In this he pleased neither party, for the rich were angry for their money and the poor that the land was not divided, and, as Lycurgus [the noted Spartan lawgiver] ordered it his commonwealth, all men reduced to equality. He, it is true . . . having reigned many years in Lacedæmon [Sparta], had got a great reputation and friends and power, which he could use in modelling his state; and applying force more than persuasion . . . was able to employ the most effectual means for the safety and harmony of a state, by not permitting any to be poor or rich in his commonwealth. Solon could not rise to that in his polity, being but a citizen of the middle classes; yet he acted fully up to the height of his power, having nothing but the goodwill and good opinion of his citizens to rely on; and that he offended the most part, who looked for another result, he declares in the words—

"Formerly they boasted of me vainly; with averted eyes
Now they look askance upon me; friends no more, but enemies."

And yet had any other man, he says, received the same power—

"He would not have forborne, nor let alone,
But made the fattest of the milk his own."

Soon, however, becoming sensible of the good that was done, they laid by their grudges, made a public sacrifice, calling it Seisacthea, and chose Solon to new-model and make laws for the commonwealth, giving him the entire power over everything, their magistracies, their assemblies, courts, and councils; that he should appoint the number, times of meeting, and what estate they must have that could be capable of these, and dissolve or continue any of the present constitutions, according to his pleasure.

A later, imaginary representation of Solon, the Athenian leader whose reforms laid the groundwork for democracy.

First, then, he repealed all Draco's laws, except those concerning homicide, because they were too severe, and the punishment too great; for death was appointed for almost all offences, insomuch that those that were convicted of idleness were to die, and those that stole a cabbage or an apple to suffer even as villains that committed sacrilege or murder. So that . . . Draco's laws were written not with ink but blood; and he himself, being once asked why he made death the punishment of most offences, replied, "Small ones deserve that, and I have no higher for the greater crimes."

Next, Solon, being willing to continue the magistracies in the hands of the rich men, and yet receive the people into the other part of the government, took an account of the citizens' estates, and those that were worth five hundred measures of fruit, dry and liquid, he placed in the first rank, calling them Pentacosiomedimni; those that could keep an horse, or were worth three hundred measures, were named Hippada Teluntes, and made the second class; the Zeugitæ, that had two hundred measures, were in the third; and all the others were called Thetes, who were not admitted to any office, but could come to the assembly, and act as jurors; which at first seemed nothing, but afterwards was found an enormous privilege, as almost every matter of dispute came before them in this latter capacity. Even in the cases which he assigned to the archon's cognisance, he allowed an appeal to the courts. Besides, it is said that he was obscure and ambiguous in the wording of his laws, on purpose to increase the honour of his courts; for since their differences could not be adjusted by the letter, they would have to bring all their causes to the judges, who thus were in a manner masters of the laws. . . . And for the greater security of the weak commons [i.e., common people], he gave general liberty of indicting [the right to sue] for an act of injury; if any one was beaten, maimed, or suffered any violence, any man that would and was able might prosecute the wrong-doer; intending by this to accustom the citizens, like members of the same body, to resent and be sensible of one another's injuries. And there is a saying of his agreeable to his law, for, being asked what city was best modelled, "That," said he, "where those that are not injured try and punish the unjust as much as those that are."

Greek History– The Classic Age, Part 1: The Fifth Century B.C.

Chapter 4

Introduction

The fifth century B.C., comprising roughly the first half of the Classic Age (ca. 500–323 B.C.), is the most famous and most written-about period in all of Greek history. This is not without reason, for indeed, in retrospect the century seems literally jammed with momentous historical developments and events.

The first of these was the establishment of full-blown democracy in Athens circa 508 B.C., by the popular leader Cleisthenes and his supporters. The city's democratic institutions expanded further in the decades that followed, thanks to the efforts of other dynamic leaders, especially Themistocles, Ephialtes, and Pericles. Though remarkable in and of itself, since it was the first known democracy in human history, this political development also significantly affected Greek affairs in the fifth century. First, freedom of expression blossomed in Athens as it had nowhere else before. This attracted talented artists and writers from around the Greek world to visit or settle in the city and helped to inspire and facilitate the cultural golden age that highlighted the century's second half. In addition, other Greek states emulated Athens and created democracies of their own; while the more conservative Sparta looked on these developments as radical, dangerous, and threatening to Greece's political stability, an attitude that helped to fuel increasing tensions between the Spartans and Athenians.

The back-to-back Persian invasions of 490 and 480–479 B.C. constitute the next crucial events of the century. After Athens and Eretria (on Euboea's southern coast) aided the Ionians in their rebellion against Persia, it was only a matter of time before the Persians would seek retribution by moving on the Greek mainland. The Athenians, led by their general Miltiades, repelled the first attack at Marathon; an alliance of several Greek states, led by Athens and Sparta, blunted the second. Perhaps the most pivotal figure in the second invasion was Themistocles, who convinced his countrymen to build a large fleet, fortified Athens's port (Piraeus), and orchestrated the decisive Greek naval victory at Salamis (which the Athenian playwright Aeschylus described in his play, *The Persians*).

Later Greeks came to call the roughly fifty years following the Persian invasions the *Pentekontaetia,* the "Fifty Years." Modern scholars often refer to it as the Age of Pericles, or Athens's Golden Age. All of these titles are meant to commemorate the Athenian achievement of artistic, literary, and other cultural splendor in this period, which is understandable; for as scholar Victor Ehrenberg remarks in *From Solon to Socrates*, "Pericles and his times have been regarded as the very fulfillment of human endeavor and cultural harmony." Yet the Fifty Years had its darker side, as it was also a time of complex political turmoil and bloody military strife among the Greek states. In addition to numerous sporadic battles, small wars, and other disorders, the period saw the rise of Athens's maritime empire, which it often held together by means of naked force, as those cities who tried to secede discovered to their extreme misfortune.

Most ominously, the period was characterized by worsening relations between Athens and Sparta and their respective federations of allies. Confrontation between these two leading Greek states was probably inevitable, since their cultures and temperaments were so different. In comparison to the liberal, energetic Athenians, who thrived on a vigorous foreign policy and domestic social, political, and artistic experimentation, the Spartans maintained a politically backward and socially repressive society. By this period, most other Greek states had long since gotten rid of their kings (chieftains) and instituted oligarchies or democracies. However, Sparta retained its kings (two ruling jointly at all times), although their powers were overshadowed in all but religious and military matters by a group of elders (ephors). Nearly every Spartan social custom and institution was part of or influenced by the *agoge,* a regimented military system designed to turn out strong, effective warriors. The system certainly achieved this goal, for well before the dawn of the Classic Age Sparta had the most widely feared land army in Greece.

In the eyes of their fellow Greeks, however, the Spartans paid a heavy price for this military distinction. The citizens of Sparta constantly worried that their agricultural serfs, or helots (the former inhabitants of the neighboring state of Messenia, conquered by Sparta ca. 650–620), who greatly outnumbered them, might rebel; therefore they expended much of their energy maintaining internal security and order. Also, distrusting change, Sparta preferred to avoid contact with most other states, especially those it deemed too liberal and unstable, like Athens. And for the most part, the Spartans came to view as frivolous most of the art, literature, monumental architecture, and material luxuries that other states took for granted; so they discouraged these things in favor of simple necessities. To the outside world, Sparta appeared not only secluded, but also small, modest, and unadorned, a look that sorely belied its real power and influence. As Thucydides put it, if Sparta

> were to become deserted and only the temples and foundations of buildings remained, I think that future generations would, as time passed, find it very difficult to believe that the place had really been as powerful as it was

represented to be. Yet the Spartans . . . stand at the head not only of the whole Peloponnesus itself but also of numerous allies beyond its frontiers. Since, however, the city . . . contains no temples or monuments of great magnificence, but is simply a collection of villages . . . its appearance would not come up to expectation. If, on the other hand, the same thing were to happen to Athens, one would conjecture from what met the eye that the city had been twice as powerful as in fact it is.

(*Peloponnesian War,* Warner translation)

These major differences between the two great powers were part of what motivated the growing animosity that finally led to outbreak of the devastating Peloponnesian War in 431 B.C. This was the final and ultimately most momentous event of the century. For it exhausted all of the combatants and sent the Greek city-states into a spiral of decline (in the second half of the Classic Age) from which they were unable to escape.

The principal contemporary literary sources for the fifth century B.C. are Herodotus's *Histories,* the major source for the Persian Wars; Thucydides' masterful history of the Peloponnesian War, which also backtracks briefly to cover the major political events of the Fifty Years; and Xenophon's *Hellenica,* which chronicles the century's last decade. Of the later ancient Greek writers who covered the events of the fifth century, the most important is Plutarch (first century A.D.), whose biographies of Themistocles, Cimon, Aristides, Pericles, Alcibiades, Nicias, and Lysander contain some information from ancient sources that are now lost. The *Library of History* (or *Universal History*) of Diodorus Siculus (first century B.C.) is sometimes helpful but on the whole less reliable.

Selection 1

The Athenians Crush the Persians at Marathon

Peter Green

This description of the Persians' first invasion of the Greek mainland (in 490 B.C.) and their decisive defeat on the plain of Marathon is by the distinguished University of Texas classicist Peter Green. He points out that some of the most influential Athenians of the early fifth century B.C. fought in the battle. These included Miltiades, who had earlier resided near the Hellespont, where he had witnessed Persian troops in action and noted their weaknesses; Themistocles, who would later become the father of Athenian naval supremacy; and Themistocles' frequent political opponent, Aristides. Green is also careful to mention that Hippias, one of Athens's former tyrants, accompanied the Persian invasion forces. Having been exiled from Athens several years before, Hippias had taken refuge at the Persian court and he hoped that this new expedition would end with his reinstatement as Athenian tyrant.

*[O*n the spring of 491 B.C.] Darius decided to test the morale of the various Greek states. While his shipyards were busy turning out fresh warships and horse-transports, he sent envoys round the Aegean and main-

land Greece, demanding earth and water in token of vassalage. Athens and Sparta refused. In Herodotus's words, 'at Athens they [the messengers] were thrown into the pit like common criminals, at Sparta they were pushed into a well—and told that if they wanted earth and water for the king, those were the places to get them from'. But all the islands, Aegina included, and a number of mainland cities, especially in the north, submitted without protest. The Thasians were told to dismantle their walls. They did so. With most of the North Aegean from Thessaly to the Dardanelles in his power, Darius felt ready to strike. Early in 490 a new fleet and army assembled near Tarsus, on the Cilician coast opposite Cyprus, and sailed westward for Ionia. Darius had replaced Mardonius with his own nephew, Artaphernes, and a Median noble called Datis. 'Their orders,' says Herodotus, 'were to reduce Athens and Eretria . . . to slavery, and to bring the slaves before the king'. The exiled Hippias also sailed with them, in high hopes—though now nearly eighty—of returning to Athens as dictator once more.

From Ionia the fleet moved westward through the Cyclades. There was to be no risk of another shipwreck off Mt Athos. Naxos, which had survived an attack ten years before, was now captured and sacked. The inhabitants of Delos heard the news and fled. Datis, who knew the value of propaganda, sent them reassuring messages: he would never, he said, harm the island in which Apollo and Artemis were born. . . . The Persian fleet advanced from island to island, commandeering troops and picking up children as hostages. At Carystus, the southernmost town of Euboea, they met with a flat refusal, upon which they laid siege to the town and began burning the crops in the surrounding countryside. Datis and Artaphernes had a fighting force of at least 25,000 men; by now their total numbers, rowers and conscripts included, were over 80,000. To transport them they had some 400 merchantmen, with a minimum escort of 200 triremes. The Carystians, understandably, gave in.

At Eretria doubt and confusion reigned. Some were for fighting it out. Others wanted to abandon their city to the Persians, take to the hills, and (like their modern descendants) harry the enemy with guerilla operations. Others again, the inevitable quislings, were secretly preparing to sell out to Datis for Persian gold. Four thousand Athenian colonists had come from neighbouring Chalcis to help defend the threatened city. One of the Eretrian leaders warned them what was afoot, and advised them to get out while the going was good. They withdrew to Athens, where their services as hoplites soon proved more than welcome. Eretria held out for a week, then was betrayed from inside the walls. In accordance with Darius's orders, all the city's temples were burnt as a reprisal for the burning of Sardis. A few days later, says Herodotus, 'the Persian fleet sailed for Attica, everyone aboard in high spirits and confident that Athens would soon be given the same sort of medicine'. . . . The Persians' immediate destination was the Marathon plain, some twenty-four miles north-east of Athens itself, on the coast opposite Eretria.

The Armies Face Off

It was old Hippias who had suggested Marathon as the Persian beachhead. Datis wanted room to use his cavalry, and Marathon offered just the right conditions—a long flat strip between the mountains and the sea, with easy through access to Athens by way of the Hymettus-Pentele gap.

There were marshes at the north-east end, and clumps of trees and scrub dotted the plain. Better still, there was a fine shelving sandy beach (lined today with dunes and umbrella pines) on which to haul up the Persian warships and disembark horses. The invasion fleet beached at the north-east end of the bay, between the marshes and the long promontory known as Cynosura, or the Dog's Tail. Here Datis had natural protection on his landward side, an easy line of retreat by sea, and good grazing for his horses. . . .

From the heights of Mt Pentele the beacon flared, telling Athens that enemy forces had landed. A fast runner was sent off to Sparta with the news. Athens was threatened; reinforcements were urgently needed. The runner, Pheidippides, left Athens while it was still dark, and reached Sparta by the following evening, having covered something like 140 miles over bad roads. . . . The Spartans were full of sympathy, but regretted that they could not put troops into the field until after the full moon—that is, on 11–12 August. To do so would have meant breaking a religious taboo, probably in connection with the Carneian Festival, sacred to Apollo. It was now 5 August. Reinforcements could not be expected for another ten days. The Spartans were, beyond any doubt, sincerely pious and old-fashioned traditionalists: we have no right, without strong supporting evidence, to accuse them of practising religious hypocrisy for political ends. Yet it is undeniably curious how often such taboos happened to fit in with their practical plans. An expeditionary force was in readiness at the frontier, prepared to move as the moon, or the luck of battle, dictated. Meanwhile the Spartan government avoided committing itself.

From the moment the fall of Eretria became known, a succession of fierce debates had taken place in the Athenian Assembly. Some were for sitting tight and holding the city against siege. Others, Miltiades in particular, insisted that the citizen-army should go out and fight. A siege would cut them off from Spartan reinforcements . . . and increase the risk of treachery within the walls. Just who might be in touch with Hippias and the Persians at this juncture no one, except the conspirators themselves, could tell; but the existence in Athens of a large pro-Persian pressure-group was an accepted fact, and those who meant to fight ignored it at their peril. When the news of the Marathon landing reached Athens, it was Miltiades' policy which won the day. Clearly he argued that their only hope—especially against cavalry squadrons—was, in modern terms, to 'contain the beach-head': that is, to prevent enemy forces from fanning out and advancing inland. A famous resolution, to 'take provisions and march', was approved by the Assembly: tradition makes Miltiades the proposer, and tradition may well be right.

So the heavy-armed infantrymen of Attica, some 10,000 strong, set off along the quickest route to Marathon, through the Hymettus-Pentele gap and along the coast, their ration-bags loaded on mules or donkeys, slaves carrying their body-armour. The commander-in-chief, or War Archon [*polemarchos*] was Callimachus of Aphidna. Miltiades, though almost certainly responsible for the strategic and tactical plan which won the battle, and earned him well-merited fame, served as one of the ten divisional commanders; among his colleagues was Aristeides, Themistocles' great rival, known as 'the Just'. When the Athenians reached the southern entrance to the Marathon plain, between Mt Agrieliki and the sea, they took up their position by a precinct, or grove, sacred to Heracles, a little beyond the Brexisa marsh. . . . By so doing they effectively blocked any Persian advance on Athens. As a defence against Datis's cavalry they felled a number of trees and set them in position across the plain, with their branches facing the enemy. At this point they were joined, unexpectedly, by a volunteer force of between six hundred and a thousand Plataeans. Plataea was a small town in Boeotia, to the north of Attica, and an old ally of Athens. Every available man there had turned out to help repel 'the Barbarian'.

For several days (7–11 August) nothing happened: the two armies sat facing one another, two or three miles apart, and made no move. Both sides, in fact, had excellent reasons for playing a waiting game. The Athenians, who possessed neither archers nor cavalry, were unwilling to operate in the open plain, where Datis's squadrons would have them at a severe disadvantage. They still hoped, too, that Spartan reinforcements might reach them in time. After four days the moon would be full, and a Spartan army—with any luck—on its way to join them. The longer the Athenians sat tight, the better their chances.

The Persians, too, had their own motives for not wishing to force an immediate engagement. If the Athenians were shy of encountering Persian cavalry, Datis and Artaphernes, conversely, had no wish to launch their own weaker infantry against Greek hoplites holding a prepared position. More important, they were in touch, through Hippias, with a group at Athens who had promised to betray the city to the Persian invader. . . . When everything was ready, the conspirators would flash a shield on Mt Pentele. . . .

Day followed day, and still there were was no sign of a Spartan army, no shield-signal from the mountain-top. Herodotus reports that the Greek divisional commanders reached a five-a-side deadlock over their immediate course of action. One group argued that the Athenian army could not possibly win a pitched battle against such odds. They were heavily outnumbered; they had no cavalry or archers, whereas the Persians were well-supplied with both; the only logical course was to fall back on Athens. Miltiades and his friends had already countered such arguments in the debate which ended with the decision to go to Marathon. If the generals did in fact fight this debate all over again, then Miltiades, it is clear, proved equally firm. Withdrawal, moreover, would be suicidal in the circumstances. Callimachus needed little or no persuasion to stay where he was. Perhaps he acted on a hunch; perhaps he had learnt something of Datis's plans from spies or deserters.

Datis and Artaphernes must have known all about those Spartan reinforcements, and the alleged reason for their delay. Once the moon was full, further waiting might prove highly dangerous. Yet there was still no signal from the pro-Persian party in Athens by 11 August. A crucial decision now faced the Persian commanders; and it looks very much as though they made up their minds to take a chance, and go ahead with their planned operation [to keep the Athenian troops occupied while Datis sailed around Attica and took the city] regardless. In that case, Datis will have sailed for Phaleron Bay on the night of 11–12 August, under cover of darkness, taking the bulk of the cavalry with him: not all, since at least some token cover would be needed for Artaphernes' holding force. This body, to be on the safe side, must have substantially outnumbered the Athenians, though not so far as to weaken the assault group: 15,000 seems a likely figure. Even so, it is clear that neither Datis nor Artaphernes expected their opponents to risk an attack without archers or cavalry: when they in fact did so, the Persians' first reaction was that the poor fellows must have taken leave of their senses.

Attack at Dawn

The Persians may have hoped to benefit by treachery, but it was the Athenians who actually did so. Some Ionian scouts serving with Artaphernes noticed the absence of Datis's task force, and slipped across to the Athenian lines before dawn, bearing a message which afterwards became proverbially famous—'the cavalry are away'. . . . Miltiades realised, as soon as he heard the news, that here was the one possible chance for Athens to snatch a victory. Even with a strong following wind, Datis could not reach Phaleron by sea in less than nine or ten hours: twelve would be a more likely estimate. He was unlikely even to begin disembarking his troops and horses till late afternoon. Artaphernes was now very short on cavalry, though he still had his corps of archers. He had also, for safety's sake, redeployed his forces no more than a mile from the Athenian lines. If the Athenians could bring him to battle and beat him, they might just get back to Athens in time to deal with Datis. Even so, it would be . . . a damned close-run thing. Battle-weary troops could hardly hope to march those twenty-four miles in much less than seven or eight hours. By nine o'clock at the latest they would have to be on the

road. Callimachus agreed with Miltiades and, as Commander-in-Chief, decided to risk an engagement. It was about five-thirty a.m.

The troops were now drawn up in battle order. Callimachus himself commanded the right wing, where he had placed his own tribal division. The left wing was held by the Plataeans. The Leontid and Antiochid tribes were placed in the centre, with the remaining Athenian divisions spread out on either side of them. It was in the centre that the toughest fighting took place. (Themistocles was a Leontid, and Aristeides an Antiochid, so they were both in the thick of it.) Now if Callimachus had massed his troops eight deep, in the normal way, the Persians would easily have outflanked him. A front of 1,250 infantrymen, allowing a yard per man, is not all that wide, and once the Athenians left their entrenched position for the open plain they would become doubly vulnerable. . . . Callimachus and Miltiades therefore made a virtue of necessity. They deliberately thinned out their centre, widening the space between each man, and reducing the number of ranks to three or four at most. Their most powerful striking force they massed on the wings. Here Miltiades' intimate and detailed knowledge of Persian military customs proved invaluable. He must have guessed that Artaphernes, like all Persian commanders, was liable to place his crack troops in the centre, and his conscript levies on the wings. To risk—indeed, to invite—a Persian breakthrough in the centre was taking a calculated risk indeed. But if Callimachus and the Plataeans could knock out Artaphernes' wings quickly, and then wheel about to reinforce their own weakened centre, the battle was as good as won.

So they faced each other on that August morning—the 12th, in all likelihood—between the mountains and the sea. It was about six o'clock, and the sun had just risen across the water, above the Euboean hills. Bronze armour glinted; feet shuffled and stamped. Then came the shrill note of a trumpet, and the Athenian ranks moved forward, marching briskly, spears advanced: men with a job of work to do. . . . Artaphernes' troops were drawn up in line, waiting for them, a stationary barrier reaching from Mt

Kotroni to the shore, archers deployed in front, cavalry—what there was of it—on the wings. As the Greeks came within range of the Persian archers (at about 150 yards distance) they broke into a double, to get through that murderous hail of arrows as fast as possible, and engage.

The Persian order of battle was just as Miltiades had anticipated. Artaphernes' best troops—Iranian guardsmen reinforced by picked tribal warriors from the eastern frontier—were placed in the centre. His less reliable units, the satellite battalions of the empire, had been relegated to the wings. Amongst these were Ionian levies: Greek arrayed against Greek, and (as the events of the previous night suggest) probably not too happy about it. The Athenians had several other advantages to compensate for their lack of numbers. Greek discipline, Greek tactics, Greek weapons and body-armour were all very much superior to those of the Persians. It was long spear against javelin, short sword against dagger or scimitar, bronze-lapped cuirasses against quilted jerkins, bronze-faced shields against wicker targets. The Athenians had a first-rate battle-plan; best of all, they were not imperial conscripts, but free men fighting to preserve their freedom.

In the centre, predictably, the Persians had the best of it. Step by hard-fought step, sweating and gasping, the Athenian hoplites were forced back. . . . Here was where the brunt of the Persian attack fell; and it was here, in the front ranks of their respective divisions, that Themistocles and Aristeides fought. Meanwhile on the wings the Greeks had carried all before them. Many of the fleeing Persians stumbled into the Great Marsh and were drowned: their total death-roll reached the staggering figure of 6,400 and it was here that they incurred their heaviest casualties. . . . Other fugitives retreated along the narrow gap between the marsh and the shore, making for the ships hauled up in the lee of the Dog's Tail.

At this critical point Greek discipline once more proved its worth. There are few things harder to control than a military rout and pursuit. Yet both Athenians and Plataeans, once victory

was secure, disengaged according to plan. 'Having got the upper hand,' says Herodotus, 'they left the defeated Persians to make their escape, and then, drawing the two wings together into a single unit, they turned their attention to the Persians who had broken through in the centre'. The tactical skill which this complex movement implies is quite extraordinary. The Persian advance was contained and halted somewhere near the great mound which marks the burial-place of 'the men of Marathon'. The Athenian and Plataean wings about-faced, and hastened back the way they had come. They did not take the Persians in the rear (tempting though this must have been) because to do so might well have meant sacrificing their own hard-pressed centre altogether in the process. Instead, they outflanked the battle in a double-pincer movement, which strengthened the Athenian line with massive reinforcements, and, eventually, brought Artaphernes' advance to a standstill. Then the tide of battle turned, and the Persian line broke. Those who could forced their way through to the sea, and retreated along the foreshore, where their ships were launched and ready for departure.

The Athenians pursued them closely, cutting down stragglers in the shallows till the water ran red with blood, calling back to their camp-followers for torches to set the Persian vessels on fire. It was during this stage of the battle the Athenians suffered most of their astonishingly few casualties: only 192 all told. Callimachus the War Archon was killed, together with one of his divisional commanders; and as they reached the Dog's Tail, Cynegirus, the brother of Aeschylus the playwright, 'had his hand cut off as he was getting hold of a ship's stern, and so lost his life'. During the last stand by the Persian centre Artaphernes had had time to get most of his other surviving troops aboard, and to save a large part of his naval squadron. He lost only seven ships to the Athenians: with the rest he stood out to sea. It was at this point—better late than never—that the long-awaited signal was flashed from the mountains above Marathon. The Persians set course for . . . Phaleron, no doubt hoping to find Athens already occupied by

Datis—or at least to arrive before the Athenian army. It was about nine in the morning, perhaps even earlier: the battle and pursuit had taken something under three hours.

The Legend More Important than the Battle?

As if they had not done enough already, the Athenians once again achieved a near-miracle. Aristeides and the Antiochid division were left behind to guard the prisoners and booty. The rest at once set off back to Athens, each man for himself: 'as fast as their feet could carry them', Herodotus says, and one can well believe it. When they reached Athens, they took up a defensive position at Cynosarges, to the south of the city, facing Phaleron and the sea. They can scarcely have got there before four in the afternoon, and Datis's squadron may well have sailed into Phaleron roads an hour or less later. Yet that hour made all the difference, in more ways than one. The reappearance of the Marathon warriors—grim, indomitable, caked with dust and sweat and dried blood—not only gave Datis pause for thought; it also, obviously, came as an unexpected shock to the . . . pro-Persian party. A lot of people in Athens must have silently switched sides in a hurry: Datis would get no help from within the walls now.

His fleet rode at anchor for a while, presumably long enough to let Artaphernes and his battered survivors rejoin the main body. Then the entire Persian expeditionary force set sail, and retreated, somewhat ignominiously, to Asia, leaving 6,400 dead and an unrecorded number of prisoners behind them. Callimachus, on behalf of the State, had vowed a kid [young goat] to Artemis for every enemy soldier killed. The Athenians were forced to pay the debt by instalments, at the rate of five hundred a year. For the time being at least, Greece was rid of the Barbarian.

After the battle came the feasting, the epigrams, the propaganda, the tall stories: almost before the dead were buried, Marathon had become a legend. Giant warriors and ancestral heroes had, men said, fought in the Athenian ranks. Offerings of Persian spoils and armour flowed in to the temples of Olympia and Delphi. Statues were set up, hymns of thanksgiving composed. Those who died in the battle were sumptuously commemorated by the mound—originally over fifty feet high—which still marks their last resting-place. . . .

Practically speaking, Marathon was no kind of final solution: it merely postponed the day of reckoning. On the other hand, this unprecedented victory gave an enormous boost to Athenian morale. It showed that a well-trained Greek army could beat the Persians *on land*—something the Ionians had never contrived to do. Psychologically speaking, the legend became almost more important than the actual battle. It also very soon turned into a rallying-cry for conservatives and traditionalists of every sort. The 'men of Marathon', the heavy-armed soldiers who had saved Athens, alone and unaided except for one Plataean contingent, were all property-owning landowners or farmers. They came in after years to embody every known or remembered conservative virtue: selfless public service, old-fashioned morality, hard work, thrift, respect for one's parents and the gods. . . .

A Spartan army, two thousand strong, was sent off as promised the moment the moon was full, on 12 August—which happened to be the day on which Marathon was fought. Herodotus says that they 'were so anxious not to be late that they were in Attica on the third day after leaving Sparta [14 August]. They had, of course, missed the battle; but such was their passion to see the Persians, that they went to Marathon to have a look at the bodies. After that they complimented the Athenians on their good work, and returned home'. Curiously, whether the Spartans acted in good faith, or missed the battle on purpose, they still played a vital part in ensuring a Greek victory. The mere fact that they were, or might be, on the move forced both Datis and the pro-Persian group in Athens to act before they were ready. From this all else followed. The gates of Athens remained closed to the invader. There was no treacherous *coup* inside the city. . . . Datis did not even land his cavalry, let alone take Miltiades in the rear; and old Hippias had lost his last chance of re-establishing the Peisistratid dynasty in Athens. He sailed away with the Persian fleet, and died on the voyage back to Sigeum. Age and disappointment between them had finished him off: he had nothing left to live for.

Selection 2

The Persians' Massive Second Invasion of Greece

Peter Levi

This concise synopsis of the second and larger Persian attack on the Greek mainland (480–479 B.C.) is by Peter Levi, a classicist at Christ Church, Oxford. He picks up the narrative of the Greco-Persian wars directly following the resounding Athenian victory at Marathon in 490 and briefly covers the important political events leading up to the huge 480 offensive. This was led by Xerxes, who had inherited the Persian throne when his father, Darius, died in 486. The inter-war years witnessed continuing struggles between Athens and its rival neighbor, the island polis of Aegina, a major strike at Athens's silver mines at Larium in southeastern Attica, and the rise in influence of the Athenian politician Themistocles (who, fortunately for Athens, convinced his countrymen to use the riches from Larium to build a new fleet of warships). Levi then goes on to describe the outcomes of the Battles of Thermopylae, Artemisium, Salamis, and Plataea.

Excerpted from *Atlas of the Greek World*, by Peter Levi. Copyright © Equinox (Oxford) Ltd. Reproduced by permission of Andromeda Oxford Ltd.

*m*emorials in marble and bronze at Marathon and Delphi can hardly express the Athenian triumph. There were poems, a famous painting, legends and written histories. Six hundred and fifty years later, travelers still believed they heard ghostly noises of armed men when they crossed the battlefield. Those who fought at Marathon were known as the "men of Marathon" for the rest of their lives. At that time the Athenians undertook the strong and splendid older Parthenon [temple atop the Acropolis], which was still unfinished ten years later, when the Persians came back. These were also the years of the early development of tragic poetry (Aischylos was one of those who had fought at Marathon). In foreign affairs the Athenians were occupied with the continuing struggle, slightly more successful now, of their city against Aegina. It is instructive that in an action in 487 BC, the Athenians still had only 50 ships and dared not attack Aegina without borrowing another 20 from Corinth.

At home, Athenian politics developed towards direct democracy. The board of state officers was now appointed by lot, and since that is no way to appoint a military commander, authority in war was given to a board of ten elected generals, one from each tribe. In 487 Hipparchos the chief magistrate was exiled, and in 486 Megakles, a nephew of Kleisthenes, followed him. In 484 it was Xanthippos, who had married Kleisthenes' niece and fathered Perikles, who was ostracized. Miltiades, the hero of Marathon, died a disgraced adventurer. One at a time, the menace of individual members of these great families was being nullified. In the same years Themistokles was active. He first held office before Marathon and was another who fought there; his family was rich and noble, though he may himself have been a half-member of it; in the end he too died in exile, having been ostracized, as governor of a Greek city in the Persian empire.

It was Themistokles who fortified the Peiraeus, perhaps in imitation of the lagoon harbors of Corinth at Lechaion, but easily surpassing Corinth by the adaptation of rocky natural advantages. In 483 and 482, when the mines of Laurion first vomited silver in quantity from a deep level, he built up a fleet of 200 ships. When the Persians struck again, in 480 BC, Athens was for the first time in its history strong enough to win a victory greater than Marathon. It was Marathon that was remembered as the example, the first turning back of Asia. But the campaign of 480 was a much more serious threat. Darius himself did not live to invade again, although he began preparations. He was distracted by a rebellion in Egypt, and in 486 he died.

Xerxes and His Forces

Xerxes succeeded his father, and by the time Egypt was settled it was 484 BC. Xerxes moved carefully and in massive force. He had a canal cut on the inland side of Athos, to avoid a repetition of the 492 destruction of the Persian fleet, and a bridge built over the Strymon; his army gathered; in 481 he came down to Sardis, and spent the winter there.

Xerxes was a doomed character. When his host at Sardis begged that the oldest of his five conscripted sons be left at home, Xerxes had the lad cut in half and marched his army through the middle. Two great bridges were built for him to join Europe and Asia; when they were blown away in a gale he had the engineers beheaded and the sea itself flogged. In order to get his army across, he had that flogged as well.

The numbers of this enormous host given by the historian Herodotos, who was a young boy at the time, are so colossal it is hard to credit them. The army included Ethiopians in leopard skins with stone-tipped arrows, Persians in coats of mail and trousers, Indians in cotton, central Asians in goatskins, men armed with clubs, or daggers and lassos, Thracians in fox-fur hats, lancers, swordsmen, archers and persons in "dyed garments and high boots." We are told of more than one and a half million infantry and 80,000 cavalry; the real number of the whole land force was more likely less than 200,000, among whom the elite troops of the Persians numbered 10,000, and the Persian fleet comprised perhaps less than 1,000 ships.

As a flash of lightning at night reveals the shapes of mountains, this invasion reveals something about the communications of the Greeks. The Spartans held a congress at the Isthmus of Corinth, attended by 31 states. Thessaly, most of Boeotia, and the smaller groups of the north stayed at home; they stood in the immediate path of Persia, and had no reason to expect the south would protect them. Argos stayed at home because of the old hatred of Sparta; the Spartans had defeated the Argives severely on their own territory well within memory, and an embassy from the congress was fruitless. So, for various reasons, were the embassies sent to Crete, Corfu and Syracuse. Only Athens and Aegina seem to have been reconciled. But an army of 10,000 Greeks occupied the vale of Tempe, between Thessaly and Macedonia, and a fleet gathered; both these forces were under Spartan command. The army at Tempe retreated at once, because it was discovered on the spot that Tempe was only one of several passes, and it was felt that the Thessalians were insecure allies to have behind one's back.

The Greeks Achieve Complete Victory

Seven thousand men under King Leonidas of Sparta took up a new position opposite the north

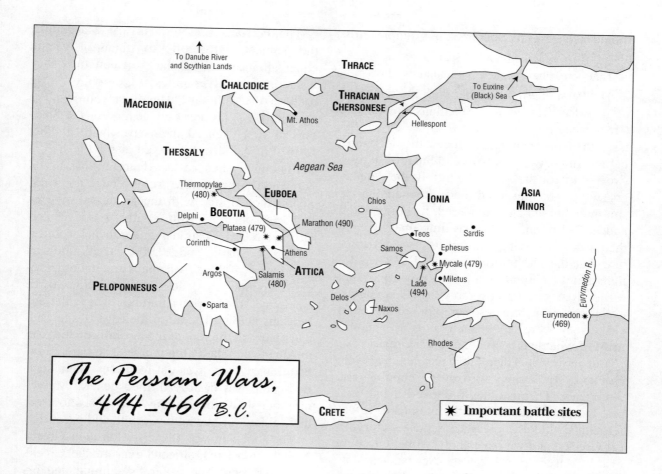

The Persian Wars, 494–469 B.C.

✴ **Important battle sites**

end of Euboea, at the top of a rocky pass above Thermopylai, the Hot Gates. The hot springs the pass is named for are still running, but the landscape has altered utterly; the river Spercheios has silted its estuary, and a coastal plain now carries the main road from north to south Greece where the ancient terrain was impassable. The army of 7,000 would have fallen back further to the Isthmus itself, but the Athenian fleet was now a crucial factor, and Athens must be defended at least symbolically. The main army in the Peloponnese refused to move, excusing itself by a festival of Apollo and by the Olympic festival. Meanwhile, the Athenians prudently evacuated their civilian population to the Peloponnese, retained half their fleet to guard their own coast, and sent half north with the other Greek ships to Artemision on the north coast of Euboea, with a rearguard at the straits opposite Chalkis. The whole Greek fleet had 280 ships. The huge con-

gregation of shipping that the Persians commanded stationed itself opposite, but on a bad shore. A tempest destroyed a large part of it.

At sea, local knowledge and seamanship favored the Greeks. On land, they suffered a disaster. There is seldom really only one route through Greek mountains. The Greeks were outflanked by the Persian elite troops, but they knew it in time, and all but 1,400 men retreated, some Thebans and Thespians, perhaps because their own country was so close, and 300 Spartans. Leonidas and his few men held the western end of the pass against the main body of the Persian army. He died, and two brothers of Xerxes died. After a ferocious and prolonged defense, the last Spartans died surrounded. The spirit in which the Spartans met their fate was one of resolute . . . courage, and a certain grim gaiety. . . . Their epitaph, almost certainly by the finest laconic poet of that or perhaps any age, Simonides, was simple; in Greek it is simpler still.

Tell them in Lakedaimon [Sparta], passer-by,
That here, obeying their command, we lie.

The Persian army together with the remnants of the fleet hunted the Athenians home. The Greek army mustered at the Isthmus, all but the last Athenians abandoned Athens, the fleet hung in the wind between Athens and Salamis. It took two weeks for the acropolis to fall, the defenders were all murdered and the sanctuaries smashed, burned and plundered. It is the broken and buried remnants of that time that are now the greatest surviving treasures of archaic sculpture, but the harmonious gaiety, the lively delight and the playful or solemn formality of that earlier time were irrecoverably lost. Sanctuaries, except those of Demeter, were not rebuilt for 50 years; they were left in their ruins as a monument of what had been done to the Greeks.

But it was at Athens that the Persians were checked. By various strokes of cunning and diplomacy, Themistokles provoked a battle at sea, between Salamis and the mainland. It was ferociously bloody, it was a complete victory for the Greeks, and we have an eyewitness account of it by Aischylos. "I saw the Aegean sea blossoming with corpses." "They smashed at men like tunny fish, with broken oars and pieces of timber." Xerxes, with an army of 60,000 men, retired into Asia, and set up headquarters in Sardis. The Persian army then reassembled in Thessaly to besiege fortified cities. Meanwhile, the Greeks were building monuments, settling accounts and distributing loot. . . . The Greeks had won a victory at sea and a moral victory on land; the retreat of those vast Persian hordes for the second time in ten years confirmed that it was worthwhile to continue to resist.

The Persians sent the king of Macedonia, their subject, with an offer to Athens of free and equal alliance; was it the Athenian fleet they wanted, or the silver mines of Laurion, or a safe road to the Isthmus? Athens stayed loyal to Sparta, but as the Persians advanced, the Spartans at first excused themselves with another festival of Apollo, and stayed inside the wall at the Isthmus. Then, at last, fearing what would happen if Athens were to surrender her fleet, Sparta moved, and with the greatest army that had ever emerged from southern into central Greece: 5,000 Spartans, 5,000 tribal soldiers subject to Sparta, and 20,000 serfs, joining an allied army of 8,000 Athenians and the other regional contingents, so that the whole force amounted to a serious number. They met the Persians below Plataiai on the edge of the Theban plains, at the foot of the last hills on the road to Athens and the Peloponnese. The Persian expeditionary force was cut to pieces, their fortified camp was destroyed, their general Mardonios perished, the leading Thebans who were their allies were taken to Corinth and executed.

The loot that was dispersed through Greece was the most magnificent treasure the Greeks had ever seen. The general's scimitar and his silver-footed throne were dedicated on the acropolis of Athens, and the Odeion of Perikles, the first roofed theater in Greece, designed for its acoustics, was an imitation made long afterward of the great audience tent of Xerxes, captured at that battle. At Delphi the memorial of the battle was the massive bronze column of three scaled snakes twisted together, with their three heads spitting outward at the top, and a golden tripod balanced on their noses.

Selection 3

An Eyewitness Describes the Battle of Salamis

Aeschylus

The Battle of Salamis took place on about September 20, 480 B.C. in the narrow strait between the island of Salamis and the coast of Attica a few miles southwest of Athens. Xerxes ordered his warships, numbering almost 600, into the strait and mounted a nearby hill to watch the conflict. He was at first confident that the fewer than 350 vessels in the combined Greek fleets (more than half of which were Athenian) would have no credible chance against his forces. To his mounting horror, however, the Greek ships steadily hemmed in the Persian galleys on one side of the strait and the greater Persian numbers proved a disadvantage in the confined space.

A detailed description of the battle was provided by the Athenian playwright Aeschylus, who actually fought at Salamis. In his play, The Persians, *first produced in 472 B.C., just eight years after the event, he includes the following scene, in which a Persian messenger brings news of the disaster to Atossa, Xerxes' mother. Although this is a dramatization, and therefore not a straightforward historical document, large sections clearly have* the ring of an eyewitness account.

a TOSSA: Now tell me how the two fleets fell to the attack.
Who first advanced, struck the first blow? Was it the Greeks,
Or my bold son, exultant with his countless ships?

MESSENGER: Neither, my queen. Some Fury, some malignant Power,
Appeared, and set in train the whole disastrous rout.
A Hellene [Greek] from the Athenian army [reportedly a servant sent by Themistocles to deceive the Persians] came and told
Your son Xerxes this tale: that, once the shades of night
Set in, the Hellenes would not stay, but leap on board,
And, by whatever secret route offered escape,
Row for their lives [i.e., run away]. When Xerxes heard this, with no thought
Of the man's guile, or of the jealousy of gods,
He sent this word to all his captains: 'When the sun
No longer flames to warm the earth, and darkness holds
The court of heaven, range the main body of our fleet

Threefold, to guard the outlets and the choppy
  straits.'
Then he sent other ships to row right round the
  isle [of Salamis],
Threatening that if the Hellene ships found a
  way through
To save themselves from death, he would cut off
  the head
Of every Persian captain. By these words he
  showed
How ignorance of the gods' intent had dazed his
  mind.

Our crews, then, in good order and obediently,
Were getting supper; then each oarsman looped
  his oar
To the smooth rowing-pin; and when the sun
  went down
And night came on, the rowers all embarked, and
  all
The heavy-armed soldiers; and from line to line
  they called,
Cheering each other on, rowing and keeping
  course
As they were ordered. All night long the captains
  kept
Their whole force cruising to and fro across the
  strait.
Now night was fading; still the Hellenes showed
  no sign
Of trying to sail out unnoticed; till at last
Over the earth shone the white horses of the day,
Filling the air with beauty. Then from the
  Hellene ships
Rose like a song of joy the piercing battle-cry,
And from the island crags echoed an answering
  shout.

The Persians knew their error; fear gripped every
  man.
They were no fugitives who sang that terrifying
Paean [battle hymn], but Hellenes charging with
  courageous hearts
To battle. The loud trumpet flamed along their
  ranks.
At once their frothy oars moved with a single
  pulse,

Beating the salt waves to the bo'suns' chant; and
  soon
Their whole fleet hove clear into view; their right
  wing first,
In precise order, next their whole array came on,
And at that instant a great shout beat on our ears:
'Forward, you sons of Hellas! Set your country
  free!
Set free your sons, your wives, tombs of your
  ancestors,
And temples of your gods. All is at stake: now
  fight!'
Then from our side in answer rose the manifold
Clamour of Persian voices; and the hour had come.

At once ship into ship battered its brazen beak.
A Hellene ship charged first, and chopped off the
  whole stern
Of a Phoenician galley [one of many ships from
  Persian vassal states]. Then charge followed
  charge
On every side. At first by its huge impetus
Our fleet withstood them. But soon, in that
  narrow space,
Our ships were jammed in hundreds; none could
  help another.
They rammed each other with their prows of
  bronze; and some
Were stripped of every oar. Meanwhile the
  enemy
Came round us in a ring and charged. Our
  vessels heeled
Over; the sea was hidden, carpeted with wrecks
And dead men; all the shores and reefs were full
  of dead.

Then every ship we had broke rank and rowed
  for life.
The Hellenes seized fragments of wrecks and
  broken oars
And hacked and stabbed at our men swimming
  in the sea
As fishermen kill tunnies or some netted haul.
The whole sea was one din of shrieks and dying
  groans,
Till night and darkness hid the scene. If I should
  speak

For ten days and ten nights, I could not tell you all
That day's agony. But know this: never before
In one day died so vast a company of men.

ATOSSA: Alas! How great an ocean of disaster has
Broken on Persia and on every eastern race!

MESSENGER: But there is more, and worse; my story is not half told.
Be sure, what follows twice outweighs what went before.

ATOSSA: What could be worse? What could our armament endure,
To outweigh all the sufferings already told?

MESSENGER: The flower of Persian chivalry and gentle blood,
The youth and valour of our choice nobility,
First in unmoved devotion to the king himself,
Are sunk into the mire of ignominious death.

ATOSSA: My friends, this evil news is more than I can bear.—
How do you say they died?

MESSENGER: Opposite Salamis
There is an island—small, useless for anchorage. . . .
There Xerxes sent them, so that, when the enemy,

Flung from their ships, were struggling to the island beach,
The Persian force might without trouble cut them down,
And rescue Persian crews from drowning in the sea:
Fatal misjudgement! When in the sea-battle Heaven
Had given glory to the Hellenes, that same day
They came, armed with bronze shields and spears, leapt from
their ships,
And made a ring round the whole island, that our men
Could not tell where to turn. First came a shower of blows
From stones slung with the hand; then from the drawn bow-string
Arrows leapt forth to slaughter; finally, with one
Fierce roar the Hellenes rushed at them, and cut and carved
Their limbs like butchers, till the last poor wretch lay dead.

This depth of horror Xerxes saw; close to the sea
On a high hill he sat, where he could clearly watch
His whole force both by sea and land. He wailed aloud,
And tore his clothes, weeping; and instantly dismissed
His army, hastening them to a disordered flight.

Selection 4

The Rise of Athens's Maritime Empire

Alan L. Boegehold

Brown University scholar Alan L. Boegehold tells here how the Delian League (or Confederacy of Delos) came into being following the expulsion of the Persians from Greece in 479 B.C. Although the alliance was originally intended to protect Greece from further Persian incursions, he explains, the Athenians almost immediately began transforming the organization into their own maritime empire, which they controlled by various means, including naked force.

"*A*thenian Empire" is a phrase in conventional use, describing a system of tribute-paying states who answered in varying ways to the authority of Athens. Originally they were autonomous members of an alliance of Greek city-states and islands formed in 478 after the battles of Plataea and Mycale [the last major battles of Xerxes' invasion of Greece] to defend Greeks against anticipated Persian invasions, and to avenge damage and injuries done by the Persians in the recent past. This alliance came under Athenian military leadership after the Spartan regent and general Pausanias disgraced himself and the Spartans withdrew from further participation in the struggle against Persia. States from

Reprinted with the permission of The Free Press, a division of Simon & Schuster, from "The Athenian Empire in Thucydides," by Alan L. Boegehold, in *Landmark Thucydides: A Comprehensive Guide to the Peloponnesian War*, edited by Robert B. Strassler. Copyright © 1996 by Robert B. Strassler.

the allied fleet asked Athens to lead them and Athens complied: she was in an advantageous position to command, employing as she did a large and active fleet and enjoying a new and singular reputation for heroism gained by her triumph at the battle of Marathon, her people's heroic evacuation of their city, and her role in the recent naval victory of Salamis.

Establishment of the Delian League

The new alliance is known as the Delian League because its members at first conducted their deliberations and established their treasury on the small centrally located island of Delos, an ancient Ionian sanctuary sacred to Apollo. Most of the island cities in the Aegean Sea and many coastal cities of Thrace and Asia Minor became members, recognizing that they were vulnerable to Persian forces and exposed to an allied Greek fleet that could either support or harry them. When the Athenian Aristides, widely known as "the Just," took command, he designed a League fund to which member states were to contribute money annually, with each paying an amount determined more or less by its size and resources. It was agreed that some nautical cities, and the major islands of Chios, Lesbos, and Samos, would contribute ships and manpower in lieu of money. All member states took an oath binding them permanently to the alliance. Although each member theoretically had an equal say in League matters, there was no major, counterbalancing force against that of Athens to attract clusters of votes in opposition. For this reason, when there was great diversity of opinion among members, any few who voted with Athens weighted the balloting enough for Athens to prevail; and there would always be some who would cooperate with her. In time the restless energy of the Athenians almost inevitably transformed their initial commanding position among equals into that of a ruling power.

The genesis and duration of the Athenian Empire can be sketched in its larger outlines from several ancient written sources. Thucydides' description of the years between the defeat of the Persians in 479 and the outbreak of the Peloponnesian War in 431—known as the "Pentecontaetia" ["fifty years"] by scholars, although it does not exactly comprise fifty years—is our most substantial account of this period, despite some surprising omissions. [The later ancient Greek writers] Plutarch and Diodorus Siculus also provide important information, and other details can be drawn from various surviving state documents inscribed on stone. And yet despite this comparative abundance of evidence for a short period of time, many elements of chronology and sequence continue to resist satisfactory ordering. There can be no doubt, however, that Athens' empire ceased to exist when her fleet was defeated and captured by the Peloponnesians at Aegospotami in 405.

After Aristides came Cimon son of Miltiades, one of Athens' greatest generals. He assumed command of the Greek forces and vigorously and successfully set about driving the Persians out of the Aegean. By the early 460s (467?), when Cimon won his most famous victory over the Persians in a combined land and sea battle at the Eurymedon River in Pamphylia [in southern Asia Minor], the Delian League comprised nearly two hundred member states and controlled not only the entire Aegean Sea but also a broad coastal strip of western Asia Minor. Many of these states benefited greatly from their membership in an alliance that suppressed piracy, en-

couraged trade and commerce, and provided employment for the poor as rowers in the fleet. Moreover, Athens generally favored democratic factions, and when oligarchs and democrats in a given state were almost equally matched in a struggle for dominance, Athenian support could prove decisive for the democrats. Democratic regimes that owed their establishment and continued existence to Athens tended to be reliable and loyal subject allies. They might have preferred autonomy, but, for many, answering to Athens was an acceptable alternative to the rule of local oligarchs. . . .

In time, may members of the League found their contributions of military service and ships onerous, and elected to pay a cash equivalent instead. Athens used these funds to improve her own properly equipped and well-trained fleet. As a result, Athens found herself in an even better position to collect tribute from reluctant allies, and such allies found themselves less able to offer serious resistance to Athenian demands. By 431, only [the Aegean island states of] Lesbos and Chios continued to supply ships of their own and to enjoy the status of privileged allies rather than subjects.

Instruments of Athenian Power

States who sought to leave the alliance found early on that Athens would not permit them to do so. Naxos (before 467) and Thasos (465–62) tried to break away but were besieged, defeated, and compelled to remain as members. When the large island of Samos defied Athens in 440, a major military campaign was mounted to subdue and punish her. The revolts of Lesbos in 428 and of Chios and other states in 411 were more threatening still, because they took place during the Peloponnesian War. Athens responded to these uprisings with increasingly firm and harsh measures designed to maintain and even to increase the nature and extent of her rule. Opponents were exiled or executed. Fines were levied, and in some cases land was confiscated and allocated to Athenian citizens. Some states that refused to become members of the alliance were compelled to join it. This odious use of imperial power, perhaps based on the presumption that those who are not with us are against us, was first employed against Carystus in Euboea around 472; it culminated in the brutal conquest of Melos in 415, and collapsed in Athens' total and calamitous failure to subjugate Syracuse two years later.

Relations with Sparta began to deteriorate when Cimon, in 462, persuaded the Athenians to help the Spartans, who were besieging Messenians and Helots at Mount Ithome. When the Spartans rudely sent the Athenians home soon after they had arrived, many Athenians were offended and blamed Cimon personally. Not long afterward they ostracized him, but they recalled him before his ten-year banishment was complete so that he could again command their forces against the Persians. He died while leading a Greek fleet at Citium on the island of Cyprus around 450. Cimon's death, together with the outbreak of open conflict with Sparta and the destruction by Persia of a large Greek fleet in Egypt in 454, may well have led Athens to increase her control over the League. In any case, she moved the League treasury from Delos to Athens in 454/3, and seems thereafter to have consulted less and less with the allies about questions of policy. In her official language, she began to refer to the allies as "all the cities that Athens rules." Pericles had reason to warn his fellow citizens in 429 that their rule over the empire was a tyranny, one that it may have been wrong to take, but which by that time was very dangerous to let go.

For some reason, Athenian military activity against Persia ceased shortly after Cimon's death. There is a persistent tradition in the fourth century that the Athenian Callias, son of Hipponicus, secured a formal peace with Persia around this time—the mid–fifth century. By the terms of that peace, it is thought that Persia agreed that her ships would not sail west of Phaselis or out of the Black Sea, and that her *satraps* (governors of Persian provinces) would not attempt to force Athenian allies to return to Persian rule. Thucydides, however, does not mention any such peace treaty, nor do other fifth-century writers. As a result, there is wide disagreement whether such a "Peace of Callias," which occupies a key place in modern (and authoritative) reconstruction of the course of the Athenian Empire, was actually made.

Athens also exerted control over her subjects through judicial agreements. Questions of justice required agreements between states—if only to determine where complaints would be heard. Often more complex questions needed to be addressed, such as the class of offense, the kind of court, and the citizenship of the perpetrator. It was normal for a state to enter into a formal agreement with another to regulate such matters, and the two would publish their own particular rules of administration. Athenians required that a larger number and variety of cases be tried at Athens than was usual in such agreements. They believed their courts were just and fair to their subjects, and indeed they complained that despite their superior power, they abided by such agreements to their own disadvantage. It is relevant to note that after 462, when Athenian popular courts entered a new era, one in which the people adjudicated a vastly wider array of suits and prosecutions, their facilities for judging, that is, courts and personnel, functioned at a level of volume and complexity higher than anything that could be found anywhere else in the Aegean basin.

Whether the allocation of legal business was consistent with perfect equity or not is a moot point. Certainly, Athens wielded various instruments of power effectively, at least during the first sixty years of its empire. An important control was her ability to modulate a robust flow of commercial traffic by sea and to pay for an abundance of goods, from basic foodstuffs to luxuries, all of which meant profit for those who did business with her. This power was used against Megara when Athens by decree barred Megarians from conducting trade in any ports of the empire or the markets of Attica. This particular prohibition proved so harmful to Megara and was considered so outrageous that its repeal was among the key Peloponnesian demands that preceded the outbreak of war. In addition, the

League treasurers (*hellenotamiai*), who were all Athenians, collected the tribute and acted as enforcers when states were slow to pay. In some locations—for example, on Lemnos, Imbros, the Chersonese, as well as at Histiaea, Aegina, Lesbos and Melos—Athens settled her own citizens as colonists or lot-holders (*clerouchs*) who turned their new land into virtual extensions of Athens, and served, if only by their presence, as Athenian garrisons overseeing the local citizens. In time, Athens also imposed on her tributary allies her own silver coinage and a system of standard weights and measures.

When the Athenians moved the League treasury to Athens in 454/3, they consecrated a sum equal to one sixtieth of each year's tribute to Athena, tutelary goddess of Athens, and used that money in various ways to enhance their city; they could now pay citizens to hold many civic offices, and they could honor Athena on the Acropolis with magnificent new buildings such as the Parthenon and the Propylaia. A fragmentary record of these appropriated sums, published as lists inscribed on marble slabs, begins in 454/3 and ends possibly in 410/409. A 5 percent harbor tax imposed on the allies in 413 may have turned out to be more practicable. . . .

Plutarch wrote that Pericles had to respond to complaints that he should not use League contributions to beautify Athens. In reply, he said that the allies contributed nothing but money, and that as long as the Athenians did their job, which was to run the war against Persia, they did not need to present any accounting to those who gave the money. This cool assessment is in its tone quite in keeping with the chilling Athenian "realpolitik" of the Melian Dialogue [the words spoken, according to Thucydides, between negotiators from Athens and the island of Melos when the Melians were refusing to knuckle under to Athens]: those who have power do what they like, those who do not, do what they must.

Selection 5

A Contemporary View of the Turbulent Mid–Fifth Century B.C.

Thucydides

Excerpted from *The History of the Peloponnesian War*, by Thucydides, translated by Rex Warner (Penguin Classics, 1954, revised ed., 1972). Translation copyright © 1954 by Rex Warner. Reprinted by permission of Penguin Books Ltd.

In his great history of the Peloponnesian War (431–404 B.C.), Thucydides (ca. 460–ca. 399) included a section on the political and military events of the Pentekontaetia, the so-

called "Fifty Years" between the end of the Persian invasions (479) and the outbreak of the Peloponnesian conflict. The following portion of the narrative covers the major events from 464 to 439. Historians sometimes refer to the conflicts of these years collectively as the "First Peloponnesian War." Whatever one calls the period, there is no doubt that its tensions and animosities constituted the long-range causes of the great war that erupted in 431.

*a*nd now [in 464 B.C.] the Spartans, finding that their war in Ithome [against the rebellious helots] showed no signs of ending, appealed for help to their allies, including Athens, and the Athenians came to Sparta with a considerable force under the command of Cimon. The chief reason that they asked for Athenian help was that the Athenians had the reputation of being good at siege operations, and, after a long siege, it became clear to the Spartans that they themselves lacked experience in this department of warfare; for otherwise they would have succeeded in taking the place by assault. This expedition was the occasion for the first open quarrel between Athens and Sparta. The Spartans, failing to capture Ithome by assault, grew afraid of the enterprise and the unorthodoxy of the Athenians; they reflected, too, that they were of a different nationality and feared that, if they stayed on in the Peloponnese, they might listen to the people in Ithome and become the sponsors of some revolutionary policy. So, while keeping the rest of their allies, they sent the Athenians home again, not saying openly what their suspicions were, but merely declaring that they had no further need of Athenian help. The Athenians, however, realized that they were not being sent away for any such honourable reason as this, and saw that in fact they had become in some way suspect. They were deeply offended, considering that this was not the sort of treatment that they deserved from Sparta, and, as soon as they had returned, they denounced the original treaty of alliance which had been made against the Persians and allied themselves with Sparta's enemy, Argos. At the same time both Argos and Athens made an alliance on exactly the same terms with the Thessalians.

Meanwhile the rebels in Ithome after ten years' fighting [an error; it was more like four] were unable to hold out longer, and came to terms with Sparta, the terms being that they should have a safe conduct to leave the Peloponnese and should never set foot in it again: if any of them was caught there in future, he should be the slave of whoever caught him. There was also an oracle from Delphi which the Spartans had and which instructed them to let go the suppliant of Zeus at Ithome. So they left the country with their wives and children, and the Athenians, because of the ill feeling against Sparta which had already developed, received the exiles and settled them in the town of Naupactus, which they had recently taken from the Ozolian Locrians.

At this time Megara also joined the Athenian alliance, abandoning her alliance with Sparta because the Corinthians were attacking her in a war concerning the frontier boundaries. Thus the Athenians held Megara and Pegae, and built for the Megarians their long walls from the city to Nisaea, garrisoning them with Athenian troops. It was chiefly because of this that the Corinthians began to conceive such a bitter hatred for Athens.

About this time [460 B.C.] Inaros, the son of Psammetichus, a Libyan and the King of the Libyans bordering on Egypt, starting out from Marea, the town south of Pharos, organized the revolt of nearly the whole of Egypt from the Persian King Artaxerxes. After taking over power himself he called in the Athenians to help him. The Athenians happened to be engaged in a campaign against Cyprus with 200 ships of their own and of their allies; they abandoned this campaign, came to Egypt, and sailed from the sea up the Nile. They gained control of the river and of two-thirds of Memphis, and then attempted to subdue the remaining third, which was called the White Castle and inside which were the Persians and Medes who had escaped and those of the Egyptians who had not joined in the revolt.

At this time, too, the Athenians sent out a fleet and made a landing at Haliae [in the western Argolid]. Here they were engaged by a force of Corinthians and Epidaurians, and the Corinthians were victorious. Later there was a sea battle . . . between the Athenian and Peloponnesian fleets, and the Athenians were victorious.

Athens Fights Aegina, Corinth, and Sparta

After this [in 459 B.C.] war broke out between Athens and Aegina, and there was a big battle at sea off Aegina between the Athenians and the Aeginetans, with the support of allies on both sides. The battle was won by the Athenians, who captured seventy enemy ships. They then landed on Aegina and started to besiege the place, under the command of Leocrates, the son of Stroebus. At this point the Peloponnesians, wishing to relieve Aegina, made a landing in the island with 300 hoplites who had previously been serving with the Corinthians and Epidaurians. At the same time the Corinthians and their allies seized the heights of Geraneia and moved down into the Megarid, believing that it would be impossible for the Athenians to come to the relief of Megara, since they had two large forces already serving abroad in Aegina and in Egypt; and, they thought, if Athens did manage to relieve Megara, she would have to withdraw her troops from Aegina. The Athenians, however, did nothing of the kind. They raised in the city a force out of the old men and the very young who had been left behind and marched to Megara under the command of Myronides. Here an indecisive battle was fought between them and the Corinthians, and when the battle was broken off, each side considered that it had had the advantage. However, after the Corinthians had withdrawn, the Athenians, who had in fact done best in the fighting, set up a [victory] trophy. About twelve days later the Corinthians, who had had to suffer the taunts of the older people in their own city, made their preparations, marched out, and put up a trophy of their own to prove that the victory had been theirs. The Athenians came out

against them from Megara, overwhelmed the contingent that was setting up the trophy, and then engaged and defeated the rest of their enemy. As the defeated Corinthians were retreating, quite a large section of their army, coming under severe pressure and being uncertain of its route, plunged into an enclosure on someone's estate which had a deep ditch all round it so that there was no way out. Seeing what had happened, the Athenians closed up the main entrance with their hoplites and, surrounding the rest of the enclosure with light-armed troops, stoned to death all who were inside. This was a very severe blow to the Corinthians. The main body of their army fell back on Corinth.

At about this time [457 B.C.] the Athenians began to build their two long walls down to the sea, one to Phalerum and one to Piraeus. And at the same time the Phocians started a campaign against Doris, the original homeland of the Spartans, containing the towns of Boeum, Cytinium, and Erineum. When they had captured one of these places the Spartans came to the assistance of the Dorians with a force of 1,500 hoplites of their own and 10,000 of their allies. This force was commanded by Nicomedes, the son of Cleombrotus, acting as deputy for the Spartan King Pleistoanax, who was still under age. The Spartans compelled the Phocians to come to terms and to give back the town which they had taken. They then began to think of their return journey. If they went by sea, across the Gulf of Crisa, the Athenians would be able to sail up with their fleet and stop them; nor did the route across Geraneia appear to be a safe one, since the Athenians held Megara and Pegae. The passes over Geraneia are difficult ones and were always guarded by the Athenians; moreover, on this occasion the Spartans had information that the Athenians had every intention of preventing them from taking this route. It seemed best, therefore, to stay in Boeotia and wait and see what the safest line of march would be. In this course they were also influenced by the fact that there was a party in Athens who were secretly negotiating with them in the hope of putting an end to democratic government and preventing the building of the Long Walls.

The Athenians marched out against them with their whole army, supported by 1,000 troops from Argos and by contingents from their other allies, making up altogether a force of 14,000 men. They made this attack partly because they thought that the Spartans were in difficulties about their way back, and partly because they had some suspicions of the plot to overthrow the democracy.

The battle was fought at Tanagra in Boeotia, and, after great losses on both sides, the Spartans and their allies were victorious. The Spartans then marched down into the Megarid, and, after cutting down some of the plantations of trees, returned home through Geraneia and past the Isthmus [of Corinth]. The Athenians, on the sixty-second day after the battle, marched into Boeotia under the command of Myronides. They defeated the Boeotians in battle at Oenophyta and conquered the whole of Boeotia and Phocis. They pulled down the fortifications of Tanagra and took as hostages a hundred of the richest people among the Opuntian Locrians. Meanwhile they finished the building of their own Long Walls. Shortly afterwards Aegina surrendered, and was forced to destroy her fortifications, to hand over her fleet, and to agree to pay tribute in the future. Then, too, the Athenians, under the command of Tolmides, the son of Tolmaeus, sailed round the Peloponnese, burnt the Spartan dockyards, captured the Corinthian city of Chalcis, and, after making a landing at Sicyon, defeated the Sicyonians in battle.

Disaster in Egypt

Meanwhile the Athenian and allied force in Egypt was still engaged, and suffered all the chances and changes of war. At first the Athenians were masters of Egypt, and the King of Persia sent to Sparta a Persian named Megabazus with money to bribe the Spartans to invade Attica and so force the Athenians to recall their fleet from Egypt. These negotiations, however, were unsuccessful, and as the money was being spent without any results, Megabazus and what remained of it were recalled to Asia. The King

then [in 454 B.C.] sent out to Egypt another Persian, Megabazus, the son of Zopyrus, with a large army. He arrived by land, defeated the Egyptians and their allies in battle, and drove the Hellenes out of Memphis. In the end he penned them up on the island of Prosopitis and besieged them there for eighteen months. Finally he drained the channels round the island by diverting the water elsewhere. The ships were thus left high and dry; most of the island was connected with the mainland, and he captured it by marching across to it on foot. So, after six years of war, this great venture of the Hellenes came to nothing. Out of the whole great force a few managed to make their way through Libya and find safety in Cyrene, but nearly all were destroyed. Egypt once more passed into the control of the King of Persia, except that Amyrtaeus, the King in the marshes, still kept his independence. Because of the size of the marshes it was impossible to capture him: also the Egyptians who live in the marshes are the most warlike of their race. Inaros, the King of the Libyans, who had been the person responsible for the Egyptian revolt, was betrayed to the Persians and crucified. Meanwhile fifty triremes from Athens and the rest of the League had sailed out to relieve the forces in Egypt. They put in at the Mendesian mouth of the Nile, having no idea of what had happened. Here they were under attack from the land by the Persian army and from the sea by the Phoenician fleet. Most of the ships were lost, though a few managed to escape. This was the end of the great expedition against Egypt made by the Athenians and their allies. . . .

Three years later [450 B.C.] a five years' truce was made between Athens and the Peloponnese. Having no Hellenic war on their hands, the Athenians, under the command of Cimon, made an expedition against [the Persians at] Cyprus with 200 ships of their own and of their allies. Sixty of these were detached to go to Egypt at the request of Amyrtaeus, the King in the marshes; with the rest they laid siege to Citium. Cimon's death, however, and also a shortage of provisions made them leave Citium. Then, when they were sailing off Salamis in Cyprus, they fought both by land and sea with an army and a fleet of Phoenicians, Cyprians, and Cilicians. They were victorious in both battles, and then went home together with the sixty ships which had returned from Egypt.

After this the Spartans engaged in the campaign known as the sacred war. They took over the temple at Delphia and gave it back to the Delphians. As soon as they had retired, the Athenians marched out, took the temple again, and gave it back to the Phocians.

Some time after this [447 B.C.] the exiled party among the Boeotians gained possession of Orchomenus, Chaeronea, and some other Boeotian towns. The Athenians, under the command of Tolmides, the son of Tolmaeus, marched against these enemy strongholds with a force of 1,000 of their own hoplites and contingents from their allies. They captured Chaeronea, made slaves of the inhabitants, and left a garrison in the town before retiring. On their way back they were attacked at Coronea by the Boeotian exiles from Orchomenus supported by Locrians, by exiles from Euboea, and by others who shared their political views. This force defeated the Athenians, killing some of them and taking others alive. The Athenians then made a treaty by which they got back their prisoners at the price of evacuating the whole of Boeotia. The exiled party among the Boeotians came back into power and the other states also regained their independence.

Not long after this [in 446 B.C.], Euboea revolted from Athens. Pericles had already crossed over to the island with an Athenian army when he received the news that Megara had revolted, that the Peloponnesians were on the point of invading Attica, and that the Megarians had destroyed the Athenian garrisons except for a few who had managed to escape to Nisaea; in making this revolt Megara had called in the aid of Corinth, Sicyon, and Epidaurus. Pericles hurried-

Pericles

ly brought the army back from Euboea, and soon afterwards the Peloponnesians, under the command of the Spartan King Pleistoanax, the son of Pausanias, invaded Attica, laying waste the country as far as Eleusis and Thria. Then, without advancing any farther, they returned home.

The Athenians, under the command of Pericles, crossed over again into Euboea and subdued the whole island. . . .

Soon after they had returned from Euboea [446–445 B.C.] the Athenians made a thirty years' truce with Sparta and her allies: Athens gave up Nisaea, Pegae, Troezen, and Achaea—all places which they had seized from the Peloponnesians.

The Rebellion of Samos

In the sixth year of the truce [440 B.C.] war broke out between Samos and Miletus over the question of Priene. After having had the worst of the fighting the Milesians came to Athens and lodged violent protests against the Samians. Their cause was supported by various private individuals from Samos itself who wished to set up there a different form of government. So the Athenians sailed to Samos with forty ships and established a democracy there. They took fifty boys and fifty men as hostages and kept them in Lemnos. Then, leaving a garrison behind in Samos, they returned home. However, some of the Samians, instead of staying on the island, had fled to the mainland. These entered into communications with the leading oligarchs still in the city and also made an alliance with Pissuthnes, the son of Hystaspes, who at that time was the Persian Governor at Sardis. They raised a force of about 700 mercenaries, and passed over into Samos under cover of night. First they made an attack on the democratic party and imprisoned most of the leaders; then they rescued the hostages from Lemnos and declared themselves independent. They handed over to Pissuthnes the troops in the Athenian garrison and the Athenian officials who had been left in Samos, and at once made preparations for an attack on Miletus. At the same time Byzantium joined them in revolting from Athens.

When the Athenians heard of this they sailed against Samos with a fleet of sixty ships. Sixteen of these were not brought into action: some had been sent to Caria to watch the movements of the Phoenician fleet; others had gone to Chios and Lesbos with orders to send reinforcements. The remaining forty-four, under the command of Pericles and nine other commanders, fought, off the island of Tragia, with a Sarnian fleet of seventy ships which was returning from Miletus and included twenty transports. The result was a victory for the Athenians.

Later they were reinforced by forty ships from Athens and twenty-five from Chios and Lesbos. Having landed on the island and established their superiority with their ground forces, they built three walls to blockade the city, which was already blockaded from the sea. Pericles then took sixty ships from the fleet anchored off Samos and sailed away at full speed for Caunus and Caria, since news had arrived that the Phoenician fleet was on its way against them. Stesagoras and others, with five ships, had actually left Samos and gone to enlist the aid of the Phoenicians. During Pericles' absence the Samians put out to sea in a surprise attack; they fell upon the Athenian camp, which had not been fortified, destroyed the ships that were posted to keep a look-out, and defeated in battle the other ships that were launched to meet them. So for about fourteen days they controlled the sea round their island and were free to bring in or take out what they wanted. But when Pericles returned they were once more under naval blockade. Later the Athenian fleet was reinforced from Athens with forty ships under the command of Thucydides, Hagnon, and Phormio, and twenty more under the command of Tlepolemus and Anticles; also thirty ships from Chios and Lesbos. The Samians made a brief effort at resistance by sea, but were unable to hold their own and were forced to accept terms of surrender after a nine months' siege: they pulled down their walls, gave hostages, handed over their fleet, and agreed to pay reparations in instalments at regular intervals. Byzantium also agreed to return to its status of a subject city.

Selection 6

The Causes of the Peloponnesian War

Raphael Sealey

Drawing frequently on Thucydides' pivotal history, Raphael Sealey of the University of

Excerpted from *A History of the Greek City States, 700–338 B.C.*, by Raphael Sealey. Copyright © 1976 The Regents of the University of California. Reprinted by permission of the University of California Press.

California, Berkeley, devotes most of this brief examination to the immediate cause of the great war that brought Athens to its knees and exhausted all of the states that took part. Corcyra (modern Corfu), an island off the Greek mainland's western coast, was a

Corinthian colony; and Epidamnus, a city located farther up that coast, in what is now Albania, was Corcyra's own colony. In 435 B.C. these states became involved in a serious dispute that drew in Corinth and Athens; and the Corinthians eventually asked Sparta to intervene. After considering this and other political crises of the late 430s B.C., Sealey speculates about some of the war's long-range causes, explaining that they are less well documented than the immediate causes and therefore more difficult to assess.

In 431 the Athenians, with their Empire and some other allies, went to war against the Spartans, whose allies included states within and beyond the Peloponnese. The ensuing struggle, the Peloponnesian War (431–404), was interrupted by some years of peace after 421 but it may be said to have lasted twenty-seven years, until Athens was besieged and yielded, giving up her Empire. . . . The causes continue to be disputed. Opinions vary between two extremes. On the one hand, some historians claim that the war was the result of a long process, namely of the growth of Athenian power ever since 478 and of the Spartan response to that phenomenon. . . . At the other extreme, some historians claim that war broke out as a result, perhaps unforeseen, of several incidents occurring and decisions taken in the second half of the 430s; these historians give primary attention to "the complaints and the disputes," as Thucydides calls them. The next step here will be to outline those incidents and the consequent diplomatic interchanges.

Athens's Troubles With Corcyra and Poteidaea

Epidamnus had been founded as a colony from Corcyra, probably in the [mid-to-late seventh century B.C.]. . . . Civil strife came to a climax there in the 430s; one party was expelled and it joined the local barbarians in harassing the city. So the Epidamnians of the city appealed to Corcyra for help and, when they were rebuffed there,

they took their appeal to Corinth. In response the Corinthians, calling to mind old grievances against Corcyra, prepared to send additional settlers and troops to Epidamnus. The Corcyreans resented this interference; they sent a fleet to support the Epidamnian exiles and to besiege the city. Thereupon the Corinthians raised a fleet from themselves and their allies and sent it in the direction of Corcyra. The two fleets met off Leucimme, a promontory of Corcyra, in 435; the result of the battle was a severe defeat for Corinth. On the same day the city of Epidamnus surrendered to the force besieging it. . . .

The Corinthians were unwilling to accept the defeat as final; they spent 434 and much of the next year building ships and gathering rowers from the Peloponnese and other parts of Greece. So the Corcyreans, fearing a new and larger expedition, sent an embassy to Athens to seek an alliance (433). The Corinthians sent a counter-embassy to dissuade the Athenians from helping Corcyra. The Athenians held two meetings of the assembly to consider the question. At the first they were as much persuaded by the Corinthians as by the Corcyreans. At the second they still refused to make an offensive and defensive alliance with Corcyra or, in Greek terms, an agreement to have the same friends and enemies, for this could obligate them to join the Corcyreans in an attack on Corinth and thereby break the Thirty Years' Peace; but they made a defensive alliance, requiring each party to come to the aid of the other, if it was attacked. Shortly afterwards the Athenians sent a force to Corcyra, but it consisted of only ten ships and it had instructions not to fight the Corinthians unless they threatened Corcyrean territory directly.

A large fleet, drawn from Corinth and her allies, proceeded towards Corcyra in 433. The Corcyrean fleet, together with the ten Athenian ships, engaged it in battle among the Sybota islands near the mainland opposite the southern end of Corcyra. As the fighting proceeded, the Athenian ships joined in the action. For a considerable time the Corinthians seemed likely to win; in particular, their left wing put the corresponding part of the Corcyrean line to flight. But late in the day twenty more ships from Athens approached the scene of fighting; the Athenians had decided that the original ten ships were too few for their task. The Corinthians, however, thought that the twenty ships were the vanguard of a larger force, and they retreated; on the next day they prepared to sail home. Thus although Athenian participation in the engagement was slight, it converted a probable Corinthian victory into an indecisive battle.

In the winter of 433/2 another incident developed and this time Athenian provocation was more apparent. The trouble concerned Poteidaea, which held the isthmus of Pallene, the westernmost promontory of the Chalcidice peninsula. Poteidaea was a colony of Corinth and it received supervisory magistrates from the mother city at regular intervals. It was also a member of the Delian League and paid tribute to Athens. Thus it was a place where Athenian and Peloponnesian claims might clash. In the winter of 433/2 the Athenians sent the Poteidaeans an ultimatum; they were required to dismantle the part of their fortifications facing Pallene, to give hostages, and to exclude the Corinthian supervisory magistrates. The Poteidaeans are recorded in the tribute quota list as paying tribute for 433/2 and indeed at a higher figure than usual. But rather than comply with the ultimatum they sent envoys to Corinth; the envoys proceeded with some Corinthians to Sparta and gained some assurance from the Lacedaemonians [Spartans] that these would invade Attica, if the Athenians attacked Poteidaea. Then Poteidaea rebelled against Athens, apparently some little time after the date in the spring of 432 when the tribute was due. . . .

When Poteidaea rebelled, some at least of the cities of Chalcidice joined the revolt and . . . set up a federal state with its capital at Olynthus. The Corinthians responded to the revolt of the Poteidaeans by sending a force, including 1,600 hoplites, under Aristeus to help them. The Athenians, however, sent 2,000 hoplites and forty ships under Callias to operate against . . . the rebels. Callias . . . defeated the Poteidaeans outside their town and began besieging it from the

side where the isthmus lay. Later the Athenians sent reinforcements under Phormion; he completed the blockade of Poteidaea by investing it from the side of Pallene. . . .

After Callias had defeated the Poteidaeans and the siege of Poteidaea had begun, the Corinthians complained to Sparta. Complaints against Athens were received from other allies too. The Spartans accordingly called a meeting of their public assembly; it heard speeches by some of the allies, by an Athenian embassy, and by some Spartans. Then the presiding ephor, Sthenelaidas, formulated the issue in a tendentious way; those, he said, who thought that the Thirty Years' Peace had been broken and that the Athenians were committing injustice were to go to one side, and those who thought otherwise were to go to the other. A large majority of the voters were of the opinion that the Thirty Years' Peace had been broken.

This decision of the Spartan assembly did not lead to immediate military action, and the subsequent delays confirm the inference that Spartan counsels were divided. The meeting of the Spartan assembly took place sometime in the summer of 432, and in consequence of the vote the Spartans invited their allies to send envoys to a congress of the Peloponnesian League. The congress met at Sparta in about the fall of the year and voted by a majority in favor of going to war. Thereafter military preparations took some time; after giving the vote of the congress Thucydides (1.125.2) comments: "A year did not pass by but less, before the Peloponnesians invaded Attica and openly went to war.". . .

The Megarian Blockade and Other Factors

Other allies of Sparta, besides Corinth, had grievances against Athens, and these deserve some attention. When the Spartans called a meeting of the assembly in the summer of 432, some Aeginetans complained privately that the Athenians had infringed their autonomy in contravention of the Thirty Years' Peace. It has been conjectured that Athens had stationed a garrison in Aegina, but there can be no certainty. More can be said about a complaint which the Megarians presented on the same occasion; the Athenians had passed a decree excluding them from the Athenian market place and from the harbors of the Athenian Empire. Thucydides mentions this decree again (1.139.1), when he relates the diplomatic interchanges which followed between Athens and Sparta in the winter of 432/1 after the congress of the Peloponnesian League; at one stage Lacedaemonian envoys bade the Athenians raise the siege of Poteidaea and respect the autonomy of Aegina, and above all they insisted that there would be no war if the Athenians repealed the decree about Megara.

Thus Thucydides gives repeal of the Megara decree as the chief demand in a Spartan ultimatum. The reader may infer that this was the issue most discussed in Athens in the weeks immediately preceding the outbreak of war. Other sources confirm this impression. Aristophanes in *The Acharnians*, a play produced early in 425, alludes (lines 515–539) to the Megara decree as if it were the sole cause of the war. It is not the business of comedy to weigh historical issues but to make jokes; even so this joke is some indication of popular belief. The fourth-century historian Ephorus treated the Megara decree as the main cause of the Peloponnesian War. Thucydides on the other hand gives far less attention to the Megara decree than to the incidents concerning Corcyra and Poteidaea. Was he overreacting to popular exaggeration of the dispute about Megara, or was his assessment just?. . .

Apart from the disputes about Corcyra, Poteidaea and Megara there may have been others. In another context Thucydides (2.68) mentions troubles arising at the town of Amphilochian Argos on the Gulf of Ambracia [on the mainland's western coast]. The Amphilochians admitted some people from Ambracia as joint settlers in their town and hence became hellenized. But after a time the Ambraciote settlers expelled the Amphilochians from Argos. So the Amphilochians of the district gained the alliance of their Greek neighbors, the Acarnanians, and these two powers appealed to the Athenians for

help. The Athenians sent them thirty ships under the command of Phormion. Directing the combined forces, Phormion captured Argos and "enslaved" its Ambraciote inhabitants, that is, he killed the men and sold the women and children into slavery. This was a severe measure and likely to offend Corinth, since Ambracia was a Corinthian colony. Thucydides does not say when Phormion's intervention took place. Dates suggested vary from ca. 437 to 432, but arguments for each date are inconclusive, since they are drawn from silence, that is, from the failure of Thucydides to mention the incident in passages where one might expect it.

Some historians have thought that particular disputes, such as those concerning Poteidaea and Megara, do not account adequately for the outbreak of the Peloponnesian War and they have looked for a more comprehensive cause. They have been influenced by their understanding of Thucydides's statement about the causes of the war. Thucydides distinguishes "the most genuine cause" from "the complaints and the disputes," and many readers have thought that his statement of "the most genuine cause" simply specified the growth of Athenian power and the fear felt by the Spartans in consequence. . . . Somewhat later in his account he returns to this theme. After recounting the disputes about Corcyra and Poteidaea and the meeting of the Spartan assembly, he says (1.88) that the Lacedaemonians voted as they did "not so much because they were persuaded by the arguments of their allies as because they feared lest the power of the Athenians might grow greater, for they saw that the greater part of Greece was already subject to them." To support this view Thucydides inserts a digression (1.89–118), which summarizes the way Athenian power had grown since 479. . . .

Even if Thucydides had not alluded to the growth of Athenian power in discussing the causes, it could be maintained that the war was caused by Athenian imperialism and the Spartan response to this. Holders of such a view can point to the growth of Athenian power in the first two decades of the Delian League and they can cite plentiful illustrations of Athenian dynamism in the First Peloponnesian War, especially in its opening years. . . .

Some judgement on the causes of the Peloponnesian War may be reached by approaching the problem from another angle. Thucydides's history of the Peloponnesian War is a model of impartiality, but it is written from an Athenian point of view, and since all subsequent studies draw heavily on it, the war has come to be called "The Peloponnesian War;" had its history been written from a Spartan point of view, it would be called "The Athenian War." Correspondingly, inquiries into its causes tend to become inquiries into Athenian behavior; the attempt is made to trace changes in Athenian policy and to find which actions of the Athenians brought about war. But an inquiry into Spartan policy is equally legitimate, although there is far less evidence; one may ask what actions of the Spartans led to war. The question is especially appropriate because the Spartans were technically the aggressors. When the Spartan assembly met in the summer of 432, Thucydides says that an Athenian embassy was present and in its speech to the Spartans it offered to submit the matters in dispute to arbitration (1.78.4). The first military action of the war was an attack by the Thebans on Plataea and in this the allies of Sparta behaved as the aggressors.

Accordingly, some importance attaches to the stated war aims of the Spartans. As already noted, in the winter of 432/1 the two sides exchanged a series of embassies and recriminations. The last Spartan embassy coming to Athens delivered a brief message, saying: "The Lacedaemonians desire peace, and there would be peace if you would let the Greeks go as autonomous states." The Greek word "autonomous" was ambiguous, but in this context the Spartan ultimatum seems to be a demand that the Athenians should disband their Empire and thereby restore full independence to their allies. Elsewhere Thucydides (2.8.4), explaining the resources of both sides at the beginning of operations, remarks: "There was much more good will towards the Lacedaemonians, especially because they had proclaimed that they were freeing the Greeks." In short, the Spartans voiced an intention of destroying the Athenian Empire, and they achieved this in 404. This amounts to saying that the Spartan war aims were unlimited.

A distinction may be drawn between "wars for limited objectives" and "total wars." In the Samian War, for example, the Athenians pursued the limited objective of bringing Samos back into their Empire; they did not seek to destroy the Samian state. But in a "total war" one side at least seeks to destroy the other as a political entity; in the Peloponnesian War the Spartans sought to destroy the Athenian Empire, although they let Athens survive. In the case of a "war for limited objectives" the historian can hope to specify causes with some precision; he begins his inquiry from the stated war aims. But in a "total war" stated war aims are vague and comprehensive and they are not intended to limit the actions of their author. So the historian can only say that such a war was caused by the whole situation preceding it.

Selection 7

The Peloponnesian War Devastates Greece

Charles Freeman

*This concise overview of the great fifth-century
B.C. war of the city-states is by scholar Charles
Freeman, author of several recent volumes
about ancient Greece and Rome.*

The Peloponnesian War began with the
declaration of war by Sparta on Athens in
431 B.C. . . . Almost immediately Athens
suffered a devastating blow when plague broke
out. Its spread was aggravated by the large number of country-dwellers who had crowded into the
city. It is possible that a quarter of the population
died, including, a year later, Pericles himself,
probably from an associated disease. This is perhaps the turning-point in the history of Athens,
the moment when the optimism expressed so confidently by Pericles begins to fade. . . .

The fundamental problem of the war was how
a naval power such as Athens could defeat land-
locked Sparta and how Sparta, with no effective
navy, could hope to capture the well-defended
Athens. The first years of the war were marked
by a series of ineffective raids on each other's
territories. Spartan troops ravaged Attica almost
every year (but could never actually storm the
city itself, which, protected by its Long Walls,
maintained open access to the sea). Athens

launched raids on the Peloponnesian coast and
one on Megara, an ally of Sparta's. Her hope
was perhaps to stimulate the helots into revolt
and destabilize Sparta's alliances. She also revived her old policy of the 450s and attempted to
win control of the plains of Boeotia. The policy
ended in failure after a decisive defeat at the
hands of Thebes and her allies at Delium [east of
Thebes] in 424.

In 425, however, the Athenians had a lucky
break that ended the stalemate. They managed
to capture a group of some 120 Spartans who
had become stranded on the island of Sphacteria
on the western coast of the Peloponnese when
their supporting fleet had been destroyed by the
Athenians. The shock effect of the Spartan capitulation was immense, not only on Sparta but
on the Greek world. Traditionally Spartans died
in battle rather than capitulate and the city's reputation was seriously damaged. Sparta was
ready to surrender and would probably have
done so immediately if a raid by a Spartan general Brasidas in 524 had not succeeded in capturing a number of Athenian cities along the
Chalcidice peninsula and the northern Aegean,
including the vital centre of Amphipolis. After
an Athenian counter-attack saw the death of
Brasidas, both sides were willing to come to
terms. The Peace of Nicias was signed in 421
with each side agreeing to give up their gains.
Amphipolis, however, chose to stay independent
of Athens.

Reprinted from *Egypt, Greece, and Rome: Civilizations of the Ancient Mediterranean*, by Charles Freeman (1996) by permission of
Oxford University Press; © Charles Freeman, 1996.

Sparta appeared, at first, the more vulnerable of the two states. Her manpower was in decline, one reason why the loss at Sphacteria was so significant, and her control over the Peloponnese seemed to be faltering. Her ally Corinth refused to sign the treaty when land she had lost was not included in it. Athens, under the influence of a persuasive young aristocrat, Alcibiades, now began interfering directly in the Peloponnese, making treaties of mutual defence with two important cities, Argos and Elis. (Elis oversaw the Olympic Games and even banned Spartan athletes from them in 420.) Alcibiades claimed later that his strategy was to force Sparta to counter-attack and risk losing everything in one battle. The battle came in 418, at Mantineia, but it was a crushing Spartan victory. It was to be another thirty years before the Peloponnesian cities risked confrontation with Sparta again.

The Sicilian Expedition

Athens' hopes of direct control of the Peloponnese now seemed thwarted, and her next move was to launch an expedition to the west, to Sicily and southern Italy, as a means of strengthening her position as a Mediterranean power. Her trading interests in the west were well established and there had been an earlier expedition to Sicily in 427. This new venture was largely the brainchild of Alcibiades. Alcibiades was a complex character, egocentric and ambitious, and shrewd enough to use his status as a successful competitor in the Olympic Games (he won the chariot race in 416) and his personal magnetism to manipulate the Assembly into support for the expedition. Thucydides considered his motives were largely personal ones, the desire to make his name as a military commander and to tap the wealth of the west for himself.

The problems involved in achieving and holding even a foothold in Sicily when the opposition of such wealthy and well-protected cities as Syracuse was bound to be aroused were immense. Yet such was the confidence of Athens that there was even talk of conquering the whole island. . . . Shortly before the fleet sailed, however, the Herms, marble pillars bearing the head of the god Hermes and an erect phallus, which were used as boundary markers and signposts and whose phallic properties were a token of good luck, were mysteriously mutilated. The hysteria that resulted and the witch-hunt that followed in the effort to find the perpetrators shows that Athens remained a deeply superstitious city despite the intellectual revolutions of the fifth century. A number of aristocrats were rounded up (and Alcibiades himself later recalled from Sicily to face trial) but the matter was never satisfactorily explained. The city was left haunted by a sense of ill omen.

The story of the expedition is Thucydides' masterpiece and deserves to be read in his own words. His account starts with a magnificent description of the fleet of 134 triremes and 5,000 hoplites setting off to the west in 415. Once the fleet had arrived in Sicily, however . . . it soon became clear that conflict with Syracuse was inevitable. There were three commanders, among them Alcibiades himself, and they disagreed as to whether to launch an immediate attack, delay until they had found more allies, or return home after making a show of strength. Alcibiades was then summoned home (to defend himself against a charge of involvement in the mutilation of the Herms), but defected to Sparta instead. His loyalties to his home community turned out to be much shallower than those to himself. By then Athens was in direct conflict with Syracuse, and another of the commanders, Lamarchus, was killed in skirmishing around the city. Nicias, who was left in charge, was the commander least committed to direct confrontation with Syracuse, whose fine position, large resources, and well-defended harbour made her a formidable enemy.

In fact, there was a time when Athens might have triumphed. Her fleet gave her the initiative at sea and she captured Syracuse's harbour. The construction of siege walls around the city was put in hand. The morale of Syracuse was, however, transformed when a Spartan commander, Gylippus, managed to infiltrate a small force into the city. Athens lost her chance. Even though reinforcements arrived from home (bringing the total commitment to half of Athens' entire navy) a land attack failed. Eventually the decision was made to evacuate the harbour, whose entrance was now blocked by the Syracusan fleet.

In one of his most gripping passages Thucydides describes the emotional impact of this decisive battle as the Athenian hoplites waited to see if they would be saved:

> As the struggle went on indecisively, the Athenian soldiers revealed the fear in their hearts by the swaying of their bodies; it was a time of agony for them, for escape or destruction seemed every moment just at hand. So long as the issue of the sea-battle was in doubt, you could have heard every kind of sound in one place, the Athenian camp: lamentation, shouting, 'We're winning!', 'We're losing!', all the cries wrung from a great army in great peril. The feelings of the men on the ships were much the same, until at last, when the battle had gone on for a long time, the Syracusans and their allies routed the Athenians and fell upon them, decisive winners, yelling and cheering, and chased them to the land. And then the Athenian sailors, as many of them as had not been captured afloat, beached their ships wherever they could and poured into the camp. The soldiers were not in two minds any more, but all with one impulse, groaning, wailing, lamenting the outcome of the battle, rallied—some of them close to the ships, others to guard the rest of their defensive wall, while the greater part of them began to think now about themselves, about how they were going to survive.

(Translation: Kenneth Dover)

A final attempt to urge the Athenians to give battle again with their surviving ships was met with mutiny and the only option left was to escape overland. The description Thucydides gives is one of his most gripping and heart-rending. The dead were left unburied. The wounded, desperate at being left, dragged themselves after their comrades as they moved off, overcome themselves by their own shame of betrayal. The plight of the retreating army, without food and with continual harassment by Spartans and Syracusans, was horrific. When they came to water the hoplites were so thirsty they rushed forward to drink even though enemy missiles rained down on them. They lay in a stream drinking what was turning into a mess of mud and blood before the final surrender. The survivors were herded back to Syracuse and then imprisoned in appalling conditions in the quarries which surrounded the city.

The Conflict Drags On

There was no doubt that this was a catastrophe. Forty thousand men may have been lost as well as half the city's fleet. Athens' democracy came under severe strain, overthrown in 411 by an oligarchical government of Four Hundred who were in favour of making peace with Sparta. The empire was also in revolt. One rebel, Mytilene, was recaptured but the island of Chios had to be abandoned after a blockade which failed. In 411 Euboea revolted and joined Sparta. However, some historians . . . among them Simon Hornblower, argue that Thucydides inflated the importance of the Sicilian disaster, partly to create a literary impact. The fact is that Athens was able to continue the war. The Four Hundred were overthrown when they tried to make peace on behalf of Athens and replaced by a semi-democratic government of Five Thousand. The navy remained loyal to the democracy throughout and gradually new ships were built. Despite some defections, the empire survived largely intact. The will to resist remained amazingly strong.

Once again, however, it looked as if there would be deadlock with neither city able to deliver a death-blow to the other. Sparta, on the advice of Alcibiades, had set up a fortified base at Deceleia, half-way between Athens and her frontier with Boeotia, which meant that Spartan soldiers could dominate and ravage land in Attica all the year round. They could also lure slaves away from Athens, and twenty thousand are recorded as escaping from the city, a severe drain on its human resources but not enough to defeat it. Somehow new resources had to be found to bring the conflict to an end.

The only major source was Persia, and in fact

The Spartans and Syracusans overwhelm the exhausted Athenian troops, whose invasion of Syracuse has ended in utter failure.

from the 420s both Athens and Sparta had been hoping to secure her support. The Athenians ruined their chances by unwisely backing two satraps [Persian governors] who were in rebellion against the monarchy and, from 411, it was Sparta who gained the money to build and equip a fleet. In return the Spartans acquiesced in the achievement of Persia's main objective since the Persian Wars, the return of the Greek cities of Asia to her control. This was the end of any pretence that Sparta was fighting for the liberation of Greece.

The closing years of the war (411–404) saw the experienced Athenian fleet locked in conflict with the newer but better-resourced Spartan one. The ambition of Sparta was now to close off Athenian supplies of grain from the Hellespont. A Spartan fleet was there in 411 and managed to capture the city of Byzantium. The Athenians were not finished, however, and won two major victories in 411 and 410 and another at Argi-

nusae (near Lesbos) in 406. Byzantium was regained in 408. In 410 the Spartans even sued for peace, but Athens refused to negotiate.

For Athens, however, a final victory remained elusive. The Spartans now always had enough resources to rebuild their fleet. In 405 the Spartans, under their commander Lysander, captured the town of Lampsachus in the Hellespont and were able to shelter their fleet in its harbour. The Athenian fleet arrived to challenge them but had to beach on the other side of the strait at Aigospotamae where there was no harbour. This left them dangerously exposed. They sailed out day after day to challenge the Spartans, who would not come out. Lysander noticed, however, that once the Athenian ships returned across the strait they were left on the beach unmanned. He launched a sudden attack achieving complete surprise. One hundred and seventy ships out of Athens' fleet of 180 were captured. When the news reached Athens, a howl of despair spread up from the Piraeus to the city as the implications were realized. With the Hellespont now under Spartan control, Athens was starved and forced into surrender (404). The Long Walls were pulled down, the fleet reduced almost to nothing, and a Government of Thirty imposed on the city by the victorious Spartans. Against all expectations, Athens had actually been comprehensively defeated, even though the Spartans did not destroy the city completely, afraid perhaps of creating a power vacuum in the area.

Selection 8

An Athenian Recalls His City's Surrender

Xenophon

The Athenian historian Xenophon (who was exiled in 399 B.C. but allowed to return to Athens in 365) chronicled the last years of the Peloponnesian War in his Hellenica. *The following excerpt from that work describes the war's climactic engagement in 405 at Aegospotami on the Hellespont where a Spartan fleet commanded by Lysander neutralized a large Athenian naval force. (Xenophon includes an anecdote in which Alcibiades, the infamous Athenian traitor, tried in vain to aid his countrymen.) With the Hellespont completely under Spartan control, Athens's life-giving grain route from the Black Sea (the Pontus) was severed. Xenophon goes on to tell how the city was blockaded and finally had to choose between starvation and surrender.*

Excerpted from *The History of My Times (Hellenica)*, by Xenophon, translated by Rex Warner (Penguin Classics, 1966). Translation copyright © Rex Warner, 1966. Reprinted by permission of Penguin Books Ltd.

*L*ysander now sailed from Rhodes along the Ionian coast to the Hellespont. His object was to intercept the [Athenian] merchant ships coming out of the Pontus and to deal with the cities in the area which had revolted from Sparta. The Athenians also set out there, keeping out in the open sea from Chios, since Asia was in enemy hands.

Lysander sailed along the coast from Abydus to Lampsacus which was an ally of Athens. He had land support from the forces from Abydus and other cities and these troops were under the command of a Spartan, Thorax by name. They made an assault on the city and took it by storm. It was a rich city, full of wine and grain and other supplies, and it was given over to the soldiers to plunder, though Lysander released all the prisoners who were free men.

The Athenians had been sailing close behind and, with their fleet of 180 ships, came to anchor at Elaeus in the Chersonese. It was here, while they were having their morning meal, that they received the news about Lampsacus. They set out at once for Sestus where they took provisions aboard and then went straight on to Aegospota-mi, which is opposite Lampsacus. The Helle-spont here is about two miles wide. It was here that the Athenians had their evening meal.

The night passed and at dawn Lysander or-dered his men to have breakfast and embark. He had the side-screens put up on the ships and made all preparations for battle, but gave orders that no one should leave his position or put out into the open sea.

Lysander's Victory

As soon as the sun rose the Athenians came up with their fleet in line of battle to the mouth of the harbour. However, Lysander did not put to sea against them, so, when it was late in the day, they sailed back again to Aegospotami. Lysander then instructed some of his fastest slips to follow the Athenians and, when they had disembarked, to observe what they were doing and then to re-port back to him. He did not allow his own men to go ashore until these ships had returned.

Both he and the Athenians did the same thing for four days. All this time Alcibiades was in his castle and he could see from there that the Athe-nians were moored on an open shore with no city behind them and that they were getting their supplies from Sestus, which was about two miles [the text is in error; it was closer to fifteen miles] away from the ships, while the enemy, in-side a harbour and with a city at their backs, had everything they wanted. He therefore told the Athenians that they were in a very poor position and advised them to shift their anchorage to Ses-tus, where they would have the advantages of a Harbour and a city. 'Once you are there,' he said, 'you can fight whenever you please.'

The generals, however—particularly Tydeus and Menander—told him to go away. 'We are in command now,' they said, 'not you.' So Alcibi-ades went away.

On the fifth day as the Athenians sailed up, Lysander gave special instructions to the ships that were to follow them. As soon as they saw that the Athenians had disembarked and had scattered in various directions over the Cherson-ese—as they were now doing more freely every day, since they had to go a long way to get their food and were now actually contemptuous of Lysander for not coming out to fight—they were to sail back and to signal with a shield when they were half-way across the straits. These or-ders were carried out and, as soon as he got the signal, Lysander ordered the fleet to sail at full speed. Thorax and his men went with the fleet.

When [the Athenian general] Conon saw that the enemy were attacking, he signalled to the Athenians to hurry back as fast as they could come to their ships. But they were scattered in all directions; some of the ships had only two banks of oars manned, some only one, and some were not manned at all. Conon himself in his own ship with seven others and also the state trireme *Paralus* did get to sea fully manned and in close order. All the rest were captured by Lysander on land. He also rounded up nearly all the crews, though a few managed to escape into various fortified places in the neighbourhood.

Conon, escaping with his nine ships, could see that for the Athenians all was over. . . . With eight ships, he sailed away to . . . Cyprus. The *Paralus* sailed to Athens to report what had happened. . . .

After making the necessary arrangements at Lampsacus, Lysander sailed against Byzantium and Calchedon. Both places submitted to him and the Athenian garrisons were allowed to go away under safe conduct. . . . Lysander sent all Athenian garrisons and any other Athenians whom he found back to Athens, allowing them safe conduct to go there, but nowhere else. He knew that the more people there were in the city and in Piraeus, the sooner the food supplies would run out. Then, leaving behind a Spartan, Sthenelaus, as governor of Byzantium and Calchedon, he sailed back to Lampsacus and re-fitted his ships.

Siege and Capitulation

It was at night that the *Paralus* arrived at Athens. As the news of the disaster was told, one man passed it on to another, and a sound of wailing arose and extended first from Piraeus, then along the Long Walls until it reached the city. That night no one slept. They mourned for the lost, but more still for their own fate. They thought that they themselves would now be dealt with as they had dealt with others. . . . Next day they held an Assembly at which it was decided to block up all the harbours except one, to repair and man the walls, and to take all other measures to put the city into a state of readiness for a siege.

While the Athenians were occupied in this way, Lysander sailed out of the Hellespont with 200 ships. Coming to Lesbos, he settled matters in Mytilene and the other cities and sent Eteonicus with ten triremes to Thrace. Eteonicus brought all the places in that area over to Sparta. Indeed, directly after the battle every state in Greece except Samos had abandoned the Athenian cause. . . .

Lysander then sent word to Agis at Decelea and also to Sparta that he was sailing to Athens with 200 ships. At the same time Pausanias, the other king of Sparta, the whole army of the Spartans and all the rest of the Peloponnesians, except the Argives, took the field. When the whole force was concentrated, Pausanias led them to Athens and camped in the Academy. Meanwhile Lysander arrived at Aegina and, gathering together as many of the people of Aegina as he could, gave the island back to them. He did the same thing for the people of Melos and for all the others who had been deprived of their own states. Then, after devastating Salamis, he anchored at Piraeus with 150 ships and closed the harbour to all merchant ships.

The Athenians were now besieged by land and by sea. They had no ships, no allies and no food; and they did not know what to do. They could see no future for themselves except to suffer what they had made others suffer, people of small states whom they had injured not in retaliation for anything they had done but out of the arrogance of power and for no reason except that they were in the Spartan alliance. They therefore continued to hold out. They gave back their rights to all who had been disfranchised and, though numbers of people in the city were dying of starvation, there was no talk of peace.

However, when their food supplies were en-

tirely exhausted they sent ambassadors to Agis, saying that they were willing to join the Spartan alliance if they could keep their walls and Piraeus, and that they were prepared to make a treaty on these terms. Agis told them to go to Sparta, saying that he himself had no authority to negotiate. This reply was reported back to the Athenians by the ambassadors and they were sent on to Sparta. However, when they were at Sellasia, near the Laconian border, and the ephors heard what their proposals would be— i.e. the same that they had made to Agis—they told them to go back again and, if they really wanted peace, to think again and return with better proposals than these. When the ambassadors got back to Athens and made their report, there was general despondency. The people saw nothing but slavery in front of them and knew that, while another embassy was on its way, many would die of famine. But still no one wanted to make any proposal offering to destroy the walls. . . .

[The moderate Athenian politician] Theramenes, with nine others, was then chosen to go as ambassador with full powers to Sparta. Lysander meanwhile sent an Athenian exile called Aristoteles with some Spartans to the ephors to tell them that he had advised Theramenes that it was they who were the only people empowered to make peace or war.

At Sellasia Theramenes and the other ambassadors were asked to define the purpose of their mission. They replied that they had come with full powers to treat for peace and the ephors then gave orders that they should be summoned to Sparta. On their arrival the ephors called an assembly at which many Greek states, and in particular the Corinthians and Thebans, opposed making any peace with Athens. The Athenians, they said, should be destroyed. The Spartans, however, said they would not enslave a Greek city which had done such great things for Greece at the time of her supreme danger. They offered to make peace on the following terms: the Long Walls and the fortifications of Piraeus must be destroyed; all ships except twelve surrendered; the exiles to be recalled; Athens to have the same enemies and the same friends as Sparta had and to follow Spartan leadership in any expedition Sparta might make either by land or sea.

Theramenes and his fellow ambassadors brought these terms back to Athens. Great masses of people crowded round them as they entered the city, for it was feared that they might have come back unsuccessful and it was impossible to delay any longer because of the numbers who were dying of hunger. Next day the ambassadors reported to the Assembly the terms on which Sparta was prepared to make peace. Theramenes made the report and spoke in favour of accepting the Spartan terms and tearing down the walls. Some people spoke in opposition, but many more were in favour and so it was decided to accept the peace. After this Lysander sailed into Piraeus, the exiles returned, and the walls were pulled down among scenes of great enthusiasm and to the music of flute girls. It was thought that this day was the beginning of freedom for Greece.

Greek History– The Classic Age, Part 2: The Fourth Century B.C.

Chapter 5

Introduction

istorians generally date the second half of the Classic Age from the fall of Athens at the conclusion of the Peloponnesian War in 404 B.C. to the death of Alexander the Great in 323 B.C. This period was largely defined by two overriding themes—the political decline of the leading city-states and the Greek conquest of the Persian Empire. The first major postwar political setback was the abolition of Athens's cherished democracy after its defeat in 404 and the installation of a Spartan-backed oligarchic council in its place. The leading figure in this ruling body, which became known as the Thirty Tyrants, was a right-wing politician named Critias. After a short reign of terror in which hundreds of people were murdered or exiled, the Thirty were deposed, Critias was killed, and democracy was restored, although it never again attained the vigor it had displayed before the great war.

The first major military event of the postwar period was the so-called "March of the Ten Thousand," which in certain ways foreshadowed the decline of both the Greek city-states and the Persian Empire. A group of Greek mercenaries followed the would-be Persian usurper Cyrus the Younger in his unsuccessful quest to dethrone his own brother and found themselves stranded in the heart of Persia. Against incredible odds, they fought their way to the Black Sea and safety, a harrowing journey that the historian Xenophon, one of their number, chronicled in his *Anabasis.* On the one hand, these adventurers represented a whole generation of men who, because of the long Peloponnesian War, knew little else but soldiering. In a sense they formed a polis unto and loyal primarily to themselves; and professional armies for hire, as opposed to local militias fighting to defend home and hearth, became increas-

ingly prevalent. The ultimate success of the Ten Thousand also proved crucial to Greek-Persian military relations in the coming years. If so small and ill-supplied a Greek army could fight its way through Asia and emerge in one piece, what damage might a far larger and better-supplied Greek force inflict on Persia?

This realization was not lost on a group of influential orators who began to call for the Greek states to unite in a Panhellenic (all-Greek) crusade against Persia. The best-known of these orators, Isocrates, declared in 380 B.C., "Consider what a disgrace it is to sit idly by and see Asia flourishing more than Europe and the barbarians [non-Greek-speaking people, in this case the Persians] enjoying a greater prosperity than the Hellenes [Greeks]. . . . We must not allow this state of affairs to go on." (*Oration to Philip,* trans. George Norlin)

For a while, though, constant bickering and rivalries among the major city-states forestalled any major move on Persia. In the wake of its victory over Athens in the great war, Sparta enjoyed political dominance in Greece. But the Spartans proved to be bullies who were fearful of other states forming alliances against them, and they grew especially worried about the Boeotian League, a group of about a dozen small cities led by Thebes. Despite repeated attempts to disband the League, Sparta eventually faced a formidable Theban army led by the shrewd military reformer Epaminondas and his stalwart colleague Pelopidas. In 371 B.C. the Boeotians shattered the myth of Spartan invincibility and Epaminondas soon went on to invade the Peloponnesus, supplanting the Spartan hegemony with a Theban one. However, he and Pelopidas turned out to be Boeotia's primary assets, and when they died prematurely in battle, Theban dominance wavered.

At the same time, the city-states were by now exhausted from decades of war. This made it possible for Macedonia's King Philip II, through a combination of diplomacy and naked force, to impose his will on the powerful mainland states in the 340s and 330s B.C. A series of impassioned speeches warning of the threat Philip posed (the *Philippics*) were delivered in vain by the Athenian orator Demosthenes, for the Macedonian king and his young son, Alexander, defeated a temporary alliance led by Athens and Thebes in 338.

It was therefore Philip, and, following his untimely death by assassination, Alexander who took up the mantle of a Panhellenic assault on Persia. Alexander's defeat of that mighty empire in an amazingly short time remains one of history's most incredible success stories. By the time that he too died an untimely death in 323 B.C., Greece and the Near East had been forever changed; and the fate of both now rested in the hands of his successors. Unfortunately, those hands would turn out to be, for the most part, grasping and self-serving.

Fortunately for historians, the amount of written evidence for the political events of fourth-century B.C. Greece is considerably greater than that for the fifth century, although numerous gaps remain. For the decline of the city-states, Xenophon's *Hellenica* is crucial. Though it covers only the period from 411 to 362 (ending with the Battle of Mantinea) and often omits or glosses over notable events and people, it is the only surviving formal history from the period. Other important works by Xenophon are his *Anabasis;* his *Memorabilia,* concerning his friend, the philosopher Socrates, who was executed in Athens in 399; and his *Constitution of the Lacedaemonians,* in which he provides information about Sparta and its institutions. Some useful historical information also derives from the surviving speeches of Athenian orators, including Isocrates, Demosthenes, Lysias, Isaeus, Aeschines, and Lycurgus; surviving inscriptions that list the terms of crucial alliances; and works by later historians, notably Diodorus's *Library of History* and Plutarch's lives of Artaxerxes, Agesilaus, Demosthenes, Timolean, Pelopidas, and Phocion.

For Philip's and Alexander's rise and exploits, the contemporary sources are few (consisting mostly of bits and pieces in the speeches of the Athenian orators). The bulk of the surviving works about them were written considerably later and therefore tend to mix romanticized or fictional accounts with the real facts. The principal source for Philip is Diodorus, who, though not always reliable, did incorporate a good deal of information from the largely lost *Philippica* (*History of Philip*) of the fourth-century B.C. historian Theopompus. The most comprehensive sources for Alexander are the *Anabasis* of the second-century A.D. Greek historian Arrian; Plutarch's *Life of Alexander;* and the Latin version of the great conqueror's career by the first-century A.D. Roman historian Quintus Curtius Rufus.

Selection 1

The March of the Ten Thousand

Stringfellow Barr

Xenophon's Anabasis *(meaning "march up-country") tells the exciting story of the so-called "March of the Ten Thousand," the adventures of a band of Greek mercenaries who had to fight their way through hostile Persian territory to reach safety. Their military campaign, the first important one of Greece's post–Peloponnesian War period, foreshadowed the last—namely Alexander's conquest of Persia in the 330s and 320s B.C.—for both involved the inability of Persian forces to withstand superior Greek armor, training, and tactics. As former Rutgers University scholar Stringfellow Barr explains here, Xenophon, an Athenian and friend of the famous philosopher Socrates, was one of many Greeks who answered the call of a Persian prince named Cyrus (or Cyros), who wanted to overthrow his brother, King Artaxerxes II. In telling how Cyrus's quest failed, leaving the Greeks stranded in the heart of Persia, Barr skillfully weaves in illuminating sections of Xenophon's own narrative.*

*I*n the spring of 401, some two years before his death, Socrates was asked for advice by one of his young friends, Xeno-

Excerpted from *The Will of Zeus: A History of Greece from the Origins of Hellenic Culture to the Death of Alexander,* by Stringfellow Barr. Copyright © 1961 by Stringfellow Barr. Reprinted by permission of HarperCollins Publishers, Inc.

phon. Xenophon had received a letter from an old family friend, a Theban named Proxenus. Cyrus, younger brother of Artaxerxes II, new King of Kings, had induced Proxenus "to get as many men as he could and join him, since he was about to attack the Pisidians, who were making themselves a nuisance to his country." So Proxenus had raised a force of mercenaries and had gone to Cyrus. If Xenophon would join him there, he promised

> to introduce him to Cyros, who was, he said, more than home and country to himself. Xenophon read his letter, and consulted Socrates the philosopher about this trip. Socrates had a suspicion that there might be some state objection to his being friendly with Cyros, because Cyros had favoured the Lacedaimonians [Spartans] in their war against Athens; so he advised Xenophon to go to Delphi and inquire of the oracle about this journey. Accordingly Xenophon went and asked Apollo what god he should sacrifice and pray to, that he might best accomplish the journey he had in mind, and come back safe and successful. Apollo named the gods to whom he must sacrifice.

> When he came back he told the oracle to Socrates. But Socrates blamed him because he had not asked first whether it was better for him to go or to stay, but just decided to go, and then asked how he could best do it. "But,"

said he, "since you did ask that, you must do what the god bids."

So Xenophon sacrificed to the gods whom Apollo's oracle had named and joined Proxenus and Cyrus of Persia in Sardis.

Battle and Betrayal

The decision was a fateful one. It was the subsidies of Cyrus that had enabled the Spartans to destroy the Athenian Empire, to starve Athens herself to her knees, to place a Spartan garrison on the holy Acropolis, and to back up the bloody Critias in his anti-democratic terror. Xenophon, then in his early twenties, son of a landowner from an estate some nine miles northeast of Athens . . . politically conservative . . . had served in the cavalry under the Thirty. Now the democracy was back in power. Now he was joining his Theban friend, to whom Cyrus the Persian was "more than home and country.". . .

The Greek mercenary force he joined at Sardis contained some 12,900 infantry, of whom 10,600 were heavy-armed. On March 6, 401, Cyrus led them eastward out of Sardis. Not even Proxenus knew that it was not the hill tribes of Pisidia whom Cyrus was leading them against but the King of Kings himself. Of the Greeks, only the Spartan Clearchus, their commander, knew.

> However, when they got as far as Cilicia [in southern Asia Minor], it seemed to be clear to all that they were marching against the king. Most of them followed for shame of one another and Cyros, although they feared the journey and went against their will; and one of these was Xenophon.

At Tarsus the Greeks balked, and some of the mercenaries even stoned Clearchus. But Clearchus cleverly succeeded in convincing them it was unsafe to turn back, and Cyrus lied about his reasons for wanting to reach the Euphrates River. Although the Greeks were still suspicious, a 50-per-cent increase in pay decided them to follow on. At Thapsacus on the Euphrates, Cyrus told the higher Greek officers the truth: they were marching against the King and against Babylon. This time it took a bonus to get

the Greeks in motion again, but they crossed the river and followed Cyrus down the left bank toward the famous city, marching through the Syrian desert with its sweet-smelling plants, hunting the wild asses, whose meat tasted like venison but was tenderer, hunting the ostrich, the bustard, the gazelle. When they neared the King's army, Cyrus made fresh promises in case of victory and then reviewed his forces. Cyrus had his Greek mercenaries, a much larger number of Asian troops, a few scythe-bearing chariots. His brother, King Artaxerxes, had a much larger force than his, more scythed chariots, but no Greek mercenary force. On a September morning at the village of Cunaxa, a few miles from the site of modern Baghdad, the Great King struck. The Greek mercenaries of Cyrus raised the paean [battle hymn], charged at the double, and completely scattered the forces opposite them. But Cyrus himself was less lucky. He managed to attack the King his brother personally, and even to wound him, but he himself was killed. Instead of attacking the Greeks, Artaxerxes then withdrew: anyhow the death of Cyrus had brought the Greek expedition to ruin. When the Greeks returned to their camp for breakfast, there was nothing to eat: the camp had been pillaged.

When the Great King sent word that they were to lay down their arms, they refused. They wanted to get home to Greece, but how? They had marched nearly 1,500 miles from Sardis. They could not possibly go back the way they had come: they lacked the necessary provisions to cross the desert. Tissaphernes, the royal governor whom Cyrus had replaced at Sardis, offered to guide them northward toward the Black Sea. And so, with Tissaphernes' army leading, the Greeks started up the left bank of the Tigris toward the great eastern mountains of modern Turkey. They reached the Great Zab, which flowed into the Tigris.

But there was distrust between the two armies. Where, wondered the Greeks, was Tissaphernes guiding them? Would they be ambushed? On the Persian side, there was fear of this desperate army of Greek mercenaries, which, like some hostile polis, moved through the heart of the Persian Empire. How get rid of them? At last Clearchus, the Spartan commander, decided to seek a conference with Tissaphernes and to try for some sort of firmer understanding. Tissaphernes invited the Greek leaders to his quarters; there he seized Clearchus, Proxenus, Menon, and two other Greek leaders and sent them to the Great King; the remainder of the delegation were massacred. Then he sent fresh demands to the Greek army to lay down their arms. . . .

When Xenophon came later to write the history of their Anabasis, their March Up Country, he pictured the army, now largely bereft of leadership:

> They could not sleep for sorrow, longing for home and parents, for wives and children, which they never expected to see again. In this state they all tried to rest.

> There was a man in the army named Xenophon, an Athenian, who was neither general nor captain nor private. . . .

Xenophon called together the officers who had served under his friend Proxenus, pointed out that the Persians had broken their oaths and thereby aligned the gods on the side of the Greeks, and said:

> They are men easier to wound and to kill than we are if the gods give us victory as before.

> Perhaps others are now thinking the same, but in heaven's name don't let us wait for someone else to come and pat us on the back and say, Go it. Here's a grand enterprise! Let us take the lead and show the others how to be brave! Show yourselves the best of officers, and as worthy to be captains as the captains themselves! Count on me, if you are willing to make the start; I will follow you, or if you order me to lead, I will not make my youth an excuse, but I think I am old enough to keep danger from myself!

With one dissenting vote, the subordinates of Proxenus chose this young Athenian to lead their contingent. Then they collected officers from the other contingents and by midnight about a hundred officers were in council. Xenophon was called on to speak. He urged them instantly to appoint new officers to replace those the army had now lost. This was done, and then they convened a general assembly of the whole army, just as the Council at Athens might have convened the Assembly of all citizens. A Lacedaemonian officer addressed them, then the newly appointed general of the Arcadian contingent spoke.

> Then Xenophon rose; he was arrayed for war in his finest dress. "If the gods grant victory," he thought, "the finest adornments are most proper for such a victory; if I must die, after grand ambitions I would meet my end in grandeur."

He insisted that with God's help there were many good hopes of safety. Someone in the audience sneezed. This was a good omen; the soldiers recognized it as such by kissing their hands to heaven; and Xenophon instantly cried:

> While we were speaking of safety came an omen of Zeus the Saviour! Then I think we should vow to this god a thanksgiving for salvation as soon as we reach the first friendly country, and vow a sacrifice to the other gods according to our ability. Whoever agrees with this, let him hold up his hand.

All held up their hands. Then they made their vow and chanted the paean. Xenophon now spoke at length. He reminded them that the Persians had come long ago to punish Athens. At Marathon the Athenians had beaten them. Then Xerxes had come by land and sea with an innumerable host. The ancestors of this audience he was addressing had beaten them. The Greeks would beat them again. No cavalry? They would need none. No provisions? They would seize provisions. Rivers impassable? All rivers could be passed if you went far enough toward the source. Even if the army could not escape, it was strong enough to settle down and defy the King, as some of the hill tribes had in fact done. . . .

Next he proposed that they burn their baggage train. All hands would be needed to fight.

But the chief thing was complete obedience to discipline. The Persians had treacherously killed the Greek leaders: the Persians must find that the Greeks could obey new leaders. He called for a vote approving his plans.

> Or if anyone has anything better, let him speak up boldly and say so, even if he is a private soldier, for our common safety is our common need.

The Journey to the Sea

The Greek army started north toward the high mountains, a Greek polis on the march, a panhellenic polis . . . a footloose polis like Athens herself, but one prepared to move much further than Salamis, into the towering, unknown mountains. . . . The army turned polis and struck out for the mysterious highlands. Their common safety was their common need; their habits of self-government bound them together, their sneezes were omens, and their trust was in Zeus the Savior.

The long ordeal began. The Persian archers could outrange the Cretan archers who served in the retreating polis. And Xenophon had been wrong about not needing cavalry. Persian cavalry constantly harassed the rear guard, which Xenophon and Clearchus' successor, the young Timasion, commanded. Xenophon concluded that slingers and horsemen must be found. Some 200 men of Rhodes were collected who understood slings and whose leaden bullets had twice the range of the stones, as big as a human fist, which the Persian slingers hurled. Horses hitherto used as pack animals were examined and some fifty were found fit for cavalry. By the time the retreating army reached the ruins of Nineveh, the Rhodian slingers and the newly formed cavalry were holding Tissaphernes at bay. The Cretans were collecting and using the spent arrows of the Persians. Moreover, in some of the villages they found lead to make bullets for the slings and plenty of gut to use in the slings themselves. The moving polis was in some sense importing the goods it required, but importing them by moving to where they were.

Sometimes it found a well-provisioned village and spent a few days there, partly to let its surgeons tend the wounded, partly to eat the good wheat meal stored there and drink the wine and let their horses feed on the stored-up barley.

It took them seven days of constant fighting to pass through the mountainous country of the wild Kurds, at whose hands they suffered more losses than all those Tissaphernes had been able to inflict. Then they started across Armenia, shadowed by Tiribazus, the King's local governor, who kept an eye on them but did not attack. It was now late autumn and the heavy snowfalls began. Once they marched through snow six feet deep. The army lost animals, slaves, soldiers.

> Men also were left behind who had been blinded by the snow or lost their toes by frostbite. It did some good to the eyes if the men marched holding something black before their eyes; for the feet, to keep them moving without rest all the time and to take off the shoes at night. But if any slept with shoes on, the straps worked into the feet and the shoes froze; for the old shoes were gone, and they had to make them of raw leather from untanned hides newly flayed.

They came to underground houses, filled with people and animals. There they got provisions, including an unfamiliar drink, beer:

> barley-wine in tubs; there were barley-grains floating on the wine at the rim, and straws lay there, large and small, without knots. If you were thirsty, you picked up one of these and sucked through it. It was very strong wine if drunk neat, and the taste was delicious when you were used to it. . . .

Through the countries of the Taochians and the Chalybeans they stumbled on until they reached a sizable city called Gymnias. Thence they marched five days to Mount Theches.

When the first men reached the summit and caught sight of the sea there was loud shouting. Xenophon and the rearguard, hearing this, thought that more enemies were attacking in front; for some were following behind them from the burning countryside, and their own rearguards had killed a few men and captured others, and taken wicker shields, covered with raw hairy oxhides, about twenty. But when the shouts grew louder and nearer, as each group came up it went pelting along to the shouting men in front, and the shouting was louder and louder as the crowds increased. Xenophon thought it must be something very important; he mounted his horse, and took Lycios with his horsemen, and galloped to bring help. Soon they heard the soldiers shouting "Sea! sea!" and passing the word along.

Then the rearguard also broke into a run, and the horses and baggage animals galloped too. When they all reached the summit then they embraced each other, captains and officers and all, with tears running down their cheeks. And suddenly—whoever sent the word round—the soldiers brought stones and made a huge pile. Upon it they threw heaps of raw hides and sticks and the captured shields. . . .

And so they sacrificed to their gods. They still had to get through the country of the Macronians, but luckily a man in the Greek army, who had been a slave in Athens, recognized these highlands as his native land and was able to negotiate safe passage. They now reached the Colchians, those distant barbarians Jason had reached when his Argonauts had sought the Golden Fleece, barbarians whose passionate princess, Medea, Euripides had immortalized. The Colchians massed their forces in order to hold a mountain pass. Xenophon formed the Greek army in company columns and prepared them to fight their way through. Then he addressed the soldiers:

"Men, these whom you see alone are left in the way, to keep us from reaching at once the place we have been seeking so long. These men, if we can, we must devour raw!"

Then the word went round to offer their prayers; they prayed aloud, and chanted the battle-hymn, and advanced.

The enemy fell into panic. In two more days the

Greeks were in Trapezus, on the shore of the Black Sea, that vast water the Greeks had always called the Euxine, the Hospitable Sea.

A modern drawing captures the moment when Xenophon and his followers reached the shores of the Black Sea.

They had left Sardis, so near the Aegean, in spring. They had fought the fateful battle of Cunaxa, outside the mighty walls of Babylon, in September. They had crossed the highlands of eastern Turkey in the dead of winter. Now it was February, and they had gained the sea, and to a Greek the sea was the road home. Meanwhile, the citizens of Greek Trapezus provided them with a market, and made them gifts. . . . After [participating in] sacrifices and games, the moving . . . panhellenic polis met and deliberated on the best way to get home.

First Leon, a Thurian, rose, and spoke as follows:

"To speak for myself, sirs, I'm tired out by this time, with packing up and marching and doubling and carrying arms and falling in and keeping guard and fighting. I want a little rest now from these hardships. We have the sea, then let's go by sea the rest of the way, lying flat like Odysseus, till we get to Hellas."

There was great cheering at this, "Good! Good!" and someone else said the same, and so said all of them. Then Cheirisophos rose, and said:

"I have a friend, sirs, Anaxibios, who is now Lord High Admiral at home, as it happens. If you will send me there, I think I shall bring you back ships of war and transports to carry you. If you want to go by sea, wait until I return; I won't be long."

On hearing this, the men were delighted and voted that he should sail, the sooner the better.

But suppose Chirisophus should fail to secure sufficient sea transport? Xenophon persuaded the army to borrow warships from Trapezus and seize merchant vessels. They would pay and maintain the crews. He also tried to organize the pillage on which the army counted for food. He persuaded the coast cities to repair the roads, so they could march to the Hellespont if they had to; and the cities acceded, because they were all fearful of this mercenary force and eager to be rid of them. When Chirisophus did not return and when they themselves failed to capture enough transports and when provisions grew scarce, they put on board the ships they had those who were sick, those over forty, the boys and women they had seized during the long march, and most of the baggage, and sent them westward to Cerasus, another colony of Sinope. The rest of the army made the journey on foot in three days. At Cerasus the generals reviewed and numbered their troops. There were 8,600 men left, about two-thirds of those who had fought at Cunaxa. The rest had been killed in action, or lost in the mountains, or had perished in the snow, or had been captured, or had died of disease. They now divided the booty. They reserved a tithe for Apollo and Artemis, and entrusted shares of it to their generals, including Xenophon. . . .

Meanwhile, Xenophon looked upon all these men-at-arms, and all those targeteers, and the bowmen and slingers and horsemen, too, and all fit from long practice—he saw all these on the Euxine, where so great a force could never have been collected without vast expense, and he thought it would be fine to found a city there, and to add territory and power to Hellas.

The army heard of his desire and murmured. They wanted to go home. But, now that their common danger had decreased, discipline was declining fast. The Greek cities of the coast were increasingly alarmed, as Sicily had once been alarmed by Athens' grand armada, with its concentration of force and its ill-defined purpose. This same combination now gave Xenophon's army of mercenaries the appearance of a very large animal with a very small brain. Repeatedly, during the summer of 400, as the army slowly made its way toward the Bosphorus, Xenophon toyed with the idea of colonizing, especially at Calpe's Haven, which lay on the Black Sea coast only a score of miles east of Byzantium, only half a day's journey by oar. He would give this brainless, thrashing animal a purpose. Xenophon later wrote:

Calpe's Haven lies halfway on the voyage between Heracleia and Byzantion. It is a promontory jutting out into the sea; the part by the sea being a sheer cliff, height where it is least no less than twenty fathoms, and facing the land a neck about four hundred feet wide. The space inside the neck is enough for ten thousand inhabitants. . . .

They encamped on the beach beside the sea. They would not camp on a place which might be turned into a city. . . . For most of the soldiers had not been driven by poverty to this expedition; but it was the fame of Cyros which had brought them, some had followers with them, some had spent money themselves, and a few others had run away from home—they had left father and mother, or even children too, hoping to return with wealth for them, since they had heard how others had made their fortunes with Cyros. Men such as these wished to return safe to Hellas.

More Treachery and Hardship

When at last they reached Byzantium and the Spartan admiral Anaxibius closed the city's gates against them, they forced their way in. Xenophon had to remind them that the Lacedaemonians now controlled Hellas. If the Lacedaemonians had but recently brought his own city, imperial Athens, to her knees, they could certainly reduce Byzantium and they could punish any mercenary army that had seized it. To everybody's relief, at that moment

> a certain Coiratadas arrived; he was a Theban on his travels, not a banished man but one with a fever for generaleering, ready with his services if army, city, or nation wanted a good commander. He came and said he was ready to lead them to what is called the Delta of Thrace, where they could get all sorts of good things; until they got there, he would find plenty of food and drink. While he was speaking, the answer came from Anaxibios: that if they were obedient they should never be sorry for it; he would report it to the authorities at home, and he would himself do all he could for them. Accordingly, the soldiers accepted Coiratadas for their general, and went outside the walls. Coiratadas arranged to be there the next day with victims for sacrifice, and a seer, and food and drink for the army. When they were outside, Anaxibios closed the gates and proclaimed that any soldier caught inside would be sold as a slave.

A new Spartan governor arrived and found 400 sick men from Xenophon's army whom his predecessor had quartered in Byzantium. The new governor promptly sold them as slaves. The Theban buccaneer, Coiratadas, who had hired the army, sacrificed repeatedly in a vain effort to get favorable auspices; then he disappeared. The generals could not agree where to lead their rootless, hungry polis next. An exiled Thracian prince named Seuthes hired the army in hopes of winning back his father's kingdom. All through the harsh Thracian winter they served him, but the pay was irregular; and so, hearing that Sparta had decided on war with their old enemy Tissaphernes and would willingly pay them well, some 6,000 followed Xenophon across the Hellespont back into Asia Minor. They passed near Troy and then marched to Pergamos. There in March, 399, Xenophon turned over his 6,000 men to the Spartan commander, Thibron. Scarce fifty miles to the southeast lay Sardis, whence Cyrus had led them bravely forth two long years before. It was an expedition that had taken them some 4,000 miles.

Meanwhile, several things had happened to Xenophon. A month before his old master, Socrates, had been condemned to death in Athens. A month later the city that condemned Socrates would condemn Xenophon himself, in his absence, to exile: had he not served under Cyrus, whose pay had enabled Sparta to destroy the Athenian Empire? According to Xenophon's own later account of the great expedition, he reached Pergamos with scarcely more worldly goods than Socrates, and had to sell his horse in order to pay his passage home. But luckily the wife of a Greek exile at Pergamos told him of a wealthy Persian who lived in a nearby castle. Xenophon led his followers against this fat prey, bagged the Persian, his wife and children, many other captives, horses, and cattle. Of this rich plunder Xenophon was voted the lion's share. But there was more booty in the Persian provinces yet to be won, and fame too: he stayed on in Persia's Aegean provinces to serve in the Spartan army.

Selection 2

Continued Rivalries Cause the City-States to Decline

Chester G. Starr

This chronicle of the main Greek political and military events of the early decades of the fourth century B.C. is by Chester G. Starr, the late distinguished veteran scholar of the Universities of Illinois and Michigan. He begins with some important observations about the underlying causes of the decline of the polis-system. Then he tells how these weaknesses took their toll, as one after another of Greece's great powers vied for dominance and succeeded only in further exhausting the already war-weary Greek states.

The political framework within which the Greeks lived and developed their civilization had been that of the city-state since the eighth century B.C. Down to 400 this political system proved essentially satisfactory. Its requirements of communal loyalty merged religious, social, political, and economic attitudes and institutions under an overriding unity; the *polis* both channeled and supported Greek art and literature.

This success had been possible partly because Greece was still a simple land. The city-states did not press too closely upon one another and, though distinct, had usually been able to sink individual differences in critical times, as during the Persian wars. When the Greek political system was emerging, the Aegean had been free from outside threats, and by the time the Persians rolled forward the Greeks had had strength enough to repel the Great King. Internal cleavages and dissensions had normally been mitigated by colonization, by the ensuing economic progress of the homeland, and by an inherited spirit of loyalty to common goals.

During the fifth century these favorable factors had begun to weaken, and during the next 100 years Greece experienced ever more serious political difficulties. On the one hand the threats to local freedom which were advanced by Persia from outside and by ambitious city-states from within made each *polis* more jealous of its autonomy. Yet on the other hand the tiny political units of Greece became closely interlinked. Politically they contracted alliances; culturally they shared an ever more cosmopolitan civilization; economically they grew dependent upon foreign trade.

The internal political climate of these states also changed markedly in the fourth century. The *polis* had been largely secularized in the materialistic, yet patriotic spirit of the Periclean age. . . . In the fourth century the changing economic and intellectual attitudes led to the professionalization of government and armies and to a concomitant weakening of the attachment of the individual citizen to his state.

The years from 404 to 336 . . . were a difficult age, marked both by chaos and by vigor. In its opening decades efforts were made to change the character of the *polis*, either by forcible unification under the aegis of a leading city-state such as Sparta and Thebes or by federal experiments. The efforts failed, and eventually an outsider, Philip of Macedonia, entered the scene to conquer all the Greeks. Taken as a whole, the developments of the age led the Aegean world straight toward that great explosion in which it conquered the Near East under the leadership of Philip's son, Alexander.

The Spartan Hegemony of Greece

Visible signs of political distress in Greece appeared during the Peloponnesian war. Long protracted, it devastated many parts of the Aegean and left Athens too weak to maintain that naval peace which had protected commerce and had kept the Persians at bay; many men had grown used to military life and to military solutions to political problems; and the ugly specter of civil strife had been unleashed in many states.

Upon the final victory in 404 Sparta might have been expected to retire once more within its Peloponnesian stronghold, for the primary requirement of Spartan policy was to maintain the strength of its citizens at home. But the world was now much changed. The bitter struggle just concluded must have suggested to Lysander and other Spartan leaders that they could no longer be safe even in their ancestral domain unless they controlled Greece; and the general moral support which Sparta had enjoyed in its war against Athenian "tyranny" may well have misled it as to the ease of this task. The principle, too, that "rule belongs by nature to the stronger" had now become a conscious belief in Greek international politics. Without much debate the Spartans decided to retain and consolidate their mastery by land and by sea, a fatal decision which eventually produced the complete ruin of

Sparta by 371.

Within the Greek states Sparta encouraged the conservative element. In some cities it installed a governor, or *harmost*, with a garrison; often it instituted a governing board of 10 oligarchs, a decarchy. Athens was placed in the hands of 30 such leaders, who varied from moderates to extreme conservatives. With the aid of the Spartan *harmost* whose garrison held the Acropolis, the extremists, led by Critias, gained power and proceeded in the next year to execute some 1500 dissidents and to exile about 5000 others. Very quickly the narrow vision of the Spartan government became evident, as did also its vacillation between ruthlessness and inaction as one wing or another of Spartan leadership dominated. Public opinion, even among the old Spartan allies, soon swung against its swelling power, especially inasmuch as Sparta forcibly collected tribute to maintain its fleet.

In those states held by Spartan representatives and local henchmen the situation often became tense. At Athens, for example, the rule of the Thirty was challenged by an exile, Thrasybulus, who first seized the frontier fort of Phyle with the connivance of the Thebans and then took Piraeus in the late spring of 403. Critias was killed in an attack on the port, and by September the extreme right had taken refuge in Eleusis. Although Lysander moved up to repress the resurgence of Athenian democracy, he was superseded by the Spartan king, who felt that blind Spartan support of the ultraconservatives was hopeless. The democrats then coalesced with the more moderate oligarchs, though the remnants of the Thirty held out at Eleusis until 401.

To make the Spartan situation worse, open war with Persia soon broke out. Immediately after their victory the Spartans had yielded to Persia the Greeks of Asia Minor, as they had promised to do in return for the subventions which had produced their fleet; but the cities of Asia Minor had supported the viceroy Cyrus, brother of the new Persian king Artaxerxes II Memnon, who made a bid for the throne.

With Spartan tolerance Cyrus raised a force of 13,000 men and in 401 marched inland to

Mesopotamia. In battle with his brother at Cunaxa, Cyrus was killed, though the Greeks defeated the Persian left wing; thereafter the Greek mercenary generals were seized in an interview with the Persians. The surviving common soldiers, the famous Ten Thousand, elected new generals, including the Athenian Xenophon, and made their way back through Armenia to the Black Sea by the spring of 400. This exploit suggested to many Greeks over the next decades that they had the strength, if united, to conquer the whole Persian empire. . . .

Immediately, however, the Greeks of Asia Minor, fearful of punishment for their support of Cyrus, begged aid from Sparta; and the Spartans, encouraged by the military lessons to be drawn from the expedition of Cyrus, tried to redeem their reputation as defenders of all Hellenes against outside control. After some skirmishing they sent a new king, the lame but popular Agesilaus (398–60), to Asia Minor in 396 with a large army of Spartans and mercenaries, the latter largely drawn from the Ten Thousand. Rather than fighting a full-scale war by land, the Persians began to construct a navy and also sent a wily Rhodian agent, laden with gold, to play upon the dissensions of Greece itself.

By 395, less than 10 years after the close of the Peloponnesian war, the Spartans once more faced war at home, which was led by Thebes, Corinth, Argos, and even Athens. Lysander was killed at the outset, and in 394 the Spartans had to recall Agesilaus from Asia Minor. Spartan naval supremacy was ended off Cnidus in the same year by the Persian fleet, which was commanded by the Athenian Conon and was partly manned by Greek rowers; thereupon the islanders seceded from Spartan rule and formed an alliance of their own.

The course of the hostilities in Greece was complicated and indecisive. One fruit was the resurgence of Athens, which rebuilt its long walls to Piraeus 394–91, reoccupied the Aegean islands of Lemnos, Imbros, and Scyros in 392, and launched a new navy in 390. Eventually the warring states sent ambassadors to the Persian satrap at Sardis, who proclaimed the terms which the Great King thought desirable:

> . . . that the cities in Asia, with the islands of Clazomenae and Cyprus, should belong to himself; the rest of the Hellenic cities he thinks it just to leave independent, both small and great, with the exception of Lemnos, Imbros, and Scyros, which three are to belong to Athens as of old.

This was the famous King's Peace of 387.

Execution of the peace was entrusted to the Spartans, whom the Persian king now trusted more than he did the Athenians; and the Persians promised to war against anyone who did not accept the terms. The chief leader of Sparta, Agesilaus, brutally used this dominant position to destroy all politically dangerous alliances. The Arcadian state of Mantinea was split up into villages; the Chalcidian league, grouped about Olynthus, was dissolved; the citadel or Cadmea of Thebes was seized by a Spartan commander in time of peace. After three years a small band of Theban patriots liberated their city in 379 and resumed the war anew. Little by little Spartan power in Boeotia was broken, and finally in 371 the main Spartan army was defeated in the decisive battle of Leuctra.

The Theban Hegemony

Sparta had ruled Greece more or less completely for 30 years. The consequences were that Greece was largely splintered, that Persia held many Greeks directly under its sway and served as arbiter for the rest, and that Sparta was utterly ruined. Whereas an Athenian orator shortly after 404 had praised Sparta "because of her innate worth and military skill," Thucydides had been very doubtful of the Spartans' ability to adapt their narrow ways to foreign rule. Later on the great analyst Aristotle looked back and observed that the Spartans "collapsed as soon as they had acquired an empire. They did not know how to use the leisure which peace brought; and they had never accustomed themselves to any discipline other and better than that of war."

The body of full Spartan hoplites had thus shrunk from about 5000 in 479 to less than 2000 at the time of Leuctra, partly through losses in war, partly through disfranchisement of those "Equals" who lost their land. All efforts to admit inferiors to the rank of "Equals" were refused by such conservatives as Agesilaus, who preferred to organize the Peloponnesian league into tax-paying districts so as to hire mercenaries. Worse yet, the Spartans became luxury-loving and corruptible. One token of the ever freer transfer of land which horrified Athenian thinkers was the fact that two-fifths of the Spartan farmlands passed into the hands of women. Through their petty and vindictive policies the Spartans had lost their great reputation even at home, and the Peloponnesian league dissolved as soon as the Thebans entered the Peloponnesus.

Thebes stepped into Sparta's place and held it for nine years. The strength of Thebes rested ultimately upon its leadership of the Boeotian league, which had been reorganized into a truly federal state embracing a number of democratic Boeotian city-states. This method of countering the separatist tendencies of the small political units was also favored abroad by Thebes. Either at this time, or earlier, similar leagues appeared in Thessaly, Aetolia, Acarnania, probably western Locris, Achaea, and above all in Arcadia, where a new center, Megalopolis ("Great City"), was built with Theban support to protect the northern neighbors of Sparta.

Theban power was also in large part an expression of the genius of its two great leaders, Epaminondas, a brilliant general and far-seeing, moderate statesman, and his collaborator Pelopidas. The latter secured Persian support, which resulted in a new peace of 367 in favor of Thebes; but in fighting in Thessaly Pelopidas was killed in 364. Epaminondas then had to face a coalition of Sparta, Mantinea, Elis, Achaea, and Athens, which resulted in the major battle of Mantinea (362). The Thebans won the day, and through the victory might have hoped to control all Greece. Epaminondas, however, had been killed. Thereafter the Greeks made peace and formed an ephemeral league to safeguard order; the real result [according to Xenophon] was "ever greater confusion and indecision in the Greek world."

Greece's Great Powers Exhausted

By 355 the major Greek city-states were politically exhausted. Sparta stubbornly refused to admit its loss of prestige but no longer had any influence. Thebes was by this date at war with its western neighbor, the Phocians, who had seized Delphi and were using the gold and silver of the sanctuary to hire whole mercenary armies. Athens, which had by land first supported Thebes against Sparta and then Sparta against Thebes, had by now lost its renewed naval position in the Aegean.

For a time, as long as its naval efforts were devoted primarily toward securing order, Athens had been able to count on wide support from the commercially oriented states; and in 378 its leader Callistratus had even formed the Second Athenian Confederacy to oppose Sparta, but not Persia. The terms of alliance included rigid safeguards against a repetition of the Athenian imperialism of the fifth century. Yet the temptations of power were too persuasive, and after the Theban collapse in 362 Athens began to abuse its position. The more liberal statesman Callistratus was condemned to death while in exile, and when he later returned to Athens was dragged from an altar and executed. The more important of the Athenian allies accordingly revolted in 357–55 and made good their independence, shattering the strength of the Confederacy.

While the Greek homeland had been searching in vain for political unity—and pulverizing itself in the search—much the same course of events had taken place in western waters. Here an extremely able and ruthless Syracusan noble, Dionysius, had seized control of Syracuse in 405 and remained master, with some vicissitudes, to his death in 367. During his autocratic rule Dionysius had beaten off great Carthaginian attacks, the first of which had enabled him to gain power, and expanded his realm to include most of the south Italian colonies as well as points in the Adriatic Sea; at various times he was allied with Sparta or Athens. But while he made Syracuse the greatest city of the west, he destroyed many Greek states and sowed dissension in others; his rule rested always on cruelty and on the employment of mercenaries drawn from native peoples as much as from the Greeks. After his death his son Dionysius II soon lost control, and Carthage once more took the offensive. Only the arrival of Timoleon, a general sent from Corinth on the appeal of Syracuse, saved the day. During 344–36 Timoleon defeated the Carthaginians, especially at the Crimisus river in 341; restored democracy in Syracuse; and rebuilt several destroyed Greek cities.

Both in Greece and in the west the political contentions of the city-states were opening the way for outside powers. In Italy the state of Rome was by this time striding forward with ever-surer steps; in the Aegean, Philip was already king of Macedonia. Nor had the developments of the first half of the fourth century B.C. all been negative. The military art, for example, had made tremendous advances in an era of incessant war. Strategic views had been much sharpened so that generals saw more clearly the main objectives and key points in a campaign; tactics had progressed as mercenary generals and soldiers became more common. Epaminondas, in particular, had made action on the battlefield more mobile and commonly had concentrated his infantry strength on a deeply massed left flank, which carried the day while the other flank was refused or conducted a holding action. Another general, the Athenian Iphicrates, had much improved the light-armed infantry (*peltasts*), armed first with javelins and then with short spears, which could in broken terrain defeat even the best Spartan hoplites.

Another factor of importance was the growing sense of Panhellenic unity, conjoined with a horror at the way the Greek states were tearing themselves to pieces externally and internally . . . and men of good will came ever more to feel that the Greeks must unite. A prominent spokesman of this group was the Athenian Isocrates (436–338), who first advanced in his *Panegyricus* of 380 the idea that the Greeks should ally themselves in a holy war against Persia, which was both rich and temptingly weak. To this theme he resorted repeatedly in the next 40 years and gained a wide audience.

Selection 3

The Thebans Challenge Spartan Dominance

Plutarch

In the fateful battle of Leuctra (in Boeotia), in 371 B.C., the Theban army crushed Sparta's phalanx, which proved to be the first major step in the collapse of the Spartan dominance of Greece. The leading Theban general,

Epaminondas, was a brilliant military tactician who had recently overhauled the Theban army. The Thebans' crack infantry unit, the Sacred Band (made up of 150 pairs of male lovers) was commanded by Epaminondas's capable colleague, Pelopidas. The following tract, composed of excerpts from Plutarch's biographies of Agesilaus and Pelopidas, recounts how Epaminondas provoked Agesilaus, one of Sparta's two kings, at a conference in Sparta; how the other Spartan king, Cleombrotus, attacked Boeotia; and how the Spartans went down to defeat.

By this time [371 B.C.] both sides had come to favour a common peace, and ambassadors from all over Greece assembled in Sparta to negotiate a settlement. One of these was Epaminondas, a man who had already gained a reputation for his culture and learning, but had not yet given any proof of his military genius. It soon became clear to him that the rest of the delegates were overawed by Agesilaus, and he alone maintained the dignity and confidence to speak out freely. Accordingly he delivered a speech not on behalf of his fellow Thebans but of Greece as a whole: in this he declared that war made the Spartans strong at the expense of all the other states, and insisted that peace should be founded upon terms of justice and equality, and that it would only endure on condition that all the parties concerned were put on an equal footing.

Agesilaus noticed that all the Greek delegates listened to Epaminondas with the greatest attention and admiration, and so he asked him whether he thought it just and equitable that the cities of Boeotia should be independent of Thebes. Epaminondas promptly and boldly responded with another question—did Agesilaus think it just and equitable that the cities of Laconia should be independent of Sparta? At this Agesilaus grew angry, jumped to his feet and asked him to state unequivocally whether he intended to make the cities of Boeotia independent, whereupon Epaminondas merely repeated his question as to whether Agesilaus intended to make the cities of

Excerpted from *The Age of Alexander: Nine Greek Lives*, by Plutarch, translated by Ian Scott-Kilvert (Penguin Classics, 1973). Translation copyright © Ian Scott-Kilvert. Reprinted by permission of Penguin Books Ltd.

Laconia independent. Agesilaus flew into a rage and seized upon this pretext to strike the name of Thebes out of the peace treaty and declare war upon her. He ordered the rest of the Greek delegates to depart now that they had settled most of their disputes. Those differences which were capable of resolution should, he said, be left to the final terms of the peace: those which were not would have to be settled by war, since it was a hard task to remove all the causes of dissension between them.

At this time Cleombrotus, the other Spartan king, was in Phocis with an army, and the ephors at once sent orders to him to lead his forces against Thebes. They also summoned a meeting of their allies, who considered the campaign a great burden and showed no enthusiasm for it, but did not dare to oppose or disobey the Spartans. . . .

The Thebans found that they had to face a new danger, that of being completely displaced from their native land, and a fear such as they had never experienced before now spread through the whole of Boeotia. It was at this time, just as Pelopidas was leaving his house, that his wife followed him on his way, weeping and entreating him to take care of his life. 'My dear,' he said to her, 'this is very good advice for private soldiers, but generals need to be told to take care of the lives of others.' When he reached the camp, he found that the Boeotarchs [Theban generals] disagreed as to what should be done: he at once gave his support to Epaminondas and voted in favour of engaging the enemy. Pelopidas did not hold the office of Boeotarch, but he enjoyed great confidence as the commander of the Sacred Band, as was only right for a man who had given his country such proofs of his devotion to liberty.

Dreams and Portents

Accordingly the decision was taken to risk a battle, and the Thebans pitched camp opposite the Spartan army at Leuctra. Here Pelopidas had a dream which disturbed him deeply. In the plain of Leuctra are the tombs of the daughters of Scedasus. These girls are known as the Leuctridae, because it was here that they were buried after they had been raped by some Spartan strangers and had later committed suicide. Their father could obtain no satisfaction from the Spartans for this brutal and lawless outrage, and so, after solemnly cursing the Spartan race, he killed himself on the tombs of his daughters, and hence for ever after prophecies and oracles continually warned the Spartans to beware of the vengeance of Leuctra. . . . This atrocity, of course, took place long before the battle.

As Pelopidas slept in the camp, he dreamed that he saw the girls weeping over their tombs and calling down curses on the Spartans, and also that Scedasus urged him to sacrifice a red-haired virgin to his daughters if he wished to conquer his enemies. Pelopidas thought this a terrible and impious command, but nevertheless he rose and described his dream to the diviners and the generals. Some of these insisted that he must not neglect or disobey the order. . . . Others took the opposite view, and argued that such a barbarous and impious sacrifice could not be pleasing to the powers above. . . . They argued that it is probably foolish in any case to believe that there are deities who delight in bloodshed and in the slaughter of men, but that if they exist, we should disregard them and treat them as powerless, since it is only weak and depraved minds that could conceive or harbour such cruel and unnatural desires.

While the Theban leaders debated this problem and Pelopidas in particular was at a loss what to do, a filly suddenly broke away from a herd of horses, galloped through the camp and stopped at the very spot where the conference was taking place. The other spectators admired above all the colour of her glossy mane, which was a fiery chestnut, the vigour of her movements and the strength and boldness of her neighing, but Theocritus the prophet, with a sudden flash of understanding, cried out to Pelopidas, 'The gods are with you! Here is your victim. Let us not wait for any other virgin, but take the gift the god has provided for you.' At this they caught the filly and led her to the tombs of the girls. There they crowned her with garlands, consecrated her with prayers and joyfully offered up the sacrifice. Then they explained to the whole army the details of Pelopidas' dream and the reasons for the sacrifice.

The Spartans Routed

During the battle Epaminondas kept edging his phalanx to the left so as to form an oblique angle to the front. His object was to draw away the right wing of the Spartans as far as possible from the rest of the Greeks, and to drive back Cleombrotus, who commanded the Spartan right, by launching an attack in which the main strength of the Theban infantry was concentrated in column on that wing. The enemy perceived his intention and began to change their formation, extending their right wing and starting an encircling movement so as to outflank and envelop Epaminondas. But at this point Pelopidas dashed forward from his position, and advancing with his band of three hundred at the run, attacked the Spartans before Cleombrotus could either deploy his wing or bring it back to its previous position and close up his ranks. His charge caught the Spartans out of position: they had not yet formed their line and were still moving about indecisively. And yet the Spartans were the most skilled and experienced soldiers in the world, and in their training they paid special attention to the problem of changing formation without falling into disorder or confusion; each man was accustomed to take any one of his comrades as his right-hand or rear-rank man, and, wherever danger might threaten, to concentrate on that point, knit their ranks, and fight as effectively as ever. But now when Epaminondas' main phalanx bore down on them alone and ignored the rest of their army, and Pelopidas with a charge of extraordinary speed and daring had already hurled himself upon them, their spirit faltered, their courage deserted them, and there followed a rout and a slaughter of the Spartans such as had never before been seen. In this battle Pelopidas, although he was not one of the generals and commanded only a few men, won as much fame for the victory and the triumph of Theban arms as Epaminondas, who was the Boeotarch in command of the whole army.

Selection 4

Philip II and the Rise of Macedonia

N.G.L. Hammond

The sudden, spectacular rise of the Macedonian monarch Philip II in the mid–fourth century B.C. and his subsequent mastery of Greece's leading city-states is one of history's most remarkable success stories. When he assumed power as a young man, his country was backward and divided. And his northern borders were threatened by Illyrians (or Dardanians), Paeonians, and other fierce tribal peoples. Yet in an amazingly short time he overcame these obstacles and forged Europe's first national standing army. As detailed in this essay by N.G.L. Hammond, professor emeritus at Bristol University, this effective fighting force enabled Philip to penetrate central and southern Greece. His first major victory in this strategic region was over the Phocians (of the city-state of Phocis, northwest of Thebes). The Phocians had recently seized the sacred sanctuary at Delphi (in central Greece), home of the famous oracle. Most members of the Amphyctyonic League, a loose alliance of nearby states who sent representatives to administer the sanctuary, objected and the so-called Sacred War ensued. The ambitious and crafty Philip,

Hammond explains, proceeded to exploit the conflict to his own advantage.

Philip took control in 359 not as king but as guardian of his nephew, Amyntas IV, a young boy. His country was on the verge of collapse, having lost 4,000 men in battle, while the victorious forces of Bardylis [king of the Illyrians] were in occupation of towns in Pelagonia and Lyncus and threatened to invade Macedonia itself in 358. Philip put heart into his army by holding assembly after assembly, rearming and training his infantry, and inspiring them with his own indomitable spirit. In spring 358 he convinced the assembly of the King's Men that they should take the offensive. In a decisive battle with almost equal numbers he inflicted a crippling defeat on Bardylis, established the east bank of Lake Lychnitis (Ochrid) as his frontier, and confirmed a treaty of peace with Bardylis by marrying his daughter, Audata. His victory freed Pelagonia, Lyncus and the other tribal states of West Macedonia, then called 'Upper Macedonia', from raiding and occupation by the Dardanians. He now invited the peoples of these states to abolish their monarchies and to enter the Macedonian kingdom with equal rights to those of the Macedonians. The invitation was accepted. . . .

By this act, which Philip must have taken

Macedonia's Philip II, pictured here, managed to unite his country's feuding highland and lowland regions into a powerful nation.

with the agreement of the Macedonian assembly, he doubled the resources and the manpower of the kingdom. It was important to raise the standard of life in Upper Macedonia to that of Lower Macedonia, and for that purpose he founded new towns there in which young men received educational and military training. As they graduated he recruited the best of them to enter the king's army and become members of the assembly as 'Macedones'. His innovations were so successful that the number of his Companion Cavalrymen rose from 600 in 358 to 2,800 in 336, and that of the Companion Infantrymen from 10,000 in 358 to 27,000 in 336. Alexander was to inherit the most formidable army in Europe.

Philip's Early Conquests

By a combination of diplomatic skill and military opportunism Philip defeated Illyrian tribes beyond his western frontier, forced the Paeonians to become his subjects, gained possession of Greek colonies on his coast, defended Amphipolis against the Athenians and Crenides—renamed Philippi—against the Thracians, and advanced his eastern frontier to the river Nestus (Mesta), all by late 354. He was fortunate in that

Athens was distracted by the war against her subject-states (357–355) and Thebes by the war against Phocis, which became the Sacred War (355–346); and he managed to make a treaty of alliance with his powerful neighbour, the Chalcidian League of city-states [on the three-fingered Chalcidic peninsula, just east of Macedonia], on condition that neither party would enter into separate negotiations with Athens. During these eventful years he confirmed an alliance with the ruling house of Larissa in Thessaly by marrying a lady of that house, Philinna, and an alliance with the Molossian royal house by marrying Olympias in 357. . . . In that year, 357, he was elected king in place of Amyntas IV.

The Sacred War was declared by a majority of the members of the Amphictyonic League, of which the Council laid down rules of conduct in religious and other matters and in particular administered the temple of Apollo at Delphi. That majority was formed by the peoples of Thessaly, Central Greece and Boeotia; but the minority included Athens, Sparta, Achaea, and later Pherae in Thessaly, which all entered into alliance with Phocis. Other states showed sympathy with one side or the other. The Phocian occupiers of Delphi survived by looting the treasures and hiring mercenary soldiers, and in 353 an able leader, Onomarchus, launched an offensive against Thebes and sent 7,000 mercenaries to support Pherae against the other Thessalians. This was Philip's opportunity; for the Thessalians asked him for help and he enabled them to win a victory. But Onomarchus came north and inflicted two defeats on Philip. He withdrew, as he said, 'like a ram, to butt the harder'. In 352 Philip and his Thessalian allies won a decisive victory over Onomarchus' army of 500 cavalry and 20,000 infantry, to the amazement of the city-states. Philip paraded his championship of Apollo. For his soldiers went into battle wearing the laurel wreath associated with the god, and on his orders 3,000 prisoners were drowned as guilty of sacrilege. He also championed the cause of liberty and federalism against the dictators of Pherae, whom he now expelled together with their mercenaries. His reward was election as President of the Thessalian League, which placed its forces and its revenues at his disposal. At this time he married Nicesipolis, a member of the leading family in Pherae.

His chief fear was a coalition of Athens and the Chalcidian League; for the Athenian fleet could then blockade his coast and the armies of the two states could invade the coastal plain of Macedonia. In 349, when the Chalcidian League violated its treaty and entered into alliance with Athens, Philip invaded Chalcidice and despite the efforts of Athens captured Olynthus, the capital of the League, in 348. He held the Olynthians responsible for breaking the religious oaths which had bound them under the treaty. He razed the city and sold the population into slavery. He destroyed two other city-states (Apollonia and Stagira) and incorporated the peoples of the Chalcidic peninsula . . . into the Macedonian kingdom.

Meanwhile the Phocians were running short of funds and so of mercenary soldiers, and the Thebans had been hammered into a condition of weakness. Who would administer the *coup de grâce* [death blow]? Envoys from most of the city-states hastened to Pella, hoping to enlist Philip on their side in 346. At that time Alexander, as a boy of ten, will have watched with interest as his father found gracious words for all of them and committed himself to none. When the envoys were on their way home to their respective states, the Macedonian army reached Thermopylae, where the Phocian leader and his 8,000 mercenaries accepted the terms offered by Philip: to surrender their weapons and horses, and to go wherever they wished. The Phocian people were now defenceless. . . .

Philip had acted as the champion of Apollo. It was for him a matter of religious conviction. He therefore entrusted the settlement to the Council of the Amphictyonic League, on which his allies in Thessaly and Central Greece had a majority of the votes, and they no doubt listened to his advice. The terms for the Phocians were mild by Greek standards (one Greek state proposed the execution of all the men): disarmament, division into village-settlements, payment of an indemnity to Apollo and expulsion from the Amphicty-

ony. In their place the Macedonians were elected members. The two votes of Phocis on the Council were transferred to the Macedonian state. . . .

Philip Deals with Southern Greece

Philip's aim was to bring the city-states into concord and set up a Treaty of Common Peace, of which Macedonia and they would be members. This . . . coincided with the tenor of a political pamphlet entitled *Philip*, which [the noted orator] Isocrates published in 346 just before the capitulation of Phocis. He advised Philip as the ruler of the strongest state in Europe to bring the city-states into concord, lead them against Persia, liberate the Greeks in Asia, and found there new cities to absorb the surplus population of the Greek mainland. The price of concord was acceptance of the *status quo*. . . . Despite Philip's offers to set up a Common Peace, Athens, Sparta and Thebes went their own way in the name of 'freedom', and Philip realised in 341 that he might have to use force rather than persuasion if he wanted to exercise control.

Athens depended for her food-supply on imports of grain from South Russia, which had to pass through the Bosporus and the Hellespont. On the European side Byzantium was able to exact 'benevolences' [tolls] from shipping at the Bosporus, and Athens through her colonies on the Chersonese (the Gallipoli peninsula) could do likewise in the Hellespont. The Asian side was held by Persia, which had put down a series of revolts on the coast of the Mediterranean and could now muster a huge fleet. Philip approached this sensitive area through a conquest of the tribes of eastern Thrace. It was during the Thracian campaign in 340 that he appointed Alexander at the age of sixteen to act as his deputy in Macedonia. From then on Alexander was fully aware of Philip's plans.

Events moved rapidly. Philip laid siege to Perinthus and Byzantium, whereupon Athens declared war. He was thwarted by Persia and Athens acting in collusion. He summoned Alexander to join him . . . and extended his control of eastern

Thrace to the Danube. During his return to Macedonia in summer 339 he had to fight his way through the land of the Triballi, a powerful tribe which captured some of his booty. In Greece another Sacred War had started, and the command of the Amphictyonic forces was offered to and accepted by Philip in the autumn. The sacrilegious state which he had to discipline was Amphissa. He took his Macedonian army and troops from some Amphictyonic states not towards Amphissa but through Phocis to the border of Boeotia, in order to threaten Thebes, which though his 'friend and ally' had been behaving in a hostile manner, and to act against Athens, with which he was still at war. The envoys which he sent to Thebes were outbid by the envoys of Athens. In violation of her treaty Thebes joined Athens and sided with Amphissa. Philip tried more than once to negotiate terms of peace, but in vain. The decisive battle was fought at Chaeronea in Boeotia in August 338. The troops of Boeotia, Athens, Megara, Corinth and Achaea numbered some 35,000; those of Macedonia and her allies somewhat less.

Alexander, in command of the Companion Cavalry, pitched his tent by the river Cephissus. When his father's tactics created a breach in the opposing phalanx Alexander charged through the gap, and it was he who led the attack on the Sacred Band of 300 Thebans [Thebes' crack infantry unit]. The Macedonian victory was total. Thebes was treated harshly as the violator of its oaths. Athens was treated generously. Alexander led a guard of honour which brought the ashes of the Athenian dead to Athens—a unique tribute to a defeated enemy—and the 2,000 Athenian prisoners were liberated without ransom. As Philip advanced into the Peloponnese, his enemies submitted and his allies rejoiced. Sparta alone was defiant. He ravaged her territory and he gave some frontier regions to his allies; but he did not attack the city. During his return northwards he left garrisons at Acrocorinth, Thebes and Ambracia. Meanwhile the Council of the Amphictyonic League reduced the restrictions on the Phocians, made the Amphissaeans live in villages and approved the acts of Philip.

The future of the city-states was in Philip's hands. He decided to create the 'Greek Community' (*to koinon ton Hellenon*), in which the states would swear to keep the peace among themselves, maintain existing constitutions, permit changes only by constitutional methods, and combine in action against any violator of the 'Common Peace', whether internal or external. His proposal, made in autumn 338, was accepted by the states in spring 337, and a 'Common Council' was established, of which the members represented one or more states in proportion to their military and naval strengths. The Council was a sovereign body: its decisions were sent to the states for implementation, not for discussion. The military forces and the naval forces at the disposal of the Common Council were defined: the former amounted to 15,000 cavalry and 200,000 infantry, and the number of warships, which is not stated in our sources, was later to be 160 triremes, manned by crews totalling some 30,000 men. Thus the Greek Community far outdid the Macedonian State in the size of the forces it could deploy. The Council had disciplinary, judicial and financial powers which were binding on the member-states. If we look for a modern analogy, we should look rather to the United States of America than to the European Community.

The next step was the creation of an offensive and defensive alliance between the Greek Community and the Macedonian State for all time. Because Macedonia was already at war with Persia, the Council declared war on Persia late in 337 and voted that the commander of the joint forces should be Philip. Within the Community his title was 'Hegemon' [supreme commander or captain-general], and the powers of his office were carefully defined. In the spring of 336 the vanguard [small leading unit] of the joint forces crossed to Asia under the command of three Macedonian generals whom Philip appointed, and arrangements were made for the stipulated forces of the coalition to follow in the autumn with Philip as overall commander.

The brilliance of Philip's political initiative, power of persuasion and effective leadership is obvious. He brought into being the combination of a newly created Greek State, self-standing and self-governing, and a Macedonian State which was unrivalled in military power. If that combination should succeed in liberating the Greek cities in Asia and in acquiring extensive territory, it would provide a cure for many of the troubles of the Greek world. [The Greek historian] Theopompus, critical of Philip in many ways, entitled his history *Philippica* 'because Europe had never produced such a man altogether as Philip, son of Amyntas'.

Selection 5

The Conquests of Alexander the Great

Thomas R. Martin

This overview of the exploits of Macedonia's Alexander III (the Great) is by Thomas R. Martin, a professor of classics at Holy Cross. Martin includes several anecdotes and details that shed light on Alexander's character, such as the fact that he kept a copy of Homer's Iliad *with him always. As Martin points out, Alexander's most immediate legacy was the chaotic scramble to carve up his newly acquired empire in the years following his untimely passing.*

a disgruntled Macedonian assassinated Philip in 336 B.C. Unconfirmed rumors circulated that the murder had been instigated by one of his several wives, Olympias, a princess from Epirus to the west of Macedonia and mother of Philip's son, Alexander (356–323 B.C.). Alexander promptly liquidated potential rivals for the throne and won recogni-

tion as king while barely twenty years old. In several lightning-fast campaigns, he subdued Macedonia's traditional enemies to the west and north. Next he compelled the city-states in southern Greece that had rebelled from the League of Corinth at the news of Philip's death to rejoin the alliance. (As in Philip's reign, Sparta remained outside the league.) To demonstrate the price of disloyalty, Alexander destroyed Thebes in 335 as punishment for its rebellion. This lesson in terror made it clear that Alexander might claim to lead the Greek city-states by their consent (the kind of leader called a hegemon in Greek) but that the reality of his power rested on his superior force and his unwavering willingness to employ it.

With Greece cowed into peaceful if grudging allegiance, Alexander in 334 led a Macedonian and Greek army into Anatolia to fulfill his father's plan to avenge Greece by attacking Persia. Alexander's astounding success in the following years in conquering the entire Persian Empire while still in his twenties earned him the title "the Great" in later ages. In his own time, his great-

Excerpted from *Ancient Greece: From Prehistoric to Hellenistic Times*, by Thomas R. Martin. Copyright © 1996 by Yale University. Reprinted by permission of Yale University Press.

ness consisted of his ability to inspire his men to follow him into hostile, unknown regions where they were reluctant to go, beyond the borders of civilization as they knew it. Alexander inspired his troops with his reckless disregard for his own safety, often, for example, plunging into the enemy at the head of his men and sharing the danger of the common soldier. No one could miss him in his plumed helmet, vividly colored cloak, and armor polished to reflect the sun. So intent on conquering distant lands was Alexander that he had rejected advice to delay his departure from Macedonia until he had married and fathered an heir, to forestall instability in case of his death. He had further alarmed his principal adviser, an experienced older man, by giving away virtually all his land and property in order to strengthen the army, thereby creating new landowners who would furnish troops. "What," he was asked, "do you have left for yourself?" "My hopes," Alexander replied (Plutarch, *Alexander* 15). Those hopes centered on constructing a heroic image of himself as a warrior as glorious as the incomparable Achilles of Homer's *Iliad*. Alexander always kept a copy of the *Iliad* under his pillow, along with a dagger. Alexander's aspirations and his behavior represented the ultimate expression of the Homeric vision of the glorious conquering warrior.

Victory Follows Victory

Alexander cast a spear into the earth of Anatolia when he crossed the Hellespont strait from Europe to Asia, thereby claiming the Asian continent for himself in Homeric fashion as territory "won by the spear" (Diodorus, *Library of History* 17.17.2). The first battle of the campaign, at the River Granicus in western Anatolia, proved the worth of Alexander's Macedonian and Greek cavalry, which charged across the river and up the bank to rout the opposing Persians. Alexander visited Midas's old capital of Gordion in Phrygia, where an oracle had promised the lordship of Asia to whoever could loose a seemingly impenetrable knot of rope tying the yoke of an ancient chariot preserved in the city. The young Macedonian, so the story goes, cut the Gordion knot with his sword. In 333 B.C. the Persian king

Darius finally faced Alexander in battle at Issus, near the southeastern corner of Anatolia. Alexander's army defeated its more numerous opponents with a characteristically bold strike of cavalry through the left side of the Persian lines followed by a flanking maneuver against the king's position in the center. Darius had to flee from the field to avoid capture, leaving behind his wives and daughters, who had accompanied his campaign in keeping with royal Persian tradition. Alexander's scrupulously chivalrous treatment of the Persian royal women after their capture at Issus reportedly boosted his reputation among the peoples of the king's empire.

When Tyre, a heavily fortified city on the coast of what is now Lebanon, refused to surrender to him in 332 B.C., Alexander employed the assault machines and catapults developed by his father to breach the walls of its formidable offshore fortress after a long siege. The capture of Tyre rang the death knell of the walled city-state as a settlement impregnable to siege warfare. Although successful sieges remained rare after Alexander because well-constructed city walls still presented formidable barriers to attackers, Alexander's success against Tyre increased the terror of a siege for a city's general population. No longer could the citizens of a city-state confidently assume that their defensive system could withstand the technology of their enemy's offensive weapons indefinitely. The now-present fear that a siege might actually breach a city's walls made it much harder psychologically for city-states to remain united in the face of threats from enemies like aggressive kings.

Alexander next took over Egypt, where hieroglyphic inscriptions seem to show that he probably presented himself as the successor to the Persian king as the land's ruler rather than as an Egyptian pharaoh. On the coast, to the west of the Nile River, Alexander in 331 founded a new city named Alexandria after himself, the first of the many cities he would later establish as far east as Afghanistan. During his time in Egypt, Alexander also paid a mysterious visit to the oracle of the god Ammon, whom the Greeks regarded as identical to Zeus, at the oasis of Siwah far out in the western Egyptian desert. Alexander told no one the details of his consultation of the oracle, but the news got out that he had been informed he was the son of the god and that he joyfully accepted the designation as true.

In 331 B.C., Alexander crushed the Persian king's main army at the battle of Gaugamela in northern Mesopotamia, near the border of modern Iraq and Iran. He subsequently proclaimed himself king of Asia in place of the Persian king. For the heterogeneous populations of the Persian Empire, the succession of a Macedonian to the Persian throne meant essentially no change in their lives. They continued to send the same taxes to a remote master, whom they rarely if ever saw. As in Egypt, Alexander left the local administrative system of the Persian Empire in place, even retaining some Persian governors. His long-term aim seems to have been to forge an administrative corps composed of Macedonians, Greeks, and Persians working together to rule the territory he conquered with his army.

To India and Back

Alexander next led his army farther east into territory hardly known to the Greeks. He pared his force to reduce the need for supplies, which were difficult to find in the arid country through which they were marching. Each hoplite in Greek armies customarily had a personal servant to carry his armor and pack. Alexander, imitating Philip, trained his men to carry their own equipment, thereby creating a leaner force by cutting the number of army servants dramatically. As with all ancient armies, however, a large number of noncombatants trailed after the fighting force: merchants who set up little markets at every stop, women whom soldiers had taken as mates along the way and their children, entertainers, and prostitutes. Although supplying these hangers-on was not Alexander's responsibility, their foraging for themselves made it harder for Alexander's quartermasters to find what they needed to supply the army proper.

An ancient army's demand for supplies usually left a trail of destruction and famine for local inhabitants in the wake of its march. Hostile armies simply took whatever they wanted. Friendly armies expected local people to sell or donate food to its supply officers and also to the merchants trailing along. These entrepreneurs would set up markets to resell locally obtained provisions to the soldiers. Since most farmers in antiquity had practically no surplus to sell, they found this expectation—which was in reality a requirement—a terrific hardship. The money the farmers received was of little use to them because there was nothing to buy with it in the countryside, where their neighbors had also had to participate in the forced marketing of their subsistence.

From the heartland of Persia, Alexander in 329 B.C. marched northeastward into the trackless steppes of Bactria (modern Afghanistan). When he proved unable to subdue completely the highly mobile locals, who avoided pitched battles in favor of the guerrilla tactics of attack and retreat, Alexander settled for an alliance sealed by his marriage to the Bactrian princess Roxane in 327. In this same period, Alexander completed the cold-blooded suppression of both real and imagined resistance to his plans among the leading men in his officer corps. As in past years, he used accusations of treachery or disloyalty as justification for the execution of those Macedonians he had come to distrust. These executions, like the destruction of Thebes in 335, demonstrated Alexander's appreciation of terror as a disincentive to rebellion.

From Bactria Alexander pushed on eastward to India. He probably intended to march all the way through to China in search of the edge of the farthest land on the earth, which Aristotle, once Alexander's tutor, had taught was a sphere. Seventy days of marching through monsoon rains, however, finally shattered the nerves of Alexander's soldiers. In the spring of 326 B.C. they mutinied on the banks of the Hyphasis River (the modern Beas) in western India. Alexander was forced to agree to lead them in the direction of home. When his men had balked before, Alexander had always been able to shame then back into action by sulking in his tent like Achilles in the *Iliad*. This time the soldiers were beyond shame.

Alexander thereupon proceeded south down the Indus River. Along the way he took out his frustration at being stopped in his eastward march by slaughtering the Indian tribes who resisted him and by risking his life more flamboyantly than ever before. As a climax to his frustrated rage, he flung himself over the wall of an Indian town to face the enemy alone like a Homeric hero. His horrified officers were barely able to rescue him in time; even so, he received grievous wounds. At the mouth of the Indus on the Indian Ocean, Alexander turned a portion of his army west through the fierce desert of Gedrosia. Another portion took an easier route inland, while a third group sailed westward along the coast to explore for possible sites for new settlements and harbors. Alexander himself led the contingent that braved the desert, planning to surpass earlier Persian kings by marching through territory that they had found impassable. There a flash flood wiped out most of the noncombatants following the army. Many of the soldiers also died on the march through the desert, expiring from lack of water and the heat, which has been recorded at 127 degrees in the shade in that area. Alexander, as always, shared his men's hardships. In one legendary episode from this horrible ordeal, a few men were said to have brought him a helmet containing some water they had found. Alexander spilled the water out onto the sand rather than drink when his men could not. The remains of the army finally reached safety in the heartland of Persia in 324 B.C. Alexander promptly began plans for an invasion of the Arabian peninsula and, to follow that, all of North Africa west of Egypt.

The Son of a God?

By the time Alexander returned to Persia, he had dropped all pretense of ruling over the Greeks as anything other than an absolute monarch. Despite his earlier promise to respect the internal freedom of the Greek city-states, he now impinged on their autonomy by sending a peremptory decree ordering them to restore to citizen-

ship the large number of exiles wandering homeless in the Greek world. The previous decades of war in Greece had created many of these unfortunate wanderers, and their status as stateless persons was creating unrest. Even more striking was Alexander's communication to the city-states that he wished to receive the honors due a god. Initially dumbfounded by this request, the leaders of most Greek states soon complied by sending honorary delegations to him as if he were a god. The Spartan Damis pithily expressed the only prudent position on Alexander's deification open to the cowed Greeks: "If Alexander wishes to be a god, we agree that he be called a god" (Plutarch, *Moralia* 219e).

Scholarly debate continues over Alexander's motive for desiring the Greeks to acknowledge him as a god, but few now accept a formerly popular theory that he sought divinity because he believed the city-states would then have to obey his orders as originating from a divinity, whose authority would supersede that of all earthly regimes. Personal rather than political motives best explain his request. He almost certainly had come to believe that he was the son of Zeus; after all, Greek mythology told many stories of Zeus producing children by mating with a human female. Most of those legendary offspring were mortal, but Alexander's conquest showed that he had surpassed them. His feats must be superhuman, he could well have believed, because they exceeded the bounds of human possibility. In other words, Alexander's accomplishments demonstrated that he had achieved godlike power and therefore must be a god himself. The divinity of Alexander, in ancient terms, emerged as a natural consequence of his power.

Alexander's overall aims can best be explained as interlinked goals: the conquest and administration of the known world and the exploration and possible colonization of new territory beyond. Conquest through military action was a time-honored pursuit for ambitious Macedonian leaders such as Alexander. He included non-Macedonians in his administration and army because he needed their expertise, not because he had any dream of promoting an abstract notion of what has sometimes been called "the brotherhood of man." Alexander's explorations benefited numerous scientific fields, from geography to botany, because he took along scientifically minded writers to collect and catalogue the new knowledge that they encountered. The far-flung new cities that he founded served as loyal outposts to keep the peace in conquered territory and provide warnings to headquarters in case of local uprisings. They also created new opportunities for trade in valuable goods such as spices that were not produced in the Mediterranean region.

Alexander's plans to conquer Arabia and North Africa were extinguished by his premature death from a fever and heavy drinking on June 10, 323 B.C., in Babylon. He had already been suffering for months from depression brought on by the death of his best friend, Hephaistion. Close since their boyhoods, Alexander and Hephaistion were probably lovers. When Hephaistion died in a bout of excessive drinking, Alexander went wild with grief. The depth of his emotion was evident when he planned to build an elaborate temple to honor Hephaistion as a god. Meanwhile, Alexander threw himself into preparing for his Arabian campaign by exploring the marshy lowlands of southern Mesopotamia. Perhaps it was on one of these trips that he contracted the malaria-like fever that, exacerbated by a two-day drinking binge, killed him.

Like Pericles, Alexander had made no plans about what should happen if he should die unexpectedly. His wife Roxane was to give birth to their first child only some months after Alexander's death. When at Alexander's deathbed his commanders asked him to whom he bequeathed his kingdom, he replied, "To the most powerful [kratistos]" (Arrian, *Anabasis of Alexander* 7.26.3).

The Athenian orator Aeschines (c. 397–322 B.C.) well expressed the bewildered reaction of many people to the events of Alexander's lifetime: "What strange and unexpected event has not occurred in our time? The life we have lived is no ordinary human one, but we were born to be an object of wonder to posterity" (*Orations* 3.132). Alexander himself certainly attained legendary status in later times. Stories of fabulous exploits attributed to him became popular folk tales throughout the ancient world, even reaching distant regions where Alexander had never trod, such as deep into Africa. The popularity of the legend of Alexander as a symbol of the height of achievement for a masculine warrior-hero served as one of his most persistent legacies to later ages. That the worlds of Greece and the Near East had been brought into closer contact than ever before represented the other long-lasting effect of his astonishing career. Its immediate political and military consequences were the struggles among his generals that led to the creation of the kingdoms of the Hellenistic world.

Selection 6

Alexander's Brilliance as a Leader

Arrian

Arrian (Flavius Arrianus) was a Romanized Greek historian who wrote during the first half of the second century A.D., *when Rome ruled the Greek world. His* Anabasis Alexandri *(meaning "Alexander's march up-country"), the most complete surviving ancient source for Alexander's career, was based largely on two contemporary histories now lost. The first was by Alexander's general, Ptolemy, who later went on to rule Egypt; the second was by one of Alexander's engineers, Aristobulus. The following tract from Arrian's work includes a description of the battle at the Hydapses River (in western India), fought against the Indian king Porus in 326* B.C. *Arrian then gives his own appraisal of Alexander's strengths and skills. Arrian's comments clearly demonstrate why Alexander acquired such a lofty reputation for great leadership, both in his own and later times.*

Once this second crossing [of the Hydapses] was successfully accomplished, Alexander again marshalled his troops. His Royal Squadron and the best of the other mounted regiments he brought round to the right wing, stationing the mounted archers in the van;

in the rear of the cavalry he posted the Royal Regiment of Guards under Seleucus, then the Royal regiment of the heavy infantry, in close touch with the other Guards divisions, according to their precedence for that day. The archers, Agrianes, and javelin-men took their position on either wing of the main body of infantry. Having thus made his dispositions, he gave orders for the infantry, nearly 6,000 strong, to follow in order of march, while he himself, with only the cavalry (numbering some 5,000) in which he thought he had the advantage over the enemy, moved forward rapidly. Tauron, captain of the archers, was instructed to advance in the rear of the cavalry with all the speed he could make.

The idea in Alexander's mind was that if Porus' army should attack in force he would . . . fight a delaying action until his infantry could come to his support; if, on the other hand, the Indians proved to be so badly shaken by the bold and unexpected crossing of the river that they took to their heels, he would be able to press hard on the retreating army, and the more men they lost during their withdrawal, the lighter his own task would subsequently be. . . .

Porus' son arrived on the scene with . . . 2,000 mounted troops and 120 chariots . . . but Alexander had been too quick for him and had already effected his final crossing from the island. Against this force Alexander first sent his mounted archers, while he himself moved on with the cavalry, thinking that Porus was on the way to engage him with the main strength of his army, and that this cavalry contingent, posted in the van, preceded the rest of the Indian troops. But as soon as Alexander received an accurate report of the enemies' numbers, he attacked at once, and the Indians, seeing Alexander there in person and his massed cavalry coming at them in successive charges, squadron by squadron, broke and fled. The Indians' losses in the action were some 400 mounted men, Porus' son being himself among the killed; their chariots and horses were captured as they attempted to get away—speed was impossible, and the muddy ground had rendered them useless even during the fight.

The Indians who did succeed in getting away reported to Porus that Alexander had crossed the river in force and that his son had been killed in the action. Porus was faced with a difficult choice, for the troops under Craterus, who had been left behind in Alexander's original position opposite the main Indian army, could now be seen making their way over the river. Swiftly he made up his mind; he determined to move in force against Alexander, and to fight it out with the King of Macedon himself and the flower of his men. Then, leaving behind a small force with a few elephants to spread alarm among Craterus' cavalry as they attempted to land on the river-bank, he marched to meet Alexander with all his cavalry, 4,000 strong, all of his 300 chariots, 200 elephants, and the picked contingents of his infantry, numbering some 30,000 men.

Much of the ground was deep in soft mud, so he continued his advance till he found a spot where the sandy soil offered a surface sufficiently firm and level for cavalry manœuvre, and there made his dispositions. In the van he stationed his elephants at intervals of about 100 feet, on a broad front, to form a screen for the whole body of the infantry and to spread terror among the cavalry of Alexander. He did not expect that any enemy unit would venture to force a way through the gaps in the line of elephants, either on foot or on horseback; terror would make the horses uncontrollable, and infantry units would be even less likely to make the at-

tempt, as they would be met and checked by his own heavy infantry and then destroyed by the elephants turning upon them and trampling them down. Behind the elephants were the foot-soldiers, though not on a front of equal extent: the various units, forming a second line, were so disposed as to fill the intervals in the line of elephants. There was infantry on both wings as well, outflanking the elephants, and, finally, on both flanks of the infantry were the mounted units, each with a screen of war-chariots.

Noting that the enemy was making his dispositions for battle, Alexander checked the advance of his cavalry to allow the infantry to come up with him. Regiment by regiment they made contact, moving swiftly, until the whole force was again united. Alexander had no intention of making the fresh enemy troops a present of his own breathless and exhausted men, so he paused before advancing to the attack. Meanwhile he kept his cavalry manœuvering up and down the line, while the infantry units were allowed to rest until they were once more in good heart for battle.

Alexander Launches His Attack

Observation of the Indian dispositions decided him against attempting an assault upon their centre, where the heavy infantry was massed in the intervals of the protecting screen of elephants, and his reluctance to take this course was based precisely upon Porus' own calculations; relying, instead, on his superiority in cavalry, he moved the major portion of his mounted troops towards the enemy's left wing, to make his assault in that sector. Coenus was sent over to the Indians' right with Demetrius' regiment and his own, his orders being that when the enemy moved their cavalry across to their left to counter the massed formations of the Macedonian mounted squadrons, he should hang on to their rear. The heavy infantry was put in charge of Seleucus, Antigenes, and Tauron, with orders not to engage until it was evident that the Indians, both horse and foot, had been thrown into confusion by the Macedonian cavalry.

Once the opposing armies were within range,

Alexander launched his mounted archers, 1,000 strong, against the enemy's left wing, hoping to shake it by the hail of their arrows and the weight of their charge, and immediately afterwards himself advanced with the Companions against the Indian left, intent upon making his assault while they were still reeling under the attack of the mounted archers and before their cavalry could change formation from column into mass.

The Indians meanwhile withdrew all the cavalry from other sections of their line, and moved it across to meet and counter Alexander's movement towards their flank, and it was not long before Coenus' men could be seen following, according to orders, close in their rear. The Indians were thereupon compelled to split their force into two; the larger section, containing the best troops, continued to proceed against Alexander, while the remainder wheeled about in order to deal with Coenus. This, of course, was disastrous not only to the effectiveness of the Indians' dispositions, but to their whole plan of battle. Alexander saw his chance; precisely at the moment when the enemy cavalry were changing direction, he attacked. The Indians did not even wait to receive his charge, but fell back in confusion upon the elephants, their impregnable fortress—or so they hoped. The elephant-drivers forced their beasts to meet the opposing cavalry, while the Macedonian infantry, in its turn, advanced against them, shooting down the drivers, and pouring in a hail of missiles from every side upon the elephants themselves. It was an odd bit of work—quite unlike any previous battle; the monster elephants plunged this way and that among the lines of infantry, dealing destruction in the solid mass of the Macedonian phalanx, while the Indian horsemen, seeing the infantry at one another's throats, wheeled to the assault of the Macedonian cavalry. Once again, however, the strength and experience of Alexander's mounted troops were too much for them, and they were forced back a second time on the elephants.

During the action all the Macedonian cavalry units had, by the exigencies of the fighting rather than deliberate orders, concentrated into a single body; and now its successive charges upon this sector or that inflicted heavy losses on the enemy. By this time the elephants were boxed up, with no room to manœuvre, by troops all round them, and as they blundered about, wheeling and shoving this way and that, they trampled to death as many of their friends as of their enemies. The result was that the Indian cavalry, jammed in around the elephants and with no more space to manœuvre than they had, suffered severely; most of the elephant-drivers had been shot; many of the animals had themselves been wounded, while others, riderless and bewildered; ceased altogether to play their expected part, and, maddened by pain and fear; set indiscriminately upon friend and foe, thrusting, trampling, and spreading death before them. The Macedonians could deal with these maddened creatures comfortably enough; having room to manœuvre, they were able to use their judgement, giving ground when they charged, and going for them with their javelins when they turned and lumbered back, whereas the unfortunate Indians, jammed up close among them as they attempted to get away, found them a more dangerous enemy even than the Macedonians.

In time the elephants tired and their charges grew feebler; they began to back away, slowly, like ships going astern, and with nothing worse than trumpetings. Taking his chance, Alexander surrounded the lot of them—elephants, horsemen, and all—and then signalled his infantry to lock shields and move up in a solid mass. Most of the Indian cavalry was cut down in the ensuing action; their infantry, too, hard pressed by the Macedonians, suffered terrible losses. The survivors, finding a gap in Alexander's ring of cavalry, all turned and fled. Craterus and the other officers who had been left on the bank of the river began to cross as soon as they saw Alexander's triumphant success, and their fresh troops, taking over the pursuit from Alexander's weary men, inflicted upon the vanquished Indians further losses no less severe.

Nearly 20,000 of the Indian infantry were killed in this battle, and about 3,000 of their cavalry. All their war-chariots were destroyed. Among the dead were two sons of Porus, Spitaces the local Indian governor, all the officers in command of the elephants and chariots, and all the cavalry officers and other commanders of high rank. The surviving elephants were captured. Out of Alexander's original 6,000 infantry, some eighty were killed; in addition to these he lost ten of the mounted archers, who were the first unit to engage, about twenty of the Companions, and 200 of the other cavalry.

The Two Kings Meet

Throughout the action Porus had proved himself a man indeed, not only as a commander but as a soldier of the truest courage. When he saw his cavalry cut to pieces, most of his infantry dead, and his elephants killed or roaming riderless and bewildered about the field, his behaviour was very different from that of the Persian King Darius: unlike Darius, he did not lead the scramble to save his own skin, but so long as a single unit of his men held together, fought bravely on. It was only when he was himself wounded that he turned the elephant on which he rode and began to withdraw. The wound was in his right shoulder, the only unprotected part of his body; no missile, as he moved here and there in the thick of the fighting, could touch him anywhere else because of the corselet [chest armor] which he wore—a corselet exceedingly tough and closely fitting, as all who subsequently saw him could observe.

Alexander, anxious to save the life of this great and gallant soldier, sent Taxiles the Indian to him. Taxiles rode up as near as he dared and requested him to stop his elephant and hear what message Alexander sent him, as escape was no longer possible. But Taxiles was an old enemy of the Indian King, and Porus turned his elephant and drove at him, to kill him with his lance; and he might indeed have killed him, if he had not spurred his horse out of the way in the nick of time. Alexander, however, far from resenting this treatment of his messenger, sent a number of others, the last of whom was an Indian named Meroes, a man he had been told had long been Porus' friend. Porus listened to Meroes' message, stopped his elephant, and dismounted; he was much distressed by thirst, so when he had revived himself by drinking, he told Meroes to conduct him with all speed to Alexander.

Alexander, informed of his approach, rode out to meet him, accompanied by a small party of his Companions. When they met, he reined in his horse, and looked at his adversary with admiration: he was a magnificent figure of a man, over seven feet high and of great personal beauty; his bearing had lost none of its pride; his air was of one brave man meeting another, of a king in the presence of a king, with whom he had fought honourably for his kingdom.

Alexander was the first to speak. 'What,' he said, 'do you wish that I should do with you?'

'Treat me as a king ought,' Porus is said to have replied.

'For my part,' said Alexander, pleased by his answer, 'your request shall be granted. But is there not something you would wish for yourself? Ask it.'

'Everything,' said Porus, 'is contained in this one request.'

The dignity of these words gave Alexander even more pleasure, and he restored to Porus his sovereignty over his subjects, adding to his realm other territory of even greater extent. Thus he did indeed use a brave man as a king ought, and from that time forward found him in every way a loyal friend. Such was the result of the battle with Porus and the Indians beyond the Hydaspes. . . .

A Man More than Human?

Alexander died in the 114th Olympiad, in the archonship of Hegesias at Athens [June 10, 323 B.C.]. He lived, as Aristobulus tells us, thirty-two years and eight months, and reigned twelve years and eight months [or more probably he was thirty-two years and eleven months old and had reigned for thirteen years when he died]. He had great personal beauty, invincible power of endurance, and a keen intellect; he was brave and adventurous, strict in the observance of his religious duties, and hungry for fame. Most temperate in the pleasures of the body, his passion was for glory only, and in that he was insatiable. He had an uncanny instinct for the right course in a difficult and complex situation, and was most happy in his deductions from observed facts. In arming and equipping troops and in his military dispositions he was always masterly. Noble indeed was his power of inspiring his men, of filling them with confidence, and, in the moment of danger, of sweeping away their fear by the spectacle of his own fearlessness. When risks had to be taken, he took them with the utmost boldness, and his ability to seize the moment for a swift blow, before his enemy had any suspicion of what was coming, was beyond praise. No cheat or liar ever caught him off his guard, and both his word and his bond were inviolable. Spending but little on his own pleasures, he poured out his money without stint for the benefit of his friends.

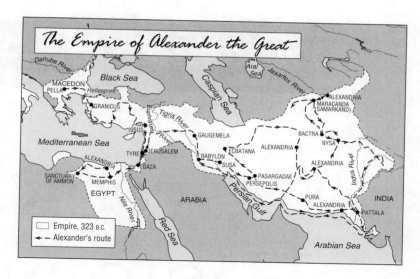

The Empire of Alexander the Great

Doubtless, in the passion of the moment Alexander sometimes erred; it is true he took some steps towards the pomp and arrogance of the Asiatic kings: but I, at least, cannot feel that such errors were very heinous, if the circumstances are taken fairly into consideration. For, after all, he was young; the chain of his successes was unbroken, and, like all kings, past, present, and to come, he was surrounded by courtiers who spoke to please, regardless of what evil their words might do. On the other hand, I do indeed know that Alexander, of all the monarchs of old, was the only one who had the nobility of heart to be sorry for his mistakes.

Nor do I think that Alexander's claim to a divine origin was a very serious fault—in any case, it may well have been a mere device to magnify his consequence in the eyes of his subjects. . . . Surely, too, his adoption of Persian dress was, like his claim to divine birth, a matter of policy: by it he hoped to bring the Eastern nations to feel that they had a king who was not wholly a foreigner, and to indicate to his own countrymen his desire to move away from the harsh traditional arrogance of Macedonia. That was also, no doubt, the reason why he included a proportion of Persian troops (the so-called 'Golden Apples', for instance) in Macedonian units, and made Persian noblemen officers in his crack native regiments. . . .

It is my belief that there was in those days no nation, no city, no single individual beyond the reach of Alexander's name; never in all the world was there another like him, and therefore I cannot but feel that some power more than human was concerned in his birth; indications of this were, moreover, said to be provided at the time of his death by oracles; many people saw visions and had prophetic dreams; and there is the further evidence of the extraordinary way in which he is held, as no mere man could be, in honour and remembrance. Even today, when so many years have passed, there have been oracles, all tending to his glory, delivered to the people of Macedon.

In the course of this book I have, admittedly, found fault with some of the things which Alexander did, but of the man himself I am not ashamed to express ungrudging admiration. Where I have criticized unfavourably, I have done so because I wished to tell the truth as I saw it, and to enable my readers to profit thereby. Such was the motive which led me to embark upon this History: and I, too, have had God's help in my work.

Greek History– The Hellenistic Age

Chapter 6

Introduction

*A*lexander's leading generals and governors, the so-called Successors (*Diadochoi*), included Perdiccas, Eumenes, Antigonus Monophthalmos (the One-eyed), Ptolemy (TAW-luh-mee), Seleucus, and Antipater, to name only a few. When they began fighting among themselves soon after his passing, the eastern Mediterranean–Near Eastern world entered a period of profound political and cultural transformation. The Greek-dominated sphere that emerged after their roughly four decades of devastating wars was far larger and more cosmopolitan than any previous Greek state or region. The Greeks came to call this sphere the *oikoumene* (ee-koo-MEH-nee), or "inhabited world." Indeed, at the time it seemed to constitute a world unto itself, geographically and culturally speaking, for nearly all of the states it encompassed had similar political, economic, and cultural institutions imposed by Greek rulers and the elite classes that supported them.

Given the fact that so much of the *oikoumene* was made up of Near Eastern lands, it was only natural that many of its institutions and customs would blend Greek and Near Eastern elements. It is this distinctive blend that modern historians single out in calling these realms Hellenistic, or "Greek-like" (as opposed to Hellenic, which refers to a culture that is solely Greek). The turbulent Hellenistic Age lasted from Alexander's death in 323 B.C. to the death of another legendary figure, Cleopatra VII, the last major Hellenistic ruler, in 30 B.C.

In overall size and geographic extent, the Hellenistic world roughly coincided with Alexander's short-lived empire, which it had superceded. It stretched from Macedonia and Epirus in the far west to the borders of India in the far east; and from the shores of the Black Sea in the north to Egypt's deserts and Nile River valley in the south. The difference was that the brave new world that emerged from the *Diadochoi* wars was divided into numerous separate and competing political states. The three biggest were the Seleucid Kingdom, established by Seleucus (ca. 358–281 B.C.), encompassing the vast lands surrounding the Persian Gulf (the central portion of the old Persian Empire) and parts of Asia Minor; the Ptolemaic Kingdom, founded by Ptolemy (ca. 360–282), consisting mainly of Egypt and parts of nearby Palestine; and the Macedonian Kingdom, created by Antigonus II Gonatas (ca. 320–239, grandson of Antigonus the One-eyed, (ca. 382–301), made up mostly of Macedonia and portions of the Greek mainland.

Sharing the *oikoumene* with these large states were a number of smaller but still influential ones. Among the most notable were the kingdoms of Pergamum (or Pergamon), located in western Asia Minor, and Epirus, lying to the west of Macedonia and facing southern Italy. Pergamum started out as part of the Seleucid realm; but about 262 B.C. it broke away, led by Philetaerus and his adopted son Eumenes, who founded the Attalid dynasty (named after Philetaerus's father, the Macedonian Attalus). Under the Attalids, Pergamum often dominated affairs in Asia Minor and became a famous cultural center, with the second-largest library in the world (next to the one in the Ptolemaic city of Alexandria).

Epirus, long a political and cultural backwater, rose briefly to prominence under its greatest king, the military adventurer Pyrrhus (319–272 B.C.). An important figure in the Successor wars, Pyrrhus's main claim to fame was his confrontation with the Romans. Asked to intercede on behalf of the Greek city of Taras (or Tarentum), in southern Italy, which was at odds with Rome, the Epirote king crossed into Italy in 280 B.C. and engaged the Roman legions in several battles. Although he inflicted heavy losses on them, he sustained equally heavy losses of his own and, unable to achieve a decisive victory, eventually withdrew from Italy, foreshadowing the following century's large-scale Greek retreat before Rome's might.

The other important Hellenistic powers included the Aetolian League (centered in western Greece) and Achaean League (in the Peloponnesus), federations of cities that had allied themselves partly out of shared backgrounds and customs, and also for mutual protection. The Achaean League, states noted scholar Peter Green in his *Alexander to Actium*, consisted of

> a group of cities united in a confederacy (*sym-politeia*), that is, with a common federal citizenship but retaining independent control of their internal affairs. This constitution has been the cause of much scholarly debate (its written terms do not survive), but the modern, if more complex, parallel of the United States is inescapable.

The Hellenistic world also featured some powerful independent city-states, two of the most successful being the island of Rhodes (off the coast of Asia Minor), which withstood the famous siege (in 305–304 B.C.) by Demetrius Poliorcetes (336–283, son of Antigonus the One-eyed); and Byzantium (on the Propontis, the waterway between the Hellespont and Bosporus straits).

Of all of these states, the Aetolian and Achaean leagues, though plagued by numerous internal weaknesses and a mutually destructive rivalry, represented perhaps the greatest hope for Greece's future. For they were at least real, if small-scale, attempts to achieve lasting unity among the old-style Greek city-states. However, the intrusion of Rome into the eastern Mediterranean sphere beginning in the early second century B.C. ended up dashing any hopes for the eventual emergence of a "United States of Greece" that might have gone on to absorb and transfigure all of Europe.

Indeed, Roman aggression ensured that the Hellenistic era would be the last period of major Greek political independence in antiquity. Having fought and defeated the empire of Carthage (centered in northern Africa) in the first two Punic Wars (264–241 and 218–201 B.C.), the Romans turned with a vengeance on Macedonia's King Philip V, who had aided Carthage in the second conflict. Within a few decades, all of mainland Greece was in Roman hands; and by the mid–first century B.C. there was only one major Hellenistic state left—Ptolemaic Egypt, whose last ruler, the audacious and capable Cleopatra, allied herself with two powerful Romans, Julius Caesar and Mark Antony. Their tempestuous relationships and struggles, set against the larger historical backdrop of Greece's fall into subjugation and Rome's rise to Mediterranean mastery, subsequently became the stuff of legend.

As for the primary written sources for the political events of the Hellenistic Age, Diodorus's *Library of History* provides a chronicle of the Successor wars up to 302 B.C. This period, along with that of the following two decades, is fairly well covered in Plutarch's biographies of Pyrrhus, Eumenes, Demetrius, the Spartan kings Agis IV and Cleomenes III, and the Achaean statesman Aratus. However, the period from 281 to 221 B.C., encompassing the heart, so to speak, of the age, is unfortunately one of the most poorly documented in all of ancient history. (Polybius's narrative of Rome's rise, which has much information about the Greek states in the late second and early first centuries B.C., begins in 221; a surviving overview of these years in a work by the third-century A.D. Roman historian Justin is very sketchy and somewhat unreliable.) A number of surviving inscriptions and papyrus fragments help illuminate this period's economic aspects, as well as those of the whole Hellenistic Age. Cleopatra's exploits, the fall of the Ptolemaic Kingdom, and other aspects of late Hellenistic times are covered in the histories of the first-century A.D. Roman historian Suetonius and the second-century A.D. Romanized Greek historians Appian and Dio Cassius.

Selection 1

Wars of Alexander's Successors

Michael Grant

Following Alexander's death in 323 B.C., a long series of bloody conflicts ensued among his leading generals, the so-called Diadochoi *("Successors") and their sons, the* Epigoni *("those born after"). As described here by Edinburgh University scholar Michael Grant, these wars ended with the emergence of three large Hellenistic kingdoms in the lands that had so briefly made up Alexander's vast empire.*

*U*nlike almost everybody else in the world, Alexander possessed the ability and genius to put his yearnings into practice to an almost immeasurable extent.

He and his helpers explored many lands, he brought the title of king into the Greek world, he helped decisively to inspire a long-lived religious cult of rulers, he founded a number of Greek cities, he issued a fine, uniform, empire-wide currency. But the everlasting legend that sprang up around his life and personality—one of the most astonishing, prolonged imaginative phenomena in the history of the world—was far more enormous than anything he himself left behind: for the implementation of his marvellous plan of partnership with the Persians re-

mained in the air—and almost everything else, too, still remained to be done. . . .

When the king was asked on his deathbed to whom he bequeathed his empire he could only reply (so it was said): 'to the strongest'. There is thus a bitter irony in the story that when a storm rages in the Aegean the mermaids emerge and cry out to passing ships, 'Where is Alexander the Great?'; and the captain cries back along the wind, 'Alexander the Great lives and rules, and keeps the world at peace.' To keep the world at peace was exactly what Alexander failed to do. On the contrary, his early death was followed by four decades of warfare between his generals.

The First Phases of the Fighting

Most of the competitors had played important parts in his army. The monarchy was at first officially represented by two kings appointed in his place, Philip III Arrhidaeus (his mentally retarded half-brother) and Alexander IV (his posthumous son by [the Persian princess] Roxane). A few of the commanders still wanted to preserve the unity of the empire that this kingship purported to represent. Most of their colleagues, however, were intent on breaking up these dominions, so as to carve out kingdoms for themselves. From a military and political viewpoint, therefore, the period of forty-two years in which the Successors fought against one another is highly confused. Moreover, although the aims of the participants were simple

Reprinted with the permission of Scribner, a division of Simon & Schuster, and by permission of Weidenfeld & Nicolson, from *From Alexander to Cleopatra*, by Michael Grant. Copyright © 1982 by Michael Grant Publications Ltd.

enough—the seizure of territory and assertion of personal status—the detailed events seem chaotic and purposeless. Nevertheless, the appearances and disappearances of the leading notable figures, and the kaleidoscopic readjustments of the relations between them, make it possible to divide the period up into a few successive, distinguishable stages.

To begin with, after Alexander was dead, the central government was partially and imperfectly represented, not by the kings who were powerless, but by three other principal Macedonian personages. Antipater, formerly one of Philip II's chief advisers, had been left in Europe by Alexander as his viceroy. Perdiccas had become Alexander's second-in-command, and after the king's death was virtually regent of the empire; it was his intention to come to some arrangement which would look legitimate, while concentrating the real power in his own hands. The third of these figures was Craterus, who had been transferred back home by Alexander with discharged Macedonian soldiers, and now became the guardian of King Philip III Arrhidaeus, perhaps under the supervision of Perdiccas.

Other officers quickly set themselves up as local rulers on their own account. Alexander's associate Ptolemy I—later known as Soter (Saviour)—arrived in Egypt as representative of Philip III Arrhidaeus, but quickly asserted his virtual independence, founding the Ptolemaic state in that country and adding Cyrenaica [the region west of Egypt] to its territory. Antigonus I Monophthalmos (One-Eyed) had served Alexander for ten years as governor of Phrygia (west-central Asia Minor), and now extended his control to the south coast of the peninsula. Alexander's former bodyguard and commander Lysimachus was given a principality consisting of Thrace and northwestern Asia Minor. Eumenes—not a Macedonian like the others, but a Greek from Cardia in Thrace—had been secretary both to Philip II and to Alexander. After the latter's death, he was installed as governor of Cappadocia in east-central Asia Minor, though the territory still had to be conquered.

In the first phase of the struggle that followed, Antipater crushed a rebellion of the Greek city-states—led by Athens—known as the Lamian War, and a revolt of Alexander's mercenaries left behind in Bactria (Afghanistan) was likewise suppressed. Ptolemy's kidnapping of Alexander's corpse and its removal to Egypt led to a war in which Perdiccas and Craterus were killed, in a Macedonian mutiny and a battle against Eumenes respectively. At the conference of Triparadisus in northern Syria (321) Antipater was made sole guardian and viceroy of the two young kings, while Antigonus I Monophthalmos, who was his friend, gained the command of the royal army in Asia. Seleucus I, later known as Nicator (Conqueror)—who had been a friend of Alexander, but was not one of his prominent generals—became governor of Babylon.

The next five years witnessed a decisive weakening of the central government, especially after the death of Antipater (319). His successor Polyperchon associated himself with Eumenes—ostensibly as champion of imperial unity—but was driven from Macedonia and most of Greece by Antipater's son Cassander; while Eumenes, expelled from Asia Minor by Antigonus I, found himself deserted by his own troops, and was put to death (ca. 316). In the previous year, Philip III Arrhidaeus had been captured and killed by Olympias, the mother of Alexander the Great, out of a desire to obtain the eventual sole rule for her infant grandchild Alexander IV.

The five years that followed saw powerful attempts by Antigonus I, supported by his son Demetrius I, to make himself sole ruler of the whole of Alexander's empire. These ambitions caused Cassander, Ptolemy I Soter and Lysimachus to unite against the pair. In 312 Demetrius I was defeated by Ptolemy I at Gaza, and Seleucus I, who had been ejected from Babylon by Antigonus four years earlier, regained the city and, with it, Alexander's eastern territories, thus laying the foundations of the Seleucid kingdom.

The Last Surviving Successors

A truce was agreed upon in 311, but only lasted for a single year. King Alexander IV was soon put to death by Cassander, who also made strenuous and partially successful efforts to master Greece and Macedonia. Antigonus I found it impossible to suppress Seleucus I (310–309); and Antigonus' son Demetrius I (in spite of a naval victory over Ptolemy I off Cyprus) failed to take Rhodes by siege, unable to live up to his nickname Poliorcetes (the Besieger). In 306 Antigonus I assumed the title of king (without naming any particular territory), and Ptolemy I and Seleucus I did likewise in 305–304. By this time it had become increasingly clear that the principal danger to all the other leaders came from the imperial ambitions of Antigonus I: but finally Lysimachus and Seleucus I defeated and killed him at 'the battle of the kings', fought at Ipsus between 75,000 men on either side (301), and won by elephants which Seleucus had obtained from the Indian king Chandragupta Maurya in return for the cession of his eastern territories. This outcome of the battle, by eliminating the only potential reunifier, meant the irrevocable dismemberment of the empire of Alexander, which was now divided into four separate kingdoms: those of Seleucus I, Lysimachus, Ptolemy I and Cassander.

Yet another, and final, phase of the wars of the Successors was still to follow. Recovering from his father's disaster at Ipsus, Demetrius I reoccupied Greece and, after the death of Cassander (297), gained control of Macedonia as well. But in 288 his Macedonian territory was simultaneously invaded by Lysimachus and Pyrrhus I of Epirus—the western neighbour of the Macedonians—with such success that Demetrius I lost his entire territories and fled to Asia Minor, where, three years later, he died of drink, supplied freely by Seleucus I. Demetrius' son Antigonus II Gonatas maintained himself precariously in Greece, but meanwhile Lysimachus, by a series of lightning actions, was greatly extending his own territories, which now included not only Macedonia itself, but also Thrace, Thessaly and a large part of Asia Minor. In 281, however, he was attacked by his former ally Seleucus I, and at Corupedium in Lydia (western Asia Minor), these two last survivors of Alexander's generals, both over eighty years of age, fought a battle that confirmed Seleucid power, since Lysimachus lost and fell: but shortly afterwards Seleucus died too, at the hands of an assassin.

The scene was now transformed by the invasion of the Balkans by the warlike Celts (Gauls). Antigonus II Gonatas triumphantly repelled them near Lysimachia in Thrace (278/277), so that many of them moved across the straits (Hellespont) into Asia Minor, enabling their victor to establish control over Macedonia. The 'Age of the Successors' was now over, and the three great Hellenistic dynasties had fully established themselves: the Antigonids in Macedonia, the Seleucids in Syria and Babylonia and lands farther east, and the Ptolemies in their empire based on Egypt.

Selection 2

The Hellenistic Kingdoms

Hermann Bengtson

In the early years of the Hellenistic era, the new states that grew up within the borders of Alexander's old empire set new patterns and standards for most Greeks. Although a few Hellenistic states (Rhodes and Byzantium, for example) were poleis in the traditional mode, most made the transition to monarchy, using the Macedonian, Egyptian, and Persian courts as models to one degree or another. According to the noted German historian Hermann Bengtson, these states' structures, rulers, and the trappings of royalty they created eventually passed on to Rome and later still to Europe. Bengtson explains how the Hellenistic rulers took steps to ensure the perpetuation of their dynasties by creating co-regencies (joint reigns of two rulers) and ruler cults, in which the family founders and some of their descendants were elevated to godhood. Bengtson mentions the members of two philosophical movements of the time. The Cynics renounced wealth, material comforts, and social conventions, claiming that this freed them to seek knowledge, truth, and harmony; while the Stoics believed that the universe is infused with a divine purpose or intelligence and that every human being, regardless of wealth or social class, possesses a small piece of that divine intelligence.

Excerpted from *History of Greece: From the Beginnings to the Byzantine Era*, by Hermann Bengtson, translated and updated by Edmund F. Bloedow. Copyright © 1988 University of Ottawa Press. Reprinted by permission of University of Ottawa Press.

*T*he Hellenistic states within Alexander's empire in Asia and Egypt owed their origins to conquest. They were "territory won by the sword" of their founders, and were bequeathed as private property within the new dynasties. In Macedonia the situation was different. Here the old military and national monarchy, which was at the same time both hereditary and patriarchal, continued up to Philip V (222/1–179 B.C.). Common to the Hellenistic states (again with the exception of Macedonia) is the absence of an ethnic character—they were states composed of various ethnic groups. Thus in the Seleucid and Ptolemaic kingdoms a numerical minority of foreigners, Macedonians and Greeks, ruled over the broad mass of the native population. The foreigners owed their positions and their social status exclusively to the favour of the king, and their rise and fall was inextricably linked with his person and his dynasty. The Macedonian officers and officials proudly appended the term "Macedonian" to their names; even the king adhered to this custom. When Alexander conquered the Achaemenid [i.e., Persian] empire he created the territorial state within the frontiers of the Greek world. All inhabitants of his empire, conquerors or conquered, were subjects of the king, although in a manifoldly graduated form.

The Founding of Royal Dynasties

The hallmark of the Hellenistic states was their territorial magnitude. It confronted the new masters of the conquered areas with completely novel problems of organisation, which were brilliantly solved by the Macedonians and Greeks. It is no accident that the period of the successors and the generation after produced an abundance of outstanding personalities. What the narrow limits of the homeland denied them, the Macedonians and Greeks found in the vast regions of Asia and Egypt—an unlimited field for political and economic planning. In addition, a large element in the population demonstrated the greatest competence in the wielding of power. At the time of the death of its founder (281 B.C.) the kingdom of Seleucus incorporated approximately 1.4 million square miles; if the very thinly populated regions of the Iranian highlands and the vast expanse of the unpopulated Persian Desert be subtracted, there would remain 207,000 square miles—in Asia Minor, northern Syria and Mesopotamia, to a large extent culturally developed regions. The territory of Ptomely I was smaller. Together with his foreign dominions, Cyrenaica, Cyprus, South Syria, parts of the Anatolian coast, islands of the Aegean and the possessions in Thrace, the area may be estimated at approximately 40,000 square miles, and the Antigonid kingdom in Macedonia and Hellas was only about 28,000 square miles. All other Hellenistic states were even smaller. The Pergamene state of the first Attalids (before the ephemeral conquest of Seleucid Asia Minor by Attalus I) was a magnified polis, similar to Syracuse under Hieron II. After the peace treaty with Rome the territory of the latter amounted to only 4,300 square miles. It is difficult to estimate the respective sizes in population. In the first century B.C. Egypt (Alexandria excepted) allegedly had 7 million inhabitants. Sources upon which to base any estimates for the remaining states are lacking, and it is preferable not to attempt to give any specific figures.

In their form and in their institutions the Hellenistic states had certain similarities, as the ruler cult, the imperial organisation and the regulation of defence. But diversity of population and traditions in many individual cases constituted major differences, so that only in a restricted sense is it possible to speak of a "unity within a multiplicity."

Alexander's conquest of the Achaemenid empire established the foundations of Hellenistic monarchy, and with this, of Western monarchy as well. Although Alexander's monarchy may appear to be the realisation of certain cosmopolitan tendencies in the Greek philosophy of the fourth century B.C. . . . in essence it was infinitely removed from the Greek ideal of rule by the surpassing individual. It was the encounter and fusion of the Macedonian military monarchy with the great monarchy of the Achaemenids and with the traditions of the ancient Babylonians and Assyrians (as absorbed by the Persians) which decisively determined the character of Alexander's monarchy. In the land of the Nile Alexander was the successor to the Pharaohs, in Babylon he acknowledged his reverence to the imperial god Marduk, while to the Persians he wished to appear as the legitimate successor to the Achaemenids. Thus all ancient world empires found something of themselves in this new universal monarchy.

What was denied Alexander, the founding of a dynasty, his marshals Seleucus and Ptolemy achieved. They lacked the most important element, legitimacy, and so used mythology to connect themselves with Zeus, Apollo, Heracles or Alexander, in order to overcome this deficiency. It was, however, primarily the Hellenistic philosophy of the Cynics and the Stoics that legitimised the new system of rule. Taking as their point of departure the Greek idea of the special rights of the outstanding individual, the philosophers justified the monarchical rule of the successors on the basis of their great capabilities, which as military leaders and statesmen they had demonstrated to the world. In addition, the monarchical idea in large measure corresponded with the Stoic world view: as Zeus ruled in heaven, so should the king in his likeness rule on earth. It is no accident that a number of Stoic philosophers in the third century B.C. were present at the Hellenistic courts, not only as friends and advisers to Antigonus Gonatas but also to the Spartan king Cleomenes III. To his subjects the king became the inspired law.

The Stoics tried to show that the monarchy fitted the rational principle in cosmic events. Transcending all the barriers of birth, race and social position, philosophy created a picture of the ideal state on earth—which found expression in the Stoic symbol of shepherd and flock. It was the patriarchal element which gave the unlimited Hellenistic monarchy its moral justification.

The most important external mark of Hellenistic royal dignity was the diadem, the wreath [usually of gold and worn on the head like a crown], which Alexander, on the model of the Achaemenids, was the first to wear. From the Hellenistic courts the diadem made its way to the Thracians, the Scythians and Sarmatians of southern Russia, and indeed as far as India. It was even worn at times by women, of whom the energetic Arsinoe II was undoubtedly the first. On the other hand, neither the first Antigonids nor Agathocles of Syracuse nor the kings of Cyprus and Sparta adopted it. Philip V, whose rule signifies the radical switch to absolutism, was the first in Macedonia to adorn himself with the diadem, as he was also the first of the Antigonids to have his image stamped on coins, long after the successors and other Hellenistic kings had done so. Other symbols of the dignity of the Hellenistic rulers were the signet-ring (at the Hellenistic courts there was also the office of Chief Guardian of the Seal), and, as the sign of the perpetuity of the royal dignity, the sacred fire which burned beside the throne. This feature was also inherited from the Achaemenid period, and the Hellenistic monarchs passed it on to the Roman emperors. Another monarchical usage was the common practice of reckoning according to the regnal years of the king in the Ptolemaic, Antigonid and Attalid kingdoms, a custom adopted by [Rome's] Augustus in counting the years of his tribunician power.

Genuinely Hellenistic is the singular form which the co-regency assumed. After Antigonus Monophthalmus in 306/5 B.C. appointed his son Demetrius co-regent with the title "King," co-regency became very common, chiefly in the Seleucid and Ptolemaic houses (Seleucus I and Antiochus I from 294/3 B.C. and Ptolemy after 285 B.C. are the first examples). Its function was clearly to secure the transition of power to the successor. In the case of the Seleucids the co-regent was on occasion (for instance, Antiochus I as crown prince) "General Governor of the Upper Satrapies," the regions beyond the Euphrates, with the official capital in Seleuceia on the Tigris. Under the later Ptolemies the co-regency was upgraded to the so-called "full co-regency" of two or more rulers, with the first instance that of Ptolemy VI and Ptolemy VIII. The participation of women in the government was an innovation. In this the line may be traced from Arsinoe II to the Ptolemaic queen Cleopatra I, then to Cleopatra II and Cleopatra III, and ultimately to the last Cleopatra. Alongside them the male members of the Lagid throne were nothing more than ciphers. The practice of consanguineous marriage [in which the partners are blood relations] in the ruling houses, often attested for the Hellenistic period, was adopted from Achaemenid custom. In the background of this practice there may have figured the intention to exclude from the very outset hereditary claims on the part of foreign dynasties. In the Hellenistic period, moreover, a kind of "society of kings" soon emerged, and marriages based on equality of birth were the rule. . . .

Rulers Transformed into Gods

At the Hellenistic courts in Alexandria, Antioch and Pella, Macedonian tradition continued in the institution of the Body Guard and the Page Corps. The terms "Relatives" of the King and "Friends," taken over in part from the Achaemenids and partly from Pharaonic Egypt, gradually became, in the form of a number of gradations, nothing more than empty court titles, a phenomenon which may be observed primarily in developments in Ptolemaic Egypt during the second century.

Common to all the Hellenistic monarchies except Macedonia we find the ruler cult. The Hellenistic royal cult is the most conspicuous expression of the absolute form of government, the very foundation of the monarchy, and all subjects, regardless of class, religion or birth, participated in it. Its roots extend back beyond the Hellenistic period above all to Alexander's demand for divine honours from the Greeks in 324 B.C.

In Egypt there was a clear distinction between the Egyptian and the Hellenistic ruler cult. In the Egyptian royal cult, obligatory only for the old native population, the *fellaheen*, the Ptolemies, like Alexander the Great . . . before them, were naturally accepted as successors to the Pharaohs. As such they—as at one time the Persian kings—bore the ancient Egyptian titles, especially the epithet "Son of Re." After the Ptolemies the Roman emperors from Augustus to Diocletian found entry into this cult, an example of how deeply rooted this tradition had become by practice over the millennia in this conservative land.

The actual Hellenistic ruler cult was not created until the second generation, in the Ptolemaic as well as in the Seleucid empire. In Egypt it was a creation of the astute Ptolemy II (later, in the second century B.C., called Philadelphus). This born statesman had his father, Ptolemy I, consecrated as "Saviour God" after his death in 283 B.C. To this cult was added that of his wife, Berenice I, after her death. Later Arsinoe II, the sister-wife of Ptolemy II, was deified after her death (9 July 270 B.C.) under the cult name of "Brother-Loving Goddess." The notion of exalting the dead into gods stems from the world of Greek ideas, and expands to making heroes of humans who possessed exceptional qualities— for instance, founders of cities and lawgivers. The Hellenistic royal cult applied equally to all subjects of the Ptolemies: Macedonians, Greeks, Egyptians or any other members of the kingdom.

Ptolemy II, however, went even a step further. He inaugurated the cult of his own person and of his sister-wife, Arsinoe II, under the name "Divine Consanguineous Couple," and thereby commanded the veneration of the living ruler. This was a measure of tremendous significance, for it exalted the king above all his subjects during his lifetime. . . . Kingship had moved into a higher realm, and the foundations of absolute rule "by the grace of God" had been laid. Sub-

sequent Ptolemies adhered to the apotheosis of the living ruler. After taking the throne they adopted a cult title under which they and their wives enjoyed such divine honours as "Beneficent Gods," "Father-Loving Gods," "Epiphany Gods," and so forth.

Uniquely Ptolemaic, finally, was the cult of Alexander the Great, created by Ptolemy I at least as early as 311 B.C. This was an imperial cult, in which not only members of the most prominent Macedonian families appeared as priests, but on occasion even the Ptolemaic kings themselves. Alexander became the imperial god of the Ptolemaic kingdom and patron of the Ptolemaic dynasty, an attempt to link the dynasty genealogically with him. Under the name "Alexander"—he is never called "God"—he appears to have been placed on the same level as the Olympian gods. In Alexandria there was a difference between the official cult and the city cult of the city's founder—Alexander. The latter may even have been created during the lifetime of the great Macedonian.

Little is known about the official cult of the Seleucids. It seems likely that Antiochus I introduced it after the death of his father, Seleucus I. He elevated him to the level of a god as Zeus Nicator, and dedicated a temple to him. Antiochus I may perhaps also have created the imperial cult of the living ruler, organised according to satrapies, and expanded at the beginning of the second century by Antiochus III.

Alongside the imperial cult demanded by the king was the cult of the Seleucids, observed by the Greek communities of the empire on a voluntary basis and very diversely organised by the individual poleis.

The Hellenistic ruler cult served well to unify the ethnically diverse empires of the Seleucids and the Ptolemies. In many instances it was also adopted by the small Hellenistic states. Even today an inscription from Nemrud Dagh testifies to the organisation of the ruler cult in the small state of the Commagenean prince Antiochus I (first century B.C.), in which Iranian and Greek elements are combined. There is scarcely a phenomenon of greater importance for the cultural development of the ancient world. The imperial cult stands at the very heart of the spiritual struggle between the Roman state and Christianity, as may be seen in, for instance, the . . . persecution of the Christians in the middle of the third century A.D.

Military and Ethnic Elements

In all three major Hellenistic states the Macedonian military assembly remained, as a residue from the time of the elective monarchy in Macedonia, which existed before the hereditary monarchy. After the era of Alexander the Great—during his Asian campaign it acted often—it survived in the major Hellenistic kingdoms until the end of political Hellenism. The Macedonian military assembly still had the important powers of formal confirmation of the new king, of appointing a guardian in case of minority, of ratifying royal testaments and, finally, passing judgment in cases of high treason. Even after the period of the successors, under the Antigonids, Seleucids and Ptolemies, the military assembly still decided issues of great political significance. Later, however, only the garrisons in Alexandria and Antioch enjoyed the rights of the military assembly. In the course of time the population of the capitals also acquired certain rights, and often in highly tumultuous scenes enforced its wishes. . . .

The individual Hellenistic states were very different in their ethnic structure, the specific traditions of the countries and the distinctive developments in the individual kingdoms. In the Seleucid empire the Persian inheritance shows particularly clearly. In its territory, stretching in 281 B.C. from the Hindu Kush to the Aegean and from the Caucasus to the Persian Gulf, dwelt an almost unlimited number of races and nationalities—Iranians (Persians, Medes, Bactrians, Parthians *et al.*), Semites (Babylonians, Syrians, Phoenicians and Jews), Anatolians, Macedonians and Greeks. As in the organisation of the Persian empire, there were three categories among the subjects of the king: the dynasts, the poleis and the *ethnoi*. The dynasts, great landlords in Asia Minor and in Iran, acknowledged Seleucid sovereignty, but were in fact all but independent, although under obligation to supply troops and to pay tribute. As well as secular, there were religious dynasties, extensive temple territories of Asia Minor and North Syria, whose lords, the high priests, commanded large numbers of followers and slaves. The Greek poleis too stood outside the Seleucid territorial administration, with only the *ethnoi*

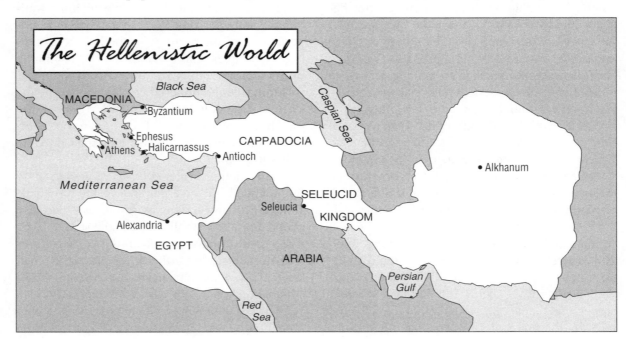

The Hellenistic World

and their territory, called "the region," subject to the immediate supervision of the king's governors. The division of the empire into satrapies, hyparchies and toparchies was in part a legacy from the time of Alexander, and beyond this undoubtedly from the Persian empire. On the whole the empire at the height of its power in 281 B.C. may have counted twenty-five to thirty satrapies.

Although the total territory continually decreased in the following decades, the number of satrapies increased, particularly in the empire's central region, in Syria and Mesopotamia. In Asia Minor as well the large administrative units were split up—a development which was given further impetus chiefly by Antiochus III.

Selection 3

Rise of the Achaean League

Polybius

In addition to monarchies large and small and a few prominent city-states, the Hellenistic powers included two federations of cities—the Aetolian and Achaean Leagues. In chronicling what was to him the recent history of Greece and Rome (from about 220 to 167 B.C.), the second-century B.C. Greek historian Polybius included a detailed account of the formation and deeds of the Achaean League, a Hellenistic federation that eventually included most of the cities of the Peloponnesus (or Peloponnese). It must be remembered that, because Polybius himself came from a patriotic Achaean family, the account, excerpted here, is far from unbiased. Still, the Achaeans consistently displayed a political reasonableness that gave their democratic alliance, and perhaps all of Greece, great future promise. Unfortunately for them, however, subsequent Roman aggressions ensured that said promise would never be fulfilled.

Excerpted from *The Rise of the Roman Empire*, by Polybius, translated by Ian Scott-Kilvert (Penguin Classics, 1979). Translation copyright © Ian Scott-Kilvert, 1979. Reprinted by permission of Penguin Books Ltd.

The Achaeans . . . have achieved a growth of power and an internal political harmony which are altogether remarkable. There have been many attempts in the past to persuade the Peloponnesians to adopt a common policy for the general advantage, but none of them ever succeeded because each of the promoters of such a union was always striving not for the general liberty but for his own supremacy. Yet in our day these ideals have made so much progress and achieved such a degree of fulfilment that not only have the Achaeans created an allied and friendly community, but they also share the same laws, weights, measures and currency, and besides these the same magistrates, council and law courts. An area which embraces almost the whole Peloponnese only differs from the situation of a single city in the sense that its inhabitants are not encircled by a single wall; in other respects whether the region is considered as a whole or city by city its institutions are virtually identical.

In the first place it is worth investigating how the name of Achaeans first came to be applied to the Peloponnesians, and was later adopted by all of them. The people who originally bore this ancestral name were not pre-eminent among the rest either for the size of their territory, the number of their cities, their wealth or their prowess in war. The Arcadian and Laconian nations [in the central and southern Peloponnesus, respectively] far exceed them in area and in population, and certainly neither of these could ever agree that any Greek people was their superior in warlike valour. How then do we explain the fact that both these peoples and the rest of the Peloponnese have been willing to exchange not only their political institutions but even their name for those of the Achaeans? Clearly we ought not to say that this is the work of chance, for that would be a very inadequate explanation. We must rather seek a cause, since no chain of events, whether expected or unexpected, can reach its conclusion without a cause. The cause, then, in my opinion is something like this. It would be impossible to find anywhere a political system or a guiding principle which allowed more equality and freedom of speech, or which was more genuinely representative of true democracy, than that of the Achaean League.

This constitution found some of the Peloponnesians ready to adopt it of their own free will; many others were induced by persuasion and argument to take part, while those who were obliged to accept it by force when the time came soon found themselves appreciating its benefits. For the community reserved no special privileges for its original members, but equal rights were granted to all states as they joined it, and in this way it soon achieved the aim it had set itself, since it was supported by two very powerful allies: the sense of humanity and of equality. It is this system, then, which we must regard as the foundation and the prime cause of the harmony which prevails in the Peloponnese, and hence of its prosperity.

These principles and this constitution had existed in their particular local form in Achaea from an early date. There is plenty of evidence of this, but for the present purpose it will be enough to quote one or two examples [Polybius first cites the case of a group of Greek commu-

nities in southern Italy who welcomed mediation by Achaean delegations during a time of disorder in the fifth century B.C.]. . . .

Later on when the Spartans, against all expectations, were defeated at Leuctra [in 371 B.C.], and the Thebans, equally unexpectedly, claimed the hegemony of Greece, all the other states were plunged into uncertainty, and above all the two peoples directly concerned, since the Lacedaemonians [Spartans] refused to admit that they had lost, while the Thebans were not entirely convinced that they had won. Here again the Achaeans were the one people in all Greece to whom both parties turned for arbitration on the matters in dispute. This could not have been on account of their strength, for they were at that time almost the weakest state in Greece, but rather on account of the general faith in their trustworthiness and high principles, and there is no doubt that this opinion of the Achaeans was universally held.

Leaders of Stature Redirect Achaean Affairs

Up to that time, however, these political principles had done no more than exist among the Achaeans. There had been no practical application of them and no significant effort to increase the power of the country, since it had not hitherto produced a statesman worthy of the system; whenever anyone had shown signs of fulfilling this role, he had been thrust into the background and hampered, either by the Lacedaemonian government, or still more effectively by that of Macedon.

But when in due course the country did find leaders of sufficient stature, its potentialities for good were immediately revealed by the fulfilment of that most glorious purpose, the union of the Peloponnese. The originator and creator of the project was Aratus of Sicyon [271–213 B.C.]. Philopoemen of Megalopolis [252–182 B.C.] championed it and finally established it, while Lycortas [Polybius's father] and his party secured its continuance for a considerable time. . . . As for the measures carried out by Aratus, I shall touch upon these only briefly . . . since he has published an honest and lucid memoir of his own career [a work that unfortunately did not survive]. . . .

The first step was taken by the cities of Patrae and Dyme, which formed a league during the 124th Olympiad [284–280 B.C.]. . . .

Because they had not entered the League but had formed it, we do not find any inscription to record that a League had been established. Some five years later the people of Aegium expelled their Macedonian garrison and joined the League, and the people of Bura, after putting their tyrant to death, followed their neighbours' example, while the next to join, almost at the same time, was the state of Caryneia. Its tyrant Iseas had seen the garrison driven out of Aegium and the tyrant of Bura killed by Margus and the Achaeans, and when he recognized that all the neighbouring cities were about to make war on him, he abdicated. He received a guarantee of his personal safety from the Achaeans and formally consented to the admission of Caryneia to the League.

Now why, the reader may ask, do I retrace the history of this period? My purpose is first of all to explain which of the Achaean cities took the initiative in the re-creation of the League and at what dates, and secondly to show that the claims which I made concerning the political principles of the League are borne out by the facts. The point at issue is first that the Achaeans always followed one consistent policy: this was to invite other cities to share in their equality and freedom of speech, and to make war on and subdue all those who either on their own account, or with the help of the Kings [i.e., the ruler, of the Hellenistic monarchies], tried to enslave any of the states within their borders; and secondly that in this manner and pursuing this purpose they finally achieved this aim, partly through their own efforts and partly with the help of their allies. It is important that we attribute to the Achaean political principle in the first place all due credit for the results to which in later years their allies also contributed. For although the Achaeans played a prominent part in the enterprises of others—especially in many conducted by the Romans which were conspicuously successful—

yet they never showed the least desire to exploit any of these successes to the advantage of any one state; in return for all the ardent support which they gave to their allies they bargained for nothing but the freedom of all states and the union of the Peloponnesians. All this will be more clearly understood when we come to examine the efforts of the League in action.

For the first twenty-five years after the reconstitution of the League among the cities I have mentioned [i.e., from 280 to 255 B.C.], a secretary and two generals were elected by each city in turn [rotating once a year]. After this they decided to elect only one general and to entrust him with the management of all the League's affairs. The first man to receive this honour was Margus of Caryneia. Then, in the fourth year after Margus' generalship, Aratus of Sicyon, who was still only twenty years of age, liberated his city from its tyrant through his personal valour and daring. He had always been a passionate admirer of the Achaean political system, and he now made his own city a member of the League. Eight years later, during his second term of office as general of the League, Aratus successfully planned an operation to seize the Acrocorinth [the acropolis of Corinth, another Peloponnesian city], which at that time was held on behalf of Antigonus, the King of Macedon. By this stroke he not only delivered all the inhabitants of the Peloponnese from a great source of fear, but he persuaded the newly liberated city of Corinth to join the League as well. Then during the same term of office he contrived to bring Megara into the League by similar means. . . .

Aratus had achieved remarkable progress in his aims within a very short space of time, and thereafter he continued to direct the affairs of the League. His designs and projects were all concerted towards one end: to expel the Macedonians from the Peloponnese, to sweep away the tyrannies, and to re-establish the freedom of the League both as a communal and an ancestral right for each member. So long as Antigonus Gonatas lived, Aratus opposed Macedonian interference in Greek affairs and resisted the perpetual lust for plunder of the Aetolians; he effectively upheld both policies, even though these two powers were so unscrupulous and aggressive that they entered into an agreement for the express purpose of dissolving the Achaean League [in 245 B.C., the Macedonians reoccupied Corinth and the Aetolians invaded the Peloponnesus].

However, on the death of Antigonus [in 239 B.C.], the Achaeans went so far as to make an alliance with the Aetolians and they supported them ungrudgingly in their war against Demetrius [II]of Macedon. So for the time being their estrangement and hostility were appeased and a somewhat more sociable and friendly sentiment grew up between the two peoples. Demetrius only reigned for ten years . . . and after this the tide of events seemed for a while to be flowing in favour of the policy for which the Achaeans had striven all along. The local tyrants of the Peloponnese were in despair, alike at the death of Demetrius, who had acted so to speak as their patron and paymaster, and at the pressure which

Aratus now brought to bear upon them. He demanded that they should lay down their authority, offering generous rewards and honours to those who agreed to abdicate, and holding over those who refused the fear of what they would suffer at the hands of the Achaeans. And so there was a general move to grant Aratus' demands, vacate the seats of power, set free the various cities, and join the League. Lydiades, the tyrant of Megalopolis, had shown rare foresight and practical sense in anticipating while Demetrius was still alive what was likely to happen, and had of his own free will laid down his authority and given his allegiance to the League. Later Aristomachus, the tyrant of Argos, Xenon, the tyrant of Hermione, and Cleonymus, the tyrant of Phlius, all likewise laid down their authority and joined the League.

These events substantially increased both the size and the power of the League.

Selection 4

Roman Armies Enter Greece

Arthur E.R. Boak and William G. Sinnigen

Eager to punish Macedonia's king, Philip V, for helping Carthage during the Second Punic War, late in 200 B.C. the Romans crossed the Adriatic Sea into Illyria (Illyricum), the Balkan region bordering Macedonia in the west. Soon afterward they entered Greece, and within only a few years managed to defeat not only Philip, but the able and energetic Seleucid ruler Antiochus III and the feisty Aetolian League (or Confederacy) as well. This synopsis of these initial Roman interventions in Greek affairs is by former University of Michigan professor Arthur E.R. Boak and former Hunter College professor William G. Sinnigen.

Excerpted from *A History of Rome to A.D. 565*, 5th ed., by Arthur E.R. Boak and William G. Sinnigen; © 1978. Reprinted by permission of Prentice-Hall, Inc., Upper Saddle River, N.J.

*D*uring the thirty-five years which followed the battle of Zama, Rome attained the same dominant position in the eastern Mediterranean that she had won in the West as a result of the First and Second Punic Wars. The explanation of Roman interference in the East and the rapid extension of her authority there lies in the political situation of the Hellenistic world at the close of the third century, one which Rome exploited by virtue of her increasingly important role as patron to states east of the Adriatic. . . .

Down to the year 201 Rome can hardly be said to have had any definite eastern policy. Diplomatic intercourse with Egypt had followed the visit of an Egyptian embassy to Rome as early as 273, but this had had no political consequences. Since that date she had come into conflict with the Illyrians and with Macedonia and had established a small protectorate across the Adriatic, but in so doing her actions had been spasmodic and had been brought about by the attacks of the Illyrians and Macedonians upon her allies or herself and were not the result of any aggressive policy of her own. The interest and outlook of Rome's agrarian oligarchy did not include Hellas [Greece] as a whole or the Greek East. This may be seen in the favorable peace terms granted Philip V of Macedonia in 205, by which Rome abandoned her formal alliances with Philip's enemies, especially the Aetolians. This is the first known instance in which Rome failed to fulfill to the letter her written agreements with her friends, and marks an important stage in the growing sophistication of her foreign policy. These actions made her very unpopular in most of Greece. Her erstwhile allies, especially the Aetolians, protested that they had been left in the lurch, while other Greek states felt antagonistic because Rome had permitted the Aetolians to treat them brutally during the recent war. Rome still found it possible to maintain friendly relations, albeit without formal and possibly entangling treaties, with Pergamon, the Illyrians, some city-states of the Peloponnesus, and possibly Athens. Rome's general attitude toward the Greek world in the period 205–201 was watchful rather than disinterested; she had no vital or definite commitments in the area except the defense of her Illyrian clients.

The Romans Turn Eastward

A combination of circumstances involving Illyria brought about the Second Macedonian War. After the peace of 205 Philip apparently misread the Roman attitude toward Greece as one of total disinterest and attempted by diplomacy to seduce the Illyrians from their connection with Rome. Just as Rome was observing the Illyrian situation with increasing disquiet in 202, the envoys of Rhodes and of Attalus I, King of Pergamon, arrived to inform the Senate of Philip's aggressions in the East and of his alleged pact with Antiochus to partition the Egyptian Empire. They requested Roman help. The Senate, basically unconcerned with what was going on in the Aegean and undisturbed by the unlikely prospect of the "alliance" between Philip and Antiochus being directed against Italy at some future date, was interested, however, in humbling the king who had stabbed her in the back during the recent war with Hannibal and who was now tampering with her Illyrian clients. It seized upon Philip's aggressions against Attalus as a possible *casus belli* [justification for war]. Roman ambassadors were sent to Greece in 201/200 to proclaim a basic change in Roman policy—protection of all Greeks against future Macedonian aggression—and to mobilize Greece under the Roman aegis against Philip. They also carried an ultimatum for Philip which they delivered to one of his generals, a demand that he refrain from war with any Greek state and that he submit his differences with Attalus to arbitration. The ultimatum revealed Rome's new aims: the reduction of Philip to the status of a client prince and the consequent conversion of Greece into a Roman protectorate. Although the Senate was apparently committed to war when these demands were not met, the Roman people as a whole shrank from embarking upon another war so soon after the close of the desperate conflict with Carthage. At first the Centuriate Assembly voted against the proposal, and at a second meeting was induced to sanction it only when the people were told they would have to face another invasion of Italy if they did not anticipate Philip's action. When the Assembly finally gave its approval, one of the Roman ambassadors whom the Senate had already sent to Greece to threaten Philip and encourage his opponents presented the formal declaration of war to the king, who was at that time engaged in the siege of Abydos on the Hellespont, whereupon the conflict began. In accordance with their instructions the ambassadors then visited Antiochus in Syria, perhaps to intercede on behalf of Egypt or to assure him of the good will of Rome so that he might not abandon his Syrian campaign and unite his forces with those of Philip in Macedonia. Roman diplomacy leading up to the war shows that at this stage of her history Rome took states unilaterally under her protection without the formality of a treaty and tended to regard her friends not as equals but as clients.

Late in 200 a Roman army under the consul Sulpicius Galba crossed into Illyricum and tried to penetrate into Macedonia. Both in this and in the succeeding year, however, the Romans, although aided by the Aetolian Confederacy, Pergamon, Rhodes, and Athens, were unable to inflict any decisive defeat upon Philip or to invade his kingdom.

With the arrival of one of the consuls of 198, Titus Flamininus, the situation speedily changed. The Achaean Confederacy was won over to the side of Rome, and Flamininus succeeded in forcing Philip to evacuate Epirus and to withdraw into Thessaly. In the following winter negotiations for peace were opened. At the insistence of her Greek allies, Rome now demanded not merely a guarantee that Philip would refrain from attacking the Hellenes but also the evacuation of Corinth, Chalcis, and Demetrias, three fortresses known as "the fetters of Greece." Philip refused to make this concession.

The next year military operations were resumed with both armies in Thessaly. Early in the summer a battle was fought on a ridge of hills called Cynoscephalae (the Dogs' Heads), where the Romans won a complete victory. Although the Aetolians rendered valuable assistance in this engagement, the Macedonian defeat was due primarily to the superior flexibility of the Roman legionary formation over the phalanx. Philip fled to Macedonia and sued for peace. The Aetolians and his enemies in Greece sought his destruction, but Flamininus realized the importance of Macedonia to the Greek world as a bulwark against the Celtic peoples of the lower Danube and would not support their demands. The terms fixed by the Roman Senate were: autonomy of the Hellenes, in Greece and Asia; evacuation of the Macedonian possessions in Greece, in the Aegean, and in Illyricum; an indemnity of 1,000 talents; and the surrender of nearly all his warships. These conditions Philip was obliged to accept (196). Soon afterwards he became a Roman ally.

At the Isthmian games of the same year Flamininus proclaimed the complete autonomy of the peoples who had been subject to Macedonia. The announcement provoked a tremendous outburst of enthusiasm among most of the Greek states. After spending some time in effecting this policy and in settling the claims of various states, Flamininus returned to Italy in 194, leaving the Greeks to make what use they would of their freedom. The dramatic proclamation of Flamininus is often attributed to the cultural philhellenism [admiration for Greek culture] increasingly noticeable at this time among the Roman ruling class. Rome's interest in Greek freedom was not sentimental, but was rather the natural result of political and strategic considerations growing out of the recent war. Rome was now merely applying throughout Greece a policy that she had previously used in Messana, Saguntum and Illyria. If the Greeks were free, from the Roman point of view they enjoyed the freedom of client states, which, as a matter of course, would pursue a foreign policy compatible with Roman interests and which would form a bulwark against any hostile action on the part of Philip or Antiochus.

Rome Defeats Antiochus and the Aetolians

Even before Flamininus and his army had withdrawn from Greece, the activities of Antiochus had awakened the mistrust of the Roman Senate and threatened hostilities. The Syrian king had completed the conquest of Lower Syria in 198. Profiting by the difficulties in which Philip of Macedon was involved, he had then turned his attention toward Asia Minor and Thrace with the hope of recovering the possessions once held by his ancestor, Seleucus I. The Romans were at the time too much occupied to oppose him. Outwardly he professed to be a friend of Rome and to be limiting his activities to the reestablishment of his empire's former extent. Eventually, in 196 he crossed over into Europe and took Thrace. The Romans tried to induce him to withdraw but were unsuccessful. Two years later Antiochus himself opened negotiations with the Senate to secure Roman recognition of his claims to Thrace and to certain cities in Asia Minor which, relying upon Roman support, refused to acknowledge his overlordship. The Roman government, cynically enough, was willing to abandon its self-proclaimed status as protector of the Greeks in Asia if Antiochus would evacuate Thrace. Since Antiochus, although harboring no designs against Rome, refused to be forced out of his European possessions, he decided to support the anti-Roman elements in Greece to force Rome to yield the points at issue. Accordingly, he willingly received deputations from the Aetolians, who were the leading opponents of Rome among the Greeks.

The Aetolians, Rome's allies in the war just concluded and greatly exaggerating the importance of their services, were disgruntled because Macedonia had not been entirely dismembered and they had been restrained from enlarging the territory of the Confederacy at the expense of their neighbors. In short, they wished to replace Macedonia as the leading Greek state. Accustomed to regard war as a legitimate source of revenue, they did not easily reconcile themselves to Rome's imposition of peace in Hellas. Ever since the battle of Cynoscephalae they had striven to undermine Roman influence among the Greeks, and now they sought to draw Antiochus into conflict with Rome.

In 192 they brought matters to a head by un-expectedly attacking some of Rome's supporters in Greece and seizing the fortress of Demetrias, which they offered to the king [Antiochus], to whom they also made an unauthorized promise of aid from Macedonia. Trusting in the support promised by the Aetolians, Antiochus sailed to Greece with an advance force of 10,000 men. Upon his arrival the Aetolians elected him their commander in chief. . . .

In 191 a Roman army under the consul Acilius Glabrio appeared in Greece and defeated the forces of Antiochus at Thermopylae. The king fled to Asia. Contrary to his hopes he had found little support in Greece. Philip of Macedon and the Achaean Confederacy adhered to the Romans, and the Aetolians were made helpless by an invasion of their own country. . . .

As Antiochus would not listen to the peace terms laid down by the Romans, the latter resolved to invade Asia Minor. Two naval victories, won with the aid of Rhodes and Pergamon, secured control of the Aegean, and in 190 a Roman force crossed the Hellespont. . . .

One decisive victory over Antiochus at Magnesia [in western Asia Minor] in the autumn of 190 brought him to terms. He agreed to surrender all territory north of the Taurus mountains and west of Pamphylia, to give up his war elephants, to surrender all but ten of his ships of war, to pay an indemnity of 15,000 talents in twelve annual instalments, and to abstain from attacking the allies of Rome. . . . He was still at liberty to defend himself if attacked. Peace upon these conditions was formally ratified in 188. This time Rome did not "free" all the Greeks as she had done in 196, since such an action would have produced too many petty states and future imbroglios [entanglements]. Some of the Greek city-states did receive their freedom, but Rhodes and Pergamon were the principal beneficiaries of the peace, which brought them an accession of territory at the expense of neighboring Greeks and non-Greeks alike. . . .

The Roman campaign of 191 against the Aetolians had caused the latter, who were also attacked by Philip of Macedon, to seek terms. The Romans demanded unconditional surrender, and the Aetolians decided to continue the struggle. No energetic measures were taken against them at once, but in 189 the consul Fulvius Nobilior pressed the war vigorously and besieged their chief stronghold, Ambracia. Since the obstinate resistance of its defenders defied all his efforts and since the Athenians were trying to act as mediators in ending the war, the Romans abandoned their demand for unconditional surrender. The Aetolians proved that they had not understood the meaning of clientship, and the Romans were determined that any peace treaty with them should express their dependent status. Peace was finally made on the following conditions: the Aetolian Confederacy was granted a permanent alliance with Rome on an unequal footing, with the obligation to support Rome against all her enemies; the Confederacy gave up all territory captured by its enemies during the war; Ambracia was surrendered and sacked. . . .

Although by her alliance with the Aetolians Rome had planted herself permanently on Greek soil and in the war with Antiochus had claimed to exercise a protectorate over the Greek world, the Senate as yet gave no indication of reversing the policy of Flamininus, and the Greek states remained friends of Rome in the enjoyment of political "independence." It was not long, however, before these friendly relations became seriously strained and Rome was induced to embark upon a policy of political and then military interference in Greek affairs, which ultimately put an end to the apparent freedom of Hellas.

Selection 5

Rome Subdues the Mainland Greek States

Max Cary

This account of the last few years of liberty for the inhabitants of mainland Greece (including Macedonia) is by the late, distinguished University of Michigan scholar Max Cary. He begins with the resistance offered to Rome by Macedonia's new king, Perseus, son of Philip V (who had signed a treaty with the Romans after they had defeated him in 197 B.C.). Cary then gives an overview of the *main events of the Third Macedonian War (171–168 B.C.), including a very clear description of the pivotal Battle of Pydna, and goes on to chronicle the demise of the Achaean League.*

Excerpted from *History of the Greek World from 323 to 146 B.C.*, by Max Cary (London: Methuen, 1968). Reprinted by permission of Underwood & Co., Solicitors, on behalf of the Estate of Max Cary.

P hilip's successor Perseus inherited the cautious temperament of the true Antigonid breed, but was trained in the self-assertive traditions of his father. His early policy was an unsteady compromise between these conflicting tendencies. At the outset of his reign he conciliated the [Roman] Senate by applying for a renewal of his father's treaty, and to the Greek cities in his dominions he was more considerate than Philip. But he placed himself in a false position by his ostentatious promises to bankrupts and political outlaws from the towns of the Greek Homeland. These appeals to the political and economic underworld brought him no solid support, while to the Romans they appeared as an attempt to overthrow their settlement of Greek affairs. Renewed visits by senatorial commissions, before whom Perseus failed to clear himself, gave rise in turn to fresh accusations from the king's malevolent neighbours. In 172 [B.C.] king Eumenes of Pergamum made a journey to Rome to present a crime-sheet against Perseus. Returning home by way of Delphi, he was all but killed by a falling rock from [Mt.] Parnassus [a tall peak near Delphi, in central Greece], and he used this incident—which may quite well have been due to natural causes—to pillory the Macedonian king as an assassin. Hereupon the Senate resolved its doubts by sending an order to disarm as an ultimatum to Perseus, and thus virtually forced on the Third Macedonian War. Like the Third Punic War, this conflict was the outcome of ill-defined suspicions rather than of clearly proved guilt.

The Third Macedonian War was a plain trial of strength between Macedon and Rome. Perseus received no Greek support save from a few minor towns of Bœotia. The Epirotes [inhabitants of the kingdom of Epirus] declared themselves sufficiently to draw Roman vengeance upon their country, but gave Perseus no effectual aid. The abstention of the Greeks was partly due to Perseus' parsimony [stinginess], which deterred him from spending the accumulated funds of the Macedonian treasury in a timely diplomatic offensive. But it is highly unlikely that he could have bought many Greek states for a war against Rome. Apart from the Greek exiles and debtors, he had on his side some political leaders who chafed at the inevitable restrictions entailed with Rome's gift of freedom to the Greeks. But the governing classes in general acquiesced in [gave in to] a Roman suzerainty [domination] which greatly added to their security, and they had not

forgotten Cynoscephalæ [the battle in which the Romans had decisively defeated Philip V]. Under these conditions a general Greek rally to Macedon was out of the question. On the other hand Perseus had scrupulously avoided those blunders of policy which had brought the Greeks into the field against Philip. The Romans therefore received no Greek assistance except from the Achæan League, which supplied a small contingent, and from Pergamum and Rhodes, which furnished a few warships and transports. Their total field force, numbering some 35,000, hardly exceeded that of Perseus.

The Romans and Perseus, having fumbled into war, spent three years in trying to fumble out of it. Though the Roman generals had a fleet at their disposal, they derived scarcely any benefit from it. For two years they made vain endeavours to force the Olympus range between Thessaly and Macedonia. In 169 the consul Marcius Philippus carried the barrier, but more by luck than by management. On the other hand Perseus' congenital cautiousness recovered possession of him on the field of battle. A victory gained by him in a cavalry action near Larissa in 171 frightened him into making two successive attempts at negotiation, and in 169 he abandoned the Olympus position before the Romans had extricated [removed] their columns from the mountain defiles. It was not until 168 that the Roman army and fleet, brought into effective co-operation by the consul Æmilius Paullus, were able to acquire a definite foothold in Macedonia.

In 168, however, the war was decided in the course of a few minutes. The battle of Pydna, in which Perseus' army was virtually annihilated, was in essentials a replica of Cynoscephalæ. Developing by chance from an affair of outposts, it began with a mass attack by the Macedonian phalanx, which Paullus, a seasoned veteran, declared to have been the most terrifying sight in his ample experience. The Roman legions, which never proved their elasticity and manœuvring power more brilliantly than on this field, fell back in good order upon higher ground, and as the momentum of the charging phalanx dislocated its ranks, they thrust themselves, company by company, into its gaps or round its flanks. The Macedonian infantry, unable to reform its line, and left unprotected by its mounted flank guards, was quickly killed off in a veritable battue.

Macedonia and Epirus Are Overrun

During the Third Macedonian War anti-Roman feeling among the Greeks had been strengthened by the failure of the earlier Roman commanders to protect the civilian population against marauding troops and by their own excessive requisitions. But Greek resentment was allayed by the exemplary discipline enforced by Paullus upon his soldiery. Besides, the massacre of Pydna relieved the Romans of all further reason for fearing the Greeks. Nevertheless the generosity . . . with which the Senate had hitherto treated Greek affairs now gave way to anxious suspicion. Though for the third time they left the Greeks free and withdrew their troops, they took precautions, wise and unwise, against future misuse of their liberty. In Macedonia they dethroned the Antigonid dynasty and set up four federal republics extending in a line from the Illyrian frontier to the river Nestus. The new federations were in themselves a justifiable experiment, for the growth of town life in Macedon had made the people ripe for a measure of self-government. Moreover, in fixing the yearly rate of war-indemnity at a mere half of the former royal land-tax, they left Macedon in a better financial position than under the Antigonids. But in prohibiting all intercourse, political or economic, between the four succession-states, they violated the legitimate sense of nationhood among the Macedonians; and in deporting to Italy not only Perseus but all the royal officials they left the republics without political leadership.

In Greece the Romans made no alterations in the governments and but few changes in the frontiers. But they took strong measures to purge the cities of declared or suspected sympathizers with Macedon. In Ætolia they furnished troops to their principal supporters, who executed five hundred antagonists after a farcical trial.

In Achæa, where a party led by Lycortas and his son Polybius (the future historian) had unsuccessfully advocated neutrality, they first demanded a judicial massacre on the Ætolian pattern; on discovering that they could not carry this point they deported one thousand suspects . . . under pretence of arranging for their trial in Italy. In Epirus the ex-consul Paullus was bidden to punish the ineffective sympathies of the people for Perseus with a systematic dragonade [persecution] in which he carried off 150,000 souls to the Roman slave-market. This utterly inexcusable brutality, which left Epirus half-desolate, was never requited [avenged] upon the Romans. Their more venial mistakes in Macedon and Achæa brought their revenge with them.

In Macedon the new federations so far proved their capacity to govern, that in 158 [B.C.] the Senate removed some of the previous commercial embargoes. But the restriction of intercourse between the four republics prevented their taking adequate measures for common defence. By a fortunate chance the Dardanians [neighboring Balkan tribesmen], having recently been engaged in a murderous war in the Balkan hinterland, were slow to seize their opportunity. But in 150 an adventurer named Andriscus, who claimed to be a son of Perseus, won enough adherents to gain successive battles against the . . . levies [troops] on either side of the river Strymon [running through central Macedonia]. From a reunited Macedon the pretender mustered sufficient troops to defeat a small Roman force which the Senate hastily sent against him. But his improvised levies were easily disposed of by an augmented Roman army under Cæcilius Metellus, and Macedon made its final surrender to Rome. After the Fourth Macedonian War the Senate did not repeat the mistake of partitioning Macedon, yet it dared not entrust the entire country to a native administration. It therefore broke with its long-standing policy of leaving Greek lands ungarrisoned and converted Macedon into a Roman province. By this act it virtually closed the book of Macedonian history.

In Peloponnesus the deportations of the Achæan suspects, far from cowing the League, drove it to open hostility against Rome. For sixteen years the Senate turned a deaf ear to the League's protests against the detention of its citizens; in 151 it released without trial the surviving remnant of the prisoners. But this act of grace came too late to appease Achaean resentment. Since the Third Macedonian War the revolutionary element, whose chief strength lay in the proletariate of Corinth, had gained steadily upon the friends of Rome and of domestic peace. . . . The stalwarts of the League fixed a fresh quarrel upon Sparta over the thorny question of its special privileges, and thus provoked a direct conflict with the Senate, to which the Spartans as usual carried their complaints. The extremist leader Diæus prepared a military execution upon Sparta without awaiting the Senate's decision, which was delayed through its preoccupation with the Macedonian and the Punic Wars. The Senate eventually answered his contumacy [stubbornness] with an order to the Achæans to restore full independence to Sparta, which desired it, and to Corinth and Argos, who had no wish to secede. With this sentence of mutilation it finally threw the League into the hands of the extremists, and the Senate's envoys barely escaped death at the hands of the Corinthian mob. In 147 the Senate endeavoured to re-open negotiations by tacitly rescinding its previous instructions, while Metellus sent a conciliatory message from Macedon. But the new Achaean general Critolaus, mistaking the Senate's overture for a confession of weakness, played off its commissioner with impudent chicanery [trickery], and the mob of Corinth hooted Metellus' envoys off the platform. To cut off the League's retreat, Critolaus had himself proclaimed dictator by tumultuary procedure. With his usurped powers he compelled the wealthier citizens to contribute heavy taxes and to set free a quota of slaves for military service; and in 146 he directed an expedition against Heracleia-ad-Œtam [a town near the strategic pass of Thermopylae, in Central Greece], which had under unknown circumstances been annexed to the League, but had

profited by the Senate's recent pronouncement to re-assert its independence. He was joined on the way by contingents from Thebes and other Central Greek towns, where the party of social revolution was in the ascendant. But while he lay before Heracleia he was taken unawares by Metellus, who put the Achaean forces to headlong rout and flung them right back upon Corinth. Meanwhile Diæus had collected a second forced levy of freemen and slaves, amounting to some 15,000 men. With this scratch force he offered a desperate resistance to Metellus' successor Mummius, who had brought up large Roman reinforcements. In a battle on the Isthmus [of Corinth, the narrow land bridge connecting the Peloponnesus to the Greek mainland] the raw Achæan levies proved once more—if proof were needed—that Greeks under firm leadership could fight without flinching; but in the face of hopeless odds they met with irretrievable defeat.

The End of Greek Liberty

In Greece, as in Macedon, the Senate decided to take no further chances. By way of upholding the sanctity of ambassadors [in 146 B.C.], it ordered the inhabitants of Corinth to be sold into slavery, and the town to be levelled to the ground. It dissolved the Achæan League and annexed its component states to the province of Macedonia. These states henceforth paid tribute to Rome and in some cases had their constitutions remodelled. Athens retained its full freedom; the small local leagues in which the states of Central Greece and Thessaly had been grouped by previous Roman action retained their autonomy under the supervision of the governor of Macedonia. Under this settlement the Greek ideal of local autonomy was in large measure realized, and for the first time in its history the country enjoyed an enduring peace. But the ideal of a United States of Greece was finally shattered, and the era of liberty and of fertile political experiment in Greek lands gave way to two thousand years of forced inertia.

Selection 6

Cleopatra: Last of the Greek Hellenistic Rulers

Peter Green

The last Hellenistic realm to maintain a semblance of independence, the Ptolemaic Kingdom, had, by the mid–first century B.C., degenerated into a third-rate power cowering in Rome's mighty shadow. This was the age of devastating civil wars and power struggles among powerful individuals, including the renowned Roman generals Julius Caesar and Gnaeus Pompeius (Pompey); Caesar's lieutenant, Marcus Antonius (Mark Antony); and Caesar's adopted son, Octavian (the future emperor Augustus). To their number must be added one Greek, who was every bit as talented and ambitious as they—Cleopatra VII, daughter of Ptolemy XII (called Auletes, "the Piper"). After she and her lover/ally Antony went down to defeat at Actium in western Greece, in 31 B.C., she became the last of the Ptolemies and the last major independent Greek ruler of antiquity. As Peter Green, of the University of Texas at Austin, points out in this excerpt from his definitive study of the Hellenistic Age, it was perhaps poetically fitting that the era's first and last great Greek figures—Alexander and Cleopatra—both became, and remain, legendary.

*O*ne of the more tempting excuses for Rome's progressively more radical, steadily less reluctant policy of intervention and eventual takeover in the eastern Mediterranean was, beyond any doubt, the patent inability of the rulers *in situ* [then in place] to manage their own affairs. This not only encouraged what Rome, and conservatives generally, saw as dangerous sociopolitical trends—mass movements by the dispossessed, encroachment by non-Mediterranean tribal elements—but, worse, proved disastrous for trade, a fault that Roman administrative paternalism could seldom resist the temptation to correct. In addition to the rampant scourge of piracy . . . a general condition of acute economic and, intermittently, political anarchy now afflicted both Syria and Egypt. Cities, local chieftains, and individuals all broke away when they could from a now highly inefficient (though no less captious and oppressive) system of central bureaucracy. Endless . . . dynastic conflicts, combined with relentless extortion (to pay for these and other excesses), had all but destroyed the countryside. . . .

Ptolemies in Egypt

Behind the last convulsive struggles of Seleucids and Ptolemies Roman policy—or, worse, free enterprise minus a policy—can always be sensed in the background. Worse still, from the viewpoint of the Greeks in particular, was the imposition of rival foreign warlords—Caesar and Pompey, Octavian and Antony—who not only fought out their own dynastic struggles on Greek soil and in Greek waters, but bled the inhabitants white for supplies, from grain to warships, and had an unnerving habit of executing those who chose the wrong (i.e., the unsuccessful) side. Roman egotism was matched, as so often, by Greek cynicism: survival became the prime objective. . . .

If Ptolemy Auletes . . . enjoyed a relatively undisturbed reign of almost thirty years (80–59/8, 55–51) in which to indulge his passion for flute playing (*Aulētēs* means "Piper") and other, less mentionable, habits, that was no tribute to his strength of character. . . . There were, in fact, two good reasons why Ptolemy Auletes, and his kingdom, survived as long as they did. To begin with, he had no serious rivals for the throne. This did not mean he was popular—far from it—but it did set his enemies a problem when it came to replacing him. At the time of his enforced exile in 59/8 . . . the Alexandrians—who had thrown him out . . . scraped the very bottom of the dynastic barrel trying to find any acceptable substitute for him.

After a little-known son of Cleopatra Selene [a former royal princess, daughter of Ptomely X] had died on them during negotiations . . . in desperation they picked on an alleged royal claimant whose chief title to consideration was the name of Seleucus. His appearance, and oafish manners, got him the nickname in Alexandria of *Kybiosaktēs*, "the Salt-Fish Hawker." The ulterior purpose of this frantic search was to find a male consort for Auletes' daughter Berenice, who had been proclaimed queen in her father's absence, perhaps at first as a temporary measure. The evidence is patchy. . . . Auletes left behind, as co-regents in his absence, his wife (and sister) Cleopatra V Tryphaena, together with their eldest daughter, Berenice IV. Two other daughters, Arsinoë and Cleopatra VII, the future queen, were barely adolescent, while the boys, Ptolemy XIII and Ptolemy XIV, were still infants. . . .

[These last members of the Ptolemaic dy-

A woodcut captures some of the splendor of the Egyptian court in the era in which Cleopatra and Antony were allies.

nasty] went out in a blaze of glory that has inspired great poetry down the ages. In the spring of 51 Ptolemy Auletes died, leaving the kingdom in his will, jointly, to his eighteen-year-old daughter Cleopatra, and her younger brother Ptolemy XIII, then about twelve. In Cleopatra the tradition of brilliant, strong-willed Macedonian queens reached its apotheosis [highest expression]. With Cyprus, Coele-Syria, and Cyrenaica gone, with the world her ancestors had known crumbling about her, with famine at home and anarchy abroad, this astonishing woman not only dreamed of greater world empire than Alexander had known, but came within an iota of winning it. . . . No one could fail to take her seriously. How far her sexual allure was exercised for its own sake, and how far in pursuit of power, we shall never know for certain. But there are one or two pointers. Like many Hellenistic queens, she was passionate, but never promiscuous. Caesar and Antony apart, we hear of no other lovers. . . . The wretched surviving iconography [surviving images of her on coins and so on]. . . suggests neither a raving beauty nor a voluptuary. . . . There is also her choice of lovers to consider. Anyone who so consistently aimed for the top is unlikely to have been motivated by nothing apart from sheer unbridled passion. . . .

She was, in short, a charismatic personality of the first order, a born leader and vaultingly ambitious monarch, who deserved a better fate than suicide. . . .

The times, however, were hard, and she was forced to make of them what she could—which was a great deal. The civil wars in Italy [between Caesar and Pompey] broke out in 49, two years after she came to the throne. She made her independent spirit clear from the start. By August 51 she had already dropped her young brother's name from official documents, despite traditional Ptolemaic insistence on titular male precedence among co-rulers. (Throughout her reign, independent or not, Cleopatra was always forced to accept either a brother or a son, however underage or otherwise ineffectual, as obligatory consort: there were some traditions not even she could ignore.) She also, exceptionally, put her own portrait and name on her coinage, again ignoring those of her brother. This, not surprisingly, alarmed the more powerful court officials in Alexandria. . . . Such behavior very soon brought opposition to a head. Certainly by 48, and in all likelihood two years earlier, a palace cabal [plot], led by Theodotus, the eunuch Pothinus, and a half-Greek general, Achillas, ousted Cleopatra in favor of her more pliable younger brother, with themselves as a council of regency. . . .

Enter Caesar

Meanwhile Pompey, defeated at Pharsalus (Aug. 48), took ship for Alexandria. He was relying, unwisely, on his position as backer, indeed as Senate-appointed guardian, of young Ptolemy XIII. . . . He seems not to have realized, till it was too late, just how far Pharsalus had destroyed his international reputation and credit. Achillas and his fellow regents were already working out their best approach to Caesar; in their eyes Pompey was nothing but a dangerous

embarrassment. They had him murdered as he stepped ashore, an object lesson for the precocious boy king, who watched this scene from the dockside, arrayed in his diadem and purple robes. Pompey's severed head was pickled, and afterwards presented, as an earnest of good will, to his conqueror, who at least had the grace to shed tears at the sight. Caesar may have been only too glad to have Pompey thus providentially put out of the way, but the circumstances of his death were appalling, and Caesar himself knew this better than anyone. At the same time the episode encouraged him in what was to prove a near-fatal Egyptian adventure. When he came ashore himself at Alexandria four days later, he was in a mood of careless and arrogant confidence, with an escort of no more than thirty-two hundred legionaries and eight hundred cavalry. His public reception was anything but ecstatic. . . . Riots followed.

Ptolemy XIII was away at Pelusium, ready to defend the frontier against his elder sister. Caesar coolly installed himself in the royal palace and began issuing orders. Pothinus the eunuch . . . brought Ptolemy back to court, but took no steps to disband his army. At this point Cleopatra, anxious not to be left out of any deal being cut, had herself smuggled through these hostile lines, like contraband, and turned up in her carpet. Both she and her brother were invited to appear before Caesar's *ad hoc* judgment seat the following morning; but by then Caesar, who was instantly captivated by Cleopatra's insistent charms, had already made her his lover, as she doubtless intended he should. Young Ptolemy instantly grasped the situation (hardly difficult, in the circumstances), and rushed out in a fury, screaming that he had been betrayed, to rouse the Alexandrian mob. . . .

The so-called Alexandrian War, which followed . . . came as near to destroying Caesar himself, let alone his reputation, as any campaign, military or political, that he ever fought. Once he had to swim from the mole to save his life, leaving his purple general's cloak behind as a trophy for the enemy. The warehouses and some part of the great Alexandrian Library went up in flames. Caesar managed to capture the Pharos lighthouse, which safeguarded his control of the harbor. Arsinoë, meanwhile, contrived to escape from the palace, fled to Achillas, and was promptly proclaimed queen by the army and the Macedonian mob, an act for which her sister never forgave her. All through that winter fighting and intrigue sputtered on. . . . [Eventually, Caesar received reinforcements and defeated his opponents.] Ptolemy XIII fled and was drowned in the Nile. Thus Cleopatra, whom Caesar had restored, officially, to joint occupancy of the throne of Egypt, now, in effect, indeed became sole ruler—although as a sop to tradition she was duly married off to her younger brother Ptolemy XIV, now aged eleven. . . .

Rather than make Egypt a province, with all the senatorial intrigue and rivalry that this was bound to entail, Caesar had every intention of shoring up the Ptolemaic regime, on his own terms. To have a son in line for the throne would by no means come amiss, whatever the status of consort and heir in Rome. Meanwhile, to placate the Alexandrians and the Egyptian priesthood, Cleopatra obligingly wed her sibling co-regent, while her younger sister, Arsinoë, languished under arrest with a charge of high treason pending against her. . . .

In July 46, after his successful African campaign, Caesar returned to Rome, to be showered with unprecedented honors, including four successive triumphs and a ten-year dictatorship. During these celebrations (Sept.–Oct.) he brought over Cleopatra and her entourage, establishing them in his own town house, a return of hospitality that caused considerable offense among conservative Republicans. . . . By then he was mulling over ideas about deification and world empire that seemed, or were thought, to include the establishment of Alexandria as a second capital, and of Cleopatra herself as some kind of bigamous queen-goddess, the New Isis, as she styled herself. Rome buzzed with gossip. . . .

Exit Caesar, Enter Antony

But the Ides of March 44 [when Caesar was stabbed to death in the Senate] put an end to all these grandiose dreams. Two weeks after Caesar's assassination, when the will was known and Caesarion [Caesar's and Cleopatra's young son], inevitably, had no place in it, Cleopatra, with more speed than dignity, and perhaps in real danger of her life, left Rome and returned to Alexandria. . . . On her arrival Cleopatra lost no time in having her sibling consort, Ptolemy XIV, assassinated, and Caesarion established, at the tender age of four, as her new co-regent. [Soon afterward, Octavian and Antony defeated Caesar's assassins and Cleopatra, like most others at the time, saw Antony as the more likely of the two to end up controlling the Roman sphere.] . . .

By the time that Antony summoned her to that fateful meeting at Tarsus, in 41, she already knew more than enough about him: his limited tactical and strategic abilities, his great popularity with his troops; his blue blood, which was so embarrassingly offset by financial impoverishment; the drinking, the . . . womanizing, . . . the Herculean vulgarity, the physical exuberance and brutal ambition, the Dionysiac pretensions to godhead. . . .

Antony was tickled by the idea of having a blue-blooded Ptolemy (his previous mistresses, not to mention his present wife, Fulvia, a powerful termagant, all seem to have been shrewishly middle-class), and by the coarse implications of all this royal finery: eight or nine years later we find him writing to Octavian, asking him why he has changed so much, turned so hostile—"Is it because I get into the queen?". . .

Both Cleopatra and Antony, then, had highly practical ulterior reasons for cultivating one another; how much personal chemistry helped the equation is hard to tell. Nor can anyone be certain how soon Antony planned to return when he left Cleopatra in the early spring of 40, or what he told her—not necessarily the same thing. Her magnetism was by no means irresistible, since in the event he did not see her for another four years. . . . Public considerations once more came first. That same autumn Antony made his peace with Octavian at Brundisium (Brindisi), cemented the alliance by marrying his fellow triumvir's sister, Octavia—a beautiful and high-minded young intellectual, recently widowed, and with three children from her first marriage. . . . Meanwhile in Alexandria Cleopatra, never one to do things by halves, bore Antony twins, a boy and a girl. His first child by Octavia, a girl, was born in 38.

Just what Antony thought he was doing at this point is not wholly clear. He may have been playing the Roman card; he may have thought he could finesse Cleopatra against Octavia, in whose company, during the winter of 38–37, he played the dutiful intellectual in Athens, attending lectures and going the rounds of the philosophical schools. . . . Octavian's growing enmity also must have turned him back toward the idea of playing winner-take-all, with Alexandria as his base. If Octavia had borne him a son, things might have been different; but she had not, and Cleopatra had. Cleopatra also held the still-impressive accumulated treasure of the Ptolemies, something that Octavian, too, kept very much in mind. . . .

So Antony left Italy and went east, with the Senate's authority to reallocate client kingdoms—a commission that, as we shall see, he proceeded to interpret in a more than liberal fashion. . . . The first thing that Antony did, on reaching Antioch, was to send for Cleopatra. After their long separation it was now that his, or their, schemes for . . . a "Romano-Hellenistic Orient" began to take shape.

Antony proceeded to lavish on the queen not only Cyprus . . . but also the cedar-clad Cilician coast, so ideal for shipbuilding, not to mention Phoenicia, Coele-Syria, and the richest spice-bearing regions of Judaea and Arabia, dispositions that not unnaturally caused vast offense in Rome, and not only because of Cleopatra's personal unpopularity there: these provincial areas were in fact not in his authority to dispose of, and the obvious purpose of their allocation to Cleopatra, Egypt itself being virtually without timber, was to provide lumber and shipyards for the creation of a large Egyptian fleet. The twin children were also now acknowledged by Antony, and officially named Alexander Helios and Cleopatra Selene, titles powerfully evocative of Hellenistic

dynastic ambition. . . .

So it came about that in 34 Antony committed himself still further to his independent Graeco-Roman dream. After a successful—and financially rewarding—Armenian campaign he celebrated a triumphal parade through Alexandria, playing the role of the New Dionysus, while Cleopatra, enthroned as the New Isis, presided over the ceremony. (Inevitably, when the news reached Rome, this occasion was misinterpreted as an unauthorized and improper Roman triumph.) Only a few days later a yet more explicit political ceremony took place. In the great Gymnasium of Alexandria, with Cleopatra once more robed as Isis, and Antony enthroned by her side, titles were bestowed upon the royal children. Ptolemy XV Caesar (Caesarion)—though carefully subordinated to the royal pair—was made joint ruler of Egypt with his mother and proclaimed King of Kings (she became Queen of Kings, a higher honor still). Alexander Helios . . . was declared Great King of what had been the Seleucid empire at its zenith. . . . His sister, Cleopatra Selene, was instated as Queen of Cyrenaica and Crete. The youngest son of Antony and Cleopatra, Ptolemy Philadelphos . . . was proclaimed, at the age of two, King of Syria and Asia Minor: he was also dressed in Macedonian royal robes. . . .

[These ceremonies] not only laid improper claim to territories that were either outside Rome's control or, worse, already under Roman administration; they also made it only too clear that Cleopatra and the formidable resources of Egypt were backing Antony's dreams. Once again the irresistible lure of world empire was in the air: the grim lessons of the past three centuries had been quickly forgotten. . . .

Enter Octavian, Exit Antony, Cleopatra, and the Hellenistic Age

In 32/1 Antony formally divorced Octavia, thus forcing the West to recognize his relationship with Cleopatra; he had already, unprecedentedly, put the Egyptian queen's head and name on his official Roman coinage, the silver denarii that enjoyed an enormously wide circulation throughout the eastern Mediterranean. These acts also terminated even the pretense of his Roman allegiance, and Octavian . . . formally declared war on Cleopatra, and on her alone; no mention was made of Antony. The whipped-up hysterical xenophobia [anti-foreign feelings] current in Rome at the time can be sensed from the (largely factitious) propaganda of such Augustan poets as Virgil and Propertius. Cleopatra was the drunken lascivious Oriental, worked over by her own house slaves . . . whoring after strange gods and foreign ways. . . . Inevitably, she was also portrayed as an indiscriminately sensual harlot, a charge that, as we have seen, was almost certainly false, though she did (it was claimed) derive a "really sensuous pleasure" from literature.

Antony became the target of more serious, and better founded, political accusations, for example that he had misused troops, acted without senatorial authorization, and given away territories that belonged to Rome. . . .

The exaggerated charges against Cleopatra also reveal fear; and though today the outcome may seem inevitable . . . at the time many must have believed that the New Isis would triumph, that Antony would indeed launch a dazzling new career of world conquest and imperial co-partnership from Alexandria. . . . Octavian's crushing naval victory at Actium, on 2 September 31—planned and won for him by his admiral Agrippa—finally put paid to Antony's ambitions. Less than a year later, after a halfhearted defense of Alexandria against Octavian's advancing army, Antony committed suicide. Cleopatra soon followed his example. . . . Once she was safely dead, admiring tributes to her noble end could be entertained without risk, while her heir Caesarion was butchered without compunction.

On 29 August, 30 B.C., Octavian officially declared the Ptolemaic dynasty at an end, thus writing finis—as we can see now—to the whole Hellenistic era of the Successors. . . . The Successors' territories, meanwhile, were absorbed into the administrative efficiency of a semi-Stoicized universal empire. No room, there, for the New Isis. Yet Cleopatra achieved her dying wish. Unlike her forebears, she knew the country she ruled; and when she had the famous asp—in fact an Egyptian cobra—smuggled to her in a basket of figs, it was in the belief that, as Egyptian religion declared, death from snakebite would, the . . . cobra being sacred, confer immortality. She was not mistaken. Only Alexander—another Macedonian—could eclipse the mesmeric fascination that she exercised down the centuries, and still exercises, upon the European imagination: the perennial symbol of what, had Actium gone the other way, might have been a profoundly different world. We end, as we began, with a legend.

Democracy, Citizenship, and Justice

Chapter 7

Introduction

Looking back on ancient Greek democracy and justice, Athens appears to dominate the scene. This is partly because Athens was for a long time the largest, most populous, and most influential city-state in Greece. Also, it acquired two widely famous and far-reaching law codes during the Archaic Age (those of Draco and Solon); and it was the first Greek state (in fact, the first state anywhere) to institute a fully democratic government. These, however, are not the principal reasons that modern historians are forced to dwell mainly on Athenian justice and democracy. The fact is that most of the substantial first-hand information about these topics that has survived the ravages of time comes from Athenian writers and other Athenian sources and describes Athens.

Other Greek states followed Athens's lead and created democratic institutions of their own; but surviving evidence describing these institutions is meager, scattered, and fragmentary. An educated guess would be that, since the Athenian model was there for all to see and learn from, many, if not most, other Greek democracies resembled that model, at least in its basics. Most, for instance, would have had popular assemblies in which citizens chose leaders and debated crucial issues; and likely all would have had courts that dispensed justice, even if their exact set-up and rules differed from those in Athens.

It is also important to realize that even among those Greek states that did not have fully developed or radical democracies, most had certain basic democratic institutions in place. By the Classic Age, the majority of non-democracies had oligarchic councils. As a rule, these councils did not have dictatorial powers and were forced to recognize a wide range of social and political rights and freedoms, at least for citizens.

Since in any Greek state only those with the legal status of citizen had political rights, it is necessary to determine first who the citizens were and what requirements they had to meet to become so. Again, most available evidence comes from Athens. Although we know that Athenian citizens possessed a formidable array of rights, the state defined the citizen rather narrowly, at least by the standards of modern democracies like the United States. Only free males born in Attica (i.e., Athenian territory) were eligible for complete citizenship rights, including the political rights to vote and hold public office (which required a minimum age of eighteen). Their female relatives were citizens too, but a special type, the *astai*—those without political rights. Slaves, who had no rights at all, could not be citizens. And neither could metics (*metoikoi*), foreigners (including both non-Greeks and Greeks from other poleis) who lived and worked in Athens. The metics were mostly merchants and tradespeople, such as potters, metalsmiths, and jewelers. By modern standards, the fact that they could neither take part in government nor own land seems unfair, for they made important contributions to the community. For instance, they provided essential goods and services, paid taxes, and served in the army when needed.

Full citizenship was thus a special and cherished right; and its loss, known as *atimia* (literally "dishonor"), the stiffest penalty delivered by the courts short of exile or death, was highly dreaded. An *atimos,* a man whose citizenship had been revoked, could not speak in the Assembly or law courts, hold public office, or enter a temple or the marketplace. And the community as a whole strictly enforced these sanctions. For example, any citizen who saw an *atimos* in a prohibited area was allowed to arrest him on the spot.

The principal public institutions that Athenian citizens ran and benefited from were, of course, those that had been established or enhanced by the democratic revolutions of Solon and Cleisthenes, in the early and late sixth century B.C. respectively. These included the Assembly, the Council (which Cleisthenes expanded from 400 to 500 members), the board of ten generals (*Strategia*), the impeachment-like process of ostracism to remove unwanted leaders, and the various law courts. Besides these polis-wide institutions, there were also local ones. For example, each of the demes (the small ward-like districts that Cleisthenes either set up or reorganized) had its own tiny assembly, which decided local political matters.

It can probably be safely assumed that most Greek states, open democracies or not, had, if not the rough equivalents of most of these institutions, at least some sort of justice system. Each such system would have undergone a steady evolution, as Athens's version did, although the specific steps and outcomes surely varied. In the dim past, when kings (or chieftains) ruled Athens, the head man must have dispensed most justice; later, when a small group of nobles ran the state, an aristocratic council, the Areopagus, did so; later still, in the early sixth century B.C., Solon revised the laws and introduced law courts of various kinds; and finally, in the late 460s, democrats led by the reformer Ephialtes (Pericles' mentor) reorganized the courts, expanding the size and powers of juries. (Certain added refinements, such as payment for jurors, came later, under Pericles.)

Combined with other democratic institutions, the right of ordinary citizens, even poor ones, to have their day in court and be judged by a jury of their peers was a singular and momentous development in human history. Many other premodern societies had laws and justice; but usually these were overseen by monarchs and aristocrats; and only rarely was government and justice in the hands of the common people themselves. In *The Murder of Herodes* noted classical scholar Kathleen Freeman remarks, Athens's democratic system,

> though it had obvious faults and made glaring mistakes, was nevertheless a remarkably intricate and effective piece of machinery, the like of which the world had never seen, for the dispensation of justice equally to all. It was typical of all Hellenic [Greek] thought, as opposed to oriental [Near Eastern] ideas of absolute obedience to a personal ruler, that in every rightly-constituted state the law must stand above human caprice and ambition. . . . In the Athenian democracy, the constitution was designed to ensure that supreme power remained in the hands of the people, whose duty it was to defend the law. No single person or group of persons must ever rise so far above his fellows as to be out of control by the people, and above the law.

The major primary sources for Greek democratic institutions and justice include Aristotle's *Athenian Constitution,* which summarizes the development of Athens's government from the days of Draco (late seventh century B.C.) to those of Pericles (mid-to-late fifth century B.C.); the few surviving writings of the lawgiver Solon; various sections of the histories of Herodotus and Thucydides (including Thucydides' re-creation of Pericles' remarks about democracy); an anonymous fifth-century B.C. document titled *Constitution of the Athenians,* which is critical of democracy; and the writings of later Greeks, especially Plutarch, whose biographies of Solon, Themistocles, Cimon, Pericles, and others contain valuable information from other ancient sources now lost. Of crucial importance, in addition, are the surviving speeches of notable fifth- and fourth-century B.C. Attic orators, including Antiphon (born 480), Lysias (ca. 458), Isaeus (ca. 420), and Demosthenes (384). Each wrote numerous court speeches for hire, either for the defense or the prosecution; these tracts contain much priceless information about law and trial procedures, as well as many other aspects of Greek life at the time.

Selection 1

Athens Establishes the World's First Democracy

Michael Grant

This excerpt from noted classical scholar Michael Grant's informative volume, The Rise of the Greeks, *outlines the major elements of the democracy instituted in the late 500s* B.C. *by the popular Athenian leader Cleisthenes and his supporters. Grant first sets the scene by explaining how Cleisthenes, a member of the aristocratic Alcmaeonid clan (or house), came to prominence. (This involved another important family, the Pisistratids, which had recently produced three tyrants in succession—Pisistratus and his sons, Hippias and Hipparchus.) Then Grant explains the new democratic reforms, including the creation of ten new tribes, some 140 demes (small community- or ward-like districts), an expanded Council (the members of which were chosen by lot, or random drawing), the Assembly of citizens, and the procedure of ostracism.*

The regime of Hippias and Hipparchus ran into difficulties. . . . The Athenian brothers' rule became harsher: and in 514 Hipparchus was murdered. His assassins Harmodius and Aristogeiton, who paid for the deed with their lives, were later honoured by a

statuary group sculpted by Antenor, and went down to posterity as the 'tyrant-slayers' who had ended the dictatorship—misleadingly, since they had failed to kill Hippias.

It was instead . . . the noble Alcmaeonid house which led the movement that brought him and his regime down. After one of their returned members, Cleisthenes . . . held the archonship in 525/524, Hippias had expelled the clan (along with others). However, Cleisthenes instigated King Cleomenes I of Sparta—with which the Pisistratids had formed close connections—to drive out the Athenian autocrat (510), which he did, allegedly by enlisting Delphic support.

Cleomenes subsequently fell out with Cleisthenes, but the Spartan's attempts to supersede him by a rival aristocratic faction-leader Isagoras, and then to restore Hippias to his dictatorial office (504), proved total failures.

On the second of these occasions the Athenians defeated the armies of two of Sparta's allies, Chalcis and the Boeotian League, on one and the same day, a double victory which greatly increased Athenian self-confidence. Boeotia, which had already fought Athens for Plataea without success in *c.*519, was not finally defeated, but Chalcis was, and the lands of its nobility were confiscated for 4,000 Athenian settlers, known as *klerouchoi* after the allotments of land (*kleroi*) that they were given. These migrants introduced a new type of colonization by retaining their Athenian citizenship (unlike settlers in normal colonies, who became citizens of their new foundation), so that although geographical distance from the mother city obliged them to create organs of local self-government they remained liable to Athenian military service, acting, when necessary, as a garrison defending the interests of Athens.

The New Tribal Units and Council

In the course, or at the end, of these excitements—perhaps in a series of several stages, from c.506 to c.500—Cleisthenes, backed by popular support . . . was granted or assumed the powers needed to prevent the destruction of his own Alcmaeonid party, which was getting the worst of the internal struggle. Armed with these powers, he asserted his authority and seized the chance to introduce the most famous constitutional reforms in Greek history.

They displayed an extraordinary complex design. . . . Cleisthenes superseded the four antique Attic tribes, which had been dominated by the nobles—and which had excluded many of the new citizens created by Solon and the Pisistratids—in favour of ten new tribes, unlinked with the old tribal past. The four old tribes were allowed to survive for religious purposes, but it was upon their ten newly created successors that the future of Athens depended. For they came to form the basis of all aspects of public life. One such aspect was military service, since each of the ten tribes was required to supply a regiment or squadron to the army, and this soldierly function of the new tribes meant that their cohesive *esprit de corps* developed rapidly. It was encouraged by religious sanctions, since each tribe was named after a mythological hero allegedly buried at Athens—except for two of the heroes, whose burial places were shown at Salamis and Eleusis. A number of foreigners and slaves were admitted into these ten Cleisthenic tribes. Their creation represented a deliberate attempt to break up the old regional, conservative allegiances. For one thing, the new tribes were not units of local government; their headquarters were in the city. And, above all, any reversion to the old regionalization was prevented by means of the ancient institution of the *trittyes* (thirds). These, . . . had probably been territorial synonyms . . . used for purposes of administration. There had been twelve of them, but Cleisthenes raised the number to thirty. That is to say, there were still three in each tribe. But each of these three *trittyes*, in every tribe, was based on a different region of Attica from the regions to which the other two *trittyes* in the same tribe belonged, so that people were 'mixed up', and opportunities for local loyalty were dissipated.

Moreover, in order to avoid any resuscitation of the old trouble-making factions of the Plain, Coast and Hill, the three regions were novel creations which by no means completely corresponded with the three old areas. The new regions were Town (*astu*, including Athens, Phaleron and Piraeus and part of the adjacent plain), Coast (*paralia*, comprising most of the former territory of the same name, but including additional coastal zones), and the Interior (comprising parts of all the former areas).

Cleisthenes also divided the ten tribes and thirty *trittyes* into demes (*demoi*), about 140 in number, which, for practical purposes, replaced the aristocratic clan and phratry organization. That antique system, it is true, continued to exist for religious purposes and functions, but the deme was now the fundamental subdivision of society. Demes from each of three new regions were included in all the ten tribes. Having originally been villages or city-wards or small towns, these demes varied greatly in size. After the initial registrations, membership was hereditary and did not depend on residence, so that the members of a deme were not concentrated in a single place.

Nevertheless, demes maintained their own list of members and members' property (and kept lists of metics [resident foreigners] as well), so that they could furnish the state with information required to enforce civic obligations—and were able, also, to exert control over the right to Athenian citizenship: to be an Athenian citizen meant being registered on the official roll of one's paternal deme. The demes also possessed their own land, social life and religious cults, as well as their own assemblies (perhaps rarely convened). Such activities, under the leadership of an annually elected *demarchos*, counterbalanced and therefore weakened the corresponding organs of the old clans and phratries. Granted the passive nature of rustic life, the wealthier and more aristocratic demesmen (and those belonging to demes near Athens) must have retained a considerable measure of authority. And yet this new local autonomy furnished not only the rich, but every Athenian citizen, with the opportunity to gain some understanding of the process of state government—without having to rely upon a local patron or a dictatorial head of government, or upon his faction.

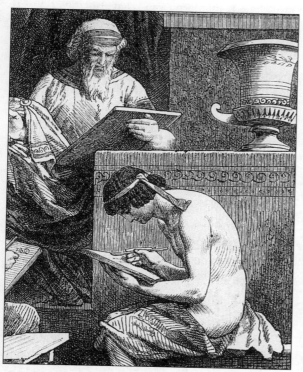

This nineteenth-century engraving depicts Solon dictating his laws, which were far less repressive than those previously enacted.

The extension of political activity and authority to the citizenry in general was given expression by Cleisthenes' new Council (later Boule) of Five Hundred members. The tradition ascribing to Solon the creation of a Council of Four Hundred

to supplement, and largely supersede, the Areopagus was probably correct. But we hear little of Solon's body, and it was the Council of Cleisthenes which dominated the future. Its 500 members comprised fifty men, over the age of thirty, from each of the ten newly created tribes. Every one of the demes that constituted each tribe was represented on the new Council in proportion to the size of its population; and in this way, the Council served as a bridge between city and countryside, while at the same time staving off the rise or revival of parties and political interest groups, and thus contributing to the creation and development of the Athenian democracy.

The Council met daily except on holidays and unlucky days. Its business was prepared by a committee manned by fifty of its own members (*prytaneis*), each group serving for one-tenth of the year. The group currently in office was on duty every day, under the guidance of one of its number, who also acted as the committee's chairman (*epistates*). Whether this system existed, in its final form, as early as the time of Cleisthenes is not clear, but the multiple duties of the Council must presumably have required some such 'agenda subcommittee' from the outset. For the Council was entrusted with far-reaching and varied deliberative and administrative duties. Moreover, it monopolized the initiative in all law-making, and possessed important judicial functions, notably the right to investigate alleged illegalities. Council members served for a year, and could serve for a second year after an interval.

The method, however, by which, in these early days of the body's existence, they were selected cannot be determined for certain. At first elected and unpaid, from *c.*450 (or 462) at least they were appointed by demesmen by lot (sortition). . . .

The lot was believed by the Athenians to possess a religious sanction, since it left the decision to the gods. At a subsequent date, this procedure came to be exalted by radicals (but reputedly deplored by Socrates) as a supreme principle of the ultra-democratic system they admired, since it gave everyone an equal chance. And democratic, in this sense, it was, though not democratic in the other sense of allowing merit every opportunity to secure its place: the lot, as critics pointed out, takes no interest in merit.

However, this system, during the subsequent centuries of Athenian democracy, did not work as badly as might have been expected. This was largely because so many ordinary citizens had received a basic political and administrative training in the various local community bodies, so that sortition could not go far wrong. But especially in the early period the method was also subjected to a very important qualification: the lot was taken only from names chosen through a previous process of voting (*prokrisis*) by the demes, so that in fact the candidates eventually chosen by lot had been drawn from a short-list of men selected by a vote, that is to say on the basis of merit. Whether this 'middle way' had been established at Athens by Solon or not . . . it must already have played a part in the arrangements of Cleisthenes.

The Assembly and Board of Generals

The Assembly, as well as the new Council, now possessed considerable powers, which had scarcely been the case before. The relative strength of these two bodies, at the time of Cleisthenes and during the decades that followed, is difficult to assess, but the task has to be attempted, because upon the answer to this question depends our estimate of the thoroughgoing character, or otherwise, of the early or incipient Athenian democracy (democracy among male citizens, that is, because women, metics and slaves were excluded).

In favour of the supposition that the Assembly held the upper hand, reference could be made to its right to amend or reject, during its forty meetings each year, the motions placed before it by the Council. Moreover, the Assembly retained in its hands certain essential functions, including the responsibility for declarations of war; and the annual change in the entire membership of the Council deprived it of the corporate feeling that might have prompted a stand against the Assembly's 'sovereign' authority. Besides, the citizen

membership of the latter body had become more articulate and more radical, and also, with the growth of the franchise [right to vote], much larger. When the herald cried out, 'What man has good advice to give the *polis* and wishes to make it known?' he was issuing a genuine invitation to the entire voting body: here was direct (not, as today, representative) democracy in action, inviting political oratory before wide, interested, participatory audiences.

All the same, it was the Council which determined what business should be placed before the Assembly, and in what shape—and it met more frequently than the Assembly (which, moreover, only voted by a show of hands). The Council also replaced the Areopagus (now or a little later) in preparing that business (*probouleusis*); and it subsequently had to see that the Assembly's decrees were carried out, so that the formula 'the Council and People decided' possessed real significance.

A second important limitation of the Assembly's powers was the establishment during these years of a board of ten generals (*strategoi*), one from each of the ten tribal regiments or squadrons, to command Athens' military forces. The *strategoi*, who at first came from noble and wealthy families, were *not* appointed by lot, because of the specialized nature of their duties, but were elected by the Assembly—and they could be re-elected an unlimited number of times.

The polemarch [war archon], as of old, still led the state's forces out to battle, and fought in a position of danger. But he and the other archons were no longer as important as they used to be. A sign of this change was the decision that they, too, like the members of the Council, should be appointed by lot, out of a select list of *prokritoi*, chosen by the demes (a system abandoned in the fifth century in favour of two successive lot-takings). Our confused sources make it difficult to determine when the archons came to be appointed in this way; 487/486 is a possible date, but on the whole it is more likely that this, too, was an arrangement made by Cleisthenes. (The date when scrutiny of candidates for archonships, and audit of their performance, were instituted was *c.* 462.)

Evidently the creation of the *strategoi* constituted a greater limitation upon the Assembly's untrammelled sovereignty than archons, with their diminished powers, were any longer able to impose. But an equally potent restriction upon that body's freedom of action, viewed as a democratic expression of the people's will, came from within its own ranks and from its own character.

For, although anyone could get up and speak in the Assembly, we also learn that anyone speaking foolishly was at once shouted down. That is to say, a fair measure of expert knowledge was needed to address not only the Council but the Assembly as well—and the only people with the time to acquire such knowledge were members of the leisured aristocratic class, so that the upper ranks of society, and the determined self-perpetuating lobbies that they formed, were still the predominant element. However, a man who thus became a leading figure in the Assembly only prevailed by personally exerting and asserting his powers of persuasion before this audience, over and over again. He did not receive automatic, pre-eminent deference because he belonged to this or that faction or class. Indeed, it was Cleisthenes' deliberate intention, we are told, to eclipse such previous factional associations or loyalties . . . fostered by the aristocratic clubs and *symposia* [all-male after-dinner drinking parties held and attended by the well-to-do] which stood at the centre of an early Greek city's political, social and cultural life (though here he was not entirely successful, since these institutions defied and survived all such attempts to eliminate them).

Cleisthenes was again thinking along similar lines, aiming at the prevention of internal factional warfare, when he introduced the extraordinary institution of ostracism. This was a method of banishing prominent politicians who had become unpopular. Any Athenian who wished such a person out of the way inscribed the man's name on a fragment of pottery (*ostrakon*), and if the total number of votes exceeded 6,000, the man whose name headed the list had to go into exile for ten years. Although no

one was ostracized until 487, Aristotle's indication that the procedure had been devised by Cleisthenes can be accepted. But he was not equally right to believe that ostracism was intended as a safeguard against the revival of dictatorship; or at least, if this was so, it was only a secondary aim, or one of the original aims, perhaps, which became overlaid. The main purpose of the process, as the course of events later showed, was to prevent clashes with and between aristocratic opponents. For there were many Pisistratid supporters still at Athens, and indeed for other reasons as well political leadership remained fragile—as Cleisthenes, himself earlier a violent faction-leader, knew only too well. So he concluded that only the temporary removal of one or other of such contestants could enable the state to survive. . . . The exile of a tiresome politician would effectively silence him; for Athenian civilization was still mainly oral, and in an oral culture if you remove a man physically he has lost his lines of communication, and can no longer make trouble. . . .

By taking these measures, he [Cleisthenes] did not, it may be supposed, foresee the huge power of the Athenian democracy in the following century. Yet he pointed firmly towards that power by vouchsafing the people, the Assembly, a glimpse of what it would eventually achieve. The contemporary description for the degree of democracy established by Cleisthenes, or existing in his time, was *isonomia*, equality under the law, replacing the aristocratic hierarchic orderliness described as *eunomia*. True, the old framework had not been destroyed, but it had been overlaid by a new one; as elsewhere, the old *thesmos*, 'ordinance' fixed by an authority, was now supplemented and partly replaced by *nomos*, law or custom adopted by a community as a result of its own decision. The *isonomia* of Cleisthenes, though it did not all come into force at once but emerged gradually, was a sophisticated, intricate and experimental array of new political institutions, adding up to the most democratic form of government that had so far been devised by human ingenuity, and establishing the essential features of Athenian society for 200 years.

Selection 2

Meetings of the Athenian Assembly

Donald Kagan

This description of how the Athenian Assembly met and conducted its business is by Yale University's Donald Kagan, a noted authority on ancient Athenian democracy. Kagan punctuates his brisk narrative with excerpts from two plays by the fifth-century B.C. comic playwright Aristophanes (one of which pokes fun at Aristophanes' colleague, the tragedian Euripides) and a speech by the great fourth-century B.C. orator Demosthenes.

At the heart of what we would call the legislative branch of the Athenian democracy was the assembly (*ekklesia*). It was open to all adult male citizens of Athens, during Pericles' lifetime perhaps as many as forty thousand men. Most Athenians lived many miles from the city and few owned horses, so attendance required a long walk to town. As a result, the number taking part was probably from five to six thousand, although some actions required a quorum of six thousand. The meetings took place on a hill called the Pnyx, not far from the Acropolis and overlooking the Agora. The citizens sat on the earth of the sharply sloping hill, and the speakers stood on a low platform. It was not easy for them to make themselves heard;

Demosthenes, the great fourth-century orator, is said to have practiced speaking by the seashore over the crashing surf to make his voice strong enough for his work on the Pnyx.

We can get some idea of the opening of these meetings from a comic version in Aristophanes' *Acharnians*, performed in 425. The first speaker is a typical Aristophanic comic hero, an old-fashioned farmer who complains about the war because it keeps him in Athens, away from his farm in the country:

It is the day of an assembly and already morning, but the Pnyx is deserted. They are chattering in the Agora, dodging the rope dripping with red dye. [A squad of slaves roamed the streets and swatted obvious shirkers with such ropes leaving red marks on their tunics. Anyone caught with such stains had to pay a fine.] Even the Presidents of the Assembly have not arrived. They will be late, and when they finally come they will push and fight each other for a seat in the front row, streaming down all together, you can't imagine how; but they will say nothing about making peace. Oh my Athens! I am always the first to make the return voyage to the assembly and take my seat. And since I am alone, I groan, I yawn, I stretch my legs, I fart, I don't know what to do, I write, pull out my loose hairs, add up my accounts, looking off at my fields, longing for peace, hating the town, sick for my village-home, which never said "buy my charcoal, my vinegar, my oil"; the word "buy" is unknown there where everything is free. And so, I have come here fully prepared to shout, to interrupt and abuse the speakers if they talk about anything but peace. But here come these noon-time Presidents. Didn't I tell you? Didn't I predict how they would come? Everyone jostling for the front seat!

Next, the herald of the assembly says, "Move up! Move up within the consecrated area!" Then he recites the formula that regularly began debate in the assembly: "Who wishes to speak?"

Preliminary Ceremony

The scene in *Acharnians* omits the prayer that began sessions of the assembly and preceded the beginning of business. We can get an idea of what that was like from the parody Aristophanes presents in another of his comedies, the *Thesmophoriazusae*. The humor in the passage derives from the hilarious idea of women holding a political assembly and from Euripides' reputation as a misogynist [woman-hater]. The herald recites the opening prayer, which included a curse on those who would subvert the democratic constitution:

Let there be silence, let there be silence. Pray to the Thesmophorae, Demeter and Kore, and to Plutus and Calligeneia and to Earth the foster mother, and to Hermes and the Graces that this present assembly and meeting may do what is finest and best, bringing advantage and good fortune both to Athens and to ourselves. And let the woman who acts and speaks best for the Athenian people and for Womankind win out. Pray for this and for good things for yourselves. Io Paean! Io Paean! Let us rejoice.

The assembly of women responds with a choral song of prayer. Then the herald recites the curse:

Pray to the Olympian and Pythian and Delian gods and goddesses, and to the other gods that if anyone plots evil against the people of Womankind or is negotiating with Euripides or the Persians to the harm of the people of

Womankind, or aims at becoming a tyrant or at restoring a tyrant, or denounces a woman for palming off someone else's baby as her own, or if there is a slave who is an accomplice in her mistress' intrigues and betrays her secret to her master, or who does not deliver messages faithfully, or if there is a lover who gets what he wants from a woman with lies but never carries out his promises . . . may he and his family die a horrible death; and pray that the gods give many good things to all the rest of you women.

Again the chorus responds with a prayerful song. Then the herald turns to business:

Listen all! Approved by the Council of Women, moved by Sostrata, Timoclea was president and Lysilla secretary: to hold an assembly on the middle day of the Festival of Thesmorphoria in the morning, when we all have most leisure; the first item on the agenda will be: what should be done with Euripides, since it is clear that he wrongs us all? Who wishes to speak?

If we put aside the jokes at the expense of women, substitute "the people of Athens" for "the people of Womankind," and add "those who bring false reports and those who deceive the people" to the list of those accursed we will be left with a fair approximation of the form in which the assembly began its business.

The People Ultimately Sovereign

But the real meetings on the Pnyx were rarely comic; they dealt with serious questions. The assembly had four fixed meetings in each of the ten periods into which the official year was divided, and special meetings were called when needed. Topics included approval or disapproval of treaties and making declarations of war, assigning generals to campaigns and deciding what forces and resources they should command, confirmation of officials or their removal from office, whether or not to hold an ostracism, questions concerning religion, questions of inheritance, and, in fact, everything else. In the second meeting of each period "anyone who wishes can address the people on whatever subject he likes, whether private or public," and the third and fourth meetings discussed "all other kinds of business," whatever that might be.

It is especially impressive for a citizen of a modern representative democracy to read of these great town meetings dealing directly with questions of foreign policy—questions that could mean life or death for those present at the debate and for their city. Many such dramatic assemblies met in Pericles' time, but the one best described took place almost a century after his death. Philip of Macedon had marched into central Greece, only three days' march from Athens, one of his greatest enemies. What to do, whether to resist or try to negotiate such terms as they could, these decisions could determine the fate of Athens and its people, and they would be decided on the Pnyx by the assembled masses. Demosthenes, leader of the resistance to Philip, gives his version of the meeting.

> It was evening when a messenger came to the presidents of the Council to report that Elatea [in nearby Boeotia] had been taken. In the midst of their dinner they got up at once and cleared the booths in the market-place . . . while others sent for the generals and called for the trumpeter, and the city was filled with commotion. At dawn on the next day the presidents called the Council to the Council House, and

> you [the Athenian people] went to the assembly, and before the Council began proceedings and made any proposal the whole people was seated up on the Pnyx. Then the Council arrived, the presidents reported the news it had received and introduced the messenger who had brought it. When he had spoken the herald asked, "Who wishes to speak?" And no one came forward. (from *On the Crown*)

To get an idea of the distance between ancient and modern democracy we need only consider how an emergency—like the seizure of an American embassy—would be dealt with today in the United States. It would probably arrive first as secret information at some bureau of the government's vast and complex intelligence service. It would be treated as highly confidential and revealed only to a few people in the White House and the State and Defense departments. Policy would be discussed in a small, closed group, and the decision made by one man, the president. If there were no leaks, the people would hear of it only when the die had been cast.

Questions no less grave than the one confronting the Athenians of Demosthenes' time arose more than once in Periclean Athens. Each time, the popular assembly held a full debate and made the decision by raising their hands in a vote determined by a simple majority. There can be no stronger evidence of the full and final sovereignty of the Athenian people.

Selection 3

The Athenian Justice System

N.R.E. Fisher

This informative overview of the Athenian justice system initiated in 362 B.C. by the democratic reformer Ephialtes is by N.R.E. Fisher, a classicist at University College, Cardiff, Wales. Before 362, everyday justice was handled by one or more archons (public administrators), often including the Thesmothetai, *six archons whose principal function was seeing that justice was carried out. The Areopagus, an aristocratic council composed of ex-archons, heard murder and arson cases;* ephetai, *courts consisting of groups of fifty-one citizens over age fifty, heard cases of accidental killing or the killing of a noncitizen; and appeals courts (*heliaia), *probably consisting of meetings of the entire Assembly, handled appeals. Ephialtes' system in a sense streamlined the old one by replacing much of it with public jury courts (*dikasteria) *somewhat similar to those in modern democracies. In covering the new system, Fisher explains the juries, prosecutors, lawsuits, penalties and their enforcement, and the responsibilities of both litigants and the state in bringing cases to court. It is important to keep in mind that not all Greek states, even those that had democracies, necessarily*

Excerpted from N.R.E. Fisher, *Social Values in Classical Athens* (London: Dent, 1976). Reprinted by permission of the author.

adopted the Athenian system in its entirety, although it is likely that most of the democracies had similar basic features. Unfortunately, most surviving records regarding laws, courts, and justice are Athenian and very little is known about other Greek justice systems.

Athenians professed to believe that the preservation of the laws was crucial to democracy and worked to the real advantages of all citizens; and that the major role here had to be played by the popular juries. A programme of re-inscribing and co-ordinating the existing laws was undertaken in the last years of the Peloponnesian War and finished by the restored democracy [after the overthrow of the Thirty Tyrants in 403 B.C.], and a distinction was drawn between 'decrees' passed by the assembly, and 'laws' of greater generality and permanence. Laws were supposed to go through more cumbersome procedure, involving a special board of 500 'legislators'; but it appears that this procedure was not used as often as it might have been, and confusion between laws and decrees was not avoided. More important as checks on hasty and ill-considered legislation were the two 'indictments', the first for 'illegality' (brought against a decree), and the second for 'introducing an unsuitable law' (against a law). These were of course used by politicians as means of reversing defeats and of attacking enemies; but they did allow more consideration of a measure's usefulness or coherence with other valid laws or decrees. These procedures demonstrate, as do many others, the use of the law courts and juries as final arbiters in legislative matters. Throughout the system the courts gave the final decisions and could not be called to account for them—and this with no weakening, in men's eyes, of democratic principles.

Juries and Prosecutors

Great care was taken to ensure that all corruption of juries was avoided, and that they were as representative as possible. A panel of 6,000 jurors was chosen each year, and as many of those as wished turned up on each day that the courts were due to sit. Juries for particular cases were extremely large; we hear of juries ranging from 200 to the full 6,000. Methods of selection of juries underwent frequent refinements. From about 378/7, a complex system involving jurors' allotment tokens and allotment machines ensured that each jury had a roughly equal representation from each of the ten tribes, that all jurors had a roughly equal chance of selection, and above all that the selections were unpredictable, made at the last minute, and free from unfair manipulation.

Various distinctions were drawn between various types of legal action; the most important is that between *dikai* and *graphai*. *Dike* is a word of wide generality in legal and moral contexts, its meaning covering 'justice', 'order', 'right', 'claim', any legal process, 'penalty' or 'revenge'. But as a technical term for a class of lawsuits it indicates that the right to bring that lawsuit was restricted to the person wronged (or his/her *kyrios* [legal guardian] where applicable). This distinguishes it from a *graphe*, 'indictment', and also from other specialized forms of procedure such as *eisangelia*, 'impeachment', and types of summary action. In all of these, prosecution was open to 'anyone who wishes', i.e. to any Athenian citizen, not necessarily a relation of the victim, nor a public official, nor belonging to a particular class.

In most cases where prosecution was open to any citizen, some notion of public concern is evident, and penalties tended to be paid to the state: these include some cases (theft, adultery and 'insult'—*hubris*) where an individual was wronged. In other cases, the law allowed a *graphe* where the victim was likely to be unable to bring a case—such as wrongs committed inside a family.

The most important thing about the *graphai* is the choice of 'anyone who wishes' as prosecutor. Firstly, the idea displays characteristic mistrust of public officials. Secondly, the institution was rightly regarded in antiquity as one of the most democratic elements in Solon's reforms. Its importance in encouraging active participation and feelings of involvement in the affairs of the *polis* and of other individuals was clearly immense, as it became clear that prosecution, as well as service on a jury, was open to all and not just to a select class.

Although the dangers of widespread corruption and of dominance by the upper classes were to some extent avoided by throwing prosecution open in this way, prosecutors in *graphai* themselves risked much criticism. One problem, affecting especially prosecutors in 'private' cases, derives from a clear conflict of values. Solon allegedly wished all citizens to feel that other people's wrongs were their business; but the great emphasis on the obligations to manage one's *oikos* [family], help one's *philoi* [friends] and harm one's *echthroi* [personal enemies], involved a conflicting attitude: that one should not interfere in the business of other people. A word meaning basically 'apt to do much', 'fond of business' (adjective *polypragmon*, noun *polypragmosyne*) when used of individuals frequently conveyed the notion of objectionable interference, busybodying and so on. Hence prosecutors not related to their victims and claiming to be acting in the best interest of the *polis* incurred much hostility if they appeared to interfere in the affairs of those neither their *philoi* nor their *echthroi*. This conflict between Solonian ideals and traditional values may be seen at many points in comedy and the speeches.

Matters were made worse by doubts about the motives of the prosecutors. In a number of public cases, prosecution was encouraged by offering a proportion of the fines or confiscation of property; and naturally enough other ways of profiting were found, such as a reward from those pleased to see an enemy attacked, or payment from those threatened with a prosecution. A special term, *sykophantes*, was applied to anyone involved in prosecutions of which one strongly disapproved, and covered prosecuting on false charges, or for money from any source, or to please someone else. It was commonly applied to politicians, especially minor or young politicians, in their constant legal contests.

Consequently, litigants when prosecuting rarely relied solely on a statement of their patriotic duty, and liked to be able to claim personal reasons for prosecuting, that they or their friends had been wronged or attacked in the courts by their opponents. Almost universally true of 'private' cases, this applies also to a large number of public cases; and defendants of course accuse their opponents of being *sykophantai*, of plotting against them with the worst of motives.

It must in practice have been extremely difficult for juries to decide on the motives of a prosecutor, and they cannot simply have assumed that all prosecutors in *graphai* were *sykophantai*. It is equally hard for us to assess the extent to which the system actually was abused by *sykophantai*, oppressing the self-effacing but innocent rich, or trumping-up charges to help their friends or harm their enemies. Some complaints must have been justified; and there is no doubt that the system encouraged the intensification of political struggles and aided the complexity of political and private friendships and quarrels. The political struggles at times assumed a strong class basis, between ostentatious democrats and real or suspected oligarchs; at other times they were rather merely between those who disagreed on foreign policy, or were competing for political position. The dangers were clearly recognized. Prosecutors in *graphai* who failed to get a fifth of the votes, or who abandoned the case, were supposed to be fined 1,000 drachmae.

A *graphe* specifically directed against *sykophantia* was also available. For all its disadvantages, the *graphe* was basic to the democratic system, and satisfactory alternatives were rarely produced even by its critics.

Bringing Cases to Court

The absence of public prosecutors is complemented by an absence of other officials at most points in the course of a lawsuit; litigants, and juries, had to do most of their work unaided.

The nearest Athens got to a police force was a board of officials (the Eleven) concerned with dealing with common criminals, such as thieves, under various summary procedures, and with the enforcement of certain penalties. These officials were supported by public slaves, the 'Scythian archers'. Such descriptions as we have of fights in streets and houses fail to show officials offering any assistance; parties have to summon help and witnesses as best they can from friends, neighbours and passers-by. Possibly officials were of more use in dealing with lower class criminals than with the rich and influential offenders we hear most about. Certainly no officials played the detective and investigative roles we are used to; individuals had to collect evidence, draw up charges and procure witnesses for their own cases.

Many *dikai* went to arbitration before a court hearing. All citizens of at least *hoplite* [infantry soldier] status served as public arbitrators in their sixtieth year. An arbitrator attempted to reconcile the parties, and if he failed, he gave judgment under oath; the losing party could then appeal and take the case to court. Other cases all involved a preliminary hearing before a magistrate to ensure that the case was admissible.

At hearings in court, litigants had normally to deliver their own speeches, no doubt written out and prepared in advance. In special circumstances such as illness or inexperience the jury gave permission for all or most of the speech to be delivered by an 'advocate', a relative or close *philos*. In a *graphe* it would naturally help if an advocate had his own reasons for *echthra*. More commonly, especially in public cases, one could call on brief character-references from one's *philoi*; here one naturally chose as advocates the most influential of those prepared to speak for one, and it appears that politicians and generals acting as advocates did attempt to use their own influence and claims for *charis* [thanks, gratitude] in the service of their *philoi* or perhaps of those who (illegally) paid them for such favours. This further example of the advantages in litigation accruing to the rich and the well connected is frequently made the object of complaints.

Equally, if not more, important, was the assistance one might get in the preparation of the speech, and advice about one's case in general. Every litigant no doubt importuned anyone he thought might be useful; but the growth of experts in this field, the 'speechwriters' (*logographoi*), skilled in legal procedure and in rhetoric, made a significant difference. Help from a speechwriter no doubt needed either a connection or money; *logographoi* earned a living, whether as a full career, or as a prelude or a sideline to a political career.

Public attitudes to advocates and speechwriters were as contradictory as those towards politicians and prosecutors. Because rhetoric and legal experience can be used to make 'the worse argument seem the better', and because a man should not interfere in another's lawsuit, speechwriters and advocates are constantly abused; and litigants and 'good' characters in comedy present themselves as simple, honest citizens unused to legal procedure and subtle arguments. On the other hand, rhetorical skill was admired for its own sake by many Athenians, as was political success; and it was argued that to be able to seek help from one's friends when in difficulties was a fair and democratic thing.

Juries got even less legal assistance. The presiding magistrate gave no legal rulings, and the laws themselves could be heard only if the litigants had them read out. If laws were conflicting or ambiguous the jury had to decide without expert advice what view to take. Again the important decisions were left to the people, unfettered by possibly corrupt officials; consequently any growth of jurisprudence, or use of precedents, tended to be sacrificed to democratic principles.

Through all the procedure of a lawsuit, opportunities for delays, obstacles and sharp practice abounded. Pleas of unavailability, countersuits, other lawsuits against one's opponent, special pleas of non-admissibility, and many other devices, could be used by experienced operators, with willing friends to bring suits and be witnesses, in order to deceive juries or to obstruct and catch unwary opponents, or even arbitrators and other officials. But, as always, the extent of abuse of the system is very hard to assess.

Penalties and Their Enforcement

Here too the main points that stand out are the extent of the involvement of individuals, and the advantages of wealth and experience in using or misusing the system. Cases were divided into two categories, depending on whether the penalty for the offence was fixed, or whether the jury could choose between a penalty suggested by the prosecutor, and one suggested, after conviction, by the defendant. Penalties available to a court were death, imprisonment, exile, total or partial loss of civic status (*atimia*), confiscation of property and fines; cumulation of penalties was possible (e.g. death and confiscation of property for homicide, imprisonment and double restitution for theft), and non-payment of fines meant loss of civic status for the man and his descendants until the fine was paid, and could involve imprisonment. In general penalties can be said to have been severe by our standards; for example death could be imposed for a variety of offences including types of theft and robbery, treason, political corruption and failure, various religious offences from uprooting sacred olives to impiety, or citing a non-existent law in court.

Some penalties paid to the state were carried out by officials. The Eleven supervised the death penalty and imprisonment. Those exiled who returned could be taken to the Eleven and summarily executed. Those who had been deprived of status could be prosecuted by 'anyone who wishes' if they exercised some forbidden right.

If fines or confiscations were not immediately forthcoming, the assistance of 'anyone who wishes' was again invited; he might make a 'denunciation' (*apographe*), submitting an inventory of the property so that it could be sold by the *polis'* auctioneers. If he did so successfully, he was entitled to three quarters of the proceeds, which seems, from the point of view of the state's finances, a sad consequence of its reliance on volunteers to prosecute.

Greater difficulties, and less state participation, obtained in private cases, where the survival of procedures of 'self-help' is very evident. A litigant awarded a sum of money, or a right to an object or property in possession of his opponent, was entitled to attempt to take possession if it was not immediately surrendered. If prevented, he could attempt to 'distrain' on other objects of roughly equivalent value. If he was prevented from distraining, his only recourse was a legal action for 'ejectment', which if successful produced an additional fine payable to the state. This system was obviously open to abuses, and given a sufficiently tough, shameless and determined opponent, could result in virtual stalemate. Equally, it could produce fights in the streets or inside people's houses, and further lawsuits and hostilities. In these enforcements state officials appeared to have rendered minimal assistance.

Selection 4

An Accused Murderer Defends Himself in Court

Lysias

The following court speech (translated by Kathleen Freeman) was written at Athens sometime between 400 and 380 B.C. by Lysias (ca. 458–ca. 380), the renowned Attic orator and speech-writer (logographos). *His client was the defendant in the case, one Euphiletus, who had been accused of murder. The circumstances were that Euphiletus's wife had been seduced by a man named Eratosthenes and Euphiletus had caught the adulterers in bed and slain Eratosthenes on the spot. According to Solon's laws, most of which were still in force in Athens, a husband was allowed to slay his wife's lover as long as the adultery was the sole reason for the act. If the slayer had some other motive for the killing, he could be prosecuted for murder; and this was how Euphiletus ended up in court; Eratosthenes' relatives accused him of arranging the meeting between his wife and Eratosthenes as part of a preconceived murder plan. Euphiletus insisted that this was a lie and that he had merely availed himself of the law as written.*

Note the skill with which Lysias structures the defense, creating a careful, detailed picture of a kind-hearted, trusting husband who is stealthily deceived by his wife and her disreputable lover. The speech also suggests to the jurors that in acquitting Euphiletus they will be sending a message to other would-be seducers and home-wreckers and thereby doing the community a service. The various sections of the speech, including the Proem (introduction), Narrative, Arguments, and Epilogue (conclusion), are standard elements of the formal rhetoric (art of persuasive speech) that the Greeks developed and the Romans adopted and perpetuated. The verdict in this case is unknown, but it is likely that Euphiletus was acquitted, for adultery was considered a serious offense among the Greeks.

The Proem

I would give a great deal, members of the jury, to find you, as judges of this case, taking the same attitude towards me as you would adopt towards your own behaviour in similar circumstances. I am sure that if you felt about others in the same way as you did about yourselves, not one of you would fail to be angered by these deeds, and all of you would consider the punishment a small one for those guilty of such conduct.

Moreover, the same opinion would be found prevailing not only among you, but everywhere throughout Greece. This is the one crime for which, under any government, democratic or exclusive, equal satisfaction is granted to the meanest against the mightiest, so that the least of them receives the same justice as the most exalted. Such is the detestation, members of the jury, in which this outrage is held by all mankind.

Concerning the severity of the penalty, therefore, you are, I imagine, all of the same opinion: not one of you is so easy-going as to believe that those guilty of such great offences should obtain pardon, or are deserving of a light penalty. What I have to prove, I take it, is just this: that Eratosthenes seduced my wife, and that in corrupting

This is a Roman copy of a Greek bust of the noted Attic orator, Lysias.

her he brought shame upon my children and outrage upon me, by entering my home; that there was no other enmity between him and me except this; and that I did not commit this act for the sake of money, in order to rise from poverty to wealth, nor for any other advantage except the satisfaction allowed by law.

I shall expound my case to you in full from the beginning, omitting nothing and telling the truth. In this alone lies my salvation, I imagine—if I can explain to you everything that happened.

The Narrative

Members of the jury: when I decided to marry and had brought a wife home, at first my attitude towards her was this: I did not wish to annoy her, but neither was she to have too much of her own way. I watched her as well as I could, and kept an eye on her as was proper. But later, after my child had been born, I came to trust her, and I handed all my possessions over to her, believing that this was the greatest possible proof of affection.

Well, members of the jury, in the beginning

she was the best of women. She was a clever housewife, economical and exact in her management of everything. But then, my mother died; and her death has proved to be the source of all my troubles, because it was when my wife went to the funeral that this man Eratosthenes saw her; and as time went on, he was able to seduce her. He kept a look out for our maid who goes to market; and approaching her with his suggestions, he succeeded in corrupting her mistress.

Now first of all, gentlemen, I must explain that I have a small house which is divided into two—the men's quarters and the women's—each having the same space, the women upstairs and the men downstairs.

After the birth of my child, his mother nursed him; but I did not want her to run the risk of going downstairs every time she had to give him a bath, so I myself took over the upper storey, and let the women have the ground floor. And so it came about that by this time it was quite customary for my wife often to go downstairs and sleep with the child, so that she could give him the breast and stop him from crying.

This went on for a long while, and I had not the slightest suspicion. On the contrary, I was in such a fool's paradise that I believed my wife to be the chastest woman in all the city.

Time passed, gentlemen. One day, when I had come home unexpectedly from the country, after dinner, the child began crying and complaining. Actually it was the maid who was pinching him on purpose to make him behave so, because—as I found out later—this man was in the house.

Well, I told my wife to go and feed the child, to stop his crying. But at first she refused, pretending that she was so glad to see me back after my long absence. At last I began to get annoyed, and I insisted on her going.

"Oh, yes!" she said. "To leave *you* alone with the maid up here! You mauled her about before, when you were drunk!"

I laughed. She got up, went out, closed the door—pretending that it was a joke—and locked it. As for me, I thought no harm of all this, and I had not the slightest suspicion. I went to sleep, glad to do so after my journey from the country.

Towards morning, she returned and unlocked the door.

I asked her why the doors had been creaking during the night. She explained that the lamp beside the baby had gone out, and that she had then gone to get a light from the neighbours.

I said no more. I thought it really was so. But it did seem to me, members of the jury, that she had done up her face with cosmetics, in spite of the fact that her brother had died only a month before. Still, even so, I said nothing about it. I just went off, without a word.

After this, members of the jury, an interval elapsed, during which my injuries had progressed, leaving me far behind. Then, one day, I was approached by an old hag. She had been sent by a woman—Eratosthenes' previous mistress, as I found out later. This woman, furious because he no longer came to see her as before, had been on the look-out until she had discovered the reason. The old crone, therefore, had come and was lying in wait for me near my house.

"Euphiletus," she said, "please don't think that my approaching you is in any way due to a wish to interfere. The fact is, the man who is wronging you and your wife is an enemy of ours. Now if you catch the woman who does your shopping and works for you, and put her through an examination, you will discover all. The culprit," she added, "is Eratosthenes from Oea. Your wife is not the only one he has seduced—there are plenty of others. It's his profession."

With these words, members of the jury, she went off.

At once I was overwhelmed. Everything rushed into my mind, and I was filled with suspicion. I reflected how I had been locked into the bedroom. I remembered how on that night the middle and outer doors had creaked, a thing that had never happened before; and how I had had the idea that my wife's face was rouged. All these things rushed into my mind, and I was filled with suspicion.

I went back home, and told the servant to come with me to market. I took her instead to the house of one of my friends; and there I informed her that I had discovered all that was going on in my house.

"As for you," I said, "two courses are open to you: either to be flogged and sent to the tread-mill, and never be released from a life of utter misery; or to confess the whole truth and suffer no punishment, but win pardon from me for your wrong-doing. Tell me no lies. Speak the whole truth."

At first she tried denial, and told me that I could do as I pleased—she knew nothing. But when I named Eratosthenes to her face, and said that he was the man who had been visiting my wife, she was dumbfounded, thinking that I had found out everything exactly. And then at last, falling at my feet and exacting a promise from me that no harm should be done to her, she denounced the villain. She described how he had first approached her after the funeral, and then how in the end she had passed the message on, and in course of time my wife had been over-persuaded. She explained the way in which he had contrived to get into the house, and how when I was in the country my wife had gone to a religious service with this man's mother, and everything else that had happened. She recounted it all exactly.

When she had told all, I said:

"See to it that nobody gets to know of this; otherwise the promise I made you will not hold good. And furthermore, I expect you to show me this actually happening. I have no use for words. I want the *fact* to be exhibited, if it really is so."

She agreed to do this.

Four or five days then elapsed, as I shall prove to you by important evidence. But before I do so, I wish to narrate the events of the last day.

I had a friend and relative named Sôstratus. He was coming home from the country after sunset when I met him. I knew that as he had got back so late, he would not find any of his own people at home; so I asked him to dine with me. We went home to my place, and going upstairs to the upper storey, we had dinner there. When he felt restored, he went off; and I went to bed.

Then, members of the jury, Eratosthenes made his entry; and the maid wakened me and told me that he was in the house.

I told her to watch the door; and going down-stairs, I slipped out noiselessly.

I went to the houses of one man after another. Some I found at home; others, I was told, were out of town. So collecting as many as I could of those who were there, I went back. We procured torches from the shop near by, and entered my house. The door had been left open by arrangement with the maid.

We forced the bedroom door. The first of us to enter saw him still lying beside my wife. Those who followed saw him standing naked on the bed.

I knocked him down, members of the jury, with one blow. I then twisted his hands behind his back and tied them. And then I asked him why he was committing this crime against me, of breaking into my house.

He answered that he admitted his guilt; but he begged and besought me not to kill him—to accept a money-payment instead.

But I replied:

"It is not I who shall be killing you, but the law of the State, which you, in transgressing, have valued less highly than your own pleasures. You have preferred to commit this great crime against my wife and my children, rather than to obey the law and be of decent behaviour."

Thus, members of the jury, this man met the fate which the laws prescribe for wrong-doers of his kind.

The Arguments

Eratosthenes was not seized in the street and carried off, nor had he taken refuge at the altar, as the prosecution alleges. The facts do not admit of it: he was struck in the bedroom, he fell at once, and I bound his hands behind his back. There were so many present that he could not possibly escape through their midst, since he had neither steel nor wood nor any other weapon with which he could have defended himself against all those who had entered the room.

No, members of the jury: you know as well as I do how wrongdoers will not admit that their adversaries are speaking the truth, and attempt by lies and trickery of other kinds to excite the anger of the hearers against those whose acts are in accordance with Justice.

(To the Clerk of the Court):

Read the Law.

(The Law of Solon is read, that an adulterer may be put to death by the man who catches him.)

He made no denial, members of the jury. He admitted his guilt, and begged and implored that he should not be put to death, offering to pay compensation. But I would not accept his estimate. I preferred to accord a higher authority to the law of the State, and I took that satisfaction which you, because you thought it the most just, have decreed for those who commit such offences.

Witnesses to the preceding, kindly step up.

(The witnesses come to the front of the Court, and the Clerk reads their depositions. When the Clerk has finished reading, and the witnesses have agreed that the depositions are correct, the defendant again addresses the Clerk):

Now please read this further law from the pillar of the Court of the Areopagus:

(The Clerk reads another version of Solon's law, as recorded on the pillar of the Areopagus Court.)

You hear, members of the jury, how it is expressly decreed by the Court of the Areopagus itself, which both traditionally and in your own day has been granted the right to try cases of murder, that no person shall be found guilty of murder who catches an adulterer with his wife and inflicts this punishment. The Lawgiver was so strongly convinced of the justice of these provisions in the case of married women, that he applied them also to concubines, who are of less importance. Yet obviously, if he had known of any greater punishment than this for cases where married women are concerned, he would have provided it. But in fact, as it was impossible for him to invent any more severe penalty for corruption of wives, he decided to provide the same punishment as in the case of concubines.

(To the Clerk of the Court):

Please read me this Law also.

(The Clerk reads out further clauses from Solon's laws on rape.)

You hear, members of the jury, how the Lawgiver ordains that if anyone debauch [morally corrupt] by force a free man or boy, the fine shall be double that decreed in the case of a slave. If anyone debauch a woman—in which case it is *permitted* to kill him—he shall be liable to the same fine. Thus, members of the jury, the Lawgiver [Solon] considered violators deserving of a lesser penalty than seducers: for the latter he provided the death-penalty; for the former, the doubled fine. His idea was that those who use force are loathed by the persons violated, whereas those who have got their way by persuasion corrupt women's minds, in such a way as to make other men's wives more attached to themselves than to their husbands, so that the whole house is in their power, and it is uncertain who is the children's father, the husband or the lover. These considerations caused the Lawgiver to affix death as the penalty for seduction. . . .

You have heard the witnesses, members of the jury. Now consider the case further in your own minds, inquiring whether there had ever existed between Eratosthenes and myself any other enmity but this. You will find none. He never brought any malicious charge against me, nor tried to secure my banishment, nor prosecuted me in any private suit. Neither had he knowledge of any crime of which I feared the revelation, so that I desired to kill him; nor by carrying out this act did I hope to gain money. So far from ever having had any dispute with him, or drunken brawl, or any other quarrel, I had never even set eyes on the man before that night. What possible object could I have had, therefore, in running so great a risk, except that I had suffered the greatest of all injuries at his hands? Again, would I myself have called in witnesses to my crime, when it was possible for me, if I desired to murder him without justification, to have had no confidants?

The Epilogue

It is my belief, members of the jury, that this punishment was inflicted not in my own interests, but in those of the whole community. Such villains, seeing the rewards which await their crimes, will be less ready to commit offences against others if they see that you too hold the same opinion of them. Otherwise it would be far better to wipe out the existing laws and make different ones, which will penalise those who keep guard over their own wives, and grant full immunity to those who criminally pursue them. This would be a far more just procedure than to set a trap for citizens by means of the laws, which urge the man who catches an adulterer to do with him whatever he will, and yet allow the injured party to undergo a trial far more perilous than that which faces the law-breaker who seduces other men's wives. Of this, I am an example—I, who now stand in danger of losing life, property, everything, because I have obeyed the laws of the State.

Selection 5

Democracy on the Local Level

Eli Sagan

Often overlooked in discussions of ancient Greek democracy are the nature and role of local political organizations. Eli Sagan, of New York's New School for Social Research, here explores politics in the demes (demoi), Athens's small community- or ward-like districts organized (or perhaps reorganized) during Cleisthenes' democratic reforms circa 508–507 B.C. Sagan suggests that the development of democratic practices in these local districts may have influenced, or at least aided in, the formation of larger, polis-wide democratic institutions in the early fifth century.

*T*he picture we get of Athenian democracy from Thucydides, Aristophanes, Xenophon, and their ilk is of a boisterous Assembly of 5,000 to 6,000 impetuous citizens voting on whether or not to go to war, execute generals, or commit genocide. The fourth-century orators (Desmosthenes, Aeschines) present a more stable and responsible picture but still one of central democracy by multitudes. The day-to-day government of the towns was a virtually unexplored area until this century. However, an extraordinary picture of town politics has been revealed, particularly since 1945, confirming . . . [that] the democratic spirit thrived in the demes of Attica. The central democratic government did not arise full grown from the lead of Zeus. It owed much to township democracy.

A Polis in Microcosm

There were 139 to 140 demes in Attica, some much larger or smaller than the average. The population of Athens varied significantly over the years, but estimates set the average number of citizens at about 30,000, giving an average deme membership of about 220. In the deme almost everyone knew everyone else on a face-to-face, daily-contact basis, a far different situation than in the city.

Each deme had its own full-participation, direct-action assembly open to every citizen. The percentage of the total citizen body attending was probably much higher than at the central Assembly in Athens, where the inhibition of walking twenty to twenty-five miles each way to attend, and the sense that 1 vote in 6,000 could not matter much, kept many from exercising their political rights. It is generally agreed that in the deme assembly each attendee had the right to vote on all issues, as in the New England town meetings. We do not know who was allowed to speak, nor for how long, but this information is also lacking for the national Assembly at Athens. We know a great deal about attendance at the national Assembly, about voting procedures and the chairmanship, but we don't know what kept discussions from getting out of hand. From the speeches that remain to us, it is clear that those with political power (Demosthenes, Cleon) could address the Assembly, but how the debate was limited we do not know. We know even less about the deme assemblies but those with superior wealth and more than usual personal force probably had greater influence, since this is true for almost all such institutions. That deme politics was a school of democracy, with all its strengths and faults, seems a more than reasonable assumption.

The activities of a deme were many and complex. [Historian David] Whitehead calls it "a *polis* in microcosm." First and foremost, citizenship in the city-state at large was determined at the deme level. A man reaching the age of political maturity was certified as a legitimate member of the *polis* in the deme of which his father had been a citizen. Family connections with particular demes were established at the time of Cleisthenes, in 508. Descendants of those original deme citizens remained politically attached to their demes, regardless of where they eventually lived; the citizenship of all sons of citizen fathers had to be attested to in the original deme of residence. Contested cases of citizenship were decided first under deme auspices.

The use of the deme name to identify a person, either in place of or with the patronymic, or father's name, grew with the emerging democratic spirit: So-and-so of Rhamnus, instead of So-and-so the son of. . . . Those with strong aristocratic connection continued to use the patronymic as an indication of high status.

Connecting deme and national politics, members of the Council (five hundred in all) were elected annually from the demes on a proportional basis. The deme of Eleusis sent eleven councillors each year; the largest deme, Acharnai, twenty-two; very small demes, like Pambotadai and Sybridai, alternated with each other, each electing one member of the Council every other year. This smacks of "representative democracy" in Athens, supposed to exemplify pure direct democracy. The problem is that our data fail us at this point. We have no indication whether those elected to the Council were given instructions at the deme level on how to vote. We do not know whether the councillors owed their election to their stand on certain issues. We cannot know, therefore, whether this was a case of representative government or merely a broad, democratic way of choosing a Council.

Every deme annually selected an executive officer, the *demarchos*. Evidence indicates that originally he was elected, but by the fourth century the demarch was selected by sortition, though we do not know how. It may have been by lot from a chosen group of people. It seems unlikely that the names of all men, rich and poor, literate and illiterate, capable and incapable, were thrown into the lottery. The question is unanswerable to date.

We do not know to what extent the demarch was responsible for religious and other festivities of the deme, but the amount of communal activity was remarkable. [As Whitehead writes] "The demes always provided a rich and varied religious diet for their members, and this is nowhere more evident than in the surviving portions of deme *fasti* or calendar of recurring festivals and sacrifices." The communal celebrations cost money and the performance of the calendar forced each deme to maintain a complex budgetary system. "The costs of cult—upkeep of temples and shrines, offering of regular sacrifices, celebration of recurrent festivals—surely represented . . . the major object of regular expenditure, and indeed the fundamental *raison d'être* [reason for being] of the budget as a whole."

The same kind of interpenetration of religion and political life—the "civil religion" if you will—pertained on the deme level as in the central polity of Athens. Many demes had local cults, involving permanent temple structures. Some were self-sufficient, but others were maintained by the deme government, which appointed priests or priestesses. The demarch might be in charge of cult money, collecting rent from leased sacred land. He might also attend to the maintenance of temples and their precincts. It was common practice for the demarch to play a significant role in offering sacrifices. In Eleusis and Myrrhinous, for instance, it was his responsibility to distribute the sacrificial meat. The burial of the unclaimed dead—those unattended by relatives or, in the case of slaves, masters—was, by law, the duty of the demarch.

The great theater of Athens, where the magnificent festival of Dionysus was celebrated, was not the only such structure in Attica. We know of seven and evidence indicates seven more demes that had their own theaters, host, among other festivals, to the rural Dionysia at which theatrical triumphs from the city were performed. It is a moving experience to sit today, looking at the sea, in the amiable theater at Thorikos, over twenty-five miles from Athens (a four- to six-hour walk), and ruminate on how rich and complex life was in the townships of ancient Attica. A democracy as powerful and enduring as Athens did not survive on city air alone.

The *demarchos* also had more mundane, secular tasks to perform. In many demes, he supervised the inscribing and erection of the stone stelai that recorded the decrees of the deme assembly. It is interesting that some demes dated their documents by reference to the incumbent demarch and not to the eponymous Archon [the official in charge of state festivals and family

matters] of the government of Athens, the accepted procedure of the national polity. Some demes used the name of a local priest or priestess, ignoring the central calendar. We have strong evidence that the theoric fund—state allowances, originally made to poorer citizens to enable them to attend the theater, later distributions from the central government to all citizens—was distributed on a deme-by-deme basis, probably by the *demarchos* himself. . . .

The annual budget of the township was a complex one; much of the deme's activity involving the collection and expenditure of funds. An office most often mentioned in the documents is that of *tamiai*, treasurers. Many demes owned land collectively and derived income by renting it out. A decree from the deme of Aixone states, "it is resolved to elect men who, with the demarch and the tamiai and the lessee of land from the deme, will sell to the highest bidder the rights to olive trees on it; and the names of the three men chosen are appended." The deme could also lend out—at interest—its own or temple funds over which it had some control. Ordinary expenditures would routinely be handled by town officials, but sometimes an extraordinary expenditure required a special appointment. A decree from Acharnai makes reference to "'elected men' who have reported what it will cost to build altars for Ares and Athena Areia."

Regardless of the time or form of government, human beings appear reluctant to pay their debts and force may be necessary to preserve the sacredness of a contract. In a speech written by Demosthenes, Euxitheus recollects his year as *demarchos* in Halimous and the enemies he made by insisting that rents and other monies due the deme be paid. The demarch was also called on to collect bad debts from individuals and enforce the obligations of citizens to the central state.

My family summers in a small township in New England, where the population increases a hundredfold in the summer, but where the year-round inhabitants number only about 700 with approximately 500 voters. Many of the permanent citizens are active in the political and economic life of the town: selectmen, assessors, building inspectors, garbage-dump supervisors, and members of the planning board, zoning board, board of health, school committee, finance committee. A hint of corruption appears every so often; factions form; money talks; lawsuits abound. But the direct democratic process reigns supreme. Many important decisions are made in the full-town meeting. An unusually large number of citizens make it their business to know what goes on in town. It is remarkable how much the demes of Attica, though dimly perceived, resonate with the knowledge and experience of this modern community.

Corruption and Accountability

The key to responsible democratic government is accountability. Without it, corruption reigns. The failure of a community to police its officers and to curb the normal amount of corruption and arrogance can only lead to degradation of a polity.... In its central government and on the deme level Athens spent an extraordinary amount of time and energy on holding officials accountable, usually at the end of their term of office. The health of the *polis* largely depended on this.....

Corruption and the fight against it were continuous on the deme level. It is amusing to observe that some demes developed a reputation for being amenable to the sale of what was not supposed to be purchasable: citizenship within the *polis*. They became the butt of the comic poets, just as our comedians could get a quick laugh by referring to the assumed political dishonesty of Jersey City or Cook County, Illinois. "Today a slave, tomorrow a Sounian" ran a joke of the second quarter of the fourth century. The deme of Potamos was equally infamous for its flexible civic virtue in regard to illegal citizenship as the comic poet Menander noted. In his court speech *Against Eubulides* Demosthenes details the corruption in the deme of Halimous. Two foreigners, Anaximenes and Nikostratos, were enrolled as Halimousioi illegally after paying bribes of five drachmas each to the conspirators. Despite this publicity, the deme maintained its easy approachability. Several years after Demosthenes' speech, an ex-slave and metic Agasikles was impeached for a successful fraudulent attempt to obtain full citizenship from the same deme.

Citizenship was not the only thing for sale. We have evidence that some of the townships, during the first half of the fourth century, "had begun . . . to 'sell' opportunities to hold sortitive city offices." [Whitehead] As a result the central government took away from the demes the privilege of filling those places, though they could still fill council seats. Some citizenship cases involved dirty politics. Euxitheus, who is the complainant in the case *Against Eubulides*, asserts that in Halimous, where he was a citizen, Eubulides and his father, the current demarch, conspired to remove Euxitheus from the citizenship roll, claiming that the written record had been lost. A vote of the deme assembly, held under oath but under questionable circumstances, excluded ten men, including Euxitheus, from citizenship. Euxitheus claimed that Eubulides initiated the action for revenge against him and that coconspirators were bribed to readmit the others expelled. The trial for which the speech was delivered took place at the Heliastic court in Athens, where, we assume, since the records do not tell us, Euxitheus' rights were restored to him.

When we contemplate the democracy of the central Athenian government, a direct polity with an Assembly of 6,000 citizens, some of them walking more than twenty miles to attend a session, juries of 1,000 or 2,000, offices filled by lottery, votes for war or peace taken in huge meetings more closely resembling an army than a voting body, we may reflect that this is "not us," that it is truly *ancient* society. The polity in the townships, on the other hand, has a familiar ring. The style of democratic participation and even the brand of petty and not-so-petty corruption echos our own experience.....

Local Pride and the Democratic Miracle

We have a single, unfortunately brief, reference in an ancient source to the feeling people had for

their demes. After the outbreak of the Peloponnesian War, Sparta invaded Attica. The city was
secure behind its walls, but the countryside was
wasted, and Pericles moved all the country folk
into the city, making it an island of refuge. The
uprooted were not happy with their displaced-
persons status, and Thucydides tells us "Deep
was their trouble and discontent at abandoning
their houses and the hereditary temples of the
ancient constitution, and at having to change
their habits of life and to bid farewell to *what
each regarded as his native city*." [italics added]

There is no political analysis from Aristotle or
anyone else on what action on the deme level
meant for the democratic spirit of the society.
We can now see enough, however, to postulate
that there may have been great similarities between ancient Athens and nineteenth-century
America as to the *meaning* of the township
democracy. If we resort to the comparative
method, [nineteenth-century French writer Alex-
is] de Tocqueville may teach us much about
Athens in his paean to township politics.

> The New Englander is attached to his town-
> ship because it is strong and independent; he
> has an interest in it because he shares in its
> management; he loves it because he has no
> reason to complain of his lot; he invests his
> ambition and his future in it; in the restricted
> sphere within his scope, he learns to rule so-
> ciety; he gets to know those formalities with-
> out which freedom can advance only through
> revolutions, and becoming imbued with their
> spirit, develops a taste for order, understands
> the harmony of the powers, and in the end ac-
> cumulates clear, practical ideas about the na-
> ture of his duties and the extent of his rights.

There is one passage in [*Orestes*, a work by
the Athenian playwright] Euripides that gives a
picture of a sturdy, right-thinking, democratic
yeoman which resembles the laconic, upright,
steady New Englander of the last century. How
much does the practice of township democracy
contribute to these characteristics?

> *But at last*
> *someone stood up to take the other side.*

> *Nothing much to look at, but a real man;*
> *not the sort one sees loafing in the market*
> *or public places, ma'am, but a small farmer,*
> *part of that class on which our country depends;*
> *an honest, decent, and god-fearing man,*
> *and anxious, in the name of common sense,*
> *to say his bit.*

It seems unlikely that our yeoman learned this
commitment to the democratic spirit—the right
and *the obligation* to say his bit for the just decision—only through the central government in
Athens. Political and social action in the deme
may have more to do with the spirit of society
than we have imagined.

Some tantalizing questions arise about the relationship of political action and ambition on the
township and the central-government level. Did
an ambitious, rising politician learn his political
ropes in deme politics? Was success at the township level the avenue to political recognition in
the central government (as some of our successful politicos proceed up the ladder from county
to state to Washington)? We cannot know but the
answer appears to be negative. It seems that the
central government in the city and political life
in the 139 to 140 demes occurred on two different levels with little interaction between the two,
especially among the political leaders. We know
the names of forty demarchs, but only two certainly held office in the central government. Of
the 250 citizens known to have held the office of
general in the fifth and fourth centuries, not one
was active in the demes. And of the 157 known
proposers of laws or decrees in the central Assembly between 403 and 322 only 3 or 4 can be
proven to have participated in deme politics.

Central political life apparently operated independently of township politics, with no need to
draw its rising stars therefrom. This may represent a social and economic hierarchical pattern.
The rich and those of noble houses would tend to
concentrate their efforts in the city. Their sons
and nephews would provide the fresh new political talent. In the demes, the local nobility and rich
peasants probably held dominant positions, but
the middling and lower-class citizens no doubt

had their say, as in New England townships.

A more important question, because its answer would shed light on the origins of democracy, is that of the historical development of the deme democracy. Cleisthenes put the final configuration on the distribution of demes, but he did not create the demes, many of which, like Eleusis, must have descended from small city-states or villages that merged at some point in the dark past to form the *polis* of Athens. What was local political life like at the time of Solon and of the tyranny of the Pisistratidai [the mid-sixth century B.C.]? It is possible that, though the central government became a tyranny, democracy still flourished in the townships. It is even possible that local democracy waxed and developed during the tyranny of Pisistratus and this evolution prepared the way for the central democratic reforms of Cleisthenes in 508 after the fall of the tyrants. We are asking, but cannot know, how much, if at all, the development of local democracy contributed to the establishment of democratic forms in the central government.

Must a healthy democratic state originate on the local level? What would a comparative study of England and Germany, for instance, reveal? The former led the modern world in democratic action; the latter encountered formidable difficulties in establishing and maintaining a free society. How much did differences in township life in the eighteenth century contribute to these two different developments? . . . For ancient Athens, the answers may never come; only the central state is visible to us before the fifth century. We have the obligation, however, to look at the modern world, to inquire of the multitude of states that have struggled for democratic forms and failed, how much this failure results from the fact that democracy is almost impossible to impose from above. The "miracle" of Athenian democracy may have had its genesis in the lowly, almost invisible, demes.

Selection 6

An Athenian Complains About Democracy's Drawbacks

The Old Oligarch

As early as the first century B.C., about three centuries after the death of the Athenian historian Xenophon, his corpus of surviving writings contained a short document titled Constitution of the Athenians. *However, modern scholars have determined that he did not write it. (Besides the fact that it is much more repetitive and awkwardly worded than anything Xenophon wrote, it is now believed to have been written in the 440s B.C., over a decade before he was born. How it came to be attributed to him remains unclear.)*

The real author, whose identity is still unknown, has been called the "pseudo- (false-) Xenophon," but is more commonly known as the "Old Oligarch." This name derives from the obvious fact that he disapproves of Athens's democratic institutions and would rather see the state revert to the kind of oligarchic rule it once had. The compliments he pays the democracy seem designed to emphasize that its creators and supporters have done a commendable and thorough job of appealing to the masses of common people; and thereby they have made democratic institutions very well entrenched and all the more difficult to get rid of. The Old Oligarch's main gripe, which he repeats in one context after another, is that democracy sacrifices the needs and rights of the "better," "cleverer" classes in favor of those of the "baser," "ignorant" commoners. On the one hand, the document corroborates what scholars have long known from historical descriptions of Pericles' battles with his political opponents; namely that some Athenians felt that the city's democracy was too liberal and radical. On the other hand, because of the author's undisguised elitist contempt for non-aristocrats and people of modest means, to modern observers the document seems to confirm democracy's strengths rather than its weaknesses. Ironically, this is the exact opposite of what he had intended.

*n*ow, as for the constitution of the Athenians, and the type or manner of constitution which they have chosen, I praise it not, in so far as the very choice involves the welfare of the baser folk as opposed to that of the better class. I repeat, I withhold my praise so far; but, given the fact that this is the type agreed upon, I propose to show that they set about its preservation in the right way; and that

Excerpted from *Athens in the Age of Pericles*, by Charles Alexander Robinson. Copyright © 1959 by the University of Oklahoma Press. Reprinted by permission of the University of Oklahoma Press.

those other transactions in connection with it, which are looked upon as blunders by the rest of the Hellenic world, are the reverse.

The Baser Versus the Better Folk

In the first place, I maintain, it is only just that the poorer classes and the common people of Athens should be better off than the men of birth and wealth, seeing that it is the people who man the fleet, and have brought the city her power. The steersman, the boatswain, the lieutenant, the look-out-man at the prow, the shipwright—these are the people who supply the city with power far rather than her heavy infantry and men of birth and quality. This being the case, it seems only just that offices of state should be thrown open to every one both in the ballot and the show of hands, and that the right of speech should belong to any one who likes, without restriction. For, observe, there are many of these offices which, according as they are in good or in bad hands, are a source of safety or of danger to the People, and in these the People prudently abstains from sharing; as, for instance, it does not think it incumbent on itself to share in the functions of the general or of the commander of cavalry. The commons [i.e., common people] recognizes the fact that in foregoing the personal exercise of these offices, and leaving them to the control of the more powerful citizens, it secures the balance of advantage to itself. It is only those departments of government which bring pay and assist the private estate that the People cares to keep in its own hands.

In the next place, in regard to what some people are puzzled to explain—the fact that everywhere greater consideration is shown to the base, to poor people and to common folk, than to persons of good quality—so far from being a matter of surprise, this, as can be shown, is the keystone of the preservation of the democracy. It is these poor people, this common folk, this worse element, whose prosperity, combined with the growth of their numbers, enhances the democracy. Whereas, a shifting of fortune to the advantage of the wealthy and the better classes implies the establishment on the part of the commons of a strong power in opposition to itself. In fact, all the world over, the cream of society is in opposition to the democracy. Naturally, since the smallest amount of intemperance and injustice, together with the highest scrupulousness in the pursuit of excellence, is to be found in the ranks of the better class, while within the ranks of the People will be found the greatest amount of ignorance, disorderliness, rascality—poverty acting as a stronger incentive to base conduct, not to speak of lack of education and ignorance, traceable to the lack of means which afflicts the average of mankind.

The objection may be raised that it was a mistake to allow the universal right of speech and a seat in council. These should have been reserved for the cleverest, the flower of the community. But here, again, it will be found that they are acting with wise deliberation in granting to even the baser sort the right of speech, for supposing only the better people might speak, or sit in council, blessings would fall to the lot of those like themselves, but to the commons the reverse of blessings. Whereas now, anyone who likes, any base fellow, may get up and discover something to the advantage of himself and his equals. It may be retorted, "And what sort of advantage either for himself or for the People can such a fellow be expected to hit upon?" The answer to which is, that in their judgment the ignorance and the baseness of this fellow, together with his good will, are worth a great deal more to them than your superior person's virtue and wisdom, coupled with animosity. What it comes to, therefore, is that a state founded upon such institutions will not be the best state; but, given a democracy, these are the right means to secure its preservation. The People, it must be borne in mind, does not demand that the city should be well governed and itself a slave. It desires to be free and to be master. As to bad legislation it does not concern itself about that. In fact, what you believe to be bad legislation is the very source of the People's strength and freedom. But if you seek for good legislation, in the first place

you will see the cleverest members of the community laying down the laws for the rest. And in the next place, the better class will curb and chastise the lower orders; the better class will deliberate in behalf of the state, and not suffer crack-brained fellows to sit in council, or to speak or vote in the assemblies. No doubt but under the weight of such blessings the People will in a very short time be reduced to slavery.

Punishing the Rich and Shifting the Blame

Another point is the extraordinary amount of license granted to slaves and resident aliens at Athens, where a blow [delivered to a slave] is illegal, and a slave will not step aside to let you pass him in the street. I will explain the reason of this peculiar custom. Supposing it were legal for a slave to be beaten by a free citizen, or for a resident alien or freedman to be beaten by a citizen, it would frequently happen that an Athenian might be mistaken for a slave or an alien and receive a beating; since the Athenian People is not better clothed than the slave or alien, nor in personal appearance is there any superiority. Or if the fact itself that slaves in Athens are allowed to indulge in luxury, and indeed in some cases to live magnificently, be found astonishing, this too, it can be shown, is done of set purpose. Where you have a naval power dependent upon wealth we must perforce be slaves to our slaves, in order that we may get in our slave-rents, and let the real slave go free. Where you have wealthy slaves it ceases to be advantageous that my slave should stand in awe of you.

The common people put a stop to citizens devoting their time to athletics and to the cultivation of music, disbelieving in the beauty of such training, and recognizing the fact that these are things the cultivation of which is beyond its power. On the same principle, in the case of the choregia [sponsorship of plays], the management of athletics, and the command of ships, the fact is recognized that it is the rich man who trains the chorus, and the People for whom the chorus is trained; it is the rich man who is naval commander or superintendent of athletics, and the People that profits by their labors. In fact, what the People looks upon as its right is to pocket the money. To sing and run and dance and man the vessels is well enough, but only in order that the People may be the gainer, while the rich are made poorer. And so in the courts of justice, justice is not more an object of concern to the jurymen than what touches personal advantage.

To speak next of the allies, and in reference to the point that emissaries from Athens come out, and, according to common opinion, calumniate and vent their hatred upon the better sort of people, this is done on the principle that the ruler cannot help being hated by those whom he rules; but that if wealth and respectability are to wield power in the subject cities the empire of the Athenian People has but a short lease of existence. This explains why the better people are punished with infamy, robbed of their money, driven from their homes, and put to death, while the baser sort are promoted to honor. On the other hand, the better Athenians protect the better class in the allied cities [those in Athens's maritime empire]. And why? Because they recognize that it is to the interest of their own class at all times to protect the best element in the cities. It may be urged that if it comes to strength and power the real strength of Athens lies in the capacity of her allies to contribute their money quota. But to the democratic mind it appears a higher advantage still for the individual Athenian to get hold of the wealth of the allies, leaving them only enough to live upon and to cultivate their estates, but powerless to harbor treacherous designs. . . .

Further, states oligarchically governed are forced to ratify their alliances and solemn oaths, and if they fail to abide by their contracts, the offence, by whomsoever committed, lies nominally at the door of the oligarchs who entered upon the contract. But in the case of engagements entered into by a democracy it is open to the People to throw the blame on the single individual who spoke in favor of some measure, or put it to the vote, and to maintain to the rest of the world, "I was not present, nor do I approve of the terms of the agreement." Inquiries are made in a full meeting of the People, and should any of these things be disapproved of, they can at once discover countless excuses to avoid doing whatever they do not wish. And if any mischief should spring out of any resolutions which the People has passed in council, the People can readily shift the blame from its own shoulders. "A handful of oligarchs acting against the interests of the People have ruined us." But if any good result ensue, they, the People, at once take the credit of that to themselves.

I repeat that my position concerning the constitution of the Athenians is this: the type of constitution is not to my taste, but given that a democratic form of government has been agreed upon, they do seem to me to go the right way to preserve the democracy by the adoption of the particular type which I have set forth.

Selection 7

An Athenian Extols the Benefits of Democracy

Pericles

In 430 B.C., at the end of the first year of the Peloponnesian War, Athens's citizenry met to hear Pericles eulogize the city's first batch of war dead. In his magnificent speech, he called on his countrymen to honor not only the recently fallen soldiers, but also their ancestors for creating a democratic state well worth dying for. One by one, he enumerated the qualities of the state and its people that democracy had fostered or enhanced. These qualities had made Athens great, he said, an example and "education" for the rest of Greece. Finally, he predicted that the greatness of democratic Athens would prove timeless and inspire awe in future generations. And indeed, in the fullness of time this profound prophecy came to pass. (Note: Pericles' speech survives in a paraphrased version in Thucydides' chronicle of the Peloponnesian War.)

I shall begin by speaking about our ancestors, since it is only right and proper on such an occasion to pay them the honour of recalling what they did. In this land of ours there have always been the same people living from generation to generation up till now, and they, by their courage and their virtues, have

Excerpted from *The History of the Peloponnesian War*, by Thucydides, translated by Rex Warner (Penguin Classics, 1954; revised edition, 1972). Translation copyright © Rex Warner, 1954. Reprinted by permission of Penguin Books Ltd.

handed it on to us, a free country. They certainly deserve our praise. Even more so do our fathers deserve it. For to the inheritance they had received they added all the empire we have now, and it was not without blood and toil that they handed it down to us of the present generation. And then we ourselves, assembled here today, who are mostly in the prime of life, have, in most directions, added to the power of our empire and have organized our State in such a way that it is perfectly well able to look after itself both in peace and in war.

I have no wish to make a long speech on subjects familiar to you all: so I shall say nothing about the warlike deeds by which we acquired our power or the battles in which we or our fathers gallantly resisted our enemies, Greek or foreign. What I want to do is, in the first place, to discuss the spirit in which we faced our trials and also our constitution and the way of life which has made us great. After that I shall speak in praise of the dead, believing that this kind of speech is not inappropriate to the present occasion, and that this whole assembly, of citizens and foreigners, may listen to it with advantage.

Power in the Hands of All the People

Let me say that our system of government does not copy the institutions of our neighbours. It is

Pericles delivers his renowned funeral oration, in which he correctly predicted that future ages would wonder at Athens's achievements.

more the case of our being a model to others, than of our imitating anyone else. Our constitution is called a democracy because power is in the hands not of a minority but of the whole people. When it is a question of settling private disputes, everyone is equal before the law; when it is a question of putting one person before another in positions of public responsibility, what counts is not membership of a particular class, but the actual ability which the man possesses. No one, so long as he has it in him to be of service to the state, is kept in political obscurity because of poverty. And, just as our political life is free and open, so is our day-to-day life in our relations with each other. We do not get into a state with our next-door neighbour if he enjoys himself in his own way, nor do we give him the kind of black looks which, though they do no real harm, still do hurt people's feelings. We are free and tolerant in our private lives; but in public affairs we keep to the law. This is because it commands our deep respect.

We give our obedience to those whom we put in positions of authority, and we obey the laws themselves, especially those which are for the protection of the oppressed, and those unwritten laws which it is an acknowledged shame to break. . . .

Then the greatness of our city brings it about that all the good things from all over the world flow in to us, so that to us it seems just as natural to enjoy foreign goods as our own local products.

Then there is a great difference between us and our opponents, in our attitude towards military security. Here are some examples: Our city is open to the world, and we have no periodical deportations in order to prevent people observing or finding out secrets which might be of military advantage to the enemy. This is because we rely, not on secret weapons, but on our own real courage and loyalty. There is a difference, too, in our educational systems. The Spartans, from their earliest boyhood, are submitted to the most laborious training in courage; we pass our lives without all these restrictions, and yet are just as ready to face the same dangers as they are. Here is a proof of this: When the Spartans invade our land, they do not come by themselves, but bring all their allies with them; whereas we, when we launch an attack abroad, do the job by ourselves, and, though fighting on foreign soil, do not often fail to defeat opponents who are fighting for their own hearths and homes. As a matter of fact none of our enemies has ever yet been confronted with our total strength, because we have to divide our attention between our navy and the many missions on which our troops are sent on land. Yet, if our enemies engage a detachment of our forces and defeat it, they give themselves credit for having thrown back our entire army; or, if they lose, they claim that they were beaten by us in full strength. . . . This is one point in which, I think, our city deserves to be admired. There are also others:

Our love of what is beautiful does not lead to extravagance; our love of the things of the mind does not make us soft. We regard wealth as something to be properly used, rather than as something to boast about. As for poverty, no one need be ashamed to admit it: the real shame is in not taking practical measures to escape from it. Here each individual is interested not only in his own affairs but in the affairs of the state as well: even those who are mostly occupied with their own business are extremely well-informed on general politics—this is a peculiarity of ours: we do not say that a man who takes no interest in politics is a man who minds his own business; we say that he has no business here at all. We Athenians, in our own persons, take our decisions on policy or submit them to proper discussions: for we do not think that there is an incompatibility between words and deeds; the worst thing is to rush into action before the consequences have been properly debated. And this is another point where we differ from other people. We are capable at the same time of taking risks and of estimating them beforehand. Others are brave out of ignorance; and, when they stop to think, they begin to fear. But the man who can most truly be accounted brave is he who best knows the meaning of what is sweet in life and of what is terrible, and then goes out undeterred to meet what is to come.

The Mighty Monuments of Empire

Again, in questions of general good feeling there is a great contrast between us and most other people. We make friends by doing good to others, not by receiving good from them. This makes our friendship all the more reliable, since we want to keep alive the gratitude of those who are in our debt by showing continued goodwill to them: whereas the feelings of one who owes us something lack the same enthusiasm, since he knows that, when he repays our kindness, it will be more like paying back a debt than giving something spontaneously. We are unique in this. When we do kindnesses to others, we do not do them out of any calculations of profit or loss: we do them without afterthought, relying on our free liberality. Taking everything together then, I declare that our city is an education to Greece, and I declare that in my opinion each single one of our citizens, in all the manifold aspects of life, is able to show himself the rightful lord and owner of his own person, and do this, moreover, with exceptional grace and exceptional versatility. And to show that this is no empty boasting for the present occasion, but real tangible fact, you have only to consider the power which our city possesses and which has been won by those very qualities which I have mentioned. Athens, alone of the states we know, comes to her testing time in a greatness that surpasses what was imagined of her. In her case, and in her case alone, no invading enemy is ashamed at being defeated, and no subject can complain of being governed by people unfit for their responsibilities. Mighty indeed are the marks and monuments of our empire which we have left. Future ages will wonder at us, as the present age wonders at us now. We do not need the praises of a Homer, or of anyone else whose words may delight us for the moment, but whose estimation of facts will fall short of what is really true. For our adventurous spirit has forced an entry into every sea and into every land; and everywhere we have left behind us everlasting memorials of good done to our friends or suffering inflicted on our enemies.

This, then, is the kind of city for which these men, who could not bear the thought of losing her, nobly fought and nobly died. It is only natural that every one of us who survive them should be willing to undergo hardships in her service.

The Family and Social Roles and Institutions

Chapter 8

Introduction

Besides religion, the major social institutions in ancient Greece included the family and other kinship groups associated with it, education, and slavery. As is still true today, the family (*oikos*) was society's smallest and most basic social unit. However the *oikos* included not only the members of the "nuclear" family common in modern Western society (parents and children), but also grandparents and other relatives, all property, including land and slaves, and the tombs of ancestors. The *oikos* was "the basis of one's security and social identity," says scholar N.R.E. Fisher in *Social Values in Classical Athens*, "and the main source of one's social and religious obligations and relationships."

The first such obligation was to make sure that the family did not die out. Since Athenian society was patriarchal (dominated by men) and patrilineal (family leadership and property passed from father to son), it was essential for the head of the family to produce a son, or if necessary to adopt one. When the head of the household had more than one son, the sons eventually established their own *oikoi,* which remained linked to the parent family through strong kinship ties.

This was the basis of the next largest social group, the clan, or *genos.* The average clan consisted of a group of families that claimed descent from a common ancestor. In the affairs of the extended family, the heads of the *gene* were usually more influential than the heads of individual households. It was common, for example, for a clan leader to arrange marriages for his various sons, daughters, nephews, nieces, cousins, and grandchildren, who might come from many different *oikoi.*

The next units in the widening social pyramid were the phratry and the tribe, both highly extended kinship groups. The typical phratry, or "blood brotherhood," consisted of about thirty clans, comprising about as many people as lived in an Attic village or a neighborhood in Athens's urban center. And indeed, many such villages and neighborhoods were dominated by one or two phratries. Often the focus of social gatherings and religious rituals, a phratry was similar to a modern religious congregation, except that the members of a phratry were related to one another. The tribe, or *phyle,* the largest single social unit, commonly consisted of three phratries.

Within the framework of the family and other kinship groups rested certain traditional roles. The father (or in the case of his death his surviving brother or son) earned the living and made and enforced the rules; the wife (or mother or daughter) ran the household and looked after the children and slaves; and the slaves did most of the menial labor. In the Classic Age, women's lives were most often highly restricted and "respectable" middle- and upper-class women rarely ventured outside the house. By contrast, poorer women often had no choice but to work or do the family shopping and so might be seen more often in the streets. The lot of women improved somewhat (and in a few areas markedly so) in Hellenistic times, when a number of women enjoyed more social mobility and economic clout.

However, the position of children and slaves remained always inferior and subordinate. Philosophers like Aristotle defended and reinforced this state of affairs. On the one hand, they claimed that children were mentally and morally inferior to adults. "Of all animals," Plato wrote,

the boy is the most unmanageable, insomuch as his fountain of reason is not yet regulated. He is the most . . . insubordinate of animals. And that is why he must be bound with many bridles. . . . Any freeman who comes in his way may punish him . . . if he does anything wrong; and he who . . . does not inflict upon him the punishment he deserves shall incur the greatest disgrace. (*Laws,* trans. Benjamin Jowett)

At the same time, the philosophers held that natural law ordained that some people should be slaves to others.

The most important pursuit of childhood (for males at least) was education. Young girls were trained at home by their mothers in weaving and other household arts, although some vase paintings suggest that at least a few girls learned to read. In Athens, young boys began attending school at about age seven. The boys attended private schools in which they learned reading and writing and eventually the verses of Homer and other poets. Boys also learned to sing and play the lyre (from teachers known as *kitharistes*) and physical education (athletic events and dancing). Some fathers had a slave or freedman (freed slave), called a *paidagogos,* escort their sons to school and supervise their behavior there.

By the late fifth century B.C., higher education in Athens could be obtained for a fee from roving teachers called sophists; they raised the ire of traditionalists, who disapproved of their use of rhetoric (the art of persuasive speaking) to make both sides in an argument seem equally valid. Beginning in the century that followed, a few young men also studied at formal university-like schools, such as Plato's Academy (where Aristotle studied under Plato).

On the whole, education in many other Greek poleis, at least the larger and more progressive ones, was presumably similar to that in Athens (although conclusive evidence for most is lacking). The major exception appears to have been Sparta. In this Peloponnesian polis, known for its tough and efficient soldiers, not only the education of boys and young men, but the whole social system was built around the *agoge,* a rigid and often harsh system of military institutions and practices. First, Spartan elders (ephors) examined all male infants; those considered too weak were condemned to exposure (*ektesis*),

being left outside on a mountainside to die.

Those Spartan boys who made it past this initial test faced years of difficult, relentless learning and training, which was subsidized and supervised by the state rather than privately run. Here, the emphasis was not on reading, writing, and other literary skills, as at Athens and other states, but on the ability to endure hardships and become a strong, fearsome soldier. (There was some instruction in dancing, patriotic songs, and poetry, but these subjects took a decided back seat to military training.) In *Ancient Greece* Sarah Pomeroy and her colleagues give the following summary of what young Spartan males endured:

> To toughen their feet, they went barefoot, and they often went naked as well. When they were 12, their hair was cut short. They . . . were each allocated only one cloak yearly to wear in all kinds of weather. . . . The boys slept in groups on rough mats that they had made themselves. To develop cunning and self-reliance, they were encouraged to supplement their food rations by stealing. Whipping awaited anyone who revealed his lack of skill by getting caught. . . . From the ages of 14 to 20 the *ephebes* (young men) performed their preliminary military service. . . . Between the ages of 20 and 30 they were permitted to marry but had to continue to live with their army groups until the age of 30. . . . Though the harsh treatment of those perceived as cowards discouraged failure, the system did not work on everyone, and some boys failed to develop as expected. . . . Life was wretched for boys who were unable to cope with the rigors of military life. . . . They were called "tremblers". . . [and] obliged to wear cloaks with colored patches and to shave only half their beards. Mocked and humiliated in public, they were despised even by their own kinsmen, whom they were believed to have dishonored.

Spartan women also received an education at state expense, the only women in all of Greece known to have enjoyed this privilege. The nature of this learning is unclear but seems to have emphasized physical fitness (probably to help facilitate having many baby boys to replenish the army ranks); some girls may also have learned reading and other skills. Spartan women managed the household, as other Greek women did. But unlike other Greek women, they were not so confined in the home and could even own land. Aristotle, who complained that female Spartans had entirely too much freedom, reported that in his day they owned two-fifths of the land in Sparta. Considering the wide gulf between the social systems of Sparta and Athens, it is not surprising that the two states distrusted each other and were almost always at odds.

Among the original sources for Greek social life and institutions are a number of major treatises by fourth-century B.C. scholars, orators, and philosophers. These include Plato's dialogues (including his *Republic,* which casts light on the society of his time while envisioning a utopian society); the *Politics* and numerous other works by Aristotle; Xenophon's *Oeconomicus, Symposium,* and description of Sparta's social-political system; Isocrates' *Against the Sophists;* and works by Demosthenes, Theophrastus, and others. Sections of many extant classical Greek plays, especially the comedies of Aristophanes and Menander, allude to various social roles, customs, and institutions, as do the works of Herodotus, Thucydides, Diodorus, and other historians. Especially helpful, as usual, is Plutarch, who provides much valuable information about social life in his *Moralia* (*Moral Essays*), as well as his more familiar biographies. (The *Moralia* and his lives of Lycurgus, Cleomenes, and Agis, for example, are major sources of information about Spartan society.)

Selection 1

The Family: Its Members and Structure

W.K. Lacey

The family (oikos) was the basic unit of ancient Greek society. As noted scholar W.K. Lacey explains in this excerpt from his book-length study of classical Greek families, every aspect of community life, from citizenship and land ownership to religion, law, and social relationships, was to some degree built around the family and its needs and tradi- *tions. Lacey discusses these needs and traditions, while identifying the various members of the family and describing their respective roles, rights, and duties to one another and to the state.*

*a*ristotle began his work on Politics by stating that it is necessary to break down communities unto their smallest parts in order to understand the different characteristics of each. The smallest unit of the state is the family, the *oikos,* which is comprised of the three elements, the male, the female and the servant. The servant is defined as that which comes under the rule of another to obtain security; to [the farmer and poet] Hesiod, says Aristotle, this is the plough-ox (the servant of the poor), to political man (i.e. man of the *polis* or city-state) it is his slave. Male and female have a natural instinct to procreate themselves successors, says Aristotle, an instinct common also to all living creatures, and this introduces into the family a fourth element, the children.

A further essential element in the *oikos* was its means of subsistence; that Aristotle agreed that this was so is proved both by his statement that the members of an *oikos* are those who feed together, and by his subsequent remark that some call the obtaining and management of possessions the whole of household management. An *oikos* that could not support its members was, to the Greeks, no *oikos* at all.

An *oikos* without children was also not fully an *oikos*. Every Greek family looked backwards and forwards all the time. It looked backwards to its supposed first founder, and shared a religious worship with others with a similar belief; it also looked forwards to its own continuance, and to the preservation for as many future generations as possible of the cult of the family which the living members practised in the interest of the dead. The son of a house was therefore (in the best period of the Greek *polis*) under a strong obligation to marry and procreate an heir for the *oikos* in order to keep the *oikos* alive, and he himself both felt that obligation and, so far as we can see, acted upon it. The other requirement, however, that the *oikos* must be able to support its members, was also not forgotten. No Greek would have accepted the idea that every man has a right to marry and beget children if he wants to; marriage was for those who could afford it. Consequently, when a father's *oikos* was not large enough to provide a livelihood for several sons, some of them would leave it to seek their fortune away from home, enlisting as mercenary soldiers or as sailors, or establishing for themselves a new home as members of a colony when their own (or another) city called for volunteers.

An *oikos* was therefore a living organism which required to be renewed every generation to remain alive; it supported its living members' needs for food, and its deceased members' needs for the performance of cult rituals. A childless *oikos* was visibly dying—no man's life-span is all that long—so we may well appreciate the joy with which a child, and especially the first-born son of a family, was received.

The Individual and the *Oikos*

The relationship between individual and *oikos* exhibits considerable variations in the different ages and communities of the Greek world. In the Homeric world [the Dark and Archaic Ages] the individual hero (the only class for which we can say anything significant) was wholly responsible for it, and wholly in command of it, in so far as his power enabled him to be. In the *polis* communities of old Greece, the ancestors' land, and their tombs, which were the evidence of their ancient ownership and the object of the family's cult, provided strong unifying bonds within which the individual lived as a member of his *oikos*. Here too every *oikos* was itself a member of one or more larger groups, the clan (*genos*), the phratry, the tribe (*phyle*), the deme, whose members were fully members of the *polis*. Membership of these larger units was secured through membership of an *oikos*, so that the individual was never free of the units to which he belonged. In the colonial settlements, especially in Ionia and Sicily, however, the individuals who went out were freed from their ancestral *oikoi* by their emigration, and however successful the attempts to foster the spirit of unity and civic-consciousness may have been, the web of family tradition and *oikos*-membership was never so strong [in such settlements], since it was not rooted in *oikoi* (lands and houses in particular) and cults which the families felt had been vested in them by right of descent from some mythical, heroic founder.

This lack of cohesiveness in society had two principal results: it made these city-states much less exclusive than those of the motherland, but it also made them politically much less stable, with the result that they came frequently under the rule of tyrants. . . . Regular features of these and similar tyrannies were transplantations of whole populations, expulsions of old citizens, and enrolments of new ones, who were often non-Greek mercenaries, and redistributions of lands, houses and other property which formed an essential part of the *oikoi* of the civic communities of old Greece. Settling down into a homogeneous and reasonably cohesive society always remained, therefore, a task whose accomplishment tended to elude them. . . .

The tightly-knit corporation of the city and the unity of the family were closely interdependent, and were the basis and the product of the greatest age of the city-states. Therefore (to return to Aristotle) the study of the family is the study of two relationships: the *oikos* as an independent unit, especially the relationships of the free members, and the *oikos* as a constituent unit of the larger units out of which the city-state, or *polis*, was composed.

The *Oikos* and Its *Kyrios*

Greek society was (and is) patriarchal: the master of the *oikos* was the head of the family, its *kyrios*, as its governor, governing the slaves as master, the children as a sort of king because of their affection for him and his greater age, his wife like a political leader, differing from normal political leadership only in that this relationship does not involve change of leaders, as self-governing states normally change their leaders, but the husband is always the head of the family.

Headship of a family, *kyrieia*, and the status of *kyrios*, is an important feature of all Greek family life. In Homer it is taken for granted, in democratic Athens it is defined by the lawyers in certain aspects; even in Sparta it is implied in the status of full citizen, *homoios*, of Spartiate rank, above thirty years old, who alone was allowed a share in political life, and to set up house and live with his wife.

Only a man could be *kyrios* of a family. This is not to say that women could not look after a man's property when he was absent on military service or abroad, whether for trade or state service. Obviously they could; we can quote as examples Penelope in Homer, who managed at least to prevent Odysseus' house being taken over during his absence. . . . Nor does it mean that when a man died his widow did not look after his possessions until his heir was established, or until the guardian to his children, if they were minors, had taken charge of their property. For such periods women were said to be in control of possessions, *kyria*, but these periods have the essential quality of the temporary, pending the return of the actual *kyrios*, or the establishment of a new one in possession of the property. Such a position does not convey the right to make decisions regarding the disposal of property, especially disposal of the essential element in the property of the *oikos*, its *kleros* or allotment of land. Before the Hellenistic Age, only at Sparta do we hear that the women had the power in their husbands' absence to dispose even of real-estate. . . .

As the *polis* never ceased to rest on an agrarian basis, so the family's lands always remained of fundamental importance. It is commonly supposed, both from what traces of early systems of land-holding survive, and from the practices adopted when colonial settlements were made, that land—arable land, that is—was initially divided into *kleroi* which were allotted to the various heads of the kinship-groups of the settlers. . . . Whether or not such *kleroi* were or had ever been equal is unknown; it was a principle of democratic propagandists that they should be equal, but it is much more likely in an early aristocratic age that the division was unequal. Aristotle declares that 'in many cities it was not even lawful to sell the *kleros* which had first been allocated'; clearly this rule was designed to prevent undue accumulations of land by individuals. . . .

In *polis*-communities only a citizen of the *polis* was entitled to own land in the domain of the *polis*; the only exceptions to this rule were a few specially privileged aliens who were explicitly granted this right. . . . It therefore follows that minors always had to have a guardian if their father had died before they were of age to assume the *kyrieia* of their property, and that every woman had to have a *kyrios* all her life. Frequently—before her marriage, while she was married, and when she had been widowed but had an adult son—a woman's *kyrios*, and the *kyrios* of the property which had been set aside for her maintenance, were the same person, but when a widow was left with an infant son, his guardian was custodian of the property, since it was held in trust for her son, who would ultimately inherit it, while control of her personal status (*i.e.,* whether she was remarried or not) reverted to her own family's *kyrios*.

Women did not in the fullest sense own landed property at any stage in Greek history (except in Sparta), but there were occasions on which a man had only female children; when this disaster occurred, the Greeks' interest in maintaining the continuity of the families was so great that they arranged for such girls to be married to their nearest agnatic relative (a father's brother—*i.e.,* an uncle—if possible) in order to re-establish the family in the next generation. Such girls were in Athens given the name of *epikleros*, a word sometimes mistranslated as 'heiress'. Heiress and *epikleros* do not correspond, since an *epikleros* never owned 'her' property, in that it was not within her power to dispose of it except through a child; conversely, however, it could not legally be alienated from her as long as she lived. The arrangements for the marriage of an *epikleros* were therefore of the deepest concern both to her relatives and to the state, and at Athens at least and at Gortyn in Crete and elsewhere we can prove the existence of elaborate legal provisions to ensure that a lack of sons did not cause a family to become extinct, and that the future of girls without brothers was not simply left in the hands of their father's kinsmen.

Men without natural heirs could also adopt sons. We do not know how early this was possible in Athens, but there are traces in Homer, so that it may have been admissible from the earliest times. An adopted son, however, was also not wholly *kyrios* of the *oikos* he inherited, since he could dispose of it only by begetting a son, and not by will. There is also some evidence that at

Athens an *oikos* did not become registered in the name of an adopted son until he had begotten a son and registered him in the *oikos* of his adoptive father, thus providing two generations of successors to the *oikos*.

Women's inability to own property and to dispose of it also had the result that households consisting of one woman or a group of women and no men were virtually unknown; households therefore often included elderly women who were either in the master's *kyrieia* or put themselves under his protection. That this was very common is certain, and it was further encouraged by law, since in Athens at least children were legally obliged to maintain their parents in their old age. The fact that her husband's mother was living in the house cannot always have been welcome to a young wife, and Plato at least thought that it was undesirable, but it did help to prevent one of the great social problems of modern times—the loneliness of the old.

The *Oikos* in the Clans, Religion, and Law

Beyond the *oikos* to which a man belonged lay the wider kinship-groups, the *genos* (in the plural *genē*), or clan, and the phratry, or brotherhood. What the origins of these groups were we do not know; members of the same *genos* traced their pedigree back to a common ancestor, but it was freely acknowledged even in ancient times that the members of the same *genos* (*gennētai*) were not necessarily kinsmen, and that outsiders had been admitted.

It was perhaps as a result of this that there were almost social class-divisions amongst the *gennētai*. There were noble houses who provided in settled conditions the political leadership of the *genē*, and who held the hereditary priesthoods, and probably considered themselves to be the genuine lineal descendants of the ancestor-hero; they were known in Athens as *Eupatridae*. . . .

An *oikos* also belonged to a phratry. The origins of phratries are also obscure; they appear once in Homer as unmistakably military units.

. . . Phratries have been explained as local self-defence groups, or as the oldest unions of a number of families, but the military group, the 'blood-brotherhood', seems to be a more satisfactory explanation. . . . *Phrater* is a form of the Indo-European word for brother by blood, one born of the same parents (as in Latin, for example, the word is *frater*), yet nowhere in the Greek dialects is *phrater* used in this sense; it is always used to mean a member of the same phratry, and different words were adopted for brothers by birth. In society the evidence comes from the rules about exacting penalties from homicides. . . . In Athenian law the duty of avenging a violent death (or securing purification) was laid on the *oikeioi*, the members of the *oikos*, failing whom it fell not on the *genos*, but on the phratry, despite the fact that the phratry played no part in determining the succession-rights to the *oikos* of the deceased. In historical times, however, in Athens the phratries had become associated with the *oikoi* and the (locally determined) demes, whose rolls comprised the citizen-registers. . . .

All Greek social groups were also religious unions, whose management lay in the hands of the head. In Athens, the cult of the *oikos* itself with its *kleros* of land, the local group of which the *kyrios* of the *oikos* was head, was that of Zeus Herkeios, and many aspects of family religion are associated with Zeus. . . .

There is no doubt that membership of associations which owned these cults was proof of genuine Athenian citizenship—Socrates for example was proud of belonging to them. On the other hand, it appears not to have been necessary to have a Zeus Phratrios, a fact which militates against the assertion that phratry-membership was necessary for full citizenship.

The common gods of all the *kleroi*, *genē* and phratries, however, were a feature of democratic societies: Aristotle in the *Politics* mentions the amalgamation of private cults as one means of making a *polis* more democratic, but the families provided the origin of the state cults, and their cults continued to exist beside the state cults. The state had its own shrines of Zeus Herkeios (in the forecourt of the Mycenaean palace on the Acropolis, under the sacred olive tree) . . . and it is clear . . . that shrines of Zeus Herkeios were to be found in individuals' courtyards. . . .

As in all primitive societies, the most important kinship-groups among the Greeks of the age of settlement were those of the most important families, whether their 'importance' lay in their military leadership or priestly functions, or (most usually) both. Communities remained essentially tribes until the interrelationships of the kinship-groups, and of the individuals within these groups, came under the regulation of a law which was not just the monopoly of the noble, priestly families, but was known—or at least knowable—to all. This common knowledge of the law was the foundation of the city-state; the dawn of Greek history in the seventh and sixth centuries BC is therefore the age of the law-givers, so-called: part of their work was political—the establishment of a constitution containing a political structure—but most of it was concerned with establishing a code of laws; that is, they tried to establish rules by which the claims of different families in their relations with other families could be regulated. These claims, like those regulated by all codes of laws, fell broadly into the two classes of property-claims and claims concerning persons. Property-claims include especially those concerning land and houses, real-estate, and the rights to acquire, own and transmit it to successors—claims, in fact, which affect primarily the family's means of subsistence. In claims concerning persons the family was concerned both because injury to persons might affect a family's ability to maintain itself (for example through the disabling of the breadwinner) and because its religious ties and honour might be affected, as for example in cases of murder, rape or seduction. Honour in this last sense certainly had religious undertones, but it had also practical, political consequences as well, since in city-states (Sparta excepted of course) a child not born in wedlock had no kinship rights or claims over property belonging to the family of its mother. The bastard, and the state of bastardy, are important subjects in Greek law, and so, in consequence, are rape, seduction and virginity. The vital importance of the family for the state is well illustrated by the fact that all legal cases affecting the family in Athens were classed as public and not private; that is to say, it was open to any person, not merely the injured party, to take the initiative in prosecuting a suspected offender, and the prosecutor was in most cases also exempt from the statutory penalties which were normally attached to a prosecutor who failed to convince one-fifth of the jury. In a state which lacked a public prosecutor it is hard to think of more active steps which could have been taken to ensure that the family was fully protected in its rights by the law.

The *Oikos* and Its *Xenoi*

An *oikos* also included outsiders who had a right to come in, or whom the master of the house accepted into the *oikos*. These may be said to have been of two classes, those who came into the *oikos* in order to serve it, and by their labour to help to sustain it, and those who came in only on a temporary basis, as visitors. The former comprised principally the slaves and the animals which worked on the farm and the beasts of burden, the latter the *xenos* (plural *xenoi*), a word which is the Greek for both host and guest. The act of sharing house and board made the slave fully a member of the family; in fourth-century Athens, and probably from very much earlier, a slave was made a member of the family ceremonially by having nuts and dried fruits scattered over him by the mistress of the house when he came into it, a ritual which also greeted the bride when she first entered her husband's house. Slaves were initiated into the cult of the family's gods, and normally took part in the family's religious festivals. The plough-ox too was regarded as an intrinsic part of the family, as Aristotle says. This statement cannot be taken too literally, nor as having that meaning in the fullest sense, but that there was a very strong bond of fellow-feeling between a peasant and his oxen is attested by the fact that the Athenians would never sacrifice a ploughing-ox, nor one which had been harnessed (*sc.* to a cart)—it was regarded as 'a farm-worker and a partner in the labours of men', and it is shown on the stage in the touching scene in Aristophanes' *Acharnians* when the peasant comes onto the stage to recover his lost plough-oxen.

The *xenoi* were a part of the Greek idea of the family, and fair treatment of (and respect for) their *xenoi* was among the 'un-written commandments' upon which the ethical standards of the *polis* were based, 'that you should honour the gods, your parents and your *xenoi*'. *Xenoi* were hereditary among the noble families, accustomed to travel away from their homesteads for trade, interest or even piracy and war, and to a lesser extent the same was doubtless true of humbler folk; it was considered scandalous to injure one with whom you had shared in table and salt, while to give shelter to a traveller from another city was a virtuous act, often (in myth) bringing reward to the doer, while to turn away a suppliant at the altar was an act that called down divine vengeance.

Selection 2

The Lives of Classical Greek Women

Eva Cantarella

Throughout most of ancient Greek history, women had no political rights and most lived highly restricted lives controlled by their fathers and husbands (although some evidence suggests that they were somewhat less restricted before and after the Classic Age). This was at least the case for most middle- and upper-class women. Many women from poorer households worked (in the fields, as laundresses, and so on) and therefore had more mobility outside the home, and also shared more household responsibilities and authority with their husbands. Most of the substantial surviving evidence, however, relates to wives and mothers from households of some means; and this is what historians must draw on in painting a general picture of Greek women's lives. Eva Cantarella, a distinguished member of the faculty at Italy's University of Parma, here summarizes the status and rights of (or lack thereof) and restrictions placed on many Athenian women in the Classic Age. As she points out, once a woman left her father's house, the only social roles open to her were wife/mother, concubine (a husband's mistress, often live-in), hetaira *(a highly educated courtesan), or common prostitute.*

Marriage, prescribed by the first laws as the center of female life, remained the focal point of the *polis'* defense and the reinforcement of its economic, social, and political security. We will therefore use marriage as the primary point of reference as we try to follow the life of Greek women in the classical period. We begin with their birth, assuming they escaped the fate of being "exposed."

Exposure (*ektesis*) of newborns was a practice allowed by law and accepted without difficulty by the social conscience. Despite Aristotle's proposal to ban it, it was still practiced in the Hellenistic period.

Posidippus (a New Comedy playwright who lived between the third and second centuries B.C.) observed that "a poor man brings up a son, but even a rich man exposes a daughter." Indeed, girls were exposed much more frequently than boys were. Girls, after all, were an expensive and unremunerative investment, not only because of the cost of supporting them as children but also because of the expense of providing them with dowries. When a girl married, the family lost her just when she was ready to fulfill her biological function of reproduction. A daughter, in other words, did not "repay" what was spent on her if she married, and if she did not marry, she continued to be a burden on the family economy.

That is why (as among all peoples who practice infanticide), girls are the most common victims. In Greece, the custom was to put the infant into a crockery pot (called *chutra*, whence the verb *chutrizein*, "to put into a pot") and abandon it on a roadside usually not far from home. The exposure of infants in Greece had the socially, and thus politically, useful function of regulating the number of the members of groups and, above all, regulating the ratio between the sexes in such a way that there would not be an excess of women who would remain unmarried. The need to marry off all eligible women gave rise to the activities of the matchmaker, a figure widely found at Athens. Even more significant was a practice that was forbidden by a law attributed to Solon, but which, one infers from the very fact that it had to be forbidden, was widespread, and perhaps never completely wiped out, that is, the drastic but effective practice of a father's selling as a slave the daughter he risked seeing turn into a "white-haired virgin."

Engagement, Marriage, and Divorce

Brought up at home by slaves if their family was well-off (in Greece, when economic conditions allowed, women did not raise their very young children themselves), girls did not stay long in their father's house. Betrothed at sometimes extremely young ages (in one famous case, at five), they waited for marriage (at age fourteen or fifteen; the man would usually be about thirty) without receiving any education, either at a school or at home. If the family was well-to-do, they learned only women's work. Their pastimes, which were certainly not aimed at intellectual development, consisted of such toys and games as dolls, hoops, balls, tops, and swings.

The ceremonies that accompanied marriage, or at least the most sumptuous, lasted for three days. On the first day (*proaulia emera*), the father of the bride made offerings to the gods, the bride sacrificed her toys to Artemis [the goddess thought to protect women in childbirth], and the bride and groom bathed in water drawn from a spring or sacred river. The second day (*gamos*), the father of the bride held the nuptial banquet, at the end of which the bride was taken to the husband's house. The third and last day (*epaulia emera*), the bride, in the new house, received the wedding gifts.

Yet none of these ceremonies constituted a legally valid wedding. Beginning in the age of Solon, the event that made a marriage valid sometimes took place many years before the actual wedding. This was the *eggue*, or "promise." It was the *eggue*, in other words, and not the wedding ceremonies, that under the law made the difference between simple cohabitation (*suneinai*) and a true marriage (*sunoikein*). The *eggue* did not signify the beginning of the marriage (which was only when the couple began to live together) nor was it legally binding (in the sense that it obliged a couple to go through with the marriage); the promise was a "condition of legitimacy" of the marriage itself, and consequently the legitimacy of the offspring depended upon it.

At Athens, the existence of a blood relationship between the bride and groom was not an obstacle to marriage, not even when the relationship was quite close, such as uncle and niece or even brother and sister. There was, however, one distinction: although marriage between consanguineous brother and sister (with the same father) was allowed, marriage between uterine siblings (same mother) was prohibited.

The logic of this rule, according to some, can be explained by history. The ban on marriage between uterine siblings would be the remnant of a matrilineal system in which the children of the same mother could not marry because they were members of the same family, while there would have been no obstacle to marriage between consanguineous siblings, because they belonged to different families. But I believe there is another explanation. When a girl married her father's son, the dowry stayed in the family. The financial advantage was, perhaps, the true reason for allowing the breaking of a taboo that could cause all the anguish dramatized in the story of Oedipus [who unwittingly marries his own mother].

The rule and its logic are not very informative. Far from being a personal relationship inspired by an emotional choice, marriage usually took place for social and financial reasons, for example, the necessity of keeping the family fortune intact (in marriage between siblings) or the desire to establish or maintain bonds with other families (in marriage with outsiders). In any case, it was the family that was valued, not the bride.

Closed off in the internal part of the house to which the men did not have access, the married woman had no chance to meet persons other than members of the household. In Athens, men even did the shopping. Wives (and, for that matter, mothers, sisters, and daughters) could not attend banquets. . . . Only the women of the poorest classes moved among men with a certain freedom, going to the market to sell bread or vegetables, or, in the demes of Attica, working the land and taking the animals to market. But for the women of the wealthiest classes, there was only one chance to meet outsiders. Certain ceremonies (public festivals and funerals) were the exceptions. The women were allowed to leave the house for these gatherings and young Athenians took advantage of them to arrange clandestine meetings. For example, Eratosthenes met the wife of Euphiletus [the defendant in a famous murder case] at her mother-in-law's funeral; he became her lover and was killed by her husband.

The empty life of the Greek woman of the upper or middle class, deprived of interests or gratifications, was not even repaid by the knowledge that her relationship with her husband was exclusive. This was not necessarily because he had a relationship with another man, though that happened often enough; quite frequently he had relationships with other women that were socially and even, in part, legally recognized.

The Athenian system provided for three pos-

This drawing of the women's quarters of an Athenian home shows the women of the house engaging in routine household duties while a slave loads a laundry basket.

sible ways to dissolve a marriage (apart from death, of course). The first, and certainly the most frequent, was repudiation by the husband, called *apopempsis* or *ekpempsis*. A husband could repudiate a wife at will, without justification. The only difficulty for him was that he had to give back the dowry. Another legal method was abandonment of the "conjugal roof" by the wife, called *apoleipsis*. Even when there were serious reasons, it was sometimes physically blocked by husbands . . . who stopped their wives from going to the archon to request the needed authorization. Finally, by the so-called paternal *apheresis*, the wife's father, for reasons of his own (usually to do with family property), might interrupt his daughter's marriage.

At Athens what marked a woman's definitive passage into the husband's family was not the marriage but the birth of the first child. Only when she gave her husband a child, did a woman enter irreversibly into the new *oikos*. Her father could end the marriage at any time up till that moment. In special cases, the woman's nearest relative had the right to do so too. The reasons for this will become clear as we look at the condition of the so-called heiress (*epikleros*), the woman who found herself the only descendant of a family without males (*oikos eremos*).

In Athenian law of succession, males enjoyed a more privileged position than females, given that the existence of male offspring and descendants excluded female offspring and descendants from succession. The only privilege the woman (called, in this case, *epiproikos*) had a right to was a dowry, a complex of goods which, at marriage, became the property of her husband. She received the dowry in lieu of sharing the family inheritance.

Sometimes, of course, there were no male descendants. Although a woman, by herself, could not inherit the patrimony (*kleros*), she was nevertheless the means by which it was transmitted to the family's males. The concern on the part of her relatives that she not marry an outsider thus becomes obvious, as does the reason why she might be made to marry her nearest relative. In fact, the hand of an heiress was often sought by several aspirants, each claiming to be her nearest relative. The solution proposed by Athenian law was that the woman be "awarded" by a special judgment to the litigant who proved that he was her nearest relative. . . .

There were only two provisions . . . that worked in women's favor. The first law, attributed to Solon, concerned the fate of a poor heiress. With no parents to give her a dowry, the heiress without money risked not finding a husband. And so grave was this danger for a woman that Solon maintained that the nearest relative, if he did not wish to marry her himself, should be obliged to provide her with a dowry. Another law, also attributed to Solon, concerned the wealthy *epikleros* (married, therefore, for her money), who risked being ignored by her husband after she had produced an heir. The husband was obliged by law to have sexual relations with her at least three times a month. This is how Athenian legislation responded to the needs of the *epikleros*. It assured her a husband, necessary for a dignified place in society, and guaranteed her a "ration" of sexual intercourse with a man she had not chosen.

Wife, Concubine, and Hetaera

Demosthenes says that the Athenian man could have three women: the wife (*damar* or *gyne*) "for the production of legitimate children"; the concubine (*pallake*) "for the care of the body," that is, for regular sexual relations; and the hetaera for pleasure. This division of three female functions (in itself extremely revealing of the male–female relationship) poses certain problems that arise from the difficulty of defining the boundaries of the role of concubine. In daily life, a man's relationship with a *pallake* (who was sometimes received into the conjugal home) was substantially identical to his relationship with his wife. It was subject to legal regulation which, on the one hand, required the concubine to be faithful, as though she were a wife . . . and, on the other hand, granted certain rights of succession to her children, though not the same as those accorded legitimate children.

This does not mean that Athenian law authorized bigamy. . . . It means that the law granted a certain status to children born out of wedlock. In other words, the law recognized and regulated the existence of concubines and established a precise hierarchy among the different stable relationships that a man might have.

The third woman in the Athenian's life, though not bound to him in a stable relationship, was more than just a casual companion. She was the hetaera. More educated than a woman destined for marriage, and intended "professionally" to accompany men where wives and concubines could not go, the hetaera was a sort of remedy provided by a society of men which, having segregated its women, still considered that the company of some of them could enliven their social activities, meetings among friends, and discussions which their wives, even if they had been allowed to take part, would not have been able to sustain. Enter the hetaera, who was paid for a relationship (including sex) which was neither exclusive nor merely occasional, as indicated by her name, which means "companion." This relationship was meant to be somehow gratifying for the man, even on the intellectual level, and was thus completely different from men's relationships with either wives or prostitutes.

Most prostitutes were of servile status, though sometimes freeborn girls who had been exposed as infants were rescued for the purpose of putting them to work as prostitutes. The profession of the prostitute (*porne*) was not forbidden by law but was the object of strong social disapproval. The law of the city concerned itself with prostitutes for only two reasons: to set a ceiling on their prices and to collect a tax on their income.

Very different from that of a common prostitute, however, was the status of the woman who sold herself not in the streets or brothels but in the temples. As in the East, sacred prostitutes (*hierodoulai*) existed in Greece too. After having been consecrated to the divinity, they sold themselves to passers-by, giving the proceeds to the temple to which they were attached.

The legal status of the *hierodoulai* is uncertain. Some maintain that they were slaves of the temple, others that consecration to the goddess made them free, though obliged to live in the temple and serve there as prostitutes. The question is irrelevant. Prostitutes in either case, the *hierodoulai* were privileged, not only for the greater protection and wealth than enjoyed by other prostitutes, but for their "sacredness," which placed them above ordinary *pornai* on the social scale. . . .

The possible social positions of women were as wives, concubines, hetaerae, or prostitutes. Which position a woman held was determined exclusively by her relationship, whether stable or occasional, with a man. And given that this relationship was constructed for the purpose of responding to male needs, the condition of woman could not have been other than it was: personally unsatisfying, nearly nonexistent socially, and regulated by a series of laws that established her inferiority and permanent subordination to a man.

Then, of course, there was women's total exclusion from any form of political participation. . . . At Athens only those who were able to defend the city in arms could be citizens (*politai*), with a sole exception. The man who committed a particularly serious crime was considered unworthy to defend the city and was declared *atimos*. Deprived of political rights, the *atimos* became not a second-class citizen but a citizen of the very lowest rank. As such he was called *astos*, to indicate his belonging to the city (*aste*) in the physical sense but his exclusion from the citizen organization. Women were called by the same term—*aste*. Until the age of Pericles, a woman's status as *aste* had no effect on the transmission of citizenship to her children. Her supposed "potential" citizenship, that is, as transmitter of it, was utterly nonexistent for centuries. Until 451–50 B.C., the year in which Pericles established that a mother had to be *aste* for her children to be *politai*, the only way for citizenship to be transmitted . . . was for the father to be Athenian.

They were iron rules, then, that the *polis* imposed on women, shutting them out and depriving them of practically every chance of freedom: rules that both considered them inferior and made them so.

Selection 3

Wedding Arrangements and Ceremonies

Sue Blundell

Nearly every major aspect of the early stages of marriage in ancient Greece was different than is common in Western societies today. As a rule, women married younger than they do today, brides played little or no part in the wedding preparations; and romantic love between the bride and groom was a rare occurrence. The following informative tract by Sue Blundell, of Birkbeck College in the University of London, examines the various steps that led to the wedding day, as well as the wedding ceremony itself.

*M*ost Athenian girls were probably married for the first time between the ages of fourteen and eighteen. Evidence is limited, but where it exists it indicates that the younger end of the age range may have been favoured: for example, the new bride in a treatise by Xenophon is aged fourteen (*Oeconomicus* 7.5); and the sister of the orator Demosthenes was to be married at fifteen (Demosthenes 27.4 and 29.43). Most men on the other hand probably married at about the age of thirty. The reasons for early female marriage are not at all clear. Since in normal circumstances most Greeks were probably keen to limit the

size of their families, it seems unlikely that the motive was the maximising of breeding potential. Perhaps in general it was the perceived need to control women that was responsible for the practice. The belief that women became wild and ungovernable at puberty, the stress on premarital virginity and the fact that the girl's father (who would have been over thirty when she was born) might die in the near future, may all have made early marriage appear desirable. A husband might also prefer a young wife whom he could educate to run the household in the way that he wished (see Xenophon, *Oeconomicus* 7.4–5). The disparity in the ages of husband and wife would have helped to foster the notion of the intellectual inferiority of the female, and would have reinforced patriarchal attitudes towards women.

A woman was legally incapable of arranging her own marriage, and this responsibility normally fell to her guardian. There is scarcely any evidence to show that the woman was allowed any say in the matter. When, for example, a speaker in a lawsuit (Isaeus 2.3–9) is describing how Menecles, a close friend of his deceased father, asked him and his brother for the hand of their sister, he remarks: 'Knowing that our father would have given her to no-one with greater pleasure, we gave her to him in marriage.' Later on, when Menecles decided that in view of their childlessness his wife ought to be given the chance to remarry, her brothers did at least insist that she herself would have to agree to the divorce; but again there is no suggestion that she played any part in choosing her new husband.

There was, however, a good chance that the bride would at least have had some social contact with her new husband. In Classical Athens, close-kin marriages were relatively common. . . . Marriages between first cousins appear to have been particularly favoured; but marriages between uncles and nieces, second cousins, cousins once removed and siblings with the same father but a different mother are also known. This tendency to look for partners within the extended family probably sprang from a traditional loyalty towards one's kinsfolk. If a man had a favour to confer in the form of a daughter and her dowry, he would prefer that it went to someone to whom he was closely related, and whose character and material resources would be well known to him.

If the extended family did not yield a suitable candidate, then a woman might be offered to a close friend of her father, as in the case of Menecles' wife. But marriages to men who were unconnected with the family also occurred, and sometimes a bride may not even have set eyes on her husband-to-be prior to their betrothal. The amount of wealth available on both sides would certainly have been an important consideration when these unions were arranged, at least among the upper classes. . . .

Love and Marriage?

Was love never a motive for marriage in Classical Athens? [Noted scholar K.J.] Dover has suggested that, while love-matches may not have existed among the upper classes, lower down the social scale segregation of the sexes would not have been feasible, and young people must sometimes have met and had love affairs. However, there is only one reference to such an affair in Classical literature, in a comedy of Aristophanes in which a young woman waits to welcome her lover while her mother is out (*Women in the Assembly* 920). There is no suggestion at all that this is expected to lead to marriage.

Certainly, there seems to have been little room for the concept of love in the official ideology surrounding marital relations in Athens. When the speaker in the [court] case against Neaera [a non-Athenian *hetaira* who was prosecuted for living with an Athenian citizen as his wife] tells his listeners 'We have courtesans (*hetaerae*) for pleasure, concubines to take care of our day-to-day bodily needs, and wives to bear us legitimate children and to be the loyal guardians of our households' (Demosthenes 59.122), his object is to distinguish between the various types of sexual relationship which an Athenian male might enter into; but at the same time he gives voice to a strictly utilitarian view of the purpose of marriage, one with which he would presumably have expected his audience to sympathise. 'Love and marriage' is a scenario which is largely absent from the imaginative literature of the Classical period. Yet, in the early Hellenistic Age, the comic playwright Menander wrote plays in which young men fell in love and were anxious to marry the objects of their affection. This was undoubtedly new as a theme, and its appearance in the theatre is indicative of the growing acceptability of privatised aspirations. It is, on the other hand, hard to believe that the experience itself was an entirely novel one. However, the fact that Menander's plots focus on the removal of the seemingly insuperable social obstacles standing in the way of wedded bliss suggests that love and marriage may not have been viewed as natural partners. Whether in the Classical Age this had led to a great deal of frustration it is impossible to say: there is certainly no indication of this in the sources for the period.

The legal definition of marriage in Athens is unclear, but it seems likely . . . that [as Cynthia Patterson argues] it should 'be understood not as a simple legal event but as a composite process', involving a number of actions or events. One of these was certainly the procedure known as *engue*, which is often translated as betrothal. It consisted of a private verbal contract made between the bride's *kyrios* [legal male guardian] and the groom (or the groom's *kyrios*, if the groom himself was not yet of age). Proof of *engue* was vital if the legitimacy of one's children was ever called into question, so that it was advisable to perform it in front of witnesses. The agreement was probably sealed by the traditional formula, 'I hand over this woman to you for the ploughing of legitimate children' (Menander, frag. 720). . . . Normally the dowry would have been transferred at the *engue*, and its monetary value agreed upon. In most cases the cohabitation of the couple probably commenced shortly afterwards, but in some situations there might be a considerable interval: Demosthenes' sister, for example, was betrothed at the age of five when her father was on his deathbed (Demosthenes 28.15). *Engue* was not apparently a legally binding contract, since the groom could withdraw at any point prior to cohabitation, on condition that the dowry was repaid.

The Wedding Celebration

Apart from *engue*, the wedding celebration (*gamos*), cohabitation (*sunoikein*), and the production of children may all have been regarded as indicators of the existence of a marriage. None of the sources provides us with a complete description of the *gamos*, the set of rituals which accompanied the handing over (*ekdosis*, literally, 'giving out') of the bride to the groom: the account which follows has been pieced together from various visual and literary texts.

At some point prior to the ceremony, a sacrifice was performed by the bride's father, and it may have been at this stage in the proceedings that the bride cut off her hair, and removed and consecrated to a goddess such as Artemis or Athena the girdle which she had worn since puberty. Both these actions were symbolic of her imminent transfer to a new status. She was then given a ritual bath in water that had been drawn from a sacred spring and carried in a special vessel known as a *loutrophoros*: if a girl died unmarried, one of these pots was often buried with her, and was sometimes represented on her tombstone. The public part of the ceremony began with a wedding feast in the house of the bride's father. At nightfall, the partially veiled bride, the groom and the groom's best friend were carried to the couple's future home in a nuptial chariot drawn by mules, accompanied by a torchlit procession of friends and relatives singing nuptial hymns.

At their destination the bride was greeted by her mother-in-law, who was carrying torches, and was formally conducted to the hearth, the focal point of her new home. Meanwhile, bride and groom were showered with nuts and dried fruits, emblems of fertility and prosperity, and a boy crowned with a wreath of thorns and acorns circulated among the guests distributing bread from a basket shaped like a winnowing fan. The presence of this child, who had to have both parents still living, signified that the proper end of the couple's union was the birth of children; but at the same time the acorns, the bread and the words that he spoke—'I escaped the bad, I found the better'—were symbolic of a prehistoric transition from a raw to a domesticated diet, and were suggestive of the dual role played by agriculture and marriage in the progress from savagery to civilisation. The climax of the proceedings came when the bride was led by the groom towards the bridal chamber, while a wedding hymn was sung by the guests. It may have been at this point that she removed her veil with a ritual gesture. On the following day, which was called the *epaulia*, gifts were presented to the couple by the bride's father and other relatives; they were carried in procession to the house, and included many items—a wool-basket, pots, furniture, jewellery, fine garments, combs, perfume—which alluded either to the domestic role or to the sexual identity of the new wife.

These ceremonies emphasised the fundamental nature of the transition in which the bride was involved. One obvious motif was that of alienation: by being veiled, the bride was converted into a non-person in her old home so that she could be reborn as a married woman in the new one. There were also suggestions of a theme of abduction: at the start of the wedding procession the bride was lifted on to the chariot by the groom; and as she was led towards her new home, and again when she was conducted around the hearth, the groom held her by the wrist, a gesture indicating control and possession. . . .

Several writers have noted that many of the

rituals performed at weddings—such as the purification and adornment of the bride, the cutting of the hair, and the procession accompanied by song—were paralleled by ones that took place both at funerals and at sacrifices. The equation between marriage and death is also to be found in literature. It stands at the core of the story of the rape of Persephone, and is frequently encountered in tragedy: when, for example, Antigone goes to her grave, her lament includes the exclamation 'I shall be married to the lord of Acheron (river of the Underworld)', and 'Oh tomb, oh bridal-chamber' (Sophocles *Antigone* 816, 891). The identification of the bride as victim, or corpse, underlined not just the critical nature of the transformation, but also the themes of loss, sorrow and helplessness. Although in the course of the ceremony the bride was pronounced 'blessed' by the assembled company, the occasion was hardly viewed, in ritual terms, as 'the happiest day of her life'. Nor, in all likelihood, would she have experienced it as such. The idea of rebirth and renewal, which was a vital element in sacrifice, was present also in a marriage, but the bride herself may not have been particularly conscious of it.

A marriage did not bring about any change in the legal or political status of the bride: she merely passed from the control of one male to that of another. Nonetheless, symbolically, socially and emotionally, this was the most important transition which she would ever undergo. She was passing from childhood into adulthood, from virginity into wifehood, and from the *oikos* in which she had grown up to the one in which she was to spend the rest of her life. The occasion may also have involved her transference from one community to another, if . . . there were as many marriages between couples from different *demes* (local communities) as there were between those belonging to the same *deme*. It would not be surprising if the experience were a traumatic one, especially since it preceded the loss of her virginity to an older man who may have been almost a complete stranger to her. Sophocles, in a fragment from one of his plays, has probably captured her feelings very well:

> It is my belief that young women in their fathers' homes lead the sweetest lives of all. For ignorance always keeps children secure and happy. But when we reach womanhood and gain some understanding, we are thrust out and sold away from our ancestral gods and our parents. Some go to live with strangers, some with foreigners, some go to joyless homes, some to unfriendly ones. And all these things, once a single night has yoked us to our husbands, we are obliged to praise, and consider a happy outcome.

Selection 4

A Wife's Duties in Marriage

Xenophon

Xenophon composed his Oeconomicus *sometime in the early mid–fourth century* B.C. *while he was living on his estate at Scillus, near Olympia. Translated variously as* The Householder *and* The Management of an Estate, *the work purports to demonstrate the efficient way to run a country estate. As Plato frequently did, Xenophon chose for a format a dialogue between two characters, one of them the martyred philosopher Socrates, whom Xenophon had known well. Although the other speaker is a country gentleman named Ischomachus, that character is clearly a thinly disguised representation of Xenophon himself.*

One of the most fascinating and engaging sections of the work concerns Ischomachus's young wife, who, through his recollections, contributes some dialogue of her own. Their conversation reveals her age when they wed (fourteen) and much information about the expectations the husband has for her and their long-term relationship. Ischomachus/ Xenophon views marriage as a partnership ordained by the gods, and he sees it as his happy duty to teach his wife about life. He also provides a rationale for making a woman

Excerpted from Xenophon, *Memorabilia and Oeconomicus*, translated by E.C. Marchant (New York: Putnam, 1923).

the overseer of the home and a detailed list of the duties she is expected to perform.

'Pray where do you spend your time,' said I, 'and what do you do when you are not engaged in some such occupation? For I want very much to learn how you came to be called a gentleman, since you do not pass your time indoors, and your condition does not suggest that you do so.'

"Smiling at my question, 'How came you to be called a gentleman?', and apparently well pleased, Ischomachus answered: 'Well, Socrates . . . as you ask the question, I certainly do not pass my time indoors; for, you know, my wife is quite capable of looking after the house by herself.'

"'Ah, Ischomachus,' said I, 'that is just what I want to hear from you. Did you yourself train your wife to be of the right sort, or did she know her household duties when you received her from her parents?'

"'Why, what knowledge could she have had, Socrates, when I took her for my wife? She was not yet fifteen years old when she came to me, and up to that time she had lived in leading-strings, seeing, hearing and saying as little as possible. If when she came she knew no more than how, when given wool, to turn out a cloak, and had seen only how the spinning is given out to the maids, is not that as much as could be expected? For in control of her appetite, Socrates, she had been excellently trained; and this sort of training is, in my opinion, the most important to man and woman alike.'

Marriage a Partnership

"'But in other respects did you train your wife yourself, Ischomachus, so that she should be competent to perform her duties?'

"'Oh no, Socrates; not until I had first offered sacrifice and prayed that I might really teach, and she learn what was best for us both.'

"'Did not your wife join with you in these same sacrifices and prayers?'

"'Oh yes, earnestly promising before heaven to behave as she ought to do; and it was easy to see that she would not neglect the lessons I taught her.'

"'Pray tell me, Ischomachus, what was the first lesson you taught her, since I would sooner hear this from your lips than an account of the noblest athletic event or horse-race?'

"'Well, Socrates, as soon as I found her docile and sufficiently domesticated to carry on conversation, I questioned her to this effect:

"'"Tell me, dear, have you realised for what reason I took you and your parents gave you to me? For it is obvious to you, I am sure, that we should have had no difficulty in finding someone else to share our beds. But I for myself and your parents for you considered who was the best partner of home and children that we could get. My choice fell on you, and your parents, it appears, chose me as the best they could find. Now if God grants us children, we will then think out, how we shall best train them. For one of the blessings in which we shall share is the acquisition of the very best of allies and the very best of support in old age; but at present we share in this our home. For I am paying into the common stock all that I have, and you have put in all that you brought with you. And we are not to reckon up which of us has actually contributed the greater amount, but we should know of a surety that the one who proves the better partner makes the more valuable contribution."

"'My wife's answer was as follows, Socrates: "How can I possibly help you? What power have I? Nay, all depends on you. My duty, as my mother told me, is to be discreet."

"'"Yes, of course, dear," I said, "my father said the same to me. But discretion both in a man and a woman, means acting in such a manner that their possessions shall be in the best condition possible, and that as much as possible shall be added to them by fair and honourable means."

"'"And what do you see that I can possibly do to help in the improvement of our property?" asked my wife.

"'"Why," said I, "of course you must try to do as well as possible what the gods made you capable of doing and the law sanctions."

"'"And pray, what is that?" said she.

"'"Things of no small moment, I fancy," replied I, "unless, indeed, the tasks over which the queen bee in the hive presides are of small moment. For it seems to me, dear, that the gods with great discernment have coupled together male and female, as they are called, chiefly in order that they may form a perfect partnership in mutual service. For, in the first place, that the various species of living creatures may not fail, they are joined in wedlock for the production of children. Secondly, offspring to support them in old age is provided by this union, to human beings, at any rate. Thirdly, human beings live not in the open air, like beasts, but obviously need shelter.

Indoor and Outdoor Tasks

Nevertheless, those who mean to win store to fill the covered place, have need of someone to work at the open-air occupations; since ploughing, sowing, planting, and grazing are all such open-air employments; and these supply the needful food. Then again, as soon as this is stored in the covered place, then there is need of someone to keep it and to work at the things that must be done under cover. Cover is needed for the nursing of the infants; cover is needed for the making of the corn into bread, and likewise for the manufacture of clothes from the wool. And since both the indoor and the outdoor tasks demand labour and attention, God from the first adapted the woman's nature, I think, to the indoor and man's to the outdoor tasks and cares.

""""For he made the man's body and mind more capable of enduring cold and heat, and journeys and campaigns; and therefore imposed on him the outdoor tasks. To the woman, since he has made her body less capable of such endurance, I take it that God has assigned the indoor tasks. And knowing that he had created in the woman and had imposed on her the nourishment of the infants, he meted out to her a larger portion of affection for new-born babes than to the man. And since he imposed on the woman the protection of the stores also, knowing that for protection a fearful disposition is no disadvantage, God meted out a larger share of fear to the woman than to the man; and knowing that he who deals with the outdoor tasks will have to be their defender against any wrong-doer, he meted out to him again a larger share of courage. But because both must give and take, he granted to both impartially memory and attention; and so you could not distinguish whether the male or the female sex has the larger share of these. And God also gave to both impartially the power to practise due self-control, and gave authority to whichever is the better—whether it be the man or the woman—to win a larger portion of the good that comes from it. And just because both have not the same aptitudes, they have the more need of each other, and each member of the pair is the more useful to the other, the one being competent where the other is deficient.

""""Now since we know, dear, what duties have been assigned to each of us by God, we must endeavor, each of us, to do the duties allotted to us as well as possible. The law, moreover, approves of them, for it joins together man and woman. And as God has made them partners in their children, so the law appoints them partners in the home. And besides, the law declares those tasks to be honourable for each of them wherein God has made the one to excel the other. Thus, to the woman it is more honourable to stay indoors than to abide in the fields, but to the man it is unseemly rather to stay indoors than to attend to the work outside. If a man acts contrary to the nature God has given him, possibly his defiance is detected by the gods and he is punished for neglecting his own work, or meddling with

his wife's. I think that the queen bee is busy about just such other tasks appointed by God."

""""And pray," said she, "How do the queen bee's tasks resemble those that I have to do?"

""""How? she stays in the hive," I answered, "and does not suffer the bees to be idle; but those whose duty it is to work outside she sends forth to their work; and whatever each of them brings in, she knows and receives it, and keeps it till it is wanted. And when the time is come to use it, she portions out the just share to each. She likewise presides over the weaving of the combs in the hive, that they may be well and quickly woven, and cares for the brood of little ones, that it be duly reared up. And when the young bees have been duly reared and are fit for work, she sends them forth to found a colony, with a leader to guide the young adventurers."

""""Then shall I too have to do these things?" said my wife.

A Wife's Duties

""""Indeed you will," said I; "your duty will be to remain indoors and send out those servants whose work is outside, and superintend those who are to work indoors, and to receive the incomings, and distribute so much of them as must be spent, and watch over so much as is to be kept in store, and take care that the sum laid by for a year be not spent in a month. And when wool is brought to you, you must see that cloaks are made for those that want them. You must see too that the dry corn is in good condition for making food. One of the duties that fall to you, however, will perhaps seem rather thankless: you will have to see that any servant who is ill is cared for."

""""Oh no," cried my wife, "it will be delightful, assuming that those who are well cared for are going to feel grateful and be more loyal than before."

""""Why, my dear," cried I, delighted with her answer, "what makes the bees so devoted to their leader in the hive, that when she forsakes it, they all follow her, and not one thinks of staying behind? Is it not the result of some such thoughtful acts on her part?"

""""It would surprise me," answered my wife,

"if the leader's activities did not concern you more than me. For my care of the goods indoors and my management would look rather ridiculous, I fancy, if you did not see that something is gathered in from outside."

"''And my ingathering would look ridiculous," I countered, "if there were not someone to keep what is gathered in. . . . But I assure you, dear, there are other duties peculiar to you that are pleasant to perform. It is delightful to teach spinning to a maid who had no knowledge of it when you received her, and to double her worth to you; to take in hand a girl who is ignorant of housekeeping and service, and after teaching her and making her trustworthy and serviceable to find her worth any amount; to have the power of rewarding the discreet and useful members of your household, and of punishing anyone who turns out to be a rogue. But the pleasantest experience of all is to prove yourself better than I am, to make me your servant; and, so far from having cause to fear that as you grow older you may be less honoured in the household, to feel confident that with advancing years, the better partner you prove to me and the better housewife to our children, the greater will be the honour paid to you in our home. For it is not through outward comeliness that the sum of things good and beautiful is increased in the world, but by the daily practice of the virtues."

"'Such was the tenor of my earliest talks with her, Socrates, so far as I can recall them.'"

Selection 5

The Hellenistic Age Brings Increased Opportunities for Women

Sarah B. Pomeroy

Here, from her widely-read and acclaimed book, Goddesses, Whores, Wives, and Slaves: Women in Classical Antiquity, *Hunter College scholar Sarah B. Pomeroy discusses the status, roles, and achievements of Hellenistic women. Some women of the period, she points out, notably those in Athens, led lives as socially restricted and economically powerless as most Greek women did in prior ages. But for many other women, steadily changing social attitudes brought varying degrees of expanded educational opportunities, legal rights, and economic clout.*

The Hellenistic world was dramatically different from that of the preceding period. Loss of political autonomy on the part of the city-states wrought a change in men's political relationships to their societies and to each other. These changes, in turn, affected women's position in the family and in society. The effect on any individual woman depended largely on her social class and the area of the world in which she lived.

The amount of information available on Hellenistic women is surprisingly large, especially in comparison with the dearth of material on Greek women in earlier periods. The abundance of information about the royal women of Greek descent during the Hellenistic era can be attributed both to the impact these memorable women had on ancient authors and to the fact that they involved themselves in the political activities of men—which are, after all, the concern of most historians. The experience of women of lesser status can also be found in public records, as some freeborn women gained more influence in political and economic affairs, besides expanding their options with regard to marriage, public roles, education, and the conduct of their private lives. Finally, the experience of women—from slaves and courtesans to queens—has been preserved in the cultural artifacts of the period. Close scrutiny of the representation of women in sculpture, vase painting, New Comedy, and other art forms yields much insight into their sexual experiences as well as into the nature of their everyday lives. The commentary of philosophers—for the most part urging the retention of traditional female roles—reveals that women's position altered as society changed during this period. . . .

Royal Marriages and Alliances

Among Macedonian ruling families, the relationship between mother and son could be much stronger and more significant than that between husband and wife. Many Macedonian kings indulged in both formal and informal polygamy, and because they often chose not to confer most-favored status on one of their wives—thereby making clear as well which of their sons was the designated successor to the throne—they fostered a climate of intrigue and struggle for power within their courts which could end in their own death at the hands of a power-hungry mother plotting on behalf of her son. The stories that have come down to us portray the Macedonian queens as ambitious, shrewd, and, in many instances, ruthless. The common elements of the tales relate the elimination—often by poison—of political antagonists and rival queens and their progeny, the murder of the husband, and the queen's expectation that she will enjoy more power in the reign of her son than she did when her husband was on the throne. Clearly, these are women competing in a traditionally male arena, and using decidedly male tactics and weapons, in addition to poison, said to be a "woman's weapon."

Aside from Cleopatra VII . . . the most powerful and illustrious of the Macedonian princesses were Olympias and Arsinoë II. Olympias is famous as the mother of Alexander the Great. At the court of her husband, Philip II, Olympias struggled against rival wives, mistresses, and their children to assure Alexander's succession to the throne of Macedonia. Though she ultimately suffered defeat and exile, she was clearly a woman of genius and determination. . . . The psychological impact that such a mother must have had on Alexander has long been a subject of historical speculation.

Alexander was proclaimed king after the murder of Philip in 336 B.C. The murder was blamed on Olympias, probably unjustly (she was in exile at the time), although she had much to gain when her twenty-year-old son succeeded his father. Two years later, Alexander set out on his conquest of the Persian Empire. While Alexander was absent on campaign, Olympias presided over the court of Macedonia. She competed for power with Antipater, whom Alexander had left at home as viceroy. Politically, Alexander supported Antipater, but he never ceased to be personally devoted to his mother.

Although the pattern of alliances of strong mothers and sons was repeated time and again . . . women were also used in passive roles by Hellenistic kings in ways that paralleled those employed by the Greek tyrants of the Archaic Age. The marriages of Macedonian princesses, for example, were often arranged by their male guardians to cement alliances between men: the guardian and the husband. These dynastic marriages were dissolved when new alliances appeared politically more attractive. However, the unilateral rejection of a queen by the husband in favor of another could result in violence, and once the disfavored bride's father or guardian became involved, marriage alliances often produced international entanglements. . . .

The Ptolemies [in Egypt] readily arranged dynastic marriages for their women. But four of the first eight Ptolemies married their sisters. The marriage of full sister and brother had never been encouraged among Greeks or Macedonians, who regarded it as incestuous, but it had been a local Egyptian custom of the royal family, to whom the Ptolemies wished to appear as successors. Moreover, brother-sister marriage eliminated foreign influences from the court. The first marriage of full brother and sister among the Ptolemies was that of Ptolemy II and Arsinoë II, who were both officially worshiped as divine during their lifetimes, reviving another traditional Egyptian custom which was also followed by their successors.

Arsinoë ruled with her brother for approximately five years, until her death in 270 B.C. As was customary in Macedonian courts, she inaugurated her reign by accusing all her rivals of treason and having them eliminated. She was the first Egyptian queen whose portrait was shown with her husband's on coins, and [the writers] Theocritus and Callimachus celebrated her in poetry. The period when Arsinoë joined her brother in the government was characterized by a dramatic improvement in the military and political affairs of Egypt; Arsinoë herself was responsible for the expansion of Egyptian sea power. Though some historians condemn her for unbridled ambition, most agree that she surpassed her brother in talent for governing Egypt. . . .

No Hellenistic queen had political power solely by virtue of birth, except when she was destined to marry her brother. Only in Egypt, during the decline of the Ptolemies, did a daughter (Berenice III), or a sister (Cleopatra VII) with her brother (Ptolemy XIII), succeed to the throne. But many women wielded power as wives or mothers, especially of weak kings, and as regents for young sons or absent husbands, or through the dynamism of personal ambition. The competent women visible in Hellenistic courts were one of the positive influences of this period toward increasing the prestige of nonroyal but upper-class women. . . .

Improved Status, More Rights

As living queens were being celebrated by poets and receiving numerous public honors, so public decrees honoring women were published in the Greek world in the Hellenistic period, and increased in frequency under Roman rule. Priestesses and women performing religious services received the most numerous honors, as they had even in Classical Athens. In the second century B.C. lengthy decrees were passed for Archippe by the assembly of Cyme in Asia Minor, detailing her generosity, including the amount she had spent on wining and dining the entire population. Even in Athens, Pericles' idea that women should not be spoken of, either for praise or blame, no longer prevailed. With aristocratic ostentation, fathers of girls who spun wool and embroidered the *peplos* [sacred robe] of Athena had decrees passed honoring their daughters' service. The names of many girls of noble families are listed.

Women were also the beneficiaries of the more generous granting (for diplomatic, economic, and cultural reasons) of citizenship and political rights by Greek cities that was a characteristic phenomenon in this cosmopolitan period. A few women obtained awards of political rights or held public office. Some were awarded honorary citizenship and the rights of proxeny (privileges granted to foreigners) by foreign cities in gratitude for services performed. In 218 B.C. Aristodama, a poetess of Smyrna, was granted honorary citizenship by the Aetolians of Lamia in Thessaly because her poetry had praised the Aetolian people and their ancestors. An inscription records the existence of a female archon (magistrate) in Histria in the second century B.C. In the first century B.C. another female magistrate, Phile of Priene, became the first woman to construct a reservoir and aqueduct. It is very likely that she was made a magistrate because she promised to contribute to the public works out of her private funds. Here we have one of the main reasons for the increased importance of women: the acquisition and use of economic power.

These women were exceptional, and most others continued to be excluded from participation in government. But since, at least from our viewpoint, under the domination of Hellenistic monarchs the implications of citizenship and its privileges were less far-reaching for men than they had been in the independent city-states of the Classical world, on the one hand the gap in privileges between men and women was much narrowed, and on the other, the men—rather than attempting to hoard them—became more ready to share with women the less-valued privileges they had.

Although the increase in the political involvement of nonroyal Greek women was slight, a slow evolution in legal status, particularly in private law, can be traced. This change can be seen more in the areas newly Hellenized through Macedonian conquest than in the old cities of the Greek mainland. . . . Lacking the traditional safeguards of the *polis*, a Greek woman might not have easy recourse to the protection of her male guardians, and hence she required both an ability to safeguard herself and an increased legal capacity to act on her own behalf.

Papyrus documents from Egypt provide abundant evidence in the field of private law, but the assumption must not be made that Hellenistic law was uniform, nor that Egyptian practices apply to other areas. . . .

Greek women in Egypt were . . . permitted to act without a guardian in some situations. A woman was permitted to write a petition to the government or police on her own behalf, since this involved neither contractual obligation nor undue publicity. In these petitions, some women exploit the notion that they are members of the weaker sex, without male defenders: one asks for special consideration as "a needy defense-

This figurine of a well-to-do Hellenistic woman holding a fan captures a popular female dress style and hairstyle of that era.

less woman"; another says she is obviously deserving of pity because she is a "working woman"; a third asks to be relieved of the obligation to cultivate state land, citing earlier decisions where women were granted exemptions solely on the basis of their sex, and adds that she is "childless and incapable of providing even for myself." Widows or mothers of illegitimate children could give their daughters in marriage and apprentice their sons. . . .

As the Hellenistic era progressed, the role of the bride's father diminished. It was common for a father to give a daughter in marriage in his role of formal guardian, but some contracts were made simply between a woman and man agreeing to share a common life. The right of the married daughter to self-determination against paternal authority began to be asserted. According to Athenian, Roman, and Egyptian law, a father was permitted to dissolve his daughter's marriage against her will. However, later, in Roman Egypt, under Egyptian law, the authority of the father over a married daughter was curtailed by judicial rulings stating that the wishes of the woman were the determining factor. If she wished to remain married, she could do so. . . .

Gains in economic responsibility outstripped women's legal competence during this period. Not only in Egypt but in other areas of the Greek world respectable women were participating more actively in economic affairs. Greek women exercised control over slaves, for they are common among the manumittors [freers of slaves] named in inscriptions. There are 123 women among the 491 manumittors listed at Delphi before 150 B.C. The records of land sales from Ceos and Tenos also list many women. There is good evidence for economic activity of women at Delos: married women, assisted by their guardians, borrowed money—suggesting that they rather than their husbands were responsible for their own debts—and wives of borrowers are recorded as "agreeing to" loans made by their husbands. At Amorgos, likewise, inscriptions show husbands making contracts concerning property with the explicit agreement of their wives. Moreover . . . a few women won public acclaim for generous contributions from their personal funds. . . .

In Athens, in contrast to some other parts of the Greek world, there was little, if any, economic or legal emancipation of citizen women. In fact, from 317 to 307 B.C., during the government of Demetrius of Phalerum, there was less freedom than in the Classical period. The legislation of Demetrius reflected the ethical ideas of Aristotle, who . . . believed that the deliberative part of woman's soul was impotent and needed supervision. Demetrius established a board of "regulators of women" (*gynaikonomoi*), who censored women's conduct and also controlled the lavishness of dinner parties. . . .

Athens remained the center for philosophy—as it had been in the Classical period—and citizen women in Athens still were by and large exposed to nothing more intellectual than practical training in domestic matters. At the opening of the Hellenistic Age, men continued to be attracted to the . . . followers of Aristotle, who explained man's public role by analogy to his place in the individual family—a microcosm of the patriarchal city-state. Theophrastus, another disciple of Aristotle, theorized that more education would turn women into rather lazy, talkative busybodies. Even the upper class, to which one would naturally look for an endorsement of schooling for women, did not educate its daughters. . . .

[However], there is evidence that in other parts of the Greek world some women were given at least a rudimentary education in athletics, music, and reading, in imitation of the time-honored curriculum for boys.

Physical education was now available to women. Athletics were an essential part of the male curriculum that was opened to women in the Hellenistic period precisely because the Classical ideal no longer prevailed. . . .

More important than the possibility of participating in . . . athletics was the acquisition of the ability to read and write. During the Hellenistic and Roman periods, we find from Egyptian papyri that some women are able to sign their names to contracts, although the number of illiterate women who have to resort to another person to sign on their behalf is proportionately higher than for men.

Not surprising against the background of increased literacy and education for women is the reemergence of poetesses. One poetess of the period won high praise. Erinna, of the Dorian island of Telos, can be compared to [the Archaic Greek poetess] Sappho. Both speak of private worlds, and both are masterful artists. . . .

Courtesans and Prostitutes

The special status accorded upper-class women continued with little relation to the attitudes toward women in less respectable areas of Hellenistic society. These women were the courtesans, who, with the exception of the royal and aristocratic women, were the most sophisticated females of their time—and the most notorious. To a large degree, however, the picture we have of the lives of prostitutes in the Hellenistic Age has been unduly embellished and enhanced by their presentation as characters in New Comedy.

New Comedy, which succeeded tragedy and Old Comedy as the national drama of Athens, and purported to hold up a mirror to life, is peopled with prostitutes. Since the scenes, by convention, are set out-of-doors, and respectable city women, especially unmarried girls, were required to stay inside, courtesans and slaves were the only females available to participate in the intrigue of this drama. In the romantic atmosphere of New Comedy one plot is repeated *ad nauseam:* a free young man is smitten with passion for a young slave woman. He intrigues to buy or steal her from the pimp who owns her and keep her as a concubine. Her father appears and identifies her as his long-lost daughter by means of trinkets she was wearing when found in infancy. When her parentage is known, she is thereby rendered freeborn, with no taint attaching from her former employment. The father explains the hardships that forced him to expose his daughter in infancy, and furnishes a dowry so that the couple can marry.

Thus the comedy has a happy ending, and the bride, now a "good" woman, can no longer figure in the adventures typical of this sort of drama. If she were a mythical heroine of tragedy, doubtless her marriage would have been of interest. But ordinary respectable women were not intended for representation: stage settings therefore were not designed for interior scenes, and the New Comedy—in true Cinderella fashion—usually closes with marriage.

Needless to say, in reality the careers of few prostitutes ended in such bliss, and the question of their parentage was, for most prostitutes, a sore point indeed. The prostitute's choice of career was often not her own: exposure of unwanted infants was widely practiced, probably more so than in the Classical period. . . . An abandoned infant automatically had slave status, unless proven freeborn. Despite the arguments of modern scholars that rearing an infant was more expensive than buying a full-grown slave, the evidence shows that some slave dealers made this investment. The fate of many of these infants, if they were female, was to work as prostitutes, thus alleviating the disparity in numbers between free males and females which exposure of females had created. These women could not, however, become legitimate wives, and many freeborn men were doomed to a life of celibacy, owing to the lack of marriageable women.

The happiest ending a slave prostitute could hope for was manumission, but even so . . . she would continue to owe service to her former mistress or master. Her children could be claimed as her master's property, perhaps to be sold to a brothel. . . .

A few prostitutes, euphemistically referred to as companions (*hetairai*), led a more glamorous life. . . . Hellenistic courtesans mingled with many of the leading men in the state; these were primarily members of the Macedonian courts. The famous courtesan Thais was rumored to have captivated Alexander, and then Ptolemy I, to whom she bore three children. Some courtesans were . . . learned. . . . Leontion, the companion of the philosopher Epicurus, rivaled Theophrastus in writing philosophy. . . .

More Frank Depictions of Female Love

The literature and visual art of the Hellenistic period, when compared with either the restrained or lewd depictions of women in the preceding ages, reveal a new interest in the eroticism of women. It is difficult from this vantage point to determine the extent to which these changed sexual mores touched the lives of respectable women, but it may be assumed by analogy with Roman women that, to a degree, some Greek women implemented the advice in the manuals for courtesans—such as Ovid's *Art of Love*—for their personal gratification.

The various portrayals of the female figure—draped, naked, or nude—in the visual arts of the Archaic, Classical, and Hellenistic periods are good indicators of changing social attitudes. . . . The most striking feature of Hellenistic art was the development of the nude female figure in sculpture. . . .

Erotic vase paintings of the Hellenistic Age also proclaim changes in sexual relationships. Earlier vases had depicted group sex scenes in stark physical surroundings. Hellenistic art shows fewer representations of male homosexual activity, and focuses instead on tender heterosexual scenes of couples in bed in a private and comfortably furnished setting. The furnishings are essential prerequisites, for a sophisticated etiquette of romance was developing which was to culminate in handbooks on the art of love. . . .

The turning inward toward a private sexual relationship, which we today take for granted, was of little interest to Greeks of the Classical period, but was fully explored in Hellenistic literature and art. This change in the relationship between the sexes can be attributed, with varying degrees of speculativeness, to a number of factors . . . the influence of philosophers, the actions of royal women, and women's increasing economic power. The polis system of such a city as Athens—requiring a marital arrangement protective of women—had changed, allowing to men a familiarity with respectable women, especially in the areas recently settled by Greeks. At the same time, a new permissiveness was granted to respectable women. In his second *Idyll*, the poet Theocritus (300–260 B.C.) describes the activities of Simaetha, a virgin, perhaps an orphan, who went to a festival chaperoned by another woman. On the road she caught sight of and fell in love with a young man. He made love to her and later jilted her. In his fifteenth *Idyll*, Theocritus shows two respectable Greek housewives in Alexandria going to see "The Loves of Venus and Adonis," where they are jostled and addressed by men in the throng. Here, it is necessary to raise the question whether nudity in the visual arts connoted not only greater freedom for but also less respect toward women.

Selection 6

Classical Views of Childhood and Children

Mark Golden

Surviving evidence suggests that child-rearing customs in ancient Greece reflected a general societal view of children that most people today would deem misguided and counter to the development of healthy self-esteem. As explained here by Mark Golden, a classicist at the University of Winnipeg, on the whole childhood was not viewed as an enviable, happy time of life, as it often is today, and adults felt little or no nostalgia for their youth. This was partly because they believed that children lacked proper reasoning powers, courage, or even a moral capacity until they were at least in their teens. And so, it was thought, young children needed to be closely watched, carefully trained, and, when necessary, harshly disciplined by parents, tutors, and other community members. There were some positive views of children too, says Golden, who cites evidence mostly from classical Athens; for instance, they were sometimes seen as possessing the ability to convey divine or natural truths in a way that most adults could not.

The child is father of the man, wrote Wordsworth. Some Greeks agreed. Childhood prodigies, signs of future superiority, were a staple of myth and biography. Achilles [Hero of Homer's *Iliad*] killed a boar when he was only six, Cyrus [II, Persia's first great king] was chosen to play king by his contemporaries at the age of ten and able to give shrewd advice at fifteen or sixteen, the always arrogant Alcibiades [the noted fifth-century B.C. Athenian politician] threw himself in front of a wagon and stopped it when playing in the street "while still small.". . . In conformity with this view, theorists of education like Plato and Aristotle stress the importance of proper training and environment from the moment of birth and even before for the development of good citizens. "The lessons of childhood marvelously grip the mind," Critias remarks [in one of Plato's dialogues], apparently quoting current wisdom. . . .

Yet there was another tendency, too, to stress the discontinuities between one time of life and another. In *The Symposium*, Plato has Diotima mention the idea that a man is the same from childhood to old age. But, she continues, though he is called the same, he does not retain the same characteristics. He is always becoming a new person . . . physically and intellectually, in his opinions and in his temperament. Aristotle, dealing with the various senses in which one thing is said to be formed from another, groups together the sayings "From day comes night" and "From the boy comes the man." This perspective informs the reflection, frequent in the orators, that there is no way to tell how a child

will turn out (a motive for the adoption of adults). It takes its most developed form in the various schemes dividing human life into two, three, four, five, six, seven, and even ten stages, based on numerology or astrology, the number of seasons or of fingers on each hand, with more or less discrete traits. . . .

It is within this context that we should situate Athenian ascriptions of characteristics to childhood and to children: a range of opinions on the relative importance of continuity and change within the course of human life. . . . Predictably, children are thought to approach adult norms more closely as they grow older; this process is marked by stages, which differ according to author and context. But children may also be regarded as so lacking in some adult qualities that they seem more closely to resemble another species altogether, or so free from others that they transcend the usual human limitations and enter into a privileged relationship with the gods. . . .

Children Seen as Intellectually Inferior

What I have called negative attributes predominate in this catalog [of childhood attributes]. Though characters in tragedy occasionally envy children their freedom from the burdens of adult life, especially those they must bear themselves, the Greeks of the classical period were generally not nostalgic for childhood. It was a privilege of the gods, or of those they especially loved, to pass through childhood quickly, to be born with many of the powers they would display when grown. So, in their first days of life, Apollo slays Python and founds his oracle at Delphi, Hermes steals his brother's cattle, Heracles kills the snakes Hera sends against him in his cradle. . . .

Children were regarded as physically weak, morally incompetent, mentally incapable. . . .

Aristotle thinks that children have free will but not *prohairesis*, "resolve, purpose," and cannot therefore be really happy or moral. But morality is also the subject of a comment by the orator Aeschines, who regards the ability to distinguish right from wrong as the mark of the adult male citizen. It was courage that children were felt to lack in particular; children might seem brave, but this was dismissed as mere ignorance and thoughtlessness. Readily frightened as they were, children were easy prey for stories about female bogies like Empousa, Gello, Gorgo, Lamia, Mormo (or Mormolyke). . . .

Intellectual incapacity is touched on far more often, and in sources of many different kinds. One of the most popular Greek proverbs, "Old men are children again," always refers, as far as we can tell from ancient commentators and extant examples, to mental incompetence. Aeschylus's Prometheus says that Hermes is "a child and even more mindless" if he expects to learn his secrets. In Sophocles, Oedipus hesitates to give his children advice because they do not yet possess *phrenes*, "wits." Old Comedy makes much ado about humor so crude only children laugh. . . . The fullest compendium of children's intellectual shortcomings comes from Plato, concerned as he is with knowledge as a key to ethical development as well. Plato (or his speakers) claims that children know little, are gullible and easily persuaded, can understand only the simplest things, talk nonsense, make unreliable judges. Some adults, we are told, tease children (and amuse themselves) by talking to them in a high-flown and mock-serious manner. . . . Superiority is expressed by saying a man makes others appear like children or less than children; inferiority is denoted by the taunt, "Even a child could refute you"; an argument is made conclusive by the clincher, "Not even a child would deny this."

Plato often groups children with women, slaves, and animals. These are also associated in Aristotle, for whom boys bear a physical resemblance to women (because they do not yet concoct semen), animals stand in the same relation to humans as children to adults, and both animals and children are as inferior to adults as bad and foolish men are to good and wise ones; as one consequence, the opinions of animals and children are regarded with equal contempt. Children are also linked with the sick, the drunk, the insane, and the wicked. No sensible person would

choose to live with their powers of reasoning, or to return to childhood once he left it. One specific weakness that Aristotle adds to Plato's list is a short memory. Children, it seems, are simply in too troubled and unstable a state to acquire knowledge and exercise sound judgment.

Of course, the child has the potential to outgrow all these limitations; as Aristotle says, he is not yet complete and whole. It is interesting, however, that the child is seldom a symbol of what is to come, and that when, as rarely, he is, the future hopes he represents are often unrealized. . . . More often, children figure in images that ignore their future capabilities in favor of their futility in the present. The child builds castles in the sand, and then whirls them away. The child chases a winged bird, which flees from his grasp. . . . Here we have a vision of childhood rich with loss and longing. But there is beauty and grace in the image as well, for children have qualities adults lack, and some of these are thought to be attractive.

Passion, Innocence, and Insight

Most prominent among the positive physical characteristics of children are the sweet smell of their breath and skin and their softness. Mentioned in contexts full of pathos by parents in tragedy, these are also discussed and explained by the philosophers. According to the *Problems* ascribed to Aristotle, a child's smell stays sweet until puberty, at which point the sweat becomes saltier and stronger-smelling. Plato explains the softness of children's bodies in an interesting account of the aging process. When they are young, creatures are formed of firmly interlocked triangles of matter. These are soft, as they are newly produced from marrow and nourished on milk. As older and weaker triangles that make up food and drink come into contact with them, they overcome these invaders and so grow. In time, however, the body's triangles begin to weaken after so many battles, and can no longer assimilate new ones to themselves. They are divided by newcomers and decay, the process that is called old age. . . . Their mode of speech also was their own. As among other species (except cattle), children have higher voices than adults. Plato's Callicles takes pleasure in listening to small children lisp. Baby talk is quoted on the comic stage and in Theophrastus's character sketches. In addition, we are told that children have dense bodies (and so suffer from leprosy less than men), are snub-nosed, get thinner in the summer, are particularly prone to head lice, and are especially likely to get dizzy if they look at things a long way off. And, sweet though their skins may be, their body products are not, a perception exploited for comic purposes.

One physical characteristic has implications for children's temperament. In a number of places in the Aristotelian *Problems*, we read that children are moister and hotter than adults. As a result, they are more hot-tempered as well, greedier and angrier than men. Aristotle elsewhere notes their passion, and regards childhood as the time when the appetite for pleasure is strongest. All this is in agreement with Plato, who says the young are "fiery," and ranges children with slaves, women, and the lower classes as those who have the most desires, pleasures, and pains. Specific pleasures include sweets—a honeycomb stuffed in a newborn's mouth might stop its crying—and music. Passionate as they are, children are energetic, unable to keep still in body and voice, susceptible to crying out or leaping about in a disorderly fashion. Because their reason is as yet uncurbed, they are treacherous, fierce . . . in short, the most difficult to manage of all wild creatures. Lack of discipline renders them changeable; Plato regards children's tendency to alter their games from day to day as dangerous. . . .

Immature and lacking in experience, children were also believed to be innocent, and so were easily associated with phenomena outside the usual areas of citizen interaction: nature and the gods. As a proverb put it, "Wine and children tell the truth"; children's chance comments might be credited with oracular force, their advice be valued for its special insight. Herodotus, who knew a good story when he heard one, passes on an excellent illustration (5.49–51). When the Greeks of Asia Minor were planning to revolt from Persian rule, Aristagoras, the tyrant of Miletus, came to Sparta to enlist the aid of king Cleomenes. At first, Cleomenes was inclined to help his fellow Greeks. But when Aristagoras unwisely revealed that the distance from the coast to the heart of the Persian empire was some three months' journey, he changed his mind. Aristagoras then turned from persuasion to bribery, and had upped the ante to fifty talents when Cleomenes' daughter Gorgo, a girl of eight or nine, cried out, "Father, the stranger will corrupt you if you don't go away." Cleomenes, pleased by his daughter's advice, left, and Aristagoras went away empty-handed; in the event, the revolt ended in disaster. . . .

A second response involves a combination that is characteristic of the Athenian attitude toward children: their limitations are recognized, they themselves are loved and enjoyed. From this point of view, clever comments and wisdom beyond their years are neither regarded as special delivery from the gods nor dismissed with contempt. Either reaction would constitute taking the children too seriously. . . . They are simply cute.

Selection 7

The Status and Treatment of Greek Slaves

Michael Grant

From his social history of Greece and Rome, distinguished and prolific classical historian Michael Grant delivers the following effective summary of the institution of slavery as it was practiced in ancient Greece. Drawing on a wide array of sources, from Homer and Hesiod to Xenophon, Plato, and Aristotle, Grant discusses the numbers of Greek slaves, how they came to be slaves, their status, varying treatment, duties and professions, and the ways that philosophers and other writers rationalized and justified the institution.

Slavery seems an appallingly inhumane institution, because its essential feature is that slaves have no independence or rights or legal personalities of their own, but are the property of their masters. Slavery was a feature of every advanced ancient civilization, not only those of the Greeks and Romans. And those Greeks and Romans who played a large part in public life or made important contributions to literature and art were enabled to do so by means of the spare time, or leisure, and financial surpluses, conferred upon them by their slaves (this was the only way in which such a surplus could be acquired).

There were various forms and nuances of ancient labour. . . . But it was slavery, chattel slavery, that was the most significant kind of unfree labour at the highest periods of Greek and Roman history. Even if never . . . predominant, it was extensive and general, and inherent in the very conception of the ancient state. Every action, belief or institution was in some way or other affected by the possibility that someone involved might be a slave. The contribution of slave labour was essential, so that it is justifiable to describe Greece and Rome as, to a large extent, slave societies, such as do not exist today, at least in the western world.

To insist on the history of the 'rights' of slaves is not very relevant. For, basically, they had none. Their total contrast with free men was a familiar rhetorical point. They were even regarded as kinless, and in Greece their marriages were unrecognised, and their owners could prevent them from taking place. The exploitation of slaves was based upon the direct use, or sanction, of force, not upon the 'free' play of economy, as in capitalist societies. This was the most extreme way in which one social group could use its power for economic advantage. Plato noted that the protection and defence of slaveholders was a crucial function of the government, and Aristotle described the master-slave relationship as one of three most basic features of the household—slaves being the best, most manageable, and most necessary property a man could possess. A slave was not expected to display virtues, and the comic dramatist Menander gave his slaves special masks, displaying mental disharmony and moral deviance, to be expected from men who were mostly non-Greeks, and therefore natural barbarians and enemies. Their treatment, of course, varied. Relying on their lack of rights, a master might vilify or beat them with immunity. Or, remembering their indispensable services, he might choose to treat them decently—within the limits of their status. The result might be warm mutual affection. . . . Or, alternatively, relations between master and slave might be deplorable.

Numbers and Status of Slaves

What percentage of the total population of the Greek *poleis* the slaves constituted has been much debated and argued; and, in any case, each state was constituted differently. One recent estimate suggests that in the classical Athens of the fifth and fourth centuries there were between 80,000 and 100,000 slaves of both sexes, representing about one-third of the total population. But some say there were more, and some less. Anyway there were a lot, and there was always a sufficient supply of them. A very large number of these slaves were foreigners—there was a general opinion that one ought not to have Greek slaves—and they were obtained by capture in war, by sale in the huge slave-markets such as Delos (of which we know too little), and by birth to those who were already slavewomen.

How far all this slavery kept down the pay of free workers—who shared so many occupations with them—remains uncertain, but it must surely have done so (although we can detect no protests from the free poor) and must have caused some contempt for free labour. Numerous slaves worked in the basic field of agriculture, but many others in industry and public works. And another disputed question is the extent to which slavery impeded technological improvement, and so industrial advance. Once again, it must surely to some extent have done so—because when so much slave labour was at hand, even if not wholly efficient, why bother

about better technology or rationalisation of production methods?

However, the slaves, although numerous, did not do *most* of Greek production. And the work they did was often in their master's household, to satisfy his needs and those of his family. Others could be hired out to a third party, or allowed to work independently, for instance as craftsmen. Others, again, had the state, not an individual, as their master. Some of these worked in mines, for instance Athens's notorious silver-mines in Laurium. That is to say they, and their functions, were varied and flexible, so that efforts to describe them as a single social 'class' must be rejected.

Slaves were at first not very numerous in Greece, but they always existed. Homeric slaves, being the products of wars and raids and piracy, were mostly women, but not all: Eumaeus, in the *Odyssey*, had been sold into slavery, and there were other male slaves as well. The households of Alcinous and Odysseus were said to possess fifty slaves each, but that is a conventional figure. In spite of the very low estimate accorded to impoverished free men, 'Zeus', remarks Eumaeus, 'takes away half a man's worth when the day of slavery comes upon him.'

Yet [the eighth-century B.C. Boeotian farmer and poet] Hesiod represented a widespread view when he saw slavery as essential to his slave-owning class. Another early writer, Aesop, was a slave himself, from Thrace, which was where so many slaves came from. He is a partly legendary figure, but seems to have written the earliest collection of fables. Whether he expressed views about the disadvantages of the slave status, or employed the slave situation to universalise the human experience, must remain conjectural.

In archaic Greece, slavery was still not very extensive. But then, in the sixth century, there was an astronomical increase. This was partly because Solon, at the beginning of the sixth century, abolished debt-bondage at Athens (though at other cities it remained in force). . . . It meant that Athens, deprived of the forced labour of its serfs, had to import many additional slaves from elsewhere to take the place of those who had thus

A nineteenth-century illustration depicts a group of Athenian slave girls socializing at a water fountain.

been released from their serf-like obligations.

When wars broke out, slaves got new chances. For one thing, a city-state's mobilisation of free urban troops for war depended on the maintenance of production by the slaves who remained at home. And, furthermore, the slaves themselves were sometimes enrolled to fight. This occurred during internal convulsions (*staseis*), but it was also not unknown in external wars. Whether slaves fought against the Persians at Salamis is uncertain, but certainly they rowed in the Peloponnesian War, notably at Arginusae (406), though this was recognised as exceptional; and they occasionally served as soldiers as well.

They also made their mark in civilian capacities too. For example, some of the leading potters and vase-painters were almost certainly, slaves. And in the labour force on the Acropolis slaves worked alongside free men. Increasing

democracy at Athens, and emphasis on the rights of poor citizens, enhanced the general reliance on slavery. That is to say, individual freedom flourished when slavery was abundant as well. At Athens there were large private workshops manned by slaves, such as those of Lysias and his brother, and Pasion—both factories for making shields. But there were also other new, upwardly mobile, opportunities for slaves (still within their slave status), although always, of course, the iron distinction which kept them apart from, and under, free men was maintained.

Why, given this new degree of possible latitude, did the slaves in classical Athens not revolt? Partly because, being foreigners from all parts, they were polyglot and multi-ethnic, possessing no degree of unity. But what they did, instead, was to run away, and fugitive slaves were always a major problem; they could count on some degree of religious asylum. During the Peloponnesian War, after the Spartans fortified Deceleia in Attica, a very large number of the slaves employed by the Athenians at their Laurium silver-mines defected to the other side.

In the following century, Athenian slaveowners displayed a tendency to replace enforced obedience by attempting to encourage spontaneous obedience, so that the legal personality of slaves began to emerge. True, people were still frightened of them, and were still eager enough to equate them with barbarians—enemies, against whose threat military training was necessary—and the 'free poor' struggled to maintain the citizen-slave distinction. Yet Athenian law came to protect slaves, in a limited way, and their killing was prohibited. Such sanctions, however, were religious or social rather than legal; and constraints on slave-masters were not so much motivated by a desire to protect the slaves as by the wish to protect the state against over-powerful slave-masters.

Slavery Rationalized by Writers and Philosophers

During the fifth and fourth centuries the writers all had their say on this theme. Herodotus, while denouncing the corporate enslavement of Greek states to the Persians, accepted *individual* slavery as the will of the gods. Euripides, as always, was more critical, observing that a good slave could have 'internal' freedom, and be a better person than a free man. He was echoing the sophists' (minority) view that slavery was *not* natural—so that it could not degrade anyone who was not 'really' a slave. A slave, that is to say, could be 'free in mind'. As Euripides causes a messenger, himself of slave status, to remark:

> It's low not to feel with your masters,
> Laugh with them, and sympathise in their
>   sorrows.
> Born to service as I am, I would be
> Numbered among the noble
> Slaves, unfree in name,
> Free in mind. Better this than for one man
> To be doubly cursed—a slave in mind
> As well as slave in the words of his
>   fellows. [*Helen* 726–733]

The comic dramatist Aristophanes, however, although he boasted of abandoning conventional jokes about slaves, did not really accept them as human beings. His conservative contemporary, known as the Old Oligarch, believed that in Athens they were too well treated!

> Unrestraint on the part of slaves and resident aliens [metics] is very prevalent with the Athenians, and it isn't permitted to beat them there, nor will a slave stand aside for you.

> I'll explain what's behind the local practice: if it were lawful for a free person to beat a slave, resident alien, or freedman, lots of Athenians mistaken for slaves would get beaten. For the populace there is no better in its clothing than slaves and resident aliens, and its appearance is no better. If someone is amazed at this too, that they let slaves live it up and in some cases to lead lives of great splendour: this too they would seem to do on considered opinion. For where there is naval power it is necessary for slaves to work for money. . . . And where there are rich slaves there is no longer any advantage in my slave's being afraid of you.

Xenophon, aware of what the sophists had said, declared that the 'real' slave is the bad (free) man, in bondage to his own faults and lusts, whereas whether one is, or is not, an actual slave, is an accident of fortune—a convenient sop to the consciences of slave-owners; who, he also, more ominously, suggested, ought to avail themselves of unpaid bodyguards against the danger that slaves presented. . . .

Something has already been said about Plato's and Aristotle's views on the subject; but it may be added that Plato felt an aristocratic contempt for slaves, as well as for other manual workers, and barbarians. He saw no theoretical justification for the view that slavery was a mere convention, and his *Laws* are severer on slaves than the actual laws of his time.

Aristotle, however, provides the only surviving ancient attempt at a determined analysis of slavery. Like Plato, he considered it perfectly right and proper that some people are slaves. Aware of men who held the opposite view, he disagreed with them, maintaining that barbarians, for example, are slaves by nature, and that men conquered in war legitimately became the property of the ruler: the rule of the free man over the slave is a necessary institution:

> The slave is not merely the slave of the master but wholly belongs to the master. These considerations therefore make clear the nature of the slave and his essential quality: one who is a human being belonging by nature not to himself but to another is by nature a slave. . . .

After a prolonged and intricate argument Aristotle comes down firmly in favour of the principle of natural slavery: 'there exist certain persons who are essentially slaves everywhere, and certain others who are so nowhere . . . it is just and proper for the one party to be governed and the other to govern by the form of government for which they are by nature fitted'.

The author of the *Oeconomica*, which was preserved under the name of Aristotle [but written by an unknown author, usually called the Pseudo-Aristotle], reflected upon the character of a slave's existence:

The slave who is best suited for his work is the kind that is neither too cowardly nor too courageous . . .

Three things make up the life of a slave, work, punishment and food. To give them food but no punishment and no work makes them insolent. And that they should have work and punishment but no food is tyrannical and destroys their efficiency. It remains therefore to give them work and sufficient food; for it is impossible to rule over slaves without offering rewards, and a slave's reward is food. . . . And since the drinking of wine makes even free men insolent . . . it is clear that wine ought never to be given to slaves, or at any rate very seldom.

Meanwhile, however, the politician Hyperides proposed that slaves should be granted citizenship in order to fight against King Philip II of Macedonia. As for Menander (342/1–293/89 BC), he is aware of the literary and comic tradition, from the slave-owner's point of view, that slaves are lazy, sex-crazed or gluttonous, and need to be beaten. But some of his slaves (who figure extensively in his plays) are also clever and resourceful schemers—useful to free men, and helping them to see themselves as they are. As for the supply of slaves, he took it for granted that piracy would remain one of the principal sources. . . .

Hellenistic Greece did not add a great deal. The slave-markets were active, because of wars and continued kidnapping by pirates, though slavery was also perpetuated by breeding. The Seleucid monarch Antiochus IV Epiphanes possessed a huge number of slaves of his own, and we hear (from a later age it is true) that they constituted one-third of the population of Pergamum. At Chios, in the third century BC, there was a slave rebellion under a certain Drimacus (this was another place where slaves were particularly abundant). In Ptolemaic Egypt the picture is mixed. There were not, it appears, a great many chattel slaves, since the free poor took their place. But we hear not only of debt-bondage but of various kinds of domestic slaves—and even of female slaves owned by women—and in the second century BC there was an Egyptian school for slaves.

In general, the idea of 'rights' for slaves began to take shape gradually, prompted by the growing individualism of the Hellenistic age. Attitudes varied, and the views of the Stoics were not altogether illiberal. True, they were somewhat contemptuous of slaves, but they did feel that the whole institution needed to be defined, and, in particular, that slaves ought to be properly treated. For slaves were allowed a capacity for virtue, seeing that moral status, the Stoics pointed out, depended on the soul, so that social status was irrelevant—and very often due to capricious fortune: the wise man alone is free, and the bad man is a slave. The actual state of slavery, that is to say, as many people felt at the time, was 'an accident': unnatural perhaps, but indispensable and a fact of life.

Selection 8

A Philosopher Attempts to Justify the Institution of Slavery

Aristotle

The Greek scholar/philosopher/scientist Aristotle (384–322 B.C.) composed his Politics *in the late 340s B.C., at about the time that he accepted the invitation of Macedonia's King Philip II to tutor the crown prince, Alexander. The work outlines Aristotle's conception of the proper form and function of the political and social institutions of the Greek polis. Tackling one of these institutions, slavery, in Book 1, he, like other ancient thinkers, accepts it as a natural state of affairs. In other words, nature designed some people to be better than others; and the "superior" ones are logically the masters of the "inferior" ones. (An important corollary of this argument is that Greeks are naturally superior to barbarians, or non-Greeks, a doctrine Aristotle was careful to reinforce in young Alexander.)*

In retrospect, Aristotle's logic in justifying slavery is faulty, in that it is based primarily on simple observation of existing circumstances rather than on moral and ethical concerns; that is, he observes that masters and slaves exist in all known societies and

concludes, erroneously, that the institution would not be so widespread if it was not what nature (or the gods) intended.

*n*ow that we have a clear idea about the parts of the state, we must first discuss management of estates, or households, since every state consists of households. The parts of this subject are the same as the parts of the household: a complete household consists of slaves and free persons.

Now, any subject must be studied by taking first the simplest elements. In the case of the household, the prime elements are the following: master and slave, husband and wife, father and children. Our task is therefore to examine each one of these three groups and to see what they mean and what they ought to be. . . .

Let us first . . . take master and slave, in order to see what is required for the basic needs of life. We want also to see if one can get a better idea about the subject than the opinions now current. Some people think that the art of being master is a sort of science: they think that management, mastership, statesmanship, and kingship are identical, as we said at the start. Others think that it is contrary to nature for there to be masters ruling over slaves; they argue that slave and free are determined purely by convention, whereas by nature there is no difference between the two. This is why the relationship is not just, since it is imposed by constraint, or force.

Property is part of the household, and the art of acquiring property is part of household management. (After all, without the basic essentials, it is impossible to exist, let alone live the good life.) Now, if we look at the arts, we see that each of them must have its proper tools or instruments in order to complete its function; so too with the manager. Instruments are either inanimate or animate; for the pilot of a ship, the rudder is an inanimate instrument, whereas the lookout man is an animate instrument, the point being that an assistant (such as the lookout man) is to be classed as an instrument in the case of the arts. Similarly, an article of property is an instrument for living; property is a number of such instruments; and the slave is an animate article of property. Every assistant is, as it were, an (animate) instrument prior to (inanimate) instruments. . . .

The term "article of property" is used in the same way as "part." Part, for instance, is not only a part of something else; it belongs entirely to that thing. The same applies to "article of property." That is why a master is merely master of the slave, but does not belong to the slave; the slave, however, is not only the master's slave, but belongs entirely to the master.

This shows us clearly what a slave is and what he can do. A human being who by nature belongs to another, not himself, is by nature a slave. One person belongs to another if, though a person, he is an article of property (he is *owned*), for an article of property is an instrument for action that can be separated from the owner.

Body and Soul

We must now see whether there is such a person as a slave by nature, and whether it is good and just for some people to be slaves or not—whether all slavery is contrary to nature. It is not hard to get the answer either by reasoning philosophically or by working from the facts.

Ruling and being ruled are not only necessary, they are also expedient. From birth onwards, the difference is noticeable; some tend to be ruled, others to rule. . . .

In cases in which we are dealing with composites, made up of several parts that form a single common whole—whether the parts are continuous or separate—a ruler and a subject can always be found. This is by nature an essential characteristic of animate things; even in things that are inanimate there is a sort of ruling principle, as with harmony in music. . . .

At any rate, animate creatures are the first cases where we can see the authority of a master and the rule of a statesman. Soul rules over body like a master; and mind rules over appetite like a statesman or king. This makes it clear that it is natural and expedient for the body to be ruled by the soul, and for the emotional part to be ruled by the mind and by the part that has reason. When both are equal, or the natural relation is reversed, all these functions are impaired.

What is true of man is also true of other living creatures. Domesticated animals are superior in nature to untamed animals; it is better for all the former to be ruled by man, since in this way they obtain security.

Also, as regards male and female, the former is superior, the latter inferior; the male is ruler, the female is subject. It must also be that the same is true for the whole of mankind. Where there is a difference between people, like that between soul and body, or between man and mere animal (this being the condition of people whose function is to use their bodies, manual labor being the best service they can give, for such people are by nature slaves), it is better for the lower ones to be ruled, just as it is for the subjects mentioned above. A man is a slave by nature if he *can* belong to someone else (this is why he does in fact belong to someone else) or if he has reason to the extent of understanding it without actually possessing it. Animals other than man do not obey reason, but follow their instincts. There is only a slight difference between the services rendered by slaves and by animals: both give assistance with their bodies for the attainment of the essentials of living.

Nature tries to make a difference between

slave and free, even as to their bodies—making the former strong, with a view to their doing the basic jobs, and making the free people upright, useless for servile jobs but suitable for political life, which is divided into the tasks of war and of peace. The opposite, however, often turns out to be the case: it happens that some have the physique of free men, whereas others have the souls. It is quite obvious that if people showed their differences in their mere physique, as the statues of the gods show the difference between gods and men, everyone would say that the inferior ones ought to be slaves of the others.

If this is true of the body, it is even more just for the distinction to apply to the soul. But it is not so easy to see the beauty of the soul as the beauty of the body. It is clear, then, that people are by nature free men or slaves, and that it is expedient and just for those who are slaves to be ruled.

Undeserved Slaves Versus Natural Slaves

It is not hard to see that people who say the opposite have some right on their side. "Being a slave" and "slave" are both ambiguous. There are also those who are slaves only by convention. Convention here means a kind of agreement by virtue of which what is captured in war is held to belong to the victors. This is said to be a just principle; but many lawyers challenge its legality on the grounds that it is abhorrent for something to be the slave and subject of what can exert superior force and is merely superior in power. There is disagreement about this, even among experts.

There is a reason for the tangled dispute between the two theories. There is a sense in which virtue, when provided with the external means, is supremely able to use force; and it is always the case that superiority occurs by virtue of having more of some good or other. This leads to the idea that force must somehow be connected with goodness, so that the disagreement on this question is only about the matter of justice. That is why some think that justice is benevolence, whereas others think that the rule of the stronger

is itself the principle of justice. But if these views are taken separately from one another, neither has any validity or persuasive force as against the view that it is superiority in virtue that entitles one to rule and mastery.

There are some who hold fast to a kind of justice, as they think—after all, convention or law is a kind of justice—when they count enslavement, as the product of war, as just. At the same time, however, they assert that it may not be just: for it is possible for the start of the war not to be just, and no one would say that the man who did not deserve to be a slave is truly a slave. Otherwise, the consequence will be that people whom we think to be really wellborn will turn out to be slaves and the children of slaves if they happen to be captured and sold.

That is why they do not mean to assert that such people are slaves, but that barbarians are. Yet, in saying that, all they are looking for is the "natural slave," as we said at the start. It is undeniable that there are people who are slaves wherever they are, and others who are never and nowhere slaves. The same applies to noble birth: our nobles regard themselves as wellborn, not only in their own country but anywhere in the world; barbarians, however, are wellborn only in their own country. They thus assume that there is a sense in which noble and free are absolute, and another in which they are not. As Helen puts it, in the play by Theodectes: "Who would dare call me a servant, when I have gods on both sides of my family tree?"

When they talk in this way, they are simply using the ideas of virtue and vice to distinguish between slave and free, wellborn and lowborn. Their assumption is that good parents produce good offspring in the same way that human beings produce human beings and animals produce animals; but although nature tries to achieve this, it is frequently unable to succeed.

There is some reason for the dispute. It is not always true that people who are slaves or free are such by nature. In cases where such a distinction does exist, it is expedient and right for one group to be slaves and the other to be masters, for one set to be ruled and the other to exercise the rule proper to it, which means to act as a master. But ruling in the wrong way is bad for both sides: part and whole, just like body and soul, have a common interest; and a slave is part of his master, an animate, even though separate, part of his body. That is why master and slave have a community of interest and friendship—provided they are what they are by nature; if they are not, but are in this position by convention, because of force, the opposite is true.

It is clear from this that mastership and statesmanship are not identical; nor are all forms of power the same, as some thinkers suppose. Statesmanship means ruling over people who are by nature free, whereas being a master means ruling over people who are by nature slaves. Management is monarchic, since every household is controlled by one person; whereas statesmanship is ruling over those who are free and equal.

A man is given the title of "master," not because he has a certain branch of knowledge, but simply because he is of a certain disposition. The same is true of the words "slave" and "free." But there could be a science of being a master and a science of being a slave. An example of the latter would be the subject taught by the man at Syracuse, who, for a fee, used to teach slaves their routine jobs. The study of these subjects could be extended to take in cookery and other kinds of service. There are different kinds of jobs, some being more respectable and others more basic; as the saying goes: "slave before slave, and master before master."

All such subjects are "sciences" fit for slaves. The science of being master is concerned with the use of slaves. A man is not master by virtue of acquiring slaves, but by using them. There is nothing great or important about this science. The master must know how to order what the slave has to know how to do. This is why people who can afford it avoid the trouble: they have a sort of steward who takes over this job, and they, the masters, go in for politics or philosophy. The art of acquiring slaves is different from both the science of being a master and the "science" of being a slave. If it is just, it is part of war or hunting. This is enough on the subject of master and slave.

The Complete History of

Religious Beliefs and Customs

Chapter 9

Introduction

Religious belief and worship was one of the most essential aspects of Greek life. Some kind of religious ritual accompanied nearly every gathering, function, or important endeavor, both private and public. No pious Greek consumed a meal, for example, without offering a portion of the food to the gods; religious ritual attended important life-cycle events such as birth, marriage, and death; a military general performed a sacrifice before a battle; and many public meetings, such as those of the Athenian Assembly, began with an animal sacrifice and prayers.

In contrast to the situation in most modern societies, in which religion is viewed as a private affair, the Greeks saw it as a public concern. It was seen as essential to a community's welfare to maintain the goodwill of the gods. And the crime of impiety (*asebeia*), lacking faith in or respect for the gods, was a serious one; for if one person offended the gods, it might bring down their wrath on the whole community. Moreover, most Greeks made a connection between religion and patriotism in their belief that certain gods favored certain cities above other cities. Each city had its personal patron deity, therefore, who, it was thought, watched over and protected that community. (Athena was the patron of Athens, for instance; Hera that of Argos; and Poseidon that of Corinth.)

Such divine favoritism was not seen to come free, of course. Rather, the gods expected something in return. The most common view was that they would provide a certain minimum level of good fortune, prosperity, and safety as long as the people upheld their oaths (made in the gods' names); made the proper sacrifices; faithfully celebrated the traditional religious festivals; and consulted the gods directly when unsure about crucial religious matters, through oracles (priestesses who acted as mediums between gods and men).

These gods (*theoi*) the Greeks worshiped were anthropomorphic, meaning that they were envisioned as having human form and attributes. The traditional stories surrounding them, the myths (*mythoi*), like the Greek language, acted as a unifying force, instilling the idea that all Greeks were, beneath the surface, kinsmen. The major gods were known as the "Olympians" because early traditions claimed they dwelled atop Mt. Olympus (in northern Thessaly), the tallest mountain in Greece. These included the familiar Zeus, Hera, Poseidon, Apollo, Artemis, Athena, and others. Supposedly, they had overthrown an earlier race of gods, the Titans, in a stupendous battle in the remote past. The Greek pantheon (group of gods) also included a number of minor gods; and also a few former mortals, most notably Heracles (whom the Romans later called Hercules), who, it was believed, became divine after their deaths.

The origins of the Olympian gods and the religious customs surrounding them are still somewhat unclear. However, studies of the surviving Linear B tablets indicate that some of these deities (including Zeus, Poseidon, Dionysus, Hermes, and others), or at least early versions of them, were part of the Bronze Age Mycenaean pantheon. Some of the basics of worship, especially sacrifice (making offerings to the gods) apparently also originated in this period. In the Dark Age and Archaic Age, following the downfall of Mycenaean civilization, some of these gods and practices were retained. And new elements were added, among them open-air altars on which to perform the sacrifices; temples (at first of wood, later of stone), each dedicated to a specific god; cult images (statues) of the gods, usually resting inside the temples; a complex and rich mythology (collection of myths) surrounding the gods; and public religious festivals to honor the gods (most were local in nature, but a few, such as that at Olympia, were panhellenic, or all-Greek).

By the 600s B.C., these diverse religious elements had coalesced into the classical Greek religion. The most visible element, the temples, underwent a spectacular transition to monumental stone architecture in the late 600s and throughout the 500s; this trend culminated in the erection of the magnificent Parthenon (dedicated to Athena) in Athens in the 440s. Because Athena and other deities were thought actually to reside from time to time within their temples, these structures were seen as sacred places. And so were the surrounding grounds, where the altars stood. (To respect a god's privacy, no worship took place inside a temple, as it does in modern churches.) A temple and its grounds together made up the god's sacred sanctuary.

The sanctuaries naturally became the focus of the religious festivals. For example, the Erechtheum (or Erechthion) temple on the Athenian Acropolis, which housed Athena's sacred wooden statue (believed to have fallen there from the sky), played a central role in Athens's most important religious festival—the Panathenaea. The huge and stately procession (parade) that opened (or closed?) the festival conveyed Athena's sacred robe, the *peplos,* which was later draped around the statue in the Erechtheum, replacing the one made for the prior festival.

On reaching their final destination near the Erechtheum, the worshipers also engaged in large-scale public sacrifice. Conforming to ancient traditions, classical Greek animal sacrifice consisted of set rituals. First, the worshipers draped flower garlands over the animal, referred to as the victim, as they led it to the altar. Next, a priest or priestess poured water over the altar to purify it and sprinkled barley grains on the victim for the same purpose. Then he or she used a club to stun the animal and a knife to cut its throat, drained the blood into a bowl, and sprinkled some of it on the altar (or over the worshipers). Finally, several priests used axes and knives to slaughter the victim. The bones and organs were wrapped in the fat and burned, generating smoke that, it was believed, rose up to nourish and appease the gods; while the worshipers divided, cooked, and ate the meat.

In addition to processions, sacrifices, and other rituals, public religious celebrations involved prayers, as did many more private occasions, such as births, marriages, travel departures, funerals, and so on. A Greek prayed standing, with his or her hands raised, palm upwards. If the god being addressed dwelled beneath the earth, the worshiper might stretch his or her arms downward or stomp on the ground to get the god's attention. Kneeling in prayer, which is common today, was seen as unworthy of a free person.

Because any Greek could pray or perform sacrifice on his or her own, there were no priests in the modern sense of full-time spiritual guides. When family members prayed together at their home altars, the head of the household led the ritual; while in larger public ceremonies, a clan or tribal leader or a leading state official usually took charge. In addition, various temples and cults (religious congregations) often had part- or full-time staffs of caretakers and specially trained individuals who initiated or aided in sacrifices and other rituals and looked after the sacred objects (*hiera*). Any of the people just described might bear the title of priest (*hiereus*) or priestess (*hiereia*).

Priest-like individuals were also involved in divination, foretelling future events by reading and interpreting various kinds of divine signs, an art that required special skills the average person lacked. For example, there was a widespread belief in omens, signs of impending good or bad fortune, which might be detected by examining animals' livers or other organs, birds' behavior and flight formations (augury), or patterns of thunder and lightening; by throwing dice or lots; by calling up the spirits of the dead (necromancy); or through astrology (connecting human behavior to the movements of the heavenly bodies). To attend to such matters, a clan might have its own priest, who inherited his part-time position from a relative. Some people also commonly consulted professional soothsayers, usually itinerant (traveling) characters who, for a price, explained the meanings of omens, dreams, and signs revealed in sacrifices.

Soothsayers also sometimes claimed to be able to interpret oracles, a form of natural divination. These were messages, almost always vague and open to interpretation, thought to have been given to humans by the gods. (The sacred sites where these messages were given, as well as the priestesses who delivered them, were also called oracles.) The most famous and revered oracles were those of Apollo at Delphi (in central Greece) and of Zeus at Dodona (in northwestern Greece).

The practices of animal sacrifice and divination were only two of the many aspects of ancient Greek religion that set it apart from most modern faiths. The Greeks also had no sacred text, like the Bible; no set, systematic moral creed; nor any universally accepted concepts of the afterlife. Regarding the latter, most Greeks believed in some form of life after death; however, these beliefs varied widely. A common early concept (which some people still clung to in classical times) was that the god Hermes guided the soul into the Underworld, the House or Realm of Hades (ruler of the Underworld) and his wife Persephone. This was viewed as a sad and dismal abode, but not necessarily a place of punishment; so it was not the equivalent of the Christian Hell.

In time, various poets introduced the concepts of post-death punishment and reward. Particularly virtuous people might be chosen by the gods to spend eternity in the lovely, ideal setting of Elysium (or Elusion), also referred to as the Isles of the Blessed; while the wicked suffered in a miserable place called Tartarus. Some versions pictured an ancient ferryman named Charon rowing souls across the black waters of the River Styx (meaning "hated"), the Underworld's outer boundary. Once across, it was not possible to leave because the fearsome three-headed dog Cerberus stood guard and devoured those who tried.

Rejecting these mostly grim views of life after death, a number of Greeks turned to religious groups that promised to show all their members the secrets of achieving happy afterlives in Elysium. These groups, which met in private gatherings rather than public festivals, were known as mystery cults (*mysteria,* from the word *mystes,* meaning "initiate"). The term "mystery" derived from the fact that both the sacred objects and the initiation ceremonies of each cult were kept secret. Perhaps the most famous were the "Eleusinian Mysteries," centered at Eleusis, in western Attica, dedicated to Demeter, the goddess who oversaw agriculture. The mystery cults remained more or less on the fringe of Greek religion during the Classic Age, when the city-states emphasized and supported traditional public rituals. But in the Hellenistic Age (323–30 B.C.), they grew and flourished. This was a time of widespread expansion of Greek culture into the Near East, and the Greeks readily absorbed various eastern gods and cults. The Egyptian cult of Osiris (ruler of the afterlife) and his mate Isis became extremely popular, partly because the Greeks identified Isis with Greek goddesses like Aphrodite, Demeter, and Athena. The melding of the identities of the gods of two different peoples (a process called syncretism) was most prominent in the case of Sarapis. This god, who was artificially created at the order of Ptolemy I, founder of Egypt's Ptolemaic dynasty, combined attributes of the Egyptian Osiris with the Greek Dionysus and Hades.

The surviving ancient sources that inform us about Greek religion are many and varied. Homer (in the *Iliad* and *Odyssey*) and Hesiod (in his *Theogony* and *Works and Days*), who wrote in Archaic times, are credited with crystallizing and setting the tone of the basic pantheon of gods and their associated myths. "Homer and Hesiod," wrote Herodotus in the fifth century B.C., "are the poets who . . . described the gods for us, giving them all their appropriate titles, offices, and powers." (*Histories* 2.53) Herodotus himself, as well as other Greek historians, including Diodorus, alluded to various myths. Another important source for the gods and myths are the thirty-three *Homeric Hymns,* composed by a series of poets between the eighth and fifth centuries B.C.; the odes of Pindar (early fifth century B.C.); the plays of the fifth-century B.C. Athenian dramatists Aeschylus, Sophocles, and Euripides; the *Argonautica (Voyage of the Argo)* by the poet-scholar Apollonius of Rhodes (third century B.C.); the second-century

B.C. poet Apollodorus's compendium of myths (the *Bibliotheca*); the first-century B.C. Roman poet Ovid's similar, more massive compendium (the *Metamorphoses*); and works by other Roman poets, notably Apuleius, Virgil, and Catullus. Information about burial customs and other religious practices and rituals comes from the speeches written for Athenian court cases by Demosthenes, Lysias, and others; Plato's *Laws;* Plutarch's *Life of Solon;* Pausanias's *Guide to Greece;* and other treatises, as well as from surviving inscriptions, tomb epitaphs, and vase- and plaque-paintings.

Selection 1

The Creation of the World and the Gods

Hesiod

The most detailed ancient Greek creation story is the one told by the eighth-century B.C. Boeotian poet Hesiod in his Theogony, *which translates roughly as* The Genealogy of the Gods. *In the following excerpts (translated by Rhoda A. Hendricks), he begins with formless chaos, as most creation myths do. Springing from chaos, he envisions natural forces and kinds of physical matter, such as earth and sea, taking the form of beings who can reason and reproduce. Thus, Gaea (or Gaia), the Earth, soon mates with Uranus (or Uranos), the Sky or Heavens, and give rise to Cyclopes and other giants and monsters, as well as the first race of gods, the Titans. The leading Titan, Cronus (or Cronos), marries his sister, Rhea, and they produce the first group of Olympian gods, including Zeus. Hesiod then proceeds to give an exciting account of the devastating war between these two divine races, as well as an atmospheric description of Tartarus, comprising the darkest reaches of the Underworld.*

irst of all Chaos came into being, and then Gaea, the broad Earth, the ever certain support of all the deathless gods who dwell on the summit of snowy Olympus, and also dark Tartarus in the innermost part of the broad-pathed earth, and also Eros [the power of love and sexual union], the fairest of the immortal gods, who relaxes the limbs and overpowers the resolution and thoughtful determination in the hearts of all the gods and all mankind.

From Chaos came both Erebus [Darkness] and Nyx, the black Night, and of Nyx there were born Aether and Hemera, the Day, whom she bore to Erebus in a union of love. And Gaea first of all brought forth an equal to herself, Uranus, the starry Heaven, to cover her about on all sides and to be an ever certain dwelling place for the blessed gods.

Gaea also brought forth far-reaching Hills, the pleasant homes of the goddess Nymphs, who

Excerpted from Hesiod, *Theogony*, translated by Rhoda Hendricks, in *Classical Gods and Heroes: Myths as Told by the Ancient Authors.* Copyright © 1972 by Rhoda Hendricks. Reprinted by permission of Continuum International Publishing Group.

dwell in the wooded valleys of the hills. Without the delights of love, she also gave birth to the barren sea, Pontus, with his swelling waves. But later she lay with Uranus and bore [the Titans, including] deep-eddying Oceanus, Hyperion, and Iapetus, also Theia and Rhea, and Themis and Mnemosyne, and gold-crowned Phoebe and lovely Tethys. After them the youngest was born, the wily Cronus, the most dreadful of her children, and he hated his vigorous father.

In addition, she gave birth to the Cyclopes [giants], who possess mighty hearts, Brontes and Steropes and also strong-minded Arges, who gave thunder to Zeus and forged the thunderbolt. They were like the gods in all other respects, but a single eye was set in the middle of their foreheads. They were given the name Cyclopes, because indeed one round eye was set in their foreheads. Strength and force and craftiness were in their deeds.

Three other sons were also born of Gaea and Uranus, huge and strong [monsters named] Cottus and Briareus and Gyges, overpowering offspring. A hundred arms rose from their shoulders, and each one had fifty heads growing out of his shoulders, set upon sturdy limbs, and the physical strength in their great frames was mighty and dreadful. They were the most terrible of the children born of Gaea and Uranus, and they were hated by their father from the beginning. As soon as each one of them was born he would hide him away in the depths of the earth and would not allow him to return to the daylight.

Uranus delighted in his evil deed, but Gaea groaned within because she was filled with distress, and she planned an evil and deceitful trick. She quickly created gray steel, forged a great sickle, and explained her plan to her beloved sons. She spoke, encouraging them, but she was grieved at heart. "My children, offspring of a sinful father, if you have the will, we shall make your father pay for this wicked outrage, for he was the first to devise shameful acts." So she spoke, but terror seized them all, and not one of them uttered a sound. Great Cronus, however, took courage and spoke these words in answer to his beloved mother:

"Mother, I shall in truth take it upon myself to accomplish this deed, since I have no feeling for my father, who bears an evil name, for he plotted shameless deeds from the first." So he spoke, and Gaea was greatly delighted in her heart. She concealed him in an ambush and placed in his hands a sickle with sharp, jagged teeth and laid before him the whole plot.

Then mighty Uranus came, bringing the night with him, and he lay over Gaea with the longing of love, spreading out at full length, and his son stretched out his left hand from the ambush, grasping the huge jagged sickle in his right hand, and quickly cut the genitals from his father's body and cast them behind him.

They did not fall from his hands in vain, for Gaea received kindly all the drops of blood that fell from them. As time rolled on she bore the mighty Erinyes and the huge Giants, shining with armor, and the Nymphs, whom they call Meliae throughout the boundless earth.

As soon as Cronus cut off the organs with the steel and threw them from the land into the swelling sea, they were carried off on the surface of the water, and a white foam from the immortal flesh rose up around them, and within the foam a maiden came into being. First she was carried close to holy Cythera, and then from there she came to seagirt Cyprus. She stepped forth as a beautiful goddess, and all about her, grass grew up beneath her delicate feet. The gods and men call her Aphrodite, and also the foam-born goddess and fair-crowned Cytherea, because she arose from the foam near Cythera, and Cyprus-born, because she was born on wave-washed Cyprus.

And Eros [pictured as either her companion or son] walked beside her, and lovely Desire followed her from the first, when she was born and when she entered the assembly of the gods. She had this honor from the beginning, and this was the destiny allotted to her among men and the immortal gods—the conversations of young maidens, and smiles, deceptions and sweet delight, love and affection, and gentleness. [Led by Cronus, the Titans overthrow Uranus, and Cronus, the new leader of the gods, decides to marry his sister Rhea.]

The Birth of Zeus

Rhea was joined in wedlock to Cronus and bore to him glorious children; Hestia, Demeter, Hera with sandals of gold, mighty Hades, who dwells in his home below the earth and has a heart without pity, and loud-sounding Poseidon, the earth-shaker, and wise Zeus, the father of both gods and men, by whose thunder the broad earth is made to tremble.

Great Cronus swallowed these children as soon as each one came forth from his mother's womb, having this purpose in mind; that not any other one of the illustrious gods should have the honor of being king among the immortals. For he had learned from Gaea and starry Uranus that it was fated that even though he was powerful he would be overpowered by his own son, through the plans of mighty Zeus. For this reason he did not keep a blind watch, but lay in wait and swallowed each infant, while unceasing grief held Rhea in sorrow.

But when she was on the point of giving birth to Zeus, the father of gods and men, she turned in prayer to her dear parents, Gaea and starry Uranus, to contrive some plan with her so that she might bear the dear child without his knowledge, and that vengeance might be taken on the father for the children whom the mighty and crafty Cronus had swallowed. They in truth heard the plea of their beloved daughter and helped her, and they told her also what was fated to happen in regard to Cronus the king and his stout-hearted son.

Then they sent her to the fertile land of Crete, when she was about to give birth to the youngest of her children, great Zeus. Mighty Gaea took him willingly from her in broad Crete to nourish and rear. There Gaea carried him in her arms and hid him in a deep cave below the depths of the sacred earth on heavily wooded Mount Aegeum. She put into the arms of Cronus, the earlier king of the gods and the mighty son of Heaven, a great stone wrapped in swaddling clothes. Thereupon, lifting it up in his hands he put it down into his stomach, merciless as he was. He did not realize in his heart that his son, undefeated and carefree, had been left alive in place of the stone, and that his own son was soon destined to overpower him by an act of force and to keep him from his honors, reigning over the immortal gods himself.

As time rolled on, great Cronus, because he was tricked by the plans of Gaea, brought his offspring forth again, vomiting up first the stone he had swallowed last. Then Zeus set the stone firmly in the broad earth at sacred Pytho [an early name for Delphi] below the valleys of Parnassus, to be a sign from heaven from that time on, a thing of wonder to mortal men. He also freed from their bonds his father's brothers [the giants and monsters], the sons of Uranus, whom his father foolishly had bound fast. They remembered to show gratitude for his kindness and gave him thunder and the blazing thunderbolt and lightning. Trusting in these, he rules over mortals and immortals. . . .

As soon as their father, Uranus, became angry in his heart with [the monsters] Briareus and Cottus and Gyges, he bound them in strong bonds because he despised their arrogant manhood and their appearance and size, and he forced them to dwell below the broad-pathed earth at the edge of the world, grieving deeply for a long time and holding great sorrow in their hearts.

The Great War in Heaven

But the immortal gods whom fair-haired Rhea bore in wedlock to Cronus, at the bidding of Gaea, brought the three back again to the light; for she told them everything from beginning to end, explaining that with the three sons of Uranus they would win victory and a splendid achievement. For the Titan gods and those gods who were born of Cronus had been fighting a heartbreaking war for a long time. They struggled against each other in mighty combat, the illustrious Titans going into battle from lofty Othrys, while the gods whom fair-haired Rhea bore in wedlock to Cronus fought from Olympus.

Thus they held heartbreaking anger against each other and had been fighting without ceasing for ten long years. Nor was there any end to the bitter struggle, but the outcome of the war was hanging in the balance.

But when Zeus had furnished Briareus and Cottus and Gyges with all that was needed—nectar and ambrosia, the things that the very gods themselves eat—the manly spirit grew strong within the breasts of all three of them.

Then the father of both men and gods [Zeus] spoke to them: "Listen to me, splendid children of Gaea and Uranus, so that I may tell you what my heart bids me say. For the Titan gods and those who are born of Cronus have already been fighting for a very long time against each other to win a great victory. Now show your great power and invincible strength by opposing the Titans in fierce combat."

Thus he spoke, and blameless Cottus answered him: "Divine Zeus, you speak of things that are not unknown to us. It was because of your thoughtful planning that we came back again from the gloomy land of darkness and returned once more from cruel bondage, O king, son of Cronus. Now, therefore, with firm resolution and prudent planning we shall fight to defend your power in fierce combat, contending with the Titans in a violent struggle."

Thus he spoke, and the gods approved when they heard his words, and their hearts longed for war even more than they had before. Then they all, both the females and the males, stirred up battle that day; the Titan gods and those who were born of Cronus, and also those mighty and powerful ones whom Zeus released from Erebus below the earth and brought back to the light. They had a hundred arms rising from their shoulders, and each had fifty heads growing out of his shoulders, set upon sturdy limbs.

These three indeed took their stand against the Titans in grim combat, holding enormous rocks in their powerful hands. The Titans, opposing them, quickly strengthened their ranks, and both sides at the same time displayed the mighty force of their hands. The boundless sea echoed and reechoed terribly, and the earth resounded loudly. The broad heaven groaned as it was shaken, and lofty Olympus [tallest peak in Greece] quivered on its foundations under the onslaught of the immortal gods. A heavy trembling reached dark Tartarus [a dark recess of the Underworld], as did the loud sound of their feet and their mighty weapons in the indescribable attack, when they hurled their dread missiles against each other. And the shouts of both sides rose to the starry heavens as they clashed with a great war cry.

Zeus, leader of the Greek gods, is depicted in this bronze statue dated to ca. 450 B.C. His right hand once held a thunderbolt.

Then Zeus no longer held his spirit in check; now his heart was filled with rage and he displayed all his power. He came from heaven and from Olympus hurling his lightning bolts without pause. The life-giving earth resounded all about with flames, and the great forest crackled on all sides with fire. All the earth throbbed with heat, and the streams of Oceanus and the barren sea were seething. The heat surrounded the earthbound Titans, and unspeakable flames reached up to the upper air, and the bright light of the flashing lightning took the sight from their eyes. A dreadful burning heat took possession of Chaos, and it seemed as if the earth and vast heaven above had come together, so great was the din as the gods opposed each other in strife. The terrible sound of fearful combat rose up, and acts of courage were displayed.

Until the end of the battle they faced each

other and fought without ceasing in a fierce struggle. And among those in the front Cottus and Briareus and Gyges stirred up bitter fighting, for they hurled three hundred rocks from their sturdy hands, one after another, covered the Titans with their missiles, and sent them beneath the broad earth. Then, when they had overpowered them by force, even though they [the Titans] were full of spirit, they bound them in heavy chains as far down below the earth as heaven is above the earth—for that is the distance from earth to dark Tartarus. A bronze anvil falling for nine nights and nine days from heaven would reach the earth on the tenth, and, in turn, a bronze anvil falling for nine nights and nine days from earth would reach Tartarus on the tenth.

Dark and Murky Tartarus

Around Tartarus stretches a wall of bronze, and night spreads about it in three rows, and, moreover, above it grow the roots of the earth and of the barren sea. In that place the Titan gods have been hidden by the plan of Zeus the cloud-gatherer under the gloomy darkness in a dank region at the extreme edge of the vast earth. There is no way out for them, for Poseidon placed on it gates of bronze, and a wall surrounds it on all sides. There Gyges and Cottus and great-hearted Briareus dwell, the faithful guardians of aegis-bearing Zeus [The aegis being a sturdy protective shield or breastplate associated with Zeus and Athena].

And there in order are the sources and ends of the dark earth and murky Tartarus and the barren sea and starry heaven, all dreadfully dark and dank, hated even by the gods. There the terrible home of dark Night stands covered over with murky clouds. Standing in front of this, Atlas, the son of Iapetus, holds up the wide heaven on his head and untiring hands without moving, where Night and Day come quite close, addressing each other in greeting as they cross the great bronze threshold. While one is coming down inside and the other is going out through the door, the house does not keep them both inside at the same time. But one is always outside the house and moves over the earth while the other is, in turn, inside the house and waits until the hour of her own journey arrives. One holds full-seeing light for men on earth, while the other, deadly Night, covered by a murky cloud, holds in her arms Sleep, the brother of Death.

There also the children of black Night have their homes; Sleep and Death, terrible gods. Never does the shining Sun look upon them with his rays, either as he goes forth into heaven or as he returns from heaven. Of these, the former, Sleep, lingers over the earth and the broad surface of the sea and is gentle and kind to men, but the other has a heart of iron, and the spirit of bronze within his breast is pitiless, and he holds fast to whatever man he has seized and is hated even by the immortal gods.

There, in the front, the echoing chambers of the god of the lower world, mighty Hades, and his wife, dread Persephone, stand, and a terrible dog guards the entrance; a dog without pity, and he has an evil habit. He welcomes those who enter with his tail wagging and his ears erect, but does not allow anyone to go out again, for he lies in wait and chews up whomever he finds leaving the gates.

And in that place dwells the goddess hated by the immortal gods, dread Styx, the eldest daughter of Oceanus, who [as a dark river] flows back into himself. She dwells apart from the gods in a splendid house overarched with huge rocks and supported all around by silver columns reaching toward heaven. Seldom does swift-footed Iris come to her with a message over the wide surface of the sea. When discord and strife appear among the immortal gods, however, and when any one of those who dwell on Olympus has spoken falsely, then Zeus sends Iris to bring the mighty oath of the gods from afar in a golden pitcher, the renowned chill water that runs down from a steep and lofty rock. . . .

And there in order are the sources and ends of the dark earth, and murky Tartarus and the barren sea and starry heaven, all dreadfully dark and dank, hated even by the gods. There, also, are gleaming entrance gates and an immovable threshold of bronze. And over this threshold and apart from all the gods the Titans live, on the other side of gloomy Chaos. But the splendid allies of loud-thundering Zeus—Cottus and Gyges—dwell in homes on the bottom of Oceanus. And, indeed, since Briareus was brave, Poseidon the heavy-sounding earth-shaker made him his son-in-law and gave him his daughter in marriage.

Selection 2

The Major Gods: Their Attributes, Attendants, and Images

David Bellingham

This overview of the most important of the many ancient Greek gods, along with their symbols, attributes, and most common images in artistic depictions, is by scholar David Bellingham, an expert on the subject matter and techniques of ancient wall painting. Most of the gods he mentions were among the Olympians, so-called because in legend they dwelled atop Mt. Olympus, in northern Thessaly. However, Bellingham also discusses a number of minor gods associated with the Olympians, such as Aphrodite's companion, Eros, Demeter's daughter, Persephone, and Hermes' son, Pan. Also identified are various attendants and followers, including Dionysus's Maenids and Satyrs.

Zeus

Son of Cronus and Rhea, he proved his superiority in single combat against Typhon and in the battle with the Titans and became king on Mount Olympus. After having a number of children with Titanesses, he married his sister Hera; although they had several important children, their marriage was far from happy, mainly owing to Zeus' tendency to lust after mortal women. A common pattern emerges in these relationships: Zeus is attracted to a woman and is compelled to visit her in disguise (his true appearance with thunder and lightning would destroy a human being); Hera discovers the affair and seeks revenge against her husband by punishing the woman or the offspring of the liaison.

Zeus (meaning 'to shine') was god of the sky in all its moods, from the clear bright light to the darkest storm. He administered justice and protected oaths sworn in his name. In art he appears as a long-haired (sometimes plaited up), mature and somewhat imposing figure; he is represented in heroic nudity as well as in full regalia; his attributes are his throne, sceptre, thunderbolt (not our modern zigzag design, but rather like an exploded fat cigar), diadem and eagle. His most important sanctuary was Olympia where all Greek states were entitled to compete in the games held in his honour every four years. A rich temple was built there in the 5th century BC which housed the gold and ivory statue of the god seated on his throne; it was made by Pheidias and became one of the Seven Wonders of the World.

Hera

A daughter of Cronus and Rhea, Hera was one of the gods to be swallowed by Cronus; when she was vomited back up by the Titan, she did not join the battle with her brothers and sisters against the giants, but was put into the care of Oceanus and Tethys. She became the permanent wife of Zeus after his relationships with other goddesses, and became the guardian of marriage and childbirth; her character in the myths reflects this role and she is constantly venting her anger at her husband's infidelities. Her children by Zeus were Ares, Hebe (guardian of youthful beauty and divine cup-bearer) and Eileithyia (goddess of childbirth); in angry response to the birth of Athene without a mother, Hera bore Hephaestus without a father.

In art Hera is depicted as a mature woman, sometimes with an elaborate crown and sceptre and holding a wedding veil aside from her head. Her most important cult centre was at Argos.

Athene

Virgin goddess of war as well as the arts and crafts and in later times of general wisdom, Athene had an extraordinary birth. Zeus had been warned by his grand-parents, Gaia and Uranus, that his first wife, Metis, would have a son who would overthrow Zeus as he had his own father. Zeus therefore swallowed Metis, who was pregnant, and forgot all about her until one morning he awoke with a terrible headache and a rattling sound in his head. Hephaestus was called in to crack open Zeus' skull to see what

the trouble was; the smith-god obliged and out jumped Athene in full armour—she became Zeus' favourite. Her titles 'Promachos' (the Champion) and 'Ergane' (Worker) reflected her dual role as a goddess of war and everyday work.

In art she appears as a tall, slim, noble woman with helmet, spear and shield and her special breastplate, the aegis, decorated with the head of the Gorgon [female monster] Medusa, worn over a long tunic. Her main sanctuary was on the Acropolis at Athens where an ancient wooden image of her was worshipped in the Erechtheion, while Pheidias constructed a huge gold and ivory statue of the goddess for the magnificent Temple of Athene Parthenos ('Virgin'), called the Parthenon. The Panathenaic Games were held in her honour every year, while every four years there was a special festival during which a new tunic was placed on the old wooden statue.

Long ago the Athenians had built up a prosperous city and desired a god to protect them. Both Poseidon and Athene wanted the honour and began to fight for it. The Athenians suggested a more peaceful way of settling the dispute: whichever of the two gods gave them the greatest gift would be awarded the city. Poseidon went first and thrust his trident into the Acropolis rock to bring forth a salt-water pool which threatened to flood the city; the Athenians protested that their rich farmland would be spoilt and asked Athene to produce a more useful gift. Athene struck the rock with her spear and immediately an olive tree sprouted; the Athenians realised that its fruit would provide them with oil for cooking, lighting and perfume and awarded the city to her protection. The marks of the trident and the sacred olive tree remained for centuries.

On one occasion Athene was bringing a huge rock to plant as a natural defensive barrier for Athens; Hephaestos saw her coming and attempted to make love to her as she flew towards the walls. She managed to fend him off and the rock fell to the ground to become the conical hill Lykabettos, while his seed fell onto the Acropolis and Erichthonius, the future King of Athens, was born. Athene not only fought with the Athenians but accompanied many Greek heroes on their adventures.

Poseidon

Son of Rhea and Cronus, god of the sea, earthquakes and horses, Poseidon received dominion over the sea when he drew lots with his brothers Zeus and Hades. His adventures often resemble those of Zeus, involving the seduction of mortal women in the guise of animals, including a ram, a dolphin and a bird; and like Zeus, he also fell in love with men, taking Pelops to Olympus as his lover and presenting him with winged horses to win a chariot-race to obtain his wife; Pelops gave his name to the Peloponnese. Poseidon was constantly fighting for dominion of places on the land including Athens, which he lost to his niece Athene, and Corinth, where Helius received the hill of Acrocorinth and Poseidon was given the Isthmus which forms the bridge to Attica. An important sanctuary was dedicated to him at the Isthmus. In art he is similar to Zeus, perhaps lacking his more domineering attitude, and identifiable by his trident; sometimes he holds a sea-creature.

Artemis

Daughter of Leto and Zeus and sister of Apollo, Artemis, like Athene, was a virgin goddess; she was given the wild areas outside city walls as her realm where she both hunted and protected the wild animals; she was also goddess of childbirth. Her encounters with men generally involve the administering of cruel punishments for their attempts to rape or spy on her. In art she appears as a beautiful huntress, usually in short tunic and bearing quiver and bow; in later art she can appear with the crescent moon on her head—a sign of her lunar associations.

When King Agamemnon was about to lead the Greek fleet to Troy to recapture his brother's wife Helen, who had been abducted by Paris, he stupidly boasted that he was a better hunter than Artemis. She punished him by refusing winds for his sailing ships unless he sacrificed his young daughter Iphigeneia to the goddess. The girl was taken to the altar but Artemis took pity on her and replaced her with a deer, carrying her away to be her priestess in the land of the barbarian Taurians where she would sacrifice all visiting strangers to Artemis.

Apollo

Son of the Titaness Leto by Zeus, and brother of Artemis, Apollo was born on the island of Delos which remained sacred to him. While still a boy, Apollo journeyed to Delphi where he killed a huge snake called Python and took control of the Pythian oracle. He appeared as a dolphin to Cretan sailors and took them to Delphi, ordering them to guard his oracle and build a temple to Apollo Delphinius (of the Dolphin). Apollo and Artemis defended the honour of their mother when Niobe, Queen of Thebes, boasted that she had more beautiful children: they shot the Niobids with their arrows.

Apollo was god of prophecy and healing, and became associated with music and cultural activities; he was worshipped as a rational god, defending intellectual pursuits, the opposite of Dionysus. He had many affairs with both male and female mortal lovers. In art he appears as a beardless handsome youth with long hair, often plaited up; he holds a bow, lyre or his sacred laurel branch.

Ares

Only son of Zeus and Hera, Ares was the god of war. He appears in art as an ordinary Greek warrior, with helmet, shield, sword and spear. His association with warfare is far from glamorous: generally we see him generating as much trouble as he can on the battlefield to cause the maximum bloodshed on both sides. His fellow Olympians do not care for him, apart from Aphrodite, who was his lover. On one occasion Hephaestus left Olympus and stayed for a while on the island of Lemnos. His wife Aphrodite called Ares into her bed, but Hephaestus had hung a net of fine wire over his bed, which fell upon them; they became completely tangled and Hephaestus invited all the other Olympians to laugh at the expense of the god of war and goddess of love. The smith god let them go free and Aphrodite returned to Cyprus and Ares returned to Thrace, a centre for his worship.

Aphrodite

The most famous account of the birth of the goddess of erotic love is that she appeared out of the sea-foam surrounding the severed genitals of Uranus; her name means 'born from foam'. Homer makes her a daughter of Zeus and the Oceanid Dione. Likewise Eros, the god of sexual desire, is her son by Ares in many accounts, though Hesiod has him welcoming the goddess ashore at her birth. Many Greeks associated her with Eastern love goddesses such as Ishtar; these were also war goddesses and this might explain Aphrodite's links with Ares, god of war. Her husband on Olympus was the lame god Hephaestus.

In art she appears at first as an attractive young woman, wearing pretty clothes and often holding a flower and a dove. Her most famous statue was made by [the fourth-century B.C. Athenian sculptor] Praxiteles for her shrine on the island of Kos, but when it was unveiled the town council rejected it, shocked by its nudity. The people of Knidos [or Cnidus, a Greek city in southern Asia Minor] bought it for their sanctuary to the goddess, placing her in a romantically positioned circular temple. The temple, which became one of the most important cult centres of the goddess, was recently discovered. . . . The statue has long since disappeared, but its base and a Greek inscription telling us the artist and subject were found. She stood with her back to the setting sun and the sea. There was a story that a man, lusting after the statue, made love to it one night; this story emphasizes her physical sexual presence in antiquity rather than the more romantic view that developed later.

The depiction of Aphrodite as a beautiful mature woman preparing to bathe influenced all later representations of the goddess. She regularly appears with Eros, who is symbolized in early art as a beautiful youth with long wings and hair, holding the bow and gold-tipped arrows with which he pierces the hearts of lovers.

In later art he multiplies into many children (Erotes or Cupids) with short wings, precursors of Renaissance 'putti'.

Aphrodite had both mortal and immortal lovers. Hermes was rejected by her, so Zeus sent his eagle to snatch her sandal and take it to Hermes, who would not return it until she had submitted. Their son was the beautiful youth Hermaphroditus with whom the Naiad [water nymph] Salmacis fell in love whilst he was bathing in her spring. As they made love, she clung to him so fast that their bodies fused into one. In art Hermaphroditus appears as a woman with male genitals.

Hephaestus

Hera probably produced this son without a father in retaliation to Zeus who had given birth to Athene without a mother. Hephaestus was rejected by Hera because of his lameness; she threw him out of Olympus into Oceanus where Thetis rescued him. When he grew up he punished his mother by making her a magical golden throne, but when she sat on it she found herself stuck fast. The gods tried to persuade Hephaestus to return to Olympus and forgive his mother; he refused until Dionysus gave him wine and led him back drunk on an ass to the great mirth of his fellow Olympians.

Hephaestus was associated with fire and the crafts of blacksmithing and metalwork and his workshop was thought to be beneath volcanoes such as Etna in Sicily. In art he often appears in a craftsman's short tunic, holding a double axe or a pair of blacksmith's tongs; his lameness is sometimes suggested by his leaning on a crutch. His temple in the Agora at Athens was close to potters' workshops and contained statues of both himself and Athene, who was also associated with crafts.

Hermes

Offspring of Zeus and one of the Pleiades [daughters of the Titan Atlas], Maia, Hermes was born in a cave on Mount Cyllene in Arcadia. He was a precocious child and, on the very day of his birth, he climbed out of his cradle and killed a tortoise outside his cave and, using the shell as a sound-box and sheep-gut for strings, invented the lyre. Later the same day, Hermes stole cattle belonging to Apollo and led them back to his cave, where he lay down in his cradle pretending innocence. Apollo eventually caught up with the thief (Hermes was later a god of thieves) and demanded the lyre in place of the cattle, in return for which he made Hermes god of herds and herdsmen. When he grew up, Zeus made him the messenger of the gods; only Hermes was allowed free passage between Olympus, the Earth and the Underworld and he escorted dead Greeks to the ferryman Charon, who for a small coin would carry the dead across the river Styx to Hades.

Hermes, like Apollo, had many love affairs. There is argument as to the mother of his most famous son, Pan, who became god of shepherds. In art, Pan appears as a lusty human figure, sometimes with goats' legs and horns and sometimes with goat's head and human body; he often plays the rustic pan-pipes. Hermes appears with his *kerykeion*, a magic wand entwined with snakes which gives him access to all places. He is often bearded and wears traveller's clothes, including a sun-hat, short tunic and cloak; his hat and boots are sometimes winged for flight.

Demeter, Persephone and Hades

Daughter of Cronus and Rhea, Demeter, goddess of corn and fertility, was seduced on earth by a prince called Iasion; their children were Plutus (Wealth) and Philomelus, who was made into the constellation Bootes ('the wagon'), which he invented. Zeus killed Iasion with a thunderbolt for presuming to love a goddess; Zeus then made love to Demeter himself and she bore a daughter named Persephone. Hades, brother of the Olympians and god of the Underworld, asked Zeus for Persephone as his wife. Zeus agreed, but, thinking that Demeter would not accept the match as she would lose her daughter forever to the Underworld, assisted Hades in Persephone's abduction. He asked Gaia to send up many lovely flowers near where

Persephone dwelt; whilst she was picking them with her friends, Hades came up from the Underworld in a chariot and took the poor girl back with him. Demeter searched the world for many days and nights in the guise of a mortal. At every town she visited, she told men the secrets of the harvest; one of these towns, Eleusis, became a centre for her mystery cult. Demeter threatened famine to the earth unless her daughter was returned; but Persephone had eaten several pomegranate seeds which meant that she would have to stay in Hades for one-third of the year, during which period Demeter refused to allow the crops to grow. Festivals were held for the return of Persephone every spring. At Eleusis, Demeter lent her winged chariot, drawn by dragons, to the youth Triptolemus; he was to use it every year to scatter seed over the earth. In art, mother and daughter sometimes wear crowns and carry torches or ears of corn.

Dionysos

Also known as Bacchus, the god of wine and vegetation, his mortal mother was Semele of Thebes, whom Zeus had taken as a lover. Jealous Hera appeared to Semele in the guise of her old nurse and dared her to demand that Zeus appear in his real form. Semele was incinerated by his thunderbolt, but Zeus salvaged the unborn boy and sowed him into his thigh; a few months later Dionysus was born and given to Hermes to entrust to the care of nymphs on Mount Nysa [the exact location of which is disputed]. When he grew up these nymphs became his female devotees, the Maenads. Hera drove him mad and he fled to the east where the oriental earth goddess Cybele cured him. He then returned to Greece, establishing his cult in different places and proved to the world that his father was Zeus.

In Classical art he appears as a beautiful youth with long hair and a thyrsos, a wand bound with ivy and topped with a pine cone; round his head he wears an ivy wreath and often carries an upturned wine cup. In later art he becomes increasingly effeminate in appearance.

His female followers, the Maenads, are human in form, but carry thyrsoi and wear skins from the animals they have slaughtered during the rites; often they wear ivy or even snakes for headbands. His male followers, the Satyrs, appear as men with horses' tails, pointed ears, and erect penises, signs of the irrational animal nature that is freed by the worship of Dionysus; we often see them drinking or in lusty pursuit of Maenads.

Hestia

The eldest child of Cronus and Rhea, Hestia guarded hearth, fire, house, family and community. She remained a virgin goddess, though both Poseidon and Apollo had wished to marry her. She rarely appears in art and has few shrines, her home being at the hearth.

Selection 3

The Nature and Forms of Greek Worship

Michael Grant

On its most basic level, Greek worship consisted of a sort of exchange between humans and the gods. The gods provided or maintained the conditions needed for human life and prosperity; and in exchange, people offered these deities compensation in the form of sacrifice. Noted scholar Michael Grant, of Edinburgh University, refers to this relationship as "reciprocal" in the following examination of Greek religious worship. Grant also lists some of the major Greek sanctuaries (sacred areas made up of the temples and their surrounding grounds) and some important religious festivals. In addition, he explains the mystery cults, singling out the most renowned of these—the cult of Demeter at Eleusis, in western Attica. It was in the rites celebrated in such local cults, he says, *and especially their promises of some kind of salvation after death, that Greek religion attained its most popular form.*

The religion of the Greeks is . . . disconcertingly difficult to comprehend. . . . It was, of course, a polytheistic religion. It had room for a large number of gods and goddesses, who, despite extensive overlapping, represented different aspects of life, mirroring the multiplicity of the human world, and were attached more or less closely to their own special shrines, although the principal deities were also recognized everywhere. Links with the ancient past were very strong, yet, as so often, we are faced with the paradox that, at the same time, the Greeks made something new out of it all.

Their debt to the past emerges most clearly in connection with the great goddesses, Hera and Demeter and Artemis. All these perceptibly, in their different ways, echo the Earth Mother or Mistress of Animals of earlier civilizations: Hera's epithet 'ox-eyed' (Boopis) and Athena's owl at Athens recall times when animal totems had been worshipped. On the other hand Zeus, the chief of the gods and lord of the sky, was a later importation, brought in during the convulsions that accompanied and followed the fall of Mycenae; and Apollo, the dread shining one, the most Greek of gods despite his apparently un-Greek name and origins, made his appearance at the same time.

The origins of Greek religion remain something of a mystery. They were sometimes attributed, unconvincingly, to Egypt, but Homer and Hesiod were credited, more plausibly, with the remarkable achievement of standardizing and welding together the Olympic gods for Greece. A strong team, too, Homer in particular makes of them, as subsequent Greeks noticed . . . a collection of perilously powerful divinities, full of vices and foibles. These failings were on human lines, since one of the most distinctive features of Greek religion, for which Homer again must take a lot of the credit, was its anthropomorphism, uniquely developed among the major religions of the world. These gods and goddesses are human beings writ large, because the Greeks, with their lively dramatic and plastic sense, were so conscious of the potentialities of men and women that they could not imagine the deities in any other shape.

In early times, at least, these divinities, while admired for their beauty and strength, were not consistently thought of as representing ethical concepts or ideals, either in their own behaviour or in their requirements from men and women, except that Zeus, various facets of whose power were described by specific epithets, expected certain basic forms of good behaviour, such as the protection of suppliants and hospitality to strangers. Other kinds of misbehaviour such as *hubris*—self-indulgence at the expense of others . . . could on occasion be punished, although the idea that the gods resented over-prosperous mortals does not clearly antedate 500 BC. But these deities could be savagely dangerous if men and women did not acknowledge them (that is what the Greek term *nomizein* means—not 'believe in') and if they were not placated; this was

an anxiety-appeasing religion of formal reciprocity, *do ut des*, I give you so that you shall give me.

Sacrifice, Sanctuaries, and Cults

Now, what they [the gods] primarily needed was sacrifice, and best of all the blood sacrifice of meat, which satisfied the guilt and exultation of the sacrificers, affirming life by its encounter with death (as well as providing welcome left-overs for food). So the principal centres of early worship were sacrificial altars, not the temples which in due course grew up behind them; altars and temples alike may well have been financed at first not only by communities but by rich individuals.

Great sanctuaries came into existence, for Zeus at Dodona and Olympia and Nemea, for Apollo at Delphi (Pytho) and Delos and Didyma and Claros, for Hera at Argos and Samos and near Croton and Posidonia, for Artemis at Ephesus, for Poseidon at Isthmia beside Corinth. The evidence for the direct continuity of such Greek sanctuaries down from Mycenaean times is conflicting or dubious (and in any case, if and when it existed, a change of deity was usually involved). But such major places of worship entered a decisive phase in the eighth century, influenced civic development and expanded enormously in the 200 years that followed. Some of the centres became famous for oracles; the oracular shrines at Dodona and especially Delphi gained enormous influence.

Around four sanctuaries, too, developed great festivals, the Olympian, Pythian, Isthmian and Nemean Games. These gatherings may perhaps have gone back to Homeric funeral games for the dead heroes, although this interpretation of their origin is disputed. In their mature form they were eloquently praised by Plato for the refreshment and 'wholeness' they bestowed on every participant. Yet their role in the unification, or otherwise, of the Greek world was contradictory. On the one hand their Panhellenic nature did something to counterbalance the particularism of individual city-states. But at the same time the contests which were the essential feature of these regular concourses formed a supreme example of the unrestrained competitiveness which so sharply kept those states apart; and it was the same spirit of competition (*agon*) that stimulated the abundant dedications of works of art to the sanctuaries, especially at Olympia and the Samian Heraeum, by cities and individuals all over the Greek world. These dedicated objects included, from the eighth century onwards, two successive types of huge bronze cauldrons, of Syrian inspiration—prestigious monumentalizations [large-scale representations] of domestic pots, decorated with ornaments which foreshadowed subsequent sculpture.

Alongside the worship of the Olympian deities was a whole range of other, more popular cults, frequently of a local or territorial character—defining the individuality of each *polis*. Such cults venerated regional or national heroes (*heroes*), notable dead men or women, historical or legendary, generally at their actual or supposed tombs. And there were also ecstatic and underworld ('chthonian', fertility) rituals: represented, for example, by the cult of Dionysus (from Thrace) and the secret Mysteries of Demeter (at Eleusis). Towards the end of the early period cults of a 'chthonian' nature attained importance because of the salvation in the afterlife which mystic initiations into their rituals could excitingly bring—excitements which had been lacking in the shadowy nullity [non-existence] of the afterlife presented, for example, by Homer.

The Mystery Religion at Eleusis

At Eleusis priestly duties were at first the hereditary prerogatives of certain families, but there and elsewhere professional priesthoods did not exist. For, despite the ever present power of Greek religion, there was no Church and no canon of orthodoxy. . . . Eleusis owed its widespread renown to the locally celebrated Mysteries (initiation rites) in honour of Demeter and her daughter Persephone (Kore, the Maiden). The cult of Demeter, in some form or another, had already been celebrated in the late Bronze (Mycenaean) Age, or at least as early as the eleventh century BC. For that seems to be the

date of the remains of a *megaron* (porched house) that was apparently the first shrine of the goddess. It was succeeded by a circular or apsed building, perhaps in *c.* 800, the epoch to which numerous female inhumations on the site, probably of priestesses, have been attributed.

The myth told how the goddess, seemingly a fusion between a pre-Hellenic underworld deity and a Mesopotamian corn-goddess, was anguished by the seizure of her daughter Persephone by Hades (Pluto), the god of the lower realm. The rape of Persephone had caused the fertility of the earth to be blasted, rather as . . . similar stories appear in Mesopotamian and Canaanite mythology.

During the course of her wanderings in search of her daughter Demeter came to Eleusis. There, the daughters of the monarch of the place, Celeus, found her seated beside a well, and took her into the royal household, where, amid miraculous happenings, she nursed the king's son. Revealing her identity to the Eleusinians, the goddess withdrew to a temple constructed for her, until Zeus agreed that Persephone might return to the upper world for two-thirds of the year. Thereupon, Demeter revived the earth's fertility, by sowing the first seeds of corn in the Rharian plain, and before ascending to Mount Olympus with her daughter she disclosed to Celeus 'the conduct of her rites and all her Mysteries'.

As the term 'Mystery'—derived from *muein*, to keep silent—suggests, the character of these nocturnal, torch-like ceremonies remained secret, in accordance with the primitive idea that outsiders should not be allowed to know the true names of a community's deities and how to enlist their aid. And besides, this was a sort of enlarged family cult to which, in theory, the head of the family admitted whom he pleased. But the Mysteries of Demeter cannot have been or remained very secret, since their later hall had room for 4,000 worshippers, and all men, women and children of Greek speech, including slaves, were eligible for initiation, provided only that they were untainted by homicide.

From such fragmentary evidence as has come down to us, it seems that the rites acted out the rape of Persephone and her mother's arrival at Eleusis to search for her, and culminated in a ritual in which the torches employed to illuminate the proceedings were thrown in the air. There also appears to have been a display and procession of models of genital organs and statuettes of men and women engaged in sexual acts, since human love-making was thought to stimulate the fertility of the crops, and by the same token obscene invectives (believed to have been the origin of iambic verse) were shouted out.

Renewal and Salvation

By *c.* 600, a few generations after the takeover of Eleusis by the Athenians, they had succeeded in elevating its cult to Panhellenic status. This widespread enthusiasm was owed, above all, to the special benefits in the afterlife which the Mysteries, embodying successive stages of initiation, were able to offer: the renewal of the crops pledged renewal of life after death, very different from the bleak prospects in the Homeric poems. 'Blessed is he who has seen these things before he goes beneath the hollow earth,' wrote [the fifth-century B.C. Boeotian poet] Pindar, 'for he understands the end of mortal life, and the beginning [of new life] given of god'—whereas for non-initiates 'everything there would be bad'. The cult also made an obvious and irresistible appeal to that submerged half of Greek society, its women, by accepting the female experiences of Persephone and Demeter as a model and source of this posthumous salvation.

For such reasons the Athenian state was eager to develop the cult under its own control, thus canalizing, beneath a guise of respectability, the ever more widespread but also suspect ideas and excitements embodied in such uncivic, mystic worships and folk traditions, so that they were able to mould the Mysteries, in their historic form, as the finest flower of Greek popular religion. The Festival of Greater Eleusinia was celebrated in the second year of each Olympiad, with lesser celebrations in the other years, and the cult was initially administered by two Athenian lay families, the Eumolpids and Kerykes, of whom the former claimed descent from the Thracian Eumolpus, believed to have been the first celebrant at Eleusis. At about the same time as this elevation of the Eleusinian cult, the grave and gay *Hymn to Demeter*—one of the most dramatically and magically exciting of the misnamed 'Homeric' Hymns—was composed, probably at Athens, to recount the myth of the goddess.

Selection 4

The Oracle at Delphi

Manolis Andronicos

Manolis Andronicos, the noted Greek archaeologist and professor at the University of Thessaloniki, composed the following highly informative description of the famous shrine and oracle of Apollo at Delphi, in central Greece. He begins with a brief historical account of the oracle, which played so crucial a role in numerous important political events and crises in the Archaic and Classic Ages. As Andronicos explains, the shrine was normally administered by the Delphic Amphiktiony. (An amphiktiony was a religious association or league of communities that all revered and collectively oversaw the shrine of a god.) But the Phokians, the inhabitants of Phokis (or Phocis), the region where Delphi was located, seized it on more than one occasion, initiating the so-called "sacred wars." Andronicos also describes in detail the oracle herself (a priestess called the Pythia) and how she delivered Apollo's prophecies to eager pilgrims.

The first diviner to occupy the Delphic oracle was the mother of the gods, Gaia. She was succeeded by her daughter, Themis. The third occupant was another daughter of Gaia, the Titaness Phoibe, who gave Apollo the surname of Phoibos [or Phoebus] as a birthday present. We have this information from the Pythia's own mouth, in the opening lines of Aischylos' [or Aeschylus's] tragedy *Eumenides*. As regards the rest of the story: how Apollo founded his first temple at Delphi, and how he slew the fearful dragon (a female serpent) near a spring, this is recounted in the ancient Homeric hymn to Apollo. In later times, men believed this serpent to have been male and even more redoubtable, none other than the famous Python, guardian of Gaia's oracle; the battle that the young god who had come from the north—from the valley of Tempe—fought against the serpent was indeed a great and terrible one. They also believed that although a god, Apollo complied to the divine rule which he himself had set: that whoever defiled his hands with the blood of murder should be sent into exile. Thus the god departed for eight years and worked in the service of Admetos, King of Pherai [in Thessaly], in order to cleanse himself of the pestilent blood of murder; then he returned, purified and clean at last, sole master of the Delphic oracle.

This is what the ancients had to say about the beginnings of the legendary oracle. But concerning the site itself, that unique site which overwhelms whoever visits it for the first time, they had another story to tell. Zeus, wishing to find the centre of the earth, let loose two eagles from the two ends of the world: the sacred birds met at Delphi, which meant that there was the "navel" of the earth. Hence, Apollo's sanctuary contained, since remotest times, an *omphalos* (navel-stone), and votive offerings in the shape of the *omphalos* were presented to the god by pious pilgrims from all over the world. The Apollonian oracle was indeed celebrated and venerated throughout the inhabited world. Not only Greeks, but barbarian monarchs as well sent envoys to consult the oracle and expressed their gratitude by dedicating sumptuous gifts and votive offerings to the god.

Such are the myths of the ancients concerning Apollo, Delphi and the celebrated oracle. However, before we come to the Delphic sanctuary and speak of the Delphic cult, we must first take a look at the place itself. . . . The visitor encounters a landscape vividly described in the Homeric hymn: "You climbed rapidly (Phoibos is being addressed here) running across the hilltops and you reached the regions of Krisa below Mount Parnassos which is covered with much snow, at the point where it forms a knee to the west, and a large rock overhangs the spot, while below a wild valley stretches out; this was the spot where the Lord Phoibos Apollo decided to have a beautiful temple . . ."

Anybody coming upon the holy site for the first time is struck with awe. . . . And there . . . in the deepest recess of the gorge and at the foot of the east rock . . . the most limpid water gushes forth: it is the water of the celebrated Kastalian Fountain where both priests and pilgrims cleansed themselves before entering the temple. On the western side, at the foot of the rock named Rhodini, Apollo's sanctuary, the most famous in ancient Greece, extends across the opening on the rising ground. And down below, the deep valley of the Pleistos river spreads out, green and silver with olive-groves, and merges with the plain of Itea stretching all the way down to the sea-coast.

Excerpted from Manolis Andronicos, *Delphi* (Athens: Ekdotike Athenon, 1993). Copyright © 1976 by Ekdotike Athenon S.A. Reprinted by permission of the publisher.

The oracle (priestess) at the Temple of Apollo at Delphi (in central Greece) swoons in preparation for her delivery of a divine message, while eager religious pilgrims look on.

The History of Delphi

The history of Delphi is inextricably bound with the history of the sanctuary and the oracle; to be more precise, Delphi only existed as a township under the shadow of the sanctuary. Archaeological excavations have revealed the existence of an insignificant settlement on the site of the sanctuary and further east, dating back to *c.* 1400 B.C. This settlement was destroyed at the end of the Mycenaean period, but came back to life . . . when Apollo's cult began to take root in that region. Hence-forward, Delphi acquired world fame and power of a kind unparalleled in Greece, although it remained a small town, sparsely populated. Over the course of 250 years, four sacred wars were waged for this small town, and at the end it caused the annihilation of the Phokians. . . .

In central Greece there existed an Amphiktyony whose seat was the sanctuary of Demeter at Anthele, a small town near Thermopylai. In the 7th century B.C., the seat of the Amphiktyony was transferred to the sanctuary of Apollo at Delphi. The Amphiktyonic League, then, declared Delphi an independent township—which meant that it no longer came under the Phokian state—and placed the sanctuary under its own protection. There existed similar Amphiktyonies in other parts of Greece as well. However, the Amphiktyony of Delphi did not consist of delegations from the city-states, but from the "nations" of the Hellenes, in other words, the ancient tribes that made up the main body of ancient Hellenism: Ainianes, Achaians, Phthiotians, Dolopes, Dorians, Thessalians, Ionians, Lokrians, Malians, Magnetes, Perrhaibians, Phokians. And so the sanctuary of Apollo became the religious and political centre of the Hellenic world—a position which no other sanctuary could claim.

During the peak period of Greek colonization

(late 8th–7th century B.C.), Greek cities that had resolved to establish a colony to some distant land first consulted the oracle as to where they should go and who should become the *oikistes*, the leader and founder of the future colony. Syracuse, Kroton, Kyrene, Thasos are among the better-known of many colonies that owed their very existence to the wise counsel of Phoibos. Several other colonies chose to name themselves after the god: Apollonia. All these cities honoured Apollo with the surname of *Archegetes*, meaning first leader. Thus the prestige and fame of the god and his oracle spread East and West, far beyond the bounds of metropolitan Greece. As early as the 7th century B.C., Midas, the legendary king of Phrygia, sent his own royal throne to the Pythian Apollo as a token of his veneration. At about the same time, another legendary king, Gyges (675 B.C.), founder of the Mermnad dynasty and ancestor of Croesus, dedicated magnificent votive offerings of pure gold to the Delphic god. Kypselos, the renowned wealthy tyrant of Corinth, built in the Delphic sanctuary the first "treasury", i.e. a small building in the shape of a temple, which had the double function of serving as a votive offering and sheltering the smaller, precious offerings dedicated by each city to the sanctuary.

The glory, power and wealth of the Delphic oracle grew steadily. However, it appears that the Phokians of Krisa decided to exploit their position as neighbours to Delphi, and levied heavy dues on the faithful who disembarked at the port of Kirrha, in Phokian territory, on their way to the oracle. Delphi then appealed to the Amphiktyony for help and the First Sacred War was declared. It was to last ten years, ending in 591 B.C. with the annihilation of the Krisaians. Kirrha and Krisa were destroyed and their territory was dedicated to the Delphic deities. The Amphiktyons then proceeded to reorganize the Pythian festival, which took place every 8 years to commemorate Apollo's return from his voluntary exile after the slaying of Python. From 582 B.C. this festival was celebrated every four years; gymnastic and equestrian contests were added to the earlier musical competition.

The sanctuary's fame spread across the world, and the offerings it received were beyond anything the boldest imagination might conceive. Croesus, the king of Lydia, famous for his wealth, sent all kinds of offerings, the most sumptuous being a lion of solid gold weighing about 250 kgs., set upon a pyramid made of 117 bricks of "white gold" (a mixture of gold and silver); in addition to that, two large kraters, one gold and the other silver, which were placed to the right and left of the temple entrance. When Apollo's poros temple was destroyed by fire in 548 B.C., not only the Greeks, but foreign sovereigns, such as Croesus of Lydia and Amasis of Egypt, made generous donations for the construction of a new temple, which cost 300 talents, the equivalent of several billions of present-day drachmae. The Alkmeonidai, the noble Athenian family exiled by Peisistratos and his sons, undertook the construction project; in excess of what was stipulated in the contract, they used marble for the facade instead of poros. . . .

About the middle of the 5th century B.C., the Phokians once again gained political power over Delphi; this led to the declaration of the Second Sacred War (447 B.C.), to restore the sanctuary's independence. In 373 B.C., a terrible earthquake uprooted huge pieces of rock and flung them on the temple of Apollo. Reconstruction started immediately, thanks to pan-Hellenic contributions, but it was interrupted in 356 B.C. by a Third Sacred War. The Phokians occupied the sanctuary for a period of ten years and confiscated not only sanctuary funds, but also a large number of valuable votive offerings. The Greeks felt highly indignant at this sacrilege. Following the intervention of Philip, king of Macedonia, the Phokians were routed, excluded from the Amphyktyony and obliged to pay a colossal indemnity (420 talents). Finally, the Fourth Sacred War broke out in 339 B.C., against the Lokrians [the inhabitants of Lokris, just west of Delphi] this time. Once again, Philip assumed leadership; after defeating the Lokrians, he proceeded to Chaironeia, where he fought the famous battle (338 B.C.), which made him master of Greece.

During the Hellenistic period, the Greek

world underwent a radical transformation. The old faith was shaken; the cities gradually lost their independence and merged within the larger context of great kingdoms. The powerful kings began to rely on their own armies rather than on divine assistance. They still consulted the oracle and sent rich gifts, but this was done in a wish to display their own wealth rather than honour the god. . . .

In 168 B.C. the Roman Aemilius Paulus defeated the Macedonians at Pydna: and at Delphi, upon the pedestal which Perseus, the Macedonian king, had prepared for his statue, the Roman set up his own equestrian figure. The hour of Rome had come. In 86 B.C., Sulla removed all the valuable offerings that had survived the Fourth Sacred War; and in 83 B.C., barbarians from Thrace plundered the sanctuary and set fire to the temple; this was the first time, according to tradition, when the flame burning since time immemorial was extinguished, depriving both Greeks and barbarians of its beneficent radiance. Nevertheless, the Delphic sanctuary still prospered; [the notorious Roman emperor] Nero removed no less than 500 statues from Delphi; and yet when [the famous Greek traveler] Pausanias visited it in the 2nd century A.D., he still found it full of masterpieces. However, when the Roman emperors were converted to Christianity, the ancient religion no longer had any place in the new State. Constantine the Great took away from Delphi innumerable works of art for the embellishment of his new capital. . . . Theodosios the Great prohibited the ancient cult and games in A.D. 394. . . .

The Method of Divination Used by the Oracle

The fame and power of Delphi was based on its oracle, which was one of the oldest in Greece. Nearly all ancient authors mention it at some point, or record some story or incident relating to it. Nevertheless, it would be a mistake to believe that we possess all the information we would wish to have, of all the details we consider necessary, concerning the procedure of divination at Delphi. A great many problems remain unsolved and numerous questions have not yet found an answer. We shall try, therefore, to set down as briefly as possible the results of recent research into the methods of divination at the Delphic oracle.

According to ancient tradition, Parnassos, the eponymous hero of Mount Parnassos, discovered the art of reading auguries [divine signs] in the flight of birds: Delphos, the hero of the city Delphi, was the first to teach entrail-reading, and Amphiktyon, the hero of the Amphiktyony, introduced oneiromancy (dream-interpretation). We also know that there existed in the Delphic sanctuary a body of priests named *Pyrkooi*, who could read auguries in the flames of sacrificial pyres. . . . The Delphic myths provide clear enough evidence that every known method of divination was practised at Delphi. But Delphi owed its fame to the oracles delivered by the Pythia, who received direct inspiration from Apollo and spoke in his name; in other words, the god of divination himself delivered the oracle, using the Pythia as a medium.

The Pythia was a woman over 50 years old. She was not necessarily a virgin, but from the moment she undertook this highest of duties— serving the god—she was under the obligation to abandon her husband and children, to move into a house destined for her alone, within the sacred precinct, to be chaste and irreproachable, and to observe certain religious rules. In spite of her age, she wore the garments of a young girl, as a mark of the virginal purity of her life. We do not know how the Pythia was selected; but it is quite certain that she did not have to belong to a noble family, like the priests and priestesses who served at other Greek sanctuaries; nor did she have to go through special training or education. She was a simple, ordinary peasant-woman, without any distinguishing mark until the moment Apollo allowed his inspiration to descend upon her. In the beginning there was only one Pythia; but when the requirements of the oracle grew more numerous, two more Pythias were added.

Until the Classical period, nobody had ever

thought of questioning the Pythia's sudden transformation and the fact that Phoibos spoke through her. All that has been written about the natural vapours emanating from the chasm in the sanctuary, or about the laurel leaves the Pythia munched and the water she drank, is but an attempt to find answers to the mystery, at a time when the faithful began to lose their faith, thinking they could explain the divine miracle with the cold instrument of reason and encompass the supernatural within a recognizable human measure. However, the ancient Greeks were certain of one thing alone: the importance of Apollo's sacred tripod, in other words, his throne, which had once been equipped with wings and carried him across land and sea. Why had Apollo chosen such an unusual throne, nobody knew and nobody dared ask; nor have any modern scholars provided a certain answer to that question. It was upon this throne that the Pythia sat in order to become the god's instrument. It was enough for her to take Apollo's place, to shed her ordinary identity, fall into a trance and deliver the divine messages in a series of mysterious, inarticulate cries. But before the Pythia took her seat upon the tripod, it was necessary to find out whether the god consented to her practising divination. A goat was therefore brought to sacrifice; but before sacrificing it, the animal was sprinkled with cold water: if it shivered from head to foot, it meant the god consented; if it did not, then the Pythia could not sit on the oracular tripod.

In early antiquity, before the 6th century B.C., divination took place only once a year, on the seventh day of the month Bysios (February–March), on Apollo's birthday. Later on it took place every month, again on the seventh day of the month, except for the three winter months, because during that time the god left the Delphic sanctuary in order to travel far away to the land of the Hyperboreans, conceding his place to Dionysos, who was worshipped next to Apollo in his own temple. On the sacred day appointed for divination, the Pythia was the first to visit at dawn the Kastalian Spring to cleanse herself. Then she burnt laurel leaves on the sacred hearth

and immersed herself in smoke. Meanwhile the priests prepared the sacrificial goat; if the god gave his consent, the animal was sacrificed on the great altar . . . in front of the temple, and thus all the pilgrims knew an oracle would be delivered that day at Delphi. In the meantime, the *Prophetai* and the *Hosioi* (priests of both Apollo and Dionysos) and certain delegates from the township of Delphi also cleansed themselves in the sacred waters of Kastalia. Finally, all the pilgrims who wished to consult the oracle similarly purified themselves at the spring.

When everyone was ready, they advanced in a festive procession towards the temple, filled with awe and anticipation. Delegates from the cities and private individuals stood outside the temple and offered the *pelanos* at the altar—a kind of consecrated bread sold on the spot at a high price, the pilgrims' first contribution to the sanctuary. Then they each advanced in turn towards the temple and placed a slaughtered animal as an offering upon the inner altar, where the undying flame burned. It was considered a great privilege to be the first to receive an oracle. . . . The priority was always retained by the people of Delphi for their own city, but second place was offered as the highest sign of honour to cities and individuals who had proved worthy of it.

The Pythia was already seated on the tripod in the *adyton* or inner shrine. The *Prophetai* stood nearby, and the pilgrim—it could only be a man—sat in a corner at some distance from her, having already posed his question to one of the *Prophetai*, either in writing or orally. The Pythia, hidden by some kind of partition, was not visible to anyone. The *Prophetes* [priest] put the question to her and she would give the god's response, deep in her trance. This was apparently unintelligible to others, but the *Prophetes* was able to comprehend it and write it down in hexameter verse; it was this written reply that was handed over to the pilgrim. The equivocal replies of the Delphic oracle have become famous in history; they were so obscure, so incomprehensible that additional divinatory gifts were required to interpret them correctly and avoid unfortunate mistakes. The case of Croesus is a good example: in answer to his question, the god said that if he waged war on the Persians, he would destroy a great power: he never suspected that . . . he would destroy his own kingdom if he fought the Persians.

Those nine days of the year when the Pythia spoke with the voice of the god must have had a tremendous impact on the pilgrims fortunate enough to be present in the Delphic sanctuary. Only a very small percentage of those who wished to consult the divine oracle had the privilege of receiving an answer within those nine days in the year when divination was performed.

For this reason, since the Archaic age, most of the pilgrims' questions were answered in a different manner: by drawing lots. This kind of divination took place every day of the year, not in the *adyton*, but in public view; it was the most common method of divination as regards simple and concrete questions, that is to say questions that could be answered by a simple affirmative or negative. But when we refer to the Pythia and the celebrated oracles delivered at Delphi, we have in mind those great days, when the god himself let his voice be heard through the mouth of the entranced prophetess.

Selection 5

Varying Beliefs About the Afterlife

Jon D. Mikalson

Because of a scarcity of solid evidence, it is difficult to ascertain how many Greeks believed in an afterlife and in which historical periods such beliefs were more prevalent. Apparently a majority in most periods envisioned some kind of existence beyond death, even if that existence was limited and/or ill-defined. As explained here by University of Virginia scholar Jon D. Mikalson, an expert on ancient Greek religion, by the middle of the Classic Age conceptions of the afterlife seem to have been highly varied and vague. In his view, even those associated with the mystery cult at Eleusis, purportedly promising salvation after death, remain poorly documented and inconclusive. Citing tomb epitaphs and excerpts from plays and other literary sources, Mikalson examines some of the most common beliefs, such as the idea that after death the soul migrated into the Underworld or floated away into the sky. His study concentrates on Athens, since so much of the surviving evidence is Athenian; however, it is a fair assumption that the Athenian view roughly reflected that of most Greeks. Mikalson concludes that by the early fourth century B.C. most Greeks, whether they believed in an afterlife or not, were more concerned with their earthly lives than with what might lie beyond death.

The Athenians' views concerning the afterlife show more variety and uncertainty than their views on any other religious topic. Differing beliefs are expressed explicitly or implicitly on such fundamental questions as whether the soul continued to exist, where the souls of the dead resided, whether the souls had perception of the life of the living, and whether the souls encountered rewards and punishments in the afterlife.

Most Attic epitaphs of this period say nothing about the afterlife. They rather, like the following two epitaphs, list the individual's virtues in this life, lament his death, and describe the sorrow of his relatives.

> Philostratus, son of Philoxenus,
> Your father's father's name you bore,
> But to your parents "Chatterbox,"
> Once their joy, now mourned by all,
> By a daimon [demon] you were carried off.
>
> Had you, by fortune's escort, attained maturity,
> We all foresaw in you, Macareus, a great man,
> A master of the tragic art among the Greeks.
> But now, in death, your reputation does remain
>   For temperance and virtue.

Such epitaphs need not be taken to demonstrate that the Athenians did not believe in an afterlife, but they do indicate, as do other sources, that Athenian popular religion was focused almost exclusively on life in this world, not in the next. Those epitaphs which do mention the afterlife speak in vague terms of the soul being with Persephone and Pluto, as in the following . . .

> It is an easy thing to praise good men.
> Abundant eulogies are quickly found.
> Now, in the chamber of Persephone,
>   The chamber shared by all,
> You, Dionysius, enjoy such praise.
> Your body, Dionysius, lies here,
> But your immortal soul is now possessed
>   By the dispenser shared by all.
> In death you left behind undying grief
> For your friends, your mother, and your sisters.

The house and chamber of Persephone and Pluto had been, of course, familiar features of the underworld since Homer, but Attic epitaphs of the fourth century describe none of the other literary features of the underworld such as . . . the ferryman Charon, or the dog Cerberus. The references to Persephone and Pluto in these epitaphs may be merely reflections of a poetic tradition with little or no basis in contemporary religious belief.

Various Destinations for the Soul

The soul of the deceased supposedly traveled from the upper world to the house of Persephone, and it was the function of Hermes Psychopompos ("Hermes the Escorter of Souls") to guide the souls on this journey. It is this belief which is implicit in the practice of burying curse tablets in graves. On these crudely inscribed lead tablets were written curses, often against opponents in legal proceedings. About three hundred have been found in Attica and published. The following . . . dating from early to mid-fourth century B.C., reflect[s] the general nature of these tablets . . .

> Let Pherenicus be put under a spell to Hermes Chthonikos and Hecate Chthonia. And I put under a spell to Hermes Chthonikos and Hecate Chthonia Galene, who associates with Pherenicus. And just as this lead is cold and is held in no esteem, so may Pherenicus and his things be cold and held in no esteem, and so may be the things which Pherenicus' collaborators say and plot concerning me. . . . And I put under a spell the soul and mind and tongue and plans of Pherenicus, and whatever he does and plots concerning me. Let all things be opposed to him and to those who plot and act with him.

Evidently the soul of the deceased was expected to hand over, like a letter, to Hermes or Persephone the messages scratched on these tablets.

Some apparently believed that the souls of the dead resided not in the underworld but in the *aither*, or sky:

> Here lies the body of Eurymachus,

But the moist air above now holds his soul
And his powerful intelligence. . . .

The belief that the soul resided in the sky, although not widely attested in sources for popular religion, was familiar enough to Athenians for Aristophanes to use it as the basis of a humorous description of a journey in outer space [*Peace*]. There was also current, at least in philosophical circles, the fear "that when the soul departs from the body it no longer exists anywhere, but is destroyed on the very day on which a man dies, as soon as it departs from the body" [Plato, *Phaedo*].

The epitaphs give no description of the life of the soul in the underworld or in the sky. In an earlier period it had been believed that a homicide victim left behind him "avenging spirits" and that these spirits harassed the murderer, but this belief does not appear current in the fourth century. . . .

Public orations for the state funerals of those who had died in war provided the occasion for outpourings of emotional and patriotic sentiments, and in our sources it is only in such orations that we have portrayals of life in the underworld. Even these portrayals are brief and bare, however. . . . Demosthenes says that the war dead "might" dwell with the good men of the past on the "Islands of the Blessed." It would appear that these orators, in their attempts to eulogize the war dead, reached beyond popular religious conceptions and introduced literary and mythological themes. The pale, almost nonexistence in the afterlife was not a sufficient reward for these new national heroes, and for them the orators had to enhance the afterlife with features from literature and mythology.

In their funeral orations Hyperides and Demosthenes each suggest that the war dead might be rewarded in the afterlife for the virtue they demonstrated in this life. Hyperides speaks directly of these rewards:

If death is like nonexistence, these men are freed from diseases and suffering and from the other things which beset the life of a human being. But if men have perception in the house of Hades and if they are cared for by the dai-

monic [element], as we suspect they are, then it is reasonable to assume that those who defended the abused honors of the gods find the greatest care from the daimonic [element].

In a very private and tender manner Hippostrate, a young girl, expresses much the same thought in the epitaph for her nurse Melitta:

Melitta, daughter of Apollodorus.
Here lies beneath the earth Hippostrate's
good nurse.
And how Hippostrate now longs for you!
I loved you so, dear nurse,
And now, for all my life,
I'll honor you, though you lie below.
If the good receive a prize in the underworld,
You now, I know, enjoy first place
with Pluto and Persephone. . . .

Each of these expressions of hope for rewards in the afterlife is limited by a condition. For Hippostrate the uncertainty is "if the good receive a prize in the underworld"; for Hyperides, "if men have perception in the house of Hades and if they are cared for by the daimonic [element]". . . . The uncertainty in each instance focuses on a different area, but it is clear that even the most positive expressions of hopes for rewards in the afterlife were riddled with doubt. Against these few instances in which hopes for rewards were expressed we must balance the hundreds of epitaphs in which the individual's virtues were listed but there is no indication of hope for rewards in the afterlife. One must, I think, conclude from these epitaphs that the expectation of rewards for virtue in the afterlife was not only very uncertain, but also very uncommon . . . that most Athenians did *not* expect to be rewarded in the afterlife for the virtues, including piety, which they demonstrated in this life.

Punishment and Rewards?

Nor did they, as a general rule, expect punishment in the afterlife for their vices and sins. In our sources it is only the aged Cephalus who, in a Platonic dialogue [*Republic*], begins to think seriously about the possible punishments after death:

When the thought of his own death approaches

a man, he feels fear and concern about things about which he did not before. The stories that are told about the things in Hades, that the man who acted unjustly in this world must pay the penalty there, are laughed at until this time, but then the fear that they may be true racks his soul. And either because of the weakness of old age or because he is now closer to Hades, he himself sees these things more clearly and is filled with suspicion and terror. . . .

Cephalus uses his wealth to square his accounts with men and gods and thereby hedges his bet in case the stories about Hades . . . might be true.

In our sources, apart from Cephalus, we find no statement of the expectation of punishment in the afterlife. It is most revealing, I think, that we do not find it in those cases where we should most expect it, that is, when speakers are attacking villainous, perjured, and impious men. In all such cases the descriptions of the expected sufferings of the malefactor stop with his death. Punishment after death is not introduced for murderers, perjurors, or perpetrators of other impious acts. The punishment might fall upon the malefactor's children, but it does not seem to have pursued the criminal himself after his death. It is also noteworthy that in the curses accompanying oaths individuals put under a curse only elements of this life such as their own lives, property, and families. . . . The conclusion must be that Athenians in the fourth century generally did not foresee such punishments for misdeeds in this life. . . .

Cephalus wishes to have, in the face of death, "sweet hope," and [the orator] Isocrates tells us that it is precisely "sweeter hopes concerning the end of life and all eternity" which initiates in the Eleusinian Mysteries received. Aristophanes portrays the initiates enjoying eternal light, music, and dancing in the afterlife. The object of Cephalus' and Isocrates' "sweet hopes" may have been something of this type, but there is no indication in the epitaphs or in the other sources for popular religion that individuals expected or hoped for this type of life after death. The secrecy surrounding the Eleusinian Mysteries may have inhibited public expression of these hopes, and the relative lack of evidence blocks our understanding of what initiation meant for an individual's afterlife. But, in any case, the silence in our sources may belie the great importance usually attributed to the Mysteries for ordinary Athenians. All we can say is that, if there was a large group of Athenians who expected a blessed afterlife because they were initiated into the Mysteries, they have very successfully concealed from us their existence.

In summary, then, the average Athenian foresaw in the afterlife, if anything, his soul residing in the underworld, in the "chamber" of Persephone. Various mythological, literary, and philosophical descriptions of the underworld were current and familiar, but none seems to have won general acceptance. And with the possible exception of initiates in the Eleusinian Mysteries, the average Athenian expected neither rewards nor punishments in the afterlife for his deeds in this life. Clearly what mattered to the average Athenian was this life, and in the fourth century he took little interest in the bleak and uncertain prospect of the afterlife.

Selection 6

Burial Rites and Customs

Donna C. Kurtz and John Boardman

The size of a person's funeral (kedeia) in ancient Greece depended in part on the wealth and deeds of the deceased. As is still true today, rich people and war heroes tended to have more splendid burial ceremonies than ordinary persons. However, certain basic funerary customs prevailed for all and regardless of how the body was handled. The two types of disposal were inhumation (burial in the ground or a tomb) and cremation (burning the body on a pyre, sometimes along with personal goods; the ashes were quenched with wine and the bones were placed in a container, which was buried). Both methods were practiced throughout antiquity. However, one or the other predominated in various periods, inhumation being the most popular in late Archaic times and the Classic Age. A funeral speech (epitaphios) was often recited at the time of burial in either case.

Some of the many other common funerary rituals and customs during the Archaic and Classic periods are examined here by scholars Donna C. Kurtz and John Boardman, from their noted book-length study of the subject. As they show, some of the customs associated with the body's formal lying-in-state (prothesis) and its conveyance to the gravesite (ekphora) are well understood. Others, for instance the perideipnon, *a meal* served at the deceased's home following the burial, are less clearly understood and scholars must use educated guesswork to reconstruct them.*

*F*or the people of Attica burial in their native land was greatly prized, and perhaps for this reason denial of burial in Attica was considered one of the greatest penalties which the State could impose. . . .

It was essential that the dead receive the customary rites of burial, but it was equally important that he receive them from the proper hands. Responsibility fell on the immediate family, and under normal circumstances it was considered improper for the dead to receive burial at the hands of one to whom he was not related. If, however, the dead had no family, or if his family could not bear the expense, the responsibility fell to a close friend or to the demarch [head of the local deme]. It seems to have been a particular duty of the son to bury his parents, especially his father, in a fitting manner. There are numerous references in literature of the Classical period to the great expense of burial, and when Plato restricts the amount which his highest class can spend on funerals, he allows the quite considerable sum of five *minae*. It is, moreover, important to remember that expense was not incurred in the furnishing of graves, for many were unfurnished and very few were rich in offerings, but in the preparation for and execution of burial and funerary rites.

It was the duty of the women of the family to prepare the body for burial. . . . Only those women who were over the age of sixty or very closely related to the dead could take part. They bathed the body, anointed it with oil, dressed and adorned it with flowers, wreaths, ribbons and jewellery. The *prothesis* took place on the day after death at the home of the dead. The significance attached to the house at which the *prothesis* took place and from which the *ekphora* began is clear from accounts, preserved by the orators, of men attempting to remove corpses from the house of death to their own homes to demonstrate that they, not the 'family', were the legitimate heirs.

The *prothesis* normally lasted one day; Plato recommended that it last only long enough to confirm death. The body was displayed on a plank-like structure with high legs—a dining couch, bed or *kline*. The body [was] wrapped in a shroud, (*endyma*). . . . Pillows—*proskephalaia*—elevated the head, and, as an added precaution against the unsightly gaping of the jaws, chin straps, *othonai*, were sometimes fitted around the head and lower jaw.

The purpose of the *prothesis* was not only to confirm death, but also to provide an opportunity for the performance of the traditional lament and for the friends and family to pay their last respects. Representations of the *prothesis* on vases and painted plaques show remarkable uniformity. The dead lies on the bier with his feet pointing towards the left, presumably towards the door, since it is from this direction that the men come in procession, raising their right hands, palm outwards—a gesture which men perform on foot and on horse, at the bier and at the grave. Women lament, tearing their hair, striking their heads and breasts. Restricting the *prothesis* to the home discouraged such displays of intense grief and turned a potentially public ceremony into a private one.

The Funeral

On the third day, before sunrise, the dead was borne out to the grave in a procession which was required by law to pass quietly through side streets. Restricting the *ekphora* to the early morning hours and banning the performance of the lament outside the house likewise encour-

This grave stele of a young fifth-century B.C. Athenian woman still bears tiny traces of its original red paint.

aged a simple family procession, not a sumptuous public cortège. . . . Vase-paintings show us the body, completely covered except for the head, being carried by pall-bearers or drawn by a cart. Men lead the procession and women follow. As at the *prothesis* the attendance of women was limited by age and family relation; even their dress was prescribed by law. When women went to the tomb, they could not travel by night unless they rode in a cart with a lamp, and they could not carry more than one obol's worth of food and drink or a basket exceeding a cubit in length. Further, they were not permitted to visit the tombs of those to whom they were not related except at the time of interment.

When the funeral cortège arrived at the grave, the body was lowered into the ground without great ceremony, and Solon expressly forbade the sacrifice of oxen at the grave. . . . We know that there was a ceremony of some sort conducted at the grave on the day of burial—*ta trita*. . . .

The traditional interpretation of *ta trita* as an independent celebration performed three days after the burial is not supported by contemporary literature, where *ta trita* and burial of the dead are regularly mentioned together. That the ceremony connected with the burial, which took place on the third day after death, should be called 'the third-day celebration' is entirely reasonable.

After the burial the mourners apparently returned to the home of the dead, which, during the period of mourning, was marked by a vessel standing outside the door—a notification of death and a warning of the *miasma* [state of pollution] which affected the house. It contained water brought from outside with which the mourners purified themselves on leaving. For the Classical period in Athens there is no evidence for the later practice of hanging a lock of hair or a branch of cypress on the door.

There are burnt deposits—ashes, bones of animals, and sherds of cups, bowls and plates—associated with some graves, and these are probably remains of food offerings made at the grave. Literary sources . . . allude to the importance of the meal, but do not describe it. Most imply that it was taken at the home of the dead, and this is in keeping with the elaborate purification of the house and the restrictions placed on those permitted entrance. Of the *perideipnon* itself we know nothing except that it was an occasion for relatives to gather, wreathe themselves and speak of the dead. . . .

The end of mourning was marked by additional ceremony. Although there is mention in later sources of a thirtieth-day rite concluding mourning, in Athens during the Archaic and Classical periods the length of time is not specified. . . .

Annual Celebrations

The end of mourning did not, however, mark the end of the family's responsibility to its departed. The annual commemorative rites, if we may judge from the number of times they are mentioned in Classical literature, were . . . important. . . . Assurance of proper performance of annual rites was reason enough for a man to adopt a son. . . . The *Genesia* deserves mention, since it is named in a fifth-century source: when Herodotus describes an annual celebration which the Issedones performed on behalf of their deceased fathers, he refers to the *Genesia* celebrated by the Greeks. Since he offers no explanation, the *Genesia* must have been known to his audience. . . . The nature of the festival is, however, not specified. . . .

Because the annual rites were so familiar, Classical sources say no more than 'the customary things were done each year'. There were probably visits to the tomb, offerings of flowers, garlands and ribbons—traditional signs of respect and reverence. Plato's description of a funeral conducted in the best taste stipulates that the annual rites must not be disregarded in the interest of economy. Not all rites were, however, performed at the grave. Each year one also did the customary things at home on behalf of the 'ancestral objects'. . . . Plato alludes to a *nomos* [law] governing the setting up of the 'ancestral objects', but precisely what they were is not clear. They were apparently handed down from generation to generation and were a necessary qualification for some public offices. Although they were portable, they were not to be uprooted, since removal or maltreatment of them not only brought censure upon the perpetrator of the offence, but also, in some way, deprived the ancestral dead of their due rites, for these 'ancestral objects' were associated with the annual offerings . . . on behalf of the dead.

Artistic Achievements

Chapter 10

Introduction

The first artistic expressions in ancient Greece were those of the Bronze Age Minoans, who inhabited Crete and some other Aegean islands. The main architectural achievements were the "palaces," or administrative-religious centers, the largest and most splendid example being that at Knossos. Many, though not all, of its architectural features were based on Egyptian and other Near Eastern models. In *Knossos: A Complete Guide to the Palace of Minos* Greek archaeologist Anna Michailidou explains:

> The overall plan of the palace appears to be an integrated complex of purpose-built rooms. It is roughly square in plan, with sides of about 150 meters, and it covers an area of 20,000 square meters. . . . Its dominant feature is the Central Court, nucleus of the whole complex and the heart of everyday life in the palace, and there was a second court on the west, facing you as you approach the site. There were several entrances on different sides, used for different purposes. . . . It was obviously a multi-storied building [having perhaps four or five levels in some places]. The building materials used were stone, wood, and clay. . . . Limestone was the commonest material for the walls . . . as well as for paving stones, piers [vertical supports] and pier bases, column-bases, door and window frames, etc. . . . Wood, a basic material in the construction of the palace, was commonly used for columns, flooring in the upper stories, roofing, stairs, door and window frames, and the doors themselves. . . . Finally, clay was used as a binding agent between the stones of the walls.

Many, if not most, of the rooms in this and other large Minoan buildings were apparently well-lit and often decorated with frescoes (paintings done on wet plaster). Minoan paintings tended to be brightly-colored, vibrant, and showed real people and animals moving through natural, informal settings (in contrast to the more idealized and formal Classical style that would develop later). Among the best surviving examples are a series of exquisite frescoes (dating from circa 1600 B.C.) discovered on the island of Thera and now on display in Athens's National Archaeological Museum. Minoan sculpture consisted mostly of small, elegant figurines rather than large-scale statues. And most pottery (except for larger jars for storage and pouring) was extremely thin and delicate, glazed, and painted either with scenes like those in the frescoes or abstract or stylized designs.

Minoan artistic styles (along with clothing styles) exerted a strong influence on those of the mainland Greek-speaking Mycenaeans. Among the principal differences: Mycenaean palaces were constructed of large blocks of stone and surrounded by massive fortification walls (although the interiors likely resembled Cretan versions); Mycenaean art emphasized more formalized military and hunting themes; and Mycenaean artisans particularly excelled at producing inlaid and embossed gold artifacts, including goblets, swords, and funerary masks.

In the Dark Age that followed the collapse of the Bronze Age civilizations, monumental architecture, wall painting, and many other arts disappeared. However, pottery continued to be made; and the first few periods into which historians and archaeologists divide the subsequent history of Greek art are named for pottery types. The main periods of ancient Greek art are the Protogeometric (ca. 1050–ca. 900 B.C.); Geometric (ca. 900–ca. 700, divided into Early, Middle, and Late); Orientalizing (ca. 720–ca. 620); Archaic (ca. 620–ca. 480); Classical (ca. 480–ca. 330); and Hellenistic (ca.330–late first century B.C.). The boundaries of these periods were usually far from distinct (as shown in the overlap of Geometric and Orientalizing), and some regions experienced a mixture of styles at various times. Protogeometric pottery was characterized by the abstract decorative designs (arcs, half-circles, concentric circles, etc.) painted onto the vases and other artifacts; Geometric featured more geometrical patterns and shapes (triangles, cross-hatching, Greek key pattern, etc.); and the term Orientalizing refers to the strong influence of Near Eastern styles in that period.

It was during the Archaic Age that monumental architecture reappeared in Greece, first and almost always foremost in the form of religious temples. These were made of wood at first, but by the late sixth century B.C. had undergone a transition to all-stone construction. Large-scale sculpture also developed in Archaic times, exemplified by stiff and formal yet elegant life-sized human figures—the *kouroi* ("young men") and *korai* ("maidens"). The most distinctive Archaic pottery style was the black-figure (featuring black figures and decorations on a reddish-orange background).

The Classical period of Greek art coincided with the political and cultural zenith of ancient Greek civilization in the fifth and fourth centuries B.C. The development of monumental architecture that had begun in Archaic times now culminated in the erection of magnificent temples and other public buildings across Greece; the most impressive and famous were those built atop Athens's Acropolis, including the immortal Parthenon. Also in Athens, sculpture of the human figure, either as part of the decoration of these buildings or free-standing, achieved larger-than-life qualities of beauty, grace, and nobility. In his *Pocket Book of Greek Art* art historian Thomas Craven describes what later came to be called the "Classical ideal":

> From the mastery of movement and anatomy, the Athenian artists proceeded to ideal forms and faces—to the creation of figures, male and female, beyond those produced by nature . . . to marbles which reveal living flesh within the polished surfaces, faces of god-like serenity, women in costumes of infinite grace.

A few statues in this period reached giant proportions, notably those of the divine Athena and Zeus crafted by the master sculptor Phidias. In addition to these wonders, huge mural-like wall paintings appeared, most notably in Athens; large theaters were constructed and the theatrical arts enjoyed their first golden age; while the most distinctive Classical pottery style was the flexible and expressive red-figure (featuring reddish-orange figures and decorations on a black background).

The last major period of Greek art, the Hellenistic, retained many Classical values, but also introduced some dramatic changes, including a new emphasis on realism and also on the individual and his or her personal qualities, emotions, and feelings. The perfect marriage of Hellenistic architecture and sculpture was the Great Altar of Zeus, erected by the Attalid ruler Eumenes II at Pergamum (in northwestern Asia Minor) in the second century B.C. It consists of a grand staircase surmounted by a massive and stately colonnaded podium; around the podium runs a magnificent sculpted frieze showing Zeus and Athena doing battle with an army of giants; the sculptors captured the sweeping movement, drama, violence, horror, and anguish of the scene with amazing skill.

The most important evidence for ancient Greek art consists, of course, of the buildings, sculptures, pottery, and paintings that have survived the ravages of time. Much can be seen today, in various states of preservation, either in museums or in their original locations. Unfortunately, however, much more has been lost than has survived. And the study of ancient written sources describing both the lost and surviving works is complicated by various factors. "First," explains Yale University art historian J.J. Pollitt, in *The Art of Ancient Greece*, "there is the fact that most of the authors who provide significant information lived *much later than the artists about whom they wrote.*" The most comprehensive written source for Classical Greek art, for instance, is the *Natural History* of the Roman encyclopedist Pliny the Elder, written in the first century A.D. "Not only is the distance between Pliny and Phidias about 500 years," Pollitt continues,

> but, as a Roman, Pliny spoke a different language and belonged to a society that was different in many ways from that of the artists who were his subject. The fact is that there are scarcely any "contemporary sources" in the extant literature on ancient art. . . . Another [complicating] factor . . . is that, with the exception of [the first-century B.C. Roman architect] Vitruvius's *de Architectura* [*On Architecture*] . . . there are *no writings which deal intentionally, directly, and exclusively with art as such.*

Thus, with the exception of Pliny's and Vitruvius's works, and the valuable guide book written in the second century A.D. by the Greek traveler Pausanias, almost all the other written references to Greek art are passing remarks made in discussions about other subjects. These appear most notably in the works of the Greeks: Herodotus (fifth century B.C.), Plato (fourth century B.C.), Aristotle (fourth century B.C.), Diodorus (first century B.C.), and Plutarch (first century A.D.); and the Romans: Cicero (first century B.C.) and Quintilian (first century A.D.).

Selection 1

The Emergence of Monumental Architecture

William R. Biers

Aside from some early developments in pottery styles, the first major form of artistic expression in Greece after the Dark Age was the development of monumental (large-scale) architecture. Specifically, the temple, at first of wood, later of stone, became the most recognizable Greek architectural form. And as University of Missouri scholar William R. Biers explains here, Greek temple architecture became a standard of artistic nobility and elegance throughout the ancient Mediterranean world; as well as in modern Western society, which has adopted the Doric and Ionic styles (or orders) for government buildings, banks, and other public structures. Biers describes the structural components and decorative elements of the two classic orders and traces their use in major temples built in late Archaic times. These structures paved the way for the erection of even greater temples, including the incomparable Parthenon, in the Classic Age.

Excerpted from William R. Biers, *The Archaeology of Greece: An Introduction*, 2nd ed., Copyright © 1980, 1987, 1996 Cornell University. Reprinted by permission of the publisher, Cornell University Press.

The seventh century is . . . the time of the development of the two major styles of Greek architecture, the Doric order and the Ionic order. The extent of outside influence involved is difficult to determine. In development and final forms these two orders are uniquely Greek and are among the major gifts of that civilization to Western art.

The best known symbol of Greek civilization is the temple. It was during the seventh century that its form was defined and the first examples appeared, built mostly of stone. The stages by which the Doric and Ionic orders of architecture were created are obscure, as indeed is their origin, and it is probable that development did not proceed evenly in all centers. Recent work has shown that Corinth may have been a leader here. . . . Certain details of decoration and probably the techniques of masonry probably came from the East. Before we look at examples of these early stone buildings, it is necessary to say something about the developed forms.

The first tentative steps toward the standard ground plan . . . had already been taken . . . with the adoption of the rectangular plan for a temple, with a colonnade or peristyle around the rectangular structure (cella) that housed the cult statue. Front and back porches (pronaos, opisthodomos) were formed by the extension and thickening of the cella walls. . . . Such porches were already in evidence in eighth-century buildings and became standard in the developed form of the plan. Once the standard form had been reached in the fifth century, it was destined to be constantly repeated with endless variations, not only in Greek architecture but to the end of antiquity and beyond. A series of rules and proportions gradually developed, which, when they were finally standardized in the fifth century, dictated the general proportions, placement, and use of the various decorative and functional members of the building. The flank columns, for instance, ideally numbered two times the number of front columns plus one; six by thirteen became the most common arrangement in the full developed Doric temple, with a colonnade that ran all the way around the cella (a peripteral temple).

The strict body of rules and relationships among the parts of the building also extended to the elevations of the buildings in the two major styles, Doric and Ionic. Both orders rely on the post-and-lintel system, familiar from Bronze Age architecture. . . . The Doric order is much the plainer of the two and may have developed somewhat earlier than the Ionic. Their origins are debated. The arguments turn on whether the individual features of each order, which are purely ornamental in stone construction, originally had structural functions when buildings were constructed of ephemeral [perishable] materials, or were derived from earlier decorative designs.

The principal characteristics of the Doric order . . . [were] the simple shaft bearing twenty channels or flutes with sharp divisions . . . between them. . . . A capital consisting of a swelling member, the echinus, is topped by a block-shaped slab, the abacus, as a transition from the vertical column shaft to the mainly horizontal upper entablature. Above the columns and supported by them is the epistyle, formed of lines of blocks that extend from column to column. The epistyle blocks are plain except for a molding along the top, which is decorated at intervals with raised panels (regulae) from which circular projections called guttae project downward. Above the epistyle is the frieze course, consisting of grooved slabs, or triglyphs, ("three glyphs," so called because each groove is called a glyph and there are two whole and two half glyphs to each unit) are separated by blank panels called metopes, which in the more elaborately decorated temples are adorned with painting or sculpture. Above the frieze comes a horizontal course and above that the roof, double pitched, with open triangular spaces, the pediments, at both ends. The pediments were often filled with sculpture. The roof is usually adorned with architectural devices, sometimes sculptured figures on the ridge or at the corners and usually with brightly painted upright palmettes [leaf-shaped decorations] and lion-head waterspouts along the eaves. The undersurface of the horizontal course (geison) above the frieze course is also ornamented with slabs (mutules) bearing guttae and placed over every triglyph and every metope.

The Doric frieze, with its triglyphs and its

regula-guttae and mutule-guttae constructions, looks like a translation in stone of wooden construction. The theory of a "petrification" [transition to stone] of previously wooden forms suggests that the triglyphs were boards secured by wooden pegs (guttae) protecting the faces of the roof beams from the weather, with the open spaces between them covered with plain slabs (metopes). Unfortunately, such evidence as we have from the earliest buildings suggests that the roof beams were probably entirely independent of the frieze course. . . .

The Ionic order is lighter and more slender than the Doric, and more highly decorated. The earliest manifestations have been found in Ionia but its specific origins are as obscure as those of the Doric. The Ionic column has an elaborately carved base—unlike the Doric, which sits directly on the stylobate [floor, foundation]—and twenty-four flutes separated by broad, flattened arrises rather than the pointed ones of the Doric column. The capital consists of two hanging volutes [scroll-like decorations]. Beneath them is an ornamental area; above is a small abacus. . . . The epistyle is generally carved, with three flat undecorated projecting bands, and the frieze is either continuously sculptured or decorated with a row of toothlike projections, known appropriately enough as dentils. . . . The vocabulary of Greek architecture is complex, with a specific name applied to each individual part. Moldings and all other minor components obey specific rules as to placement, shape, and ornament. . . .

Some paint was used for details above the columns of Greek temples and as backgrounds for sculpture. The backgrounds of metopes, friezes, and pediments were generally painted solid red or blue to help the sculpture stand out. The same colors were used for the mutules, triglyphs, regulae, and many of the moldings. The alternation of these two colors against the bright white of the building must have had a striking effect in the bright Mediterranean sunlight.

Early Monumental Temples

The establishment of the Doric order in permanent materials can be traced to Corinth. Recent excavations both at Corinth itself and at the nearby sanctuary of Poseidon on the Isthmus of Corinth, at a site known as Isthmia, have recovered the remains of large stone temples beneath the later temples. Both sites were destroyed by fire, the latter in the fifth century, the one at Corinth in the sixth. The Corinthian building is known so far only as scattered remains of wall blocks and tiles that belong to a primitive form of roofing known from some other sites. The invention of terra cotta tiles, again probably at Corinth, must have been an important step in the development of the stone temple, as their weight necessitated more support than could be given by the generally flimsy construction of earlier buildings. Investigations of the Corinthian building give it the early date of about 680 [B.C.] or a little later and suggest that the temple consisted only of a masonry cella. . . .

Terra cotta decorations apparently developed over the course of the century. Some have been associated with a temple of Apollo that was erected about 630 at Thermon, in northwest Greece. Its ground plan is similar to the restored ground plan of the early temple at Isthmia, with five columns across the ends, fifteen on the flanks, and an interior row to hold up the roof. The building measured 38.23 by 12.13 meters. The peristyle, probably originally of wood, was replaced in stone at a later date. . . .

To the seventh century also belongs the second temple of Hera on Samos, which replaced the earlier temple after the middle of the century. Still very long (37.88 by 11.65 meters), this building had six columns on each end and eighteen on each flank. New here is the deepening of the colonnade on the east end, which became a typical feature of large temples in Ionia, emphasizing the front of the building. . . . The interior represents a great improvement, with the supports for the roof now next to the walls on either side rather than down the middle of the building like a spine. The temple was built of stone and wood and doubtless was Ionic, although little except a fragment of a sculptured frieze is preserved.

On the mainland, the Doric order developed rapidly, and by the end of the century the ground plan more closely approached the proportions that became standard in the fifth century. The new investigations at Tegea [in the central Peloponnesus] have revealed the remains of a large temple, probably with a peristyle of six by eighteen columns. . . . The building's walls were of mud brick in a framework of wooden beams, with slabs of local marble to reinforce the lower portions, at least in one place. The external colonnade was probably of wood, as was the entablature. . . . Burned in 394, this early temple probably belongs to the last quarter of the seventh century. At Olympia the better-preserved temple of Hera was one of the last of the large temples to have major portions constructed of ephemeral materials. The temple, built around 600, was constructed of limestone to a height of a little over a meter, then continued up in mud brick. All the rest of the structure was originally of wood, except for the tiled roof and its terra cotta ornaments. . . . The original wooden columns were replaced as they wore out; one is recorded to have been still standing in the second century of the Christian era. . . .

The Sixth-Century Transition to All-Stone Temples

Progress was fairly rapid in the development of the temple plan and elevation in the sixth century. Increasing prosperity permitted the use of costly and more permanent building materials. The first large all-stone temple erected was the temple of Artemis on Corfu, the ancient Kerkyra, a large island off the west coast of Greece. Although very little of this building is preserved, the remains indicate an overall measurement of 49.00 by 23.46 meters, making it one of the most ambitious buildings built to this time. . . .

The temple of Artemis, also known as the Gorgon temple because of the central figure on its west pediment, is important not only for its structural character but also for its sculptural decoration. Both pediments seem to have contained the same scene; that on the east front is preserved only in fragments but the west pediment is almost completely preserved. The style

of the sculpture, an early attempt to fill the triangular pedimental space, indicates that the temple was built about 580 [B.C.].

The middle of the century witnessed the replacement of the seventh-century temple at Corinth by a new building, probably dedicated to Apollo and erected perhaps between 560 and 540. There were now six columns across the front and fifteen on each flank, the columns considerably less squat than those of the Gorgon temple and their abaci less swelling and more upright in contour. The columns, of which seven are still standing, are monoliths, or cut from one block of stone rather than being made up of drums. . . .

The temple of Apollo in Corinth shows some architectural refinements that became common in the next century and were carried out with great precision in the Parthenon. Here there is indication of a slight but measurable convex curve to the columns, called "entasis," a horizontal curvature of the stylobate and of the columns to the level of the capitals, and a slight inward inclination of the corner column. These refinements are generally considered to have been undertaken to overcome optical illusions that would have been engendered by strict adherence to right angles and straight lines. . . .

By the end of the Archaic period the Doric canon had been established in its main outlines in the temple of Aphaia at Aigina, some of whose pediment sculptures survive. Built of limestone, originally stuccoed, the temple was dedicated to a local goddess and is quite small, with a stylobate measuring 28.8 by 13.7 meters. . . . The interior had superimposed rows of Doric columns on each side, forming a two-storied colonnade, which was converted after the initial construction to support a floor or walkway between the columns and the walls of the cella at the level of the epistyle. From this time on, the two-storied interior colonnade became a part of the Doric canon. . . .

Gigantic temples were erected in the East during the sixth century; those on Samos and at Ephesos were famous. In these buildings the decorative quality of the Ionic order was fully exploited. The influence of the East is to be seen in the complicated ground plans, with the doubling and sometimes tripling of the rows of columns to give the effect of a dense forest of supports. On Samos the sanctuary of Hera continued to expand with the addition of new buildings and a monumental gateway or propylon. At the same time a great new temple (105.00 by 52.50 meters) was begun about 570 by the local architects Rhoikos and Theodoros. With twenty-one columns on each side, eight on the front, and ten at the rear arranged in two rows . . . the building was one of the largest of the Archaic period. It had a deep pronaos and a long cella with two rows of interior supports. The same essential plan was elaborated in an even longer (112.20 by 55.16 meters) and more heavily decorated building built by the tyrant Polykrates (538–522). Twenty-four columns now stood on each flank, with eight at the front and nine at the rear. Work continued on the building well into the third century, but it was never completed.

More famous and even longer than the Heraion on Samos was the temple of Artemis at Ephesos, which was constructed in the middle of the century and measured some 115 meters in length and 50 in width. . . . The building had eight columns at the front and nine at the rear, with twenty-one on each flank. It was burned down in 356 [B.C.], traditionally at the time of the birth of Alexander the Great. Rebuilt on the same plan, it was classed as one of the wonders of the ancient world in Hellenistic and later times, along with the Pyramids of Egypt and other monuments of artistic ingenuity.

Selection 2

The Practical but Beautiful Works of the Master Potters

Thomas Craven

One of the earliest of all art forms, ceramics (pottery-making), produces objects that are practical, artistically beautiful, or, under ideal conditions, both. Ancient Greek potters achieved that ideal. The late, noted art historian Thomas Craven here examines the major Greek pottery styles employed before and during the Classic Age, including geometric, black-figure, and red-figure. He also names and describes the major kinds of vessels the potters produced.

he master potters of the world were the Greeks. In variety, design, productivity, and the adaptation of beautifully made objects to everyday use, they have left . . . us . . . many thousands of examples of their highest skill. . . .

The tradition of Greek pottery had its historical origin in the palaces of Crete . . . as early as 2500 B.C. During this luxury-loving age, a school of superb geometrical vase-making was followed by free, or anti-symmetrical, pottery, the motifs of which were largely biological—plants, jellyfish, octopi, and other small fauna. In the ninth and eighth centuries B.C., there was a return to geometrical design, in some respects memorable, but for the most part monotonous and unimaginative. The basements of museums have innumerable exhibits of this period in the glass cases behind the mummies and the plaster casts. The resurgent geometrical style was applied to large urns and vases of every shape and capacity. Generally speaking, it was a scheme of ornamentation in which single, or concentric circles predominated, the circles broken, or crossed by tangential lines, and interlacings, to divert the eye from round-and-round tracings. Between the circular bands, on the larger vases, were crude pictures of naval engagements and funeral processions—events noticed ceremonially at the double gate of Athens, the Dipylon gate, which gave its name to the style. The color scheme of the ninth and eighth century vases consisted of reddish-brown figures, accentuated by white or black touches, against a ground of pale yellow or buff tones.

For a full century, from 600 to 500 B.C., the potters labored in the black-figure style—that is, with dark linear figures set against an earthen-red ground. The figures were drawn in the archaic tradition; but decoratively as pattern-components placed on the belly of an urn, they put modern ceramists to shame. The black-figure style is . . . indeed, in design and proportioning, a beautiful form of ceramics. The word ceramics, incidentally, comes from the name of a locality near Athens where potters' clay was obtained—but it is hardly in the same class as the red-figure ware. Before looking at the classic style, it will be useful to review the geometrical shapes first employed by the Greeks.

A beautiful black-figured vase, made in Attica during the Classic Age, shows artisans at work in a bootmaker's shop.

For storing or carrying wine and other liquids, the *amphora*, a vase with a narrow neck and handles on each side below the neck, was in common use. The water jar was the *hydria*, a vessel equipped with three handles and broader at the shoulder than the *amphora*. The *crater,* broad-rimmed with short cylindrical supports, was the mixing bowl and a favorite vase in Renaissance Florence. Varieties of the *crater*, such as the cup and the bell, were popular and in constant demand.

Black-figure vase-painting was followed, about 500 B.C., by a different method which simply reversed the traditional procedure. The reversed technique was the far-flung red-figure style, in which the ground was covered with lustrous black pigment and the figures composed in red, in the natural terra-cotta tones of the clay, or brightened by some warm earth tones. The red-figure style was enormously fecund [fertile], and vase-painters enjoyed a fame second only to that of sculptors. Boldly they signed their works, and today you may see inscriptions in capital letters on many of the objects. I wondered about those inscriptions until I was proficient enough to translate them, and more often than not, they were shameless bouquets from the master potter to an apprentice chosen because of his physical comeliness. They read as a rule something like this: *Young Skouras Is a Handsome Lad*; or *That Boy Aristophanes Is the Playmate of Zeus*; or *Erysipelas is the Apple of My Eye*.

Beyond the Practical

The Greeks made pottery for utilitarian [useful, practical] purposes, but as in all their works of art, they would tolerate nothing this side of perfection; and even in the mass production period at Athens, after the Peloponnesian War, and in the colonies, they never duplicated a design or stole a motif. The problems occupying them in their pottery and their domestic implements were identical, though on a more modest scale, with those of temple-building and carving—infinite simplicity, free but perfect proportioning, functionalism, or the adaptation of shape and form to intended purpose—and above all others, a beautiful sense of fitness which was never corrupted by melodramatic tricks or sensationalism.

The wares of the Greek ceramists were part and parcel of the routine life of the people. Vases were designed to hold flowers and fruits, or as decanters for wine, or as storage jars. Beautiful cups were fashioned for drinking purposes and all sorts of table china were decorated with religious scenes. The ceremonials in the temples and at *al fresco* [outdoor] altars necessitated a great variety of sacred vessels; the holy olive oil given as a prize in the Panathenaic games required a container of impeccable artistry, as did those of other festivities such as a special form of *amphora*, with a long neck, which held the water for the bridal bath—and was also used as a monument for those who died unmarried. The exquisitely shaped *lecythus*, a bell-mouthed, narrow-necked, single-handed vase, was filled with fragrant oils and buried with the dead or left at the grave side.

To a large extent, the vases and pottery in use today are derived from Greek models, whether they come from the celebrated designers of Sweden and France, or from the factories owned by the dime stores. With the classic Athenians, ceramic art in its decorative aspects was purely decorative in most cases, but with the masters, it was also a medium for the delineation, on a small scale, of the mural paintings of the great decorators. In fact, the murals of the *Stoa* [a long, columned building in the Athenian Agora], by Polygnotus, are known solely from the small-scale adaptations on vases and urns.

The Greeks, as a matter of course, ornamented their vases and household implements with subject matter of a religious nature—or with scenes from decisive battles in which the issue turned on the will of the gods. . . .

I do not wish to imply that all the religious motifs employed by the old potters were executed in a spirit of reverence. The religion of the Greeks was open to all manner of excitements from profound worship to pure sensuality, and on many of the choicest examples of vase-making, you may see fiercely amorous satyrs approaching reclining maidens in attitudes which would never pass a modern censor. The most prevalent subjects are variations on the power and personal habits of the gods, or on the Homeric and Persian wars. In hundreds and hundreds of vases you will see the Amazons holding their own against undersize *hoplites*; Heracles dining with Athena, or diverting himself with female warriors, the gods feasting, relaxing, or plotting trouble on earth, revelers headed by Dionysus, satyrs pursuing maenads, and young athletes in training or in competition. . . .

The Greeks, proceeding from black figures to red, and from archaic postures and draftsmanship, to the free and cultivated and precise style of the fourth century B.C., created the most beautiful linear designs ever drawn upon pottery. Their drawings at the peak of the classic period, both on a black ground, and in rarer examples now more valuable than any other ceramics, on a white ground, have been admired and adapted by western artists. . . .

In the mature, classic vase-painting, the old artists did not attempt to produce realistic effects, or the modern technical devices of three-dimensional figures, seen in perspective. They were linear artists working on clay and they knew all the secrets of linear decoration. When [English poet] John Keats, writing in the first quarter of the nineteenth century, gazed at a Grecian urn, he was not primarily concerned with the red figures on a black ground, nor with the quality of the line drawings, nor yet with the difficulties attending a decorative scheme on a rounded surface. He was moved and inspired by the Greek feeling for the freshness of the world, and the calm, sacrificial joys of an artistic people. Thus he wrote, when observing the pictures on the urn.

Who are these coming to the sacrifice?
To what green altar, O mysterious priest,
Lead'st thou that heifer lowing at the skies,
And all her silken flanks with garlands drest?
What little town by river or sea shore,
Or mountain-built with peaceful citadel,
Is emptied of its folk, this pious morn?
And, little town, thy streets for evermore
Will silent be; and not a soul to tell
Why thou art desolate, can e'er return.

Selection 3

Structures for the Ages: The Periclean Building Program

Plutarch

The construction of the Parthenon and other temples and public buildings in Athens in the second half of the fifth century B.C. marked the height of Greek artistic achievement in the Classic Age. Under the overall inspiration and guidance of the energetic statesman Pericles, the great sculptor Phidias, the master architects Ictinus and Callicrates, and many other gifted artists enjoyed unprece-dented freedom of expression and financial backing. Most ancient accounts describing how this remarkable building program was carried out have been lost. We are therefore fortunate to have the following brief but informative excerpt from Plutarch's Life of Pericles. *Plutarch begins with the controversy over where Pericles got the money for the building program (much of it came from the Delian League treasury); then he describes the near-elimination of local unemployment, the wide variety of workers and artisans, and the principal structures and their architects.*

Excerpted from Plutarch, *Lives*, translated by John and William Langhorne (Worcester, MA: Isaiah Thomas, 1804).

The chief delight of the Athenians and the wonder of strangers, and which alone serves for a proof that the boasted power and opulence of ancient Greece is not an idle tale, was the magnificence of the temples and public edifices. Yet no action of Pericles moved the spleen of his enemies more than this. In their accusations of him to the people, they insisted that he had brought the greatest disgrace upon the Athenians by removing the public treasures of Greece from Delos and taking them into his own custody; that he had not left himself even the specious apology of having caused the money to be brought to Athens for its greater security and to keep it from being seized by the barbarians; that Greece must needs consider it as the highest insult, and an act of open tyranny, when she saw the money she had been obliged to contribute toward the war lavished by the Athenians in gilding their city and ornamenting it with statues and temples that cost a thousand talents, as a proud and vain woman decks herself out with jewels.

Pericles answered this charge by observing that they were not obliged to give the allies any account of the sums they had received, since they had kept the barbarians at a distance and effectually defended the allies, who had not furnished either horses, ships, or men, but only contributed money, which is no longer the property of the giver but of the receiver, if he performs the conditions on which it is received. He declared that as the state was provided with all the necessities of war, its superfluous wealth should be laid out on such works which when executed would be eternal monuments of its glory, and which, during their execution, would diffuse a universal plenty—for, as so many kinds of labor and such a variety of instruments and materials were requisite to these undertakings, every art would be exerted, every hand employed, almost the whole city would be in money and at the same time be both adorned and supported by itself.

Indeed, such as were of a proper age and strength were wanted for the wars, and well rewarded for their services, and as for the mechanics and meaner sort of people, they went not without their share of the public money, nor yet did they have it to support them in idleness. By constructing great edifices, which required many arts and a long time to finish them, they had the right to share in the distribution of money from the treasury—though they stirred not out of the city—along with the mariners and soldiers, guards and garrisons. For the different materials, such as stone, brass, ivory, gold, ebony, and cypress furnished employment to carpenters, masons, braziers, goldsmiths, painters and turners. The conveyance of these artisans by sea employed merchants and sailors, and by land cartwrights, wagoners, carriers, rope-makers, leather-cutters, road-makers and iron-founders, and every art had a number of laborers ranged in proper subordination to execute it, like soldiers under the command of a general. By the exercise of these different trades, plenty was distributed among persons of every rank and condition. Thus works were raised of an astonishing magnitude, inimitable beauty and perfection, every architect striving to surpass the magnificence of design with the elegance of execution—and the most wonderful circumstance was the speed with which they were completed. Many edifices, each of which would seem to have required the labor of several successive ages, were finished during the administration of one prosperous man.

It is said that when Agatharcus the painter [hailing from Samos] valued himself upon the celerity [swiftness] and ease with which he dispatched his pieces, Zeuxis [a Greek painter from Italy] replied: "If I boast, it shall be of the slowness with which I finish mine." For ease and speed in the execution seldom give a work any lasting importance or exquisite beauty, while on the other hand the time which is expended in labor is recovered and repaid in the duration of the performance. Hence we have the more reason to wonder that the structures raised by Pericles should be built in so short a time and yet built for the ages, for as each of them as soon as finished had the venerable air of antiquity, so now that they are old they have the freshness of a modern building. A bloom is diffused over them which preserves their aspect untarnished by time, as if they were animated with a spirit of perpetual youth and unfading elegance.

Pericles appointed Phidias superintendent of all the public edifices, though the Athenians had then other eminent architects and excellent workmen. The Parthenon, or temple of Pallas [Athena], whose dimensions had been a hundred feet square, was rebuilt by Callicrates and Ictinus. [The architect] Coroebus began the Temple of Initiation at Eleusis, but only lived to finish the lower rank of columns with their architraves. Metagenes of Xypete added the rest of the entablature and the upper rows of columns, and Xenocles of Cholargus built the dome on the top. The long wall, the building of which Socrates says he heard Pericles propose it to the people, was undertaken by Callicrates. [The comic playwright] Cratinus ridicules this work as proceeding very slowly:

"'Tis long since Pericles, if words would do it,
Talked up the wall; yet adds not one mite to it."

The Odeum, or music-theater, which was likewise built by the direction of Pericles, had within it many rows of seats and pillars. The roof was of a peculiar structure, after the model, we are told, of the King of Persia's pavilion. Cratinus, therefore, mocks him again in his play *Thracian Women*:

"As Jove, an onion on his head he wears,
As Pericles, a whole orchestra bears:
Afraid of broils and banishment no more,

He tunes the shell he trembled at before!"

Pericles at this time exerted all his interest to have a decree made appointing a prize for the best performer in music during the Panathenaea, and as he was himself appointed judge and distributor of the prizes, he gave the contending artists directions in what manner to proceed, whether their performance was vocal, or on the lute or lyre. From that time on the prizes in music were always contended for in the Odeum.

The vestibule [entranceway, i.e., the Propylaea] of the Acropolis was finished in five years by Mnesicles the architect. A wonderful event that happened while the work was in hand, showed that the goddess was not averse to the work, but rather took it into her protection, and encouraged the people to complete it. One of the best and most active of the workmen, missing his step, fell from the top to the bottom and was bruised in such a manner that his life was despaired of by the physicians. Pericles was greatly concerned with this accident, but in the midst of his affliction the goddess appeared to him in a dream and informed him of a remedy which he applied, and the patient soon recovered. In memory of this cure he placed in the citadel near the altar a brass statue of the Minerva of Health. The golden image of the same goddess was the workmanship of Phidias, and his name is inscribed upon the pedestal. Through his friendship of Pericles, Phidias had the direction of everything, and all the artists received his orders.

Selection 4

Architectural Perfection Achieved in the Parthenon

Manolis Andronicos

The crowning achievement of Pericles' great building program in the second half of the fifth century B.C. was the monumental Parthenon temple, dedicated to Athens's patron goddess, Athena. Though now in an advanced state of ruin, enough of it remains to convince most modern experts that it was the most perfectly executed structure ever raised by human hands. In time, it became the chief eternal symbol not only of the remarkable city that erected it, but of the glories of ancient Greek civilization as a whole. This detailed examination of the temple, which was designed by Ictinus (or Iktinos), Callicrates (or Kallikrates), and Phidias (or Pheidias), is by the noted Greek archaeologist Manolis Andronicos.

The Parthenon is undoubtedly the most magnificent monument of Periklean Athens, and reflects in the sphere of architecture the advanced form of democracy attained by the city. The temple is dedicated to the goddess Athena . . . and the form of the Parthenon as conceived by Perikles and his advisors is fundamentally and indissolubly linked with the goddess and was a magnificent statement of the achievements of the city at the height of its power.

The architects of the Parthenon were Iktinos and Kallikrates, and the sculptor Pheidias exercised a general supervision of the work and had a decisive voice in determining the plan of the temple. Iktinos and Pheidias, both experienced artists, were clearly influenced by contemporary intellectual trends, and introduced a number of creative innovations. The temple of Athena Parthenos was a unique and inspired combination of elements from both the Doric and Ionic orders, and the result was a new architectural form which may properly be called Attic. The creation of a work like this demanded vision in its conception and consummate skill in the designing and building of it. It also required the expenditure of enormous sums of money which only Periklean Athens could have met in so short a space of time: for work on the Parthenon began in 447 B.C., and the temple itself was finished nine years later in 438 B.C., though it was a further six years before the pedimental sculptures designed by Pheidias were in position.

The Structure's Measurements and Proportions

This achievement is all the more impressive in view of the sheer scale, as well as the quality, of the work. The stylobate [floor, foundation] measures 30.88 m. × 69.50 m., making the Parthenon the largest Doric temple ever completed anywhere in the Greek world. . . . It is also the only Greek temple built entirely of marble, and the only Doric temple in which all 92 metopes bore relief decoration [the metopes of other temples bore either paintings or a mixture of paintings and reliefs]. The measure of the architectural achievement, however, is to be sought not so much in the statistics of the building as in the exquisite quality of the work, and the artistic inspiration that has transcended the material used in it. For the first time in Greek architecture, the temple ceases to be simply a monument standing within a space and creates its own internal space, which in turn imposed the external form. The demand for internal space apparently derived from the intention of Pheidias to erect a huge, 12 m. high, gold and ivory statue of Athena in the *cella* [main interior chamber], consideration that had a decisive effect on the plans. . . . The *cella* is 19 m. wide—comparable with those in the enormous temples of Ionia—and occupies approximately 5/7 of the total width of the temple.

This fundamental consideration, however, is incorporated into the general design in such a way that it ceases to be an externally imposed requirement and becomes an integral part of the architectural form. The proportions of the building are governed by a general mathematical principle: the ratio of the width of the stylobate to its length is 4:9, while the diameter of the columns is 1.905 m. and the intercolumniation [space between the columns] 4.296 m.—again a ratio of 4:9. The same ratio holds for the height of the temple to its width (13.72 m: 30.88 m = 4:9), and the width of the temple proper to its length, while the ratio of the width of the temple to its height is 16:81, or $4^2:9^2$.

There are 8 columns along the short sides, which is a number very rarely found; the long sides have 17, however, and conform to the classical principle that they should be one more than double the number on the short sides. To this end, the columns are narrower than usual (ratio of diameter: height=1:4.48) and they are set unusually close together (the intercolumniation is 2.25 m. at the bottom; in the case of the temple

of Athena Aphaia on Aegina it is 2.65, and for the temple of Zeus at Olympia, 2.32). The slenderness of the columns is reinforced by the lightness of the entablature, which is 3.295 m. high, that is, only 1.73 × the diameter of the columns (compared with 1.99 for the temple on Aegina and 1.81 for that at Olympia). The closeness of the columns of the *pteron* [colonnade running around the temple's perimeter], which means that the entire colonnade has to be viewed as a single, indivisible unit, is further emphasised by the narrowness of the porticoes between the *pteron* and the temple proper (their width is less than half the intercolumniation), and by the hexastyle colonnades in front of the *pronaos* [front porch] and the *opisthodomos* [back porch], which create the impression of a dipteral temple like those in Ionia.

The compact and forceful exterior form thus created stands in deliberate contrast to the spaciousness of the interior. The mathematical width of the *cella* noted above (19 m.) was not of itself enough to create this impression of space. It was aided by an imaginative innovation on the part of the architects: the interior double colonnades are connected by a transverse colonnade at the end of the *cella*, which has the effect of breaking the line of the axis of the central aisle and emphasizing the width. At the same time it established a background on three sides for the gold and ivory statue which stood a few metres in front of the transverse colonnade.

In addition to these brilliantly conceived solutions to the basic architectural problems posed by the building, a series of imperceptible refinements were incorporated into the structure from which the Parthenon derives an inner dynamism. These refinements fall into two categories: the use of curvature and of inclination. The former is observable in the stylobate, the epistyle, the triglyphs, the *geison* and the pediments, and includes the *entasis* of the columns (the thickening that occurs in each column from about 1/3 of the way up). The surface of the stylobate is not perfectly horizontal, as the statics of the building require, but is curved so that the mid-point of the sides is 0.11 m. higher than the horizontal, and the mid-point of the ends 0.06 m. higher. The same curvature is applied in the superstructure. Inclination [deviation from the vertical] is found in all those elements of the building that should properly be vertical—that is, the columns and walls. The columns of the *pteron* all lean inwards by 0.07 m., and the four corner columns, which form part of two sides, lean diagonally by 0.10 m. The inner surfaces of the walls are vertical, while the outer incline inwards, so that they narrow towards the top. The outer planes of the temple are not parallel, therefore, but converge slightly so that the shape of the building is rather like that of a pyramid, in which there is a movement upwards and inwards.

The brilliance of the artistic conception behind this design is matched by the feat of engineering required to realise it in practice. The differences in the angles and surfaces throughout the building that resulted from the use of curvature and inclination meant that there is not a single stone in the entire structure that is cubic in shape (they are all trapezoidal), and that almost every stone was a different shape and was designed to occupy a unique position. The dimensions of each piece therefore had to be calculated with great accuracy, and the assembly of them required extreme mathematical precision.

The Sculptures

The sculptures with which the Parthenon was decorated were in no way inferior to the quality of the architecture. Pheidias had revolutionary ideas and Perikles gave him the means to apply them. Pheidias decided to adorn all 92 metopes of the temple with reliefs, something no Greek city had hitherto dared to attempt, for the cost of such a project would have been prohibitive. The themes selected were derived from the mythical and legendary struggles of Athena and the Athenians: the Gigantomachy—the battle of the Gods against the Giants in which martial Athena fought bravely—was depicted on the eastern side; the Amazonomachy—the fight of the Athenians led by Theseus against the Amazons [the famous legendary warrior women] who had reached the very hill of the Areopagos—was

represented on the western side. The southern side told the story of the Centauromachy—the battle of the Lapiths and their king Peirithoos who with his friend Theseus overcame the terrifying Centaurs [creatures half-man and half-horse]. The northern side contained scenes from the Trojan War related to Attic heroes, including the sons of Theseus, Demophon and Akamas, who had joined Agamemnon in the great expedition. The metopes adorned the exterior of the temple and suffered severe damage with the passing of centuries. Most of those that have survived (largely from the southern side) are now exhibited in the British Museum.

The metopes provided Pheidias with ample space to record the age-old myths of Attica. . . . This was a grand theme giving any master scope enough to display his talents. Yet it was not enough for Pheidias. With Perikles and other inspired poets and philosophers of their intimate circle, spurred on by the vision of an Athenian democracy at its most creative moment, Pheidias conceived a daring and unique plan: he would immortalize Athens in marble, its people, the youths, the maidens, the men, and their gods, all in a single composition, on the happiest and most celebrated day in their lives when the joyous Athenians, with their hearts beating as one, climbed in procession up the Acropolis to worship their beloved goddess Athena Parthenos amidst all the gods who joined them in the celebration. Pheidias had often seen the splendid procession on the occasion of the Great Panathenaia in the heart of summer towards the end of July (the 28th day of [the Attic month] *Hekatombaion*), beneath the brilliant sun of Attica, moving in wave after wave of people behind the sacred vessel upon whose mast hung the *peplos* of Athena, woven by the maidens of Athens to be handed to the priests of the goddess. This vibrant vision, a living image of Athenian democracy, inspired the hearts of its leading men. Perikles praised the glory of Athens in his *Funeral Speech* when he called upon the citizens to be "lovers" of such a unique city whose power and glory were reflected in its remarkable works. (And it is certain that Perikles must have glanced with pride at the Parthenon, which had only then been completed, when he delivered his speech.) . . .

But Pheidias was sculptor; and a hymn is not easily rendered in stone. One had to combine the mind of a genius, the experience of a craftsman and the daring of a pioneer to achieve this feat. To express his vision in marble the space available in the metopes or the pediments of the Doric temple was far too limited. And so he introduced a new element to the Doric edifice by adding a feature that traditionally was part of the Ionic order: a frieze, an uninterrupted zone of marble slabs on which he could carve his vision in relief. A suitable architectural space was needed for this additional feature and the inspired artist unhesitatingly placed the frieze above the temple proper, that is above the architrave of the *pronaos* and the *opisthodomos* and over the side walls. . . . He thus had at his disposal an area measuring 160 metres in length and 1.06 metres in height. In this space he unfolded the picture of a Panathenaic procession in truly remarkable fashion. Starting out from the southwestern corner the procession moves in two directions: from the end of the western side the horsemen move towards the north, and from the northwestern edge the procession continues along the north side towards the northeastern end. The other wing of the procession advances along the southern flank from the southwestern to the southeastern end. The two gracefully moving streams of people, the northern and southern, converge at the centre of the eastern side where the gods are seated in divine majesty. . . . The sections of the frieze running along the eastern and western sides of the temple are the most remarkable both in conception and execution. Of these only the western section has survived *in situ* [in its original position]. But its location makes it difficult for the observer to see it at close enough range and appreciate the incomparable perfection of the sculptures. . . . Of the rest of the frieze, several slabs, in fact some of the very best, are now housed in the Acropolis Museum. But by far the greatest number along with what has survived of the pediments are today the pride of the British Museum, which purchased them from Lord Elgin in 1816.

The temple was finally completed in 438 B.C., when the famous gold and ivory statue of Pheidias Athena was set up. . . . The only portions of the temple not then completed were the sculptures of the pediments. These two vast compositions were the high points in Pheidian art, for they could be more easily enjoyed than any other sculptural work by all the citizens of Athens. Pheidias himself and his most talented assistants Alkamenes and Agoraktitos worked on the figures of the gods and heroes who were represented in the two pediments. On the eastern pediment Pheidias related the birth of Athena who sprang in full armour from the head of Zeus. Zeus was seated in the centre, while on either side the gods were arranged in a happy and harmonious assembly. In the two corners were the chariots of Helios, the sun god, and of Selene, the moon goddess, the former mounting from the ocean, the latter descending into the ocean. The western pediment depicted the dispute between Athena and Poseidon for the possession of their beloved city. Poseidon produced water by striking the rock with his trident and Athena made an olive-tree grow. Athena was judged the winner of this divine contest. The two deities occupied the centre of the pediment. To the right and left were their chariots and the mythical ancestors of the Athenians, the families of Kekrops and of Erechtheus. What had been spared in the passage of countless centuries, by weathering and destruction at the hands of man, was removed by Lord Elgin. These pieces, the priceless survivals of the finest creations of Classical sculpture, are now displayed in special rooms of the British Museum.

Selection 5

Wonders of the World: Phidias's Statues of Athena and Zeus

Pausanias

Besides the exquisite, slightly-larger-than-life stone and bronze figures that adorned cities and temples, a few Greek sculptors created gigantic statues of the gods. Next to the towering bronze Colossus of Rhodes, built in the early Hellenistic Age to commemorate that state's delivery from the siege of the warlord Demetrius, the two most famous such statues were the Athena in the cella of Athens's Parthenon temple and the Zeus in the cella of that god's temple at Olympia. The latter was revered as one of the "Seven Wonders" of the ancient world, along with such monuments as Egypt's Great Pyramid and the "Hanging Gardens" of Babylon.

Both the Athena and Zeus were designed and executed by the fifth-century B.C. Athenian master Phidias (or Pheidias), widely viewed as the greatest sculptor of antiquity. The Athena, a standing figure, was probably about thirty-eight feet high; while the Zeus, which sat on a throne, was two or three feet taller. Each statue consisted of a huge wooden core, roughly carved to the desired

Excerpted from Pausanias, *Guide to Greece*, vol. 1, *Central Greece*, translated by Peter Levi (Penguin Classics, 1971). Translation copyright © Peter Levi, 1971. Reprinted by permission of Penguin Books Ltd.

shape, which was covered by sheets of ivory to represent flesh and of gold and other precious metals to represent garments. And each held a human-sized statue of a goddess in one hand.

Sadly, these magnificent creations were destroyed in late antiquity. Only a few miniature copies of the Athena and a handful of brief written descriptions of the two statues have survived to give some idea of what they looked like. The second-century A.D. Greek traveler Pausanias visited both temples and jotted down the following accounts of the statues in his famous guidebook. He makes reference to numerous mythological characters portrayed in the works, including: Medusa, one of the Gorgons, hideous female monsters; Erechthonios, a legendary king of Athens whom the later Athenians pictured as a serpent; Niobe, whom the gods Apollo and Artemis punished after she insulted their mother; Heracles (or Herakles), the heroic strongman known for his adventures and superhuman labors; Achilles, the warrior hero of Homer's Iliad, *and Penthesileia, an Amazon (warrior woman) whom he slew; and the Hesperides, the daughters of Darkness, who were said to guard a tree that bore golden apples.*

*a*s you go into the temple called the Parthenon, everything on the pediment has to do with the birth of Athene; the far side shows Poseidon quarrelling with Athene over the country. The statue is made of ivory and gold. She has a sphinx on the middle of her helmet, and griffins worked on either side of it. . . . The griffins are wild monsters like lions with wings and the beak of an eagle. . . . The statue of Athene stands upright in an ankle-length tunic with the head of Medusa carved in ivory on her breast. She has a [statue of the goddess] Victory about eight feet high, and a spear in her hand and a shield at her feet, and a snake beside the shield; this snake might be Erichthonios. The plinth [base] of the statue is carved with the birth of Pandora. Hesiod and others say Pandora was the first woman ever born, and the female sex did not exist before her birth. . . .

The temple and the statue to Zeus [at Olympia] were built from spoils when Elis and the local people who joined the rebellion captured Pisa [Elis's neighbor, which had originally hosted the games]. It was Pheidias who made the statue, as an inscription written below Zeus's feet bears witness:

Pheidias the son of Charmides from Athens has made me. . . .

There are columns inside the temple . . . with upper galleries by which you can approach the statue, and a way up to the roof by a spiral staircase.

The god is sitting on a throne; he is made of gold and ivory. There is a wreath on his head like twigs and leaves of olive; in his right hand he is holding a [statue of the goddess] Victory of gold and ivory with a ribbon and a wreath on her head; in the god's left hand is a staff in blossom with every kind of precious metal, and the bird perching on this staff is Zeus's eagle. The god's sandals are gold and so is his cloak, and the cloak is inlaid with animals and flowering lilies. The throne is finely worked with gold and gems, and with ebony and with ivory. There are animals painted on it and figures worked on it: and four Victories dancing on the four feet of the

This reconstruction of the interior of the Parthenon incorrectly depicts an altar and worshipers. Sacrifices and other ceremonies took place outside the temple.

throne, with two more at the bottom of each of the four feet. On the two forward feet the Theban children are being carried off by sphinxes and under the sphinxes Apollo and Artemis are shooting down Niobe's children. Between the feet of the throne there are four bars stretching right across from one foot to another; the first begins with seven figures, but the eighth, no one knows how, has become indecipherable: they could be representations of the contests of antiquity, as in Pheidias's time the boys' contests had not been instituted. They say the one tying the ribbon round his head looks like Pantarkes, an Elean adolescent who was Pheidias's boyfriend, and who in fact won the boys' wrestling at the eighty-sixth Olympics. On the other bars is Herakles' regiment fighting the Amazons. The number of figures on both sides is twenty-nine, and [the Bronze Age Athenian hero] Theseus is serving with Herakles' allies. The throne rests not only on the feet but also on four columns standing between them. It is impossible to get underneath the throne. . . . At Olympia there are barriers like walls to keep you out. The part of these barriers facing the doors is only coloured blue, but the rest of them have paintings by Panainos. One of them is Atlas holding up heaven and earth, with Herakles standing by ready to take over the weight. . . . Also Herakles' struggle with the Nemean lion. . . . Finally in these paintings Penthesileia is breathing her last breath and Achilles is holding her up, and there are two Hesperides carrying the apples which legend says they were set to guard. Panainos was Pheidias's brother, and the battle of Marathon in the Painted Colonnade at Athens is also by him. On the topmost part of the throne above the statue's head Pheidias has carved three Graces and three Seasons. Epic poetry tell us they were among Zeus's daughters, and Homer has written in the *Iliad* that the Seasons were given charge of heaven like some kind of royal palace guards. The stool under Zeus's feet, which in Attica they call a *thranion*, has golden lions worked on it and Theseus fighting the Amazons, the first Athenian act of valour outside civil war. On the platform that holds up Zeus and all the decoration that goes with him there are golden figures of the Sun mounting his chariot, and Zeus and Hera and . . . with a Grace, followed by Hermes, who in turn is followed by the Hearth goddess [Hestia], and then Eros welcoming Aphrodite as she rises from the sea, and Persuasion crowning Aphrodite with a wreath; Apollo with Artemis is worked on it, Athene and Herakles, and right at the end of the platform Amphitrite and Poseidon, and the Moon who I think is driving a horse; some people have said the goddess rides on a mule and not a horse and they tell some silly story about the mule.

I know the recorded measurements of the height and breadth of Zeus at Olympia, but I find myself unable to commend the measurers since the measurements they give fall a long way short of the impression this statue has created in those who see it, who say even the god himself bore witness to the art of Pheidias: when the statue was completely finished, Pheidias prayed to the god to make a sign if the work pleased him, and immediately a flash of lightning struck the pavement at the place where the bronze urn was still standing in my time.

The paving in front of the statue is not made of white stone but black, with a rimmed circle of Parian stone running round it to stop the oil poured out there, as oil is good for the statue at Olympia, and oil is what keeps the ivory from taking harm in the marshy atmosphere of the Altis [the Olympic sanctuary]. What the ivory needs in the statue called the Parthenon in the upper city at Athens is not oil but water, the upper city being dry because of its extreme height, so that the ivory statue is longing for water and dampness.

Selection 6

Hellenistic Art Emphasizes Realism and Emotion

John G. Pedley

University of Michigan scholar John G. Pedley begins this informative essay by explaining the factors that made Hellenistic society, and with it the Hellenistic arts, different from those of the preceding Classic Age. Among other things, the new art had an unprecedented look of realism, infused with aspects of emotionalism, drama, and often pathos and/or violence; and like the age itself, it emphasized the importance of the individual person. Pedley's treatment is comprehensive, covering architecture, including the rise to prominence of a new order, the Corinthian; sculpture, including the monumental altar at Pergamum (or Pergamon), perhaps the greatest artistic triumph of the era; as well as wall painting, mosaics, and pottery.

The Hellenistic period is wholly different from preceding periods in many ways. Huge kingdoms have replaced the city-states of Greece, which retreat into semi-obscurity. Mighty kings required new types of architecture for which there was literally no space in cities like Athens. So centers of architectural innovation are outside traditional Greek lands, as are the vital centers of sculptural pro-

duction. Yet the legacy of Greece is evident everywhere. The world changed rapidly, with new interests and new outlooks. Realism in sculpture, to the point of caricature, came to the fore, as did individualism and interest in psychological portraits. There are new expressions of movement, of drama, and violence. Renewed interest in science and scholarship led to the foundation of the great libraries of Alexandria and Pergamon. There are new religions, great increases in population, and intensified commercial contacts. This whole great world, with all its diversities of peoples, traditions and attitudes, was unified by the language of its all too plentiful bureaucracies, Greek.

Architecture

In the early years of the third century BC a certain Philetairos took over the citadel of Pergamon in western Asia Minor and established the Attalid dynasty. He and his successors . . . radically altered this citadel and established it as the capital of a Hellenistic kingdom of great power and wealth. . . . . . They were philhellenes to the core. And they built a city distinguished enough to challenge Athens and Alexandria for architecture, sculpture, books, and learning. This city, or its upper part on the crown of the hill, was built . . . with new precepts in mind. Lower down the hill was a huge gymnasium and a sanctuary of Demeter, and much domestic architecture, but it is the architectural treatment of the top of the hill,

1000 feet (300 m) high, which is of most interest.

Here, the Attalid planners used the dramatically steep landscape to frame and show off important buildings. In the plan the theatre is prominent. This aptly underscores the theatricality of setting, which governed the position and appearance of major buildings. . . .

On the lowest terrace was a colonnaded agora, with stoas on three sides, surrounding an open space, and providing sheltered walkways in front of shops and offices on two storeys. . . . On the next terrace up was the monumental altar of Zeus built in an open court. This altar was an enlargement of a type already well known in the Greek East, consisting of a wide flight of stairs between projecting wings leading to a level platform. The altar was lavishly decorated with relief sculpture, and though several sculptors worked on it, its style is uniform. . . . The third terrace supported the Temple of Athena, one of the earliest buildings of this citadel complex, and a colonnaded court. The temple stood at the west side, at an oblique angle to the court but in line with the (later) altar of Zeus one terrace below. From this court, access was possible to the great library which housed many books and a collection of classical Greek paintings and sculpture. It challenged that of Alexandria for preeminence. . . .

A great fortification wall protected the citadel. The urban plan within, which arranged buildings on different lines on a terraced hilltop, was entirely new. It is the planning of the terraces, the coordination of the natural setting with man-made spaces, and the placement of buildings which made the upper city of Pergamon so dynamic and novel. Terraces and colonnades appeared to lead upward to the skies; the more down-to-earth realized that they led to the palace of the king and the barracks of his soldiers.

The Temple of Athena was built in the second quarter of the third century. It is a small Doric building measuring only about 24 × 13 yards (22 × 12 m), but there are new features. Columns of the peristyle are set further apart than before and are slimmer. Column heights are now 6.98 times lower diameters. Thus the bulk of the building is diminished and the airiness and lightness of the elevation are stressed. The columns were left unfluted, except directly beneath the capitals. The Doric order is rare in Hellenistic temple architecture, and Ionic is more popular. Corinthian would gradually become the order favored by Roman architects.

For temple architecture of the Ionic order, we turn to other sites in Asia Minor, Magnesia and Didyma. Creative architects working in the Ionic order tended to write about their systems of proportions and methods of planning in learned commentaries, passages of which have come down to us in the writings of the Roman critic, Vitruvius. One of these scholarly architects was . . . Hermogenes, famous for his temples at Teos, another site in Asia Minor, and at Magnesia.

Hermogenes' Temple of Artemis at Magnesia was raised above ground level by a podium of seven steps, and yet more light and air were admitted to the peristyle by wide spaces between the columns and by their slender form. Hermogenes was keen to relate the plan of the cella building to the peristyle columns, and these are aligned on the axis of the cella walls, and not on their outer faces. Such precision could only have derived from a drawing on a drafting board. . . .

More complex was the new Temple of Apollo at Didyma begun around 330 BC and left unfinished. . . . This huge and surprising temple . . . was raised high on a podium of steps and measured about 120 × 56 yards (110 × 51 m). The Ionic columns of the peristyle stood almost 66 feet tall, with ten on the façade and 21 on the flank in a double colonnade. A dozen more columns, with variously carved bases, stood in the porch. . . .

Dramatic effects, whether in urban planning or spatial organization in individual buildings, are a hallmark of Hellenistic architecture. Another is the detailed interest in the proportions of architectural members and their relationships to one another, and the recording in scholarly commentaries of preferred solutions. This seems to be the case, at any rate, with the Ionic order. Doric seems to have been out of favor for big new temples, though popular among architects for large utilitarian buildings like stoas, where its simple forms could be repeated rapidly and easily. The potential convenience and brilliance of Corinthian was only slowly being realized.

The Corinthian order was used for the first time on the exterior of a fullscale building on the Temple of Olympian Zeus at Athens. This temple had been begun by the Peisistratid tyranny in the sixth century BC, but it got no further than the stylobate before their demise. In the second quarter of the second century BC, King Antiochus IV commissioned a Roman architect, Cossutius, to build it using the Corinthian order. The enormous building, measuring around 118 × 45 yards (108 × 41 m), was planned to have triple rows of eight columns at front and back, with two rows of 20 columns on either flank. Examples of the Corinthian capitals were carried off to Rome after the Roman general, Sulla, sacked Athens in 86 BC. . . . Work was not finished on this huge temple project until the emperor Hadrian's rule in the second century AD.

Antiochos' generosity was matched by that of others, and during the second century BC Athens enjoyed a period of prosperity. Architectural growth was particularly apparent in the Agora. . . . The east side of the Agora saw the construction of the Stoa of Attalos, king of Pergamon from 159 to 138 BC, a gift from him and his wife to the Athenians. It is a large (about 126 × 22 yards: 115 × 20 m) two-storeyed structure, purpose-built for shopping. There were 21 shops behind the double colonnade on each floor, 42 in all. Marble, for the façade and the columns, and limestone were the materials used. There was wide spacing of the columns for ease of access and congregation, and variety in the use of the orders. Doric was used for the exterior on the ground level, Ionic for the interior. On the second level, Ionic columns on the exterior were linked by a balustrade, while the interior colonnade introduced a new capital type called Pergamene, which was derived from the Egyptian palm capital. Columns of the interior colonnades were left unfluted, as was the lower part of the Doric colonnade since commercial traffic was likely to damage the column flutes. Enough of the stoa was preserved in later structures for

it to be restorable with accuracy. The stoa now serves as a museum. . . .

Sculpture

Diversification of form, and of psyche [i.e., of the emotions and their appeal], presented in a realistic manner, are hallmarks of Hellenistic sculpture. The great variety of types, new and old, of poses and gestures and groups, taken in some instances to the point of caricature, has been explained by the influence of the new worlds opened to Greek artists by the conquests of Alexander. Yet much of what is new in Hellenistic sculpture was already implicit in the work of the great fourth-century [B.C.] sculptors—Praxiteles, Skopas, and Lysippos—who had consistently striven towards greater realism of human experience and expression. Lysippos' recognized enthusiasm for expanding the views of figures, his interest in mental states, his enthusiasm for surprise, for dramatic postures, for portraiture, and personification were especially influential.

The period may conveniently be divided into three chronological phases, though there is much difficulty in dating some pieces and agreement between scholars is often hard to find. The first chronological phase down to about 250 BC may be seen as a period of transition, in which revolutionary approaches appear alongside those that are conventionally Classical. The High Hellenistic phase, spanning a century from around 250 to 150 BC, follows and is typified by the style of sculptures from Pergamon. This style is often described as "Hellenistic baroque." The whole period from around 300–150 BC was seen by ancient critics, notably [the roman writer] Pliny (*Natural History* 34.52), as a dreadful mistake in terms of art. Thus, the phases of Hellenistic sculpture perhaps most admired today were least admired by critics in the first century BC, who evidently preferred Classical restraint, moderation, and ideal types. The Late Hellenistic phase, from around 150 BC onwards, saw a resurgence of Classicism, which corresponded with the Roman conquest of Greece and the shipment of countless Greek statues from Greece to Italy. Copies, adaptations, and variants of Greek originals then proliferate in answer to the demands of Roman patrons. At the same time, the baroque trend was not bred out, but continued with some vigor and, doubtless, the disapproval of Pliny and his friends.

As to the subject matter, the standing male figure remained in use for images of gods and for commemorative statuary, and the draped female figure continued to be popular. But these were no longer the dominant types. Variety and diversity were called for, and the sculptors' vocabulary expanded accordingly. Interest in realism produced true-to-life portraits and images as individual as the aged fisherman and the drunken old woman. It also provided statues representing natural states of mind, the striving athlete or the sleepy satyr. Interest in eroticism produced sensuous statues of the nude Aphrodite, images of coupling satyrs and nymphs. . . . Interest in humor produced caricatures of dwarves, slaves, and hunchbacks considered in this brutal age to be amusing, or statues of smiling, almost laughing, children evidently enjoying a natural and real, desirable, state of mind. . . . Interest in emotion produced intense images of suffering, anguish, pain, brutality, anxiety, or pleasure. Thus, the range of subject matter was enormously wide.

The period of transition in the first half of the third century BC saw several innovations which derived from Praxiteles' startling creation of the nude Aphrodite of Knidos. She was often copied throughout the Hellenistic period, but new variations were also introduced. The Capitoline Venus, a Roman copy of an original of the early third century BC, changes the goddess from a distant, confident figure into a more immediate, self-conscious, and seductive type. The gestures of arms and hands, rather than cloaking the female parts of the anatomy, actually draw attention to them. . . .

More revolutionary is a work of a pupil of Lysippos, Eutychides, who created an image of the Tyche (Fortune) of Antioch shortly after the foundation of that city, around 300 BC. . . . The Tyche appears as a draped female seated on a rock. She wears a crown, which represents the fortifications of the city, and in her right hand carries a wheatsheaf, symbolizing the fertility of the land. . . .

Also entirely new is the posthumous portrait of the Athenian orator Demosthenes by Polyeuktos, erected in the Athenian Agora around 280 BC. The original was bronze, but again it is marble copies which have survived. Demosthenes faces forward with his arms lowered and his hands joined in front of him. His expression is thoughtful. The psychological portraiture is new, whereby the personality of an individual is revealed in the posture, set, and condition of the body, as well as in the facial expression. . . .

The baroque style of the High Hellenistic phase is characterized by dramatic effects, achieved by complex postures, gestures, and groupings, and by the intensity and variety of emotional representation. . . .

The group of the Gaul and his Wife is a Roman marble copy of a bronze dedication associated traditionally with the dedications made by King Attalus I (241–197 BC) at Pergamon to celebrate victories over the Gauls. The defeated Gaul prefers suicide to surrender. He has already killed his wife in order to prevent her becoming a slave. The barbarian is portrayed as the noble hero. The group is completely carved in the round, affords many viewpoints, and effectively contrasts the vigorous and still vital male body with the female collapsing in death. Baroque is the twisting posture, the exaggerated musculature of the torso, and the high drama of the moment. The original of the group may date to around 220 BC.

The high point of this style is reached in the decoration of the great altar of Zeus at Pergamon, traditionally assigned to the reign of Eumenes II (197–159 BC). . . . The altar stood on a platform, with wings projecting forward at north and south on either side of a broad staircase. The platform supported an Ionic colonnade, while the podium below was decorated with a sculptured frieze 7 feet 7 inches (2.30 m) high. Here a colossal battle of gods and giants was depicted in local marble. The frieze consisted of some two hundred figures in such high relief and so sharply undercut that they appear almost in the round. Figures writhe and struggle, even up the steps towards the altar. Stressed moments are emphasized by tense bodies, violent postures, exaggerated muscles of torsos, legs, and arms, breathing open mouths, and deepset eyes, furrowed brows, and shocks of unruly hair. Swirling drapery enhances the dramatic effect. Zeus and Athena overthrow giants, whose faces are grim with horror and anguish. . . .

Contemporary with this baroque style are studies in the bizarre (caricatures and grotesques, for example), the erotic (hermaphrodites, groups of maenads and satyrs, and Aphrodite, Pan, and Eros, for example), and studies in realism. The athlete is now shown, not like the Charioteer from Delphi of the fifth century BC in the moment of glory after the race, but in the throes of the competition. The bronze Boy Jockey, recovered from a shipwreck off Cape Artemision and doubtless intended for the art market or a patron in Rome, is shown in midcontest. Astride his horse, he leans forward, one hand holding the reins and the other perhaps a whip as he urges his mount forward. There is no exaggeration of anatomy or of expression; the lightframed, wiry, boyish body and the concentration of mind are equally successfully rendered. . . .

The Late Hellenistic phase witnessed a renewed interest in Classical sculpture. With the Roman conquest of Greece came Roman enthusiasm for Greek culture, and not least for statuary of the fifth and fourth centuries BC. Greek statues were shipped off to Italy; Roman patrons commissioned agents to find statues suitable for their gardens or their libraries or gymnasia. Wealthy Romans came to Greece to see the sights and to be educated. Less wealthy Romans and Italians came to Greece and the east to make their fortunes, and the island of Delos became a center for their activities. Trade of all kinds flourished, and Greek sculptors turned readily to the Roman market and its taste. . . .

Of the second half of the second century BC, is the marble Aphrodite of Melos (Venus de Milo), found on the island of Melos and now in the Louvre in Paris. She is over lifesize (around 6 feet 8 inches—2.04 m tall), and stands with the left leg sharply forward, bent at the knee and turning. . . . The face is Late Classical in type,

and the anatomy, too. Though proportions are changed and she is higher-waisted than the Aphrodite of Knidos, the similarity is there. The new proportions, the twisting spiral of the figure between feet and hips, and the precarious drapery introduce new and distinctly Hellenistic notes, but the influence of the Classical is clear. . . .

Wall Painting, Mosaics, and Pottery

Direct evidence for Hellenistic wall paintings is almost as scarce as it was for the fifth and fourth centuries BC, and we may reasonably suspect that what has survived is not necessarily of the first rank. At Vergina, in Macedonia, some impressive chamber tombs were discovered. Both their façades and interiors are decorated with a series of paintings. The façade of a tomb dated to about 300 BC shows Rhadamanthys, a Judge of the Dead, cloaked and leaning on a staff. . . .

On the edge of the Greek world, at Kazanlak in Bulgaria, a vaulted tomb also from about 300 BC has been found, the vault painted with friezes of figures and chariots. The standing and seated figures are drawn from the vocabulary of Greek types. . . . The chariot and horses careering around the dome show experiment in illusionistic perspective, and precede their counterparts in Roman paintings at Pompeii by some three hundred years. Yet the figures are flat, the use of color is unimaginative, and the draftsmanship is clumsy. This is the work of a provincial Greek artist, but is nevertheless an important survivor.

Perhaps the most important innovation of Hellenistic wall painters was a greater use of landscape. There were landscape elements on the fourth-century tomb at Vergina and schematic landscape features appear even earlier. . . . It is overshadowed by a magnificent series of paintings known as the Odyssey Landscapes found in a house on the Esquiline in Rome. They show episodes from Odysseus' adventures set in the most dramatic landscapes. They are Late Hellenistic (first century BC) in date. But are they Greek (Hellenistic) or Roman? What precursors can be found? The elements in the painting of Macedonian tombs are evidence that landscape themes were under study, but nothing yet found prepares us for the . . . brilliance of the conjunction of narrative and illusion in the Odyssey landscapes. Odysseus journeys through the countryside encountering many challenges and companions. But he and his human counterparts are diminutive by comparison with the mountains, rocks, trees, the sky, and the sea. Nature herself is the real focus for the painter, so that the physical world itself becomes as important as the myth which Odysseus represents. Strong accents of light and shade emphasize the grandeur of nature, the brushwork is rapid and impressionistic. . . . It is difficult to believe that this phenomenon made its first appearance, fully mature, in the first century BC. Many sensitive commentators take the view that these landscapes are Roman adaptations of earlier, second-century BC Hellenistic paintings and that the

three-dimensional representation of landscape as a grand setting for narrative or for its own sake began then.

Literary sources tell us that Romans copied Greek paintings, but it seems they preferred paintings of the fourth century BC, since Hellenistic paintings of the third and second century BC are seldom mentioned. . . . The presence on the walls of Pompeii and Herculaneum of several versions, different in details, of a particular painting both argues the existence of a prototype and suggests the difficulty of identifying what the original looked like. . . . Perhaps, too, Roman paintings which show either Hellenistic sculptural types or large-scale landscape elements are reflections of Hellenistic paintings.

Tessellated mosaics had replaced pebble mosaics by about 250 BC, and houses at Delos provide good examples from the second century BC. Figured panels . . . with humans, animals, or

A detail from the Nile Mosaic shows a boat and oarsman. Mosaics often provide modern scholars with hard evidence for details of everyday ancient life.

groups could be worked separately, and inserted into a framework of abstract designs, of which the wave pattern remained popular. Most mosaics, however, for reasons of economy were made solely of abstract designs. Other examples from Pergamon show panels with figures shaped with strong accents of light and shade. One master craftsman here, Sosus by name, became famous for his illusionistic panels, notably one of birds drinking at a basin, and another of an unswept floor with the residue of a dinner party still on it.

Much larger mosaics decorated the floors of public buildings. At Praeneste (Palestrina), some 25 miles (40 km) east of Rome, is the sanctuary of Fortuna. Built in the second century BC, it echoes developments elsewhere in the Hellenistic world. Multiple terraces on a hillside and extensive use of colonnades remind one of Pergamon. . . .

The so-called Nile Mosaic which dates from around 100 BC . . . shows a Hellenistic adaptation of an old Egyptian motif. It was probably copied in Praeneste from a prototype created in Alexandria. The Nile and its denizens, human and animal, are the subject of this polychrome mosaic. The southern regions of Egypt are shown at the top . . . and the more populated estuary at the bottom. The river winding its way through the landscape is the thread which unites the whole scene. The interest in the life of the river is panoramic. The lower part depicts ships of all kinds: oared warships, sailing boats, fishing boats, and skiffs on the river populated by crocodile, hippopotamus, birds of all kinds, fish large and small, and water buffalo. Many buildings viewed from many angles stand on the banks. Soldiers gather under an awning outside an imposing columned building, a bugler sounds off, women loiter in a pergola, a peasant rides a donkey by. In the upper, more distant part, landscape elements take precedence over architecture, boats, and humans. Though there are hunting parties of tiny figures, this is the domain of wild animals, real and fantastic, most identified by Greek inscriptions. Rocks, trees, bushes, birds, and serpents are their companions. The knowledge of the river and the range of life it sustained is both encyclopaedic and fanciful. Scholarly interest in detail, the enthusiasm for landscape motifs, the great variety of boats and buildings and the varied views are all characteristically Hellenistic.

At the end of the fourth century BC painted pottery gave way to mold-made bowls with relief decoration. These pots at first probably imitated bowls made of precious metals. They are conventionally called Megarian bowls, but were in fact manufactured all over the Hellenistic world, and enjoyed great commercial success from the third century BC down into the first. The decoration is usually floral, but occasionally figures, and even mythological scenes, appear. . . . This technique of making pottery was picked up by the Romans in the first century BC, and resulted in the production of the most successful of Roman tablewares, Arretine. . . .

Painting on a light ground [i.e., background] continued on Panathenaic amphoras until the end of the third century BC, and a new shape, the *lagynos* (a squat jug with a long neck), is habitually decorated with brown paint on a thick white slip. The decoration most often shows garlands of wreaths, but sometimes also different objects related to feasting. The shape may have originated in Asia Minor, perhaps near Pergamon, and lasted till the first century BC. More ambitious were vases, essentially white-ground, with molded additions. At Canosa in south Italy in the third century BC, burials often included unusual pottery shapes to which fully three-dimensional attachments (horse heads and necks, for example) were fixed . . . all painted in blue, pink, and yellow on a white ground. At Centuripe in Sicily, also in the third century BC, a similar practice was followed. The polychrome burial vase, extravagant in shape and with molded additions (heads, architectural moldings), shows a seated woman flanked by two attendants. Pink, blue, yellow, and red are painted on the white ground. All the painting was done after the vessel was fired, so that these colors are notoriously fugitive [faded or missing]. This technique was quite different from the Greek red-figure of the fifth and fourth centuries BC, and this style represented, in fact, the final episode in the history of Greek vase painting.

Theater and Drama

Introduction

*G*reek drama and theater developed with relative suddenness and enjoyed their greatest flowering in Athens in the brief period spanning the late sixth through late fifth centuries B.C. Although the exact origins of these literary and visual arts are and will likely always remain uncertain, scholars have managed to piece together a likely scenario for their inception. At least by the eighth century B.C., the Greeks had developed elaborate rituals attending worship of the fertility god Dionysus, including a kind of poetry and ceremony called the dithyramb. This special form of verse, which the worshipers sang and danced to, eventually became the chief highlight of the religious festivals dedicated to the god. Apparently the dithyramb told the story of Dionysus's life and adventures, as set down in various myths the Greeks had inherited from earlier times.

As time went on, the dithyrambic ceremony expanded to include other gods, as well as human heroes, and took on increasingly dramatic form. A priest and a selected group of worshipers stood in front of the rest of the congregation and, to the accompaniment of flutes, cymbals, and other instruments, enacted a god's or hero's story through song and dance. In a way, then, the priest and his assistants were the first performers and the rest of the congregation their audience. Another advance occurred when priests began elaborating on and offering their own versions of the accepted story lines; this made them, in a sense, the first playwrights. A piece of evidence supporting this scenario for tragedy's origins is that the dithyramb was also called "goat-song" because some of those involved in the ceremony dressed as satyrs (creatures part-man and part-animal, usually a goat or horse). The term "tragedy" (*tragoidia*) most likely developed from the Greek words *tragos,* meaning goat, and *odi,* meaning song.

Another important source for drama was epic poetry, especially the epics of Homer. At first, bards like Homer merely stood before an audience (probably mainly aristocrats initially) and recited these tales. In time, however, such recitations became more formal and attached to religious festivals. An important turning point came in 566 B.C. when the Athenians instituted Homeric recitation contests—the *rhapsodia.* (The performers were known as *rhapsodes.*)

Not long afterward, perhaps about the year 534 B.C., Athens instituted a large-scale annual religious festival—the City Dionysia—in Dionysus's honor. The festival featured a dramatic competition involving both formal dithyramb and *rhapsodia.* The contest's first winner was a poet named Thespis, who is credited with transforming these traditional presentations into the first example of what later came to be recognized as a theatrical play, part of a new art form called tragedy. Thespis's novel idea was to impersonate, rather than just tell about, the story's heroes. In detaching himself from the chorus and playing a character, he became the world's first actor.

In a sense, then, Thespis created the formal art form of theater almost overnight. In setting up regular interplay between actor and chorus, he introduced the basic theatrical convention of dialogue; he also experimented with ways of disguising himself so that he could portray different characters in the same dramatic piece. He eventually decided to don a series of masks, which became another standard convention of Greek theater. In addition, Thespis apparently helped to define the role of the audience. By enlarging the dithyramb into a piece of art and entertainment, he transformed the congregation into a true theater audience. (For these innovations, Thespis became a theater immortal; actors are still called "thespians" in his honor.)

Play performances became increasingly elaborate, dramatic, and expensive. And the City Dionysia festival accordingly developed into a major holiday attraction that the populace eagerly awaited each year. Covering several days at the end of March, the festival was open to all Greeks. The state financed the theater building and its maintenance, paid fees to the actors (and possibly the playwrights), and also provided the prizes for the dramatic contests. All other expenses of play production, including costumes, sets, musicians, and the training of the choruses, were the responsibility of the backers, the *choregoi,* well-to-do citizens whom the state called on to help support the festival. These men were chosen by lot (random drawing) each year and each *choregus* was assigned to a specific playwright. Meanwhile, the playwrights not only wrote the plays, but also acted in them, trained the choruses, composed the music, choreographed the dances, and supervised all other aspects of production.

On the first day of the competition, the playwrights, their *choregoi* and choruses, along with important public officials, took part in a stately procession that wound its way through the city streets. The colorful parade ended up in the Theater of Dionysus (near the southeastern foot of the Acropolis), which seated about 14,000 spectators. In the days that followed, each of three playwrights presented three tragedies. (Tragedy was still the main dramatic form, as comedy was not yet well-developed or popular; when comedies eventually began to be performed at the City Dionysia in 501 B.C., they took place at night, after day-long presentations of tragedy.)

The settings of the plays were left mostly to the audience's imagination. In the fifth and fourth centuries B.C., as a rule the action of the plays took place outdoors, in front of a house, palace, temple, or other familiar structure. The scene building (*skene*) that stood behind the actors, redecorated appropriately by the playwright-producer, represented the fronts of these buildings. Interiors could not be shown, and there is no solid evidence for the use of movable painted scenery like that in modern theaters.

As time went on, Greek theatrical producers introduced various mechanical devices to enhance both setting and atmosphere. Perhaps the most common was the *eccyclema,* or "tableau machine." Violent acts were almost always committed "indoors," and therefore offstage and out of sight, and the audience learned about them secondhand from messengers or other characters. Sometimes, however, to achieve shock value, a doorway in the *skene* would open and stagehands would push out the *eccyclema,* a movable platform on rollers. On the platform, frozen in a dramatic, posed tableau, would be both the murderer and the victim, usually depicted in the seconds immediately following the crime.

One major advantage Athenian audiences enjoyed over modern ones was the fact that at the time drama and theater were new institutions that existed nowhere else in the world. Theatrical conventions and ideas that today seem run-of-the-mill were, in fifth-century Athens, fresh and exciting. And it was in this stimulating, creative atmosphere that some of the greatest playwrights of all time worked their magic. Of the four fifth-century B.C. master playwrights, three—Aeschylus, Sophocles, and Euripides—produced mainly tragedies. The essence of tragedy, as these writers developed it, was the struggle of human beings to reconcile the existence of both good and evil.

Early playwrights like Thespis and Phrynichus had set the basic form and tone of tragedy. But it was not until the early fifth century B.C. that Aeschylus, the first major theatrical innovator after Thespis, raised the art of tragedy to the level of great literature. Born about 525, as a young man Aeschylus witnessed Athens's steady rise toward political, military, and cultural greatness. And one of the epic events connected with that rise became the major theme of his *Persians,* written circa 472. The oldest surviving complete tragedy, the play depicts with a compelling sense of immediacy the sweeping Greek victory over Persia in the naval battle of Salamis in 480.

Of the ninety plays Aeschylus reportedly wrote, eighty-two titles are known, but only seven complete manuscripts survive. Besides the *Persians,* these are *Seven Against Thebes* (written 467 B.C.); the *Oresteia,* a trilogy consisting of

Agamemnon, The Libation Bearers, and *The Eumenides* (458); *The Suppliants* (ca. 463); and *Prometheus Bound* (ca. 460). Aeschylus won his first victory in the City Dionysia contests in 484 and went on to win twelve more times.

One of Aeschylus's great innovations was the introduction of a second actor. Until his time, following the tradition established by Thespis, playwrights made do with one actor; but this limited them to telling fairly simple stories with a few characters, which the lone actor attempted to portray using different masks. The addition of a second actor significantly expanded the story-telling potential, since it allowed the depiction of twice as many characters.

The second great fifth-century B.C. tragedian was Sophocles, Aeschylus's junior by some thirty years. Born around 496 at Colonus, then a village just outside Athens's city walls, Sophocles was the most successful dramatist ever to present plays in the Theater of Dionysus. In his first victory in the City Dionysia, in 468 (for a play titled *Triptolemus,* now lost), he defeated Aeschylus; and he went on to win first prize at least eighteen times. (According to ancient sources, he sometimes won the second prize, but never the third.)

In retrospect, Sophocles' impact on the theater, in his own time and for all times, was nothing less than extraordinary. To begin with, his output of plays was huge—reportedly 123 in all. Unfortunately, only seven of these have survived: *Ajax* (ca. 447 B.C.), *Antigone* (ca. 441), *Oedipus the King* (ca. 429), *The Women of Trachis* (ca. 428), *Electra* (ca. 415), *Philoctetes* (ca. 409), and *Oedipus at Colonus* (406). Sophocles, a master of characterization, was the first playwright to use a third actor, which further increased the amount of character interaction in drama. The result of this development was a reduction in the importance of the chorus, the size of which he fixed at fifteen members.

Born in 485 B.C., the third great Greek tragedian, Euripides, had his first plays produced in 455. Of a total of some 88, nineteen have survived: *Alcestis* (438), *Medea* (431), *Children of Heracles* (ca. 430), *Hippolytus* (428), *Andromache* (ca. 426), *Hecuba* (ca. 424), *The Suppliant Women* (ca. 422), *Heracles* (ca. 422–417), *Madness of Heracles* (ca. 420–417), *Electra* (ca. 417–413), *Ion* (ca. 417), *The Trojan Women* (415), *Iphigenia in Taurus* (ca. 414), *The Phoenician Women* (ca. 412– 408), *Helen* (412), *Orestes* (408), *The Bacchae* (405), *Iphigenia in Aulus* (ca. 405), and *The Cyclops* (date unknown). Euripides won the dramatic competitions only five times and was far less popular in his own day than either Aeschylus or Sophocles. This was primarily because Euripides' plays often questioned traditional and widely accepted social values.

In exploring how humans shape their own values and destinies, Euripides also depicted ordinary people in highly realistic ways. Many Athenians saw this mode of expression as too undignified for the tragic stage, which they felt should show more heroic, larger-than-life people and themes. Thus, Euripides was far ahead of his time, and later scholars came to see him as the first playwright to deal with human problems in a modern way.

The fourth fifth-century B.C. theatrical great, Aristophanes, was a comic playwright. The exact origins of comedy are uncertain; but it is likely that it developed out of some of the same religious rituals that tragedy did. Most of the early Dionysian processions, including the dithyramb, were serious in nature. In time, however, some of these processions featured revelers dressed in animal costumes, particularly those depicting goats and horses. These worshipers in their satyr outfits danced, sang, and exchanged off-color jokes with onlookers. That such processions were one important source of comedy (*komoidia*) is supported by the term's root words—*komos,* meaning "revel," and *aeidein,* meaning "to sing."

Although comedies first appeared on the program at the City Dionysia in 501 B.C., they did not receive official recognition, including government support for production and prizes, until 487. The most creative period for Greek comedy, often referred to as the Old Comedy, lasted from about 450 to 404 B.C. The comic playwrights typically presented highly topical humor and poked fun at people of all walks of life, but especially politicians, generals, and other leaders. This constitutes one of the best illustrations of the extraordinary degree of freedom of speech (*parrhe-*

sia) allowed under Athenian democracy.

Aristophanes, who lived from about 445 to 385 B.C., was the undisputed master of the Old Comedy. Ancient writers attribute forty-four plays to him, but only eleven have survived: *Acharnians* (425), *Knights* (424), *Clouds* (423), *Wasps* (422), *Peace* (421), *Birds* (414), *Lysistrata* (411), *Women Celebrating the Thesmophoria* (411), *Frogs* (405), *Women in the Assembly* (392), and *Plutus* (382). Throughout his career, Aristophanes used biting satire to poke fun at the leaders and institutions of his day, usually depicting them in fantastic or absurd situations.

The theatrical reign of Aeschylus, Sophocles, Euripides, Aristophanes, and their contemporaries was short-lived. In 404 B.C., Athens went down to defeat in the conclusion of the horrific Peloponnesian War and the golden age of Athenian culture more or less ended. The City Dionysia and its competitions among playwrights continued, to be sure. But the era of extraordinary innovation and enormous creative output was over.

Likewise, the comedies of the immediate postwar era were fewer, tamer, and less innovative and inspired. It is possible that the despair, depression, and disillusionment of the Athenians and other Greeks following the great war dampened both the comic playwrights' creative zeal and audiences' appreciation for humor. Later, from the 320s to about 260 B.C., the New Comedy, dominated by the popular Menander, thrived. On the one hand, it was more realistic and down-to-earth than the Old Comedy and just as popular; but it was also far tamer and less topical, satiric, and inventive.

Meanwhile, in Menander's day and long afterwards, some of the plays of the fifth-century B.C. masters continued to be performed. Unfortunately, many others were lost and with the disintegration of Greco-Roman civilization in late antiquity, Greek theaters went dark for many centuries. In time, however, the few surviving works of these masters were rediscovered and staged anew, awing and delighting modern generations, who saw in them a transcending universality and a literary quality never surpassed. Indisputably, this handful of gifted individuals had managed to create, in a stroke, the model for great drama and theater for all times.

Selection 1

Greek Playwrights Draw Mainly on Traditional Myths

Michael Grant

Because ancient Greek drama evolved from religious ritual, it was only natural that its principal themes would be drawn from myths—the stories of the gods, around whom such rituals revolved, and the humans who had supposedly interacted with them in past ages. Scholar Michael Grant, of Edinburgh University, here explains how Attic (i.e., Athenian) drama incorporated the gods mentioned in the works of the early poets Homer and Hesiod. He points out that, since Greek audiences were already familiar with the stories of these gods, the playwrights did not need to burden their texts with lengthy exposition (explanatory or background information). He then discusses Aeschylus's trilogy, the Oresteia, *as a prime example of the use of myth in classic Greek drama.*

*T*he genre by which myth took on new life [was] Attic tragedy. How the development occurred has been endlessly and, in the lack of decisive evidence, inconclusively discussed. But there appears to be a basis of truth in Aristotle's statement that tragedy evolved in the hands of those who led songs of rejoicing, accompanied by dances in honour of the god Dionysus. . . .

Although, with a few remarkable exceptions, Dionysus did not provide the themes of the plays, some of the earliest of them may have dealt with his story. But in any case the subject-matter of tragic drama was at all times closely related to religion. Indeed, the ecstatic [highly emotional, frenzied] . . . nature of the Dionysiac faith left its mark by the creation of an urgent, intense, religious spirit absent from our own drama. . . . It was the wine-like intoxicant of spiritual surrender which—to varying extents that we cannot now estimate—assisted the actors to interpret these plays, and the audiences to participate in their performance. They were more understanding audiences than any other western dramatists have known; for this was an epoch in which a small and gifted society, with slave-labour to support its shared traditions and culture, truly entered into the achievements of its great writers and artists.

Myths Employed to Illuminate Universal Problems

The subject-matter of the Athenian plays dealt with solemn fundamental matters concerning the relationship of mankind with the gods. That is to say, the subjects were mythological. The myths handed down from the Homeric and Hesiodic poems, as well as many more besides, had been retold by lyric poets writing in the intervening period. . . . And now remarkable further developments of this mythical material were on the way. . . . Greek drama was a sophisticated symbol of profound, consciously appreciated issues, illuminating the universal problem through the individual case; just as the sculptors and vase-painters of this epoch, employing the same mythological themes, likewise attained new grandeur.

The Attic playwrights altered and transfigured the myths (as Shakespeare made use of Plutarch, the English chronicles, and the Italian romances), employing them as a traditional but elastic framework which gave the fullest scope for their originality. To Greek audiences these myths, although still capable of numerous variations (even at the hands of a single author), were familiar enough to enable much explanation to be saved. The tragedian could therefore concentrate on the essence of his task, which was the poetic, religious recreation of the past in the present. For the myths were the past to the Greeks, were real, and were therefore credible. Indeed distance aided contemplation, since although the first great tragedian Aeschylus was successful with his topical *Persae* [*The Persians*] about the battle of Salamis, his rival Phrynichus had earned condemnation for a tragedy about a painful contemporary happening, the capture of Miletus by the Persians. Universality was more easily attained by the treatment of myths instead, since they avoided any such concrete situation undetachable from topical events.

Yet, even in an age in which leading thinkers, with startling rapidity, were changing from mythopoeic to rational attitudes, mythology still gave expression to what engrossed or troubled people, and continued to provide the subject-matter for the great creative dramatists—rather as artists of the fourteenth century AD constantly repainted Biblical scenes and gained by doing so. Likewise, the Boeotian lyric poet Pindar of this same period (518–438 BC) interwove in almost all his odes—as an intimate part of his thought—some illuminating myth, in order to add surprise, universality and a moral (in tones either urgent or relaxed) to a topical occasion. . . .

The historical development of tragedy explains what to us is one of the most unfamiliar features of this mythological drama, the prominent place it allows to the chorus and to choral odes. Alien to our own conventional realism, these odes were utilized (in different ways) by all the Attic tragedians; the choruses who pronounce them vary all the way from central figures in the play to peripheral observers. The chorus complements, illustrates, universalizes, or dramatically justifies the course of events; it comments or moralizes or mythologizes upon what happens, and opens up the spiritual dimension of the theme or displays the reaction of public opinion. . . . So the twelve, or later fifteen, singers and dancers of the chorus played a vital part in the perpetuation and transfiguration of the myths which was tragedy's achievement. . . .

Poetry depicts the larger passions, and the permanent and universal themes enshrined in the myths, more effectively than prose. Indeed all the world's greatest plays, mythological or otherwise, have been in poetic language. Poetry rises beyond the limitations of the theatrical framework, and gives drama the opportunity to understand and present the great issues of life in a dimension which neither science nor theology can attain. The methods of the theatre are at once subtle and direct, and in the Greek open-air stage and the long daily sessions they had to be raised to the highest degree of dramatic vividness. Thus in Attic tragedy, although certain unfamiliar conventions such as the chorus seem to us to hold up the action, and although incident and movement are sometimes scarce in comparison with the physical activity of an Elizabethan or modern play, there was an immense economy and a concentrated, irremediably speeding fe-

rocity of thought and meaning. The myths made this possible. Much of the action, as the audience knew, had already happened before the play began. This . . . directed their eyes upon the sharply explicit foreground in which fundamental problems were presented in the most vigorous and concrete form.

Aeschylus's Use of Myths

Out of the ninety plays attributed to Aeschylus, and performed from c. 499–6 BC until his death in 456, seven have come down to us. We have not enough secure dates to draw any useful conclusions about the chronological development of his art; but his most important technical innovation was the introduction of a second actor, which created the possibility of a dramatic situation or conflict. Aeschylus is also responsible for a new seriousness, a lofty intellectual tone conveyed through a densely charged style of massive grandeur and stiffly gorgeous, exuberant complexity. For [English poet] Robert Browning, as for others,

Aeschylus' bronze-throat eagle-bark at blood
Has somehow spoilt my taste for twitterings.

In veiled, oracular speech, loaded with a multiplicity of daring, inventive words and symbols, he mobilized his imaginative power to write into the myths almost incommunicable cosmic and human truths.

One of the most famous of the mythological cycles elaborated by the tragedies relates to the gory tale of the House of Pelops and Atreus. These stories were located at Argos by Aeschylus, as earlier (in the *Odyssey*) at its neighbour and forerunner Mycenae. Perhaps the . . . tradition echoes a real Mycenaean ruling house, whose alleged foreign origin may reflect early immigration from Asia Minor. After grim preliminaries in previous generations, the story comprises six crimes: the seduction by Thyestes of Aerope, the wife of his brother Atreus; the murder by Atreus of Thyestes' children (whose remains were set before their own father to eat); the abduction to Troy, by Paris, of Helen the wife of Atreus' younger son Menelaus; the sacrifice by Agamemnon (Menelaus' brother) of his own daughter Iphigenia; the murder of Agamemnon, on his return from Troy, by his wife Clytemnestra and her lover Aegisthus . . . and the murders of Clytemnestra and Aegisthus by her offspring Orestes and Electra.

The plays in Agamemnon's trilogy known as the *Oresteia* deal successively, as has been seen, with the death of Agamemnon, the deaths of Clytemnestra and Aegisthus, and the termination of the blood-feud by divine intervention. This is the only surviving trilogy of any tragedian; it may have been accompanied by a satyr-play about the wanderings of Menelaus.

Parts of the story must be very ancient—the sacrifice of Iphigenia, for example, no doubt goes back to times of human sacrifice. The *Odyssey* had held up the fate of Agamemnon as a warning and contrast to the destiny of Odysseus, and hinted at the murder of Clytemnestra by Orestes. But the paucity of references to this story in the two principal Homeric poems shows that Aeschylus was too modest if he described his subjects as "slices from the great banquet of Homer." The tragic implications of Agamemnon's story are far from Homeric, reflecting rather the religion and morality of the guilt-culture which followed and largely superseded the shame-culture of *Iliad* and *Odyssey*.

From the later seventh century BC onwards, the theme inspired artists; sculptural reliefs from the sixth-century Treasury of the Heraeum on the river Silerus in south-west Italy show Orestes killing Aegisthus, and Clytemnestra forcibly restrained—perhaps by Orestes' nurse—from attacking her son. The lyric poet Stesichorus (though transferring the scene to Sparta) introduced much of the material subsequently used by Aeschylus. . . . The subject-matter of such myths seemed to [the famed English writer] H.G. Wells, in *The New Machiavelli,* "the telling of incomprehensible parricides . . . of gods faded beyond symbolism, of that Relentless Law we did believe in for a moment, that no modern western European can believe in." Nevertheless, the *Oresteia* displays one of the world's outstanding arts in all its glory, presented to a vital, responsive community by an idiosyncratic genius of inexhaustible poetic versatility and strength. [English poet Algernon] Swinburne described the plays as "probably on the whole the greatest spiritual work of man."

Selection 2

Choruses, Masks, Costumes, and Acting Styles

James H. Butler

Modern playgoers are accustomed to certain common stage conventions, such as the curtain rising, costumes, make-up, and certain accepted and popular acting styles. Similarly, ancient Greek theater had its own conventions, which are examined here by former University of Southern California scholar James H. Butler. Some of these, like the use of the chorus and masks, which the Greeks took for granted, would seem strange to most modern audiences.

The Chorus

*W*hen Greek drama was in its most productive period, the chorus was an extremely effective and powerful theatrical instrument. It functioned as an ideal spectator helping audiences and actors to relate emotionally to what was happening in the plays by providing symbolic action that reinforced the relationship. The chorus also continually focused attention where it needed to be directed. The chorus often took an active part in the action of a play by questioning and counseling the characters. The singing, recitative [chanted lines], and dancing of the chorus as they delivered choral odes helped to establish the proper mood to blend in with the action which had just been depicted or was about to be depicted. . . .

The size of the tragic chorus (*choreutai*) prior to the advent of Aeschylean drama, which might have used a chorus of 50 in the earliest plays and only 12 in the latest, has not been established. Sophocles increased it to 15 members, where it remained. The *choreutai* in satyr drama numbered 12, while Old Comedy used a chorus of 24 sometimes split into two groups, as in *Lysistrata*. The size and importance of comic choruses dwindled much faster than the others.

Choreutai were amateurs trained and choreographed by playwrights. Later this task was turned over to *chorodidaskaloi* (chorus teachers). Choral discipline was achieved through long and arduous practice in singing the odes and in performing the steps, patterns of movement, and *cheironomia* [symbolic gestures] of the dances. These were accompanied by music composed and played by a single flute player. . . .

The usual tragic and comic choruses entered singing the *parodos* (entrance song) and led by a flute player. They were grouped in a rectangular marching formation composed of ranks and files—three by five for tragedy and four by six for comedy. Once in position in the orchestra, they turned and faced the spectators, still singing and gesturing. Entrance procedures, however, often varied from this convention according to plot requirements.

During the ensuing episodes the chorus worked out from this formation, reacting with suitable movements and gestures to the unfolding words and actions of characters. The *koryphaios* (chorus leader) entered directly into the action and carried on dialogue with the actors. Choral odes were sung and danced appropriately guided by the meters of the odes. The chorus remained in the orchestra, with a few exceptions, until the play was finished, when it left, marching in rectangular formation.

Choruses in Old Comedy were very active in dancing and singing; some members engaged in dialogue with actors; others at times broke up into smaller groups and sang and danced. . . .

Sileni (horse-men) or satyrs (goat-men) or a blend of the two led by Silenus, an attendant to Dionysus, formed the chorus for satyr drama. Double flute music accompanied the lively and grotesque *sikinnis* (satyric dance).

Masks

All actors wore masks. It is thought that this feature was a carryover from deity worship as practiced in several parts of ancient Greece. The wearing of masks helped to enhance the mystical quality inherent in theatrical performances. It also made it easier for actors to double in roles. Thespis introduced plain linen masks which were perfected by his successors. The addition of colored and terrifying masks is attributed to Aeschylus. Painted masks with open mouths and attached hair (probably human) suitably arranged for the roles depicted were worn by all actors and chorus members. Made of molded, stiffened linen, carved wood, or tooled leather, they were large enough to fit snugly over the actor's entire head, yet were light enough to be worn comfortably.

This drawing reconstructs a scene from a Greek theatrical comedy of the Classic Age. Note the use of elaborate masks to represent general character types, in this case an "old man" and a "mischievous slave."

Mask-makers created portrait masks which were often extremely lifelike; the mask of Socrates in *The Clouds* was so realistic that he is reputed to have stood up in the theatre "so that the audience could see his likeness to the actor." They also created masks of historical personages, legendary figures, and gods. Comic and satyr masks were often exaggerated, grotesque, and amusing. Old Comedy choruses of wasps, birds, frogs, and other creatures afforded mask-makers great opportunities for exercising their creative talents.

Information on Hellenistic masks is fairly extensive. Not only did they become conventionalized and stereotyped, but the forehead part (*onkos*) of tragic masks was lengthened. This elongation gave them an archaic appearance and added a few inches of height to the actors who wore them.

In his *Onomasticon* (a thesaurus of terms),

Julius Pollux, a Greek scholar and rhetorician of the second century A.D., lists and describes a number of masks. The 28 masks for tragedy he divides into the following categories: 6 for old men, 8 for young men, 3 for male servants, and 11 for women of varying ages. The 44 masks for comedy were divided into: 9 for older men, 11 for younger men, 7 for male servants, and 17 for women of varying ages. To these must be added a whole series of special masks and 4 satyr masks. Fortunately, it is possible to check Pollux's description of several masks against numerous monuments of marble and terra-cotta masks and figurines of actors, mosaics, wall paintings, friezes, and vase paintings—all showing actors wearing masks.

This evidence points up the typing of characters prevalent in Hellenistic and later Roman drama. The age, occupation, and general condition of a character could be determined almost instantly by his or her complexion, contour of face, color and amount of hair, shape of beard, hair-dress, eyebrows, shape and size of mouth, lips, and nose as depicted on the mask.

Costumes and Acting Styles

The principal actors in classical tragedy wore a woven linen or woolen chiton (tunic) which had wrist-length sleeves, was highly colored and ornamented with designs, and reached to the ground. It was encircled by a girdle worn high, just under the breast. Soft boots laced up the front and a mask covering the face completed the costume, the origins of which may date back to Dionysian and Eleusinian cult worship. But whatever its origin, this type of dress made it easier for men to disguise themselves as women because it covered more of the body than did the clothing worn in daily life. It also favored quick costume changes, a necessity for actors doubling in roles. The high-soled boot (kothornos), which added a few inches of height to the major tragic actors, came into use in the high-stage Hellenistic theatres. The rather archaic appearance of tragic actors, with their special costumes and masks, helped to lend dignity and awe to their performances.

All minor characters wore ordinary chitons. They consisted of an oblong piece of cloth wrapped or draped around the body. This was the basic dress for everyday wear of men and women alike. The himation (another oblong piece of cloth) was draped over the upper part of the chiton for outdoor wear. Travelers wore the chlamys, a short mantle attached to the left shoulder.

Great use was made of emblems and insignia in costume embellishment and also of hand properties. Old men carried staffs, and warriors were equipped with armor. Crowns of olive or laurel meant the wearer was bringing good tidings, and crowns of myrtle indicated festivity. Zeus and Athena wore an aegis, a warlike shield or breastplate with a Gorgon's head in the center. Hermes wore winged shoes. . . . Hercules (Herakles) appeared in a lion's skin carrying his club. Kings wore crowns and carried sceptres.

And Apollo had his bow.

Comic and tragic choruses dressed in a wide variety of costumes suitable for their nationality, occupation, or function in plays. The animal and bird choruses in several of Aristophanes' plays were strikingly costumed.

Sileni and the satyr choruses wore a shaggy undergarment resembling the hide of an animal and equipped with a tail. In addition, the sileni had huge phalluses [penises] and often wore animal skins.

Old Comedy actors were provided with a colored, tight-fitting, knit undergarment resembling old-fashioned union-suit underwear. It was grotesquely padded at the belly and the rump. Their chitons were cut short in order to display the red-leather phallus sewn onto the undergarment. Middle and New Comedy actors wore everyday clothing. The colors had symbolic meaning: white was worn by old men and slaves, gray or black indicated parasites, and red or purple was the color for young men.

In performance Greek plays combined dramatic action, poetic dialogue, dancing, and singing. Portions were delivered in spoken dialogue, segments were chanted in recitative, and still other pieces were sung and danced to the accompaniment of flute music. There are some superficial similarities between modern music-dramas or musical comedies and classical Greek plays. However, the latter followed a tighter pattern or structural framework, had a greater thematic thrust, and employed different artistic conventions for each genre. Eventually, the musical and choral portions were subordinated to the dramatic elements, and finally largely disappeared in late tragedy.

Greek tragic acting had simplicity, vigor, and dignity. It contained elements from its ritualistic past as well as certain pageantlike qualities. Clear articulation, careful observance of verse rhythm and meter, appropriate gestures, and skillfully executed movements were qualities ranked highest by audiences. Comic acting was vigorous, lively, and unrestrained. Presentational rather than illusionistic, it was directed to the audience as much as possible.

Selection 3

The Nature of Greek Tragedy

D.W. Lucas

In this enlightening essay, D.W. Lucas, formerly of King's College and Cambridge University, discusses the general tone and structure of Greek tragedy, at times citing Aristotle, who composed an extensive analysis of the genre (in his Poetics*) in the fourth century* B.C. *Lucas also conveniently identifies the major components, literary devices, and effects of typical Greek tragedies (although, as he points out, all of these things were not necessarily to be found in every tragedy). These include the* hamartia, *or tragic error committed by the hero; the* peripeteia, *an unexpected turn of events that brings that error to the fore; the* anagorisis, *the hero's recognition of his error; and* catharsis, *a release of emotional tension (or an emotional cleansing) generated by watching a tragedy.*

I t is well for anyone who proposes to describe and criticize tragedies to make clear from the start what meaning he attaches to the word tragedy. . . . To an Athenian anything was a tragedy which was produced at the tragic contests and was not a satyr-play. To us the word suggests a serious play with an unhappy ending. Accordingly we must accept

Excerpted from D.W. Lucas, *The Greek Tragic Poets* (New York: Norton, 1959). Copyright © 1959 by D.W. Lucas. Reprinted by permission of Routledge.

under the heading of Greek tragedy a number of plays with more or less happy endings, a few of which, notably the *Helen* [by Euripides], are not conspicuously serious. Aristotle, whom it is impossible to keep out of this discussion, regarded plays with unhappy endings as the most truly tragic. He would no doubt have justified the inclusion of serious plays with happy endings on the ground that they arouse, at least during part of their performance, the same emotions of pity and fear as a play with an unhappy ending. . . . All the same we are justified in regarding tragedy in the modern sense as significantly different from any play that ends happily because it contains an assertion that men in this world can be overtaken by undeserved catastrophe. Not every one would admit that catastrophe is really the last word, but the end of tragedy is apparent catastrophe, and it is one out of proportion to the deserts of the sufferers, because the mere fact that the play is serious makes it unlikely that the characters will be so worthless that they may be said to deserve all they get. None the less the degree of guilt attaching to them may vary greatly between tragedy and tragedy. We need only compare [Shakespeare's] *Macbeth* and *Othello*.

Aristotle's View of Tragedy

It is open to question how far tragedies of different periods and different societies can be judged by the same standards. The Greek tragic form certainly has many peculiarities of its own, not least important its comparative brevity. Aristotle had read far more Greek drama than we ever shall, and is allowed even by those who admire him least to have possessed remarkable powers of generalizing, so that it is natural to start from his account. But it should be remembered that in making his generalizations he took little account of Aeschylus, and that he seems to have regarded the heroic legends which were the raw material of tragedy with an indifference in no way characteristic of the previous century when the tragedies were composed.

Tragedy, says Aristotle, is a representation of a serious action performed by characters sufficiently like us to arouse our sympathy but better than we are. The action shows the change in the hero's fortunes, a change in the best type of tragedy from good to bad. The unity of the play depends on there being a causal connection between the episodes of the play such that we are shown a series of events each of which is a necessary or probable consequence of what has gone before. With this demand for logic and emphasis on causality is connected the famous claim that poetry is more philosophical than history; logic is the same on the stage as in the world, and the logical connections between actions and events can be revealed more clearly in the simplified relations of drama than in the complex confusions of real life, where the forces involved are more numerous and less calculable.

In order that this sequence of events may be necessary or probable the hero, unless he is a purely passive victim, must himself take the initial step. Since this step will lead eventually to catastrophe it will usually be taken in ignorance of the consequences. This is the celebrated *hamartia*; it may be both mistaken and wrong, as it was in the case of Ajax [the hero of Sophocles' play of that name]; more often it is only mistaken, as with Oedipus [the main character of Sophocles' *Oedipus the King*], whether we regard his error as being his misconception of his parents' identity or his actions in killing a man who turned out to be his father and marrying a woman who was his mother. And here the error is the more striking in that Oedipus, in

consequence of the oracle, was trying to avoid doing these very things. This brings us to what, in Aristotle's view, were two very important features of a well constructed play, *peripeteia* and *anagnorisis*, or recognition. If the hero begins the action under a misapprehension a moment must come, often just before the catastrophe, when he realizes his mistake and its consequences, and the situation is then transformed. Since it frequently happens in Greek tragedy that the vital misapprehension relates to the identity of one of the characters, recognitions are an important feature and often coincide with the *peripeteia*. At the climax of the *Oedipus*, the hero recognizes himself as the son of Laius and his wife as his own mother.

Of the hero Aristotle has little to say; he has indeed no word to describe him. He is merely the character who experiences a change of fortune. For although the action arises out of some initiative of the hero's, the course the action takes is not, in most plays, closely connected with the hero's personality, and even his original initiative is often a response to a force intruding from outside. . . .

The emotions aroused by tragedy are largely painful. Why do we of our own free will expose ourselves to this pain? To this question there is not, and there is not likely to be, an agreed answer. The reactions of an audience at a dramatic performance are complex, and individuals vary widely in their responses. Accordingly it is a mistake to seek . . . a single answer to this problem. In the first place we like excitement, and our faculty of readily identifying ourselves with one of the parties to a contest, whether a football team or a dramatic hero, makes this emotion easily accessible. In excitement there is liable to be an element of pain. It is a price which the young especially, the class which according to Plato is most addicted to tragedy, are ready to pay. Excitement is often present in high tragedy, though a drama which offers no more than excitement is merely melodrama. Yet there is little in the *Poetics* which is not a recipe as much for melodrama as for tragedy; the technical devices on which Aristotle lavishes most careful attention belong as much to one as to the other, and there remains a doubt whether he was not more fascinated by what the *Oedipus Rex* has in common with melodrama than by the qualities which raise it to a higher level.

But the tragic character, little though the Greeks had to say about him, is something more than the victim of exciting vicissitudes [variations]. His full stature can be revealed only in adversity; that is why tragedy has to be tragic. Only when the difficulties are most overwhelming, the threat of catastrophe overpowering, can his potentialities be realized. Quality can not be known in the last resort except through the ordeal that tests it. Nor is it right to think of action and character in isolation, because it is in relation to the action that the character is conceived; unfortunately it is rarely possible to talk about anything without separating it from other things with which it is in fact united.

Nearly everyone is prepared to risk some pain for the sake of excitement; many people are ready to undergo a sharper pain in order to share the vision of human greatness at full stretch which the tragic poet can communicate. Again we need not be particularly surprised. The literature of catastrophe has always been highly popular. We have a natural curiosity about the behaviour of ordinary people in extraordinary situations. One of the humbler functions of literature is to widen our knowledge, to increase our emotional range, and to enrich our lives with vicarious experience. Most of us, so far, have not come face to face with the more spectacular forms of catastrophe, with shipwreck, plague, or conflagration. We naturally wonder how people behave, how we should behave, in the circumstances. Fewer, but still a large number, wonder how human beings of a higher temper would behave in trials still more terrible. Tragedy can show the very extreme of human grandeur.

Emotional Release

It is a common experience to find that the emotional stress of seeing a tragedy is followed by a sense of calm and tranquillity: 'calm of mind, all passion spent'; or again, 'what may quiet us in a death so noble'. That this should be so is not surprising. The emotional experience may be intense, but it ends abruptly at, or soon after, the fall of the curtain, whereas the disasters of real life continue to cast their shadow for months and years. It is not strange that the easing of emotional strain should be noticeable and agreeable. However, far-reaching conclusions have been drawn from this effect of tragedy, usually in connection with Aristotle's theory of *catharsis*, which [English epic poet John] Milton had in mind when he wrote the phrases quoted above. That the effect of tragedy is cathartic is still for many the starting point for all consideration of the subject. . . .

A more hazardous inference from the sense of calm and reconciliation which may follow the seeing or reading of tragedy is that the reconciliation may be implicit in the tragedy itself, as a true picture, so far as it goes, of the universe, that behind the apparent tragedy there is harmony and that somewhere, somehow, good is triumphant. When such a vindication of the universe is part of the writer's purpose and grows out of his belief, we may no doubt be left with a sense of the higher harmony. But such a play will hardly be a tragedy in the normal sense of the word; this is very relevant to the tragedies of Aeschylus, which often end with reconciliation. It is in the nature of tragedy that it should raise, directly or indirectly, the problem of divine justice. The answer may not be a denial, but it will not be a confident affirmation. Hence the question has been raised, and variously answered, whether tragedy is possible, in the full sense of the word, within a system of Christian belief. . . . It is not, since to the Christian, as to Plato, success and disaster are things not very momentous, and a drama that reaches its conclusion in this world cannot be complete. The only real tragedy is the tragedy of the lost soul.

Akin to this is the question how far the tragic poet was, of set purpose, a teacher. It is commonly asserted that he was, but this assertion has called forth contradiction; the idea that tragedy is a didactic [instructive] art can arouse distaste. Possibly Aristophanes' famous line,

'Boys have a master to teach them, but the teachers of men are poets' (*Frogs* 1055), has been too freely quoted. Many of the claims made for the instructiveness of poetry both in the *Frogs* and in Plato's *Ion* are pretty ridiculous. Yet such claims were an attempt to rationalize the general feeling that poetry was important, and poets wise. If this had not been widely believed Socrates would not have turned to the poets in the expectation of finding men wiser than himself (*Apology* 22B). But about the middle of the fifth century the poets began to suffer from the competition of other and more professional teachers. By the end of the century poetry was coming to be regarded mainly as entertainment. For Aristotle the theatre was a source of pleasure, salutary pleasure it is true; and though he allowed poetry to be more philosophical than history, he certainly thought it a great deal less philosophical than philosophy. Yet so far as the ordinary man was concerned, for long it was the poets who discoursed on fundamental problems of human suffering and divine justice, who delivered the homilies which no one in the ancient world expected from a priest. Indeed, in any age to touch on the ultimate mysteries without in a sense teaching is not possible for a poet who takes his work seriously. A tragedy by its very nature is a commentary on life. But all this is very far from meaning that the poet began from an edifying idea which he worked up into a play. It means that the play would be set within a framework of accepted ideas which would receive fresh strength and significance from the play. And it was not without relevance that it was performed in honour of a god and in a place sacred to him on an occasion of great solemnity.

Selection 4

Oedipus Receives the Prophecy of His Own Downfall

Sophocles

Here, from Bernard M.W. Knox's acclaimed translation of Sophocles' masterpiece, Oedipus the King, *is the pivotal scene between Oedipus, king of Thebes, and the blind prophet Tiresias. The power of the scene derives from the ironic fact that both Tiresias and the audience (or reader) know that Oedipus is the murderer of the former Theban king, Laius, Oedipus's father. Only Oedipus does not realize that he himself is the criminal whom he has vowed to bring to justice. (Nor at this point does he realize that Laius was his father, or that his wife, Jocasta, is also his mother.) Oedipus cannot fathom that he, who years before outsmarted the monstrous Sphinx by solving its riddle (and there-*

by saved Thebes from the creature) could be the guilty party. Note that Tiresias's predictions that Oedipus will scream aloud, see darkness, and feel his way to foreign soil all end up coming true; for later, when Oedipus discovers the truth, he screams like a wounded animal, blinds himself, and becomes an outcast who must wander from city to city. The play, which many have called the greatest tragedy ever written, reminds all people in all ages that no one, no matter how mighty, can escape his or her own fate. Moreover, as Oedipus learns the hard way, every individual is responsible for his or her own actions and must pay for all mistakes in the end.

CHORUS LEADER

The man who sees most eye to eye with Lord Apollo is Tiresias and from him you might learn most clearly the truth for which you are searching.

OEDIPUS

I did not leave *that* undone either. I have already sent for him, at Creon's suggestion. I have sent for him twice, in fact, and have been wondering for some time why he is not yet here.

CHORUS LEADER

Apart from what he will say, there is nothing but old, faint rumors.

OEDIPUS

What were they? I want to examine every single word.

CHORUS LEADER

Laius was killed, so they say, by some travelers.

OEDIPUS

I heard that, too. Where is the man who saw it?

CHORUS LEADER

If he has any trace of fear in him, he won't stand firm when he hears the curses you have called down on him.

OEDIPUS

If he didn't shrink from the action he won't

Reprinted with permission of Pocket Books, a division of Simon & Schuster, from Sophocles, *Oedipus the King*, translated by Bernard M.W. Knox. Copyright © 1959, and renewed, © 1987, by Bernard M.W. Knox.

be frightened by a word.

CHORUS LEADER

But here comes the one who will convict him. These men are bringing the holy prophet of the gods, the only man in whom truth is inborn.

[*Enter Tiresias, from the side. He has a boy to lead him, and is accompanied by guards.*]

OEDIPUS

Tiresias, you who understand all things—those which can be taught and those which may not be mentioned, things in the heavens and things which walk the earth! You cannot see, but you understand the city's distress, the disease from which it is suffering. You, my lord, are our shield against it, our savior, the only one we have. You may not have heard the news from the messengers. We sent to Apollo and he sent us back this answer: relief from this disease would come to us only if we discovered the identity of the murderers of Laius and then either killed them or banished them from Thebes. Do not begrudge us your knowledge—any voice from the birds or any other way of prophecy you have. Save yourself and this city, save me, from all the infection caused by the dead man. We are in your hands. And the noblest of labors is for a man to help his fellow men with all he has and can do.

TIRESIAS

Wisdom is a dreadful thing when it brings no profit to its possessor. I knew all this well, but forgot. Otherwise I would never have come here.

OEDIPUS

What is the matter? Why this despairing mood?

TIRESIAS

Dismiss me, send me home. That will be the easiest way for both of us to bear our burden.

OEDIPUS

What you propose is unlawful—and unfriendly to this city which raised you. You are withholding information.

TIRESIAS

I do not see that your talking is to the point. And I don't want the same thing to happen to me.

OEDIPUS

If you know something, in God's name, do not turn your back on us. Look. All of us here, on our knees, beseech you.

TIRESIAS

You are all ignorant. I will never reveal my dreadful secrets, or rather, yours.

OEDIPUS

What do you say? You know something? And will not speak? You intend to betray us, do you, and wreck the state?

TIRESIAS

I will not cause pain to myself or to you. Why do you question me? It is useless. You will get nothing from me.

OEDIPUS

You scoundrel! You would enrage a lifeless stone. Will nothing move you? Speak out and make an end of it.

TIRESIAS

You blame my temper, but you are not aware of one *you* live with.

OEDIPUS

[*To chorus*]

Who could control his anger listening to talk like this—these insults to Thebes?

TIRESIAS

What is to come will come, even if I shroud it in silence.

OEDIPUS

What is to come, *that* is what you are bound to tell *me*.

TIRESIAS

I will say no more. Do what you like—rage at me in the wildest anger you can muster.

OEDIPUS

I will. I am angry enough to speak out. I understand it all. Listen to me. I think that *you* helped to plan the murder of Laius—yes, and short of actually raising your hand against him you did it. If you weren't blind, I'd say that you alone struck him down.

TIRESIAS

Is that what you say? I charge you now to carry out the articles of the proclamation you made. From now on do not presume to speak to me or to any of these people. *You* are the murderer, *you* are the unholy defilement of this land.

OEDIPUS

Have you no shame? To start up such a story! Do you think you will get away with this?

TIRESIAS

Yes. The truth with all its strength is in me.

OEDIPUS

Who taught you this lesson? You didn't learn it from your prophet's trade.

TIRESIAS

You did. I was unwilling to speak but you drove me to it.

OEDIPUS

What was it you said? I want to understand it clearly.

TIRESIAS

Didn't you understand it the first time? Aren't you just trying to trip me up?

OEDIPUS

No, I did not grasp it fully. Repeat your statement.

TIRESIAS

I say that you are the murderer you are searching for.

OEDIPUS

Do you think you can say that twice and not pay for it?

TIRESIAS

Shall I say something more, to make you angrier still?

OEDIPUS

Say what you like. It will all be meaningless.

TIRESIAS

I say that without knowing it you are living in shameful intimacy with your nearest and dearest. You do not see the evil in which you live.

OEDIPUS

Do you think you can go on like this with impunity forever?

TIRESIAS

Yes, if the truth has power.

OEDIPUS

It has, except for you. You have no power or truth. You are blind, your ears and mind as well as eyes.

TIRESIAS

You are a pitiful figure. These reproaches you fling at me, all these people here will fling them at you—and before very long.

OEDIPUS

[*Contemptuously*]

You live your life in one continuous night of darkness. Neither I nor any other man that can see would do you any harm.

TIRESIAS

It is not destiny that I should fall through you. Apollo is enough for that. It is *his* concern.

OEDIPUS

Was it Creon, or you, that invented this story?

TIRESIAS

It is not Creon who harms you—you harm yourself.

OEDIPUS

Wealth, absolute power, skill surpassing skill in the competition of life—what envy is your reward! For the sake of this power which Thebes entrusted to me—I did not ask for it—to win this power faithful Creon, my friend from the beginning, sneaks up on me treacherously, longing to drive me out. He sets this intriguing magician on me, a lying quack, keen sighted for what he can make, but blind in prophecy.

[*To Tiresias*] Tell me, when were you a true prophet? When the Sphinx chanted her riddle here, did *you* come forward to speak the word that would liberate the people of this town? That riddle was not for anyone who came along to answer—it called for prophetic insight. But you didn't come forward, you offered no answer told you by the birds or the gods. No. *I* came, know-

nothing Oedipus, *I* stopped the Sphinx. I answered the riddle with my own intelligence—the birds had nothing to teach me. And now you try to drive me out, you think you will stand beside Creon's throne. I tell you, you will pay in tears for this witch-hunting—you and Creon, the man that organized this conspiracy. If you weren't an old man, you would already have realized, in suffering, what your schemes lead to.

CHORUS LEADER

If we may make a suggestion—both his words and yours, Oedipus, seem to have been spoken in anger. This sort of talk is not what we need—what we must think of is how to solve the problem set by the god's oracle.

TIRESIAS

King though you are, you must treat me as your equal in one respect—the right to reply. That is a power which belongs to me, too. I am not your servant, but Apollo's. I am not inscribed on the records as a dependent of Creon, with no right to speak in person. I can speak, and here is what I have to say. You have mocked at my blindness, but you, who have eyes, cannot see the evil in which you stand; you cannot see where you are living, nor with whom you share your house. Do you even know who your parents are? Without knowing it, you are the enemy of your own flesh and blood, the dead below and the living here above. The double-edged curse of your mother and father, moving on dread feet, shall one day drive you from this land. You see straight now but then you will see darkness. You will scream aloud on that day; there is no place which shall not hear you, no part of Mount Cithaeron here which will not ring in echo, on that day when you know the truth about your wedding, that evil harbor into which you sailed before a fair wind.

There is a multitude of other horrors which you do not even suspect, and they will equate you to yourself and to your own children. There! Now smear me and Creon with your accusations. There is no man alive whose ruin will be more pitiful than yours.

OEDIPUS

Enough! I won't listen to this sort of talk from

This red-figure painting, executed on an Athenian wine cup by the so-called Oedipus Painter, shows Oedipus confronting the fearsome Sphinx.

you. Damn you! My curse on you! Get out of here, quickly. Away from this house, back to where you came from!

TIRESIAS

I would never have come here if you had not summoned me.

OEDIPUS

I didn't know that you were going to speak like a fool—or it would have been a long time before I summoned you to my palace.

TIRESIAS

I am what I am—a fool to you, so it seems, but the parents who brought you into the world thought me sensible enough. [*Tiresias turns to go*.]

OEDIPUS

Whom do you mean? Wait! Who is my father?

TIRESIAS

This present day will give you birth and death.

OEDIPUS

Everything you say is the same—riddles, obscurities.

TIRESIAS

Aren't you the best man alive at guessing riddles?

OEDIPUS

Insult me, go on—but that, you will find, is what makes me great.

TIRESIAS

Yet that good fortune was your destruction.

OEDIPUS

What does that matter, if I saved Thebes?

TIRESIAS

I will go, then. Boy, lead me away.

OEDIPUS

Yes, take him away. While you're here you are a hindrance, a nuisance; once out of the way you won't annoy me any more.

TIRESIAS

I am going. But first I will say what I came here to say. I have no fear of you. You cannot destroy me. Listen to me now. The man you are trying to find, with your threatening proclamations, the murderer of Laius, that man is here in Thebes. He is apparently an immigrant of foreign birth, but he will be revealed as a native-born Theban. He will take no pleasure in that revelation. Blind instead of seeing, beggar instead of rich, he will make his way to foreign soil, feeling his way with a stick. He will be revealed as brother and father of the children with whom he now lives, the son and husband of the woman who gave him birth, the murderer and marriage-partner of his father. Go think this out. And if you find that I am wrong, then say I have no skill in prophecy.

[*Exit Tiresias led by boy to side. Oedipus goes back into the palace.*]

CHORUS

Who is the man denounced by the prophetic voice from Delphi's cliffs—the man whose bloodstained hands committed a nameless crime? Now is the time for him to run, faster than storm-swift horses. In full armor Apollo son of Zeus leaps upon him, with the fire of the lightning. And in the murderer's track follow dreadful unfailing spirits of vengeance.

Selection 5

Aristophanes and the Old Comedy

C.M. Bowra

The heyday of Athenian Old Comedy, of which Aristophanes was the chief and most famous exponent, was the second half of the fifth century B.C. It was vulgar, flamboyant, and farcical; at the same time it was highly topical and political, as it poked fun at the leading citizens of the day, many of whom sat in the audience and watched themselves lampooned. This thoughtful expert synopsis of the Old Comedy and Aristophanes' plays is by the late, widely respected classical scholar C.M. Bowra.

Just as tragedy grew from ritual and dances connected with the mysteries of suffering, so comedy grew from rites connected with the mysteries of fertility and procreation. . . . When comedy first appears in a definite form, it belongs entirely to Athens and is, like tragedy, associated with Dionysus. It has become the natural counterpart of the most serious of arts and has for its province mockery and ribaldry [vulgar humor]. It is performed at fixed festivals; a prize is given for the best comedy; its authors are known and quoted. It has become an art, and its origins are forgotten. It found maturity later than tragedy, and its climax was reached in Aristophanes (450–385 B.C.), whose extant eleven plays were all produced after the outbreak of the Peloponnesian War. He is the only comedian from whom any complete plays survive, but he seems to have summed up in himself the main qualities of his predecessors and to be entirely representative of this surprising art.

In construction and manner Greek comedy is far removed from all subsequent comedy. Its form keeps some of the traditional elements. There is the chorus dressed to represent what the poet likes—frogs, birds, old men, women, wasps. It commonly gives its title to the play and is of great importance both for the management of the action and for the expression of the poet's opinions on topical subjects. The chorus-leader has a speech to make in which he is the poet's mouthpiece and talks on morality or poetry or politics or whatever is uppermost in the poet's mind. This is a survival of the old topical joking. The action is varied and vivid, and we find the best and oldest jokes, not excluding those scenes of beating and bullying which lie at the heart of farce. Nor are the ithyphallic origins [i.e., references, both verbal and visual, to traditional rituals that featured worshippers carrying replicas of erect penises] neglected. Greek comedy is frankly improper, and some of its best jokes are unwelcome on the modern stage. It is also enormously topical. Well-known figures of Athens are made the object of constant ridicule. There is always a debate or dispute in which some important issue is

Excerpted from C.M. Bowra, *Ancient Greek Literature* (New York: Oxford University Press, 1960). Reprinted with permission of the publisher.

discussed. All these elements belong to tradition; they are religiously observed and incontinently enjoyed. But Aristophanes combined them into a structure of transcendental farce. The old buffoonery and jesting are but the details of his impossible and magnificent plots and are transferred to a world of pure fancy. He creates fantastically unreal scenes, and peoples them with prominent figures compelled to perform the most ludicrous actions, or he fills a topsy-turvy world with ordinary men and women of his own creation and confronts their plain sense with situations of absurd improbability.

In the hey-day of their greatness the Athenians were willing to have jokes made at their expense and tolerated almost any criticism of their politics and habits. The comedians were allowed to portray public men on the stage without being prosecuted for libel. At times they were thought to go too far, and then they were fined, as Aristophanes was by Cleon, for disgracing the city before the allies and strangers. Aristophanes took full advantage of this liberty for deriding what he did not like and expressing his own views on public policy. With considerable courage and remarkable consistency he kept the same moderate outlook throughout his career and urged his countrymen not to fight Sparta and not to treat their allies as subject tributaries. He drove his points home by making his political opponents as ridiculous as he could make them and by inserting sound pieces of political advice into his work. It says much for the Athenian democracy that it bore his criticism even when it was at war, and at least in the early years of fighting he said exactly what he pleased.

Poking Fun at Politicians and War

The earliest of his surviving plays, the *Acharnians* (425 B.C.), is a satire on the war-party and the generals. In short and vivid scenes the war is made to look absurd, and without any appeal to pathos its hardships are brought home and shown to be unjustified. . . . Crammed with topical allusions and jokes, the dialogue somehow keeps to the point, and each new diversion is complete in itself. All is united by the mockery of war as opposed equally to sanity and enjoyment. But the atmosphere of farce does not prevent us from seeing how much good sense underlies the structure. The causes of war are exposed in a speech which must have seemed admirably true to many hearers, and throughout the poet pleads adroitly for his own cause by making the militarists something less than human. His own sympathies are with his hero, a perfectly sensible and hard-bitten farmer who with great adroitness faces the problem for himself and solves it.

The *Knights* (424 B.C.) is not written with such gusto and shows traces of a more bitter temper. It is an attack on the demagogue [popular politician] Cleon . . . and incidentally a tolerant and amused criticism of democracy. Once again public figures appear on the stage, this time, the generals, Nicias and Demosthenes, who were later to perish together in Sicily. But the chief figure is Cleon. . . . Nicias is made timorous and respectable, Demosthenes courageous and adventurous but rather too fond of his drink. . . . Cleon is treated unmercifully. He is shown to be violent, vain, dishonest, a receiver of bribes and notoriously revengeful. Fancy and fact are irretrievably intermingled, but the characters emerge with admirable clarity. Their main lineaments must have been true to life, or the poet would not have secured the effect he wanted. His aim was chiefly to discredit Cleon, who stood for a policy and methods of which he profoundly disapproved. He had received hard knocks, and he hit back hard in return.

These two plays are the only cases where Aristophanes presents contemporary political characters on the stage. He followed them by another play, the *Clouds* (423 B.C.), in which he held up to ridicule a figure which has played a greater part in the imagination of posterity than any of the Athenian demagogues or generals. Socrates has been sanctified by Plato, but for Aristophanes he represented all the worst features of the Sophistic Movement [in which sophists, traveling teachers, offered to teach rhetoric and other subjects in return for a fee], on which the *Clouds* is a brilliant, if rancorous, attack. By contrasting the destructive effects of the new education with an idealized picture of traditional Athenian life he has no difficulty in discrediting the Sophists. Into the character of Socrates he throws all the disagreeable qualities he can find, making him a greedy and dirty old impostor, muttering mumbo-jumbo or proposing preposterous scientific conundrums [riddles]. His disciples are either lousy students, bent down as if looking for truffles, or unprincipled young blackguards who can prove the worse the better reason and think nothing of beating their fathers. The plot is held together by the relations of an old-fashioned father and a modern son, and its lesson is made clear by the long and partisan argument between the Right and the Wrong Logic. The moral is driven home by the destruction of Socrates' "Thought Factory" at the close.

The contrast between two generations is the theme of the *Wasps* (422 B.C.), though here the rôles are reversed. The characters are all imaginary, and the play is a good-humoured skit on an old Athenian's passion for sitting on juries. . . .

In the *Peace* (421 B.C.) and the *Birds* (414 B.C.) . . . Aristophanes gave full play to his adventurous wits and created delicious worlds of fancy. The *Peace* is a political fantasia. An Athenian farmer, tired of war, flies to heaven on a dung-beetle to find that in disgust with men the gods have moved higher and that War is in possession of Olympus and has buried Peace in a cave. . . .

The *Birds* carries the same principles to confident mastery. Conceived throughout with a poet's fancy, this story of two adventurers who cozen the birds into making an empire in the sky for them is full of extraordinary life and beauty. It may perhaps be a skit on the absurd ambitions which were rife in Athens at the time of the Sicilian Expedition, but the temporary occasion is quite transcended. Scenes of great charm, where the poet reveals an unrivalled appreciation of birds and their ways, are mingled with short skits on familiar types from Athens. . . .

The renewal of war and the sense of impending failure which hung over Athenian life affect-ed Aristophanes as it affected the great tragedians. . . . And in the *Lysistrata* (411 B.C.) he made a brilliant and outspoken exposition of his opinions. His theme is that the war must be stopped, and he preaches it in a farce, where the women get peace by depriving their husbands of their conjugal rights [i.e., refuse to have sex with their husbands until the war stops]. Such a subject could not help being bawdy, but Aristophanes' gaiety and ingenuity keep the tone at a level where the bawdiness is purely farcical. His women are brilliant debaters and have a sound political sense. They know the real needs of life and are determined to get them. . . . The *Lysistrata* is a great play, admirably contrived with vivid scenes and real characters. Its moral is proclaimed in plain words, and nowhere does Aristophanes show his political sincerity better than where he asks for a real confederacy of allies instead of a tyrannical empire. Without being in the least solemn he drives his points home.

The Old Comedy's Last Days

The *Lysistrata* is Aristophanes' last pronouncement on politics. The psychology of a war-oppressed people did not allow him to continue his lessons, and he may himself have felt that they were useless. Seeking another object for his wit he found it in [his colleague, the tragic playwright] Euripides. He had already presented Euripides on the stage in the *Acharnians*, but now he devoted the greater part of two plays to him. The *Thesmophoriazusae* (411 B.C.) is a well-constructed farce built on Euripides' treatment of women. The women are determined to revenge themselves on him for the harsh things he has said of them. He sends his secretary disguised as a woman to plead his case, but the disguise is detected and a crisis arises which is solved by Euripides making his own terms with the enemy. . . . The play is written with great good humour, and if some of the characters presented can hardly have been pleased, they could comfort themselves with the absence of rancour and self-righteousness. Even Euripides wins the day, though perhaps not in a way consistent with his dignity.

In the *Frogs* (405 B.C.) Aristophanes breaks new ground and writes a fantasy out of literary criticism. Written immediately after the death of Euripides, the *Frogs* is an attempt to assess his moral and poetical value. Nowhere except in the *Birds* is Aristophanes so emphatically himself. . . . After admirable scenes of farce the climax is reached in the great scene where [the tragic playwright] Æschylus and Euripides are examined in person to see which is more worthy to be brought back to life. . . . Euripides is, of course, worsted, and his defeat is marked by some harsh words at his expense. There was something in his character and influence that riled Aristophanes, who after scoring legitimate points off his art dismisses him as a rogue.

With the *Frogs* the great days of Aristophanes and the Old Comedy ended. The defeat of Athens by Sparta closed the conditions under which Old Comedy was possible. It was too expensive for an impoverished generation, and its outspoken criticism was ill-suited to the broken confidence of a defeated people. Aristophanes survived well into the fourth century and continued to write, but neither the *Women in Parliament* nor *Wealth* has the force and brightness of his earlier work. The *Women in Parliament* is interesting as a skit on the ideas of the equality of sexes and community of property which Plato preached in the *Republic*. Aristophanes may well have read an early draft of the book or have heard its ideas in conversation. . . . *Wealth* shows a similar lack of spirit, but has an interest because it shows Aristophanes dealing with a subject suited to the time and points forward to the different art of the New Comedy. The plot is an allegory. Wealth from being blind and indiscriminate in the distribution of his favours is made to see, and the good all become rich. The simple idea must have appealed to the penniless Athenians of the day . . . and there are plenty of moral maxims. It points forward to a new age.

The unique character of the Old Comedy makes it hard to judge its value. It can be compared with no other form of art, least of all with subsequent comedy. In it farce and fantasy are somehow raised to poetry, but it is impossible to

Aristophanes, pictured here, was the master of the Greek Old Comedy, which often poked fun at community leaders.

say how far the success was due to the individual gifts of Aristophanes and not to the tradition. Its claim is that despite its topical character, despite the many quips whose point is irretrievably lost or only elucidated with great effort, it remains amusing and delightful. Many of the jokes enjoy perennial youth. Aristophanes was a master of words, and in his dialogue he uses all the weapons of comedy, newly coined monstrosities, the language of the streets and the fields, dialect and official language, topical gibes and bits of old songs. His puns are as good as puns can be, but his parodies are the work of genius. . . .

On the other hand, he was far from being a bigoted reactionary. In politics he was a man of the centre and he relentlessly opposed the military party. Partly from a real love for the great past, partly from common sense, he preferred the Athens of his youth to any alternative suggested by generals or philosophers. . . . Aristophanes was content with the good things of life, and for them he fought unwearyingly against quacks, bullies, boasters, and all those who thought they had the right to interfere with other men's enjoyment.

Selection 6

A Comic Play Ridicules the New Education

Aristophanes

In his play, Clouds, *Aristophanes humorously attacks the new brand of education making headway in his day, specifically the sophists, who taught rhetoric and other subjects for a fee. Although Socrates was not a sophist, Aristophanes, who disapproved of the eccentric philosopher, portrays him as the worst kind— an atheistic, dishonest quack running a bogus school, the "Think-Shop." A farmer named Strepsiades enrolls in hopes of mastering the art of dishonest argumentation so that he can evade his creditors. In the following scene, from a sparkling new translation by Boston University scholar Jeffrey Henderson, Socrates initiates the gullible Strepsiades into the school's loony cult that worships the Clouds (represented by the chorus) as gods.*

OCRATES
    Why have you come?
STREPSIADES

Reprinted by permission of the publishers and the Loeb Classical Library from *Aristophanes: "Clouds," "Wasps," "Peace,"* edited and translated by Jeffrey Henderson (Cambridge, MA: Harvard University Press, 1998).

Anxious to learn public speaking. You see, I'm being harried and plundered by debts and cantankerous creditors, and having my property foreclosed. . . . Whatever fee you may charge, I'll swear to you by the gods to pay in cash.
SOCRATES
What do you mean, you'll swear by the gods? First of all, gods aren't legal tender here.
STREPSIADES
So, what do you swear by? Iron coins, as in Byzantium?
SOCRATES
Would you like to know the truth about matters divine, what they really are?
STREPSIADES
I certainly would, if it's actually possible.
SOCRATES
And to have converse with the Clouds, our own deities?
STREPSIADES
Yes, very much.
SOCRATES
Then sit down upon the sacred sofa.
STREPSIADES
All right, I'm sitting.
SOCRATES

Now take hold of this, the wreath. . . . All this is our procedure for initiands [initiates].

STREPSIADES

And what's in it for me?

SOCRATES

At speaking you'll become a smoothie, a castanet, the flower of orators. Now don't move. (*Socrates sprinkles flour on Strepsiades*)

STREPSIADES

By Zeus, you won't trick me! You mean getting dredged is how I'll become flour?

SOCRATES

The old man must keep silence and listen to the prayer. O Lord and Master, measureless Air, who hold the earth aloft . . . and ye Clouds, awesome goddesses of thunder and lightning, arise, appear aloft, o Mistresses, to the thinker! . . . Come then, illustrious Clouds, in an exhibition for this man. . . . Hear my prayer, accept my sacrifice and enjoy these holy rites.

CHORUS

(*from afar*)

Clouds everlasting,
let us arise, revealing our dewy bright form,
from deep roaring father Ocean
onto high mountain peaks
with tresses of trees, whence
to behold heights of distant vantage,
and holy earth whose crops we water,
and divine rivers' rushing,
and the sea crashing with deep thunder.
For heaven's tireless eye is ablaze
with gleaming rays.
So let us shake off the rainy haze
from our deathless shape and survey
the land, with telescopic eye.

SOCRATES

Most stately Clouds, you have clearly heard my summons. (*to Strepsiades*) Did you mark their voice and, in concert, the bellowing thunder that prompts holy reverence?

STREPSIADES

I do revere you, illustrious ones, and I'm ready to answer those thunderclaps with a fart; that's how much I fear and tremble at them. And right now, if it's sanctioned, and even if it isn't, I need to shit!

SOCRATES

Don't be scurrilous [coarse and abusive] and act like those hapless comedians! Now keep silence, for a great swarm of gods is on the move, in song. . . .

STREPSIADES

Then hail, Mistresses! And now, almighty Queens, if you've ever so favored another man, break forth for me too a sound that spans the sky!

CHORUS LEADER

Hail, oldster born long ago, stalker of erudite arguments, and you too, priest of subtlest hogwash, tell us what you desire; for we would pay no attention to any other contemporary sophist of celestial studies except for Prodicus [a contemporary of Socrates and a scientist widely viewed as a genius], for his wisdom and intelligence, and you, because you strut like a popinjay through the streets and cast your eyes sideways and, unshod, endure many woes and wear a haughty expression for our sake.

STREPSIADES

Mother Earth, what a voice! How holy and august and marvelous!

SOCRATES

That's because they are the only true goddesses; all the rest are rubbish.

STREPSIADES

Come now, by Earth, doesn't Olympian Zeus count as a god with you people?

SOCRATES

What do you mean, Zeus? Do stop driveling. Zeus doesn't even exist!

STREPSIADES

What are you talking about? Then who makes it rain? Answer me that one, first of all.

SOCRATES

These do, of course! And I'll teach you how, with grand proofs. Now then: where have you ever yet seen rain without Clouds? Though according to you, Zeus should make rain himself on a clear day, when the Clouds are out of town.

STREPSIADES

By Apollo, you've nicely spliced that point with what you were saying a moment ago. And imagine, before now I thought that rain is Zeus pissing through a sieve [i.e., a strainer]! But tell me who does the thundering that makes me tremble.

SOCRATES

These [the Clouds] do the thundering, by rolling around.

STREPSIADES

In what way, you daredevil?

SOCRATES

When they fill up with lots of water and are forced to drift, by natural compulsion sagging down with rain, then run into one other, and become sodden, they explode and crash.

STREPSIADES

But who is it that forces them to drift? Doesn't Zeus?

SOCRATES

Not at all; it's cosmic whirl.

STREPSIADES

Whirl? That's a new one on me, that Zeus is gone and Whirl now rules in his place. But you still haven't taught me anything about the thunder's crash.

SOCRATES

Didn't you hear me? I repeat: when the clouds are full of water and run into one another, they crash because of their density.

STREPSIADES

Come now, why should anyone believe that?

SOCRATES

I'll teach you from your own person. Have you ever gorged yourself with soup at the Panathenae [the great religious festival honoring Athena] and then had an upset stomach, and a sudden turmoil sets it all arumble?

STREPSIADES

By Apollo I have! It does carry on terribly and shake me up, and like thunder that bit of soup crashes and roars terribly, gently at first, *pappax pappax*, and then stepping up the pace, *papapappax*, and when I shit it absolutely thunders, *papapappax*, just like those Clouds!

SOCRATES

Now then, consider what farts you let off from such a little tummy; isn't it natural that this sky, being limitless, should thunder mightily?

STREPSIADES

So that's why the words are similar, *bronte* "thunder" and *porde* "fart"! But now explain this: where does the lightning bolt come from, blazing with fire, that incinerates us on contact and badly burns the survivors? It's quite obvious that Zeus hurls it against perjurers.

SOCRATES

How's that, you moron . . . you mooncalf! If he really strikes perjurers, then why hasn't he burned up Simon or Cleonymus or Theorus, since they're paramount perjurers? On the other hand, he strikes his own temple, and Sunium headland of Athens, and the great oaks [oak trees being sacred to Zeus]. What's his point? An oak tree certainly doesn't perjure itself!

STREPSIADES

I don't know; but you seem to have a good argument. . . .

SOCRATES

Then I take it you will now believe in no god but those we believe in: this Void, and the Clouds, and the Tongue, and only these three?

STREPSIADES

I wouldn't speak a word to the other gods even if I met them in the street; and I won't sacrifice to them, or pour them libations [liquid offerings], or offer them incense.

CHORUS LEADER

Then tell us frankly what we can do for you, because nothing bad will happen to you if you honor and respect us and seek to be smart.

STREPSIADES

Well then, Mistresses, I ask of you this very small favor: that among the Greeks I be by a hundred miles the very best speaker.

CHORUS LEADER

Done! You will get that from us, so that from this moment on, no one will carry more motions in the assembly than you.

STREPSIADES

No speaking on important motions for me, please! That's not what I desire, only twisting lawsuits to my own advantage and giving my creditors the slip.

CHORUS LEADER

Then you shall get what you crave, for it is nothing grand that you desire. Now be resolute and commit yourself to our agents here.

Selection 7

Menander and the New Comedy

Robert Flacelière

The Athenian New Comedy, which flourished in the late fourth century B.C. and well into the third, was less vulgar and also less political and topical than the Old Comedy. Like many other cultural aspects of the Hellenistic Age, the New Comedy focused on realistic portrayals of human beings and their everyday lives, emotions, and problems, though in this case in light-hearted, humorous ways. Common characters and situations included clever slaves who attempt to outwit their mean or naïve masters, self-important soldiers and other authority figures who prove to be shallow windbags, siblings separated at birth who later find one another, long-lost sons and daughters who are reunited with their parents, and so on. This examination of the most popular comic playwright of the era, Menander, is by the noted French scholar Robert Flacelière.

*n*ew Comedy lasted from about 336 to 250 [B.C.]. . . . It is distinguished from the classical comedy of Aristophanes by certain technical innovations, the most obvious of which are the introduction of a prologue, in the manner of Euripides, and the diminished

Excerpted from Robert Flacelière, *A Literary History of Greece*, translated by Douglas Garman (Chicago: Aldine, 1964). English translation © 1964 by Elek Books Ltd.

role of the Chorus, which . . . tends to be restricted to singing and dancing between the acts, a kind of intermission unrelated to the subject of the play. But a more important difference is apparent in the subject matter and the way it is treated, which reflect the tremendous change that had taken place in the social and political life of Greece [in the first seven decades of the fourth century B.C.]. . . .

Social behaviour had become much more urbane and refined. As Aristotle says in the *Nicomachean Ethics*:

> One of the signs of good breeding is to speak and hear only what befits a free and distinguished person. . . . This may be seen by comparing the comedy of the old days with that of today. One used coarse words to make people laugh; the other expresses itself by implication; from the point of view of seemliness, the difference between these two methods is considerable (IV, 13).

In addition, heterosexual love and marriage play a much greater part in the New Comedy than in all Greek literature of earlier times. Indeed, the imaginative freedom of the ancient comedy ceased to appeal to the literary taste of the fourth century. . . . It was a time of prose writers, of moral and philosophical reflection; poetry was still acceptable, provided it conformed to common sense. There was a growing interest in studies of character and behaviour, as may be seen from the work of [the philosopher-scholar] Theophrastos, which appeared about 319. Menander was then twenty-three, and he and Philemon were the two outstanding representatives of the New Comedy. . . .

Philemon was not a native of Athens though it was there that he made his name. Born in 361, he was only a year short of a hundred when he died. As the rival of Menander he was often successful, but though we have the names of sixty of his comedies, only fragments have survived. . . .

But the star of the New Comedy was the Athenian Menander, who was born in 342 and died fifty years later, in 292. He was a pupil of Theophrastos [at the Lyceum, the school Aristotle had founded]. . . . Good looking and elegant, he appears to have shown very little interest in politics. He led a peaceful and studious life with the courtesan [high-class prostitute] Glykera at his villa at Piraeus, writing prolifically. . . .

Like Euripides, Menander was more appreciated by posterity than by his contemporaries, and he often had the disappointment of losing the prize to Philemon, who was certainly less talented. But, in the third century, the criticism of Aristophanes of Byzantium raised him to the front rank of Greek poets, alongside Homer. He even became so famous that one of his lines is quoted by St Paul in the New Testament and Athens ordered a bronze statue of him by the two sons of [the noted sculptor] Praxiteles to be erected in the theatre of Dionysus. There are several busts of him in existence, most of them probably inspired by this statue, which was executed at a time when both sculptors and painters were much concerned to provide a likeness. . . .

Menander wrote quickly, and with unusual facility. [The first-century Greek biographer] Plutarch records that, one day, a friend, meeting him in the street, said to him: 'The feast of Dionysus will soon be here, Menander. Haven't you written your comedy?' To which the poet replied: 'My comedy is finished: I've got the whole plan of it in my head—all that remains is to write the words.' In thirty years of creative activity, he wrote a hundred and eight comedies, an average of three or four plays a year.

Until 1898 Menander was only known to us from passages quoted by other writers, from what the ancients had said of him, and from Latin comedy, for both [of the Roman comic playwrights] Plautus and Terence took a lot from his work. . . . Then a series of papyrological discoveries in 1898, 1905 and 1957, revealed one whole play, the *Misanthrope* [or *Bad-Tempered Man*] (*Dyskolos*), and considerable parts of several others: the *Arbitration*, the *Woman of Samia*, the *Hero*, the *Beauty whose Hair was Cut*, and the *Flatterer*. . . .

The *Misanthrope* and the *Arbitration*

The *Misanthrope* . . . is chronologically the earliest of those known to us otherwise than by name, for . . . it was performed at the Lenaean festival in January 316. Menander was then twenty-five, but had already been writing for the theatre for five years.

The god, Pan, emerges from a grotto sacred to him and to the Nymphs, to speak the prologue, which sets the action at Phyle, in Attica, and describes the themes: Cnemon, an old curmudgeon, who lives with his daughter and an old servant near the grotto and is separated from his wife and from Gorgias, her son by a previous marriage:

Pan: So assiduously does the girl venerate my companions, the Nymphs, that we have decided to look after her. There is a young man, the son of a wealthy citizen, who has come to hunt in the neighbourhood with a friend. I have inspired in him a violent passion for the girl. That, broadly speaking, is the situation: as for the details, those you may learn, if you have a mind to.

The lover, Sostratos, sends his slave to Cnemon who is digging, but before the slave can give him the message he is chased away by a hail of pears and clods of earth. Sostratos' reception is not much better, though he does succeed in making the acquaintance of Gorgias, who decides that his intentions are honest, since the wealthy Sostratos asks nothing better than to be allowed to marry the poor girl. Gorgias agrees to help him, though it proves to be difficult. Because of a dream she has had, Sostratos' mother decides to offer a sacrifice to Pan and the Nymphs at their grotto, and sends her slave and a cook ahead with the sheep that is to be slaughtered (every sacrifice was followed by a meal). As they have nothing to cook it in, they try to borrow a pot from Cnemon, but he refuses and angrily drives them away. . . .

Cnemon's old servant drops a bucket down the well and in trying to rescue it drops a spade too. To retrieve his precious tools Cnemon lowers himself down the well, but the rope breaks and he thinks his end has come. Then Gorgias manages to pull him out, with the help of Sostratos, and the old man realizes that it is Gorgias, to whom he never speaks, who has saved his life. He therefore agrees to let his stepson decide who his half-sister shall marry; to the delight of Sostratos, who in turn persuades his father to let his sister marry Gorgias. The sacrifice then becomes the occasion for a double betrothal. Cnemon, who is lying on his bed covered with bruises, has to put up with the sarcasm and brutal jokes of the slave and cook he had beaten.

The plot is lively and well contrived. The scenes follow one another in rapid succession, with only four breaks, during which there is singing and dancing by the Chorus, 'a band of merry-makers, rather the worse for drink'. But the important thing is the drawing of the characters, especially Cnemon's, the only one of the leading parts that is not sympathetic. Even when he is rescued from the well he remains as surly as ever, and only wants to be left alone, though in Act IV he relents slightly: 'My great mistake was to believe that I could do without other people, and didn't need anybody's help. Now I see that death can catch you unawares, and I realize I was mistaken' (*Dyskolos*, 713 ff.).

The *Arbitration*, of which we only have rather more than half, belongs to the poet's maturity and was one of the plays most enjoyed by the Ancients. Charisios is married to Pamphile and loves his wife. But, after only five months of marriage, she secretly has a child, which she ex-

poses, leaving with him a gold ring and some jewels. Charisios, however, getting to hear of it, abandons his wife and goes to live with a courtesan, Habrotonon. Meanwhile, the child has been found by a slave, Daos, who hands him over to a poor charcoal burner called Syriscos, whose wife wants to have a child to bring up. Daos, however, has kept the jewels for himself and when Syriscos demands them Daos refuses to hand them over. They take the matter to an arbitrator, who turns out to be Pamphile's old father, Smicrines. Daos insists that he owes nothing:

It is Syriscos who owes thanks to me for granting his request. . . . I freely gave you part of what belonged to me. If you want to, keep it. If you don't, and are regretting that you ever accepted it, give it me back. What is certainly not fair is that you should have the lot, both the part I freely gave you, and the part I want for myself. [Syriscos agrees that what Daos says is correct, but he says to the arbitrator:] Against Daos, sir, the child itself has a case. Wife, fetch me the baby (*he takes it in his arms*). It is he, Daos, who demands the necklace and other things by which you can be recognized. He says the jewels were given to him, not to provide a living for you, and I have a claim to them as well, because I'm your guardian: he appointed me such by handing you over to me. The point that has to be decided is this: are these jewels and gold to be kept for the child, as his mother intended, until he is grown up; or is this thief to keep them because he happened to be the first to find them? And here is another point to be considered, sir. It may be that the child is better born than we are, and that though we bring him up he will refuse to do our kind of work. He may be forced by his nature to do deeds worthy of a free man: to hunt the lion, to carry arms, to run in the races. You've been to the theatre, so you must know what happens. What about heroes like Neleus and Pelias? Weren't they found by an old goatherd who wore a sheepskin like me? And when he found out they were high born, didn't he tell them, and give them a little wallet with things in it they could be recognized by? And instead of being goatherds they became kings (*The Arbitration*, 125 ff. and 157 ff.).

The old man's naïvety is charming, imagining that life in the great world is like some tragedy he happens to have seen. Daos is obliged to give up the jewels, and finally, thanks to the good-hearted Habrotonon the child is identified by them as the son of Pamphile and, even more surprising, of Charisios as well. For the gold ring turns out to be his: one night, during the feast of the Tauropolia, he had begotten the child on his future wife when it was too dark for them to recognize one another; and the unknown man, from whom Pamphile had snatched his ring as she tried to defend herself, had, indeed, been Charisios. As happy an ending to a romantic intrigue as anyone could wish, which Menander took from a lost tragedy by Euripides, the *Alope*.

Characters Drawn from Life

Almost invariably, the subject of Menander's plays is thwarted love, either before or after marriage, though he plays a hundred variations on it. Yet it is not only to the skill and variety of his plots that Menander owes his reputation; it rests above all on that subtle insight into every shade of feeling, every aspect of personality, thanks to which his characters have the vitality of men and women drawn from life. The language they speak is simple, relaxed and natural, yet full of zest, like the easy conversation of witty, well-educated people. He has a marvellous gift for portraying human beings in all their diversity. His work is the exquisite expression of that genuinely human wisdom that had slowly matured in the privileged conditions of Attic civilization. True, he lacks the purely comic quality of Aristophanes, very rarely does he make one want to laugh out loud; but the human situation which he presents with such truth and delicacy, and with such admirable good humour, is always entertaining and delightful.

The Complete History of

Literature, Philosophy, and Science

Chapter 12

Introduction

The debt that modern Western literature owes the Greeks is staggering. Ancient Greece not only produced the first examples of Western literature, but went on to establish virtually all of the literary forms and disciplines in use today. These include various kinds of poetry, philosophy, scientific inquiry, historical writing, tragic and comedic drama, oratorical prose (speech-writing), literary criticism, and prose fiction, including the novel. Europeans began to rediscover the surviving Greek (and some Roman) examples of these genres in the fourteenth century, in large degree inspiring and providing models for the rebirth of learning and high culture known as the European Renaissance.

The actual birth of Greek literature occurred sometime in the eighth century B.C. with the appearance of Homer's epic poems, the *Iliad* and the *Odyssey*. And it turned out to be a singularly auspicious and momentous delivery. One might expect that works composed during the last throes of a long dark age of illiteracy and cultural backwardness would be short, crude precursors of more ambitious and developed literature to come. Yet the case is just the opposite. The two epics are long, majestic, highly evolved literary masterpieces, critically acclaimed by the ancient and modern worlds alike as supremely brilliant in both conception and execution. From at least the early sixth century B.C. on, the Greeks viewed the more than 15,000-line *Iliad* and the 12,000-line *Odyssey* as vital sources of literary, artistic, moral, social, educational, and political instruction, as well as practical wisdom. These works also served as a culturally unifying force, the common property of all Greeks, emphasizing their shared cultural identity. Homer's influence and reputation in the ancient world became so great, in fact, that he overshadowed all other writers and people came to refer to him simply and reverently as "the Poet."

The late eighth-century B.C. Boeotian poet Hesiod (see Chapter 9) was another revered early master of epic poetry. "Hail, daughters of Zeus!" he wrote. "Give me sweet song, to celebrate the holy race of gods who live forever." (*Theogony* 104–106) The Greeks believed that a person's talent at singing, acting, writing poetry, or other artistic endeavors was a gift endowed by Zeus's daughters, the Muses. And Hesiod was convinced that these deities had given him the gift of "sweet song" one day while he was tending his sheep. The result was his *Theogony,* a systematic account of the creation and the genealogy of the Greek gods; and the *Works and Days,* which deals with the concepts of justice and hard work, illustrated by the day-to-day running of a farm and the planting of crops according to the calendar.

Greek epic poetry is typically long and deals with heroic themes. By contrast, lyric poetry consists of much shorter verses or songs, usually about everyday life or personal emotions, and was originally meant to be recited to the accompaniment of a solo instrument, at first the lyre. A number of different forms of shorter poems developed in the late Archaic Age. (Some modern scholars collectively label them all lyric, while others prefer to categorize them as separate types). Written in various meters (rhythms), these included elegiac poems (or elegies), iambic poems, and choral poems, the latter written to be performed at religious festivals by choirs of men, boys, or girls. There were many different subdivisions of these forms. Among the types of choral poetry, for example, were paeans (hymns of praise), funerary laments, and victory odes (*epinikia*); the fifth-century B.C. Theban poet Pindar was the widely acknowledged master of victory odes, which he composed to honor the winners of the Olympic and other major athletic contests.

Late Archaic times also saw the development of early Greek philosophy and science, although at this time no clear distinction yet existed between the two. Beginning about 600 B.C., the Greeks began to develop a systematic and in some ways almost modern approach to the study of science. The Egyptians and Babylonians had earlier amassed a great deal of scientific observation and data. But before the rise of the Greek philosopher-scientists, people everywhere, including Greece, attributed natural forces and phenomena, as well as control over human destiny, to various gods, spirits, and other supernatural elements. Because this seemed neatly to explain how the world worked, the kind of scientific questioning, research, and experimentation taken for granted today was almost unheard-of.

In seeking the underlying principles of nature, the Greeks largely removed the gods and other supernatural elements from scientific study and discussion. As modern scientists do, they tended to see the heavenly bodies and other facets of nature as material objects obeying natural laws rather than as personalized beings. "It was assumed, for the first time in history," noted scholar Rex Warner remarks in *The Greek Philosophers*, "that the investigator was dealing with a universe that was a 'cosmos'—that is to say an orderly system governed by laws which could be discovered by logical thought."

In the sixth and fifth centuries B.C., a few generations of Greek truth-seekers inquired into diverse aspects of nature. And in so doing they laid the groundwork for most of the major scientific disciplines, including astronomy, physics, chemistry, biology, and medicine. The first of these, Thales of Miletus (flourished ca. 600), attempted to understand how the cosmos works by identifying its *physis,* that is, its nature or underlying physical principle. He concluded that all matter is based on water; however, his pupil, Anaximander (ca. 611 to 547 B.C.), rejected this idea and postulated that the *physis* is a less tangible substance, which he called "the Boundless."

In the years that followed, other thinkers attempted to penetrate the secrets of nature and the cosmos, including, among many others, Pythagoras (sixth century B.C.), Anaxagoras (ca. 500–ca. 428), and Democritus (ca. 460–ca. 357). Democritus developed an early version of the atomic theory, postulating that all matter is composed of tiny, invisible particles called atoms. Modern scholars label all of these thinkers "Presocratic" because they predated the Athenian philosopher Socrates. His life and teachings mark an important turning point, namely the beginning of a major separation between Greek philosophy and science.

Socrates was opposed to the study of nature, advocating that dwelling on the physical, mechanical aspects of things diverted one's attention from what was really important. This, he said, was an understanding of the meaning of such ethical concepts as goodness, wisdom, and justice, and how human beings should best apply them to improve themselves and society. Socrates, who left no writings of his own, made a profound impression on two of his followers, Plato and Xenophon, who later described him and his ideas in their own writings.

Plato (427–347 B.C.), and later Plato's own student, Aristotle (384–322), also concerned themselves heavily with ethical concepts and the human condition. In his dialogue *Meno,* for example, Plato explores the question, "Can virtue be taught?" However, these two literary and philosophical giants did not confine themselves strictly to ethics, as Socrates had done. They each turned out a vast array of works covering a wide range of subjects, from politics to literary criticism. They also carried on important scientific researches or speculation. Plato's *Timaeus,* for instance, deals with the formation of the universe; and Aristotle made huge strides in the fields of biology and zoology, including an ingenious system for classifying animals.

Meanwhile, other philosophic-scientific giants flourished in the fifth and fourth centuries B.C. The emerging field of botany was dominated in this period by Aristotle's colleague and friend, Theophrastus, who produced voluminous writings about nearly all aspects of the plants known in his time. And paralleling and benefiting from the biological studies of Aristotle and Theophrastus were the equally impressive accomplishments of Greek physicians and medical researchers. Highly respected medical schools arose, the two most celebrated being those at Cnidus and Cos (both located just northwest of the Ionian island of Rhodes). The Cos school, overseen in the second half of the fifth century B.C. by Hippocrates, later called the "Father of Medicine," produced hundreds of writings on such topics as anatomy, surgery, treatment by diet and drugs, diseases of women and children, and medical ethics. The most important contribution of this and the Cnidus school was a major separation of medical theory from religion and philosophy and the firm establishment of medicine as a true scientific discipline.

The fifth and fourth centuries B.C. also produced important writings in other genres. These included the great tragedies and comedies of the Athenian dramatists, as well as the ground-breaking histories of Herodotus, Thucydides, and Xenophon. In addition, professional speech-writers, among them Antiphon (ca. 480–411) and Lysias (ca. 458–ca. 380), composed masterful tracts for court litigants. And the fourth century saw a flowering of oratorical prose, with the political pamphlets of Isocrates (436–338), who called on Macedonia's King Philip II to lead a panhellenic crusade against the Persians; and the fiery anti-Philip speeches (the *Philippics*) of the Athenian orator Demosthenes (384–322), who for a long time was the only leading Greek voice warning of the threat Philip posed to the city-states.

The next era of Greek philosophy, science, and literature roughly coincided with the Hellenistic historical period (323–30 B.C.), in which the Greek world expanded into the Near East and the city-state system largely gave way to large monarchies. Philosophy, increasing its separation from science, reached in new directions. A host of new movements (or schools of thought) attempted to teach ordinary people how to cope with the violence and uncertainty that characterized the times and to find some modicum of right-living and happiness. A few went so far as to preach near or complete withdrawal from everyday society. The most famous of these movements were those of the Stoics, Epicureans, Cynics, and Skeptics.

Science made huge strides in the Hellenistic Age. The main focus of research shifted from mainland Greece to Ptolemaic Alexandria, which became the known world's cultural and learning center. There, Herophilus of Calchedon (early third century B.C.), established the Alexandrian medical school. He and his pupil Erasistratus made significant advances in the field of anatomy and physiology. Other important Alexandrian researchers included Euclid (early third century), whose *Elements* remains the most important book on geometry ever written; Eratosthenes (mid–third century), who measured the earth's circumference with amazing accuracy; and Hipparchus (mid–second century), who compiled a massive star catalogue and invented latitude and longitude.

Another Hellenistic scientist, Archimedes (ca. 287–212), is acknowledged as the greatest mathematician and inventor of ancient times. In the theoretical realm, Archimedes discovered important mathematical formulas pertaining to the volumes of spheres, cylinders and other solid figures, as well as the basic principles of floating bodies. In the practical arena, he experimented with levers, pulleys, and other simple machines, demonstrating their principles in large-scale and, at the time, astonishing real-life applications, the most famous being devastating weapons of war.

Hellenistic Alexandria was also a literary center of note. Apollonius Rhodius (ca. 295–215 B.C.) revived the genre of epic poetry with his *Argonautica*, about Jason and his quest for the Golden Fleece; while his contemporaries, Callimachus and Theocritus, produced hundreds of shorter poems of high quality that exerted a strong influence on later Roman poets. Meanwhile, another contemporary, Zenodotus, restored, collated, and created new editions of earlier poetic classics, including Homer's epics; and a later Alexandrian, Aristarchus of Samothrace (early second century B.C.) wrote numerous commentaries and criticisms of earlier classics, including works by Homer, Hesiod, Pindar, and Herodotus.

Most of these works were intended for a small number of well-educated, "highbrow" readers. But thanks to the rapidly expanding educational opportunities in the Hellenistic period, for the first time in history a fairly sizable general reading public was developing. To meet the increasing demand for materials for readers of limited or average educational levels, hack writers proliferated. Thereafter, literature consisted of two types: high-quality works that appealed to a limited audience, and popular pulp for the masses.

Greek philosophy, science, and literature continued to flourish in the Roman period (the centuries following Rome's eclipse of the last independent Greek states in the first century B.C.). Noteworthy was the philosophy of Plotinus (ca. A.D. 205–270). He envisioned a hierarchy (ascending ladder) of realities, each of which gives rise to and controls the one below it. His beliefs are often labeled Neoplatonism (i.e., a newer variation on Plato) because the highest of the realities on his mystical ladder roughly corresponded to Plato's idea of the ultimate in "goodness."

In the sciences, Galen of Pergamum (129–199) ranked with Hippocrates as one of the two greatest physicians of antiquity. A voluminous writer, Galen left behind elegantly-composed treatises covering every area of medical inquiry, as well as perceptive commentaries on the works of Plato, Aristotle, and Theophrastus. Meanwhile, the brilliant astronomer-geographer Ptolemy (Claudius Ptolemaeus, ca. 100–ca. 178) produced the *Mathematike Syntaxis* (in later ages called the *Almagest*). The ideas set forth in this complex and comprehensive explanation of the movements of the heavenly bodies around a stationary earth became a dogma that was largely accepted by Western scholars until the fifteenth century.

Two of the more prominent and prolific Greek literary figures of the Roman era were Lucian of Samosata (ca. 115–ca. 181) and Plutarch of Chaeronea (ca. 46–ca. 120). Lucian wrote numerous prose works, including speeches, letters, essays, stories, and dialogues, most of them satiric, humorous, clever, and entertaining. His *True History* (which is anything but true!), for example, describes some travelers' fantastic adventures, including a voyage to the moon and an excursion to the Underworld, where they meet Homer, Herodotus, and other past notables. Plutarch was a biographer and moralist with an elegant, thoughtful, and engaging writing style. His large corpus of surviving works includes a series of some fifty biographies of famous Greek and Roman figures, including Solon, Themistocles, Pericles, Alexander, Demetrius, Fabius Maximus, Julius Caesar, and Cicero. Though these are not straightforward histories, Plutarch had access to many ancient sources that are now lost; so modern historians are forever in his debt for the considerable body of largely accurate historical information that he preserved about the eras preceding his own time.

Selection 1

Homer and His Epic Poems

Michael Grant

Greek literature, and indeed all of Western literature, begins with Homer's Iliad *and* Odyssey. *The first of these masterful epic poems revolves around the wrath of Achilles, the most formidable warrior among the Greek chieftains who besieged the city of Troy (in northwestern Asia Minor); while the* Odyssey *follows the adventures of another of these chieftains, the crafty Odysseus (king of the island kingdom of Ithaca) in the decade following Troy's fall. This highly informative examination of "the Poet," (as the ancients referred to Homer) and his timeless works (including brief synopses of their plots) is from* The Rise of the Greeks, *by the prolific and popular classical historian, Michael Grant.*

a number of cities in the eastern Aegean area claimed to be the birthplace of Homer, to whom the *Iliad* and *Odyssey* were ascribed, and internal evidence from the poems—especially their vivid, varied similes—indicates that this coastal area was the region of their origin (that the two works were the work of the same poet, which is sometimes denied, will be affirmed below).

The most convincing claims to Homer's birthplace were those of Chios and Smyrna, and despite the contradictory and fragmentary nature of our sources . . . it seems probable that, although he may have been born at Smyrna, he lived and worked on Chios. There (according to Ephorus [a fourth-century B.C. Greek historian who wrote a work describing Greek cities]) he lived for a time at the northern village of Bolissus (Volissos), later the dwelling-place of the guild of the Homeridae, devoted to reciting his poetry, who claimed to have originated from his descendants. In the seventh century the poet Semonides . . . ascribes a passage of the *Iliad* to 'the man of Chios', and at about the same time the Pythian (Delphic) section of the Hymn to Apollo . . . speaks of him as a supreme poet who 'dwelt in rocky Chios' and was blind. . . .

The poems seem to have reached their final, or nearly final, form in *c.*750/700 BC—more than 200 years, that is to say, after the arrival of the Ionians upon the island of Chios, and half a millennium later than the supposed events that their poet purported to describe. Whether these works preceded or followed the very different *Works and Days* and *Theogony* of Hesiod remains uncertain. Shorter lays by earlier anonymous or at least unknown poets, which were evidently combined and amended by Homer to form parts of the *Iliad* and *Odyssey*, may already, before his time, have been amalgamated [combined] into longer units, pointing the way towards the two complete epics that subsequently emerged during the vast period that extended between the alleged date of the Trojan War and the time of eventual compilation and composition. But on the whole it seems more likely that the amalgamation of these shorter works into the majestic, complex structure of the two great epics should be regarded as the specific achievement of Homer.

During the intervening centuries, the bards who gave performances had been illiterate, but the vanished songs that they sang had been orally transmitted from one generation to another. They no doubt included numerous recurrent formulas which served as mnemonic [memory-aiding] guides and landmarks to help the impromptu singers; and such formulas—epithets, phrases and word groups ('rosy-fingered dawn', 'wine-dark sea'), in addition to whole set themes and action sequences—continued to abound in the *Iliad* and *Odyssey*. Indeed, their 28,000 lines include 25,000 of these repetitive formulaic units.

Exhaustive efforts, with the aid of every archaeological technique, to date the objects, institutions, customs and rituals described in Homer's poems have produced mixed results, leading, above all, to the conclusion that he was not concerned to reproduce the features and values of any actual society which existed, or had existed, at any specific date. For, whereas his verses include certain allusions, of a more or less garbled character, to the Mycenaean way of life that had come to an end so long ago—notably, in large parts of the *Iliad*'s Catalogue of Achaean Ships—there are other, more numerous (though far from systematic) references to the poet's own eighth-century surroundings. On the other hand, a number of further elements derive neither from recollections of the long-past Mycenaean age nor from phenomena existent in the poet's own time . . . and are timeless.

Homer was apparently assisted towards his supreme achievement by a stroke of fortune: for his lifetime seems to have coincided with the reintroduction of writing into the Greek world. In this situation the poet, providentially personifying the impact of a literate upon an illiterate culture, may have utilized this new technique in person, and committed his verses to writing (or, more probably, dictated them to others who could write)—an opportunity which helped him, beyond measure, to create coherent, monumental poetic structures far beyond the reach of his oral predecessors.

Nevertheless, it was the antique oral tradition of which he himself was still the heir, and he no doubt composed his poetry for (and perhaps partly while) reciting or chanting aloud, accompanying his words with a simple form of lyre. . . . These performances may have taken place at noblemen's feasts or at a major festival. . . . On such an occasion, one of the two epics could have been recited in about fifteen two-hour sessions, that is to say during the course of three or four days. . . .

After centuries of controversy, it can still be argued . . . that the *Iliad* and *Odyssey* were the work of one poet, namely Homer. Certainly, the *Odyssey* reflects a way of life different from, and later than, the way of life delineated in the *Iliad*. Nevertheless, that presents no serious obstacle to the traditional attribution of both works to a single poet (the differences are no greater than those separating *The Tempest* from *King Lear* [both by Shakespeare]). Perhaps the *Iliad* was written when Homer was young, and the *Odyssey* when he was older. But that, once again, is not an inevitable deduction, since the fact that he was telling of things that purported to have happened in two different decades (both remote from himself in time—and both, also, largely products of his own imagination) need not mean that the two poems must likewise belong to widely separated decades of his own life,

although arguments based on language, ideas and structure have been put forward to suggest that this may have been the case. . . .

The *Iliad*: Its Plot and Characters

The *Iliad* narrates events that supposedly took place at some distance to the north of the poet's own home-country, in the neighbourhood of Ilium (Troy) on the Asian mainland, overlooking the Hellespont (Dardanelles). The poem describes a brief and late stage in the siege of Troy by the combined armies of numerous states of the Achaeans (as Homer calls these pre-Dorian peoples of the Greek homeland), commanded by Agamemnon, king of Mycenae. In association with his brother Menelaus of Sparta, he had prompted the leaders of other Achaean states to join this naval expedition against the Trojan monarch Priam because Paris, one of Priam's sons, had abducted Menelaus' wife, the beautiful Helen.

For nine years the Greek troops have been encamped beside their fleet outside the walls of Troy. But they have not, so far, been able to capture the city, although they have seized and plundered a number of neighbouring towns, mainly under the leadership of Achilles, prince of the Myrmidons of Thessaly, the most formidable and unruly of Agamemnon's allies. The loot from one of these townships provokes a quarrel between Achilles and his commander-in-chief. The dispute concerns Chryseis, a girl whom the Achaeans have made captive. She has been allocated to Agamemnon as his prize, but he is reluctantly compelled to return her to her father Chryses, in order to propitiate [appease] the anger of Apollo. . . . Agamemnon seeks compensation by taking possession, instead, of a girl named Briseis, who was one of the prizes of Achilles, whereupon Achilles furiously withdraws from the battle against the Trojans, taking his Myrmidon followers with him. This is the wrath which forms the first word of the poem, and it is a wrath, as Homer pronounced, which enveloped countless other

Achaeans in disaster.

A truce between the two armies, designed to enable Menelaus and Paris to settle their dispute by single combat, comes to nothing, and the war is resumed. Lacking the aid of Achilles, however, the Achaeans find themselves hard-pressed, but Achilles still refuses to help, despite an offer of handsome amends from Agamemnon. A rampart the Achaean soldiers are forced to construct around their ships and living quarters is stormed by Priam's son Hector. At this juncture Achilles relents to the extent of allowing his beloved older friend and associate Patroclus . . . to lead the Myrmidons to the rescue of their endangered compatriots. Patroclus is successful, but he dashes too far ahead, and meets his death at the hands of Hector beneath the city walls.

Thereupon, convulsed by grief and fury, Achilles himself finally enters the fray once again, throws the fleeing Trojans back into their city, slays Hector and savagely ill-treats his corpse, thus carrying his anger beyond the bounds of humanity. However, the dead man's father, Priam, in his sorrow, is prompted by Zeus to visit Achilles in his camp at night, in order to appeal for the return of his son's body. Achilles concedes his request, and the poem ends with Hector's funeral, amid an uneasy truce.

Excavations confirm that the small but advantageously located fortress of later Bronze Age Troy ('Troy VIIA') was destroyed in *c*.1250/ 1200. Its destroyers *may* have been products of the Mycenaean culture from the Greek mainland—speaking a form of Greek—though this cannot be confirmed. But the Mycenaean civilization itself (together with the form of writing that it practised) collapsed not long afterwards, and it was not, as we saw, until five hundred years later that the *Iliad* and *Odyssey* assumed approximately their present shape.

Nevertheless, this great distance of time did nothing to frustrate Homer's unparalleled descriptive talent. With lively yet disengaged comprehension, each personage is depicted as a distinct individual. The most arresting is Achilles, who possesses in extreme degree all the virtues and faults of a Homeric hero, and most completely embodies the heroic code of honour. A hero, as reconstructed by Homer . . . dedicated his entire existence, with all the aid that his birth and wealth and physical prowess could afford him, to an unceasing, violently competitive, vengeful struggle to win applause, together with the material goods which were its standard of measurement, by excelling among his peers, especially in battle, which was his principal occupation . . . .

Yet the *Iliad*, at times, seems to debate rather than lay down such principles of heroic conduct. This lust and zest for fighting, which at its zenith seemed to elevate the heroes to a pinnacle not too far short of the gods, is overshadowed by pathos: for they still have no way of escaping the mortal, fatal destiny that awaits them.

This destiny is identified with (or occasionally overrides) those very gods themselves, who, as Herodotus pointed out, were given their names, domains and human appearances by Homer and Hesiod. Amoral, unedifying, they squabble sordidly as they divide their support between the two warring sides in the Trojan War, and strike out viciously in sporadic, frightening, often unpredictable interventions. That is partly why a sense of the fragility of all human endeavour pervades the *Iliad*. The gods never die, but death pounces, in the end, upon men and heroes on earth, becoming the ultimate test of merit, the final and most searching ordeal and fulfilment. Achilles knows he has not long to live: and when, at the deeply moving end of the poem, he meets old Priam, whose son Hector he has slain, the exultant din of war has faded into misery and compassion.

Hector, although he made military mistakes and was inferior to Achilles, had been a noble hero (and a noble enemy of the Greeks), in whom warlike and elegiac elements are blended together. Agamemnon and Menelaus are flawed. There are authentic women in the *Iliad*. The last meeting of Andromache with her doomed husband Hector is poignant. As for Helen (transformed from a moon-goddess into the most seductive of human beings), she was responsible for everything, since it was only because of her that the war had ever taken place.

The *Odyssey*: Its Plot and Characters

The *Odyssey* tells of Odysseus' return to his home on the island of Ithaca from the Trojan War. His mythical wanderings lasted for ten years, but the action narrated concerns only the last six weeks of this time. At the outset of the poem, he has come to the island of the goddess Calypso, who compels him to stay there as her lover for nearly eight years, in spite of his longing to get back to Ithaca. There, in the meantime, his son Telemachus has grown up, and his home is filled with uninvited guests, the suitors of his wife Penelope. Eating and drinking at the expense of their absent host, they continually urge her to marry again and eventually insist that she must now choose one or another of themselves.

Odysseus owes his troubles to the enmity of Poseidon, for in the course of his travels he had blinded the god's son, the Cyclops Polyphemus.

While Poseidon is away, however, the other gods and goddesses are convinced by the hero's staunch patron, Athena, that they should show him pity and render him assistance. She directs Telemachus to visit Pylos (the kingdom of Nestor [one of the Greek leaders of the Trojan expedition]) and Sparta (to which Menelaus and Helen had by now returned home) in order to seek information about his father's whereabouts. Meanwhile, Zeus commands Calypso to release her captive. He constructs a raft and sets out, but Poseidon creates a storm, and his ship is wrecked. Eventually, after terrible experiences, he is cast up on the coast of Scheria, inhabited by a well-conducted people, the Phaeacians. On reaching the shore he encounters the princess Nausicaa, and she leads him to the palace of her father, the king of the Phaeacians, Alcinous.

During a banquet in Odysseus' honour, the hero describes his travels and adventures since leaving captured Troy. He tells of his perilous en-

This dramatic modern rendering shows Odysseus and his men escaping from the blinded Cyclops Polyphemus, who hurls huge stones at them.

counters with Lotus-Eaters, Polyphemus, the wind-god Aeolus, the cannibal Laestrygones, the witch Circe, the phantoms of the dead (at the end of the earth, or in the underworld of King Minos?), the Sirens, monstrous Scylla and the whirlpool Charybdis. And Odysseus describes, too, how his men had eaten the cattle of the sun-god Helios, paying for this sacrilege by a storm which destroyed them, so that only he himself had survived to make his way to the island of Calypso, and thence later to come ashore on Scheria.

Soon afterwards, despite continuing divine wrath, the Phaeacians arrange his transportation to Ithaca, where, unheroically disguised as a grimy beggar, he discovers how Penelope's suitors have been behaving in his absence. Guided by Athena, Telemachus gets back to the island from Sparta, and so Odysseus and his son, reunited, plan the destruction of their unwelcome guests. In Odysseus' palace, there is no recognition of the returned hero except from his dog (which thereupon closes its eyes in death) and his nurse Eurycleia. Penelope, once again pressed by the suitors to remarry one of their number, proposes an archery contest, allegedly to enable her to make her choice, but no one except Odysseus can string his own mighty bow. He himself, however, contrives to get hold of the weapon, and lets fly a volley of arrows to massacre the suitors. Then Penelope identifies her long-lost husband, and Odysseus rules his island kingdom once again.

Although tacked on to traditions of the Trojan War in order to justify its epic form, the *Odyssey* is founded on a standard folktale: the story of the man who is away for so long that he is believed to be dead, and yet eventually, after fantastic adventures, returns home and rejoins his faithful wife. Dozens of other wondrous ancient stories, often displaying near-eastern analogies, are transformed and incorporated into the fabric of this most exciting of poems.

The *Odyssey* resembles the *Iliad* in its commendation of physical courage, and a savage pleasure in bloodshed is by no means lacking. However, there has been a shift (if the *Odyssey* is the later of the two poems) from the doom-fraught heights of passionate heroism towards quieter virtues such as endurance and self-control and patience, while love of comrades and of honour now seems to take second place to love of home and wife—the other type of woman, who menaces male society, being rejected in the person of Circe. In a picture that oscillates between kingship and the aristocratic regimes which sometimes or often, it would seem, succeeded monarchical systems, our attention is engaged by the social and family lives of the noble landowners, living on their estates. And stress is placed on good breeding, courtliness and hospitable guest-friendship, with its elaborate web of gifts and countergifts. Nor are humbler folk, such as beggars and suppliants, ignored; more distinctive than the dim soldier-assemblymen of the Iliad, they are individually protected by a Zeus who is concerned, to this extent, with morality. . . .

This archetypal wanderer, the formidable, unconquerably strong and enduring Odysseus, cleverer and more resourceful, too, than any other Homeric hero—not so much 'cunning' as capable of analysing any situation and forming rational decisions accordingly—is the permanent exemplar of the complete man who has struggled against all the hazards of life and has vanquished them, one after another—thus finding out many things, and discovering himself. For all Odysseus' sturdy independence, however, a novel note in Greek thinking (and religion) is struck by the exclusive, protective companionship, admiring and often humorous, that is lavished upon him by the goddess Athena.

The magical Circe, too, is vividly delineated, and so is amorous Calypso, the pair whose sexual domination over Odysseus for a time shockingly reversed, in the Greek view, the natural process. But fully developed personalities are for the first time accorded to females who are human beings and not witches, notably Nausicaa and, above all, the complex, ingenious and resolutely chaste Penelope. Women, it is true, are often still not much more than masculine chattels, dependent on their husbands' prowess. Yet they play a major part in the social system, since they are able to link powerful families in alliance, evoking rich presents.

Moreover, watching and enduring on the sidelines, they possess minds and characters of their own, interpreting the significances and consequences of masculine actions. Less of a sexual chauvinist than almost any other male writer of antiquity, Homer gives his women some freedom. Agamemnon and Odysseus had departed leaving their wives in charge of their kingdoms; and the subsequent infidelity of Agamemnon's wife Clytemnestra—which was to become the theme of Aeschylus' *Oresteia*—posed a crucial threat to the male-dominated social system.

Once composed, the *Iliad* and *Odyssey* in due course became the property of a guild or clan of reciters, practitioners of the most skilled Ionian craft of the age. These, as we saw earlier, were the Homeridae prototypes and models of those professional reciters of poetry the rhapsodes, named after the *rhabdos* (baton) which they held in their hands instead of singing to the lyre. Possibly, in origin, singers of Homer's own circle, the Homeridae, claimed to be his descendants, and belonged to the island of Chios. But they and the rhapsodes after them also travelled . . . so that knowledge of the *Iliad* and *Odyssey* spread rapidly.

And indeed, throughout the entire subsequent millennium of ancient history, these two poems, perhaps slightly modified under the Pisistratid dictators of Athens—and then divided into twenty-four books each in the third century BC—supplied the Greeks with their greatest civilizing influence, and formed the foundation of their literary, artistic, moral, social, educational and political attitudes. For a long time, no histories of early times seemed at all necessary, since the *Iliad* and *Odyssey* fulfilled every requirement. They attracted universal esteem and reverence, too, as sources of general and practical wisdom, as arguments for heroic yet human nobility and dignity, as incentives to vigorous (often bellicose) manly action, and as mines of endless quotations and commentaries: the common property of all Greeks everywhere.

Selection 2

The Great Age of Greek Lyric Poetry

Jacqueline de Romilly

Various forms of early non-epic Greek poetry are, for the sake of convenience, sometimes lumped together under the general heading "lyric." This, however, is not strictly accurate, since there were distinct differences among these forms. Technically, lyric poems were intended to be recited or sung to the accompaniment of a lyre (harp) and use a wide variety of meters, or rhythms. Each line of Greek poetry consists of a number of metrical "feet," each foot made up of a set sequence of syllables. As suggested by the prefix hexa-, meaning six, a line of hexameter has six feet; and similarly, a line of pentame-

ter has five feet. These two meters were used in epic poetry, but also in elegiac poetry (i.e., elegies), shorter poems that usually (but not always) deal with love and other human emotions. On the other hand, iambic poetry utilizes trimeter, each line having three groups of syllables. Aristotle thought that iambic meter was nearest in rhythm to ordinary speech, and it was, not surprisingly, the commonest meter of tragedy and comedy. The following synopsis of non-epic Greek poetry (i.e., the shorter poetic forms that followed the epics of Homer and Hesiod) in its period of greatest flowering—roughly the early seventh through mid–fifth centuries B.C.—is by former Collège de France professor Jacqueline de Romilly.

*F*rom the eighth to the fifth centuries there were many poets in Greece, known to us for the most part from quotations in later works. Unlike Homer and Hesiod they . . . used a variety of meters, composing fairly short works that were meant to be sung. Because the instrument in most common use was the lyre, the poetry it accompanied came to be called "lyric"—a term that later outgrew this narrow and technical meaning. Alongside this poetry sung to the lyre, either by an individual or by a chorus, various other forms existed, including "elegy" (usually sung to the flute) and "iambic" poetry (so called from the name of the meter), which was recited to the accompaniment of special instruments. Such poems were not novelties at the time; already in the Homeric epics we find references to occasional poetry such as paeans, wedding songs, or dirges [funerary laments]. In the archaic age, however, the genre struck a new vein of personal expression; and this phenomenon was not confined to any one region of Greece.

Indeed, the multiplicity of geographic centers

Excerpted from Jacqueline de Romilly, *A Short History of Greek Literature*, translated by Lillian Doherty. Copyright © 1985 by The University of Chicago. Reprinted by permission of the publisher, The University of Chicago Press.

was a major feature of the new poetry, already visible in Hesiod. It corresponds to the development of new city-states. Asia Minor was still a prolific region, producing Callinus, Mimnermus, Phocylides, and Anacreon. But the islands put forward their own favorite sons and daughters: Archilochus was born in Paros and emigrated to Thasos; Alcaeus and Sappho were natives of Mytilene [on the island of Lesbos]. Soon the mainland cities were to be reckoned with as well: Solon was an Athenian, Theognis a Megarian, Pindar a Theban; and even before their time Sparta had adopted poets from abroad, such as Alcman. Where choral lyric was concerned, the influence of Greek Italy was far from negligible in the sixth century. Stesichorus was a Sicilian; Ibycus came from Rhegium (on the Italian coast opposite Sicily); Bacchylides and Pindar composed odes for Hieron, a tyrant of Syracuse. . . .

Remarkably, this poetry, which encompassed a variety of genres and developed in diverse cities, manages to reflect a number of common features of the period as a whole, in which political institutions throughout Greece were evolving in similar ways. Just as the centers of Greek cultural life were multiplying, the different strata of society were becoming more autonomous. The old hereditary monarchies had disappeared, and city-states in the fullest sense were coming into their own. Within the cities, wealth was no longer confined to the old aristocracies. New men rose to power, founding regimes in which rule was not hereditary (the tyrannies); still later, democratic regimes appeared. Whether or not it was associated with the political struggles, poetry became more personal, as in Hesiod's case. Henceforward all poets did as Hesiod had done, and still more emphatically: they spoke of themselves, of their loves or their adventures, or of what they hoped for their cities in war and in peace.

Yet in the midst of this renaissance age, a theme was found that reconciled the exaltation of the individual with that of the city, and the old aristocratic values with the growth of new states throughout Greece—praise of victorious athletes. The Olympic Games were established at the beginning of the eighth century, and the other major games at the beginning of the sixth. In its celebration of athletic victors, choral lyric—which marks the last stage of development of this kind of poetry—exalted at one and the same time a hero, a city, and an ideal conception of life.

Diverse as the lyric poets were, most had in common the sense that they were imparting a kind of wisdom. From the brief moralizing verses we find quoted here and there to the great visions of Pindar, we can see a distinctive moral thought emerging in the course of these three centuries of turmoil, liberation, and discovery. Beginning with Hesiod, the dominant strand in this thought is the idea that the gods will punish the excesses, or *hubris*, of men.

The Earliest Poets

Iambic poetry is an exception to the general rule. The meter in itself has a somewhat sharp and pungent quality, which lends itself to satire . . . and Aristotle observes (in the *Poetics*, 1448b) that this meter was commonly used for satiric or comic exchanges. His description perfectly fits the best-known of the iambic poets (who also composed "elegiac" verse), Archilochus. Since Archilochus is one of the earliest Greek poets (he seems to have lived in the first half of the seventh century), and since practically no other iambic poets are known to us, I have placed iambic verse earlier in this account than would otherwise be warranted.

Archilochus was born in Paros; but his father Telesicles had led a group of Parian settlers to the richer island of Thasos. . . . But his was the life of an adventurer rather than that of a warrior in the heroic mold. Indeed, his originality lay in his rejection of the Homeric tradition, both social and poetic, in order to embrace its opposite. Speaking in the first person, he idealizes nothing; he is a realist who refuses to glamorize war and makes a boast of rejecting the heroic code. He tells, for example, of abandoning his shield near a bush: "But I saved my life. Let the old shield rot! I'll buy another just as good."

In the same way Archilochus refuses to glamorize love—to say the least. When the man who

had promised him his daughter Neobule in marriage changed his mind, Archilochus attacked the whole family in verse, including his former betrothed, whom he branded an "old courtesan." Pindar called Archilochus "the insulter"; a few fragments of his epodes, in very bad condition, suggest that his verses could be quite obscene. This did not prevent Archilochus from having his own brand of morality ("I know how to love those who love me, and hate my enemies"), as well as a crude popular wisdom, with a tone sometimes reminiscent of fable. . . .

In meter, Greek elegy is closest to Homer and Hesiod, since it consists of alternating lines of . . . hexameter and . . . pentameter. We should not judge its content by the modern meaning of the term "elegiac," which stems from the Latin elegists. The first Greek elegies, in fact, were war poems.

The earliest poets in this tradition are Callinus, Tyrtaeus, and Mimnermus. Callinus seems to belong to the first half of the seventh century; his apparent source of inspiration was the heroic tradition. Tyrtaeus, who lived at Sparta in the seventh century, is likewise known to us for several elegies combining an exhortation to warlike courage and a glorification of death in battle. Mimnermus, by contrast, is known for poems that have nothing warlike about them. An Ionian who lived about the year 600 or a little before, Mimnermus sang of the shortness of life and enjoyed retelling episodes from the myths.

Unlike iambic poetry, elegy continued into the classical period. Toward the end of the archaic age, two poets whose work is better known to us used the elegiac form—Solon and Theognis. The contrast between their work and that of their predecessors is revealing: instead of a warlike zeal still close to the epic model, we have in Solon and Theognis the testimony of two men who took part in, and pondered, the political struggles of their time.

Theognis probably lived about the middle or the second half of the sixth century, though some scholars date the beginning of his career as early as 630. He was from Megara (probably the mainland city of that name). A collection of over

1200 lines of his elegiac poetry has survived [a portion of which is]. . . . addressed to a young man named Cyrnus. All are morally impeccable ("Be prudent, and seek neither honors, prestige, nor fortune by base or unjust actions"). . . . He bewails the evils of the age, especially the fact that "those who once were gentlemen have become nobodies" and cannot even hold their own. The only refuge is in friendship—when it is constant—and in a wisdom difficult to attain. Theognis is a fierce and rousing witness to the bitterness of aristocrats who saw themselves being dispossessed in favor of people for whom they had nothing but scorn.

Solon was involved in the same struggles but was able to rise above them, and his poems radiate an earnest attachment to the common good. We know of his career from these poems and from such later works as Aristotle's *Constitution of Athens* and Plutarch's *Life of Solon*. An Athenian, born about 640, Solon was appointed archon in 594. He took courageous measures to stem social upheaval (among others, the abolition of enslavement for debt), and many Athenian laws are attributed to him; he was seen by many as one of the fathers of Athenian democracy. . . . His poems (of which we have only fragments, some iambic and some elegiac) reflect both his political and his moral ideals, which were inseparable.

The moral standard he proposes is close to that of Hesiod. Solon wants no riches unless the gods give them, for he knows what damage hubris can cause. . . . He also knows that Zeus will punish this offense sooner or later. The idea of divine will is ever-present in Solon. In contrast to Hesiod, however, he deals mainly with the application of this standard to the city-state. He trusts that Zeus and Athene will preserve his city; but only if it is not ruined by the folly of its own citizens, who are ready to opt for hubris and injustice if they think they can turn a profit. To ward off these evils he proposes the ideal of . . . good laws, which will put an end to harmful desires. To help others achieve this ideal, Solon describes his own attitude during the time of crisis when he was in power: "To the people I gave just as much power as was necessary, without reducing or overextending their privileges. As for the powerful, whose wealth was a source of envy, I took care that they too should be shielded from indignity. I stood firm, covering both factions with a sturdy shield, and I let neither seize an unjust victory over the other". . . .

Personal and Choral Lyric Poetry

Throughout ancient times, the island of Lesbos produced lyric poets of exceptional ability. The island had been home to the early poets Terpander and Arion, of whom we know very little. Toward the end of the seventh century and the beginning of the sixth (i.e., roughly during Solon's lifetime), Lesbos produced two great poets, whose fame and literary influence were substantial. The two were contemporaries, one a woman and one a man—Sappho and Alcaeus. Both were members of the local aristocracy and may well have known one another. Living in a troubled age, each experienced exile; but Sappho, unlike Alcaeus, took no part in politics. Both also enjoyed a highly civilized and pleasure-filled way of life. . . . Finally, both wrote in a direct, concrete, and spontaneous style that cannot leave the reader indifferent.

Sappho represents the feminine side of this poetry, not only because she was herself a woman but because she lived among women (young girls to whom she taught her art) and it was women that she loved. Love is never far to seek in her poems. Among her works are wedding songs (or *Epithalamia*) and a *Prayer to Aphrodite*. There are fleeting glimpses of the graceful girls in whose midst she lived; there are also burning descriptions of erotic feeling. On this subject Sappho was quoted and emulated for centuries—and with good reason, for the emotional intensity of some of her lines is remarkable. A famous example reads: "My tongue is severed; a subtle fire steals suddenly under my skin; . . . my ears are filled with sound; sweat pours down my body; trembling seizes me; I turn paler than the grass". . . .

It is because of her that women who love women are called "lesbians." But, most important, we owe to her the creation of "lyric" poetry as we still understand that term; and the Latin lyrists, in their love poetry, all echo her. Sadly, only meager fragments of her work have survived. . . .

The poems of Alcaeus survive in much the same state. But his subject matter contrasts with Sappho's, for he tended to celebrate the pleasures of life *not* inspired by love. He wrote hymns to the gods. . . . Along with this religious vein, however, we find two major themes in Alcaeus that seem more characteristic, more revealing of his personality. First, there are the drinking songs, in which the joys of wine are associated with all occasions and all seasons. . . . Then there are the political poems . . . giving a passionate commentary on current events. . . .

With Anacreon, an Ionian from the small town of Teos who lived in the mid-sixth century, we move closer to the Greek mainland. Anacreon's patrons were tyrants: after spending some time in Abdera, on the Thracian border, he lived first at the court of Polycrates of Samos and then with Hipparchus, tyrant of Athens. Thus he called no one city his home. His genius was that of the court poet, amiable, sophisticated, fond of banquets and beautiful boys and girls—in a word, fond of love, though the love he celebrates lacks the personal and passionate note struck by Sappho. Anacreon composed light odes and epigrams; we possess many fragments, though all are quite short. . . .

Personal lyric inevitably ran the risk of becoming insipid; this was not the case with choral lyric, however. Choral poetry appeared first in Sparta, where Terpander, a native of Lesbos, had gone to found a school of choral lyric. We know that one other such school existed. It was in Sparta too that Alcman (who apparently came from Sardis) distinguished himself as a choral poet in the seventh century. He wrote songs for girls (*Partheneia*), which engaged the young singers in spirited exchanges but were not lacking in moral advice and denunciations of hubris. . . .

At the end of the seventh century, with Stesichorus (whose name means "director of chorus-

es"), we follow choral lyric to Sicily (Himera). Stesichorus wrote hymns to various heroes of the epic cycle. His poem about Helen . . . inspired Euripides' *Helen*. . . . Unfortunately, only a few brief fragments of Stesichorus survive. . . .

In the second half of the sixth century, choral lyric seems to have found a new strain with Simonides of Ceos. Born near Athens, he lived in that city at the court of the tyrant Hippias; later he moved to Syracuse, where he was a guest of the tyrant Hieron. His life was long and his literary output extensive, including dithyrambs, songs of praise, dirges, epigrams, and "epinicia," or odes for victorious athletes, a genre he seems to have pioneered. His tone is generally lofty and he does not hesitate to moralize, somewhat in the vein of Solon; he also sings of the shortness of life and the caprices of fortune. . . . Simonides gave choral lyric the same breadth that Pindar, forty years his junior, would later achieve. At the same time, we can see in Simonides' case, as in that of Solon, the definitive placing of the poet within the city-state that was to characterize the whole of the fifth century.

Pindar and Bacchylides

Pindar's work is better preserved than that of any of the poets I have discussed since Hesiod. His poems fill not just a few pages, but a volume or more in modern editions. Even so, we have an incomplete and one-sided view of his work, for only his epinician odes have survived, though he also wrote hymns to the gods, processional hymns, choral songs for young girls, threnodies, and songs of praise (panegyrics). Of his work in these genres we have only a few fragments. On the other hand, the epinicia have been well preserved. They are grouped, according to the contests involved, into Olympian, Pythian, Nemean, and Isthmian odes. From this corpus we can form an idea of his life, his thought, and his talents.

Like Hesiod, Pindar was a Boeotian; he was born near Thebes, apparently in 518, and was clearly of noble birth. . . . As early as 498, his victory odes had earned him public notice (the *Tenth Pythian*, honoring a Thessalian, was composed in that year). His fame soon spread throughout Greece. He wrote many odes for victors from Aegina, and composed a paean to the island itself. Shortly after 476 he moved to Sicily, where he frequented the courts of two famous rulers, Theron (tyrant of Acragas) and Hieron (tyrant of Gela and Syracuse); many of the odes are in honor of Sicilian victors. Still later, he returned to the Greek mainland. He found appropriate words of praise for Athens (the famous lines beginning, "You of the violet-crowned brow . . ."); he also received commissions from Corinth, Rhodes, and Cyrene (Libya). . . .

Most striking to us, perhaps, is the very considerable place Pindar occupied in the Greek world of his day, even though that world was engaged in life-and-death struggles. To understand Pindar, we must first of all realize that his poetry, though written in celebration of athletic feats, was anything but purely "occasional" verse. Pindar never *describes* the feats he praises, nor does he tell us anything about the victors' lives. He aims at once for the highest meaning of the victory, its universal and symbolic implications for the whole of human life. He reaches this higher plane by associating the individual victory with a myth and with a moral teaching.

The openings of his poems are, in the truest sense of the word, brilliant. Often they invoke glory, divinity, gold—and these three are one, for glory is a gift of the gods and shines like gold. Sometimes the next phrase or two recall the victor's earlier successes or those of his relatives. But then, gathering all his forces, Pindar leaps without transition into the world of myth. . . .

It is clear, for one thing, that he sees instructional value in the myths. Unlike the epic poets, he does not *tell* the stories but merely evokes them by means of a few dazzling images; nor does he adhere to precise chronological order. Such evocations always yield either a reflection on the meaning of the world or a piece of advice. . . . The Argonauts' quest, in *Pythian* 4, has Cyrene as its point of departure; but its import—at least a part of its import—is to highlight the luminous figure of Jason with his resplendent blond curls, as he agrees to end the old feud with his uncle and embark on his quest: for "the fates stand aloof when there is hatred between those who share one blood." Pindar means on this occasion to recommend moderation and reconciliation to the king of Cyrene. . . .

On top of this, Pindar is self-conscious about the importance of his art. His asides on the subject are not confined to the power of music but extend to the making of a good poet and the role he should take in society. We even find references to Pindar's disputes with rival poets. All such observations confirm and contribute to the untrammeled quality of his poems. Yet this freedom he allows himself is justified insofar as the nature of poetry and the poet's responsibilities are proper concerns of ethics in general. Pindar's comments about poetry are related to the other moral judgments he expresses in his odes.

To reduce his work to a series of moral judgments, however, would be to distort it seriously. It consists, in the first place, of images—examples of all that is most beautiful and brilliant in human life. It celebrates the aristocrat's enjoyment of festivals and feasts. Yet these beauties and pleasures are always bathed, as it were, in a religious light; the gods grant them and preside over them. This is the source of sublimity in Pindar's lyrics, even when his images are most concrete. For example, at the beginning of *Pythian* 1, as he celebrates the power of music, he ascends in one sustained movement from the human to the divine sphere: "Golden lyre, common possession of Apollo and the dark-haired Muses, at your voice the rhythmic steps of dancers open the festival; and singers obey your signal when, vibrant with music, you cause to ring out the first notes of the preludes that lead choruses. You know too how to extinguish the eternal fire at the tip of the thunderbolt; and Zeus's eagle sleeps, perched on the scepter of the god." The thought that the gods exist is ever present in Pindar, expressed with a respect. . . .

At the same time, this perpetual confrontation between man and the gods dominates Pindar's philosophy and his ethics. He shares with the other poets of the archaic age a vivid sense of man's vulnerability; but, unlike them, he also has a sense of what man can become by the gods' grace. He makes this point repeatedly, but most brilliantly at the end of *Pythian* 8: "Creatures of a day! What is each of us? What is he not? Man is the dream of a shadow. But when the gods cast a ray of light on him, a great brightness surrounds him, and his life is sweet". . . . Pindar's continual references to the gods make for the grandeur of his odes, giving each victory song a hymnlike quality. . . .

In the realm of politics, as elsewhere, Pindar's thought is frankly conservative; where Solon struggles against inequity, Pindar asks only for harmony and peace. . . .

By respecting such virtues, man can hope to win the goodwill of the gods and a measure of prosperity. But there is also a way for him to earn an immortality of his own—glory—endorsed and generated by the work of the poet. So the poet's responsibility is great; he must never stray from the truth, for it is up to him to save from oblivion those who deserve to be remembered. . . . This conviction of Pindar's accounts for the majestic quality of his poems. . . .

Pindar found a rival in a man ten years his junior, Bacchylides. Bacchylides was a nephew of Simonides and, like him, a native of Ceos. It must have been his uncle who introduced him to Hieron; we know that the tyrant extended his patronage to both Pindar and Bacchylides. The younger poet's work was little known until the last years of the nineteenth century, when newly discovered papyri yielded fifteen of his epinician odes, along with some paeans and dithyrambs. His art, as revealed by these works, is much simpler than Pindar's: his panegyrics are truly poems of praise, his thought is clearly expressed, and Homer's influence is palpable. In a way, the fragments of Bacchylides seem to signal the transition from early lyric to tragedy; some of his dithyrambs include dialogues . . . and some were

This engraving is based on an old bust of the poet Pindar, whose odes immortalized many of Greece's winning Olympic athletes.

written entirely in dialogue form. . . .

Indeed, with Bacchylides we are nearing the end of the line of lyric poets. A few more names could be cited, including that of a woman, Corinna (not to mention Timocreon, who attacked Themistocles); but the great age of lyricism is past. One reason, undoubtedly, was that triumphs in sport occupied a lesser place in an age when the outstanding developments were intellectual; a more important reason was the growth of democracy, causing aristocratic festivals to be eclipsed by an art form whose audience and judges were to be the body of assembled citizens.

Selection 3

Early Greek Philosophy

Charles Freeman

Classical historian Charles Freeman here summarizes the earliest Greek philosophers and their principal ideas. In general, these thinkers are usually referred to as the Presocratics because they preceded the Athenian philospher Socrates. He rejected inquiry about the natural, physical world and preoccupied himself instead with ethical questions, such as: What is goodness? and How can someone attain virtue? This set the course of much of later philosophy, which increasingly dealt with ethical questions.

By contrast, the Presocratics did attempt to explain the meaning and underlying principles of the physical world; and in this respect, they were the first scientists as well as the first philosophers. (Philosophy and science did not become totally separate disciplines until much later.) As Freeman explains, most of these thinkers can be roughly grouped into distinct schools of thought. They included the Ionians (from Greek Ionia, i.e., the western coast of Asia Minor)—Thales, Anaximander, and Anaximenes—who searched for nature's underlying substance (physis); *the Eleatics—Parmenides and Zeno—who suggested that the only real things are those that the human mind can conceive and that the visible, changeable world of everyday life is an illu-sion masking an invisible, unchangeable reality (an idea that later influenced Plato's theory of Forms); the Pluralists—Empedocles, Leucippus, and Democritus—who saw the* visible *world as the true reality and attempted to explain its structure in material, mechanical terms (as, for instance, a sub-group, the Atomists, foreshadowed the modern atomic theory with their suggestion that material objects are composed of tiny, individual particles called atoms); and the Pythagoreans—followers of Pythagoras—who viewed the* physis *as numbers or mathematical relationships.*

*I*n 585, according to the historian Herodotus, a battle between the Medes and the Lydians had been brought to a sudden halt when the sky darkened with an eclipse of the sun. The combatants were so overawed that they made peace with each other. An equally remarkable fact, however, was that the eclipse was said to have been predicted by one Thales, a citizen of the Ionian city of Miletus. It is impossible to say now, from the fragmentary sources, whether Thales had genuinely predicted the eclipse or simply provided an explanation for it after it had happened. He may have been simply passing on material gathered by Babylonian astronomers, and his own picture of the cosmos, described below, would hardly have provided him with a means of prediction. However, the moment is often seen as the birth of Greek philosophy, with Thales . . . its founding father.

There is no one reason why Greek philosophy should have begun in the Ionian world. The

Excerpted from *Egypt, Greece, and Rome: Civilizations of the Ancient Mediterranean*, by Charles Freeman. Copyright © 1996 by Charles Freeman. Reprinted by permission of Oxford University Press.

cities of the Asian coast were the most prosperous of the sixth-century Greek world. Miletus was the richest of all and, like many of the others, had had a tyrant. After he had been overthrown a civil war had broken out. One of the factions in the war was known as 'The Perpetual Sailors,' and this underlines the fact that many Milesians must have travelled abroad in search of trade—to Egypt, for instance, and equally to some of the opulent and sophisticated civilizations of the east. Here they would have had the opportunity to observe different cultures and absorb the varying intellectual traditions of these surrounding peoples. This in itself may have shaken conventional assumptions and liberated fresh ways of thinking.

The Ionians

The names of three early thinkers of Miletus survive: Thales and two followers, Anaximander and Anaximenes. All were recorded as practical men. Thales had been involved in politics and had some engineering skills. Anaximander made a map of the known world. Anaximenes was remembered for his skills of observation of everyday things, such as how an oar broke through water and scattered phosphorescence. Philosophy, in fact, may have been only a secondary interest for them. What survives of their thought is very fragmentary and subject to continuing debate. They appear to have shared a belief that the world-system, the *kosmos*, was subject to a divine force which gave it an underlying and orderly background. Where they got this idea, which is a far cry from the Homeric world of gods, is unknown—possibly from eastern mythology. It proved fundamental to the speculations which followed.

Thales is known for his prediction of the eclipse, but he also seems to have been the first man to look for the origins of the *kosmos*. For Thales the basis of all things was water, on which the earth itself floated. There were Egyptian and Semitic creation stories in which the initial state was a waste of waters, but Thales may also have picked water because of its demonstrable importance to all human life.

What Thales appears to have been suggesting is that everything stems from this one originating source. It is not clear, however, whether Thales thought that all existing things could be broken down back into water or whether they had changed irreversibly into their new forms. . . .

Anaximander, a contemporary of Thales', concentrated on a problem which arose directly from Thales' speculation, the difficulty of understanding how a particular physical entity (fire is an example given) can possibly come from something which seems to be an opposite to it, water. The very fact that he spotted the problem and tried to find a reasoned solution to it is significant in itself. Anaximander's solution was to imagine an indeterminate substance from which everything developed. He called it 'the Boundless.' Anaximander saw 'the Boundless' not only as the origin of all material but with the separate function of surrounding the earth and keeping everything in balance. He seems to have believed that not only could water and fire never merge into each other but that they, like other opposites such as 'the dry' and 'the wet,' were actually in conflict with each other, and only an overriding force, 'the Boundless,' could keep them in check.

Anaximander's other contribution was to propose how the earth existed as a stable and unmoving object in space. Thales had argued that the earth rested on water, but this left the problem of what the water rested on. Anaximander proposed that there is no reason why anything which exists at the centre should necessarily move from that position. It cannot move in opposite directions at the same time and will thus always remain suspended in the centre. If this is Anaximander's argument (it is only recorded as such by Aristotle two hundred years later), then it is the first instance in natural science of what is known as the principle of sufficient reason (the principle that nothing happens without a reason).

What Anaximander did not explain was the process by which one form of matter, 'the Boundless,' became another. Was there a boundary between 'the Boundless' and the rest of the physical world or was 'the Boundless' in some form identical with the physical world? It was left to the third of the Milesian thinkers, Anaximenes, to suggest a solution. Anaximenes argued that the world consisted of one interchangeable matter, air, from which all physical objects derived. The transition of steam into water and then into ice provided an example. Harder substances, such as rock, consisted of air which had been condensed even further. For Anaximenes, air also had a spiritual quality. It was a substance which existed eternally whatever it might be temporarily transmuted into. Its special position could be seen from its importance in sustaining life, and here Anaximenes drew on a popular conception that death occurred because air had withdrawn from the human body.

If the universe did originate from one substance, the problem was how to reconcile this with the enormous diversity and sense of constant change that any observer of the physical world is confronted with. The question of diversity and disorder was posed by one of the most complex of the early philosophers, Heraclitus, who, like his forerunners, was an Ionian, from the city of Ephesus to the north of Miletus. He was active about 500 BC.

Heraclitus' work survives in about a hundred fragments, as if he wrote not in continuous prose or verse as other philosophers did but in a series of short and penetrating observations. . . . He explored the contradictions he perceived in the physical world. Salt water is drinkable for fish but undrinkable and deadly for men. Two very different properties exist in the same substance. The road which leads upwards also leads downwards. A stream remains a single entity even while the water which makes it up is constantly changing. In many cases a concept is intelligible only because there is an opposite to it. The concept of war is only meaningful if there is also one of peace. They are mutually dependent on each other, as also are night and day, winter and summer. Heraclitus went on, however, to argue that there was an overall coherence, *harmonie* (the Greek word meant the coming together of two different components to make a structure greater than its parts), in this world. What appears to be diversity in nature is in fact part of a natural unity. The opposites provide tensions but all is reconciled by a divine force, God. . . .

The Eleatics

Heraclitus was one of those who was happy to derive his ideas from the world he could observe around him. 'All that can be learnt by seeing and hearing, this I value highest,' as he put it in one fragment. The approach taken by his contemporary and philosophical rival Parmenides could not have been more different. Parmenides was born about 515 BC in Elea, a city in southern Italy which had been founded by exiles from another Ionian city, Phocaea. He may have been consciously challenging Heraclitus when he discarded observation about the physical world in favour of taking a lonely path towards finding truths based only on reason. The physical world, Parmenides argues, in the earliest piece of sustained philosophical argument to have survived, is made up only of what can be conceived in the mind. That and that alone exists. . . . What cannot be thought of has no existence whatsoever and nothing more can or need be said about it. Parmenides goes on from here to argue that what exists—a piece of rock, for instance—can only exist in that state. It cannot be conceived of in any pre- or post-rock state because then it would not have existed as it does now and what did not exist cannot be spoken of. Therefore, the rock and by analogy all existing things are unchangeable, caught in a perpetual present. Parmenides goes further to argue that as nothing cannot exist there cannot be empty space between objects—all things that exist are joined as one indivisible substance. The logical conclusion, therefore, is that the world is composed of one unchanging substance. This immediately contradicts what the senses have to say and opens up a chasm between the findings of reason and those of observation.

Parmenides' pupil Zeno went on to explore the paradoxes exposed by Parmenides' reasoning. One is that of the arrow in flight. To the senses the arrow appears to be moving. Yet logically, Zeno argued, it was not. The argument goes as follows. Everything is at rest when it is 'at a place equal to itself.' At each moment of time the arrow is always at 'a place equal to itself.' Therefore the arrow is always at rest. Equally a runner cannot run across a stadium until he has crossed half its length. He cannot reach half its length until he has covered a quarter and a quarter until he has covered an eighth and so on. Logically, he can never reach the end of the stadium.

Parmenides had shown that if a single incontrovertible starting-point can be taken, then it is possible to proceed deductively to demonstrate some contingent truth. This was a crucial step in the development of philosophical argument. His conclusions were deeply unsettling in themselves and acted to stimulate further thought across the Greek world. Plato, for instance, acknowledged the influence of Parmenides when he argued that there are unchanging entities, the Forms, which can only be approached through reason.

The Pluralists

One reaction to Parmenides was to enquire more closely into what it was that actually made up material objects. Empedocles of Acragas, for instance, who was at work in the mid-fifth century, aimed to reinstate the senses as a valid source for knowledge. Objects, he suggested, were not unchanging as Parmenides had argued. They come into being in their different forms according to a different mix of four elements, earth, water, air, and fire. Forces of what he called love and hate caused the perpetual disintegration and reformation of different materials but the four elements remain constant. (This theory continued to be influential in Europe as late as the seventeenth century.)

An alternative explanation to the problem of material objects was to assume that they could be divided into tiny particles which were themselves indivisible. (The Greeks used the word *atomos* for such a particle, hence 'atom'). The concept originated with the mid-fifth-century Leucippus, a native of Abdera, a small town in the northern Aegean founded by settlers from Ionia. Leucip-

pus broke completely with Parmenides to assert that 'nothing' *could* exist (a good statement then as now from which to start a philosophical argument) in the sense that there could be empty space between things. If this was accepted, matter did not have to be joined together in one undifferentiated mass and objects could move as there was empty space to move through. Leucippus and his younger contemporary Democritus, also from Abdera, went on to argue that the physical world was made up of atoms which were of the same substance but differed in shape and size. These atoms move at random (exploiting the empty spaces), but atoms of like size or shape tend to be attracted to each other and form material objects (Democritus even postulated that some were conveniently provided with hooks). So the world as it exists takes shape. Every object is made of the same substance arranged differently according to the form of its constituent atoms. Where the Atomists differed from earlier cosmologists was in their belief that the formation of the world was random. There is no mention of a guiding force behind it. The only things that exist are atoms and the empty spaces between them. This was the first developed statement of materialism, the theory that nothing which can be directly grasped by the senses exists beyond the material world. . . .

The Pythagoreans

A very different approach was provided by Pythagoras, another Ionian in origin, a native of the island of Samos. He was forced into exile in southern Italy, probably about 525 BC. Very little is known about Pythagoras' life, although a mass of later legend attaches to it. He was clearly a charismatic figure and drew around him a band of devoted followers who continued in existence long after his death and who inspired other similar groups in the cities of southern Italy. It has proved virtually impossible to distinguish between what Pythagoras himself taught and what was added later by the Pythagoreans. 'Pythagoras' theorem' of the right-angled triangle, for instance, seems to have had no direct connection with him (and was probably known, in essence, to the Babylonians many hundreds of years earlier).

The one teaching which is most likely to have been Pythagoras' own is that of the transmigration of the soul. Pythagoras appears to have believed that the soul exists as an immortal entity separately from the body. The body is simply its temporary home, and on the death of one body it moves on to another. What kind of body it moves on to depends on its behaviour in each life, for the soul is not only immortal, it is rational and responsible for its own actions. It must never let itself be conquered by the desires of the body. If it does then it will suffer in the next. Likewise, through correct behaviour it can move on to a happier existence. The Pythagoreans were therefore ascetics [people who reject material comforts and practice strict self-discipline], but unlike many with this leaning they never cut themselves off from the world. In fact, many Pythagoreans became deeply involved in politics, though the austerity of their beliefs often aroused opposition.

Although direct proof of any association of Pythagoras with mathematics is lacking, he is often linked with the theory that the structure of things rests on numbers. A single string spanning a sounding-box sounds a note when plucked. Halve the length of the string and pluck it again. The note is one octave higher. Metals mixed in certain proportions form new metals. The relationship between the parts of a 'perfect' human body can be calculated mathematically. Is it possible to argue from this that mathematical forms exist unseen behind all physical structures? The possibility that they do and can be grasped by a reasoning soul was to be taken up by Plato. The study of mathematics was to be the core of the education given to his aspiring philosophers.

The varied arguments of the early Greek thinkers were invigorating but deeply unsettling. Faced with the seeming absurdities of Parmenides' deductions, philosophy could be dismissed as no more than an intellectual game. It could be argued that 'truth,' if the concept could be said to exist at all, was something relative, dependent on the inadequate senses of individual observers or the ways in which they con-

structed their reasoned arguments. In the sixth century another Ionian, Xenophanes, had already made a similar point in a famous statement about the gods:

> Immortal men imagine that gods are begotten and that they have human dress and speech and shape. . . . If oxen or horses or lions had hands to draw with and to make works of art as men do, the horses would draw the forms of gods like horses, oxen like oxen, and they would make their gods' bodies similar to the bodily shape they themselves each had.

If the gods, to take Xenophanes' example, are the construction of human minds, it is a short step to argue that other concepts—goodness or justice, for instance—might also be. The fundamental question is then raised as to whether there could ever be any agreement over what the gods, or justice or goodness, might be. This was to be the central issue tackled by Socrates and Plato in the late fifth and early fourth centuries. . . .

The Search for Understanding

The success of Greek philosophy lay in its critical and argumentative approach to an extraordinary range of questions. As [scholar] Bernard Williams [in his article in the anthology *The Legacy of Greece*] has pointed out:

> In philosophy the Greeks initiated almost all its major fields—metaphysics, logic, the philosophy of language, the theory of knowledge, ethics, political philosophy and the philosophy of art. [Williams here is only referring to the concerns of modern philosophers—he might have added mathematics and science, included as 'philosophy' by the Greeks.] Not only did they start these areas of enquiry but they progressively distinguished what would still be recognised as many of the most basic questions in those areas.

It is worth noting that Williams concentrates on the Greeks as question *askers*. They did not always come up with very effective answers. There were good reasons for this. First, their speculations often ran far ahead of what their senses could cope with. It is sobering to realize that no Greek astronomer had any means of exploring the heavens other than his own eyes. (There were instruments developed for measuring angles, but they still depended on the naked eye for their use.) Aristotle's theory of spontaneous generation, the idea that life could come from nowhere, which lingered on as a misconception until the nineteenth century, arose largely because he had no way of seeing small objects. Not the least of the Greeks' philosophical achievements was, however, to recognize this inadequacy of the senses. The fifth-century philosopher Democritus got to the core of the problem when he constructed a dialogue between a mind and the senses. 'Wretched mind, taking your proofs from us (the senses), do you overthrow us? Our overthrow will be your fall.'

'Early Greek philosophy,' writes [noted scholar] Martin West:

was not a single vessel which a succession of pilots commanded and tried to steer towards an agreed destination, one tacking one way, the next altering course in the light of his own perceptions. It was more like a flotilla of small craft whose navigators did not all start from the same point or at the same time, nor all aim for the same goal; some went in groups, some were influenced by the movements of others, some travelled out of sight of each other.

In short, the Greek world of the sixth century fostered an intellectual curiosity and creativity which took many forms. The Archaic age deserves to be seen as one where a particular attitude of mind took root. . . . It involved the search for an understanding of the physical world free of the restraints imposed by those cultures which still lived in the shadow of threatening gods.

Selection 4

Hippocrates and Greek Medicine

Philip Wheelwright

Greek medical theory and practice in the fifth and fourth centuries B.C. constituted an important aspect of philosophic-scientific inquiry. Just as the Ionian, Pythagorean, and Pluralist philosophers searched for the physical principles underlying the natural world, the members of the medical school founded by Hippocrates sought to understand the physical realities of health and disease. In particular, the Hippocratic belief that health and disease have natural causes and can be manipulated by human intervention marked a giant step away from supernatural explanations and toward a rational scientific approach. Philip Wheelwright, formerly of the University of California, Riverside, here outlines the major Hippocratic ideas and methods.

*I*n addition to and largely independent of the explicit philosophical theories—the recognized philosophers and schools of philosophy . . . there are always present in any culture various marks of implicit philosophy. By implicit philosophy is meant that which expresses itself not so much in definite propositions and arguments supporting them, but rather as the not fully probed assumptions, overtones, and outcomes of modes of living and shared aspirations. Ancient medicine, in particular, is often thus implicitly philosophical. Medical practice may give rise, in a reflective physician, to wonder about the essential nature of the human body, and hence about the human mind, which appears to have been generated out of the body's more developed activities and yet is able to win some degree of control over it. Thus medical theory on the one hand is rooted in human needs, sometimes needs of the greatest urgency, while on the other hand it points toward unsolved questions about human life which in their fuller implications are metaphysical.

The most considerable body of medical writings that has come down from ancient Greece is that associated with the name of Hippocrates (460–390 B.C.). On his native island of Cos Hippocrates founded what was probably the first school of medicine dedicated unflinchingly to the investigation and application of scientific principles. The extant writings of that school constitute what is called the Hippocratic Corpus; although their individual authorship is undiscoverable in most cases, they are apparently typical expressions of the methods employed by that school of physicians and of their resulting speculations. At any rate, for convenience and by accepted custom, we shall use the name of Hippocrates when referring to the authors of the excerpts.

Although Hippocrates never organized the philosophical principles of his thinking, and although it is impossible to be sure how much of the Corpus was written by the master himself and how much by medical disciples, we can best think of his philosophy as resting upon a pair of complementary propositions: (a) *Health is the natural state, disease is unnatural*; and (b) *Disease, no less than health, is governed by natural causes*, which it is the task of the physician to understand. Are these two propositions contradictory? In discovering the sense in which they are consistent from Hippocrates' point of view, and are to him equally important sides of the truth about human organisms, we take an important step into an understanding of his philosophy.

To describe health as "natural" has for Hippocrates a very specific meaning. Living nature is telic [purposeful], it moves toward certain discoverable biological goals. Referring to the cycle of births and deaths which marks the career of every living species Hippocrates postulates that each organism tends by nature to play its part in that cycle in a healthy manner, appropriately to the species of which it is a member, unless something hinders. When a creature is injured or falls ill, provided that its departure from normal is not unduly severe, it tends by the force of its own living nature to heal the injured part and to restore the balance that is health. Since this is so, the role of the physician as Hippocrates conceives it is not to manipulate the patient as one would handle something inanimate, but to remove, both from within and from outside the patient's body, obstructions to healthy recovery. The essential relation is not dyadic [two-fold], he holds, but triadic [three-fold]: the physician, the patient, and the disease.

Defining the Physician's Task

But if there is one sense in which health is the natural state, there is also a sense in which disease likewise is a part of nature. For the possibility of understanding disease lies, Hippocrates insists, in the fact that disease is not entirely haphazard, however it may appear superficially, but follows patterns of development which in general, if not always in detail, can be traced. What, then, is the physician's task with respect to it? Hippocrates defines that task in terms of arranging the bodily and environmental conditions so that the disease can go through its own peculiar cycle as expeditiously and safely as possible. Proper food and drink, calmness of mind and body, suitable exercise, and the like, are among the chief ways in which the bodily conditions can be made as favorable as possible to the speedy and firm completion of the cycle through illness and back again to health.

When illness begins it is marked by an excess of some bodily element over the rest—say an excess of heat, as in a fever, or of moisture as in dropsy. This excessive element is an intruder and a usurper: it must be either expelled or sent back to its proper place in the bodily complex. The physical body contains within itself the forces of healing, which act generally by a process called *pepsis*, which can be translated both as coction or cooking and as digestion. The physician must learn its character and role with respect to the particular patient and disease with which he is concerned. The wise physician will know when to try to aid and accelerate the peptic process and when to let it alone. The situation differs in different organisms; the physician cannot work by strict rule, but must watch for the "opportune moment" (*kairos*) when the situation is exactly right for the exercise of his art. There comes at some point the "crisis" (*krisis*), the moment at which the balance is ready to be tipped either way—so that the patient succumbs to the disproportionate mixture or so that the healthy forces begin to regain their ascendancy and the patient begins to recover. Since health was regarded as a right proportion of the elements in the organic body, and any ailment or disease as a disproportion, it was logical to regard the *krisis* as somehow marking a change, or the beginning of a change, from disproportion to proportion. Such a change involves, by Greek medical logic, a "washing away" (*katharsis*, *katharmos*) of the superfluous elements that caused the disproportion and the reestablishment of the new "blended maturity" (*krasis*) which is health.

But what precisely is it that by becoming excessive or defective produces variations of health? What is it that gets washed away, catharated, as a step in the curing of illness, or gets built up by proper regimen? To ask this question is to ask, in Aristotle's later terminology, about the nature of the "material cause." What are the material factors, the bodily ingredients, whose right proportion constitutes health? The Pythagorean physicians at Crotona conceived such ingredients in terms of pairs of contrary qualities, explaining health accordingly as a right proportion and blend of moisture and dryness, of cold and heat, etc., in the body. The physicians who were influenced by Empedocles, in the so-called Sicilian school of medicine, conceived their problem in terms of the four basic substances: too much earth in the human body and psyche was taken to be the cause both of constipation and of general lethargy, too much water as causing either catarrhal [inflammation and discharge from the nose and throat] and other discharges or in extreme cases dropsy [swelling caused by an accumulation of fluids], too much fire as causing both bodily fever and ecstatic mental genius. Hippocrates criticized both of these medical groups for making assumptions which could not be sufficiently tested and for seeking their explanations in areas too remote from the perceptible facts of bodily life. What we actually find within the body, he said, are "flowing juices"; which he classified (on the basis of such physiological observations as it was then possible to make) as blood, yellow bile, black bile, and phlegm. The Greek word for flowing juice was *chymos*, which later got taken into the Latin language as "*humor*," and the subsequent "doctrine of humors" in European medical theory had a long and quaint history. But the Greek word in Hippocrates' time meant simply "that which flows"; and the doctrine as he and his followers developed it represents in essence a first step toward a science of physiological chemistry.

Selection 5

Socrates and Plato Examine the Human Condition

Michael Grant

The life and teachings of Socrates marked a great watershed in the evolution of Greek philosophy. He devoted his life to studying and questioning the beliefs and behavior of his fellow citizens and to seeking definitions for ethical concepts such as goodness and justice, all aimed at the practical end of achieving "right living" and thereby happiness. In his view, "the unexamined life is not worth living." Plato, one of Socrates' pupils and one of the most influential thinkers in history, immortalized his mentor in many of his dialogues, works in which two or more characters (one of them often Socrates) seek definitions and truths about a wide variety of issues and concepts. Noted Edinburgh University scholar Michael Grant here summarizes Socrates' life and ideas and then provides a useful overview of Plato's major works, while explaining the influences that shaped his thought.

Reprinted with the permission of Weidenfeld & Nicolson and of Scribner, a division of Simon & Schuster, from *The Founders of the Western World: A History of Greece and Rome*, by Michael Grant. Copyright © 1991 by Michael Grant Publications Ltd.

Socrates (*c*.470–399), a contemporary of [the Greek physician] Hippocrates, wrote nothing himself, and it is very hard to disentangle his true opinions from what Aristophanes, Xenophon and Plato wrote about him. He was on close terms, it appears, with Pericles's friends, and in his youth listened to Archelaus, an Athenian pupil of the philosopher-scientist Anaxagoras. But then Socrates turned away from cosmology, and spent the rest of his life enquiring into a matter which had begun to interest some of his predecessors, namely human behaviour: and what he particularly tried to do was to define what makes it right or wrong.

The most important of his beliefs was the conviction that there is an eternal and unchanging *absolute standard* of right and wrong—in conformity with which we must try to make our souls as good as possible. To do this, however, we must listen to our consciences, and use our brains to work out what is, indeed, right and wrong. For *virtue is knowledge:* know yourself, for no one does wrong willingly. This was a striking, if logically dubious, conclusion, and so was the 'teleological' belief (probably attributable to Socrates, as his followers maintained) that all nature works towards a purpose.

He himself, he ironically declared, knew

nothing, but—with the exception of the two dogmas that have just been mentioned—he tried to arrive at the truth through rational enquiry, pursued by the 'Socratic method' of cross-questioning. Although scrupulous in observing his city's religious observances, he deplored immoral myths, and claimed, on occasion, to be guided by a divine sign or voice (*daimonion*).

His physical stamina was remarkable, and despite his love of irony, which could cause offence, he was genial and charming and kind, and possessed a varied and devoted circle of friends. Many of them came from the younger members of the upper class; Socrates never thought highly of the democratic form of government practised at Athens, and said so. When, therefore, this democracy was revived, after the end of the Peloponnesian War, he found himself brought to trial on a capital charge (399). The real, underlying accusation, however—his undemocratic political views—could not be admitted, since an amnesty was by this time in force. It was therefore declared, instead, 'that he does not believe in the gods in whom the city believes, but introduces other and new deities; also that he corrupts the young.' He was found guilty by 281 votes to 220. At that juncture, as earlier, he could have got away from Athens, but did not avail himself of this opportunity, since he regarded it as his civic obligation to remain in the city. Instead of escaping, therefore, he made a speech in court, suggesting that he should be maintained for life as a public benefactor. The jury felt insulted by what sounded like flippancy, and he was condemned to death. And so he drank the poisonous hemlock, and died. Eternally significant because he perished in the cause of freedom of conscience, he created the gigantic and potent Socratic legend.

One of his pupils was Plato (*c.*429–347), who, disgusted by his teacher's condemnation and execution, fled, after Socrates' death, to join other philosophical leaders elsewhere, Euclides of Megara and Archytas of Taras (Taranto) in South Italy.

Archytas, who successfully ruled his powerful city from *c.*380 to *c.*345, revived and rejuvenated the philosophical school of Pythagoras, and was himself virtually the founder of mathematical mechanics: mathematical calculation alone, he observed, is able to breed confidence among men and prevent strife. Plato absorbed Archytas's writings in this field, appreciating their application to ethics and the social order, and other Pythagorean features perceptible in Platonic dialogues bear witness once again to the same man's influence. Plato also paid three visits to Sicily, hoping to purify and philosophize the political life of Syracuse, under Dionysius I (405–367) and his nephew Dionysius II (367–357/6). These expeditions, however, were humiliating failures, especially on the last occasion, in 361, when he was detained and had to appeal to Archytas to secure his release.

Questions Posed in the Dialogues

After the first of the three Sicilian visits Plato had founded his Academy at Athens, where he taught, when not travelling, from that time onwards. Several of his works are related to the trial of Socrates, in an imaginative fashion which does not invite too keen a search for strict historical truth. *The Apology* [not in dialogue form] is an idealized account of Socrates' trial, and a moving defence, in effect, of his entire life work. *Crito* discusses why Socrates, by his behaviour in court, threw his life away, and raises the whole question of what is right and wrong in relation to the state. In *Euthyphro*, Socrates is made to declare that true religion is not subservience to arbitrary demands but cooperation in the noble tending of the soul. In *Phaedo*, on the last day of his life, he is credited with the hypothesis that the immortality of the soul is a reasonable doctrine. Here, once again, is a doctrine Plato had probably learnt from Archytas.

Other Platonic dialogues, which do not deal directly with Socrates's trial and death, nevertheless present him, imaginatively, as the principal interlocutor [member of the discussion], devoting himself to questionings that are 'aporetic' (full of puzzles). The *Charmides* shows him

*This famous painting by the eighteenth-century French artist Jacques Louis David (dah-VEED)
dramatically captures the moment when Socrates prepares to drink poison hemlock.*

talking to a young man of that name, Plato's purpose, indirectly, being to clear him of the accusation that he corrupted Athenian youth. *Charmides* seeks to define temperance or self-control (*sophrosyne*), and *Laches* likewise attempts to reach a definition of courage. *Menexenus* (385) is amusingly scathing about the epoch of Pericles, whose mistress Aspasia talks with Socrates about the Corinthian War. But that war had taken place in 395–387, long after both Aspasia and Socrates were dead—which is a warning against attempts to regard Plato's dialogues as historically authentic.

Meno asks us to consider whether virtue is teachable or not. This is, of course, relevant to the sophists . . . about whom Plato has a lot of interesting, and often rather unfair, things to say, since he disapproves of their amoral attitudes and their frivolous logic-chopping (rebuked in *Euthydemus*), not to speak of their acceptance of

fees. True, *Protagoras* offers a not wholly unjust picture of the teacher of that name. But one of his colleagues is less respectfully treated in *Greater* and *Lesser Hippias*, and in *Gorgias* Socrates is made to maintain that the rhetoric taught by the eminent sophist of that name was no more than an expedient knack, far removed from the absolute standard our conscience ought to enjoin upon us.

Amid a homosexual aura (though that, we are told, had not been Socrates's personal taste), the dramatic, subtle and witty *Symposium* professes to record the various speeches in praise of Love (Eros) delivered—in accordance with the oratorical tradition of such gatherings—at a banquet in honour of the tragic playwright Agathon. But the main purpose of the work is to show . . . how love, at first excited by a beautiful body, can finally and rapturously rise to a super-sensuous, transcendental passion for abstract beauty itself, which only the intellect can apprehend. *Cratylus*, though roughly of the same date, turns to an entirely different subject. It amounts to our first etymological treatise, concluding that language . . . is a genuine instrument of thought, capable of expressing even the most ideal kinds of thinking with accuracy, and therefore of vital assistance in enabling us to get at the truth. . . .

And then there are dialogues in which Socrates is no longer the central figure. In the abstruse [difficult to understand] . . . *Timaeus* his place is taken by an astronomer of that name, from Locri Epizephyrii in south-east Italy, who returns to the Parmenidean attitude, treating the mutable temporal world as only a pale imitation of unchanging eternal being. A monotheistic god is introduced as the intelligent, effective director of this whole providential, moral order, although he, or it, sometimes operates in incomprehensible and apparently aberrant fashions. In *Sophist* the principal spokesman is an unnamed follower of Parmenides (from his home town, Elea): yet, in spite of the *Timaeus*, the Parmenidean theory that the material world is a mere illusion is rejected after all. And then, *Philebus*—in which Socrates reappears as principal speaker—sums up Plato's final thoughts on ethics and the good life, which is a matter, he concludes, of both intelligence and pleasure, with intelligence occupying the major role.

Plato was impressed by Socrates's insistence on absolute standards, which he himself linked with the belief . . . variously discussed in his own works, that even if our senses are not a mere illusion there is a divine and unchanging reality transcending them. This was the doctrine that lay behind the Theory of Forms (*ideai*) which appeared again and again in Plato's thinking, though in his later dialogues it assumed a modified and less clear-cut shape. These Forms, apprehended by the intellect and crowned by the highest Form of all, the Form of the Good, are permanent, unvarying, eternal realities—which have given Plato his renown as the archetypal idealistic philosopher—in contrast to the shifting, imperfect, material phenomena (perceived by the senses) which 'participate' in the Forms, or, as Plato later said, 'imitate' them.

One can see why he is so fascinated by Parmenides's rejection of these material phenomena as unreal, in contrast to the eternal realities. But Plato himself, for all his insistence on those immutable realities, does not himself join in any such rejection, for he finds a bridge between them and the material world: and that bridge is the soul, as envisaged by Socrates as present in all individual persons, in whom it reflects the whole macrocosm [larger world] of the universe and enables its possessors to reach upwards and grasp the unchanging principles by which the universe is governed. Moreover, like Socrates once again, he adopts the teleological view that everything has its purpose, seeing the well-being of the individual soul, at its greatest and best, as the natural end (*telos*) of all movement and endeavour.

Plato's Political Views

Such were the various motivations that prompted Plato not only to intervene himself, disastrously, in the political affairs of Sicily, but also to earn the lasting interest of the western world by conceiving and offering theoretical views on political matters, and particularly on what might be the nature of a state's ideal constitution.

His major statements on such themes, widely separated in date, were the *Republic* (*Politeia*), *Statesman* (*Politicos*) and *Laws*. The ten books of the *Republic* (380s or 370s BC), blending politics, ethics and metaphysics in a complex, intoxicating spirit of crusading passion, are concerned with the nature of justice. It is shown, in a series of discussions led by Socrates, to be beneficial to all concerned, rationally defensible, and morally imperative: so that Thrasymachus's counter-definition of the concept as the advantage of the stronger is refuted.

Plato's imaginary ideal state is governed by guardians, who are presided over by a 'philosophical king' (for whom Archytas served as a model), and possess their wives, children and property in common. There will be three classes of citizens, each performing its proper function, and persuaded to do so, if necessary, by 'noble lies'. All political change is an illness (assuming its most virulent form in tyranny), and educational innovation is wrong, too, since it leads to cultural licence—of which poetry is an extreme example, being an imitation alien from truth, whereas mathematics, on the other hand, provides the ideal subject of instruction.

Plato's *Statesman* (360s), bringing back the *Sophist's* Eleatic interlocutor, reaffirms the evils of tyranny, but, as an alternative, considers democracy inferior to elective monarchy. The *Laws* settles, in what some have seen as a disillusioned afterthought, for a second-best state. Communism is, in practice, abandoned, and a mixed constitution seems a suitable compromise. A hierarchy [ladder of authority] of functionaries, directed by a meticulous system of checks and balance, culminates in thirty-seven Guardians of the Law. But there is also to be a Nocturnal Council, presiding over a House of Corrections where delinquents are argued with or, if that proves useless, put to death. For citizens must maintain unwavering obedience to the rules. And these, incidentally—in the true spirit of the Greek *polis*—take for granted a continual state of undeclared war between one state and another, so that peace is a meaningless term.

Utilitarianism, the theory that action is right if it achieves the greatest good of the greatest number, has claimed Plato as its founder, owing to his desire to secure the welfare of the whole community. Yet as his *Statesman* and other writings showed, he was no friend of the democrats, any more than his master Socrates had been. Furthermore, his desire that people should be governed by Reason—and that they should be induced, if necessary, to accept this government by coercive means, since reasoning is not their natural inclination—prompted him to recommend the enforcement of authoritarian regulations: including, for example, rigorous controls of the teaching of music, art, and . . . poetry, so as to leave no room for emotional licence.

Our own minds, however, are easily distracted from the distaste that we may feel for such views, owing to Plato's superlative mastery of Greek prose, displayed by a potent, graceful, versatile style, ringing all the changes from humorous lightness to heartfelt solemnity. Plato employs the dialogue form with alluring skill, unpacks a wealth of sparkling, poetical metaphors, and shows himself a master of mythical and allegorical narrative, which he utilizes to convey otherwise scarcely expressible profundities.

Selection 6

A Friend Remembers Socrates

Xenophon

As a young man, the noted soldier, historian, and country gentleman Xenophon was a follower of the controversial Athenian philosopher Socrates. Supposedly, Xenophon met Socrates in the street when the older man stopped him and asked where he could find certain common goods. After the boy told him, Socrates asked, "Where can one find brave and good men?" for which Xenophon had no ready answer. Intrigued, in the years that followed the young man spent many hours listening to and learning from Socrates.

*Away in Asia when Socrates was tried and condemned to death (399 B.C.), Xenophon pieced together what had happened from friends and ever after remained sad and troubled over the loss of his former mentor, whom he called, "All that a truly good and happy man must be." (*Memorabilia *4.8.11) This explains his motivation for writing three separate works about his old friend— the* Symposium, Apology, *and* Memorabilia. *The following excerpt from the opening of the* Memorabilia *begins with the outright dismissal of the charges that had brought Socrates to trial. Then Xenophon tells how the philosopher rejected speculations about the cosmos, which had long preoccupied other thinkers; recalls some of the typical ethical questions that concerned him; describes his self-discipline and how he urged others to achieve personal excellence; and how unscrupulous characters like Alcibiades (who became a traitor to his homeland) and Critias (who became one of the hated Thirty Tyrants) followed Socrates only to improve their speaking and arguing abilities and thereby to further their own selfish political ambitions.*

? have often wondered by what arguments those who drew up the indictment against Socrates could persuade the Athenians that his life was forfeit to the state. The indictment against him was to this effect: *Socrates is guilty of rejecting the gods acknowledged by the state and of bringing in strange deities: he is also guilty of corrupting the youth.*

First then, that he rejected the gods acknowledged by the state—what evidence did they produce of that? He offered sacrifices constantly, and made no secret of it, now in his home, now at the altars of the state temples, and he made use of divination with as little secrecy. Indeed it had become notorious that Socrates claimed to be guided by 'the deity': it was out of this claim, I think, that the charge of bringing in strange deities arose. He was no more bringing in anything strange than are other believers in divination, who rely on augury [foretelling the future through interpreting the behavior of birds], oracles, coincidences and sacrifices. For these men's belief is not that the birds or the folk met by accident know what profits the inquirer, but that they are the instruments by which the gods make this known; and that was Socrates' belief too. Only, whereas most men say that the birds or the folk they meet dissuade or encourage them, Socrates said what he meant: for he said that the deity gave him a sign. Many of his companions were counselled by him to do this or not to do that in accordance with the warnings of the deity: and those who followed his advice prospered, and those who rejected it had cause for regret. And yet who would not admit that he wished to appear neither a knave nor a fool to his companions? but he would have been thought both, had he proved to be mistaken when he alleged that his counsel was in accordance with divine revelation. Obviously, then, he would not have given the counsel if he had not been confident that what he said would come true. And who could have inspired him with that confidence but a god? And since he had confidence in the gods, how can he have disbelieved in the existence of the gods? Another way he had of dealing with intimate friends was this: if there was no room for doubt, he advised them to act as they thought best; but if the consequences could not be foreseen, he sent them to the oracle to inquire whether the thing ought to be done. . . .

Students of Human Nature

Moreover, Socrates lived ever in the open; for early in the morning he went to the public promenades and training-grounds; in the forenoon he was seen in the market; and the rest of the day

Excerpted from Xenophon, *Memorabilia and Oeconomicus*, translated by E.C. Marchant (New York: Putnam, 1923).

he passed just where most people were to be met: he was generally talking, and anyone might listen. Yet none ever knew him to offend against piety and religion in deed or word. He did not even discuss that topic so favoured by other talkers, "the Nature of the Universe": and avoided speculation on the so-called "Cosmos" of the Professors, how it works, and on the laws that govern the phenomena of the heavens: indeed he would argue that to trouble one's mind with such problems is sheer folly. In the first place, he would inquire, did these thinkers suppose that their knowledge of human affairs was so complete that they must seek these new fields for the exercise of their brains; or that it was their duty to neglect human affairs and consider only things divine? Moreover, he marvelled at their blindness in not seeing that man cannot solve these riddles; since even the most conceited talkers on these problems did not agree in their theories, but behaved to one another like madmen. As some madmen have no fear of danger and others are afraid where there is nothing to be afraid of, as some will do or say anything in a crowd with no sense of shame, while others shrink even from going abroad among men, some respect neither temple nor altar nor any other sacred thing, others worship stocks and stones and beasts, so is it, he held, with those who worry with "Universal Nature." Some hold that *What is* is one, others that it is infinite in number: some that all things are in perpetual motion, others that nothing can ever be moved at any time: some that all life is birth and decay, others that nothing can ever be born or ever die. Nor were those the only questions he asked about such theorists. Students of human nature, he said, think that they will apply their knowledge in due course for the good of themselves and any others they choose. Do those who pry into heavenly phenomena imagine that, once they have discovered the laws by which these are produced, they will create at their will winds, waters, seasons and such things to their need? Or have they no such expectation, and are they satisfied with knowing the causes of these various phenomena?

Such, then, was his criticism of those who meddle with these matters. His own conversation was ever of human things. The problems he discussed were, What is godly, what is ungodly; what is beautiful, what is ugly; what is just, what is unjust; what is prudence, what is madness; what is courage, what is cowardice; what is a state, what is a statesman; what is government, and what is a governor;—these and others like them, of which the knowledge made a "gentleman," in his estimation, while ignorance should involve the reproach of "slavishness."

So, in pronouncing on opinions of his that were unknown to them it is not surprising that the jury erred: but is it not astonishing that they should have ignored matters of common knowledge? For instance, when he was on the Council and had taken the counsellor's oath by which he bound himself to give counsel in accordance with the laws, it fell to his lot to preside in the Assembly when the people wanted to condemn Thrasyllus and Erasinides and their colleagues to death by a single vote. That was illegal, and he refused the motion in spite of popular rancour and the threats of many powerful persons. It was more to him that he should keep his oath than that he should humour the people in an unjust demand and shield himself from threats. For, like most men, indeed, he believed that the gods are heedful of mankind, but with an important difference; for whereas they do not believe in the omniscience of the gods, Socrates thought that they know all things, our words and deeds and secret purposes; that they are present everywhere, and grant signs to men of all that concerns man.

I wonder, then, how the Athenians can have been persuaded that Socrates was a freethinker, when he never said or did anything contrary to sound religion, and his utterances about the gods and his behaviour towards them were the words and actions of a man who is truly religious and deserves to be thought so.

No less wonderful is it to me that some believed the charge brought against Socrates of corrupting the youth. In the first place, apart from what I have said, in control of his own passions and appetites he was the strictest of men; further, in endurance of cold and heat and every kind of toil he was most resolute; and besides, his needs were so schooled to moderation that having very little he was yet very content. Such was his own character: how then can he have led others into impiety, crime, gluttony, lust, or sloth? On the contrary, he cured these vices in many, by putting into them a desire for goodness, and by giving them confidence that self-discipline would make them gentlemen. To be sure he never professed to teach this; but, by letting his own light shine, he led his disciples to hope that they through imitation of him would attain to such excellence. Furthermore, he himself never neglected the body, and reproved such neglect in others. Thus overeating followed by over-exertion he disapproved. But he approved of taking as much hard exercise as is agreeable to the soul; for the habit not only insured good health, but did not hamper the care of the soul. On the other hand, he disliked foppery and pretentiousness in the fashion of clothes or shoes or in behaviour. Nor, again, did he encourage love of money in his companions. For while he checked their other desires, he would not make money himself out of their desire for his companionship. He held that this self-denying ordinance insured his liberty. Those who charged a fee for their society he denounced for selling themselves into bondage; since they were bound to converse with all from whom they took the fee. He marvelled that anyone should make money by the profession of virtue, and should not reflect that his highest reward would be the gain of a good friend; as though he who became a true gentleman could fail to feel deep gratitude for a benefit so great. Socrates indeed never promised any such boon to anyone; but he was confident that those of his companions who adopted his principles of conduct would throughout life be good friends to him and to one another. How, then, should such a man "corrupt the youth"? Unless, perchance, it be corruption to foster virtue. . . .

Among the associates of Socrates were Critias and Alcibiades; and none wrought so many evils to the state. For Critias in the days of the oligarchy bore the palm for greed and violence: Alcibiades, for his part, exceeded all in licentiousness and insolence under the democracy. Now I have no intention of excusing the wrong these two men wrought the state; but I will explain how they came to be with Socrates. Ambition was the very life-blood of both: no Athenian was ever like them. They were eager to get control of everything and to outstrip every rival in notoriety. They knew that Socrates was living on very little, and yet was wholly independent; that he was strictly moderate in all his pleasures; and that in argument he could do what he liked with any disputant. Sharing this knowledge and the principles I have indicated, is it to be supposed that these two men wanted to adopt the simple life of Socrates, and with this object in view sought his society? Did they not rather think that by associating with him they would attain the utmost proficiency in speech and action? For my part I believe that, had heaven granted them the choice between the life they saw Socrates leading and death, they would have chosen rather to die. Their conduct betrayed their purpose; for as soon as they thought themselves superior to their fellow-disciples they sprang away from Socrates and took to politics; it was for political ends that they had wanted Socrates.

But it may be answered: Socrates should have taught his companions prudence before politics. I do not deny it; but I find that all teachers show their disciples how they themselves practise what they teach, and lead them on by argument. And I know that it was so with Socrates: he showed his companions that he was a gentleman himself, and talked most excellently of goodness and of all things that concern man. I know further that even those two were prudent so long as they were with Socrates, not from fear of fine or blow, but because at that time they really believed in prudent conduct.

Selection 7

Why Philosophers Should Rule

Plato

In his Republic, *often deemed his masterpiece, Plato envisions an ideal society that is, in his view, more efficient and just than any of those so far devised by human ingenuity. He states that ordinary men are unfit to rule because they have not been properly educated, more specifically in a moral sense. Only philosophers, he says, have been enlightened by the "blinding light" of the true knowledge of moral precepts, especially goodness and justice, and how these should be fairly applied to all members of the community.*

To illustrate why philosophers are the best suited of all people to rule, in Book Seven Plato presents a fascinating analogy, usually referred to as the "Myth of the Cave," excerpted here. Through the character of Socrates (who converses with a character named Glaucon), Plato describes ordinary people as living in a state of unenlightened ignorance. He likens that state to a group of pitiful individuals chained inside of a dark cave. They wrongly assume that the distorted images perceived by their senses in the cave are the real world because they are completely unaware that a wider, well-lit world of "reality" and "truth" exists beyond. Only when a person with a mind

trained to see and understand the light (i.e., reality and truth) leads them up into the daylight will they, like him, become enlightened. That trained person, of course, is the philosopher. (Later in the dialogue, Plato explains that the way to train oneself is to master subjects that deal with abstract ideas, such as arithmetic, geometry, and astronomy; finally, the soul will be liberated and capable of comprehending the Idea, or true nature, of concepts like goodness.) Thus, Plato concludes, only philosophers, who have achieved true enlightenment, are fit to rule.

"**n**ext, then," I [Socrates] said, "take the following parable of education and ignorance as a picture of the condition of our nature. Imagine mankind as dwelling in an underground cave with a long entrance open to the light across the whole width of the cave; in this they have been from childhood, with necks and legs fettered, so they have to stay where they are. They cannot move their heads round because of the fetters, and they can only look forward, but light comes to them from fire burning behind them higher up at a distance. Between the fire and the prisoners is a road above their level, and along it imagine a low wall has been built, as puppet showmen have screens in front of their people over which they work their puppets."

"I see," he said.

"See, then, bearers carrying along this wall all sorts of articles which they hold projecting above the wall, statues of men and other living things, made of stone or wood and all kinds of stuff, some of the bearers speaking and some silent, as you might expect."

"What a remarkable image," he said, "and what remarkable prisoners!"

"Just like ourselves," I said. "For, first of all, tell me this: What do you think such people would have seen of themselves and each other except their shadows, which the fire cast on the opposite wall of the cave?"

"I don't see how they could see anything else," said he, "if they were compelled to keep their heads unmoving all their lives!"

"Very well, what of the things being carried along? Would not this be the same?"

"Of course it would."

"Suppose the prisoners were able to talk together, don't you think that when they named the shadows which they saw passing they would believe they were naming things?"

"Necessarily."

"Then if their prison had an echo from the opposite wall, whenever one of the passing bearers uttered a sound, would they not suppose that the passing shadow must be making the sound? Don't you think so?"

"Indeed I do," he said.

"If so," said I, "such persons would certainly believe that there were no realities except those shadows of handmade things."

"So it must be," said he.

"Now consider," said I, "what their release would be like, and their cure from these fetters and their folly; let us imagine whether it might naturally be something like this. One might be released, and compelled suddenly to stand up and turn his neck round, and to walk and look towards the firelight; all this would hurt him, and he would be too much dazzled to see distinctly those things whose shadows he had seen before. What do you think he would say, if someone told him that what he saw before was foolery, but now he saw more rightly, being a bit nearer reality and turned towards what was a little more

real? What if he were shown each of the passing things, and compelled by questions to answer what each one was? Don't you think he would be puzzled, and believe what he saw before was more true than what was shown to him now?"

"Far more," he said.

"Then suppose he were compelled to look towards the real light, it would hurt his eyes, and he would escape by turning them away to the things which he was able to look at, and these he would believe to be clearer than what was being shown to him."

"Just so," said he.

Forced into the Sunlight of Reality

"Suppose, now," said I, "that someone should drag him thence by force, up the rough ascent, the steep way up, and never stop until he could drag him out into the light of the sun, would he not be distressed and furious at being dragged; and when he came into the light, the brilliance would fill his eyes and he would not be able to see even one of the things now called real?"

"That he would not," said he, "all of a sudden."

"He would have to get used to it, surely, I think, if he is to see the things above. First he would most easily look at shadows, after that images of mankind and the rest in water, lastly the things themselves. After this he would find it easier to survey by night the heavens themselves and all that is in them, gazing at the light of the stars and moon, rather than by day the sun and the sun's light."

"Of course."

"Last of all, I suppose, the sun; he could look on the sun itself by itself in its own place, and see what it is like, not reflections of it in water or as it appears in some alien setting."

"Necessarily," said he. . . .

"Very good. Let him be reminded of his first habitation, and what was wisdom in that place, and of his fellow-prisoners there; don't you think he would bless himself for the change, and pity them?"

"Yes, indeed.". . .

"Then again," I said, "just consider; if such a one should go down again and sit on his old seat, would he not get his eyes full of darkness coming in suddenly out of the sun?"

"Very much so," said he.

"And if he should have to compete with those who had been always prisoners, by laying down the law about those shadows while he was blinking before his eyes were settled down—and it would take a good long time to get used to things—wouldn't they all laugh at him and say he had spoiled his eyesight by going up there, and it was not worth-while so much as to try to go up? And would they not kill anyone who tried to release them and take them up, if they could somehow lay hands on him and kill him?"

"That they would!" said he.

"Then we must apply this image, my dear Glaucon," said I, "to all we have been saying. The world of our sight is like the habitation in prison, the firelight there to the sunlight here, the ascent and the view of the upper world is the rising of the soul into the world of mind. . . . At least, what appears to me is, that in the world of the known, last of all [i.e., the object of our search], is the idea of the good, and with what toil to be seen! And seen, this must be inferred to be the cause of all right and beautiful things for all, which gives birth to light and the king of light in the world of sight, and, in the world of mind, herself the queen produces truth and reason; and she must be seen by one who is to act with reason publicly or privately."

"I believe as you do," he said, "in so far as I am able."

"Then believe also, as I do," said I, "and do not be surprised, that those who come thither are not willing to have part in the affairs of men, but their souls ever strive to remain above; for that surely may be expected if our parable fits the case."

"Quite so," he said.

"Well then," said I, "do you think it surprising if one leaving divine contemplations and passing to the evils of men is awkward and appears to be a great fool, while he is still blinking—not yet accustomed to the darkness around him, but compelled to struggle in law courts or elsewhere about shadows of justice, or the images which make the shadows, and to quarrel about notions of justice in those who have never seen justice itself?"

"Not surprising at all," said he.

"But any man of sense," I said, "would remember that the eyes are doubly confused from two different causes, both in passing from light to darkness and from darkness to light; and believing that the same things happen with regard to the soul also, whenever he sees a soul confused and unable to discern anything he would not just laugh carelessly; he would examine whether it had come out of a more brilliant life, and if it were darkened by the strangeness; or whether it had come out of greater ignorance into a more brilliant light, and if it were dazzled with the brighter illumination. Then only would he congratulate the one soul upon its happy experience and way of life, and pity the other; but if he must laugh, his laugh would be a less downright laugh than his laughter at the soul which came out of the light above."

"That is fairly put," said he.

Unenlightened Versus Enlightened Rulers

"Then if this is true," I said, "our belief about these matters must be this, that the nature of education is not really such as some of its professors say it is; as you know, they say that there is not understanding in the soul, but they put it in, as if they were putting sight into blind eyes."

"They do say so," said he.

"But our reasoning indicates," I said, "that this power is already in the soul of each, and is the instrument by which each learns; thus if the eye could not see without being turned with the whole body from the dark towards the light, so this instrument must be turned round with the whole soul away from the world of becoming until it is able to endure the sight of being and the most brilliant light of being: and this we say is the good, don't we?"

"Yes.". . .

"Very well," said I, "isn't it equally likely, indeed, necessary, after what has been said, that men uneducated and without experience of truth could never properly supervise a city, nor can those who are allowed to spend all their lives in education right to the end? The first have no single object in life, which they must always aim at in doing everything they do, public or private; the second will never do anything if they can help it, believing they have already found mansions abroad in the Islands of the Blest [the pleasant region of the Underworld]."

"True," said he.

"Then it is the task of us founders," I said, "to compel the best natures to attain that learning which we said was the greatest, both to see the good, and to ascend that ascent; and when they have ascended and properly seen, we must never allow them what is allowed now."

"What is that, pray?" he asked.

"To stay there," I said, "and not be willing to descend again to those prisoners, and to share their troubles and their honours, whether they are worth having or not."

"What!" said he, "are we to wrong them and

Plato, pictured here, explores the elusive, deceptive nature of reality in the "Myth of the Cave" (from his Republic).

make them live badly, when they might live better?"

"You have forgotten again, my friend," said I, "that the law is not concerned how any one class in a city is to prosper above the rest; it tries to contrive prosperity in the city as a whole, fitting the citizens into a pattern by persuasion and compulsion, making them give of their help to one another wherever each class is able to help the community. The law itself creates men like this in the city, not in order to allow each one to turn by any way he likes, but in order to use them itself to the full for binding the city together."

"True," said he, "I did forget."

"Notice then, Glaucon," I said, "we shall not wrong the philosophers who grow up among us, but we shall treat them fairly when we compel them to add to their duties the care and guardianship of the other people. We shall tell them that those who grow up philosophers in other cities have reason in taking no part in public labours there; for they grow up there of themselves, though none of the city governments wants them; a wild growth has its rights, it owes nurture to no one, and need not trouble to pay anyone for its food. But you we have engendered, like king bees in hives, as leaders and kings over yourselves and the rest of the city; you have been better and more perfectly educated than the others, and are better able to share in both ways of life. Down you must go then, in turn, to the habitation of the others, and accustom yourselves to their darkness; for when you have grown accustomed you will see a thousand times better than those who live there, and you will know what the images are and what they are images of, because you have seen the realities behind just and beautiful and good things. And so our city will be managed wide awake for us and for you, not in a dream, as most are now, by people fighting together for shadows, and quarrelling to be rulers, as if that were a great good. But the truth is more or less that the city where those who are to rule are least anxious to be rulers is of necessity best managed and has least faction in it; while the city which gets rulers who want it most is worst managed."

"Certainly," said he.

"Then will our fosterlings [pupils] disobey us when they hear this? Will they refuse to help, each group in its turn, in the labours of the city, and want to spend most of their time dwelling in the pure air?"

"Impossible," said he, "for we shall only be laying just commands on just men. No, but undoubtedly each man of them will go to the ruler's place as to a grim necessity, exactly the opposite of those who now rule in cities."

"For the truth is, my friend," I said, "that only if you can find for your future rulers a way of life better than ruling, is it possible for you to have a well-managed city; since in that city alone those will rule who are truly rich, not rich in gold, but in that which is necessary for a happy man, the riches of a good and wise life: but if beggared and hungry, for want of goods of their own, they hasten to public affairs, thinking that they must snatch goods for themselves from there, it is not possible. Then rule becomes a thing to be fought for; and a war of such a kind, being between citizens and within them, destroys both them and the rest of the city also."

"Most true," said he.

"Well, then," said I, "have you any other life despising political office except the life of true philosophy?"

"No, by heaven," said he.

"But again," said I, "they must not go awooing office like so many lovers! If they do, their rival lovers will fight them."

"Of course they will!"

"Then what persons will you compel to accept guardianship of the city other than those who are wisest in the things which enable a city to be best managed, who also have honours of another kind and a life better than the political life?"

"No others," he answered.

Selection 8

Aristotle Expands the Frontiers of Knowledge

Michael Grant

Aristotle's importance in the history of Western philosophy and scholarship was memorably summarized by former St. John's College scholar Renford Bambrough: "The range and power of his achievements place him without question in the shortest of short lists of the giants of Western thought. To many generations of thinkers he was known simply as 'The Philosopher.' [The Italian writer] Dante . . . honored him with the proud title of 'master of those who know.' . . . In the study of ethics, politics, and literary criticism he set standards . . . by which his successors two thousand years later may still be severely judged. . . . There is no problem in any of the branches of . . . philosophy . . . on which his remarks do not continue to deserve the most careful attention from the modern inquirer." The following systematic and comprehensive overview of Aristotle's life and major works is

*by classical historian Michael Grant, the au-
thor of numerous widely read studies of Greek
and Roman civilization.*

*A*ristotle (384–322 [B.C.]) was born at the
Ionian colony of Stagirus in Chalcidice
(Macedonia). He was the son of Nicomachus . . . who was the physician of the Macedonian King Amyntas III (393/392–370/369),
and probably first inspired Aristotle's interest in
physical science and biology. But Nicomachus
died when his son was still a boy, and he was
sent, at the age of seventeen, to study at Plato's
Academy at Athens, where he remained for
twenty years, first as a student and then as a
teacher and researcher.

After Plato's death, however, he and another
prominent figure at the Academy, Xenocrates,
moved away from Athens. This may have been
partly because the city was at war with Macedonia, with which he enjoyed such close ties. But
Aristotle was also said to have disapproved of
the policy of Speusippus, who had succeeded
Plato as the Academy director. . . .

He and Xenocrates made their way to Atar-
neus in north-western Asia Minor, ruled over by
Hermeias (*c*.355–341), who was a former member of the Academy, as well as a friend of Philip
[II, King of Macedonia], and had encouraged a
group of Platonists to found a philosophical
community and school at Assus. Aristotle joined
this group, marrying Hermeias' niece and adopted daughter Pythias. Then he spent two years at
Mytilene on the island of Lesbos (345–343), and
subsequently moved to Mieza, near the Macedonian capital Pella, where he reputedly . . . took
charge of the education of Philip's thirteen-year-
old son Alexander (III the Great).

In 340, however, this appointment . . . was terminated and Aristotle may have gone home to
Stagirus. But in 335 he returned to Athens, as a
resident alien (metic) and founded his school the

Reprinted with the permission of Weidenfeld & Nicolson and of
Scribner, a division of Simon & Schuster, from *The Classical
Greeks*, by Michael Grant. Copyright © 1989 by Michael Grant
Publications Ltd.

Lyceum . . . where his group, at first somewhat
informal, was known as the Peripatetics owing to
the covered court (*peripatos*) round the building,
in which instruction and discussion took place.
Alexander's viceroy Antipater was Aristotle's
friend, but after Alexander's death (323), when
an anti-Macedonian policy prevailed at Athens,
Aristotle was accused by the Athenians of impiety (as Socrates had been) and moved out of the
city, leaving [the scholar-philosopher] Theophrastus to direct the Lyceum. He settled at
Chalcis in Euboea, but suffered from digestive
troubles, and died in the following year.

Aristotle Sets Rules for Logical Inquiry and Argumentation

His writings were of unparalleled scope and dimensions; and out of a vast number of treatises
no less than forty-seven have survived.

Their basis was logical reasoning; for although Aristotle, unlike other ancient thinkers,
did not regard logic as a science, he located it in
the forecourt of the sciences, as a necessary preliminary to them all.

His *Organon* (Instrument, Tool) on the subject consists of six studies. *Categories* describes
and classifies terms and phrases, offering ten
basic forms of statements on Being. . . . *On Interpretation* . . . discusses the parts and formulations of a sentence. The eight books of *Topics*
are concerned with a survey of propositions, indicating the ways in which probable statements
can be made—without involvement in contradictions—by the methods of dialectic [logical
argument], as established by the sophists and by
Plato. A sequel, however, the *Sophistical Refu-
tations*, warns against the deceptive inferences
into which the arguments employed by the
sophists can lead.

Aristotle's word for the study of reasoning is
'analytics', the art of discourse, rather less general than 'logic'; and the most significant parts
of the *Organon* are the *Prior* and *Posterior Analytics*, containing two books each. The former
work reviews the general principles of inductive
inference, while the *Posterior Analytics* applies

these methods of proof and definition to the nature and validity of knowledge (epistemology), indicating that there is a proper method of constructing generalizations, applicable to all the sciences, and explaining how language can and should be employed for this purpose.

Aristotle stresses the novelty of his logical writings, and even if, contrary to what has sometimes been claimed, he did not *invent* the discipline of logic . . . he was perhaps the first to comprehend the importance, not only of the content of statements, but of their form, and their formal relation to each other. This was a major breakthrough, for no one had ever before offered a general account of what is valid in argument and what is not. Written with lucid precision and clarity, and displaying sensitiveness to the structures and connections that lie beneath the surface of languages, his *Organon*, even if it seems outdated to logicians today, is by far the most important collection of writings on this theme that has come down to us from the ancient world.

Such was the instrument with which Aristotle tackled the entire field of knowledge. Plato had believed that nature is governed by general laws; and Aristotle added the conviction that this whole panorama can be reasoned out and comprehended. For such a massive investigation he recognized, for the first time, that each of the various sciences is a separate, departmental field of enquiry, and he divided these sciences into three groups: theoretical (*theoria*), seeking knowledge of the truth; practical (*praxis*), dedicated to good behaviour; and productive (*poietike*), devoted to the creation of something beyond the activity involved. The groups sometimes merged into one another, but Aristotle wrote treatises of outstanding significance under each of these three headings. . . .

All Things Exist for a Purpose

In the theoretical field, a group of fourteen of Aristotle's treatises is known as the *Metaphysics*. . . . In these works Aristotle examines the nature of reality, that is to say its causes, the principles of existence, and the essential substance of the universe. He discerns a hierarchy [a ladder of authority] of existences, each imparting form and change to the one next below it.

At the apex of the scale is the 'Unmoved First Mover', identified with God, an eternal activity of thought, free from any material admixture, imparting causal motion to the universe through a process of attraction related to love. This is a concept which Plato had already suggested, but it forms a basic feature in Aristotle's thought. It reveals his fundamentally religious attitude, and has appealed to devout people through subsequent ages, though they have been somewhat put off by the complexities he introduced, notably a suggested multiplication of Movers, created by adding fifty-five more to account for the movement of the heavenly bodies and constitute an ordered gradation in which the First Mover stands at the summit. . . .

Aristotle's interpretation of the First Mover that stood at the head of this hierarchy raises awkward questions, which his lifelong struggle with these problems was not able to solve, and which may have prompted him, in later life, to push the whole idea into the background. For example, this Mover did not create the universe, and does not (like the god later envisaged by the Stoics) pervade or direct or rule it, remaining, on the contrary, indifferent to its existence—so that Aristotle proves not to be such a 'religious' thinker after all, since his universe is not god-centred. Yet how, then, are events to be explained, if the First Mover does not control them?

The eight-book *Physics* would be better known as 'Lectures on Nature'—since its subject matter extends into metaphysics and the philosophy of science. The work examines the components of the things that exist by nature—which . . . is discussed along with other fundamental concepts such as time and space and change and matter. . . .

Aristotle basically rejected, or came to reject, Plato's doctrine [of the Forms, ideal models of objects from the visible world, which are mere imitations of the Forms]. What he saw and disliked in this view . . . was what he regarded as its transcendentalism: the distinction, inherited from Parmenides, between what is 'real' in an absolute sense (eternal, unchangeable) and what is mere matter (*hyle*), comprising the products of our sense-perceptions, and therefore only 'real' in a secondary and inferior sense of the word. Aristotle did not reject the Forms altogether, but preferred to regard them as immanent in concrete, perceived material objects— enabling the true, underlying nature of those objects to be comprehended; that is to say he refused to allow the Forms any independent, transcendental existence on their own account. . . .

There remained, then, the unsolved problem of identifying and defining the principle which enables Forms to realize themselves in matter— the principle, that is to say, which makes the world go round. Aristotle identified this process as *kinesis*, movement, including both quantitative growth and qualitative change, which, together, represent the transition of a thing's potentiality (*dynamis*)—enabling it to become something else—to its actuality (*energeia*).

Aristotle's *Physics* identifies four categories, known somewhat misleadingly as the 'Four Causes'. Three of the 'Causes' have just been mentioned, material, Form, and movement. But he also identified a fourth 'cause', namely *telos*, the end or aim or purpose for which something comes into being, and the reason for its existence. Plato (and apparently Socrates before him) had gone a long way towards this 'teleological' view, maintaining that everything exists for an end, and a good end at that. But to Aristotle this concept is of central importance, and colours the whole of his thinking.

For not only, he maintained, do all things exist for an end, but an inborn impulse impels them to try to achieve that end as completely as possible: in other words, it impels them to attain self-fulfilment, to realize the full potentialities of their Form. This natural sequence of events . . . is another sign of what might be called the religious character of Aristotle's thinking, which dominated western thinking up to the sixteenth century and beyond, but will disappoint those who seek wholly scientific explanations of the universe. However, it also disappointed nine-teenth-century religious thinkers as not being teleological *enough*, because, granted that Aristotle saw the universe as moving towards natural *ends*, it did not seem to him that nature exhibits any discoverable, providential *purpose*. . . .

On the Heavens, in four books, expounds the movement of heavenly and sublunary bodies, defining and distinguishing and organizing Plato's conceptions. The spherical shape of the earth was known to Aristotle, but he still believed it to be the centre of the universe. *On Generation and Corruption* (or *On Coming into Being and Passing Away*) interprets evolution in terms of a cyclical series of transformations. The four books *On Meteorology* deal mostly with phenomena relating to the weather, although comets, meteors and the nature of the sea are also discussed.

The First Biologist

However, living things absorbed Aristotle's interest to the greatest extent, and it is here that his characteristic concepts are most at home. In the field of biology, it was his intention to cover the entire realm of nature. But he assigned the vegetable kingdom to his pupil Theophrastus, while himself undertaking the zoological part of this huge project (though perhaps with Theophrastus' help).

His *History of* (or rather, *Enquiry into*) *Animals* is an introductory collection of facts about animal life, in four books, dealing with the anatomy, physiology and habits of all sorts of animals, fishes and birds, with emphasis on the adaptation and evolution of their organs. *On the Parts* (*Members*) *of Animals* is again in four books. There are also studies *On the Generation* (*Reproduction*) *and Gait of Animals*—of which the former, comprising five books, earned praises from Darwin—and a further treatise *On the Movement of Animals*. . . .

Biology was Aristotle's key science, as mathematics had been Plato's, and in this field he was at his triumphal best. . . . Virtually the earliest of all biologists and zoologists, he displayed marked originality and . . . patience. His imposing analyses of more than five hundred species, sketching out the entire canvas, and filling most of it in, as well, were built up from a tremendous wealth of carefully sifted data, his own and others', for the organization of which he founded a library (equipped with a large museum collection) which was the model of all subsequent libraries in the ancient world.

Some of the information and interpretation that he provides has been shown in later epochs [eras] (and especially from the nineteenth century onwards) to be erroneous, but an enormous amount remains valid; and parts of his discussions seem uncannily ahead of their time. Aristotle himself sums up his biological and zoological research methods. 'If ever the facts about bees', he remarks, 'are fully grasped, then credit must be given rather to observations than to theories, and to theories only if what they affirm agrees with the observed facts.'. . .

On the Soul, in three books, is not concerned with the human soul alone, but with all stages of animate life, the soul being interpreted as the internal principle—not immaterial, as Plato had suggested—which is united with the body and holds it together and endows it with life. But the human soul is above those of animals and plants, because it alone has the power of thought (*dianoetikon*). Equipped with this gift, a soul is the ordered microcosm [small world] that mirrors the macrocosm [large world] of the universe. . . . This elaborate and subtle analysis of the soul's functions represents the final stage of Aristotle's psychological ponderings, and no part of his philosophy has exercised a greater effect on later thought.

His Approach to Ethics

The ten books of the *Nicomachean Ethics*, the most famous of all studies of morality, is named after Aristotle's son, Nicomachus, and may be his edition of his father's lectures. Much of the work is written in a semi-popular fashion, endeavouring to reconcile philosophy with the outlook of the educated public—in a boringly middle-aged manner, some say today, while others find the tone bracingly commonsensical.

Better described as 'On Matters of Character' (which is what *ethos* means), the *Nicomachean*

Ethics deals with a 'practical' science, being a study of the Good, that is to say of *being* good, the end (*telos*) towards which conduct should be directed. In Book I this is identified with happiness or well-being (*eudaimonia*), 'an activity of the soul in accordance with reason', and the next five books define the character of such activity. Pleasure, honour and wealth are rejected as the foundation of *eudaimonia*, and the absoluteness of Plato's moral values . . . is abandoned in favour of a more realistic and pragmatic diversity. For Aristotle insists that we should start with what we find at hand, and try to perfect tendencies that are already in existence; and since, therefore, our lives are not entirely lived on a spiritual and intellectual basis, there is room not only for the virtues relating to that exalted pitch but also for qualities of character, such as courage and high-mindedness and patience and gentleness and endurance of fortune. . . .

His ethical approach is once again, as one might expect, teleological: he wants to find out what human beings *are for*—to identify the functions for which nature intends them. . . .

Excellence, as Aristotle saw it, comes as a result of deliberately selecting the Mean, a middle course. The Greeks—prone to extremes—admired this idea, of which a great deal is heard in their folklore, and in their tragedies, and in Plato: and the Mean became one of Aristotle's best-known doctrines. Human beings must choose an intermediate course between two opposite sets of extreme behaviour. . . . Although difficult to justify in logical terms, this is not, as some have assumed, a mere exaltation [glorification] of mediocrity, but a proposal probably derived from medical analogies—that it is up to each individual to seek to achieve the precise blend and proportion of qualities that is appropriate to his or her self.

Aristotle's Political Views

Aristotle exalted contemplation, but saw community life as the practical ideal: for him, as for Plato, ethics and politics are one . . . politics being the central concern of humankind, since Plato had been right to maintain that people are only parts of the society to which they belong: indeed the state, Aristotle maintained, is logically prior to the individual.

Even if this belief in the centrality of politics and priority of the state, despite acceptance in some quarters even today, is questionable, Aristotle thought more deeply about the political structure of Greek society than anyone ever before, and wrote about the subject at great length. His *Politics*, although it has reached the world in a somewhat incoherent and disorganized form, remains our most ample and searching investigation into the political conditions of ancient Greece.

The treatise approaches the topic from the viewpoint of the city-state, which provided, Aristotle assumed, the fullest life for its individual citizens. Thus they are biologically defined . . . as *zoa politika*, city-state beings, social animals whose natural, highest goal (*telos*) is to live in a *polis*. A discussion of slavery which follows adopts the view that the servitude of slaves to the free, and of barbarians to Greeks, is a condition of nature. Book II offers a historical survey of politics, examining a number of 'model' constitutions, especially those of Sparta, Crete and Carthage, and discussing various legislators. There are references to Plato, and they recur in Book III, which discusses healthy constitutions (monarchy, aristocracy and moderate democracy) in contrast with degenerate and undesirable types (tyranny, oligarchy—that is to say, government by a few, not selected for merit—and radical democracy or crowd rule).

Books IV–VI analyse various defects that damage political life, and the ways of eliminating them. It is taken for granted that every state includes, within itself, two parties, divided on economic lines, and perpetually at daggers drawn with one another. Books VII and VIII go on to depict the *best* sort of state. Like Plato, Aristotle regards education, under state control, as the first essential—but an education, this time, which although still predominantly ethical, nevertheless trains a person's emotions and body as well as his intellectual and moral capacities.

Further studies of 158 Greek city-state constitutions are now lost, except for the greater part of the *Athenian Constitution* which has been unearthed on a papyrus. Though derived, somewhat hastily, from sources of varying quality, this treatise contains a useful and succinct [concise] account of the political system of Athens and its earlier historical development. The work may or may not have been written by Aristotle himself—these 'constitutions' were perhaps parcelled out for composition to his students—but it reflects the aristocratic, anti-democratic bias which he shared with Plato. It is ironical that Athens, the leading democratic city-state, should owe so much of its fame to two convinced anti-democratic writers who flourished in its midst. . . .

His governing class, an exemplification of the Mean, would consist, for the sake of stability, of an aristocracy of intellect and virtue, comprising basically the middle class: those citizens who enjoyed moderate prosperity, and did not feel discontented enough to want political convulsions or imprudent adventures. Citizenship would be restricted to a smaller minority than actually possessed this privilege at Athens; agricultural labourers and artisans and shopkeepers would not be allowed to become citizens at all, because manual labour makes a person coarse (*banausos*) and leaves no time for a citizen's duties, which require leisure. . . .

Works on Rhetoric and Drama

His *Rhetoric*, in three books, comes under the heading of 'productive' writings, aimed at creating something that is worth while. It considers the methods of persuasion open to the orator, and how they can be reduced to rule. The first of its three books investigates the logical proofs and arguments derived from dialectical techniques. The second turns to psychological and ethical factors, discussing how the speaker can induce his audience to look upon him favourably and how he can whip up their emotions. The third book reviews matters relating to stylistic clarity, appropriate tone, correct arrangement, and forms and figures of speech. . . .

The *Poetics* is a study of poetry. Although an 'imitation' like other arts . . . poetry, Aristotle indicates, is more 'philosophical' than history, because it tells general truths, whereas history is limited to particular facts; and he does not therefore, like Plato, regard the poetic art as an always too dangerous stimulant, but sees that it can be instructive and beneficial as well.

Originally, the complete work dealt with epic, tragedy and comedy, but as it has come down to us tragedy is the principal theme. An analysis of tragic drama indicates the component elements of a play . . . and its purpose, which is defined as 'effecting the proper purgation (or purification) of the emotions through terror and pity' (or 'horror and misery'): a process which will offer a cathartic outlet to the emotions of the audience and thereby cause them pleasure. Notes on certain characteristic features of tragedies are also included, such as the 'reversal' (of fortune) and 'recognition' (or discovery) and the mysterious fatal 'flaw' (*hamartia*), which brings great men like Sophocles' Oedipus down. A brief discussion of epic poetry, and the rules which should apply to it has also survived and epic and tragic poetry are compared.

In spite of its fragmentary character, and the suspicion that Aristotle was temperamentally unsuited to appreciate either tragedy or epic to the full, his *Poetics* remains the earliest and also the most important of all Greek contributions to literary criticism—which he provided with a vocabulary of its own, and many permanently valuable definitions. In subsequent centuries the work became influential and famous, inspiring numerous editions and commentaries (especially after its initial separate printing in 1526) and exercising a dominant influence, in particular, upon the French classical drama of the seventeenth century. For the French theatre was founded upon a doctrine of dramatic unities which was thought to be found in Aristotle's treatise, though in fact the only unity which it lays down is unity of action. . . .

A Passion for Investigation

It is disconcerting . . . that [the first-century B.C. Roman orator and writer] Cicero tells us of the sparkling style and 'golden flow' [of Aristotle's writing style], because such praises are scarcely merited by the treatises that are still extant. Their language displays a concise and knotty pungency, providing an efficient vehicle for philosophical argument and scientific description, but dry and formal, and indeed at times pedantic [narrow and bookish], so that to read Aristotle is arduous. The brilliant, golden essays admired by Cicero have vanished: whereas those of his studies that have come down to us . . . for the most part seem to have been 'esoteric', unpolished and unrevised, pieces intended not for general circulation but for employment within the student body of the Lyceum.

Most of the surviving works of the fourth-century B.C. philosopher Aristotle are dry, formal lectures; nevertheless they contain the bulk of his main ideas.

However, what survives does seem to include the most important works Aristotle wrote. Their gigantic range might be thought to show him as the creator of an entire, coherent, comprehensive, encyclopaedic system, and it is as a systematizer that he has often been regarded. Nevertheless, although he did, indeed, systematize a huge range of existing knowledge, he still remained, at heart, a tentative, probing, dialectically minded explorer and researcher, making acute (though sometimes distorted) use of what others had provided, and yet continually moved by his own personal, unceasing sense of wonder. For Aristotle was a man whose master passion for the acquisition of knowledge kept him always ready, with intellectual humility, to look at a point of theory again and again, and try to handle it better all the time—on the basis of newly acquired data. . . .

And when he came down to earth, his Ionian passion for investigation of natural phenomena—despite inevitable shortcomings by modern standards—illuminated innumerable subjects with his robust yet inspired passion for orderliness, displayed by inexhaustible classifications, but also, at the same time, accompanied by an unremitting responsiveness to the complexity and variety of nature and human beings. . . .

Aristotle was the man who established the major and still accepted divisions of philosophy; and whereas Plato gave leading categories their names, Aristotle added numerous, more detailed, definitions. And it is from him that philosophers and scientists, of one generation after another, have derived their philosophical terminology which has entered into the inherited vocabulary of educated men and women, so that we employ these terms continually without any longer recalling their source.

He has been seen throughout the ages as the supreme scholar pursuing the life of the intellect for its own sake; and his posthumous prestige has been more enduring than any other thinker's. Although there is little point in trying to draw up a list, in order of merit, of the astonishingly numerous personages of genius who lived during the fifth and fourth centuries BC, it is impossible to think of any whose contribution to the world was greater than Aristotle's.

Selection 9

New Philosophies Thrive in the Hellenistic Age

Sarah B. Pomeroy, Stanley M. Burstein, Walter Donlan, and Jennifer T. Roberts

Numerous new philosophical movements emerged in the widening Greek world of Hellenistic times (323–30 B.C.). Thinkers in the preceding Classic Age had concentrated mainly on theoretical concepts, often exploring the nature of reality or the moral roles and duties of subjects and rulers within the polis. By contrast, the new philosophies tend-

ed to address the practical problems of everyday life, suggesting how people might cope with them; and these schools of thought appealed to people of all social classes, rather than primarily to the intellectual elite, as most earlier ones had. Distinguished Hunter College scholar Sarah B. Pomeroy and her colleagues provide this concise over-

view of the major Hellenistic philosophical movements: Stoicism, Epicureanism, Cynicism, and Skepticism.

The altered temper of [Hellenistic] . . . times was evident . . . in new developments in the realm of philosophy. Though they had much to say to ordinary men and women, and continue to be studied today with interest by people of varied social and economic backgrounds, Classical philosophers like Plato and Aristotle directed their teachings to affluent men of leisure who were interested in improving their political activities in the autonomous poleis. Hellenistic philosophies, on the other hand, were designed to help people cope with a world over which they had little control.

The Stoics

Like the establishments of Plato and Aristotle, two of the most important schools of Hellenistic thought flowered in Athens. These were Stoicism and Epicureanism. Born in Citium in Cyprus, Zeno (335–263 BC), the founder of Stoicism, was a friend of [the Macedonian ruler] Antigonus Gonatas and spent many years in Athens, where he lectured on the terrace known as the Stoa Poikile ("Painted Porch"). For this reason his followers received the name of Stoics (i.e., "Porchers").

Zeno's philosophy reflected the realities of the new political order. According to Zeno, the earth stood at the center of the universe with Zeus its prime mover. Just as cosmic motions never changed and Zeus remained king of the gods, so monarchy was the divinely ordered system of government. Revolution, consequently, violated the natural organization of the world, whereas patriotism and public service harmonized with the cosmic order. Serenity, the Stoics believed, was impossible without the confidence that one

Excerpted from *Ancient Greece: Political, Social, and Cultural History*, by Sarah Pomeroy et al. Copyright © 1998 by Sarah Pomeroy, Stanley Burstein, Walter Donlan, and Jennifer T. Roberts. Used by permission of Oxford University Press, Inc.

had fulfilled one's duties to others, and Stoicism entailed a large dose of humanitarianism.

Zeno urged his followers to attain an inner tranquillity that was proof not only against agonizing pain—hence our word "stoical"—but against excessive pleasure as well. He did not, however, advocate withdrawal from the social and political realm as did some of his contemporaries. Instead, he encouraged Stoics to uphold justice—but not to engage in any serious attempts at reform. Thus, while in principle Stoics considered slaves just as free as their owners, they made no attempt to abolish slavery. It was considered enough for slaves to be made aware that, deep inside, they enjoyed no more or less freedom than their masters and mistresses, who might be themselves "slaves" to greed or lust. Because they rejected excessive pleasure, moreover, Stoics embraced sex only for purposes of procreation. Their acceptance of a hierarchical sociopolitical order [a social-political system with increasingly higher levels of authority] and their rejection of sexual pleasure are two important arenas in which Stoicism anticipated the teachings of early Christianity.

The Epicureans

In keeping with their belief in an orderly universe, Stoics believed that life was rational and could be planned. A very different position was taken by Epicurus (341–270 BC), a native of Samos who moved to Athens, where he established in his home a school called The Garden. Epicurus even included women among his students. Adopting the atomic theory first put forward by Leucippus and Democritus, he rejected the determinism of the early atomists. Though he agreed that atoms fell in straight lines from the sky, he added a new element. Epicurus argued that the multiplicity of substances in the universe arose from periodic swerves in the atoms' paths, causing them to collide at a variety of angles. Like the domains continually carved out and altered by Alexander's successors, the entire universe combined by chance, and would perish and regenerate by chance as well.

This construction left little room for the gods,

and in fact Epicurus contended that though the gods must exist since people saw their images in dreams, they had no interest in humans. In the Epicurean system, the gods lived serene, untroubled lives, indifferent to such staples of Greek religious and social life as prayers, offerings, and rituals. (The good news was that the horrific punishments associated with the underworld were fictions; the bad news was that nobody on Olympus was interested in listening to complaints, offering solace, or avenging injustices.) After death, the atoms that had comprised the soul and body of each person merely dissolved.

In the absence of eternal rewards and punishments, Epicurus viewed happiness on earth as the purpose of life, thus winning for himself the name of history's first humanist philosopher. He defined happiness as the attainment of *ataraxia*, an untroubled state free from excessive pleasure and pain, much like the serenity advocated by Zeno. Unlike Zeno, however, Epicurus advocated withdrawal from a wide variety of activities that might bring pain, both the risky quest for love or money (which the Stoics would also see as problematic) and participation in politics (which the Stoics praised). For Epicureans, anything that might threaten ataraxia was to be avoided. Though in modern parlance the label "Epicurean" connotes indulgence in pleasure, particularly in the pleasures of fine dining, Epicurus actually counseled moderation in food and drink in order to avoid indigestion and hangovers. Unlike the Stoics, Epicureans approved of sex as long as it did not entail falling in love, with all the attendant pitfalls.

Cynicism and Skepticism

Despite their substantial differences over sex and politics, Stoics and Epicureans shared a common goal: attaining tranquillity in a turbulent world. A similar aim characterized two other schools of thought that evolved around the same time, Cynicism and Skepticism. The principal theorist of the Cynic movement was Diogenes of Sinope (c. 400–325 BC), who encouraged his followers to become self-sufficient by shedding the trappings of civilization for the naturalness of animals.

Denying that humans had needs different from those of other mammals, Diogenes scandalized contemporaries and earned himself the name of the Cynic ("dog," "*kuōn*" in Greek) by brazenly maintaining that people should follow instincts just as animals do—urinating or masturbating in public, for example. The heirs to the Cynics' rejection of civilized norms were the Skeptics, who also shared the Epicureans' disillusionment with public life. Skepticism, associated with the name of Pyrrhon of Elis (c. 365–275 BC), became popular around 200 BC. Stressing the impossibility of certain knowledge, Skeptics urged people to withdraw from the world around them. The quest for truth, after all, was hopeless, as was the quest for power. Today, the words "skeptical" and "cynical" are linked when we talk about people who are not easily persuaded. In this respect the philosophies we associate with the Hellenistic world (though Cynicism began in the fourth century) contrast sharply with those of Plato and Aristotle, who really believed that knowledge was possible and could be gained through education.

While Athens continued to serve as a magnet for intellectuals, it is significant that the center of philosophical speculation in the Hellenistic era shifted not only away from Athens but also away from mainland Greece in general. The best-known Stoic thinkers, for example, came from places like Cyprus and Syria, while Tarsus, Alexandria, and Rhodes became the most famous Stoic university towns. In time Stoicism took root firmly in the Roman empire, where it anchored the minds and souls of many men and women seeking to cope with the decadence and autocracy of the imperial government.

Almost as remarkable was the fate of Sparta. After a century-long decline that saw the number of Spartiates [Spartan citizens] dwindle to fewer than a thousand and tensions between rich and poor become acute, two reformer kings, Agis IV (262–241 BC) and Cleomenes III (260–219 BC), revitalized Sparta's "Lycurgan" institutions [the strict military-social system established by the legendary lawgiver Lycurgus with the intention of creating an austere society with a powerful army]. Debts were canceled, land was redistributed, and the traditional Spartan educational system, the *agōgē*, was reestablished. For a brief while, Sparta became the Stoic model state. The Stoic notion that individual suffering is part of some great natural scheme and should be borne without lamentation struck a responsive chord in Spartans, and the idea that austerity was preferable to self-indulgence reverberated with Spartan ideals as well. For a few years Spartan arms were invincible and the city seemed on the verge of dominating the Peloponnesus again. Greek intellectuals trumpeted once more the virtues of the Lycurgan system. Their dreams of Greek renewal were shattered when the joint forces of Macedon and the Achaean League crushed the Spartans at Sellasia in 222 BC. As the fate of Sparta revealed, not even the strongest polis could resist indefinitely the power of the Macedonian kingdoms that strove to subdue them or to use them as pawns in their own diplomatic and military struggles.

Selection 10

Inventions and Discoveries of the Hellenistic Scientists

Michael Grant

The Hellenistic Age (323–30 B.C.) witnessed not only the proliferation of new philosophical doctrines, but also an acceleration of the separation of science from philosophy. A multitude of scientific discoveries opened up new vistas of research and learning. Especially noteworthy were those supported by the Ptolemies at Alexandria, which quickly became the most cosmopolitan city and most prestigious learning center in the known world. Here, from his well-informed study of the Hellenistic Age, Michael Grant, of Edinburgh University, chronicles the leading scientists of the era, including the mathematician Euclid, the mechanical genius Archimedes, the medical researcher Herophilus, the geographer Eratosthenes, the astronomer Hipparchus, and many others.

M athematics, astronomy, geography and medicine flourished in the Hellenistic Age as never before. For one thing, while (as Plato complained) the old city-state governments had never spent much money on research, the new monarchs felt differently. So the richer among these kings proceeded to establish more permanent foundations for learning, among which the Museum at Ptolemaic Alexandria, with its subsidized scholars, was outstanding. Admittedly, royal patronage was limited and unsystematic, and often had military purposes in mind— but not always, for mathematics and medicine were among its principal beneficiaries.

Indeed, the outstanding mathematician Euclid was one of the first men of learning to reside in Alexandria (*c.* 300 [B.C.]). His great textbook, the *Elements*, contained thirteen books (1–6 on plane geometry, 7–9 on the theory of numbers, 10 on irrationals, 11–13 on solid geometry). By this choice of subject, Euclid was preserving the tradition of Plato, many of whose pupils had continued to stress mathematical learning. Mathematical *Elements* had also been compiled by earlier scholars: but Euclid superseded them all. He did so by incorporating everything of value that they had said, so that his own work was, in essence, the summing up of all previous Greek mathematics: the culmination, closure and stocktaking of the classical epoch that had gone before, for the benefit of the new Hellenistic world of the present and future. Euclid's *Elements* are remarkable for the sagaciously chosen five hundred axioms or theorems from which he logically and systematically deduces the results of this past activity. His proofs are rigorous and compact, his presentations symmetrical, elegant and crystal clear. The western world learnt from the *Elements* how to reason at the highest point of exactitude. No other human creation has ever demonstrated so clearly how knowledge can be derived from rational methods alone, and no book except the Bible has enjoyed so long a reign.

Strato of Lampsacus (d. *c.* 269) confirmed the separation between philosophy and science, and converted the Lyceum—of which he succeeded Theophrastus as the head—from the former to the latter. He felt strongly that the processes of nature must be explained by natural causes, not by any god or providence; and he asserted the primacy of systematic experiment over logical proof. Ctesibius, who worked at Alexandria in the same period, gave these views a practical shape and twist. Not an outstanding theoretician himself, but a mechanical genius and inventor, he was the first to construct devices employing the action of air under pressure, and created a pump equipped with plunger and valve, a water-organ, and the first accurate water-clock, in addition to improvements in artillery. We know of Ctesibius' work from his third- or second-century follower Philo of Byzantium (writer of a compendium of technology, and *Seven Wonders of the World*), and from the mathematician and inventor Hero of Alexandria, who probably lived in the first century AD. Both were serious mechanical experts, though both, at the same time, shared a great love of gadgets and devices.

The Pioneering Archimedes

Archimedes of Syracuse (d. 212) was the most far-sighted Greek mathematician of all time, a wholly original genius who advanced far beyond the frontiers of knowledge into the unknown, and was declared by [the French literary great] Voltaire to have an imagination finer than Homer's.

In solid geometry—fascinated by its logical consistency—he outstripped Euclid, and broke entirely new ground. He was consumed by a revolutionary determination to measure first, and only demonstrate afterwards. And what he measured, above all, was curvilinear area and volume: his work on the geometry of spheres and cylinders and on cones and conic sections was outstanding. Indeed, out of all Archimedes' multifarious activity, this remained the achievement of which he was evidently proudest. For he requested the sculptors of his tombstone to engrave on it a cylinder circumscribing a globe, with the ratio 2:3 written between them. This referred to his discovery that the ratio of the volume of a sphere inscribed in a cylinder to the volume of the cylinder, and the ratio of the surface of the sphere to the cylinder's surface, are as two is to three.

Archimedes' rigorous methods for determining areas and volumes led him close to the procedures of the first seventeenth-century practitioners of the integral calculus (the branch of mathematics that deals with variable quantities, and is based on the concept of the limit). He also devised a system for expressing large numbers, which no classical Greek had achieved: his *Sand-Reckoner* shows an understanding of the nature of a numerical system far in excess of the achievement of any other ancient mathematician.

His *Plane Equilibrium* can be regarded as the pioneer scientific treatise on the first principles of mechanics, which deals with the behaviour of matter under the action of force. His pioneer work in mechanics is illustrated by his alleged remark: 'give me a place to stand [i.e., with a long enough lever] and I will move the earth'. He also built further on earlier researches to produce an epoch-making work on statics (the area of mechanics dealing with bodies at rest and forces in equilibrium) and hydrostatics (the study of the equilibrium of liquids and the pressures that they exert at rest). Indeed, he virtually invented the whole science of hydrostatics, and gave it a theoretical basis. One of his discoveries was that a body immersed in water is buoyed up by a force equal to the weight of the water displaced. According to one of the legends that proliferated round his career, this conclusion dawned upon him in his bath, whereupon he ran home without his clothes, crying *heureka, heureka*—'I have found it'.

Archimedes was also an outstanding engineer. By this time the lever, pulley, wedge and windlass were already known; but he himself was plausibly credited with the discovery of a screw (*cochlias*) for raising water, which is still used in many countries to irrigate land. Popular history also ascribed to him the invention of wonderful war-machines used against the Romans in their siege of Syracuse. It was during that siege that he lost his life, for while he was engaged in drawing a mathematical figure in the sand a Roman soldier ignored his request not to interrupt his process of thought and stabbed him to death.

Geographers and Astronomers

About twelve years younger than Archimedes was Eratosthenes of Cyrene (*c.* 275–194), who worked at Athens and then became head of the Alexandrian Library. Part scientist, part humanist, he was a polymath [someone with knowledge of a wide range of subjects] who (despite the sneers that this versatility always evokes) rivalled Aristotle, or Leonardo da Vinci, in the breadth and range of his knowledge and work. But his particular achievement was in the field of geography, which had received such a mighty stimulus from the conquests of Alexander. Dicaearchus of Messana (*c.* 300), for his *Life of Greece*, had made a map of the world, and Eratosthenes revised it, using his mathematical knowledge (and observation that the sunlight strikes different parts of the earth at different angles) to determine the earth's circumference with a high degree of accuracy. He was the first systematic geographer, whose *Geographica* contributed more than any other single study by anyone else to an accurate delineation of the surface of the world.

Greek mathematical geography was largely based on astronomy, and this was the branch of applied mathematics that especially fascinated the Hellenistic world. The first Greek constructor of a mathematical scheme to explain the apparent movement of the heavenly bodies had been Eudoxus of Cnidus (*c.* 390–340), an acquaintance of Plato. . . . Heraclides Ponticus of Heraclea on the Black Sea (*c.* 388–315) put forward a new planetary system, apparently suggesting that the earth (which was now recognized to be spherical) revolves on its axis.

It was Aristarchus of Samos, however, a pupil of Strato, who achieved far more enduring fame early in the third century BC by his discovery that the earth revolves round the sun. Seleucus of Seleucia on the Tigris (?*c.* 150) supported Aristarchus' heliocentric view, but Hipparchus of Nicaea (*c.* 190–after 126), the greatest astronomer of antiquity, felt unable (like almost everyone else) to accept this conclusion because the known facts were insufficient to make any decision possible: we must abide, he felt, by the facts of observation—which could not confirm the immense distances required for Aristarchus' cosmos. Nevertheless, Hipparchus improved observational techniques out of all recognition, displaying a special talent for the selection of relevant data, which included Babylonian and Alexandrian records of eclipses, in addition to his own remarkably exact findings. He thus became the first to evolve a satisfactory theory for the motion of the sun and moon. Moreover, in the words of the Roman polymath Pliny the elder, Hipparchus 'did a bold thing, that would be reprehensible even for God—he dared to schedule the stars for posterity, and tick off the heavenly bodies by name on a list thus bequeathing the heavens as a heritage to all humankind, supposing anyone could be found to claim the legacy!'

Hellenistic astronomy lacked the close environmental control needed for the infinite repetitiveness of laboratory experiments, and the optical and other instruments at its disposal were limited. Yet its discoveries, and the developments of scientific method that accompanied them and made them possible, had been extraordinary. The sophistication of these techniques is illustrated by an astronomical clock, or calendrical computer, of c. 75–50 BC, found at the island of Aegilia or Ogylus, now Anticythera, between the Peloponnese and Crete. In this most complex of all the scientific objects that have come down to us from antiquity, an elaborate system of no less than thirty bronze dials and cogwheels is applied to the plotting of the movements of sun, moon and stars.

Advances in Medicine

Medicine, too, made notable advances during the Hellenistic Age. The science was, of course, by no means new; for example, a vase-painting of 480–470 had displayed a whole series of medical procedures that were already in operation. Traditionally, the best-known medical centres of Greece were the shrines of Asclepius, hero and god of healing, especially at Epidaurus and Cos (founded c. 350). The sanctuaries included sanatoria, where healing took the form of incubation (sleeping in the temple and receiving guidance by dreams), described by the fifth-century poet of the Old Comedy, Aristophanes. Many of the recorded cures display this element of miraculous intervention or auto-suggestion; but use was also made of dietetic régimes, baths and exercise.

How far the leading doctors of the day derived their science from the priests is hard to discover,

but it seems likely that the foundation of the Cos temple was due to the disciples of Hippocrates, the greatest of all Greek physicians. Hippocrates, who was born on that island in the latter half of the fifth century, revolutionized medicine: researching, teaching and practising at many centres in the Greek world, he introduced reason into medical science at about the same time as Socrates was performing a similar function for philosophy. The Hippocratic Oath, however, prescribing the ethics of a doctor in memorable terms, seems, in its present form at least, to have been composed after 400; and the fifty-eight works in the Hippocratic Corpus likewise seem mostly to have been written at that time or, more usually, in the Hellenistic Age, of which they thus form one of the major achievements.

The various Hippocratic advances meant that the Greeks could now employ a system of medicine based not only on theoretical principles but on gradually accumulated observation. Moreover, Greek medicine managed to maintain itself as an autonomous subject, because of its obvious social relevance. Salaried public physicians had already been known earlier, but were now to be found much more widely. . . .

Nevertheless, the Hellenistic epoch witnessed practical developments in medicine fully worthy of the theoretical studies that were being undertaken during the period. Their most important centre was now the school founded at Alexandria, which, above all, developed the science of anatomy. The creation of this branch of medicine owed much to ancient Egyptian learning. It also owed a very great deal to its royal patrons, the Ptolemies, who in addition to paying the staff of the Alexandrian Faculty (linked in some way with the Museum), gave them opportunities, hitherto unavailable, for the dissection of human bodies by providing the corpses of criminals for the purpose. It was due to these facilities that anatomy, backed by much-improved surgical methods and instruments, led the way in Hellenistic medical research.

Thus Herophilus of Chalcedon, who had moved to Alexandria in the first half of the third century, employed dissection in order to transform knowledge of the brain, eye, duodenum, liver and reproductive organs. Though an eminent scholar, he was chiefly guided by the practical tasks and problems facing doctors, of whose obligations to the public he had a particularly high conception. Erasistratus, his younger colleague and perhaps pupil, made important discoveries in relation to digestion and the vascular (circulatory) system (though understanding of the circulation of the blood still lay in the future). If Herophilus is to be called the founder of anatomy, Erasistratus was the creator of physiology. Though a cautious clinical practitioner, he blended his careful, quantitative observation with flashes of bold, even rash, speculation. He was also the father of psychiatry: the first man to realize the existence of diseases of the nervous system and their possible causes.

Herophilus and Erasistratus represented the high-water mark of Hellenistic biology and medicine. After their deaths, dissection appears to have ceased. At this period, too, the profession became divided into warring sects, of which Dogmatists and Empiricists were among the best-known. The Dogmatists, followers of Herophilus, claimed to follow the classical Hippocratic methods of deduction, arguing that knowledge of the human condition and of what causes diseases is indispensable and can be obtained only by the employment of reasoning and conjecture to supplement experience. The Empirical school, on the other hand, were contemptuous of such abstract reasoning about what is invisible and preferred to base their conclusions on direct observation of patients' visible symptoms, rather in the spirit of contemporary philosophers who were concentrating on practical guidance of the individual. Thus Serapion of Alexandria (c. 200–150)—the school's founder (or second founder after Philinus of Cos, c. 250)—pronounced that it is not the cause but the cure of sickness which concerns the physician, not how we digest but what is digestible.

The scientific history of the Hellenistic Age

terminated with Posidonius of Syrian Apamea (c. 135–50 [B.C.]). His works, like those of so many of his predecessors, are now lost: but he was evidently a polymath on a scale even more stupendous than Eratosthenes. Settling in Rhodes, and developing many contacts with Rome, he devoted himself not only to history but to every branch of science, not excluding ethnology [the study of differences in human cultures]. One of his motives was at long last to bring philosophical and scientific studies together again. Another was to illustrate his Stoic conviction that heaven and earth and all parts of the cosmos continually exchange influences with one another—and to suggest that this mutual 'sympathy' made the anti-scientific bias of most of his fellow-Stoics seem altogether misguided.

The observations Posidonius made and recorded on his widespread travels encouraged him to try to determine the distance and magnitude of the sun, to calculate the diameter of the earth, to draw a new map of the world, and to give an accurate description of the life and currents of the ocean, demonstrating the dependence of the tides upon the phases of the moon. When Aristotle had written of meteorology, he limited it to the study of the processes, conditions and phenomena of the atmosphere. But Posidonius, interpreting the same science much more widely, saw it as explaining the whole structure of the outer and upper world, within the context of a universal system which harmoniously blends matter, mind and spirit.

His almost unlimited range made him vulnerable to charges of superficiality. Yet he was the most learned man of his time; and people admiringly called him 'the athlete', with good reason. It was Posidonius' enormous achievement to collect and reshape a vast quantity of inherited Hellenic and Hellenistic erudition in a huge variety of fields, and to hand on the whole of this massive material to the Roman world and the Renaissance.

Selection 11

The Fabulous Inventions of Archimedes

Plutarch

Though he much preferred his studies of abstract mathematical concepts, the great Greek Hellenistic scientist Archimedes of Syracuse (ca. 287–212 B.C.) sometimes found himself coerced into producing mechanical inventions. He probably studied at Alexandria as a young man and then returned to his native city of Syracuse (in Sicily), where he lived at the court of King Hiero (or Hieron) II. It was Hiero who pushed Archimedes to create ingenious mechanical devices, the most famous of which were weapons of mass destruction. In 214 B.C., in a subsidiary conflict of their larger war with Carthage (the Second Punic War), the Romans began besieging Syracuse, and Archimedes rose to the challenge. The first-century A.D. Greek writer Plutarch describes Archimedes' awesome and exciting defense of Syracuse in his biography of Marcellus, the Roman commander. As Plutarch relates, Marcellus greatly respected Archimedes and wanted to put him to work for Rome; but the great inventor died in the siege, robbing the world of one of its most original thinkers. Plutarch also includes valuable information about the inventor's character and personal pursuits.

Excerpted from *Makers of Rome: Nine Lives*, by Plutarch, translated by Ian Scott-Kilvert (Penguin Classics, 1965). Translation copyright © 1965 by Ian Scott-Kilvert. Reprinted by permission of Penguin Books Ltd.

Marcellus directed a fleet of sixty quinquiremes [large warships], which were equipped with many different kinds of weapons and missiles. In addition he had built a siege-engine which was mounted on a huge platform supported by eight galleys lashed together, and with this he sailed up to the city walls, confident that the size and the imposing spectacle of his armament together with his personal prestige would combine to overawe the Syracusans. But he had reckoned without Archimedes, and the Roman machines turned out to be insignificant not only in the philosopher's estimation, but also by comparison with those which he had constructed himself. Archimedes did not regard his military inventions as an achievement of any importance, but merely as a by-product, which he occasionally pursued for his own amusement, of his serious work, namely the study of geometry. He had done this in the past because Hiero, the former ruler of Syracuse, had often pressed and finally persuaded him to divert his studies from the pursuit of abstract principles to the solution of practical problems, and to make his theories more intelligible to the majority of mankind by applying them through the medium of the senses to the needs of everyday life. . . .

However this may be, Archimedes in writing to Hiero, who was both a relative and a friend of his, asserted that with any given force it was possible to move any given weight, and then,

Archimedes, pictured here with a compass and a diagram of Syracuse.

carried away with enthusiasm at the power of his demonstration, so we are told, went on to enlarge his claim, and declared that if he were given another world to stand on, he could move the earth. Hiero was amazed, and invited him to put his theorem into practice and show him some great weight moved by a tiny force. Archimedes chose for his demonstration a three-masted merchantman of the royal fleet, which had been hauled ashore with immense labour by a large gang of men, and he proceeded to have the ship loaded with her usual freight and embarked a large number of passengers. He then seated himself at some distance away and without using any noticeable force, but merely exerting traction with his hand through a complex system of pulleys, he drew the vessel towards him with as smooth and even a motion is if she were gliding through the water. The king was deeply impressed, and recognizing the potential-

ities of his skill, he persuaded Archimedes to construct for him a number of engines designed both for attack and defence, which could be employed in any kind of siege warfare. Hiero himself never had occasion to use these, since most of his life was spent at peace amid festivals and public ceremonies, but when the present war broke out, the apparatus was ready for the Syracusans to use and its inventor was at hand to direct its employment.

Repelling the Roman Onslaught

When the Romans first attacked by sea and land, the Syracusans were struck dumb with terror and believed that nothing could resist the onslaught of such powerful forces. But presently Archimedes brought his engines to bear and launched a tremendous barrage against the Roman army. This consisted of a variety of missiles, including a great volley of stones which descended upon their target with an incredible noise and velocity. There was no protection against this artillery, and the soldiers were knocked down in swathes and their ranks thrown into confusion. At the same time huge beams were run out from the walls so as to project over the Roman ships: some of them were then sunk by great weights dropped from above, while others were seized at the bows by iron claws or by beaks like those of cranes, hauled into the air by means of counterweights until they stood upright upon their sterns, and then allowed to plunge to the bottom, or else they were spun round by means of windlasses situated inside the city and dashed against the steep cliffs and rocks which jutted out under the walls, with great loss of life to the crews. Often there would be seen the terrifying spectacle of a ship being lifted clean out of the water into the air and whirled about as it hung there, until every man had been shaken out of the hull and thrown in different directions, after which it would be dashed down empty upon the walls. As for the enormous siege-engine which Marcellus brought up, mounted on eight galleys as I have described, and known as a *sambuca* because of its resemblance to the musical instrument of that name, a stone weighing a hundred pounds was discharged while it was still approaching the city wall, immediately followed by a second and a third. These descended on their target with a thunderous crash and a great surge of water, shattered the platform on which the machine was mounted, loosened the bolts which held it together, and dislodged the whole framework from the hulks which supported it. Marcellus, finding his plan of attack thus brought to a standstill, drew off his ships as quickly as possible and ordered his land forces to retire.

After this he held a council of war and formed a new plan to move up as closely as possible to the walls under cover of darkness. The Romans calculated that the cables which Archimedes used for his siege-engines imparted such a tremendous velocity to the missiles they discharged that these would go flying over their heads, but that at close quarters, where a low trajectory was required, they would be ineffective. However, Archimedes, it seems, had long ago foreseen such a possibility and had designed engines which were suitable for any distance and missiles to match them. He had had a large number of loopholes made in the walls, and in these he placed short-range weapons known as scorpions, which were invisible to the attacker, but could be discharged as soon as he arrived at close quarters.

So when the Romans crept up close to the walls expecting to surprise the enemy, they were again greeted by a hail of missiles. Huge stones were dropped on them almost perpendicularly, and it seemed as if they were faced by a curtain of darts along the whole length of the wall, so that the attackers soon fell back. But here too, even while they were hurrying, as they hoped, out of danger, they came under fire from the medium-range catapults which caused heavy losses among them: at the same time many of their ships were dashed against one another, and all this while they were helpless to retaliate. Archimedes had mounted most of his weapons under the cover of the city walls, and the Romans began to believe that they were fighting against a supernatural enemy, as they found themselves constantly struck down by opponents whom they could never see.

Marcellus, however, escaped unhurt from this assault and afterwards made fun of his own siege-experts and engineers. 'We may as well give up fighting this geometrical Briareus [a mythical giant with a hundred hands],' he said, 'who uses our slips like cups to ladle water out of the sea, who has whipped our *sambuca* and driven it off in disgrace, and who can outdo the hundred-handed giants of mythology in hurling so many different missiles at us at once.' For the truth was that all the rest of the Syracusans merely provided the manpower to operate Archimedes's inventions, and it was his mind which directed and controlled every manoeuvre. All other weapons were discarded, and it was upon his alone that the city relied both for attack and defence. At last the Romans were reduced to such a state of alarm that if they saw so much as a length of rope or a piece of timber appear over the top of the wall, it was enough to make them cry out, 'Look, Archimedes is aiming one of his machines at us!' and they would turn their backs and run. When Marcellus saw this, he abandoned all attempts to capture the city by assault, and settled down to reduce it by blockade.

Why Archimedes Preferred Theoretical Science

As for Archimedes, he was a man who possessed such exalted ideals, such profound spiritual vision, and such a wealth of scientific knowledge that, although his inventions had earned him a reputation for almost superhuman intellectual power, he would not deign to leave behind him any writings on his mechanical discoveries. He regarded the business of engineering, and indeed of every art which ministers to the material needs of life, as an ignoble and sordid activity, and he concentrated his ambition exclusively upon those speculations whose beauty and subtlety are untainted by the claims of necessity. These studies, he believed, are incomparably superior to any others, since here the grandeur and beauty of the subject matter vie for our admiration with the cogency and precision of the methods of proof. Certainly in the whole science of geometry it is impossible to find more difficult and intricate problems handled in simpler and purer terms than in his works. Some writers attribute this to his natural genius. Others maintain that a phenomenal industry lay behind the apparently effortless ease with which he obtained his results. The fact is that no amount of mental effort of his own would enable a man to hit upon the proof of one of Archimedes's theorems, and yet as soon as it is explained to him, he feels that he might have discovered it himself, so smooth and rapid is the path by which he leads us to the required conclusion. So it is not at all difficult to credit some of the stories which have been told about him; of how, for example, he often seemed so bewitched by the song of some inner and familiar Siren that he would forget to eat his food or take care of his person; or how when he was carried by force, as he often was to the bath for his body to be washed and anointed, he would trace geometrical figures in the ashes and draw diagrams with his finger in the oil which had been rubbed over his skin. Such was the rapture which his work inspired in him, so as to make him truly the captive of the Muses [goddesses of the arts and intellectual pursuits]. And although he was responsible for many discoveries of great value, he is said to have asked his friends and relatives to place on his tomb after his death nothing more than the shape of a cylinder enclosing a sphere, with an inscription explaining the ratio by which the containing solid exceeds the contained. [In 75 B.C., 137 years after Archimedes' death, the famous Roman politician and orator Cicero discovered the inventor's tomb, which had been forgotten and become overgrown by brambles.].

Syracuse Falls

Such was Archimedes's character, and in so far as it rested with him, he kept himself and his city unconquered. But while Syracuse was being blockaded, Marcellus did not remain idle. . . . He overran a large part of Sicily, persuaded a number of cities to revolt from the Carthaginians, and defeated his opponents wherever he en-

countered resistance. Some while afterwards he captured a man named Damippus, a Spartan who had attempted to escape from Syracuse by ship. The Syracusans were anxious to ransom him, and during the numerous meetings and negotiations that followed, Marcellus noticed a particular tower which was carelessly guarded and into which he could infiltrate men unobserved, since the wall in its immediate vicinity was easy to climb. During his visits to parley with the Syracusans he had the height of the tower carefully measured and scaling ladders prepared. Marcellus chose a moment when the Syracusans were celebrating a feast-day in honour of Artemis and had given themselves up to drinking and other festivities. Before they knew what he was about, he had not only seized the tower but also occupied the adjacent wall with his troops and forced his way through the Hexapyla, the gate at the north-west corner of the city. When the citizens discovered what had happened, and while they were running to and fro in confusion and attempting to muster their forces, Marcellus ordered his trumpets to be sounded from all sides at once. The Syracusans fled from the sound in terror and imagined that the whole city had already been captured. . . .

Not long afterwards the rest of the city was captured by treachery and given over to plunder, except for the royal property, which was handed over to the Roman treasury.

But what distressed Marcellus . . . was the death of Archimedes. As fate would have it the philosopher was by himself, engrossed in working out some calculation by means of a diagram, and his eyes and his thoughts were so intent upon the problem that he was completely unaware that the Romans had broken through the defences, or that the city had been captured. Suddenly a soldier came upon him and ordered him to accompany him to Marcellus. Archimedes refused to move until he had worked out his problem and established his demonstration, whereupon the soldier flew into a rage, drew his sword, and killed him. According to another account, the Roman came up with a drawn sword and threatened to kill him there and then: when

Archimedes saw him, he begged him to stay his hand for a moment, so that he should not leave his theorem imperfect and without its demonstration, but the soldier paid no attention and dispatched him at once. There is yet a third story to the effect that Archimedes was on his way to Marcellus bringing some of his instruments, such as sundials and spheres and quadrants, with the help of which the dimensions of the sun could be measured by the naked eye, when some soldiers met him, and believing that he was carrying gold in the box promptly killed him. At any rate it is generally agreed that Marcellus was deeply affected by his death, that he abhorred the man who had killed him as if he had committed an act of sacrilege, and that he sought out Archimedes's relatives and treated them with honour.

Farming, Commerce, and Trade

Chapter 13

Introduction

Modern scholars often speak of ancient Greece's "economy" or the economies of Athens, or Corinth, or Macedonia, or other individual ancient cities and kingdoms. But this use of the word economy is very informal, a kind of shorthand to denote the general realm of finances and making a living. It does not suggest that any of these ancient political entities had a large-scale, diversified economic system in place, or a formal set of financial goals, or even an accepted theory about how a state might become financially prosperous. The fact is that no ancient Greek city or kingdom had any of these essential features of the economies of modern industrialized nations. As noted historian M.I. Finley states in his classic book *The Ancient Economy*:

> Ancient society did not have an economic system which was an enormous conglomeration [assembly] of interdependent markets. . . . There were no business cycles in antiquity; no cities whose growth can be ascribed . . . to the establishment of a manufacture. . . . The economic language and concepts we are all familiar with . . . tend to draw us into a false account. For example, wage rates and interest rates in the Greek and Roman worlds were both fairly stable locally over long periods . . . so that to speak of a "labor market" or a "money market" [implying ups and downs driven by changes in supply and demand] is immediately to falsify the situation. For the same reason, no modern investment model is applicable to the preferences of the men who dominated ancient society. . . . Equally important, few [financial] records were normally retained once they had served their immediate purpose. Hence no time series [studies of economic trends over time] was available in antiquity, in either the public or the private sector. . . and without a time series there can be no reasoning by figures, no statistics.

Without statistics to study, the ancient Greeks could not plan financial strategy very far ahead or formulate theories about how to improve financial systems. So they tended, at least most of the time, to perpetuate the status quo, to utilize the same agricultural, industrial, and commercial practices their ancestors did.

This tendency to stick with traditional economic customs is illustrated by the fact that throughout antiquity land remained the principal basis of local economies. As many people in modern developing countries continue to do, most Greeks made their living by growing crops, raising livestock, or trading the various commodities produced on farms and estates. In the Bronze Age, many, if not most, small farmers were peasants who worked lands owned or run by the state. By contrast, the Dark and Archaic ages witnessed the rise of independent farmers, who owned their own lands and exploited them to their personal advantage. A few landowners were wealthy. As a rule, they tended to be absentee landlords who lived in the urban centers and relied on hired managers (bailiffs) to look after their estates. Most landowners, however, were small farmers, who also made up the bulk of the local military militias.

The staple crops were cereal grains (especially barley and wheat), lentils, olives, grapes (for both eating and making wine), figs and other fruits, and vegetables. And the most common animals raised were sheep and goats, although pigs, horses, and other sorts of livestock were important in certain areas (for example, Thessaly was known for its horses). Although most city-states were more or less self-sufficient in these products, some of the larger ones had to import certain essentials. An often-noted example is that of Athens, which in the Classic Age imported well over half of its grain from the fertile fields of Greek cities lying along the coasts of the Black Sea.

This trade in grain was only part of a vast commercial maritime network that stretched across the Mediterranean, Aegean, and Black seas. Foodstuffs (including olive oil and wine) remained major cargo items throughout ancient times; however, hundreds of other products were also traded, including textiles, pottery, marble, timber, papyrus, and various personal luxuries. In some cases, imported goods were vital necessities because mainland Greece lacked certain important or popular products. For example, there was little iron ore in Greece, so that crucial metal was imported from the Black Sea region or other areas; and similarly, papyrus came mainly from Egypt, purple dye from Phoenicia (along the coast of Palestine), and carpets from Persia.

Indeed, the diversity of regions Greek traders visited, and also the great distances they often traveled, are impressive. Recent archaeological finds have revealed that as early as the late Bronze Age, Greek (Minoan and Mycenaean) ships traded regularly with ports in Italy, Egypt, and Palestine. The Greek commercial world significantly expanded in Archaic times as widespread colonization created new markets—in Spain, southern France, northern Africa, and elsewhere—with direct ties to the motherland. And the Hellenistic Age proved to be another period of significant expansion. During and after the wars of the Successors, new Greek cities sprang up in the Near East and tapped into trade routes stretching to Arabia, India, and other distant lands.

Some of this maritime trade was sponsored by the governments of cities or kingdoms, especially in Hellenistic times, when the great monarchies competed for the fattest shares of the international commercial markets. But more often, importing and exporting was a lucrative but risky *private* business directed by the local merchants and shippers of various states. Often, they received the backing of local businessmen who were willing to take the risk that a cargo would make a profit. (These backers are often referred to as bankers, though this is a loose term, for no large corporate lending institutions in the modern sense yet existed; "private lenders" would be a more accurate description.)

Unfortunately, very few formal written sources describing Greek economic activity have survived from antiquity (and it is doubtful that a great many were produced in the first place). The best known example is Xenophon's *Oeconomicus,* dating from the early-to-mid fourth century B.C. Translating roughly as *Estate-Manager* or *Management of a Household,* it has nothing to do with economic theory. Rather, it explains how a country gentleman (like Xenophon himself) should run his estate, including the duties of his wife and slaves and tips on planting and harvesting grains, fruits, and other crops. In the years that followed, numerous other writers wrote similar books of advice for estate owners, most of which are now lost. For the most part, modern scholars must rely on other diverse and informal sources for information about Greek agriculture, industries, trade, and other economic topics. These include some of the court speeches written by Athenian orators (for instance, Demosthenes' *Against Sdenothemis* deals with fraud among merchants and traders); occasional short discussions or references in various histories and philosophical treatises (most notably the first book of Aristotle's *Politics*); inscriptions in stone; papyrus fragments (which sometimes contain partial cargo manifests, contracts, etc.); the remains of shipwrecked cargo vessels; and to a lesser extent vase paintings and coins.

Selection 1

Trade in Greece's Bronze Age

Michael Wood

Michael Wood, author of the acclaimed study In Search of the Trojan War, *here discusses the surprisingly widespread and vigorous trading network that existed in the Greek Bronze Age. The Minoans, he says, centered at Knossus and other Cretan palaces, traded with regions as far afield as Anatolia (Asia Minor), Italy, the coasts of Syria and Palestine, and Egypt. And after the Mycenaeans overran the Minoan sphere (ca. 1420–1400 B.C.), they too carried on commerce with these areas. Needless to say, the curtailment of most of this commerce in the thirteenth century B.C., attending the collapse of Mycenaean civilization, was one of the principal factors in the onset of Greece's Dark Age.*

*n*ow in earlier times the world's history had consisted so to speak of a series of unrelated episodes, the origins and results of which being as widely separated as their localities, but from this point onwards history becomes an organic whole: the affairs of Italy and Africa are connected with those of Asia and of Greece, and all events bear a relationship and contribute to a single end.

Polybius, *World History*

So Polybius, the late-second-century-BC historian of the wars between Rome and Carthage, assessed the significance of the rise of Rome. In fact, the more we discover about the Late-Bronze-Age world the more we find that the unity of the eastern Mediterranean had its roots much further back in time than Polybius thought: roots in the sense of the cultural and commercial relations between the Aegean world, western Anatolia, Crete and the Near East in the Bronze Age. Men had travelled on the sea since Neolithic [Old Stone Age, i.e., pre–Bronze Age] times, populating islands and exploiting their natural resources as far as their technology allowed. By the end of the Bronze Age land and sea routes had been established between these different areas which were to persist for millennia. Hence, as most experts believe, Mycenaean merchants were resident in Cyprus and in Ugarit [a city on the coast of Syria] in the fourteenth and thirteenth centuries BC, and may have been active elsewhere, as for instance at . . . Sarafend in south Lebanon where a remarkable tomb of this period has been found. The importance of these routes meant that as early as the Middle Bronze Age connections had been established between the different regions of the eastern Mediterranean, and by the Late Bronze Age their destinies were to a certain extent bound up. . . .

Trade was on an organised footing in the Near East even before the Greeks came to the Aegean world, and its influence crept westwards. There were already Assyrian merchant communities at Kanesh in Anatolia in 1800 BC, living in their own quarter, over an acre in extent, bound by treaty, their caravan routes stretching across to the western sea. . . . Kings controlled commerce early, for it was the best way of bringing in surplus income and luxury products. The tremendous detail of the Linear B archives at Knossos and Pylos shows that Mycenaean kings of the thirteenth century BC had precisely that control. Among their imports were ivory, cumin, coriander and Cypriot copper, products which came by sea; perhaps there were even tiny foreign communities at Mycenaean Knossos, with people like the 'Egyptian' and the 'Lykian' mentioned in the tablets, and Pijamunu and others whose names are Anatolian. . . .

We can add to this picture Greek ships sailing to Amurru in Syria with goods bound for Assyria in the Euphrates valley. . . . They may have exported olive oil to Egypt where the olive does not thrive; their pottery appears on Near Eastern sites so extensively that one wonders whether it had some sort of snob value—or is it simply a mark of Greek commercial expertise? Is the ubiquitous [widely visible] stirrup jar just the 'Coke' bottle of its day?

To Greece came slaves from Asia Minor (and Africa?). The Knossos tablets mention cyperus seed from Cyprus, sesame, cumin, gold, and purple dye from Syria—all known by their Semitic names. Copper was a major economic need (it came of course from Cyprus, whose very name indicates its origin) and for this reason throughout the Bronze Age—bronze is made by alloying tin with copper—Cyprus was of central importance in the Mediterranean, the main entrepôt between the Greek and Aegean world on the one hand, and Syria, Ugarit and the Near East on the other.

Remarkable evidence of such trade has been uncovered recently in the first of what are likely to prove numerous Bronze-Age wrecks on the dangerous southern shore of Turkey. Off Cape Gelidonya a thirteenth-century-BC shipwreck brought to light fragments of up to 100 copper in-gots, each weighing about 50 lb, clearly the main cargo of a boat heading westwards into the Aegean from Cyprus. Among the wreckage was a large toolkit of picks, shovels, axes, blades, an anvil, two mortars, storage jars, whetstones and so on. Perhaps belonging to the merchant himself were a spit, a set of weights, bronze wire, a lamp, a reed basket, a personal razor and mirror, Egyptian scarabs and a Near Eastern cylinder seal which the owner possibly used as his personal seal: a marvellous insight into the life of one of the individual captains or traders who crisscrossed the Aegean in the Late Bronze Age. . . .

Minoan and Mycenaean Traders

The path by which the Mycenaeans had come to dominate Aegean trade seems broadly clear. After the Old Assyrian trade network across Anatolia disintegrated, the Minoans of Crete seem first to have grown in commercial enterprise in the Aegean between the eighteenth and fifteenth centuries BC. This is what Thucydides alleged in his account of [the legendary King] Minos' domination of the Cyclades, and archaeology is proving him right. British excavations at Phylakopi on [the Aegean island of] Melos showed a Minoan 'colony' there. . . . In the Cyclades, Amorgos, Thera, Siphnos and Delos have produced evidence of Minoan trading connections and even, as on Delos and Keos, the exporting of Minoan textile techniques. By the sixteenth century BC the Cretan influence is extremely marked on mainland Mycenaean pottery and especially in the craftsmanship of such Mycenaean masterpieces as the shaft grave daggers and cups. Westwards the Minoans reached southern Italy and Sicily . . . and eastwards they planted settlements in Rhodes, Kos, Samos and even on the coast of Asia Minor at Iasos and Miletus: the last named gave Minoan traders access to the hinterland of Anatolia. Further afield Minoan merchants dealt with Syria and Egypt, and their ambassadors are portrayed in Egyptian wall-paintings: Keftiu (Cretan) ships were evidently a common sight in Near Eastern ports, and the Minoans were the

These vases at Akrotiri (on the Cycladic island of Thera) may have come from Minoan Crete, which shipped goods throughout the Bronze Age Aegean sphere.

middlemen in the trade westwards. . . .

In Ugarit, finely built chamber tombs have been excavated, suggesting that the Minoan settlers there were people of wealth and sophistication, at ease in a multiracial and multilingual city. The Mycenaeans had already started to encroach into this world before they destroyed the power of the Minoans and occupied Knossos in around 1420 BC. In the previous century or so their own wares reached Melos and Naxos in quantity, and a certain amount went to Keos and Delos; further out, Minoan ware was still dominant. But after the sack of Knossos Mycenaean pottery is found right across the Cyclades. . . . Greek settlers seem to take the place of Minoan ones, at least as the ruling or commercial élites. By the thirteenth century BC Mycenaean pottery is all over the Aegean and found in quantities throughout Syria, Palestine and Egypt. . . .

It is evident that we are dealing with no small-scale or casual trade over the Aegean and Eastern Mediterranean as a whole, but with a commerce central to the economy of the Late-Bronze-Age palaces. As we would have guessed from the meticulous detail of the Linear B archives, the palaces were geared to efficient production. . . .

The conspicuous consumption [constant use of a wide range of products] of the great [Mycenaean] palaces and their estates in their heyday relied on overseas trade, and with their fragile economies they needed their world to remain relatively static in order to preserve their social and political order. They needed a continued supply of bronze, that is, of copper from Cyprus and of tin, in order to make the weapons with which they equipped their fighting forces. They needed a continued supply of slaves from Asia Minor, from Miletus, Cnidus, Halicarnassos

(Zephyrus), Chios and Lemnos, to work their estates, not only producing for their own consumption, but making a surplus—textiles, oil or whatever for export. . . . They needed to make constant armed raids overseas or into neighbouring territories in order to seize not only slaves but also treasure and booty with which to reward their armed followers, on whose strong arm their power rested. This is a condition of all early kingships. They needed, in short, a stable Aegean and Eastern Mediterranean world in order for their trade routes to exist, and for their markets to be accessible.

Selection 2

Why Land Was the Basis of Greece's Economy

Alfred Zimmern

Citing Thucydides, Xenophon, and other Greek writers, the late, distinguished classical scholar Alfred Zimmern here explains that the economic life of ancient Greek communities revolved around the ownership and/or use of land. He concentrates primarily on Athens, since that is where most of the evidence comes from. In addition to the importance of the land, Zimmern outlines the three main types of land use (pasturage for goats and sheep; raising grain and other crops; and fruit production, including olives) and takes a brief look at the landowners themselves.

*H*ow did the fifth-century Athenian make his living as a private individual? secondly, how did the Athenian State support itself? what was the economic basis of its civilization and achievements? These questions are easily asked; but they are not so quickly answered. . . . We must go back to the economic foundations of Greek society, to the origins and development of the City State, and to its ordinary humble working citizens, and so build up, layer by layer, the economics of the Athenian Empire.

Let us go back, then . . . with Thucydides for our guide, to the beginnings of Greek society, to the days before the Greeks had settled down into the routine of City State life. We shall find here some elements in their economy which remained stable and persistent, and others which, with advancing civilization, they were able later to discard or to develop. . . .

Thucydides has left us, on the first page of his book, a vivid imaginative sketch of the economic life of the earliest Greeks in their scattered villages just after the chaos of the great migrations. 'It is evident,' he says, 'that in ancient times the country now called Hellas had no settled population; on the contrary, migrations

Excerpted from Alfred Zimmern, *The Greek Commonwealth: Politics and Economics in Fifth-Century Athens*, 5th ed. Copyright © 1961, 1966 by Oxford University Press. Reprinted by permission of Oxford University Press.

were of frequent occurrence, the several tribes readily abandoning their homes under the pressure of superior numbers. Without commerce, without safe communications either by land or sea, cultivating no more of their land than they required for bare subsistence, destitute of capital, never planting their land with fruits (for they could not tell when an invader might not come and take it all away, and when he did come they had no wall to stop him), they thought little of shifting their dwellings, and consequently neither built large cities nor attained to any other kind of greatness.'

There is very little here which is common to the society of Periclean Athens. It is Greek life reduced to its barest elements. There is no trade, no travelling, no vine and olive, no security, not even organized warfare from a settled citadel; yet one permanent element stands out. These men made their living, so far as they made it at all, and did not merely rob it, by cultivating the soil. They lived by the land.

Work Worthy of a Free Man

This is the one abiding fact about the economy of the Greeks, from their earliest days down to the fifth century. . . . There were many possible ways in which a Greek could make a living, but there was only one which seemed entirely natural and traditional—work on the land.

The Greek writers who discuss the question of livelihood (and, in spite of what is often said, Greece did produce 'economists') are unanimous upon this subject. All of them preach work on the land. No other occupation which fills the family store, says Xenophon, in his glowing eulogy of the farmer's life, is at once so pleasant and so healthy, and so worthy of a free man. Agriculture, says Plato, is a more natural art than politics itself, for it 'co-operates with Nature', like medicine and physical training. And Aristotle, heedless of the life of the steppe and the forest and the fiord, actually regards agriculture of the Greek sort as the normal life of all mankind. Be that as it may, it was at any rate the right and proper occupation for the Greek father of a family. Ever since his ancestors had established

themselves, centuries back, in their little enclosed plains and valleys, and gradually dropped, as Thucydides describes for us, from the old seminomadic life into settled and stationary ways, he had been used to thinking of himself as attached, first as the member of a tribe or brotherhood and then as a father of a single household, to a definite piece of land from which he drew his living. Greek civilization is, in a sense, urban; but its basis is agricultural, and the breezes of the open country blow through the Parliament [i.e., Assembly], and the market-place. The landed tradition is the strongest and most persistent force in the inherited social economy of Greece.

It is necessary to emphasize this in order to understand to the full how fundamentally different their economy is from ours. It is not our cloistered Hellenists and city-dwellers but our shepherds and yokels who, in their daily occupations and habits of housekeeping, touch most nearly the ancient Greek—not merely the Greek of the unsettled early days and of the quiet Middle Ages, but the alert and enterprising citizen of fifth-century Athens. . . .

We must not think of work on the land as it is practised, in these days of machinery and organization . . . by up-to-date farmers and market-gardeners nearer home. We must think of it as what it was until a few years ago, the most stable and conservative of all economic occupations. The trader and the manufacturer rely upon their own skill and enterprise, and can transform and diversify what they handle. The shepherd and the farmer wait upon Nature's pleasure, and look, not to improvements in method, but to favouring skies and kindly gods. They learn to be patient and contemplative, and pleased with the day of small things; they form in every society the great bulwark of Use and Wont. The Greeks, being by tradition shepherds and farmers, were brought up conservatives.

There is another reason why it is not easy for us, approaching him as economists, to understand the Greek farmer. He did not want to grow rich. He worked on the land for a livelihood and for his city, not in the hope of high prices and an ultimate fortune. His object was to provide for his household and, if need be, to help to provide also for the community; but he had no thought of amassing wealth. The great landed fortunes so familiar to us from the eighteenth century were unknown in Greece; or if not entirely unknown, so abnormal and odious as to fall outside the limits of a general picture. If a Greek citizen owned what seemed a disproportionately large amount of the land of the community, the public opinion of the marketplace clamoured that it should be taken away from him and 'redivided'. If a trader or a craftsman was over-wealthy nobody complained, and perhaps nobody knew. At any rate his being rich did not appear to make others poorer. But in a small City State, where land was visibly limited in amount, every additional acre to the large proprietor seemed clearly to mean an acre less for the small men. So the Greek farmer had every reason, both from tradition and policy, to eschew [avoid] the dreams of avarice [greed] and develop the other sides of his nature. His pleasant household and old farm buildings and the familiar gods of the near fields and springs, together with the orderly rows of gnarled olives which his great-grandfather planted, meant more to him than all the riches his cosmopolitan younger brother might be bringing home from the Western seas. For his philosophic aim (however little he might know of it) was to be a harmonious nature, with every part of his being working together for good.

Shepherds and Landowners

How did the Greek draw his living from the land?

Under settled City State conditions he had three sources of livelihood: pasture, tillage, and fruit. Of the shepherd . . . his life was at once the most traditional and the most harmonious; for it was the life of his earliest ancestors, and was the most completely removed from the influence and interests of the city. Only one small economic tie kept him in touch, on his high pastures, with the City World below. He had not enough to eat unless he filled his store from the lowlands. . . . The shepherd and his family needed bread as well as milk and cheese: and it was this that saved them from becoming nomads. . . .

If times were unsettled they came down from the highlands and stole it; but as the City State extended its strong arm they learnt to barter for it with milk food, for which the men below, as they grew in numbers, had an ever-increasing need. Yet even when he was thus incorporated in the economy of the City State, the shepherd continued to lead a life apart, the most old-fashioned, and also, as Aristotle says, the laziest of Greek mankind; for shepherds 'get their subsistence without trouble from tame animals, and since their flocks have to wander from place to place in search of pasture, they are compelled to follow them, cultivating a sort of living farm'. No doubt Greek shepherds, whether they were slaves or citizens, were as open and courteous then as now, and as eager for the latest news of doings in the city. . . . But the main body of them, who spent the summer months on the high mountain pastures, were so removed from city life that they remained outside and unaffected by the economic development we have to follow. Only when war broke out and the frontier pastures became unsafe, did they come down into the plain and join the ranks of their fellows, if so entitled, as citizen soldiers.

Fruit and tillage, the orchard and the ploughed field, belong together, and are looked after from one hearthfire by the proprietor. So far as we can tell, tillage everywhere predominated: for the tradition was that every state must provide its own grain. Even where, as in fifth-century Attica, the growth of population had made this plainly impossible, more corn was probably raised than oil, and the country dwellers at any rate bought little food from the town. In the time of Pericles probably at least one third of the corn consumed in Attica was homegrown, and, in spite of other interests, the soil of Attica was the best farmed in Greece. Those who know how sterile it is now will appreciate the labour spent on it by these Athenian farmers who had so much else to do and to think about.

To whom did the land belong and by what tenure was it held?

Nearly all of it in the normal Greek State was in the hands of small proprietors, who worked the soil themselves. We are not concerned here with serfdom such as existed in Sparta and Thessaly. That was . . . an abnormal condition. . . . The overwhelming majority of the Greek States, like Athens from Solon's day onwards, were cultivated by freeholders. They worked the land with their households, dividing up the estate at death among their sons. . . . Nearly every citizen in an ordinary Greek State was a landowner, whether the piece he owned was large or small, enough to live on or only to starve on. When in 403 it was proposed at Athens, the leading commercial state, to limit the citizenship to owners of land or houses, we are told that only 5,000 citizens would have been excluded by the law, and most of these were probably returned colonists. . . .

Tenancy [renting or leasing the land], in our sense of the word, was therefore practically unknown in Greece. Out of the numerous inscriptions preserved which deal, in one way or another, with land, there are only 'a very small number of contracts made between individuals'.

When a Greek is a tenant at all he is a tenant for a public body: he is cultivating land for the State or for a god or for some brotherhood or association; in other words he is doing for the landlord what the landlord is unable to do for himself. A great number of such inscriptions have come down to us. It is worth while quoting one, to give an idea of how the system worked. It relates to a piece of land which belonged to the town of Poiessa (Grassland) in the island of Ceos, and runs as follows:—

Gods!

Land belonging to the City of Poiessa.

§ 1. The occupier is to pay on the tenth of the month of Bacchion 30 drachmas; if he does not pay he must leave.

§ 2. He is to bring his money to Poiessa.

§ 3. He is to give back the house in good repair and with the roof on.

§ 4. He is not to cut down the fruit trees.

Selection 3

A Greek Farmer Describes Planting and Harvesting

Xenophon

The Athenian-born Xenophon was not only a soldier and historian, but also a country gentleman-farmer who took great pride in his estate. His Oeconomicus (The Management of a Household) *presents his views on how such an estate should be properly run. It is valuable in part because it contains a detailed discussion of Greek farming techniques,* *which is in the form of a dialogue, with Xenophon's old mentor Socrates the chief character. The philosopher recollects a conversation he had with a man named Ischomachus, who seems to represent Xenophon himself, or at least voices his views. In the following excerpt, we find Socrates questioning Ischomachus about the correct methods of plant-*

ing and reaping grain, separating out the chaff, and planting fruit trees.

"'T hen, Socrates, let me refresh your memory on the subject of agriculture; but where do you wish me to begin? For I am aware that I shall tell you very much that you know already about the right method of farming.'

"'First, Ischomachus, I think I should be glad to learn, for this is the philosopher's way, how I am to cultivate the land if I want to get the heaviest crops of wheat and barley out of it.'

"'Well, you know, I take it, that fallow [i.e., unplanted land] must be prepared for sowing?'

"'Yes, I know.'

"'Suppose, then, we start ploughing in winter?'

"'Why the land will be a bog!'

"'How about starting in summer?'

"'The land will be hard to plough up.'

"'It seems that spring is the season for beginning this work.'

"'Yes, the land is likely to be more friable [easier to break up] if it is broken up then.'

"'Yes, and the grass turned up is long enough at that season to serve as manure, but, not having shed seed, it will not grow. You know also, I presume, that fallow land can't be satisfactory unless it is clear of weeds and thoroughly baked in the sun?'

"'Yes, certainly; that is essential, I think.'

"'Do you think that there is any better way of securing that than by turning the land over as often as possible in summer?'

"'Nay, I know for certain that if you want the weeds to lie on the surface and wither in the heat, and the land to be baked by the sun, the surest way is to plough it up at midday in midsummer.' . . .

Sowing

"'And now as to the time for sowing, Socrates. Is it not your opinion that the time to sow is that which has been invariably found to be the best by past experience, and is universally approved by present practice? For as soon as autumn ends, all men, I suppose, look anxiously to God, to see when he will send rain on the earth and make them free to sow.'

"'Yes, Ischomachus, all men have made up their minds, of course, not to sow in dry ground if they can help it, those who sowed without waiting to be bidden by God having had to wrestle with many losses.' . . .

"'But,' said Ischomachus, 'when we come to the question whether sowing is best done early or very late or at the mid-season, we find much difference of opinion, Socrates.' . . .

"'For my part, Ischomachus, I think it is best to sow for succession throughout the season. For in my opinion it is much better to get enough food at all times than too much at one time and not enough at another.'

"'Here again, then, Socrates, pupil and teacher are of one opinion; and, moreover, you, the pupil, are first in stating this opinion.'

"'Well now, is casting the seed a complicated problem?'

"'By all means let us take that also into consideration, Socrates. I presume that you know as well as I that the seed must be cast by the hand?'

"'Yes, I have seen it.'

"'Ah,' he said, 'but some men can cast evenly, and some cannot.'

"'Then sowers no less than lyre-players need practice, that the hand may be the servant of the will.'

"'Certainly. But suppose that some of the land is rather light and some rather heavy?'

"'What do you mean by that?' I interrupted. 'By "light" do you mean "weak," and by "heavy," "strong"?'

"'Yes, I do.' . . .

"'If after putting in the seed you plough it in again as soon as the blade appears when the land is obtaining plenty of nourishment from the sky, it makes food for the soil, and strengthens it like manure. If, on the other hand, you let the seed go on growing on the land . . . it's hard for weak land to yield much grain in the end. It's hard, you know,

Excerpted from Xenophon, *Memorabilia and Oeconomicus*, translated by E.C. Marchant (New York: Putnam, 1923).

for a weak sow to rear a big litter of fine pigs.'. . .

"'But the hoers, now, Ischomachus, why do you put them on the corn?'

"'I presume you know that in winter there is a heavy rainfall?'

"'Of course.'

"'Let us assume, then, that part of the corn is waterlogged and covered with mud, and some of the roots are exposed by flooding. And it often happens, you know, that in consequence of rain weeds spring up among the corn and choke it.'

"'All these things are likely to happen.'

"'Then don't you think that in such circumstances the corn needs prompt succour?'

"'Certainly.'

"'What should be done, do you think, to succour the part that is under the mud?'

"'The soil should be lifted.'

"'And the part that has its roots exposed?'

"'It should be earthed up.'

"'What if weeds are springing up, choking the corn and robbing it of its food, much as useless drones rob bees of the food they have laid in store by their industry?'

"'The weeds must be cut, of course, just as the drones must be removed form the hive.'

"'Don't you think, then, that we have good reason for putting on men to hoe?'

"'No doubt.'. . .

"'However,' I continued, 'after this comes reaping, I fancy. So give me any information you can with regard to that too.'

Reaping

"'Yes—unless I find that you know just what I do about that subject too. You know, then, that the corn must be cut.'

"'I know that, naturally.'

"'Are you for standing with your back to the wind when you cut corn, or facing it?'

"'Not facing it, no! I think it is irritating both to the eyes and to the hands to reap with cornstalks and spikes blowing in your face.'

"'And would you cut near the top or close to the ground?'

"'If the stalk is short, I should cut low down, so that the straw may be more useful; but if it is

long, I think it would be right to cut in the middle, in order that the threshers and winnowers may not spend needless trouble on what they don't want. I imagine that the stubble may be burnt with advantage to the land, or thrown on the manure heap to increase its bulk.'

"'Do you notice, Socrates, that you stand convicted of knowing just what I know about reaping too?'

"'Yes, it seems so; and I want to know besides whether I understand threshing as well.'

"'Then you know this much, that draught animals are used in threshing?'

"'Yes, of course I do; and that the term draught animals includes oxen, mules and horses.'

"'Then do you not think that all the beasts know is how to trample on the corn as they are driven?'

"'Why, what more should draught animals know?'

"'And who sees that they tread out the right corn, and that the threshing is level, Socrates?'

"'The threshers, clearly. By continually turning the untrodden corn and throwing it under the animal's feet they will, of course, keep it level on the floor and take least time over the work.'

"'So far, then, your knowledge is quite as good as mine.'

"'Will not our next task be to clean the corn by winnowing [separating the chaff from the grain by use of a current of air], Ischomachus?'

"'Yes, Socrates; and tell me, do you know that if you start on the windward side of the floor, you will find the husks carried right across the floor?'

"'It must be so.'

"'It is not likely, then, that some will fall on the grain?'

"'Yes, it is a long way for the husks to be blown, right over the grain to the empty part of the floor.'

"'But what if you start winnowing against the wind?'

"'Clearly the chaff will at once fall in the right place.'. . .

"'However, is the planting of fruit trees another branch of agriculture?' I continued.

Planting Fruit Trees

"'It is, indeed,' answered Ischomachus. . . .

"'I don't know what kind of soil to plant in, nor how deep a hole to dig, nor how broad, nor how much of the plant should be buried.' . . .

"'Come then, learn whatever you don't know. I am sure you have seen the sort of trenches they dig for plants.'

"'Yes, often enough.'

"'Did you ever see one more than three feet deep?'

"'No, of course not—nor more than two and a half.'

"'Well, did you ever see one more than three feet broad?'

"'Of course not, nor more than two feet.'

"'Come then, answer this question too. Did you ever see one less than a foot deep?'

"'Never less than a foot and a half, of course. For the plants would come out of the ground when it is stirred about them if they were put in so much too shallow.'

"'Then you know this well enough, Socrates, that the trenches are never more than two and a half feet deep, nor less than a foot and a half.'

"'A thing so obvious as that can't escape one's eyes.' . . .

"'Now suppose the holes are dug; have you ever noticed how the plants for each kind of soil should be put in?'

"'Oh, yes.'

"'Then assuming that you want them to grow as quickly as possible, do you think that if you put some prepared soil under them the cuttings will strike sooner through soft earth into the hard stuff, or through unbroken ground?'

"'Clearly, they will form roots more quickly in prepared soil than in unbroken ground.'

"'Then soil must be placed below the plant?'

"'No doubt it must.' . . .

"'Then it turns out that on these points too your opinion agrees with mine. But would you merely heap up the earth, or make it firm round the plant?'

"'I should make it firm, of course; for if it were not firm, I feel sure that the rain would make mud of the loose earth, and the sun would dry it up from top to bottom; so the plants would run the risk of damping off through too much water, or withering from too much heat at the roots.'

"'About vine planting then, Socrates, your views are again exactly the same as mine.'

"'Does this method of planting apply to the fig too?' I asked.

"'Yes, and to all other fruit trees, I think; for in planting other trees why discard anything that gives good results with the vine?'

"'But the olive—how shall we plant that, Ischomachus?'

"'You know quite well, and are only trying to draw me out again. For I am sure you see that a deeper hole is dug for the olive (it is constantly being done on the roadside); you see also that all the growing shoots have stumps adhering to them; and you see that all the heads of the plants are coated with clay, and the part of the plant that is above ground is wrapped up.'

"'Yes, I see all this.'

"'You do! Then what is there in it that you don't understand? Is it that you don't know how to put the crocks on the top of the clay, Socrates?'

"'Of course there is nothing in what you have said that I don't know, Ischomachus. But I am again set thinking what can have made me answer 'No' to the question you put to me a while ago, when you asked me briefly, Did I understand planting? For I thought I should have nothing to say about the right method of planting. But now that you have undertaken to question me in particular, my answers, you tell me, agree exactly with the views of a farmer so famous for his skill as yourself! Can it be that questioning is a kind of teaching, Ischomachus?'"

Selection 4

How the Greek Grain-Shipping Business Worked

Lionel Casson

Although almost all Greek city-states in the Classic Age grew their own grain, many of the larger cities needed to supplement their local harvests by importing grain from other regions. Perhaps the most conspicuous example was Athens, which fed its large population largely with grain imported from fields rimming the Black Sea. For centuries, Greek businessmen and ship captains maintained a vast trading network to obtain supplies of essential foodstuffs, and many kinds of luxury goods as well. In this tract from his fascinating book, The Ancient Mariners, *a classic of its kind, former New York University scholar Lionel Casson explains how these enterprising individuals plied their trade, taking major financial, as well as physical, risks on a regular basis.*

It was the Persian wars that launched Athens on her career as a center for shipping. Before this time cities on or off the coast of Asia Minor, such as Chios or Miletus, played the key roles in the trade of the east and Corinth in that of the west. Aegina, a little island right at Athens' door, had a merchant marine that tramped all over the Mediterranean; when

Reprinted with the permission of Scribner, a division of Simon & Schuster, from *The Ancient Mariners*, by Lionel Casson. Copyright © 1959, and renewed © 1987 by Lionel Casson.

King Xerxes was organizing his attack on Greece and was scouting the Dardanelles, the first thing that met his eye was a convoy of ships from Aegina going through loaded with South Russian grain. But when, in the wake of the victories over the Persians, Athens created an empire which ensured her special privilege in the Greek cities of the Aegean, filled her treasury, and enabled her to build up a navy that could police the seas, the Peiraeus [Athens's port] was gradually transformed into an international entrepôt [trading and market center]. And Athens maintained her commercial domination despite the stunning defeat in the Peloponnesian War. Geographically she stood in the center of the Greek world: any trader who put in and unloaded would be sure to find a return cargo and not have to go home in ballast. She had one of the few good natural harbors in the eastern Mediterranean; her coinage was still one of the best there was and was accepted in every port; there was capital available among her businessmen for investment in maritime ventures. So the Peiraeus hummed with activity.

Cargo Vessels Criss-Cross the Seas

Far and away the biggest business in Athens was the importing of grain. The ancient Greek lived principally off bread and porridge; if supplies

As a merchant ship loaded with cargo departs from the Piraeus bound for some foreign port, workers (lower right) prepare to load another vessel.

weren't unloaded regularly on the quays of the Peiraeus the populace faced hardship. The same was true of most of the larger Greek cities. Intense commercial competition took place in this age, with many a clash of interests; it was not over markets in which to sell surplus products but over access to supplies essential for keeping a city going: grain for food, wine to drink, and olive oil which, by itself, did in those days what soap and butter and electricity do for us. Athens grew olives; wine could be got nearby; but the most important, grain, was available in quantity in only three places, all of them far overseas: Egypt, Sicily, and South Russia. In the Peloponnesian War Sparta starved Athens into submission by destroying her fleet and blockading her port; a little over half a century later King Philip of Macedon, the able father of Alexander the Great, went about achieving the same result by occupying the city of Byzantium and closing the gates of the Bosporus, thereby cutting access to South Russian grain.

So, to feed themselves, Athens and the other major Greek cities required trade on an international scale. But it is necessary to get the nature and extent of their commercial activity in proper focus. The history of the Greeks in the fifth and fourth centuries B.C. is so important for its great contributions to the civilization of the West that we tend to lose sight of the actual size of the nations and the number of people involved. Athens, by far the greatest city of Greece, was politically and culturally a mighty place, but her population was certainly not more than 300,000, slaves and foreign residents included—in other words what in the United States would qualify as a center of quite moderate size. Less than 100,000 tons of grain, some 800 average-sized boatloads, were enough to feed her for a year, and some of this, though relatively very little to be sure, was grown in her own fields. The activity in importing grain was intense—the actual shipping had to be crowded into the summer sailing season— but the totals involved were small. The day of huge corporations and government in business on a large scale lay ahead. Most of the commerce was in the hands of small traders who operated with partners when they couldn't scrape up enough cash on their own, who handled one cargo a year, and who traveled on the ship along with their goods to make sure that everything went off without a hitch. But though the operations were small in scale, they were widespread. The banker or merchant at the Peiraeus had business contacts in Marseilles [in southern France] or Syracuse or Byzantium. Once, during a period of acute grain shortage around 330 B.C., Cleomenes, Alexander the Great's governor in Egypt, cornered the market on his country's supplies. In Rhodes, a port of call for all ships from Egypt, he was able to establish a headquarters where his agents could collect, from contacts all over, the latest quotations and, as the loaded freighters arrived, divert them to whatever spot was offering the highest price.

It usually took four men of business, each playing a specific role, to bring a cargo from the wheatfields of South Russia or Egypt or Sicily to the miller at Athens: shipper, shipowner, banker, and wholesaler; in many cases it took a pair or group of partners to provide the capital for each of the roles. The shipper practically always worked on credit and generally with a chartered vessel. He contracted with a shipowner for a ship or space on one and then borrowed money from some banker like Pasion [a rich Athenian merchant] to pay for the freight charges and a load of merchandise. Those who owned their own ships pledged them as security, but most put up the cargo they intended to buy. Obviously they must have been by and large men of integrity, for the banker never saw his security until months after the loan was made, when the vessel with its load finally docked at the Peiraeus. Interest for this service ran high, 22½ to 30 per cent for the four to five months of the sailing season, that is, between 67½ and 90 per cent per annum; but that was only natural. There was no insurance in those days; the banker assumed total responsibility—if the vessel failed to come back he, not the shipper, lost everything—so his reward had to be big enough to compensate for all risks. And these were considerable because, alongside the purely maritime ones, there was the ever present possibility of seizure by hostile men-of-war or attack by pirates. The same risks plus the lack of any system of insurance made the shippers and shipowners anxious to work as much as they could

with borrowed funds even when they had some of their own; in this way they limited their personal loss when a venture ran into trouble.

Whether a shipper hauled grain to Athens from Sicily or the Crimea [a peninsula in the northern Black Sea] or Egypt, the voyage was difficult and slow one way, quick and easy the other. This is because of the prevailing winds in the eastern Mediterranean and Black Sea, which during the ancient mariner's sailing season are prevailingly from the north; in the Aegean, for example, summer northerlies were so constant that the Greeks called them the Etesian, "annual" winds. . . . A skipper leaving Athens on the Black Sea run had to fight his way out there but could boom home with a following breeze. For those who handled Egyptian grain, the reverse was true: they sailed downhill before northerlies from Athens to Rhodes and before northwesterlies from there to Egypt but had to work into them all the way back, and the best course they could lay was a roundabout one by way of Cyprus; it helped somewhat that between Egypt and Rhodes they were willing to sail all year round. A skipper headed for Sicily had the wind behind him only as far as the southern tip of Greece and from that point on he had to tack; conditions were, of course, just the reverse on the homeward leg. An ancient freighter could make between four and six knots with the wind, only two or a bit more against it. This meant that the round trip to Egypt or the Crimea involved about three weeks at sea, to Sicily about two.

After a vessel arrived at the Peiraeus and the customs and port charges were paid, a shipper unloaded in the "Long Colonnade" and stood by while the wholesale grain dealers, who in turn sold to millers or consumers, bid for portions of his cargo. He had to get a good price, for this was his one chance to make a profit: what with the time consumed at sea and in loading up, generally only one round trip was fitted in the short sailing season; if the price had fallen between the time he purchased his cargo and the day he arrived at the Peiraeus, he had to swallow the loss and wait until the following year to recoup. When he finally collected from the wholesalers, he paid principal and interest to the banker and chartering charges to the shipowner and pocketed as profit what was left.

Honest and Dishonest Shippers

In a system of credit such as this, a great deal depended on the integrity of the shipper. The Athenians realized this and, though in other fields they were free and easy in making loans, even to the extent of turning over cash without papers or witnesses, when it came to maritime loans they nailed everything down hard and fast in a written contract that tried to anticipate all contingencies. But businessmen are the same in all ages and places, and the Peiraeus saw its share of shady operations. One favorite was to pledge a cargo for a loan from one banker and then, by repledging the same security, collect further loans from others. If a man could load, transport, and sell a cargo quickly enough to pay off the creditors in short order, there was a fair chance the fraud would never be discovered. If a shipper, after negotiating a series of loans in this way, could inveigle [coax] a shipowner into entering a deal to arrange a convenient shipwreck, either real if the boat wasn't worth much or pretended if it was, both could clear in one season more money than they could possibly make in years of legitimate business.

The great orator Demosthenes is best known for the fighting political speeches he made before the Athenian Assembly. In private life he was a lawyer, and his clients included a number of bankers who had lent money at one time or another to shippers who turned out to be unfortunate credit risks. In the gallery of rogues whom Demosthenes sued, the most lurid without question were a pair named Zenothemis and Hegestratus. Zenothemis was a shipper and Hegestratus a shipowner, a partnership which, if dishonest, could prove disastrous to a banker. Both came from Marseilles; like so many of the men who did business at the Peiraeus they were foreigners. The transaction involved in the case began as a perfectly legitimate one. Protus, a shipper of Athens, got a loan from a banker named Demo, putting up as collateral a cargo of Sicilian grain which he was to buy at Syracuse. He chartered space on Hegestratus' ship, left Athens, arrived at Syracuse, bought his grain, loaded it aboard, and was ready to leave. So far everything was fine. But at this point Hegestratus and Zenothemis swung into action. Each made the rounds of the local bankers, raising as many loans as he could; when asked about collateral each would glibly describe the cargo of grain that lay in the ship at the quay, merely omitting the slight detail that it wasn't his. When they had collected a sizable amount of cash in this way they sent it off to be cached in their home town of Marseilles.

This was one of those swindles in which a shipowner had to take part, since it was essential to the scheme to get rid of the grain: if that ever arrived at Athens and was sold by Protus, in the normal course of events the word would get back to the lenders at Syracuse and they would sooner or later catch up with the culprits. Zenothemis and Hegestratus laid their plans carefully. They waited until the ship was two or three days out of Syracuse en route to Athens and was coasting along not too far from the island of Cephallenia [off Greece's western coast]. On a dark night Hegestratus, leaving his partner to chat on deck with the passengers, stole down to the hold clutching a handsaw, made his way to the ship's bottom planking, and started to saw away energetically. Apparently Zenothemis' diversion on deck wasn't loud enough, because some of the passengers heard the noise below, went down to investigate, and caught Hegestratus redhanded. He rushed on deck and, without breaking his stride, went straight over the side, intending to grab the ship's boat, which was being towed behind, and cut loose; obviously he and his partner had in mind to use this means of saving their skins if the scuttling had gone off as planned. In the dark he missed it and, as Demosthenes comments, "met the end he deserved." Zenothemis, who was a quick thinker, tried a last-minute tactic: he raced about the deck hollering that the ship was going to go down at any minute and exhorting officers, crew, and passengers to climb into the boat and abandon ship. This might have worked except that Protus called to the crew that he would reward each one of them handsomely for bringing the vessel in and they stuck by their posts. When the voyage finally ended at the Peiraeus, Zenothemis was far from through. At Athens he decided to claim that the grain was really his and, when Protus and his banker took it over, hired a sea lawyer to sue the two of them for return of "his property." It's clear that Demosthenes, who represented the Athenian banker, had a tough case on his hands, especial-

ly since the creditors at Syracuse, realizing that they had been swindled and that they could recoup only if Zenothemis could acquire some assets, were zealously supporting the latter's story. What is more, it seems that at the end even Protus made a deal with Zenothemis, since the price of grain had dropped by the time he arrived and, after paying off his debt and interest and the rewards to the crew, he faced a good-sized loss on the whole transaction. We don't know what the court's decision was, for all that is preserved is the speech Demosthenes wrote for his client.

Selection 5

Common Foods and Eating Customs

Andrew Dalby

This informative essay is by Andrew Dalby, an authority on ancient Greek gastronomy (foods and eating customs). He begins by describing the various places Greeks ate meals, including town halls and outdoor public sacrifices, as well as in the home. Regarding home eating, he makes the point that men sometimes gave dinner parties for their male friends, while the women of the house often ate separately. After describing various other eating customs, Dalby lists the most common foods consumed by average Greek diners, including their desserts.

Excerpted from *Siren Feasts: A History of Food and Gastronomy in Greece*, by Andrew Dalby. Copyright © 1996 by Andrew Dalby. Reprinted by permission of Routledge.

*F*amilies often must have eaten at home, but only the briefest descriptions are to be found. If sacrificing and eating fresh meat, families might eat at shrines. . . . Men formed dining clubs which could assume political importance: evidence for them comes from historical sources and occasional inscriptions, but there is no full description of such a dinner. The state acted as celebrant at general religious festivals and as host for entertainments at the town hall. . . . Workers, soldiers and those engaged in some communal activities ate away from home, these 'working' meals sometimes being provided for them. . . . Travellers who could not call on acquaintances had to eat at inns. Some members of a household spent the whole day away from home, taking food with them if there was to be no communal ration. . . . Women, household slaves and children . . . certainly ate independently of their menfolk. Women lunched with one another, as we have seen, though respectable women did not go out to dinner in the evening.

Meal times are variable, but a midday meal was usually called *áriston,* 'lunch'. . . and an evening meal *deîpnon,* 'dinner'. The latter was perhaps typically the biggest meal of the day, and for some the only meal.

Dinner Parties

Families who were sacrificing, especially if celebrating such an event as a betrothal or wedding, but on other occasions too, invited guests to their meal. Men of the socially approved age . . . pursued courtship by entertaining. Men entertained male guests at home, and might also celebrate some public achievement, athletic or political, with a sacrificial dinner or a party for friends. *Hetairaí* [high-class prostitutes], and other women not of the proper status to be citizens' wives, might be guests at such entertainments, at home or at a shrine. These were evening and night activities: a dinner might become a drinking party, a *pótos,* or one more elaborate and organised, a *sympósion.* . . . But dinner parties and drinking parties were surely (in Athens as in most societies) less ubiquitous [widespread] than their frequent occurrence in memoirs and fiction would suggest. . . .

When no strange men were in the house, women need not retreat to 'women's quarters': they could lunch at leisure, indoors or in a courtyard. But the classical Athenian house, and the conviviality within it, were very inaccessible to the uninvited visitor. Women at home were invisible to law-abiding outsiders. House doors were commonly locked, and interiors divided into several rooms. One of these was the *andrón,* the 'dining room.'. . . It was in this room, customarily, that men entertained others to meals and drinking parties at home. Its ground plan was laid out to accommodate a certain number of couches around the walls. *Andrônes* can be recognised archaeologically by the location of the door (always off-centre), by the

length of the walls (so many couch lengths plus one couch width) and often by floor details recognisably linked to the intended placing of couches and tables. They were one-purpose rooms, more clearly so than any other room in normal houses; how frequently they were used is quite unknown. Women of respectable Athenian households did not come into contact with male guests and had no reason to enter the *andrón* when it was in use. In all the narratives of men's dinners and *symposia* from the fifth and fourth centuries there is not one certain indication of the presence of a woman of the household, and there are several explicit signs that they were elsewhere.

Similar rooms to these *andrónes* are found in certain municipal buildings, which are thus identified as *prytaneîa*—places for municipal eating—and in buildings at shrines. But many country shrines had no buildings, and certainly vase-paintings suggest that open air meals, otherwise resembling meals in dining rooms, were quite imaginable; a few literary references, scattered in time and place, and one or two paintings from Pompeii, imply that an awning (often translated 'tent') might be a regular amenity.

The high Greek dining couch was a specialised piece of furniture. It is a standard feature of vase-paintings of banquets and must have been standard in the purpose-built dining rooms just described. On the vase-paintings, with few exceptions, the rule is one diner per couch: a second person on a couch will be a woman (or occasionally a beardless young man) often offering the male diner some more or less intimate service or performing it. But not all lived in such style as to own a house with a room dedicated to dining; not all could have afforded to own all those couches. The less well-off, when they entertained, are perhaps more likely than the rich to have done so at shrines, and to have taken rugs and cushions with them. . . .

We know that at Athenian dinner parties the guests were limited in number. It is easy to count the couches that would fit in the purpose-built dining rooms of Attica . . . whether private, municipal or religious: that was exactly how the size of a reception room was customarily measured. Seven couches was a common size; five to eleven couches was the usual range, or in other words hardly more than twenty participants. . . . The intimate scale was part of the nature of Greek dining and entertainment, and was built in architecturally, for in the larger of known dining rooms the layout would have produced the effect of two to four groups dining or drinking simultaneously. . . .

The picture that can be drawn of dining and festivity in other classical Greek cities is by no means so complete as the Athenian. Athenians were, however, sufficiently impressed by the contrast between their own way of life and that of the Spartans to describe the latter relatively fully. The evidence is not straightforward, however. We can read satire on Sparta and its ways, from a city that was always Sparta's rival and frequently its enemy; also we can read strong praise, from Plato and Xenophon, philosophers and moralists whose admiration for Spartan discipline and education was almost unbounded. A fictional Spartan speaks:

> Still, I think the lawgiver at Sparta was right to enjoin the avoidance of pleasures. . . . The custom that makes men fall deepest into great pleasures and improprieties and into all foolishness, this has been ejected by our law from every part of the country: neither in the fields, nor in the towns that the Spartiates control, will you see a *sympósion* and all that goes with it to incite men to pleasure. There is not a man who would not punish with the greatest severity a drunken reveller; he would not get away even if a festival of Dionysus were his excuse—like the time when I saw [drunken revellers] on carts in your country [Athens], while at Taras, our own colony, I watched the whole city getting drunk at the Dionysia. There is none of that with us.

(Plato, *Laws* 636e–637c)

The full citizens, the Spartiates, were above over-indulgence in food and drink, or so it was claimed. But the principal difference in this field between Sparta and Athens was that whereas the communal or municipal dining of Athenians seems (to judge from surviving literature) to have been of little importance, male Spartiates dined in common all the time. Where and in what circumstances their womenfolk ate, no one knows. Communal meals, *syssítia*, were by no means unique to Sparta. Cretan cities, close to Sparta in dialect, were also close in social customs and there too men ate communally. . . .

Outlandish though they seemed to other Greeks . . . from our perspective the customs of Sparta can be seen to belong to the same spectrum as those of Athens. Athenians, like Spartans, had fixed opinions on dining together, on equal contribution to hospitality, on the separation of the sexes, on the ages at which boys began to dine as men. Spartans, like Athenians, celebrated religious occasions with food, drink, music and dance, as we know not only from the early poetry of Alcman but also from descriptions of what were evidently well-established festivals dating from the classical period or soon after it.

But every Greek city was different from every other in government, in laws, in religious observance and in other customs. Sacrifice and food preparation were naturally a major source of income at places of pilgrimage and festival. Delians were nicknamed *eleodytai*, 'table-divers', and . . . Elis, where Olympia stood, was said to be the origin of a school of cooks. Distinctions in food behaviour are among the most quickly noticed of all social peculiarities. Greeks noticed such differences among themselves: the women of Miletus, for example, who 'are not to share food with their husbands nor to call their own husbands by name' (Herodotus, *Histories* 1.146.3).

What People Did and Did Not Eat

They also noticed how they were differentiated from other peoples—from 'barbarians'—by food customs, food choices and food avoidances. Herodotus was told that after sacrifice in Egyptian temples the animal's head would be cut off, cursed and if there was a market at hand with Greek traders, sold to them. If there was not, it would be thrown in the river. . . . Greeks themselves admitted to few food avoidances, though they considered dolphins sacred, were doubtful of turtle and tortoise, seldom ate dog and very seldom horse. Of animals that were eaten at all, nearly all parts were considered acceptable food. . . . Some Greeks, though not all, ate brain; Pythagoras, it was later said, included heart among his odd list of forbidden foods. . . .

Lentils, barley and wheat formed the staple foods (*sîtos*: 'food, staple food, army food supply') of classical Greece: the lentils as soup, the barley as a mash or biscuit, the wheat as loaves, though both of the cereals could also be prepared as gruel or porridge. In addition to the older traditional forms in which these staples were eaten, sweet cakes multiplied in classical menus. Wheat . . . did not grow well in most parts of Greece and was the most expensive and the most unreliable of the three staples. Lentils and barley had been known in Greece even earlier than wheat: they were available almost everywhere. . . .

With these staples were eaten . . . vegetables, cheese, eggs, fish (fresh, salted or dried), and less frequently meat. In classical Greece the fresh meat of domestic animals formed a sacrifice, butchered with appropriate religious ritual. But the eating of meat once sacrificed, including the eating of offal and sausages, required no further ceremony. The domestic animals that were most commonly eaten—sheep, goats and pigs—had a long prehistory in Greece. Small and large game birds supplemented the native domesticated quail and the domestic fowl. . . . Cheese (in Greece normally sheep's and goats' milk cheese) had long been made. The number of species of vegetables in use had gradually grown. The number of species of fish that were exploited no doubt remained fairly constant once deep-sea fishing had become a common practice. . . .

To this structure, when meals were at their most elaborate, there were many supplements. Appetisers, not different in kind from the usual relishes but selected from those that had the most piquant flavour, preceded the meal. Wreaths and perfumes were distributed among guests as they gathered.

After the meal, wine, *oînos*, was drunk, a single taste of unmixed wine at the moment of the libation, followed by plenty of wine mixed with water. Now clean tables—'second tables'—were brought, on which cakes, sweets, nuts and fresh and dried fruit were served to accompany the wine. These delicacies were called *tragémata*, 'what one chews alongside wine' (a convenient translation is 'dessert'). . . .

One of the two most important changes in the diet of Greece since early neolithic times has been the introduction of wine: it has for at least the last three millennia been the customary drink of the country, often heavily diluted with water. The other has been the cultivation and regular use of olives. Wild forms of both grape and olive were found and probably used earlier in Greece, but the newly cultivated grape and olive of later prehistoric times were of enormous potential importance to the diet. Both provided cooking media and flavourings, the olive with its oil, the grape with its juice both unfermented and fermented into wine. It is a challenging hint of conservatism at the centre of the menu that grape, wine and olive were not visibly present in the main course of a classical Greek meal. Whatever the use of olive oil in cooking, and as a medium for sauces, olives themselves were eaten only before the meal as an appetiser. Whatever the use of must and wine in cooking, wine was served to diners only after they had eaten, and raisins also appeared then, with the second tables. And in general, the lists of *propómata*, 'appetisers', and of *tragémata* that can be extracted from the writings of comic poets and dieticians alike show a readiness to innovate that was not nearly so evident with the staple diet and its chief accompaniments in the main course.

Meat was eaten 'less frequently'. How frequently is 'less frequently'? The balance is difficult to judge. . . . Although the evidence is not strong, it is likely that vegetables, fish and perhaps cheese, and not meat, accompanied the majority of meals in Greece for many millennia.

Selection 6

Local Industries, Banking, and Financial Dealings

W.G. Hardy

In this examination of how financial affairs worked in a Greek city in the Classic Age, former University of Alberta scholar W.G. Hardy concentrates on Athens, since that is where most of the surviving evidence comes from. He begins with the local artisans who manufactured various goods in small shops that often doubled as their homes. Then he describes the retail sellers (middlemen), who were mostly metics (foreigners living in Athens), the bankers and traders, and also the well-to-do local citizens who helped the community function by providing it with financial support.

Until the Peloponnesian War, many Athenians were still on the farm and many city-dwellers held property in the country. . . .

Yet Periclean Athens was, after all, one of the major trading-centres of the Mediterranean. This pre-eminence was won and maintained by bankers, wholesale traders, and merchant-skippers, but above all by her craftsmen.

Craftsmen Run Small Shops

Today, north of the Acropolis, there is a narrow street called Shoe Lane. If you walk down it, on

both sides of you are shoes and boots and still more boots and shoes. Shoe Lane is a sort of vestigial reminder of industry in ancient Athens. There were shoemakers, metal-workers, dyers, tanners, jewellers, stonemasons, and a host of other craftsmen. But instead of mass-production in huge factories crammed with machinery, Athenian shoes, pots, sausages, hoes, axes, and the like were turned out by workers in small shops. These shops were often both the plants for manufacturing the goods, and the outlets for selling them. Often, as in much of the Near East today, they were also the homes of the craftsmen. Most of these small plants were run by a man and his apprentices, aided by a slave or two. To make the situation still more confusing from a North American point of view, all the workers of one craft lived side by side. The potters of Athens, for instance, all crowded together in the Cerameicus. . . .

If you will allow your imagination to roam for a moment, you can hear the hammers of the sweating metal-workers ring and see their forges glowing; or you can stroll through a narrow street in the Cerameicus and watch a potter moulding a lump of clay on his spinning wheel or a vase-painter drawing a design. It may be a picture of Achilles killing Hector or of men dicing or of a riot of Maenads and Sileni. But there is one important point to remember. Those vases piled around you, about the artistry of which we rave today, were manufactured not for show-pieces but for sale in one of the most fiercely competitive markets of the ancient world. Attic pots had to be good pots. Their beauty of form and design is incidental, though not accidental. They were made by craftsmen who took pride in their handiwork.

In addition to direct sales from producer to consumer, there were a swarm of retail traders, called *kapeloi*. They were to be found in the stalls of the Agora, or market-place, or in the shops round about. We read of confectioners, slave-dealers, fishmongers, vintners, and the like, and of pedlars who carried goods out through the countryside. To the Greek, however, a middle-man was always faintly suspect as a parasite on the body public. Thus, Aristotle says of retail trade in his *Politics* that it is a 'kind of exchange which is justly censured; for it is unnatural and a mode by which men gain from one another'.

Most of the retail traders were *metics,* that is, resident aliens. The craftsmen were a mixture of *metics,* slaves, and Athenian citizens. In their hands, then, was the bulk of the production and much of the retail trade in Athens. We ought to note that there was a special 'potters' market'.

Such craftsmen-cum-shopkeepers were not, so to speak, tied to a time-clock or to punching a single button on an assembly-line. They were freemen who took time off whenever they liked. Socrates, the teacher and inspiration of the philosopher Plato, was a stonemason. Yet in the Platonic dialogues we find him in the gymnasia or in the streets or at the festivals or at dinners, continually questioning the people he met in an insatiable search for truth. There was only one Socrates. Yet it is clear that his fellow-craftsmen were, on the whole, more interested, as long as they could make a simple living, in recreation or in politics or in discussion or in a stroll with a friend, than in piling up possessions. Yet these were the men who executed the perfect and in-

The remains of the once busy Athenian marketplace (Agora) and the well-preserved Temple of Hephaestos, as seen from the north rampart of the Acropolis.

tricate workmanship of the Parthenon, the Hephaesteion . . . and the Erechtheum [three famous temples in Athens]. . . .

For the building of such imperishable monuments as the Parthenon, which took nine years to complete, the State hired quarrymen, transport-workers, carpenters, masons, goldsmiths, and sculptors. Sometimes a piece of work was let out on contract. At other times the men were paid directly by the State. Sculptors got the same wage as masons. So did slaves.

The whole picture of basic Athenian industry, except for the silver mines, implies a different set of values from our own. The craftsmen knew their trade, whatever it was, though their tools were of the simplest. Yet, in general, they seem to have preferred a full participation in the life of the city to being tied too long to any manual occupation or to getting ahead financially. From the Erechtheum inscriptions of 409 B.C. we know that the usual rate of pay was a drachma a day. . . . From other references in Greek authors it can be estimated that it cost a single man about 120 drachmai a year. . . to live, and a married man with two children double that amount.

The major point, though, is that the Athenian workmen could, and apparently did, have plenty of leisure time. It would take a single man only a little more than two days of work a week to earn a living.

In passing, it ought to be mentioned that there were a few cases of mass-manufacturing. In Plato's *Republic* the discussions are supposed to take place in the Peiraeus at the home of Cephalus, a rich *metic*. Cephalus, we learn, manufactured shields and employed, apparently, 120 men. Moreover, the silver mines at Laureion were let out by the State to individuals who worked them by means of slaves. Nicias, the rich man and general who, more than any other single individual, was responsible for the disaster which befell the Athenians in Sicily, is said to have rented out a thousand slaves to the silver mines.

Traders and Bankers

Apart from these few instances, the craftsmen of Athens supplied most of the home market. In the case of the potters, they also furnished an important article for export. Pottery was the dinnerware of the ancient world; but it was also used for storing every kind of liquid and dry goods—and pottery was always getting broken. So there was a fierce competition between Corinth and Athens for the pottery market of the Mediterranean. In the fifth century B.C., Attic red-figured vases won the battle.

For its export trade which, in addition to pottery, consisted chiefly of the export of olive-oil, wine, figs, and armour, Athens needed bankers, wholesale traders, and merchant-skippers. Most of these were *metics*.

Sparta periodically expelled all foreigners within her boundaries. Athens, under Pericles, encouraged strangers to settle. *Metics* could not vote or hold office and had to be represented in the law-courts by an Athenian. Yet they paid taxes which included a special head-tax per family of 12 drachmai. . . . They were selected for liturgies [obligations to provide financial support for certain community functions] . . . and served in the army and navy. Like the Athenian citizens they seem to have been proud of the city, and they were of tremendous assistance to banking and foreign trade.

The primary function of the bankers, or tablemen as they were called, was to change coins. By Periclean days, they were also well advanced in taking in money on deposit and in making loans. Pasion, the famous fourth-century B.C. banker, began life as a slave to a banker. Then he married his master's widow and took over the bank. At his death his assets were fifty talents [300,000 drachmai]. . . . Of this amount eleven talents, or somewhat more than a fifth, were on deposit.

The minimum interest rate was twelve per cent. On loans on ships or on ships' cargoes the rate ran up to twenty or thirty per cent; this because of a provision that if a ship was lost at sea or captured by pirates the loan was cancelled. Aristotle, again, has hard words for the banker. 'The most hated sort [of moneymaking] and with the greatest reason,' he writes, 'is usury, which makes a gain out of money itself. . . . For money was intended to be used in exchange, but not to increase at interest.'

Without the banker the wholesale trader or *emporos* would have found it difficult to operate. The method of the *emporos* was to buy a large consignment of goods and to hire space on a ship for it to be taken from city to city in search of a market. If successful, the wholesale trader would come to own his own ship and would become a merchant-skipper or *naukleros*. No sailing was done in winter. But each spring the merchant-skippers would load their round-bellied tubs—a Greek merchantman could carry only about 7,000 bushels of wheat—with olive-oil and wine in Attic jars and with the finest of Attic vases. Shields, spears, and helmets might be part of the cargo. So might jars filled with beads, necklaces, and other trinkets—this for trade with backward people.

Then the skipper would set out for a season's adventuring from port to port. He might, for example, unload at Massalia, now Marseilles [in southern France] and take on hides and cheese, trade these at Carthage for rugs and cushions, exchange these at Naucratis in Egypt for ivory, papyrus, and linen, and so on. Or he might move into the Black Sea to bring back, finally, a cargo of wheat. Meanwhile, that same spring, other ships would be setting out from Miletus, Syracuse, Cyrene, Corinth, Carthage, and the other Mediterranean ports, with the same sort of trading venture in mind. Everywhere there would be warehouses in which the merchants could display their goods. Everywhere they would have to pay customs dues—at Athens these were two per cent on all exports and imports—and harbour tolls.

It was in this somewhat hit-or-miss but adventurous fashion that the trade of the ancient world was carried on. By this method the products of all known countries flowed into the Peiraeus, the port of Athens. The combination of her trade supremacy and the tribute from her empire made Athens one of the richest of the Greek cities of her day.

It was a very modest wealth from the modern point of view. The total annual state revenue of Periclean Athens in peace-time was probably close to 1,000 talents. . . . In terms of its purchasing power today . . . that is about the annual budget of a fair-sized Canadian city.

During the Peloponnesian War the tribute from the empire was raised and resort was had to the *eisphora,* or direct property tax. Even in peacetime, though there were no schools, hospitals, or old-age pensions to drain the public purse, the treasury had to take care of the public festivals such as the Panathenaea and the two Dionysia—which were drama festivals—and of the huge program of non-productive public works, such as the Parthenon. In addition, from 17,000 to 20,000 of the 43,000 citizens 'ate state bread'—that is, they were on public service and were paid for it.

Their pay was not large. Jurymen, for example, got two and later three *obols* a day. . . . *Hoplites* received four *obols* . . . a day, sailors and marines only three *obols.*

And so one might go on. Athens could scarcely have balanced her budget, had it not been for the liturgies. These were of various kinds, of which two are of particular interest. In the *choregia* a rich man was picked to collect, maintain, instruct, and equip one of the many choruses needed, for (among other forms of art) the drama. This might cost him as much as half a talent. . . . The *trierarchia* was more expensive. In it a rich man had to pay the cost of operating a *trireme* for a year. The cost was between two-thirds of a talent to a talent.

All citizens who owned property worth more than three talents . . . were subject to the liturgies. In the first years of the Peloponnesian War, the generals were able to find 400 *trierarchs* a year.

The liturgies were a capital tax on the rich, both citizens and *metics.* Yet we learn that in Periclean Athens the holders of them competed against each other to provide the best-trained chorus or the most splendidly equipped *trireme.*

The Athenians were not in love with poverty. Pericles himself in his *Funeral Speech* observed: 'We think it no disgrace to confess to poverty but a disgrace to make no effort to overcome it.'

But the whole training of an Athenian encouraged him to put simple recreations and an active life of the imagination above possessions; and he also took it for granted that citizenship involved duties as well as rights.

Selection 7

Agriculture, Industry, and Trade in Hellenistic Times

Max Cary

In this excerpt from his detailed study of the Hellenistic Greek world, the late, distinguished scholar Max Cary explores that world's economic structure and activities. As he points out, the era following Alexander's death witnessed greatly expanded markets and economic horizons for the Greeks. He begins by explaining how the Hellenistic Greeks developed agriculture, focusing mainly on Ptolemaic Egypt, where most of the solid evidence comes from. Then he discusses manufactured products and how they were traded throughout the Mediterranean and Near Eastern shipping lanes, often under the watchful eyes of rival Hellenistic governments.

Hellenistic agriculture derived a considerable stimulus from the great increase in the knowledge of plants and herbs that followed upon Alexander's conquests. This new information was reproduced in systematic form in the botanical works of Theophrastus, which in turn gave rise to an extensive literature of practical manuals. The kings of Pergamum were the chief patrons of the technical authors on husbandry, but the principal field of practical experiment was in Egypt, where the

Excerpted from *History of the Greek World from 323 to 146 B.C.*, by Max Cary (London: Methuen, 1968). Reprinted by permission of Underwood & Co., Solicitors, on behalf of the Estate of Max Cary.

first two Ptolemies proved themselves the greatest land-improvers in Greek history. In addition to the maintenance of existing dykes and canals the Ptolemies carried out extensive reclamations in districts which had fallen into neglect under Persian rule. Their greatest undertaking was the construction of a canal and sluice, by which Nile water could be conveyed across a low intervening ridge to the Fayum, the basin of a dried-out lake near Memphis. By this engineering exploit they reclaimed a large expanse of irrigable land, which became the principal area of settlement for Greek husbandmen: of the hundred villages which sprang up in it, more than half bore Greek names. On this land, and wherever else wastes were reclaimed, the cultivators received rights of hereditary tenancy and paid reduced taxes during the first years of their lease. . . .

The Ptolemies allowed the native fellahin . . . to retain their holdings, and did not interfere with their traditional system of cultivation. The Egyptian method of tillage, which was based on a simple rotation of wheat (on the prepared land) and vegetables (on the fallow), was well suited to the conditions of the country, and had enabled it to export grain before the Greek conquest. But the Greek government kept the peasantry under strict supervision. It prescribed the acreage to be tilled for each kind of crop; it stocked the arable farms and supplied seed from pedigree plants, exacting an oath from the cultivators that they would use none other; and it required them to remain on their land from sowing to harvest. Those who disobeyed these rules were liable to summary eviction, for the natives were not given a fixed lease, but held their plots by a precarious tenancy. In addition to this superintendence of routine cultivation the Ptolemies made experiments with improved seeds on selected plots. . . .

Before the Macedonian conquest the pastoral industry [raising of livestock] of Egypt had been of small importance, despite the abundance of suitable grazing land and the mild winter climate, which rendered stall-feeding quite unnecessary. Under the Ptolemies, who had special need of mounts for their cavalry and of wool for their textile factories, pasturage underwent great extension and improvement. In the Fayum wide tracts of irrigation land were turned into ranches and sown with artificial grasses. The herds, which were provided by the king and remained royal property, were kept up to a high standard by the importation of Milesian rams and other pedigree animals; the herdsmen too were largely drawn from Greek lands.

But the Ptolemies, in true Greek fashion, gave special attention to plantation husbandry. In order to encourage the formation of vineyards and olive groves, they granted heritable leases and reduced taxation to settlers who would undertake to convert reclamation-land into orchards. They imposed a frankly protectionist tariff—an unusual instrument of finance in ancient times—on luxury oils and wines from Greece, and prohibited importation of such brands as Egypt itself might produce. Greek colonists accordingly introduced the vine into every part of Egypt, and acclimatized the olive more particularly in the Fayum. Among the most zealous planters was Apollonius, who laid out a large nursery at Memphis and stocked his other estates with its produce. Besides transplanting many varieties of garden fruit and at least eleven species of vine, he made an attempt to establish standings of fir-timber for the benefit of the Alexandrian shipyards.

In the Seleucid and Attalid monarchies the cultivation of the arable lands was left in the hands of the natives, who might be peasant pro-

prietors or (as commonly in Asia Minor) serf tenants. But wherever Greek colonists went they took the vine with them, so that viticulture became a flourishing industry as far east as Persia. The cultivation of vine and olive also prospered in the older centres of the Aegean area: indeed, the vintages of Thasos, of Cnidus, of Cos and of Rhodes, and the oil of the west coast of Asia Minor, never enjoyed a greater reputation. . . .

Manufactures

Among the various forms of production manufacturing probably underwent the fewest alterations in the Hellenistic period. Despite the influx of Persian money into Greek lands, social fashions passed through no profound change, and the scientific discoveries of the age had little effect on technical processes. The only notable inventions were by-products of the genius of Archimedes, the "Archimedean screw," which served to raise water from mines, and the compound pulley. The staple of Greek craft production was still its fine ceramic ware (with moulded instead of painted decorations), though this was partly displaced by glass ware and silver plate. Besides silver ware, fashion also created a greater demand for textiles of the finer sort. Though wool remained the standard dress material, silk came into favour, and a new clothing industry was established at Cos, where thread was spun from the wild silk-worm of Asia Minor. The spread of education and of the habit of reading caused a great increase in the production of papyrus and of books. Among the heavy industries quarrying and building received an impetus wherever Greek colonies were founded or Oriental cities were reconstructed in Greek style.

While the articles of manufacture underwent little change, there was a considerable displacement in the seats of industry. In the Greek Homeland Athens remained the chief centre of the ceramic industry until c. 250; but little is heard in Hellenistic times of Corinthian bronze ware. Among the Italian Greeks the Tarentines held their own as producers of fine textiles, and they introduced the new style of moulded and ribbed pottery into the western world. . . . Among the older towns of Asia Minor Miletus benefited by the demand for good cloths and retained her industrial ascendancy; but new textile centres were established at Pergamum, whose kings took a personal interest in the weaving industry, and ... the busiest of all the manufacturing towns was Alexandria, where a regular fever of work laid hold of the population. In addition to the paper-making industry, of which it held a natural monopoly, it developed the old Egyptian crafts of casting and cutting glass, and of ornamentation with coloured metal glazes; it became the chief centre of toreutic art in silver, while its bric-à-brac permeated the villages of Egypt and was exported as far as the Black Sea. Glass and silver crafts had another important centre in Syria. Thus the prevailing tendency in the Hellenistic period was for industry to spread from Greece Proper to the Levantine [Near Eastern] capitals.

The effect of the conquest upon native eastern industries may best be studied in Egypt. ... If native industries were not much disturbed by competition from Greek capitalists, they were brought under a strict government control. A large number of Egyptian industries were converted into monopolies, under which all manufacturers had to pay a special licence. ... The production of oil was wholly forbidden save in the government's own factories, where the workers were tied down to their task like serfs and kept under the most rigid supervision. A similar system was applied in quarries and mines, where the labourers were indentured to remain at their posts for stated periods. ...

The Ptolemaic experiment of operating factories with government capital was imitated at Pergamum, where the Attalids manufactured fine textiles by the labour of state slaves. Probably, too, the parchment industry which they set up to break the Egyptian monopoly of papyrus was an instance of direct state enterprise. The Hellenistic world also offers several examples of municipal socialism. The city of Miletus—perhaps in anticipation of the kings of Pergamum—owned its textile workshops and their slave-weavers. Rhodes and Cnidus produced in municipal factories the jars which their merchants required for

their extensive export trade in wine. Even Sparta engaged in municipal industry, for the tiles used by the tyrant Nabis for the strengthening of the city walls were baked at a public kiln.

Transport

The economic progress made in the Hellenistic period is seen most clearly in the history of its commerce. The age was one of intensified traffic, for not only were the political obstacles lessened, but its natural difficulties were reduced by technical improvements. It is true that communications by land were not much developed by the Hellenistic governments. In Greece metalled roads remained as rare as ever. In Asia the Seleucids and Attalids maintained and at points extended the fine trunk roads of the Persian empire. In Egypt the Ptolemies furnished the desert tracks between Nile and Red Sea with ... water-points and police pickets; they organized a special corps of teamsters for the caravans, and they made experiments with camel-transport. But the road-work of Hellenistic kings is not to be compared with that of Roman emperors.

On the other hand, Hellenistic governments expended considerable care on their harbours. At Alexandria a bleak roadstead was converted into a safe and commodious meeting-point for Mediterranean and Nile traffic. On the inland side a fresh-water lake fed by an arm of the Nile was connected by a new cut with the Mediterranean; on the sea-front a mole was built to the off-shore island of Pharos, so as to provide a sheltered basin on either side. On the island Ptolemy I's architect Sostratus erected the famous lighthouse, a huge tower from whose summit a flare of pine-wood, projected seaward by lenses, marked the site of the harbour at a distance, it is said, of over thirty miles. Though the sea-walls of Alexandria found no rival in the ancient Mediterranean, save at Ostia under the Roman emperors, they were copied on a smaller scale at numerous other Greek ports. Towns situated at a natural sea-inlet ran out breakwaters from either side of the bay and extended the city-walls on to these, so as to make the harbours proof against weather and pirates. The improved accommodation thus provided made it practicable for Hellenistic shipwrights to increase the displacement of their craft, so that vessels capable of carrying 10,000 talents (250 tons) became normal for cargo-transport. A further aid to navigation was provided by Timosthenes, an admiral of Ptolemy II, who wrote a practical manual "On Harbours.". . . Despite better conditions of seafaring, the Greeks continued to lay up their ships for the winter; but in the summer they ventured out more freely than before on open seas and unfamiliar routes.

By their conquest of Egypt and Mesopotamia the Greeks came into possession of two natural centres of river-traffic. On the Euphrates [River, in Persia] the Seleucids . . . founded a busy river-port at Seleucia-on-Tigris. . . . In Egypt the Ptolemies found a ready-made system of inland navigation, and under their rule much of the traffic remained in native hands. But the Nile now became much more than a vehicle for local commerce. It carried the surplus produce of Egypt, and the merchandise brought by caravans from the Red Sea, to Alexandria for consumption or re-export. . . .

In the West the Carthaginians kept their general monopoly of sea-borne trade; and after 200 B.C. the semi-Italian town of Puteoli displaced Tarentum and Syracuse as the chief mart for eastern trade with Italy. Delos displaced Athens as the principal clearing centre of the Aegean area, and became an important entrepôt for the trade in grain. Greek commerce with the Black Sea remained brisk in the third century, for despite competition from Egypt Russian grain still found good markets in the Aegean lands, but it eventually fell off when the cultivation of the corn-lands was endangered by invasions from the hinterland [i.e., from central Asia]. The chief gainers by the new economic order were the stations on the trade routes to the East. At the entrance to the Aegean Ephesus [on the western coast of Asia Minor] acquired a new importance as the main terminus of the overland roads from the Asiatic continent, and Rhodes became a focus of sea-borne trade from the Levant to the Aegean, the Black Sea, and Sicily. Alexandria made one fortune by exporting the overplus of Egypt, another as the entrepôt between the Mediterranean and eastern waters. On the Syrian coast Tyre and Sidon, though overshadowed by Alexandria, retained a share of the Arabian and Indian trades travelling overland. The commercial development of Antioch was stifled in the third century by the loss of its port of Seleucia to the Ptolemies; but in the second it assumed its natural function as the terminal point of traffic from Mesopotamia and opened a brisk trade with the Aegean area. Seleucia-on-Tigris supplanted Babylon as a distributing centre for water-borne traffic from the Persian Gulf. . . . The destruction of Corinth in 146 removed one of the oldest of Greek commercial centres, but its trade was diverted rather than suppressed. In the later second century the Piræus enjoyed a . . . summer of prosperity; Delos became a rendezvous for merchants from Palestine and even from Arabia, and the collecting-point for the slave traffic to Italy.

A rough index of the relative volumes of Hellenistic and of classical Greek commerce is furnished by the fact that the customs revenue of Rhodes *c.* 170 B.C. was five-fold that of Athens in 400 (the rate of duty in either case being probably 2 per cent). Athenian trade, it is true, was then in a "slump"; even so, this figure proves that Hellenistic trade was on a different scale from that of the preceding period.

Athletic Training and Competition

Introduction

*A*ll available evidence suggests that formal, organized athletic competitions originated in ancient Greece. By at least the early Archaic Age (ca. 800–700 B.C.) and probably earlier, the Greeks had come to be fascinated, and in some cases perhaps even obsessed, by taking part in or watching athletic competitions. They came to use the word *agon,* meaning a "contest" or a "struggle," to describe them (as well as other kinds of contests, such as battles and lawsuits). And during the years that followed, a significant physical culture (social institutions and customs surrounding physical fitness and athletic training) grew up in many, if not most, Greek communities. By the Classic Age, the gymnasium, in which men received both physical and academic training, had became a common feature of most Greek city-states.

The importance most Greeks placed on athletics is revealed by the fact that they did not view them simply as a leisure pastime; rather, training for and competing in public games was a serious matter. In *Greek Athletics and the Genesis of Sport* David Sansone, of the University of Illinois, Urbana, remarks:

> What is remarkable about Greek sport is the seriousness with which it was taken as a cultural and even religious phenomenon. . . . It is not unusual for a dramatist like Aeschylus to draw his metaphors, or for a philosopher like Plato to select his illustrations, from the realms of chariot racing or wrestling. Indeed, in the hands of the most distinguished [Greek] poets and artists, sport becomes itself the subject of great art. Everyone is familiar, for example, with Myron's statue of a discus-thrower.

A major reason the Greeks took athletic contests so seriously is that these events originated as part of formal religious worship. During early religious festivals at the gods' sanctuaries, worshipers marched in formal processions and performed sacrifices of plants and animals; and in time worshipers added musical and athletic contests to these rituals. The musical *agon* often consisted of competitions on various musical instruments and poetry recitations; and the athletic *agon* eventually included several running, jumping, and throwing events that are today termed "track and field," along with wrestling, boxing, and horse and chariot racing. In all of these sacred contests, the participants dedicated their creative or physical skills and prowess to the local sanctuary's god or gods.

In time, hundreds of local sacred games were held across the Greek world. But by the end of the sixth century B.C., four of these had emerged as preeminent. They were not only the most prestigious such events, but also international (panhellenic, or "all-Greek") rather than local in character, drawing competitors and spectators from city-states far and wide. The greatest of all, of course, was the Olympic festival (honoring Zeus), held at Olympia every four years (beginning in 776 B.C., at least according to tradition). The others included the Pythian Games (honoring Apollo), held at the sacred shrine at Delphi in the third year after each Olympics; the Isthmian Games (honoring Poseidon), staged every two years at his sanctuary on the Isthmus of Corinth; and the Nemean Games (honoring Zeus), held at two-year intervals at Nemea (a few miles south of Corinth).

Together, these "big four" festivals, in which sports contests became by far the chief attraction, made up the so-called *periodos,* or "circuit" (also known as the Crown Games or Period Games). Another highly popular and prestigious festival featuring athletic events was the Panathenaea ("all the Athenians"), held at Athens every four years in honor of Athena. Because these events drew people from all across the Greek world, they, like the Greek language and the worship of the Olympian gods, served to bind all Greeks together. "The sites of the four main games," noted scholar Vera Olivova writes in *Sports and Games in the Ancient World*,

> became focal points for the whole Greek world. Amid the fertile variety of the city-states, free of pressure from any central power, it was here that a sense of national identity arose in a purely natural and spontaneous way, through awareness of a high level of shared culture both intellectual and physical, and through a sense of superiority over the slaves and over the neighboring barbarians [non-Greeks]. The outward symbol of this superiority was a strong, tanned, well-developed naked body. It became an ideal for all Greeks, distinguishing them from other peoples, and an object of admiration at all panhellenic festivals.

Considering the energy, enthusiasm, and reverence the Greeks lavished on athletic contests, it is perhaps easy to fall into the trap of imagining that they were driven primarily by the love of sport. In fact, modern scholars long supposed that Greek athletes began as "gentleman amateurs" who received no monetary awards and competed mainly out of a "noble" spirit of athletic comradeship. In this scenario, professionalism later crept in and corrupted the games' "pure" amateur spirit (an idea that led the early organizers of the modern Olympics to ban professional athletes). The supposed proof was that at the four ancient circuit festivals—at Olympia, Delphi, Isthmia, and Nemea—the victors received only crowns of leaves.

In reality, this theory is purely a myth; for the modern concept of amateur athletics did not exist in ancient Greece. Although crowns of vegetation were indeed the sole prizes awarded at the circuit games, many athletes were subsidized by well-to-do patrons; and winning athletes always received numerous financial and other awards when they returned to their home cities. These often included valuable bronze tripods, ornamental cups, and jars of olive oil, which the athletes could sell for a profit, as well as cash awards. Moreover, all of the other hundreds of local festivals that featured games gave such prizes outright.

These awards were substantial. In late fifth-century B.C. Athens, for example, a winning runner at the Panathenaea received one hundred jars of olive oil, having a total worth of about 1,200 drachmas. Since the average Greek worker earned about one drachma per day (about 300 drachma per year) in the late fifth century, an athlete could receive the equivalent of four years' salary by winning a single footrace. And often that was only the beginning. Like many other communities, Athens awarded native sons who had been victorious in the circuit games free meals for life. What is more, the most successful athletes were glorified almost as gods, as poets like Pindar and Bacchylides composed odes and sculptors like Myron molded statues in their honor.

Such valuable prizes and honors were surely the principal inducement for men to train and compete in the games, especially the most prestigious ones. The idea of competing mainly out of simple love of sport and the desire to share good fellowship with other athletes, win or lose, is strictly a modern concept. To ancient Greek athletes, in fact, winning was imperative and defeat shameful. "In the Olympic Games you cannot just be beaten and then depart," writes the first-century A.D. Greek philosopher Epictetus, "but first of all, you will be disgraced . . . before the whole world." (*Discourses* 3.22.52) Even more powerful is Pindar's description of four losers at Delphi, "to whom the Pythian feast has given no glad homecoming. . . . They, when they meet their mothers, have no sweet laughter to cheer them up. . . . In back streets they cower, avoiding their enemies; disaster has bitten them." (*Eighth Pythian Ode* 83–88)

Thus, unlike modern athletes, who often compete against the clock or measuring tape in an effort to set records, Greek athletes cared little how far they threw or how fast they ran. Beating the competition and winning first place was almost always the single-minded goal. This desire to win at nearly any cost sometimes led to cheating and bribery. In one celebrated case, in 388 B.C. a boxer named Eupolius, from Thessaly, bribed three rivals to let him win first place at Olympia. About half a century later, an Athenian supposedly won the Olympic pentathlon the same way. Yet there is no evidence to suggest that such corruption was common at Olympia. Moreover, however widespread corruption may have been in Greek athletics, most of the competitors, as is true today, were probably honest and fair. And the vast majority of both contestants and spectators thoroughly enjoyed and benefited from attending the various festival games, which greatly enriched society.

Thanks to the survival of various forms of ancient evidence, modern scholars have been able to piece together a fairly accurate reconstruction of the development and staging of Greek athletic contests. First, there is Homer's *Iliad,* which contains the world's first literary description of athletic games. Other important ancient writers about athletics were, of course, Pindar and Bacchylides (both fifth century B.C.), who composed numerous odes for victorious athletes; the Greek traveler Pausanias (second century A.D.), who in his famous guidebook described Olympia and other games sites and also provided anecdotes about famous athletes; the Greek writer Philostratus (second century A.D.), whose treatise, *On Athletics,* describes in detail most of the standard ancient athletic events; and the Greek physician Galen (second century A.D.), whose works provide valuable information about athletes' training, diet, and injuries. Other kinds of evidence include archaeological studies of the remains of ancient stadiums, arenas, gymnasiums, and so on; assorted fragments of lists of athletic events and winners; and scenes painted on pottery or carved into stone showing athletes training and competing.

Selection 1

Legendary Heroes Race Their Chariots

Homer

The earliest written reference to Greek athletic competition consists of the funeral games given by the hero Achilles to honor his fallen comrade, Patroclus, in Book 23 of Homer's Iliad. *Homer likely lived in the eighth century* B.C., *so competitions such as those he describes must have existed for at least a century, and more likely several centuries, before that time. The following excerpt, from E.V. Rieu's well-known translation, is the exciting chariot race. As happens often in the siege of Troy preceding these*

Excerpted from *The Iliad*, by Homer, translated by E.V. Rieu (Penguin Classics, 1950). Translation copyright © E.V. Rieu, 1950. Reprinted by permission of Penguin Books Ltd.

games, the gods (in this case Apollo and Athena) unashamedly intervene to help their favorites achieve victory.

And now they all mounted their chariots and cast their lots into a helmet, which Achilles shook. The first lot to jump out was that of Antilochus son of Nestor; then came that of King Eumelus, followed by that of Atreus' son, the spearman Menelaus. Meriones drew the fourth starting-place, and the last fell to Diomedes, the best man of them all. They drew up side by side and Achilles showed them the turning-point, far away on level ground. He had posted the venerable Phoenix, his father's squire, as an umpire there, to keep an eye on the running and report what happened.

The Race Begins

At one and the same moment they all gave their horses the whip, shook the reins of their backs and set them going with a sharp word of command. The horses started off across the plain without a hitch and quickly left the ships behind. The dust that rose from underneath their chests hung in the air like a storm-cloud or a fog, and their manes flew back in the wind. At one moment the chariots were in contact with the fruitful earth and at the next were bounding high in the air. The heart of each driver as he stood in his car and struggled to be first was beating hard. They yelled at their horses, who flew along in a cloud of dust.

But it was not till their galloping teams had rounded the mark and were heading back to the grey sea that each man showed his form and the horses stretched themselves. The fast mares of Eumelus now shot out of the ruck, and next came Diomedes' stallions of the breed of Tros, close behind, with very little in it. It looked as though at any moment they might leap into Eumelus' car. They were flying along with their heads just over him, warming his back and his broad shoulders with their breath. In fact Diomedes would have overhauled Eumelus then and there or made it a dead heat, if Phoebus Apollo, who was still angry with Tydeus' son, had not knocked the shining whip out of his hand.

Diomedes, when he saw Eumelus' mares going better than ever and his own horses slowing down for lack of anything to spur them on, was so angry that the tears poured down his checks. But Athene had had her eye on Apollo when he fouled Diomedes. She sped after the great mail, gave him back his whip and put fresh spirit in his horses. Moreover she was so enraged that she chased Eumelus too and used her powers as a goddess to break the yoke of his chariot, with the result that his mares ran off on their own and the shaft crumpled up on the ground, while Eumelus himself was flung out of the car and came down by the wheel. The skin was taken off his elbows, mouth and nose; his forehead was bruised; his eyes were filled with tears, and he was robbed of speech. Meanwhile Diomedes swept round the wreckage with his powerful horses, having left the others well behind. Athene filled his pair with strength and let their master triumph.

Next after Diomedes came red-haired Menelaus, Atreus' son; and next again Antilochus, who was shouting at his father's horses and urging them to spurt like Diomedes' pair. 'Show me your best paces now,' he cried. 'I am not asking you to race that pair ahead, the gallant Diomedes' horses. . . . Why are you hanging back, my friends? I tell you frankly what you can expect. No more attentions from King Nestor's hands for you! He will slit your throats without a moment's hesitation if you take it easy now and leave us with the smaller prize. So after them full tilt! Trust me to find a way of slipping past them where the track is narrow. I shall not miss my chance.'

His horses, taking their master's threat to heart, went faster for a little while, and very soon Antilochus, that veteran campaigner, saw a place where the sunken road grew narrow. It ran through a gulley: water piled up by the winter rains had carried part of it away and deepened the whole defile. Menelaus was in occupation of the track, making it difficult for anyone to come abreast of him. But Antilochus did not keep to it. He drove a little off it to one side, and pressed Menelaus hard. Menelaus was alarmed and shouted at him: 'You are driving madly, Antilochus; hold in your horses. The track is narrow here. It soon gets wider—

you could pass me there. Be careful you don't hit my chariot and wreck us both.'

But Antilochus, pretending that he had not heard him, plied his lash and drove more recklessly than ever. They both ran on for about the distance that a quoit will carry when a young man casts it with a swing of the arm to test his strength. Then Menelaus' pair gave way and fell behind. He eased the pace himself, on purpose, fearing that the powerful horses might collide in the road and upset the light chariots, in which case their masters, through their eagerness to win, would find themselves rolling in the dust. But red-haired Menelaus managed to give the other a piece of his mind. 'Antilochus,' he cried, 'you are the most appalling driver in the world. We were mistaken when we thought you had some sense. Well, have it your own way; but all the same, you shall not carry off the prize till you have answered on your oath for this affair.'

Then Menelaus turned to his horses. 'Don't stop,' he shouted at them. 'Don't stand and mope. That pair ahead of you will weaken in the leg far sooner than you. They are neither of them as young as they were.' His horses, frightened by their master's reprimand, sped on with a better will and soon were close behind the other pair.

Who Is in the Lead?

Meanwhile from their seats in the ring the spectators were looking out for the horses, who were rapidly approaching in a cloud of dust. Idomeneus the Cretan King was the first to see them. He was sitting well above the rest on high ground outside the ring, and when he heard a driver shouting in the distance he knew the voice. He also recognized one of the leading horses, who showed up well, being chestnut all over but for a round white patch like the full moon which he had on his forehead. Idomeneus stood up and called to the other spectators: 'My friends, Captains and Counsellors of the Argives; am I the only one who can see the horses or do you see them too? It seems to me that a new pair are leading, and the driver also looks different. Eumelus' mares, who were ahead on the outward lap, must have come to grief out

there, for I certainly saw them leading at the turning-post and now I cannot see them anywhere, though I have searched the whole Trojan plain. Perhaps Eumelus dropped his reins: he couldn't steer his horses round the mark and had an accident as he was wheeling. Yes, that is where he must have been tossed out and smashed his chariot, while his mares went wild and bolted. But do get up and have a look yourselves. I cannot be quite sure, but the leading mail looks like an Aetolian to me, yes, one of our Argive kings, the son of horse-taming Tydeus, Diomedes himself.'...

By now Diomedes was very close. He was driving with the whip, swinging his arm right back for every lash, and making his horses leap high in the air as they sped on to the finish. Showers of dust fell on their driver all the time, and as the fast pair flew over the ground the chariot overlaid with gold and tin came spinning after them and scarcely left a tyre-mark on the fine dust behind.

Diomedes drew up in the middle of the arena, with the sweat pouring to the ground from his horses' necks and chests. He leapt down from his glittering car and leant his whip against the yoke. Sthenelus, his gallant equerry, made short work of the prizes. He took possession promptly, giving the tripod with the ear-shaped handles to his exultant men. . . . Then he unyoked the horses.

Antilochus son of Nestor was the next man to drive up. He had beaten Menelaus not by any turn of speed but by a trick. Yet even so Menelaus and his fast horses came in close behind. . . .

Meriones, Idomeneus' worthy squire, came in a spear-throw behind the famous Menelaus. His long-maned horses were the slowest pair in the race, and he himself was the poorest racing-driver.

The last of them all to arrive was Admetus' son Eumelus. He was dragging his handsome chariot himself and driving his horses in front of him. When he saw this, the swift and excellent Achilles was sorry for the mail. He stood up in the ring and made a suggestion: 'The best driver of the lot has come in last. Let us give him a prize, as is only fair. Make it the second, for of course Diomedes takes the first.'

Selection 2

The Sacred Games at Olympia

Judith Swaddling

The games held every four years at Olympia (in the northwestern Peloponnesus) comprised the most prestigious and popular athletic competition in antiquity. Judith Swaddling, of the Department of Greek and Roman Antiquities at the British Museum, here provides important background information on the ancient Olympic festival and games. She describes the physical setting of the site and also the structures that made up the sacred Olympic sanctuary (the Altis, dedicated to Zeus). She also tells about how the games came to be (including the legends the Greeks passed on about their founding), the Olympic truce, the organizers (from the city-state of Elis), how the athletes trained, and the grand procession from Elis to the Altis.

Swaddling then provides a general program of the activities and athletic events of the festival's five days, approximately the way scholars think they occurred by the late Classic Age. The footraces included the stade *(about 600 feet); the* diaulos *(two* stades *in length); the* dolichos *(about twenty-four* stades *in length); and the* hoplitodromos *(a race in armor, about two* stades *in length). There was a horse race for jockeys who rode*

bareback and two chariot races—the tetrippon *(for four-horse chariots) and* synoris *(for two-horse chariots). The three combat events were wrestling, boxing, and the* pankration *(a rough-and-tumble combination of wrestling and boxing). In addition, the pentathlon consisted of five events: discus throw, javelin throw, broad jump, wrestling, and the* stade; *and there were boys' versions of many of these same events. (It should be noted that some other events were introduced but later discontinued; for instance, the* apene, *a race for mule-carts, first appeared on the program in 500 B.C., but was dropped in 444 B.C.)*

Every fourth year for a thousand years, from 776 BC to AD 395, the pageantry of the Olympic festival attracted citizens from all over the Greek world. They flocked to Olympia, the permanent setting for the Games, in the early years coming in their hundreds from neighbouring towns and city-states, and later in their thousands by land and sea from colonies as far away as Spain and Africa. . . .

The Altis and the Olympic Truce

The Games were held in honour of the god Zeus, the supreme god of Greek mythology, and a visit to Olympia was also a pilgrimage to his most sacred place, the grove known as the Altis.

There is no modern parallel for Olympia; it would have to be a site combining a sports complex and a centre for religious devotion, something like a combination of Wembley Stadium and Westminster Abbey.

Olympia is situated in a fertile, grassy plain on the north bank of the broad river Alpheios, just to the east of its confluence with the Kladeos, which rushes down to meet it from the mountains of Elis. In ancient times the area was pleasantly shaded with plane and olive-trees, white poplars and even palm-trees, while vines and flowering shrubs grew thickly beneath them. Rising above the site, to the north, is the lofty, pine-covered hill of Kronos, named after the father of Zeus. Successive waves of peoples who passed through the area in prehistoric times each observed the sanctity of this hallowed area. Modern visitors to the site often express surprise that the Games were held in such a remote area,

but in antiquity, the river Alpheios was navigable, and Olympia was easily accessible both from the sea (it was about fifteen kilometres from the coast) and by means of inland routes converging on the site. The hill of Kronos must always have been a conspicuous landmark in the surrounding terrain.

The clearing within the grove at the foot of the hill was once associated with fertility rites. . . . Gradually, as the worship of Zeus became predominant, people began to honour him at simple altars in the grove and hung their offerings—primitive terracotta and bronze figurines of men and animals—on the branches of nearby trees. With the establishment of the Games, this sanctuary grew and flourished. From the sixth century BC onwards the Altis was gradually adorned with temples, treasuries, halls, elaborate altars and literally hundreds of marble and bronze statues. The statues, some of which were several

Pilgrims from many Greek states eagerly make their way toward the Olympic sanctuary at Elis in the northwestern reaches of the Peloponnesus.

times life-size, were mostly victory dedications to Zeus for athletic and military achievements, and were set up by both states and individuals. There were also monuments erected in honour of benefactors, and offerings of costly materials given by wealthy tyrants and princes. Most remarkable of all the spectacles at Olympia was one of the 'Seven Wonders of the World': the resplendent thirteen-metre-high gold and ivory statue of Zeus within his magnificent temple. The statue was the work of Pheidias, the great sculptor of the fifth century BC.

As regards the origin of the Olympic Games, one can, as often in Greek history, either believe the legends, of which there are many, or look for a more down-to-earth beginning. According to the poet Pindar, Olympia was virtually created by Herakles, the 'superman' of Greek mythology. He made a clearing in the grove, laid out the boundaries of the Altis and instituted the first games in honour of Zeus. His purpose was to celebrate the success of one of his twelve labours, the cleaning of the cattle stables of King Augeas of Elis, which had been achieved by diverting the river Alpheios from its course. It is more likely, however, that athletic festivals like the Olympic Games developed from the funeral games which were held in honour of local heroes. Pelops . . . was the local hero of Olympia, and his grave and sanctuary were situated within the Altis. It is interesting that he was said to come from the east, for many people believe that it was in Asia Minor that the first organised athletic contests took place, when the Greek communities established there became prosperous enough to devote their leisure time to sport. At that time mainland Greece was still unsettled by wars and migrations.

The traditional date for the establishment of the Olympic Games was 776 BC, but competitions appear to have been held on an unofficial basis long before this. King Iphitos of Elis, a shadowy figure who lived around the ninth century BC, is said to have reinstituted the Games on the advice of the Delphic Oracle. The king had asked the Oracle how to bring an end to the civil wars and pestilence which were gradually de-stroying the land of Greece, whereupon the priestess advised that he should restore the Olympic Games and declare a truce for their duration. Whether this is true or not the Olympic Truce was a major instrument in the unification of the Greek states and colonies.

In order to spread the news of the Truce before the beginning of the Olympic festival, three heralds decked with olive wreaths and carrying staffs were sent out from Elis to every Greek state. It was the heralds' duty to announce the exact date of the festival, to invite the inhabitants to attend and, most important of all, to announce the Olympic Truce. In this way they came to be known as the Truce-Bearers, *Spondophoroi*; they served not only as heralds but also as full-time legal advisers to the Eleans. Originally the Truce lasted for one month but it was extended to two and then three months, to protect visitors coming from further afield. The terms of the Truce were engraved on a bronze discus which was kept in the Temple of Hera in the Altis. It forbade states participating in the Games to take up arms, to pursue legal disputes or to carry out death penalties. This was to ensure that pilgrims and athletes travelling to and from Olympia would have a safe journey. Violators of the Truce were heavily fined, and indeed on one occasion, Alexander the Great himself had to recompense an Athenian who was robbed by some of his mercenaries whilst travelling to Olympia.

The Olympic Games are the oldest of the four panhellenic or national athletic festivals which composed the *periodos* or 'circuit' games. The other three were the Pythian Games at Delphi, held in honour of Apollo, the Isthmian Games held at Corinth for Poseidon, and the Games at Nemea, which, like the Olympics, were in honour of Zeus. A major distinction between the Greek games and our own is that all major and minor athletic festivals, of which several hundred had been established by Roman times, were celebrated under the patronage of a divinity. The god was believed to bestow on the athletes the physical prowess which enabled them to take part in the Games. Accordingly, the athletes prayed to the deity and promised offerings should they be victorious.

The Olympic festival was celebrated once every four years in accordance with the Greek calendar, which was based on the lunar month. It was always timed so that the central day of the festival coincided with the second or third full moon after the summer solstice. This may well indicate the assimilation at some stage of the Games with fertility rites which celebrated the harvesting. It is often asked why the Greeks should have chosen the very hottest time of the year, mid-August or mid-September, for such strenuous exertion. Apart from the lunar associations it surely made sense to hold the Games at the one time during the year when work on the land was at a standstill. By then the crops were gathered and there was a lull in which men were eager to relax and celebrate the end of a hard year's work. . . .

The Stadium

The stadium did not exist during the early years of the Olympic Games. The athletes made use of an open level stretch of ground with a line drawn in the sand to mark the start (giving rise to our term 'starting from scratch'). As the races were held in honour of the god Zeus, it was appropriate that the finishing line should be close to his altar. The spectators stood on the lower slopes of the hill of Kronos.

These simple arrangements were adequate for the first centuries of the Olympic Games. Gradually various improvements were made and a rudimentary stadium was constructed within the Altis. It had shallow banks and a rectangular track, for, unlike ours, all ancient races were run on the straight. Eventually, around 350 BC a magnificent new stadium was constructed and it was situated, significantly, outside the Altis boundaries. By this time the games, although still part of the religious festival, had become established in their own right. Originally Zeus had been glorified for granting powers of strength and physical endurance to the athletes; now the athletes were becoming increasingly professional and beginning to gain recognition as cult figures themselves. Thus the removal of the stadium from the sacred precinct was a development in religious as well as athletic history.

The track in the stadium was of clay, levelled and lightly covered with sand. It had stone sills towards each end which marked the start and finish of the races. To preserve some of the religious significance of the games it was desirable for all races to finish at the western end of the course, so that the runners still ran towards the heart of the Altis as they had done in the early days. Races consisting of an even number of lengths were therefore started at the western end. The course was separated from the embankment by a ridge of stone blocks, to the outside of which was a channel that conducted water round the stadium, discharging at intervals into basins for the refreshment of spectators who stood all day in the blazing sun without any shelter.

The length of the track at Olympia is six hundred Olympic feet, 192.28 metres. According to mythology, Herakles fixed the distance of the original race (and ultimately of the stadium) by placing one foot in front of the other six hundred times. An alternative explanation was that Herakles was able to run this distance in one breath before pausing to take another. Thus it has been suggested that 'stadium' was derived from the Greek word 'to stand.' All ancient stadia were approximately six hundred feet in length but most places used a local standard of measure, causing a slight variation in the length of each stadium.

The ground rose naturally in the east and artificial embankments were constructed in the north, west and south, requiring an immense amount of labour. In this way a surprising total of between forty and forty-five thousand spectators could be accommodated. To afford spectators an uninterrupted view of the race the two long embankments were designed so that they were three metres further apart at the centre than at the ends. This arrangement is found in other ancient stadia and was copied in the modern Olympic stadium in Athens. . . .

Preparation and Training

The Olympic Festival lasted for five days but the preparations took virtually the whole of the preceding year. Strangely, there is no firm evidence that the sports facilities at Olympia were used during the period between the festivals. Local villagers may have exercised there but they would have been few in number. Much hard physical labour was therefore required to get things ready. Any undergrowth that had sprung up had to be cleared. The courses had to be dug and levelled and the sand pits prepared. Repairs and general tidying up of the buildings and monuments in and around the sanctuary were also necessary.

The most important officials at the Games, who were known as the *Hellanodikai*, commenced preparations ten months before the games were due to start. Their name means literally 'judges of the Greeks', reflecting the national character of the Games. In the early years of the festival they had been referred to merely as *agonothetai*, 'games organisers'. They had their own special residence in Elis called the *hellanodikaion*. The Hellanodikai were chosen by lot, and although their numbers fluctuated, there were ten for most of the history of the Games. One of them acted as the overall supervisor while the rest were divided into three groups, each presiding over different events. The first group organised the equestrian events, the second the pentathlon, and the third the remainder of the competitions. Throughout the ages the Olympic judges were renowned for their impartiality. They wore robes of purple, the royal colour serving as a reminder of the time when King Iphitos controlled the Games and officiated as the sole judge. The athletes, too, had to be in strict training in their home towns during the ten months prior to the Games and they had to swear to this effect.

For at least one month before the festival prospective competitors in the Games were required to reside at Elis and train under the strict supervision of the Hellanodikai. There were three gymnasiums at Elis and in addition the local market place was stripped and used as a practice track for the horse races. This period of compulsory training at Elis was enforced by the Eleans probably to demonstrate their absolute control over the Games. Their authority had been contested in the past particularly by their neighbours the Pisatans [the residents of the region of Pisa], but eventually the Eleans established supremacy. During this month the judges were fully occupied with various tasks: they disqualified those who were not fit, checked on parentage and Greek descent, and resolved any disputes concerning the classification of men and boys, horses and colts. The training was renowned for its harshness: the athletes had to observe a strict diet, carry out a gruelling regime of exercise and obey every word of the Hellanodikai. It is not certain when the period of compulsory training was introduced, but since it required the athlete to be away from home for a considerable time he had to be fairly affluent. Sometimes his father or brother would accompany him to Elis but more often a private trainer had to be employed. By this time the era of the amateur athlete was clearly coming to a close.

Two days before the festival began the whole company set out from Elis, which was roughly fifty-eight kilometres from Olympia. First came the Hellanodikai and other officials, then the athletes and their trainers, horses and chariots together with their owners, jockeys and charioteers. They followed the Sacred Way along the coast, stopping to sacrifice a pig and to perform other rites at the fountain of Piera on the boundary between Elis and Olympia. They spent the night at Letrini and the next day wound their way along the valley of the Alpheios towards the Altis.

Meanwhile people from all walks of life had been making their way to Olympia. Princes and tyrants from Sicily and southern Italy sailed up the river in splendid barges; ambassadors came from various towns, vying with each other in dress and paraphernalia. The rich came on horseback, and in chariots; the poor came on donkeys, in carts and even on foot. Food-sellers came loaded with supplies for there was no town near Olympia. Merchants flocked in with their wares. Artisans came to make figurines that pilgrims could buy to offer to their god. Booths and stalls were set up; tents and huts were erected, for only official delegates were given accommodation in the magnificent guest-house known as the *Leonidaion*. Most visitors looked for a suitable spot to put down their belongings and slept each night under the summer skies. . . .

The Olympic Program

Day One   **Morning** Swearing-in ceremony for competitors and judges in the Bouleuterion (Council-House) before the altar and statue of Zeus *Horkios* (Zeus of the Oaths).

Contests for heralds and trumpeters held near the stadium entrance.

Boys' running, wrestling and boxing contests.

Public and private prayers and sacrifices in the Altis; consultation of oracles.

Afternoon Orations by well-known philosophers and recitals by poets and historians.

Sightseeing tours of the Altis.

Reunions with old friends.

Day Two   **Morning** Procession into the hippodrome of all those competing there.

Chariot- and horse-races.

Afternoon The pentathlon: discus, javelin, jumping, running and wrestling.

Evening Funeral rites in honour of the hero Pelops.

Parade of victors round the Altis.

Communal singing of victory hymns.

Feasting and revelry.

Day Three   **Morning** Procession of the Hellanodikai (Judges), ambassadors from the Greek states, competitors in all events and sacrificial animals round the Altis to the Great Altar in front of the Temple of Zeus, followed by the official sacrifice of one hundred oxen given by the people of Elis.

Afternoon Foot-races.

Evening Public banquet in the Prytaneion.

Day Four   **Morning** Wrestling.

Midday Boxing and the *pankration*.

Afternoon Race-in-armour.

Day Five   Procession of victors to the Temple of Zeus where they are crowned with wreaths of wild olive by the Hellanodikai, followed by the *phyllobolia* (when the victors are showered with leaves and flowers).

Feasting and celebrations.

Selection 3

Nudity in Greek Athletics

Waldo E. Sweet

In this fascinating tract from his well-known book about Greek sports, noted scholar Waldo E. Sweet examines the important issue of nudity in Greek athletics. He begins by presenting the evidence for and against the competitors wearing loincloths, including quotes from the works of Homer, the fifth-century B.C. historian Thucydides, the second-century A.D. traveler Pausanias, and others. He eventually concludes that the athletes did compete in the nude. Finally, he describes how they might have avoided injuring their genitals, since they apparently did not use athletic supporters.

O ne of the unusual features of Greek athletics is that the participants are almost always shown nude in vase paintings and statues. Many modern Americans find it difficult to believe that the Greeks would not have used some kind of protection for the genitals, like the modern athletic supporter.

One explanation could be that the athletes did wear shorts or an athletic supporter of some kind, but the artist preferred to paint or sculpt the entire body. In Greek vase paintings there are many artistic conventions, for instance showing the head in profile but the body in frontal position, or a head in profile with eyes full face. There is seldom any body hair represented; the

fingers may be straight and inflexible, and the toes are often extra long. During some periods athletes were portrayed with extra large thighs. Not depicting apparel seems plausible as an artistic convention. Secondly, the ideal male of many vase painters was the pre-pubescent boy rather than the mature male. Consequently artists commonly "youthened" the figures, to employ a modern scholar's felicitious [apt] phrase. Even mature males were shown with immature genitals, which would not need protection.

Homer represents his heroes as putting on a loincloth before competing in boxing or wrestling (*Iliad* 23.683; 23.685; 23.710). In the *Odyssey* (18.67) the hero "tucked up his rags around his middle" before boxing with the beggar Iros. Several vases show a type of athletic supporter that might possibly have been used by Homeric heroes; however, these vases pose a problem. There are only about a dozen of them, all by the same potter or by a member of his Athenian workshop. Furthermore, on all of these vases, a white loincloth has been painted over the incised outline of the genitals. None of these vases was discovered in Greece proper. It looks as though the vases may have been painted over for a modest clientele.

The modern generally accepted explanation for the use of loincloths in ancient Greece runs as follows. The Homeric heroes wore loincloths while competing in athletics, but in the fifteenth Olympics (720 BC) Orsippos of Megara, a competitor in the stade, decided he could run faster without a loincloth. He boldly discarded it and stepped bare-bottomed into history. This view is based chiefly on an inscription found at Megara.

It is a poem, generally thought to have been written by Semonides, who lived in the seventh-to-sixth century BC:

> The Megarians, obeying the word of Delphi, set me up, a magnificent memorial to brave Orrhippos [Orsippos], who . . . was the first of all the Greeks to be crowned *gymnos* [naked or lightly clothed] at Olympia, since before everyone had competed in the stade wearing loincloths. . . .

In describing Megara, Pausanias seems to have seen the inscription, for the resemblance in his text is very close:

> Nearby is buried Orsippos. At a time when it was the ancient custom of the athletes to compete in the games with a loincloth, he won at Olympia in the stade running *gymnos*. . . . I think that his loincloth slipped off with his consent, since he knew that a man who is *gymnos* can run more easily than one wearing a loincloth.

> If Semonides wrote this, he wrote it two centuries after the alleged event. We must consider whether Semonides was piously perpetuating an unsubstantiated legend. In fact, we must regard with caution *all* data from the days of the early Olympics. . . .

The reputation of the historian Thucydides (late fifth-century BC) is such that we would expect him to be clear and accurate, but he is not. He says the following:

> The Spartans were the first to exercise *gymnoi* and to disrobe in public and rub themselves with olive oil after they had exercised while *gymnoi*. Formerly, even in the Olympics, athletes competed with a loincloth around their genitals, and it is not many years since they stopped. People who hold contests in boxing and wrestling and are not Greek, especially those in Asia Minor, do wear loincloths when they compete. . . .

Plato [in his *Republic*] represents Sokrates as also saying that the custom of exercising nude was fairly recent:

> We remind these people that it was not very long ago that the Greeks thought, as the barbarian nations still think, that it was shameful and ridiculous for men to be seen *gymnoi*. And when first the Cretans and then the Spartans began to engage in athletics, it was possible for wits to make fun of the whole business. . . .

So far, the testimonia could be interpreted to mean that *gymnos* is not "naked" but rather "lightly clad"; that is, the athletes could have been wearing shorts or loincloths. The following passage from Dionysius of Halicarnassus (first-century BC) describes a religious procession in Rome:

> After the chariots came the competitors in both the light and heavy events, *gymnoi* for the rest of their bodies but with their genitals covered. This custom was still observed in my time in Rome, just as it had been originally by the Greeks. It is now ended in Greece, and the Spartans ended it. The person who first removed his clothing and ran *gymnos* in the Olympics was Akanthos, a Spartan, in the 15th Olympics. Before that time all the Greeks considered it shameful to appear in the games with their bodies entirely *gymna*, as Homer testifies, the oldest and most trustworthy authority, when he presents his heroes wearing loincloths. . . .

There seems to be no way of deciding which of these versions, if any, is true. There is no agreement about who dropped his loincloth, or in what event, or in what games. The date of 720 BC is contradicted. We do not know whether dropping the loincloth was seen as an advantage or a hindrance. There are only two points on which there is agreement:

1. In Homeric times the athletes wore loincloths.

2. In the classical period athletes competed nude. . . .

The Need for Athletic Supporters?

Neither visual nor literary references give us any reason to believe that Greek athletes in classical times wore any kind of athletic supporter. It is true that there are a few scattered examples of athletes wearing a sort of boxer shorts, but this cannot be considered as showing that wearing shorts was common in classical times.

If the loincloth was not used, perhaps protection was furnished by infibulation, which was the practice of tying a thong around the foreskin of the penis. We are not told the purpose of infibulation, but it is seen on three types of people: athletes, revelers, and the mythological creatures called satyrs. There are many examples of infibulation in vase painting and statues, mostly from the period between 600 BC and 300 BC. Here is what Phrynichos, a lexicographer of 11 AD, says:

> *Kynodesmai* [dog's leash]: The cords with which the inhabitants of Attica roll back and tie up the penis. They call the penis a *kyon* [dog]

(and the word *desmos* means a leash). . . .

The fact that the most common use of infibulation is among athletes suggests that it may have been used as a protection for the genitals. But to modern athletes who are accustomed to wearing a jockstrap in almost all forms of athletics, the amount of protection that infibulation would give seems quite inadequate. At best it gives protection to the glans of the penis, but none to the testicles, one of the most vulnerable areas of the body. At best, infibulation would keep the penis from uncomfortably slapping against the body while doing an activity such as jumping jacks.

At this point we had found that the theory of athletes wearing shorts was surely untenable, and that infibulation would give no protection to the testicles. First, how much protection do modern athletes need? A short questionnaire

Young athletes train in a local gymnasium for an upcoming festival competition. The two at lower left are in the final stages of a boxing match.

446   THE COMPLETE HISTORY OF ANCIENT GREECE

was distributed to members of the athletics staff and the Department of Classical Studies of the University of Michigan, asking among other things what events in the ancient Olympics would necessitate wearing equipment like a jockstrap. Of forty respondents, only six thought no protection would be needed. We have also talked with about a dozen nudists. While conceding the need for protection in a sport like football, they do not believe that most other sports require such support.

One dedicated nudist reported in a letter that he and his friends found that "during vigorous physical activity the scrotum and penis retract into a tight, compact bundle, close to the body and removed from (danger of) injury." He went on to say that his son was required to wear a jockstrap while playing soccer. It was his opinion that this "almost universal requirement" was followed in order to avoid criticism if injury occurred: "The coach can then maintain that all the usual steps were taken to prevent injury." The muscle that lifts or drops the testicles is called the cremaster muscle. The Greek physician Galen, in describing it ("Usefulness of the Parts" 15.336), says it has voluntary motion. Sumo wrestlers in Japan strengthen this muscle by exercise, often beginning in childhood. . . .

Personal experience in running nude proved to this writer that absolutely no discomfort occurred and the genitals did in fact retract. It is quite likely that many or even most Greeks did without any protection for the genitals. Modern opinion on how much protection the ancient Greeks would need may not be valid. For example, most modern runners would need the protection of shoes in running long distance, but in August 1960 in Rome, the Olympic marathon was won by the barefoot Abebe Pikila from Ethiopia.

Selection 4

A Victorious Athlete Is Glorified in Verse

Pindar

The renowned Greek poet Pindar (ca. 518–ca. 438 B.C.) composed a large number of epinikia, *odes honoring victorious athletes. The one presented here, the* Sixth Nemean Ode *(referring to the games held at Nemea, in the northwestern Peloponnesus, which were dedicated to Zeus), celebrates one Alkimidas of Aegina. This young man won the boys' wrestling about 461 B.C. It is likely that his family commissioned Pindar to write the verses, which were performed by a choir in Alkimidas's home town. Note that the poet begins with a sweeping statement about the gods and how a few humans, notably gifted athletes, might emulate them. Pindar is noted for starting many of his odes with grand or philosophical statements. The rest of the ode honors Alkimidas by setting his victory amid a rich tapestry of prior games winners (including the boy's own ancestors) and mytho-*

logical references (including the Muses and Graces, minor goddesses said to inspire humans with talent and grace).

I

ingle is the race, single
Of men and of gods;
From a single mother we both draw
    breath.
But a difference of power in everything
Keeps us apart;
For the one [humanity] is as Nothing, but the
    brazen sky [abode of the gods]
Stays a fixed habitation for ever.
5   Yet we can in greatness of mind
Or of body be like the Immortals,
Tho' we know not to what goal
By day or in the nights
Fate has written that we shall run.

Even now Alkimidas gives visible witness
That his race is like the fruitful fields
Which change about
10 And now give men abounding life from the
        soil,
Now rest again and pick up strength.
He has come from Nemea's well-loved
        Games,
A boy in the struggle,
Who follows thus calling from Zeus;
He has been revealed a hunter
And had good sport in the wrestling.

15 He plants his feet in the kindred tracks
        [follows in the footsteps]
Of his father's father, Praxidamas;
For he, an Olympian victor,
First brought twigs from Alpheos to the
        Aiakidai;
He was crowned five times at the Isthmus,
20 Thrice at Nemea,

And saved [his father] Sokleidas from
    oblivion,
Who was first of [his grandfather]
    Hagesidamos' sons.

II

To his delight three prize-winners
Reached the peak of prowess by tasting of
    toil.
With good fortune from God
25 Boxing has proved no other house
To hold more crowns in the heart of all
        Hellas [Greece].
I hope with this big word
To hit the mark as with a shot from the bow.
    Come, Muse, waft straight to him
The glorious gale of your words;
For when men pass away,

30 Songs and tables bring back
Their noble achievements for them [i.e.,
        their deeds will be remembered in these
        verses].
Of these the Bassidai have no lack.
A clan renowned of old,
They convoyed their own hymns of praise
And could give the Pierians' ploughmen
        [i.e., the poets]
Many a song of their lordly doings.
In rich Pytho [at the Pythian Games at
        Delphi] one from the blood of this land,
35 His hands bound in the boxing-strap,
Kallias, won, the favourite

Of gold-haired Leto's children;
And at Kastalia in the evening
The Graces' loud song shed flame on him.
The bridges of the unwearying sea [i.e., the
        Isthmus of Corinth, site of another
        famous sports competition]
In the Feast of the Dwellers Around
40 And the slaughter of bulls in the second year
Honoured Kreontidas in Poseidon's acre,
And the Lion's grass crowned him in victory
Under the shaggy ancient hills of Phleious.

Excerpted from *The Odes of Pindar*, translated by C.M. Bowra (Penguin Classics, 1969). Translation copyright © C.M. Bowra, 1969. Reprinted by permission of Penguin Books Ltd.

III

45 For tellers of tales
Wide avenues open on every side
To grace this glorious island.
For the Aiakidai gave them
A surpassing destiny
And revealed their great acts of prowess.
Their fame flies far over the earth and across
the sea.
It leaped even to the Ethiopians [Africans
living south of Egypt]
50 When Memnon came not home.
Heavy for them was the fight into which
Achilles fell [in Homer's *Iliad*]
When he came down from his chariot to the
ground

And slew the son of the shining Dawn [the
Trojan champion Hector]
With the edge of his furious sword.
This theme men of old found a road for
traffic;
I too follow and make it my care.

55 But the wave that rolls at times at the ship's
keel
Is said most to trouble every man's heart.
On my willing back I shoulder a double
burden
And have come to tell the news
Of this twenty-fifth prayer answered

From the Games which men call holy.
60 Alkimidas, you have added it
To your illustrious race.
Twice the flowers of the Olympian Festival
By the precinct of Kronos [i.e., Zeus's
sanctuary beside the Hill of Kronos at
Olympia]
Were stolen from you in your boyhood
By the wanton fall of a lot [i.e., twice when
lots were drawn to decide the order of the
matches, your draw put you at a
disadvantage].
To a dolphin in the sea
65 I would match Melesias [an Athenian trainer
who coached Alkimidas] for quickness,
Charioteer of hands and strength.

Military Customs and Warfare

Chapter 15

Introduction

War was a regular feature of ancient Greek life. It is unknown how often the Bronze Age Greek kingdoms fought one another; but the facts that the Mycenaeans heavily fortified their palace-centers, that their graves were filled with weapons, and that their surviving paintings often depict armor-clad warriors suggest that they did so frequently. The Classic Age certainly saw its share of death and destruction. The back-to-back Persian invasions of 490 and 480 B.C. were followed by a long period of rivalry and bloodshed among the Greek city-states. This unrest culminated in the disastrous Peloponnesian War (431–404), after which Sparta and Thebes grappled for supremacy and then Macedonia's Philip and Alexander pursued their own conquests, first of Greece, then of Persia. (As an indicator of how constant the fighting was in this era, Athens was at war with one foe or another fully three-quarters of the time.) Then, following Alexander's death, came the devastating wars of the Successors, more fighting among the Hellenistic kingdoms, and finally the Greeks' desperate and ultimately unsuccessful struggles against the encroaching power of Rome.

During these numerous conflicts spanning many centuries, the nature of warfare itself underwent a steady evolution. Although firm evidence is lacking, the chariot and composite bow, used together, appear to have been the major offensive weapons in late Bronze Age land warfare. In the middle of the second millennium B.C., the Egyptians, Assyrians, Hittites, and other ancient Near Eastern peoples developed battlefield tactics in which masses of chariots carrying archers charged one another. The culmination of this mode of fighting was the great battle at Kadesh (or Qadesh, in southern Syria), fought ca. 1285 between the Egyptians and Hittites, in which thousands of chariots took part. In such battles, foot-soldiers followed, supported, and mopped up after the charioteers and archers.

The Mycenaeans, who had frequent contact with and were influenced by the Near East in this period, likely used at least a modified form of such warfare. Although Greece has few flat plains large enough to contain massed chariot charges, smaller versions, involving several dozen and perhaps occasionally a few hundred chariots, were certainly viable. The Linear B inventory lists from the palace of Knossus (in northern Crete) list some 340 chariot frames and 1,000 chariot wheels, suggesting a heavy use of chariots. And a formidable, extremely protective, and very heavy suit of bronze armor (not unlike that of a medieval knight) was discovered in 1960 at Dendra (near Mycenae, in the northeastern Peloponnesus). On the one hand, such armor was much too expensive for use by average infantrymen, and must therefore have been worn by a few elite (perhaps aristocratic) fighters. Also, such heavy, inflexible armor would have been impractical, even self-defeating, for an ordinary foot-soldier; whereas it would have been very practical as protection against a rain of arrows for a man standing on a chariot. Bronze Age Greek warriors undoubtedly also frequently fought man-to-man with swords and spears, for numerous remnants of such weapons from that era have been found.

After the fall of the Bronze Age kingdoms, warfare, like society itself, was for a long time smaller-scale and less organized. The chariot was no longer a major offensive device, as shown by Homer's epic poems (which in large degree describe Dark Age battles, *not* those of Mycenaean times). In the *Iliad*, chariots are used primarily to ferry the principal warriors to and from the battlefield, where they then fight one-on-one.

In Archaic times, with the rise of city-states with militia made up of citizen-farmers, a new, much more organized form of warfare evolved, built around soldiers called hoplites. Hoplite warfare was a disciplined, highly specialized system characterized by the panoply, the extensive and very heavy array of arms and armor wielded by each participant. For this reason, hoplites were designated as "heavy infantry," a common term in Western warfare ever since. The basic element of a hoplite's panoply consisted of his shield, the *aspis* (or *hoplon*), which was about three feet in diameter and weighed roughly seventeen to eighteen pounds. It was gently concave with a wooden core reinforced on the outside by a coating of bronze (although sometimes by layers of ox hide).

The panoply had other protective features, beginning with a breastplate, or cuirass, which protected the hoplite's torso. Cuirasses were sometimes made of bronze, but the most common type in the Classic Age was the *linothorax* , composed of several layers of linen or canvas glued together to form a stiff shirt. (It was often reinforced with metal scales.) The hoplite also wore a bronze helmet. The most popular type of helmet in the late Archaic Age and on into the Classic Age was the "Corinthian," which had eye-slits and breathing spaces for the nose and mouth. A hoplite also wore bronze shin-guards called greaves, which were often molded in the shape of leg muscles (usually exaggerated). His panoply was completed by his weapons, the principal one a thrusting-spear about seven feet long. He also carried an iron sword about two feet long (in a scabbard of wood covered by leather), a back-up weapon used primarily when the spear was lost or broken.

The armored hoplites fought in a special formation called the phalanx, a long block of soldiers several ranks deep. A depth of eight ranks was most common, but on occasion there might be more than eight or as few as three or four ranks. By the beginning of the Classic Age, the Athenian phalanx, which was similar to those of most other city-states, consisted of ten divisions (*taxeis*), each with its own commander (*taxiarchos*). Each division broke down into several sub-divisions called *lochoi,* each *lochos* perhaps consisting of 100 men and supervised by a junior officer (*lochagos*). The *taxiarchoi* and most other officers fought in the front rank, as did the *strategoi,* the generals to whom these officers reported.

The traditional phalanx was an extremely effective offensive unit in its heyday (ca. 700–ca. 350 B.C.) for two reasons. First, it afforded its members a high degree of protection. When assembled in open order, they stood about five to six feet apart; but in close order, perhaps two to three feet apart, the mode most often adopted when closing with an enemy, their uplifted shields created a formidable unbroken protective barrier. The other factor that made the phalanx so formidable was its tremendous and lethal forward momentum. As the formation made contact with an enemy's lines, the hoplites in the front rank jabbed their spears at their opponents; at the same time, the hoplites in the rear ranks pushed at their comrades' backs, pressing them forward at the enemy. This maneuver was known as the *othismos,* "the shoving."

As lethal as the traditional phalanx was, it still had room for improvement. This is shown by the tactical innovations introduced in the fourth century B.C. by the Theban general Epaminondas (who deepened his phalanx and had it attack in an oblique, or slanted, formation that focused on crushing the strong right wing of an enemy's formation). And Epaminondas's contemporary, Macedonia's King Philip II, soon introduced the frightening "Macedonian phalanx." Its members wielded long battle pikes (*sarissas*) that projected from the formation's front, creating an almost impenetrable wall of wood and metal. About this formation, which Philip's son Alexander and his own Hellenistic successors adopted in their turn, the second-century B.C. Greek historian Polybius writes, "So long as the phalanx retains its characteristic form and strength, nothing can withstand its charge or resist it face to face." (*Histories* 8.29.1)

Yet Polybius also goes on to explain the phalanx's disadvantages. Not the least of these was that it was very rigid and inflexible, and if it lost "its characteristic form" (due to obstructions on the battlefield or other causes), it fell apart and became almost useless. In the second century B.C., the Romans, whose military formations were much more flexible, were able to neutralize the phalanx in fairly short order.

During the Classical and Hellenistic eras, Greek generals often supported the phalanx with other military elements. Cavalry (*hippeis*) played little part in battle for a long time and came into common use only in the late fifth century B.C. during the Peloponnesian War. Even then, it was not employed in large-scale shock action (direct charges on infantry), mainly because horses were not plentiful in most parts of southern Greece; and saddles and stirrups had not yet been invented, so that riders had difficulty staying on swiftly moving horses. In this period, the Greeks used cavalry mainly to protect the phalanx against enemy skirmishers (javelin throwers and archers), to chase down escaping enemy hoplites after the phalanxes had fought, and to rescue their own injured or escaping hoplites. In the fourth century B.C., however, Philip and Alexander developed their cavalry (led by an elite corps, the *hetairoi,* or "Companions") into a shock force that bore down on and broke up some enemy infantry units. This "softened up" the enemy for the attack of the phalanx that followed.

This "one-two" punch, so to speak, was part of Philip's and Alexander's highly effective use of an integrated (combined and interrelated) arms system consisting of several diverse elements working together to achieve overall victory. In addition to the phalanx and cavalry, they used light-armed troops (skirmishers), including archers, slingers, and peltasts (*peltastai,* who got their name from their characteristic small round or crescent-shaped shield, the *pelta*). Peltasts carried small bundles of javelins. Their chief tactic was to approach the enemy, throw their weapons, and then run away.

Later the Hellenistic armies featured these same elements (with various modifications) as well as battle elephants, which first came into vogue in the late fourth century B.C. Hellenistic times also saw advances in siege warfare. Alexander's successful sieges of Halicarnassus (334 B.C.)

and Tyre (332) and Demetrius Poliorcetes' unsuccessful but spectacular siege of Rhodes (305–304) elevated the capture of walled fortresses and cities to a high art. And during the Hellenistic Age, defensive fortifications designed to resist large siege engines became much more sophisticated.

The same era also witnessed a proliferation of the use of mercenaries (hired soldiers). The city-states had used mercenaries in the Classical Age, but mainly in supplementary or supporting units. (It was common, for example, to import archers from Crete, slingers from Rhodes, and peltasts from Thrace.) The Hellenistic states, by contrast, manned their armies, including their phalanxes, *primarily* with mercenaries.

Meanwhile, naval warfare also underwent its own evolution. In the early Archaic Age, the main warship appears to have been the pentekonter, with fifty rowers who all sat on the same level, or bank. About 700 B.C. or so, the bireme appeared. With two banks of oars, it was shorter, more powerful, and more maneuverable than the pentekonter. The most revolutionary change occurred in the sixth century B.C. with the addition of a third bank of oars, producing the trireme (*trieres*), which remained the principal Greek warship for some time to come.

Such warships were impractical for long-term naval strategy because they could not remain at sea for long periods. This was mainly because they lacked eating and sleeping facilities, which meant that they had to be beached at least once a day. Naval strategy was therefore of a short-term nature, mainly concerned with how to win an individual battle. The tactics were fairly simple. Most often a warship, which was outfitted with a bronze "beak" on its prow, tried to ram an opposing ship and thereby to sink it. One common maneuver was first to attack at an angle and shear off the enemy's oars, leaving that side of the hull open to ramming. Another tactic was to use grappling hooks or ropes to lock two ships together; the hoplites from one vessel then boarded the other and fought hand-to-hand.

In the fourth century B.C. and on into Hellenistic times, larger warships appeared. These big galleys could deliver much larger volleys of missiles (from archers, catapults, and mechanical dart-throwers) than triremes could; but the principal battle tactics remained, as before, ramming and boarding.

The ancient sources of information about Greek warfare are many and varied, except for the earliest periods. For the Bronze Age, scholars have only the scattered, deteriorating remains of fortresses, weapons and armor, wall paintings, and inventories on the Linear B tablets. The first written source, Homer's *Iliad,* is of course fiction rather than history; but it likely describes fairly accurately some aspects of warfare in the Dark and early Archaic ages. For hoplite battles in the Classic Age, including weapons, formations, and tactics, the works of the Greek historians Herodotus (fifth century B.C.), Thucydides (fifth century B.C.), Xenophon (fourth century B.C.), Diodorus Siculus (first century B.C.), and the Greek biogra-

pher Plutarch (first century A.D.) are the principal written sources. Most of what we know about Philip's army and military tactics comes from Diodorus, and about Alexander's from the histories of the Greek Arrian (second century A.D.) and the Roman Quintus Curtius Rufus (first century A.D.). For the armies of the Hellenistic Age, Diodorus and Plutarch provide some information, as does the Greek historian Polybius (second century B.C.), whose comparison of the Macedonian phalanx and Roman legions is invaluable. Also, a few handbooks on military matters have survived from this era, notably those of the Greeks Aeneas Tacticus (late fourth century B.C.) and Philo of Byzantium (late third century B.C.). And as always, archaeological evidence (the remains of fortresses, weapons, armor, warships, and so on) often helps either to support or cast doubt on statements made by the ancient writers.

Selection 1

Late Bronze Age Warfare

William Taylour

Very little for certain is known about the strategies and tactics of the warfare practiced by the Bronze Age Minoans and Mycenaeans. As archaeologist William Taylour points out in this excerpt from his well-known study of the Mycenaeans, the warfare Homer depicted in his Iliad *was likely more like that of the late Dark Age and early Archaic Age than of Mycenaean times. However, some idea of how Bronze Age warriors fought can* *be deduced from examining surviving fortifications at Mycenaean citadels like those at Mycenae and Tiryns (in the northeastern Peloponnesus), Pylos (in the southwestern Peloponnesus), and Knossus (or Knossos, in northern Crete); scattered remnants of Mycenaean armor and weapons; and artistic representations of warriors and their gear in surviving paintings and sculptures.*

a strong impression created by the monuments is of the dominant accent placed upon war by the Mycenaeans. It would almost seem as if they loved strife for its own sake. This element in their nature is conspicuous from the very first, as witness the rich and varied warlike equipment buried in the earliest of the Mycenaean tombs, the Shaft Graves. On the stelae that at one time marked the position of these graves chariot scenes are frequently recorded, in which the dead king triumphs over his foes. On fragments of a silver rhyton [drinking vessel shaped like a horn] from Shaft Grave IV the siege and assault of an enemy town are depicted, and from the many surviving pieces of fresco-painting of a later period one knows that scenes of combat decorated the walls of the palaces. But the most impressive monuments of this warrior race are to be seen today in the great citadels of Mycenae and Tiryns.

The military aspect of the Mycenaean civilization is borne out by the tablets, particularly in regard to armaments. Of importance in the military sphere . . . are the *hequetai*, the Followers. One of their functions seems to have been to act as intelligence officers and to send back vital information by their charioteers to headquarters (the king). Their activities are implied in the group of Pylos tablets concerned with 'guarding the coastal regions'. As the capital city had no real fortifications, early warning of an enemy raid or threatened invasion was essential.

Chariots

The chariot figures prominently in the records both at Knossos and at Pylos. . . . These are described as being serviceable and unserviceable. The fact that the wheels are listed separately shows that they were dismounted from the chassis when the chariot was being 'garaged'. The reverse operation of mounting them is described by Homer: 'Swiftly Hebe put on the chariot the curved wheels of bronze . . .'; as a rule, however, the wheels were of willow or elm. One series of Knossos tablets gives a full muster roll: chariot, charioteer, his cuirass [chest armor], and a pair of horses. The chariot carried two men, as is clear from frescoes, vase paintings, and sealstones. The wheels are four-spoked and the axle is placed centrally under the carriage. . . .

In the *Iliad* the chariot was merely a means of transport to bring the hero to the battlefield and to convey him swiftly thence, should the combat not end as heroically as anticipated. This is unlikely to have been its role in Mycenaean times, and an older tradition is hinted at in the Iliad when the sage Nestor describes the charge of a hundred chariots that took place in his father's time, something more akin to a cavalry charge though there are few parts of Greece that are suitable for such a manoeuvre. It was the use of such tactics and the possession of the chariot that no doubt enabled the otherwise peaceable Egyptians to build up an empire from the sixteenth century BC onwards. In Greece about this very time the earliest representation of a chariot appears on the Shaft Grave stelae and we may suppose that it was this new instrument of warfare . . . that assured the rulers of Hellas of dominion over the inhabitants. Similarly the use of the chariot may have been an important contributory factor in their conquest of Crete in the fifteenth century BC; at any rate the chariot first appears there about that time.

Defensive Armor

The cuirass or coat of mail appears on the Knossos chariot muster roll, but the ideogram [picture symbol] for this is not the same as the one depicted on the Pylos tablets, neither is the word used for describing it. At Pylos the Classical word *thorax* is used and the ideogram bears some resemblance to the corslet portrayed on the Warrior Vase belonging to the end of the Mycenaean era. The Knossos cuirass, on the other hand, is remarkably like a bronze coat of mail found in a chamber tomb at Dendra (Midea), which is attributed to the . . . end of the fifteenth century [B.C.], and this is but a little earlier than the presumed date of the Knossos tablets. This unique find reminds us of how much must have perished of which we could have but little conception were it not for the record of the tablets. The later type of corslet as shown on the Warrior Vase appears to be made of leather, but the earlier kind on the Knossos tablets is specifically stated to be of bronze. Bronze has a good chance of withstanding the destruction of time but it is also a valuable metal and it seldom escaped the attention of the tomb-robber.

There are two pieces of armour of which the tablets make no mention, the shield and the greave [lower-leg protector]. These are surprising omissions, which are due no doubt to chance. Although no actual example of a shield has survived, it is fairly well documented from its representation on Mycenaean works of art. The Lion Hunt dagger-blade from Shaft Grave IV shows two different kinds of shield, the figure-of-eight and the 'tower' shield; the latter is also portrayed in a battle scene on a gold signet ring from the same Shaft Grave. The great size of these body-shields precludes them from being made of anything heavier than leather and indeed it is known that the figure-of-eight shield was made from an oxhide; this is apparent from the Fresco of Shields, a recurrent theme in wall decoration which has been found in the palaces of both Knossos and Tiryns, and recently in a room in the neighbourhood of the Cult Centre at Mycenae; the dappled design of the shields reproduces the colouring of the animal hide. . . . From the fourteenth century onwards, the whole Mycenaean armoury undergoes a change. Contacts with the East increase and influences from that quarter are reflected in new styles of weapons both of offence and defence. The large body-shield, which figured prominently in single combat and in the chase, is now replaced by the small round shield that was better adapted to collective fighting. But as a sacred symbol and as an ornament the figure-of-eight shield survived for at least another two centuries. . . . As is shown on the Warrior Vase, the shield was carried on the left arm. This factor was taken into account in the design of a Mycenaean fortress. At Mycenae the main gate and the postern gate are guarded by bastions so placed as to harass the unprotected (right) side of an attacking force.

The 'well-greaved Achaeans' is a recurring phrase in the *Iliad*. Only four examples of greaves in bronze are known. Three of them are late Mycenaean . . . the fourth belongs to the end of the fifteenth century. It was found in the same tomb as the coat of mail referred to above.

Bronze greaves therefore were in use for the early part and the end of the Mycenaean period, and probably for the whole of it but, as has been noted, bronze does not often survive. The infantry on the Warrior Vase are clearly wearing a leg protection of some sort and there are several examples in fresco painting of men . . . who are obviously equipped in similar manner. It is likely that the material was felt or leather.

A purely Greek contribution to armour is the boar's tusk helmet. It is fully described by Homer, yet this type of helmet had gone out of use long before his day; it does not survive the Mycenaean period. There are many illustrations of it in Mycenaean art: it is worn by warriors depicted on gems and seal-stones. . . . It was definitely an article of luxury, some thirty to forty pairs of boar's tusks being required to complete one helmet. Numerous fragments of these tusks have been found in tombs all over Greece. The boar's tusks, neatly cut into oblong plates and pierced at the shorter ends with holes, were sewn on to a frame of conical shape presumably of leather. The direction of the curve of the tusks was made to alternate in each successive row, of which there were generally four to five. This scheme is clearly reproduced in the ivory reliefs. The crown of the helmet was either adorned with a plume or terminated in a knob. Neck-guards and chinstraps are also shown in the ivory reliefs. . . .

Offensive Weapons

The main weapons of offence in the Mycenaean armoury were the spear, the sword, and the bow. The earliest style of spearhead is of unusual form and but sparsely represented. The bronze blade has a shoe-socket cast on one or both sides of it, into which the split point of the wooden shaft is inserted. . . . The more normal type of spearhead, in use throughout the whole of the Mycenaean age, was a narrow leaf-shaped blade with a strong mid-rib and a socketed base which was secured to the wooden shaft by a metal collar. The origin of this type seems to be Cretan. Several long, heavy spears of this kind were buried with the Shaft Grave kings and its use with the chariot is depicted on the stelae. It is brandished in single combat in battle scenes portrayed on signet rings of the same period. It also appears as a weapon of the chase in the Lion Hunt dagger. Not many examples of it have survived from the latter part of the Mycenaean period but that it still retained its importance in warfare is confirmed by the fact that it is the only weapon portrayed on the Warrior Vase. . . .

At the beginning of the Mycenaean period the most significant weapon of offence was the rapier [sword], of which there are such abundant examples in the Shaft Graves, every warrior being equipped with a far greater number than he would have needed during his turbulent life. All are of fine workmanship and some of them richly and elaborately decorated, such as to suggest trophies rather than practical weapons. They have rounded shoulders, short tangs [pointed ends], and pronounced mid-ribs which are usually semicircular in section. The short tang would make the weapon liable to break away from the hilt. The realization of this weakness would account for some examples having longer tangs. . . . Alongside these rapiers in the Shaft Graves is found another kind (Type B), less well represented than Type A. . . . The main difference between the two weapons is that Type B has square or pointed shoulders and a shorter blade. It may possibly have developed from the flanged dagger, of which there were several examples in the earlier Grave Circle, but it can also trace its an-

cestry to the Near East. A variant of Type B is the horned sword or rapier, the pointed shoulders being extended to form two horns. . . .

There are but few representations of the use of the bow in the archaeological record on the mainland and those few show exclusively scenes of the chase. The Lion Hunt dagger-blade is an example. From such sources, therefore, it could be assumed that the bow did not play an important part in Mycenaean warfare; but a fragment of a steatite vase from Knossos portrays a bearded Archer who from his dress appears to be a Mycenaean, and at Knossos two large deposits of bronze arrowheads (or javelin points?) were found. Bronze arrowheads are coupled with spearheads on the Pylos tablets and there is mention of bow-makers. Only the singlestave bow, or 'self-bow', is portrayed. There is no evidence to support the existence of the composite bow which is used by Odysseus in the slaying of the suitors [in Homer's *Odyssey*]. . . . The arrowheads are made of flint or obsidian, usually with a hollow base so that their form recalls that of a bishop's mitre [hat]. They are beautifully fashioned. . . . Archers as well as stone-slingers are depicted on the Siege Rhyton fragments, but these are not Mycenaeans but the enemy.

Brief mention should be made of the rowers listed on two Pylos tablets. There were more than 500 of them. This is our only reference to a possible navy. Representations of ships are few and mostly very schematic.

Selection 2

The Development of Hoplite Warfare

Victor D. Hanson

One of the crucial developments of Greece's Archaic Age was the advent of land warfare in which hoplites (heavily-armored infantrymen) fought one another in the formidable battlefield formation known as the phalanx. A typical phalanx consisted of about eight files (rows) of soldiers, each file lined up behind another and protected by a tightly packed array of upraised shields. The sight of two such formations smashing together and attempting to overrun each other must have been awesome and frightening; and when a Greek phalanx met a less well-armored, less cohesive formation of non-Greek troops, the outcome was almost always a stunning Greek victory. The following description of what he calls the "hoplite reform" (i.e., revolution) is by the distinguished California State University scholar Victor D. Hanson, from his masterful The Western Way of War: Infantry Battle in Classical Greece. *Supporting his narrative with passages from Polybius (whom he abbreviates Pol.), Aristotle, Homer (Hom.), Xenophon (Xen.), Thucydides (Thuc.), and Plutarch (Plut.), he explains the origins, armor, tactics, advantages, and disadvantages of hoplites and the phalanx.*

Sometime in the late eighth or early seventh century B.C. infantrymen in Greece gradually began to arm themselves with body armor, round shield, and thrusting spear, and so chose to get close and jab the opponent head-on rather than fling javelins from afar, advancing and retreating like the ebb and flow of native warriors whom Europeans encountered in nineteenth-century Africa and South America. The era of mounted fighters of the Greek Dark Ages (1200–800) who dismounted to throw the spear was also now over, for warfare no longer was the private duels of wealthy knights. On the left arm of this new warrior rested a round wooden shield some three feet in diameter, the *hoplon*, so radically different in concept from its cowhide predecessor that it was from this piece of equipment that the infantryman eventually derived his name, "hoplite." [Another possible derivation of the term hoplite is the word *hopla*, meaning "heavy equipment."] By the aid of an interior forearm strap and an accompanying handgrip, the hoplite could manage the unusually great weight of this strange shield, warding off spear blows solely with the left arm, or at times resting its upper lip on his left shoulder to save strength. In this way he could both protect his own left flank and, if formation was well maintained, offer some aid to the unprotected right side of the man to his left in the ranks. Yet, despite the shield's great weight and size, well over half a man's height, its round shape offered poor protection for the entire body, unlike the rectangular model of the later Roman legionary or the body shield of the earlier Dark Age warrior; there was little chance that a hoplite could save himself from most of the traditional sources of attack on the front and rear. The hoplite's shield offered no material advantage over earlier models in isolated skirmishes or individual duels. Even more importantly, the shield could not be easily slung over the back, as previous shields had been, to protect those who turned and ran—although this was a small drawback, since these fighting men now had no other intention but to stand firm together and push constantly forward.

We do not really know whether the use of this new equipment spawned a radical change in battle tactics, or vice versa. Yet it is at least clear that better success at warding off blows and striking home with the spear was accomplished by having the men mass in column, usually eight ranks in depth. There they could find mutual protection from an accumulation of their shields to the front, rear, and side—if care was taken to moderate and account for the natural tendency to drift rightward as each man sought cover for his own exposed, unshielded right flank in the shield of his neighbor. Although there was an accompanying loss of firepower overall, as every rank to the rear of the first three primary rows was effectively out of the initial action (the spears of these men in the middle and rear not immediately reaching the enemy), the added weight and density of the formation were believed to offer a crucial stabilizing force, in both physical and psychological terms, for the few men who first met the terrible onslaught of the enemy.

What followed this initial collision was the

A hoplite, seen in full battle gear (left) and also in an "at ease" posture, without helmet and greaves.

push, or *othismos*, as ranks to the rear put their bodies into the hollows of their shields and forced those ahead constantly onward. Some recent scholars have branded this image of a mass thrusting contest as ridiculous and absurd. Yet careful compilation of ancient descriptions of Greek warfare make it certain beyond a doubt that this was precisely what happened in hoplite battle; it soon degenerated into an enormous contest of pressure, as men used their shields, hands, and bodies in a desperate, frantic effort to force a path forward. Xenophon, an eyewitness of the last age of purely hoplite battle, remarked that any troops who were suspect belonged in the middle of the phalanx, so that they would be surrounded by good fighters at the front and rear "in order that they might be led by the former and *pushed* by the latter." (Xen. *Mem.* 3.1.9) The key, as the successful Spartan general Brasidas reminded his men, was to maintain formation always, to stay in rank, and to preserve the cohesive protection offered by the accumulation of shields. . . .

The actual social and political sequence of events at the end of the Greek Dark Ages that led to this movement toward the armament and subsequent tactics of hoplite battle cannot and will not be known, given the nature of our sources. But surely by the early seventh century B.C. the so-called hoplite reform—if we may use such a dramatic term—must have attracted a growing number of farmers, who now became restless at the idea that anyone might traverse their own small parcels of land. (Hoplite farmers usually owned properties outside the city walls of between five and ten acres.) It makes sense that the solidarity and, more importantly, the success of their wartime experience in the phalanx . . . reflected a growing confidence in their new, emerging function in the government of the Greek city-state as owners and producers of food. By the late seventh century B.C. the security of most of Greek society depended on the arms and armor that each such landholder possessed, hung up above his fireplace, and the courage which he brought into battle when confronted with an army of invasion encamped on his or his neighbors' farms.

As long as these unlikely fighters, heavily armed men in bronze armor, held their assigned places in the ranks of the phalanx, they were virtually impregnable from attack by any lighter armed, mobile infantry or by charges of heavy cavalry—provided that the ground was flat and free of obstruction. Because the great plain of Boiotia met these criteria, the legendary fourth-century Theban general Epameinondas once called it "the dancing floor of War." (Plut. *Mor.* 193 E. 18) The phalanx (which Aristotle reminds us must break its ranks when "crossing even the narrowest ditch" [Pol. 1304]) then must first find such a battlefield, and only thereafter seek out its enemy. Polybius was correct in his famous comparison between the Roman legion and the Greek phalanx, when he remarked of the advantages of the Greeks that "nothing can stand in the way of the advance of a phalanx, as long as it maintains its customary cohesion and power." (18.30.11) Success, especially when depth increased and width diminished accordingly, required that the vulnerable flanks be protected by cavalry, skirmishers, and above all, rough terrain. Even well-trained enemy archers and slingers were seldom a threat if the hoplites stayed on level ground and could be brought to close quarters quickly. When infantrymen lumbered across the last 150 yards of no-man's-land and came into the range of the ancient arrows and other hand-propelled missiles, which could wound their arms, legs, faces, and necks, and at closer ranges penetrate their body armor, the "window of vulnerability" lasted not more than a minute. These airborne attacks, far from turning aside the onset of heavily armored men, most likely served to incite their anger and to guarantee a furious collision of leveled spears. In short, for nearly three hundred years (650–350) no foreign army, despite any numerical superiority, withstood the charge of a Greek phalanx. The battles at Marathon (490) and Plataia (479) demonstrate this clearly: relatively small numbers of well-led, heavily armed Greeks had little difficulty in breaking right through the hordes of their more lightly equipped and less cohesively ranked adversaries from the East.

The extraordinary integration of civilian and military service within the city-state also explains much of the Greek success. In most cases, men were arranged within the phalanx right next to lifelong friends or family members, and fought not only for the safety of their community and farmland but also for the respect of the men at their front, rear, and side. Small landholders and craftsmen with their own armor on their backs were liable to be called up from the city's muster rolls for military service any summer after their eighteenth birthday until they turned sixty. In the fifth and fourth centuries, battle broke out in the Greek world nearly two out of every three years, so the chances were good that a man would have to leave his farm, take up his arms, fight in repeated engagements, and fall wounded or die one summer's day in battle. Military service rarely was confined to peacetime patrols or to drill, and consequently hardly any figure in fifth-century Greek literature refers to his past tenure as a hoplite but rather only to the specific battles at which he fought. . . .

In this world of perennial battle, fighting in the ranks of the phalanx required utmost courage, excellent physical condition, and endurance, but little specialized training or skill with weapons. The spear and shield, even when used in unison with other men in the crowded conditions of the column, were still much simpler to handle than either the bow or the sling or even the javelin. . . . Pericles, in his famous funeral oration after the second year of the Peloponnesian War, castigated the Spartan system for its excessive (and unnecessary) attention to hoplite drill (Thuc. 2.39.1), and Aristotle likewise seems to imply that the Spartans were just about the only soldiers in Greece who felt it necessary to train at all for battle. (Pol. 1338 b27) . . . All this would explain why on occasion we read of extreme cases in Greek history where men fought in the phalanx with virtually no training. These soldiers were not exactly "hoplites"; nevertheless, they were provided with heavy armor and ordered to fight as infantrymen with no experience or idea of hoplite combat. . . . And the hoplite class of independent small farmers, as they have for centuries since, had little free time or desire for constant drilling. Yet they came to battle with an abundance of courage, if not controlled recklessness, and possessed a spirit of camaraderie with those of the same class and background. . . . These men were natural hoplites, in short, awesome soldiers turned loose to battle on their own turf, the farmlands of Greece, men to whom Pericles in his famous funeral oration was no doubt referring when he said they "would rather perish in resistance than find salvation through submission." (Thuc. 2.42.4)

The Formula for Battlefield Success

Throughout the seventh, sixth, and on into the fifth century in Greece, a hoplite army of invasion quickly offered a challenge to pitched battle once it had made its way into the flatland of the enemy; indeed, its very occupation of precious farmland was an invitation to battle. Attacks against the walls of an enemy community were rarely successful, perhaps because siegecraft was both expensive and its techniques—the battering ram, artillery, and movable armor—were either unknown or not well understood. Only late in the fifth century and, more frequently, in Hellenistic times does one find the occasional successful siege. Nor were night engagements an option. At times the sheer daring of an attack after darkness could bring results, but more commonly it ended in chaos, misdirection, and disorder in the ranks. (Hom. *Il.* 2.387) . . . Instead, once an invading army had crossed the border, either the defenders usually marched out from their walled cities promptly to contest this occupation of their farmland, or they simply submitted to the terms dictated in order to clear the intruder from their property as quickly as possible. . . .

The psychological turmoil among the influential, landed class of hoplites within the city walls, peering out at an enemy running among their ancestral fields, was generally felt to be enough either to draw the citizen body out to fight or, better yet, to make them simply give up. In this strange ritual of agricultural poker, a few cities, usually closely tied to the sea, occasionally persuaded their citizens to "ride out" an enemy invasion and not hazard battle, but only when they had men of vision and daring—men like Pericles of Athens who could at least convince all but the hoplite class to stomach foreigners on Attic soil. When this was the case, they suffered little agricultural damage of any lasting consequence from enemy ravagers and kept their city free and their infantry—though perhaps not their pride—unhurt. Oddly, few of the city-states understood, or rather wished to understand, the advantages that this unaccustomed inactivity within the walls could achieve. Such self-control was very rare during the age of the classical hoplite, as most Greeks felt that revenge in the old form of pitched combat was the most honorable and expedient way of resolving an insult to their sovereignty. Their tradition, their duty, indeed their desire, was for a ritualistic collision, head-on, with the spears of their enemy to end the whole business quickly and efficiently.

This paradox of Greek warfare—the threat of such a relatively ineffective tactic as crop destruction being successful in drawing men out to fight—helps to explain the frequency of pitched battle between mutually consenting hoplites throughout the Greek world. Yet, if battle was so incessant among the small city-states of classical Greece, how did the social fabric endure the frequent death and destruction year after year and such a vast amount of collective time and labor seemingly wasted on defense? The answer must lie again in the sheer simplicity of phalanx tactics and strategy, a mode of battle that did not require extensive peacetime drill and training or public expenditure on arms and provisioning. More importantly, until the late fifth century, there was no need for the expense of extended campaigns, with men marching for months on end, fighting in battle after battle. The enemy was usually nearby, on the other side of a range of mountains, no farther than a few hundred miles at most. Once the invader arrived in the spring, the entire "war," if that is the proper word, usually consisted of an hour's worth of hard fighting between consenting, courageous hoplite amateurs, rather

than repeated clashes of hired or trained killers. The harvest demands of the triad of Greek agriculture—the olive, the vine, and grain—left only a brief month or two in which these small farmers could find time to fight.

Nor was combat fatal to most combatants; annihilation of entire armies was rare in the classical age, as the nearly uniform adoption of the panoply—the Greeks' bronze breastplate, shield, helmet, greaves, spear, and sword—ensured protection from repeated attacks. (It was left to the Hellenistic Greeks to record staggering deaths in battles between huge phalanxes of poorly protected infantry.) After the clash between the front ranks of armored infantry determined the direction of momentum and one side made an inroad into the ranks of the other, battle degenerated into a massive pushing contest as rank after rank struggled to solidify and increase local advantages until the entire enemy's formation was destroyed. Yet, if the defeated could somehow maintain enough cohesion, a fighting withdrawal of sorts was possible. A great number died only when there was a sudden collapse, a collective loss of nerve, when the abrupt disruption of the phalanx sent men trampling each other in mad panic to the rear, either in small groups or, worse, individually to save themselves from spear thrusts in the back. Even when one side was swept suddenly off the battlefield, casualties in such a disaster remained low by modern standards, well below 20 percent of the original force—a "tolerable" percentage as long as such a decisive engagement entailed both the beginning and end of the "war." However, several such repeated clashes . . . would have bled a small city-state white in short order.

Long-drawn-out pursuit was also rare; unlike Napoleon, the victors were not aiming for the complete destruction of an enemy army. Indeed, pursuit of fleeing hoplites was not even crucial: most victorious Greek armies saw no reason why they could not repeat their simple formula for success and gain further victory should the enemy regroup in a few days and mistakenly press their luck again. Besides, it was always good propaganda for a Greek general to profess no taste for slaughtering fellow Hellenes from the rear after the issue of battle had already been decided face-to-face. . . . When told of the slaughter of Corinthians by his Spartans, the legendary old battle veteran and king of fourth-century Sparta, Agesilaos, was supposed to have remarked, "Woe to you, Greece, those who now have died were enough to have beaten all the barbarians in battle had they lived." (Xen. *Ages*. 7.6) Both sides were usually content to exchange their dead under truce. The victors, after erecting a battlefield trophy or simple monument to their success, marched home triumphantly, eager for the praise of their families and friends on their return.

Selection 3

Greek Naval Warfare

F.E. Adcock

Naval strategy and tactics often made crucial contributions to overall victory in ancient Greek warfare. The crushing Greek defeat of the Persians at Salamis (480 B.C.), for example, proved a major turning point in King Xerxes' attempted conquest of Greece, partly because it left his land army without the customary support of its ships. And Sparta's defeat of the Athenian navy, in 405 B.C. on the Hellespont, cut off Athens's supply of grain from the Black Sea, forcing its eventual surrender. This thoughtful synopsis of Greek warships, including their structural features, tactics, strategic use, and advantages and drawbacks, is from noted scholar F.E. Adcock's classic book on Greek warfare.

*n*aval warfare, in a strict sense, begins when ships not only carry men on warlike expeditions, but also are themselves instruments of war. This they may be either as a means to enable the fighting men on board to attack the crews and fighting men of other ships with missiles or boarding parties, or as a means of injuring other ships by being driven against their hulls or oarage. In the Heroic Age [i.e., Bronze Age] ships appear as transports, the servants of land warfare. They carry the Achaeans to the coasts of Troy, and they lie on the shore awaiting the day of return, or carry raiding parties to collect plunder or supplies. There is no hint in the *Iliad* that the Trojans had ships which might have forced the Achaeans to fight at sea. The Heroic Age ships may use oars as well as sails, and in the post-Heroic Age ships become capable of fighting against each other. When that happens, the art of naval warfare begins.

It is roughly true to say that ships are now built to sail with the occasional use of oars, or to be rowed with the occasional use of sails. The second type prevails as ships of war, and by the seventh century there are ships which can manoeuvre against each other. For boarding or the use of missiles they have a kind of deck which can carry fighting men. But, besides that, the construction of these oar-driven ships leads to a strengthening of their bows by bulkheads on either side of the forward end of the keel. These coalesce [come together], as it were, into a ram which can be propelled against the hull or oarage of an enemy ship. What was, to begin with, a means of overcoming the resistance of the waves as ships were rowed at sea, or of protecting them against rocks as they came to land, becomes the means of direct conflict between ships, and the ram may be further armed with a kind of spear.

In the seventh and sixth centuries, to judge from the archaeological evidence, ships used in warfare were more and more adapted to the use of the ram at the expense of the deck which carried fighting men. Thus fighting by boarding or missile weapons was sacrificed to greater speed and capacity for manoeuvre. This was achieved by increasing the number of oarsmen, by increasing the length of the ship and reducing its height above the water, and abandoning whatever deck or superstructure there had been. Thus the penteconter, driven by twenty-five oarsmen on each side of the ship, became the standard ship of war and the standard method of combat was the use of the ram. I may add that throughout this period there seems to have been a transient use of ships with two banks of oars, probably borrowed from the Phoenicians, but this device for increasing oarage, and so increasing speed, may have been found unsuitable for the open sea and so was abandoned.

A critical examination of the slight literary evidence does not refute, but in some measure confirms, the deductions that follow from the archaeological evidence. Then came a notable invention. The penteconters had served the ends of trade for distant voyages as well as those of war. Now some unknown shipwright in the second half of the sixth century [B.C.] devised a vessel that was a warship and nothing else, and a warship of far greater power than the Greeks had known before. It was the trireme, which for nearly two centuries ruled the waves in Greek naval warfare, and continued to be used for centuries later.

It is certain that the trireme was rowed by many oarsmen—as many as a hundred and seventy—each rowing one oar, and yet was not much longer than the penteconter with its fifty rowers. It could not be much longer, for that would put too great a strain upon the keel. . . . A ship was produced that was swift and capable of manoeuvre, a ship that gave great scope for skilful rowing and steering, the ship itself being a kind of composite weapon, with mind directing matter to the confusion of the enemy.

Fleets appear in which ship fights ship. Soon after the middle of the sixth century we find this happening at the battle of Alalia, for the Phocaean penteconters which fought in that battle got their rams bent or were disabled in the fighting. But the first battle in which large forces of triremes can be discovered seeking to exploit their capabilities is the battle of Lade in 494, which really decided the fate of the Ionian Revolt. For a time before the battle the Ionians had practised manoeuvres that imply nimbleness and a general homogeneity in the ships. The Persian fleet prevailed because of desertions on the Greek side, so that the battle of Lade was no test of what Greek triremes could do.

Fourteen years later came the Great Persian War and, in the meantime, Athens had built a large fleet of warships of the new model. But it cannot be assumed that their rowers and steersmen had yet reached the full mastery of their instrument. Some at least of the Persian ships were probably more skilled in manoeuvre, and the Persian fleet had an advantage in numbers. In the first meeting of the two fleets, that in the Gulf of Artemisium, the Persians seem to have had rather the best of it, and it may be doubted if the Greeks used their ships to the fullest advantage. For victory they had to wait for the crowning mercy of Salamis, won by surprise, a determined onset, and the confusion of their enemy. . . . It was not the Athenians alone who won the battle—their kinsmen had charged as bravely,—but the new Athenian navy had justified the foresight of Themistocles [commander of the Athenian ships], made good his strategy, and turned back the tide of war.

Athenian Naval Superiority

In the year after Salamis the naval war was carried across the Aegean. From now on for thirty years the Athenian fleet and the squadrons of her allies needed to be used in amphibious operations and would have to meet ships which probably had a higher freeboard. Their admiral Cimon made a change in the trireme by making it broader in the beam and giving it a kind of bridge along its length so that it could carry more fighting men. With these ships he was very successful, but by the middle of the century . . . the Athenians were reverting to the older tactics of ramming and had improved upon them. The fleets of the Confederacy of Delos had become more predominantly Athenian, and those ships which were provided by the Allies would be brought into line with Athenian construction and practise. Not only had the Athenians the best ships, but the best oarsmen and, even more important, the best steersmen. Before the Peloponnesian War began there was a marked difference between the tactics and skill of the Athenian navy and those of other Greek states, so that . . . the Athenians noted that they fought more as in a land battle with boarding and the use of missile weapons.

Such methods as these had, by then, become out of place in the best naval circles. With the development of ship fighting against ship had come in the discovery of tactics which might exploit superior speed or capacity for manoeuvre. For example, the Greek word for circumnavigation was given the technical meaning of sailing round a ship or a line of ships so as to be able to attack the stern or a weak point in the side of enemy vessels. And there was something more direct. . . . This was the breaking through an enemy line by rowing between two opposing ships and then wheeling round to take one or other of them at a disadvantage before it could manoeuvre to meet this attack. This manoeuvre plainly called for high speed and, even more important, brilliant steering promptly supported by skilful oarsmanship. It was therefore, above all, the tactical device of highly trained crews in ships of the most skilful construction. A variant of this manoeuvre was to make the attacking trireme swerve so that its projecting bulkheads might sweep away the oars on one side of an opposing ship, while, just before the impact, the oarage of the near side of the attacking ship was drawn inwards out of harm's way. If this device succeeded, the victim was so crippled that it was out of the fight at the best, and destined to be sunk later at the worst. Of all these tactical manoeuvres the Athenians became masters in the heyday of their naval skill. . . .

The first ten years of the [Peloponnesian] war indeed mark the zenith of Athenian skill at sea, even if the fleet that set out on the Sicilian Expedition, six years later, was the finest that ever sailed from the Piraeus. It was never to return. In the relatively confined space of the Great Harbour at Syracuse the swifter, more lightly built Athenian triremes were at a disadvantage against enemy ships more suited to survive when ship met ship prow to prow. We may conjecture that the peace which preceded the Expedition permitted the Corinthians to hire more skilled oarsmen, and at last a Corinthian squadron in Greek waters was able to meet an Athenian force on equal terms. The disaster at Syracuse swept away so many fine ships and crews that the unchallengeable supremacy of Athens at sea disappeared. . . . And the indiscipline and carelessness that left the last Athenian fleet open to a surprise at Aegospotami [on the Hellespont, where it was defeated in the final, decisive battle of the war in 405 B.C.], made Athens helpless at sea and therefore helpless altogether.

The period of Athenian naval ascendancy was the most striking of the periods for which the Greeks found the word *thalassocracy*—the command of the sea. Pericles, always perhaps more an admiral than a general, realized . . . and perhaps overestimated, the scope and effectiveness of sea power, especially in time of war. It could secure the safe transit of food from the south of Russia to the wharves of the Piraeus. It could greatly hinder enemy trade passing up the Saronic Gulf, or along the Gulf of Corinth so long as there was a naval station near its entrance. It could convoy Athenian armies to any part of the Athenian Empire and carry raiding forces to any point on and off the coast of the Peloponnesus.

Triremes Overshadowed by Larger Ships

So far thalassocracy in war. But triremes and fleets of triremes had limitations which it is easy to forget. They could not carry food and water for long voyages or afford reasonable comfort for the crowded crews. They were blind at night and had poor means of communication at sea. They lay low in the water, and even if they were proceeding under sail they had not tall masts to help them watch out for the enemy or signal to each other. When they were operating as fighting fleets and nothing else, they carried too few marines to secure a landing on a hostile coast without serious risk. They might, in favourable conditions, blockade a harbour, but they could not blockade a long coastline. . . . Warships were expensive to maintain, for their crews were large, and their losses in men in any hard-fought battle were not easily replaced, even granted that superior skill might enable comparatively small fleets to be sure of victory. The ships themselves rapidly deteriorated unless they were well housed whenever they were not on active service, and they had much to fear from bad weather when they were. For they were frail. . . . However suited triremes were to manoeuvre against their own kind, they were less effective against sturdy sailing merchant ships, for if a trireme rammed a merchant ship it might not survive its success: a merchantman with a following wind could give a trireme a long chase, and merchantmen could take to the open sea for great distances while triremes must keep fairly near to land. All this must be remembered, and it may be a matter of some surprise that triremes ruled the waves for as long as they did.

In the fourth century fleets were smaller, but, even so, it was a great strain on Athens to recover from her relative weakness at sea in the middle third of the century. And though triremes never quite lost their usefulness, they gradually ceased to be the standard ship of the line. . . . By the time of Alexander the Great there was coming into service the successor to the trireme, the quinquereme, and, quite soon, ships of even greater power. These ships are defined by numerical designations which indicate the ratio of their oar power, however it was applied. They may be called, for instance, fivers, sixers, seveners and so on. Quinqueremes were now rowed by long oars or sweeps in one single row with five men pulling each oar; ships of higher denominations are rowed with more men to an oar or also more oars, however they are grouped. . . .

What is common to the larger ships is that they are called *cataphracts*, which means that the rowers were covered in and protected by an overhead deck. This deck may have added to the strength of the ship's structure so that it could resist the strain of so much more oarage power. Besides that, it made it possible to have a platform for large boarding parties of troops who might be one hundred strong or more, compared with the fourteen marines on an Athenian trireme in the Peloponnesian War. The rowing would require many oarsmen but most of them less skilled than in the heyday of trireme tactics. Manoeuvre would be slower and less resourceful. On the other hand, from Alexander onward it was easier to find well-trained infantry than skilled oarsmen. . . . And it is interesting to observe that in his great naval victory of Salamis in Cyprus, Demetrius [the "Besieger," son of Alexander's general Antigonus] adopted the land tactics of the day, and struck home with his left wing and then rolled up the enemy line exactly as generals were seeking to do with their striking force of cavalry. All this did not mean that lighter and swifter vessels lost their value for war and for the policing of the seas, and, on occasion, there appeared fleets of triremes and of lesser craft which operated with the great ships or in place of them. . . .

Short- and Long-Term Naval Strategy

I may now turn to the application of naval warfare in the field of strategy rather than of battle tactics. It is worth observing that if the comparative invisibility of ancient ships limited the value of command of the seas, this very invisibility could be used to gain a strategical advantage or to achieve surprise. Surprise is highly valued by all good judges of war, and the power to achieve it is one criterion of military or naval resourcefulness. Yet surprises are not common in Greek or Macedonian war by land or sea. It is on the whole true that the art of reconnaissance and the gathering of intelligence was not a strong point of fleets or armies in antiquity. To achieve surprise usually needs good intelligence, just as does the capacity to guard against it. Even so, it is to me surprising that armies and fleets were not oftener the victims of a well-planned surprise. I can only conjecture that ancient commanders . . . were reluctant to initiate the bold movement and take the calculated risk that often leads to catching the enemy unawares. . . .

But there is a strategy which depends on the use of fleets and their power of moving troops quickly and quietly. Thus in the early years of the fifth century the Spartan king Cleomenes manoeuvred his Argive opponents out of a strong position by transshipping his troops under cover of darkness to the opposite coast so that he could advance on Argos from another side and force the enemy to meet him there. Further, the dependence of fleets on land led to combined operations by armies and fleets, which afforded scope to the strategist. Thus in the Great Persian War the stand of [the Spartan King] Leonidas at Thermopylae had for its prime object the bringing about a naval battle in limited sea room so as to give the Greek fleet the hope of a victory which might halt the Persians' advance by land. The hope was not fulfilled, and Leonidas and his Spartans died in vain.

More fruitful was the shrewd strategy which posted the Greek fleet at Salamis on the flank of a Persian advance whether by land or sea. A Greek fleet at Salamis presented to the Persians the problem which an English fleet near Plymouth presented to the Spanish Armada as it sought to move up the Channel to reach the Prince of Parma in the Low Countries. The Persians tried to solve the problem by an attack which proved their ruin; the Spaniards disregarded it with no greater success.

In a yet wider field of naval strategy the island of Cyprus was an island of strategical importance. . . . That importance lay mainly in its geographical position. It was too far from the Greek waters of the Aegean to come within the scope of Hellenic politics or economics; but it lay near enough to the coast of Phoenicia to hamper the development of Persian naval strength, which was mainly based upon the sea power of that coast. Thus, if Cyprus was firmly controlled by Greek naval power, it went far to protect the eastern Aegean from the intrusion of Persian fleets. . . . [Later, in the mid–fourth century B.C., Cyprus] became independent, so that it could be of strategic value to Alexander and later to Antigonus I. It was in the waters of Cyprus that his son, Demetrius, won a great naval victory, and by then it had become the objective of the naval policy of the Ptolemies, for it served the ends of their sea power and was the halfway house between Egypt and her possessions in the Levant [Palestine]. In fact it does not cease to be disputed between naval powers until the general decline of the Hellenistic navies had set in late in the third century.

An even more important objective of Athenian naval policy was to secure for her commerce the passage of the Bosporus and the Dardanelles [i.e., the Hellespont]. Throughout the fifth and fourth centuries the corn that came to Athens from the northern shores of the Black Sea in return for Attic wares was a vital part of her food supply. Athens could not afford to see a hostile power in control of the Straits. These waters and the two islands of Lemnos and Imbros, the outer guard of the Dardanelles, were the constant preoccupation of Athenian diplomacy in peace and of Athenian strategy in war. During much of the fifth century this side of Athenian naval policy was merged in the general control of her Empire by sea. But it becomes clearer again in the last decade of the Peloponnesian War. For when her enemies got a footing on the west coast of Asia Minor the naval war tended to gravitate towards the Dardanelles. Her opponents had not failed to observe their importance, and . . . the final irreparable defeat of the Athenian navy in those parts made certain the surrender of Athens. . . .

Finally, the maintenance of naval power required access to the material for ships—above all, the heavy timber that was rare in the Mediterranean world,—and hides and pitch that were needed in shipyards. And these could be secured by naval power. As the author of the *Constitution of Athens* says: "If a city is rich in wood for shipbuilding, where will it be able to dispose of it without the permission of the ruler of the sea? And the same is true of iron or bronze or sailcloth, which very things are what ships are made of. And those who rule the sea can say where they are to go." The naval requirements of Athens are reflected in her negotiations with Macedon in the fifth century in her desire to secure a prior claim on the relevant exports of that country. So too in Hellenistic times the ambition of Egypt to be a great naval power was one cause of her desire to control Syria, where she could find the heavy timber which Egypt does not produce.

Selection 4

The Macedonian Army Developed by Philip and Alexander

Peter Connolly

The army that Macedonia's King Philip II and his son, Alexander III ("the Great"), developed in the fourth century B.C. was the most formidable one produced up to that time in the Mediterranean world. First, the Macedonian phalanx, with each of its members wielding a long pike (sarissa), was even more lethal than the traditional hoplite version. Also, Philip and Alexander placed a new emphasis on using infantry, cavalry (now often employed in "shock action," or direct charges on infantry), and various other supporting elements in a highly coordinated system, each element playing a key role in winning a battle. With some modifications and additions (notably elephants), this was the military system utilized by Alexander's successors and other Hellenistic generals in the third and second centuries B.C.

Noted military historian Peter Connolly here provides an informative synopsis of the various elements of the Macedonian military system and how Alexander used them in the field. Connolly regularly refers to the major ancient sources on the topic—Xenophon (Greek, fourth century B.C.); Polybius (Greek, second century B.C.); Diodorus Siculus (Greek, first century B.C.); Arrian (Greek, second century A.D.); and Justin (Roman, second or third century A.D., who quoted the now lost work of the earlier Roman historian Pompeius Trogus, who himself consulted the now lost works of the fourth-century B.C. Greek historian Theopompus, a contemporary of Philip and Alexander).

E ven before Philip's accession, the Macedonian cavalry was probably the best in Greece. It was drawn from the aristocracy and, as its name, the Companions, implies, it may have originated in a mounted royal bodyguard.

The infantry, which was raised from the peasantry, was a far different matter, lacking in discipline, training and organisation. Philip imposed an austere code of training and discipline on his army, compelling them to make regular forced route marches with full equipment and baggage to harden them against the rigours of war. He banned the use of wheeled transport and allowed only one servant to every ten men to carry the hand mills and ropes. The soldiers were forced to carry 30 days' rations on their backs when they set out on campaign. The cavalry too were restricted in the number of their servants, being allowed no more than one each. In this way Philip was able to keep the size of his baggage train and the number of his camp followers, two factors which were a constant cause of worry to any army, to a minimum.

The Macedonian Phalanx

Philip reformed his heavy infantry into a phalanx, no doubt based on the Theban model. When he took over the army it was organised in units of ten. This is confirmed by his restriction of servants to one to every ten men, and by the fact that a file in Alexander's army was called a *dekas*. At some stage he adopted the Greek system of using multiples of eight. . . . It is inconceivable that it took place earlier in Alexander's reign because of the sheer scale of his activities. One must conclude that it took place in the reign of Philip and probably well before he came into

Excerpted from Peter Connolly, *Greece and Rome at War*. Copyright © Peter Connolly, 1981, 1998. Reprinted by permission of Greenhill Books Ltd.

conflict with the Greeks, i.e. between 359 and 345. However, it is not until 323 BC, when Alexander was drafting Persians into his depleted Macedonian army, that we are given the first glimpse of the structure of the new phalanx.

Arrian says that each file (*dekas*) consisted of 16 men. This mixed Macedonian/Persian file was commanded by a *dekadarch* who served in the front rank. Behind him came first a man on double pay and then a 'ten stater' man; this man was getting less than double pay but more than the rank and file. Behind the three Macedonians came 12 Persians, and bringing up the rear another 'ten stater' man. These four Macedonians can be none other than the officers of the normal file. . . .

Philip raised the dignity of his newly formed phalanx by calling them 'foot companions'. The phalanx was divided into *taxeis* after the fashion of the other non-Spartan armies. Each *taxis* was a territorial unit recruited from a specific area of Macedonia. In Alexander's time it seems likely that there were 12 of these *taxeis*, each 1,500 strong: six were left in Macedonia and six taken on the invasion of Persia.

Of the subordinate division of the *taxis* we have practically no information. The existence of a 256-strong unit called a *syntagma* (or *speira*), which was subdivided into four *tetrarchies*, in the armies of the successors suggests a common origin which has to be Alexander's army. If this were the case, then each *taxis* would be divided into six *syntagmata*. . . .

In the later armies the *syntagma* was the smallest independent unit of the phalanx, having its own administrative staff, and it must surely have been allotted the same position in Alexander's army.

At the battle of Gaugamela [in 331 B.C.], Alexander opened gaps in his phalanx to let the Persian scythed chariots through. This could easily be done by withdrawing alternative *syntagmata* and placing each behind the *syntagma* on its right. If the phalanx was 16 deep this would leave gaps about 15m wide, and, if eight deep, gaps 30m wide.

The passage about the *dekas* in Arrian throws an interesting sidelight on the pay structure of

In a battle between Greeks and non-Greek tribesmen, a Greek phalanx crushes the opposition. Later, Philip II added progressively longer pikes, creating the dreaded Macedonian phalanx.

the phalanx. In the file there were not only 'double pay' and 'ten stater' men, but there might also be men who were receiving extra as a reward for bravery. The *dekadarch* must have received triple pay. This increasing rate of pay would have continued up through the officer structure. A similar system existed in the Roman imperial legions.

The *taxeis* had an order of precedence for each day so that each in turn would serve in the position of honour on the right wing.

The new phalangite [phalanx soldier] was armed with a long, two-handed pike (*sarissa*). Theophrastus, a contemporary of Philip and Alexander, claims that the longest *sarissa* was 12 cubits (c. 5.4m) long. Polybius claims that, in his day, it was 14 cubits (c. 6.3m) and that it had originally been 16 cubits (c. 7.2m). Scholarly opinion favours the figure given by Theophrastus, but this is mainly because it is generally be-

lieved that the later phalanx was much heavier than the earlier version. Bearing in mind Polybius' extraordinary knowledge and deep research into these matters, the author believes that Polybius' figure has to be considered seriously.

The *sarissa* may have been made in two parts joined by an iron sleeve. . . . The cornelian cherry tree was the commonest wood used in making spears, and certainly the Macedonian cavalry spears were made from it. . . . A 12-cubit pike with a shaft just under 4cm in diameter would weigh about 6.5kg, and Polybius' later 14-cubit one about 8kg. It is small wonder that Polybius comments on the great weight of the *sarissa*, making it difficult for the phalangite to carry palisade stakes.

It seems certain that the Macedonian phalangites were not restricted to the use of the *sarissa*, but, as occasion demanded, used other weapons. They could hardly carry on siege warfare with the pike, at least certainly not with a pike of that length. Several times both Diodorus and Arrian imply that they used javelins.

It is uncertain how the early Macedonian phalangite was armed. At the time of Polybius [second century B.C.] he probably wore greaves, a helmet and either a metal cuirass if he was a front ranker, or a linen cuirass if he served in the other ranks. He also carried a round shield about 60cm in diameter. There seems to be no real reason for supposing that he was much differently armed in the days of Philip and Alexander. Certainly Arrian refers to the lighter-armed part of Alexander's phalanx, implying that there must also be a heavier-armed part. It seems possible that those in the rear ranks, excluding the *ouragoi* [officers in the rear ranks], wore no body armour at all. . . .

Diodorus seems to imply that equipment was supplied free. This appears to be supported by the late 3rd-century Amphipolis inscription which lists fines to be imposed for the loss of items of equipment. This could only be operable if the equipment was supplied free.

As ever-increasing territories came under Philip's control, he was able to introduce new units into his army such as the Paeonian, and later the Thessalian, cavalry. At Chaeronea in 338 he was able to muster 30,000 infantry and 2,000 cavalry. When Alexander invaded Asia five years later, his total strength had risen to 44,000 infantry and 6,500 cavalry, but this now included contingents from the Greek states.

Alexander's Infantry and Cavalry

Diodorus gives a breakdown of Alexander's army: 12,000 infantry and 1,500 cavalry were left in Europe and 32,000 infantry and 5,100 cavalry transported to Asia Minor. This invasion force was made up of 12,000 Macedonian infantry reinforced by 7,000 from the allied states, 5,000 mercenaries, 7,000 infantry drawn from the frontiers of Macedon and 1,000 archers and Agrianian javelineers. These last were drawn from the mountainous northern frontier of Mace-

don. The 5,100 cavalry were made up of 1,800 Macedonians, 1,800 Thessalians, 600 Greeks and 900 Thracian and Paeonian scouts. . . .

The 12,000 Macedonian infantry accompanying Alexander were composed of the 9,000 Companions, already described, and 3,000 *hypaspists*. The 12,000 left in Europe seem likely also to have been composed of phalangites and *hypaspists* divided in the same proportion.

The *hypaspists* (literally shield-bearers) were slightly lighter infantry than the foot companions but fought alongside them in battle. They were usually drawn up between the phalanx and the cavalry. Their job was probably to protect the very vulnerable flanks of the phalanx. It seems likely that they were armed as the traditional hoplite with spear and Argive shield. Their name may well go back to a period when they formed a body of squires to the Companion cavalry. It was probably Philip who developed them as fully fledged infantry units, but they are not mentioned before the time of Alexander. The *hypaspists* were organised into battalions (*chiliarchies*) 1,000 strong. The first of these, the *agema*, was the king's bodyguard.

Towards the end of Arrian's life of Alexander, he mentions a unit in Alexander's army called the silver shields (*argyraspides*). He does this in such a way as to imply that they were the èlite troops and that everybody knew about them. According to Justin they were a regiment of veterans formed by Alexander after his expedition into India. They are mentioned several times by Diodorus as accompanying Eumenes after the death of Alexander. In 317 they were 3,000 strong and had the same officers as the *hypaspists*. Diodorus goes on to speak of their great prestige and how not one of them was under 60 years old. . . .

Alexander's Companion cavalry, which accompanied him on his expedition into Asia, was divided into eight territorial squadrons (*ilai*). Each *ila* was commanded by an *ilarch*. The first of these squadrons, which was larger than the others, was known as the royal *ila* and was regularly commanded by Alexander.

These *ilai* fought in a wedge-shaped formation, an innovation that was introduced by Philip. It has been suggested that in total there were 15 squadrons of Companion cavalry and that seven were left in Macedonia. These were the 1,500 cavalry mentioned by Diodorus. If this is the case, then each unit should be just over 210 strong, and the royal squadron 300. This last figure is very attractive as it is the traditional size for this type of èlite unit, e.g. the Spartan *hippeis* and the Theban Sacred Band. It also recommends itself as it is an exact figure from which a wedge can be formed. For units between 200 and 300 these are: 210, 231, 253, 276 and 300. The ideal figure for the other squadrons must be 210. At the end of the first year in Asia, reinforcements of 300 were received which, if one allows for losses, probably brought the seven *ilai* up to 231.

Obviously the *ilarch* could not expect to have the exact number in his squadron and would have left gaps in the rear rank. The great advantage of this wedge formation is that, having broken through, which was of course its prime function, it could then deploy or . . . explode laterally.

The Companion cavalry were armed with long spears (also called *sarissae*) with shafts made from cornel wood. . . . It could be used either for the traditional overhand thrust, or couched using an undergrip, but that it would be impossible to change grip in battle as it would require two hands to do so. . . . In wedge formation, the Companion cavalry could be used as shock troops against infantry. . . .

Alexander's Thessalian cavalry was also 1,800 strong. Unfortunately we do not know how many units there were nor their strength. We do know that their strengths differed and that the *ila* from Pharsalus was the largest and the best. The Thessalians were drawn up in a rhomboid formation that was introduced by Jason of Pherae about 375 BC. This diamond-shaped formation implies that the Thessalians too could be used as shock troops. According to Polybius the charge of the Thessalian cavalry was irresistible whether in *ilai* or in mass, but they were useless for skirmishing.

The 600 Greek cavalry who accompanied Alexander should . . . have formed five *ilai* of 128 men each. They would have formed up in a square 16 wide and eight deep. Owing to the length of the horse, twice the space was needed per horse down the files as it was along the ranks, so that it was in truth a square formation.

Polybius states that eight was the maximum practical depth for cavalry drawn up in block formation. Drawn up eight deep he says that 800 cavalry would occupy one *stade*. In other words two paces are allowed per horse in the ranks. The most effective depth must have been four deep.

Both the Thessalian and Greek horsemen were armed with spears. The 900 Thracian and Paeonian mounted scouts were armed with javelins. Their prime job was to scout ahead of the army to check for ambushes and to make contact with the enemy. Alexander also used them a great deal for skirmishing. . . .

When Alexander distributed the booty after the battle of Gaugamela, Macedonian cavalrymen received three times more than the Macedonian infantrymen, and the allied cavalry two and a half times as much. This probably reflects the comparative pay rates.

In the cavalry, as in the infantry, there was an order of precedence for each day and the first *ila* to be called out took up the position of honour.

Our main source of knowledge of cavalry equipment during the 4th century is Xenophon, who wrote [his *Cavalry Commander*] some 50 years before the time of Alexander. He recommends that a cavalryman should wear a cuirass with protection for the thighs, a guard for the left arm and a Boeotian helmet with all-round vision. An excellent example of one of these helmets, maybe even belonging to one of Alexander's troopers, was found in the Tigris. The thigh protection was probably the *pteryges*. The left arm guard, used in the absence of a shield, seems to have been in vogue only in his own day. He suggests a bronze chest plate (*peytral*) and face guard (*chamfron*) for the horse. No examples of horse armour from this period have yet been discovered. Xenophon also prefers the use of the curved *kopis* to the normal two-edged sword, and javelins rather than spears [since javelins were thrown, whereas spears were used to thrust and jab]. . . .

On the March and in Battle

In most respects the army of Alexander carries on in much the same way as that described by Xenophon 50 years earlier. Orders are given by trumpet. The army deploys from column of march into battle line. They still do not build proper fortified camps, although Alexander sometimes constructs a ditch and palisade. In the face of the Persians at Gaugamela, Arrian says that he had no proper defences to his camp. Like the Greeks at Plataea, he camped with his army in battle order.

On the march advance scouts were sent out ahead and, since they are referred to explicitly as advance scouts, by implication there should also be flank scouts. When approaching the enemy near the Granicus, Alexander threw out a screen ahead of the army consisting of the scouts, reconnoitring parties, the Balkan lancers and 500 light-armed troops. In this respect the Macedonians were far ahead of the Greeks. . . . [Most earlier Greek] armies and fleets approached each other undetected because of lack of scouting or other intelligence systems. The most notable example was at Mantinea [418 B.C.] where neither the Spartans nor the Argive and allied army knew that the other was less than five kilometres away.

Scouts in the sense of intelligence seekers seem to have come into use only about the time of Xenophon [early fourth century B.C.], but even so they seem to have been little used in Greece. Although Alexander, and presumably Philip, made good use of these scouts, later armies seem to have fallen back into the old ways and the Roman republican armies were no better. . . . At Cynoscephalae in 197 BC neither the Macedonian army under Philip V nor the Romans under Flamininus had the slightest idea where the other was, in spite of the fact that both could have placed scouts on the high ground in sight of both armies. . . .

Alexander normally drew up his army with the phalanx in the centre, the strongest cavalry, including the Companions, on the right and the weakest on the left. The *hypaspists* were placed at the right end of the phalanx. The right wing was further reinforced by the archers and *agrianes*. The whole line would usually be drawn up obliquely with the right wing advanced and the left held back. The first attack would always come from the advanced right wing with Alexander himself at the head of the Companion cavalry.

This was Alexander's version of the Theban tactic [the method of having the army advance with one side slanting backward, developed in the 370s B.C. by the Theban general Epaminondas]. It was adapted especially for use against the fast-moving, light-armed Persian troops. . . . Arrian is inclined to underestimate the importance of the phalanx in Alexander's battles and to treat the struggle in the centre as a sideshow. Only when the phalanx is in trouble and Alexander manages to relieve it does Arrian report its activities. This must be because he is writing a life of Alexander and wishes to concentrate on the hero of his story. In fact the cavalry is only the sledgehammer which shatters the cohesion of the Persian forces. It is the phalanx which must win the battle. Alexander may be the most successful commander of all time but he can hardly be considered the best. He left it to his generals to win the battle whilst he was off chasing the Persian cavalry. Although he had obviously read Xenophon's *Anabasis*, he learned nothing from the fate of Cyrus the Younger who was killed by a stray arrow whilst leading his cavalry. Polybius, whilst not directly criticising Alexander, says that a general who leads his troops is seen by them all but sees none of them.

For minor expeditions Alexander used only part of his army. These expeditionary forces were mainly light and fast moving. Alexander normally commanded them himself. They usually consisted of half the Companion cavalry, the *hypaspists*, the *agrianes*, the archers and one or two *taxeis* of the phalanx. Sometimes men were selected from the whole phalanx rather than taking whole *taxeis*. On one occasion at least he chose the lightest armed of the phalanx. Marching night and day these forces could cover as much as 90km a day.

Selection 5

Hellenistic Sieges, Fortifications, Mercenaries, and Battle Elephants

John Warry

The early part of the Hellenistic Age was dominated by Alexander's Successors, who battled for control of his former empire. These men were essentially warlords who built up personal kingdoms that were mostly unstable, rising, falling, or changing size and allegiance on a regular basis. (One of the more colorful of these warlords, Demetrius Poliorcetes, often found himself without a kingdom and roamed about with his troops like a pirate.) Although these men still used the Macedonian phalanx, cavalry, peltasts, and many other military units employed by Alexander, their warfare and that of their Hellenistic descendants became best known for its advances in siege methods and defensive fortifications, the use of mercenary (hired) troops on a larger scale than ever before, and the deployment of battle elephants. Former Cambridge University scholar John Warry here examines these special aspects of Hellenistic warfare, beginning his narrative with a look at the offensive and defensive capabilities of Rhodes, the island state that

managed to withstand Demetrius's siege, perhaps the most famous of ancient times.

One Greek constitutional state which continued to prosper and grow strong in a world of warlords was Rhodes. . . . The cities of the island formed a federation, with a newly-founded capital city and a central government. Each member city, however, preserved a large measure of local autonomy.

Rhodes had grown rich by carrying corn and other cargoes in its ships; Alexander's destruction of Phoenician Tyre rid the island state of a dangerous trade competitor. At the same time, the Macedonian mastery of the entire Persian empire and the consequent abolition of political frontiers in the eastern Mediterranean threw open new coasts and harbours to Rhodian vessels. In the time of Alexander's Successors, Rhodes managed to hold a balance of power and ingeniously preserved its independence. The Rhodians flattered and conciliated the contending dynasts around them, refusing to enter into any alliance with one against another. This in itself would not have been enough to secure the island's liberty if Rhodes had not possessed a strong navy of its own. Such a navy, however, the Rhodians were wise and bold enough to maintain. In their moderate form of democracy, the rowing crews of the ships were recruited from the poorer classes, while the officers were drawn from wealthier families. They did not need to rely upon mercenaries, either to serve in or command their navy.

Rhodes was, in fact, the successor of Athens as the leading Greek naval power. As at Athens, such power was dependent largely upon civic patriotism. But as a comparatively small island, Rhodes enjoyed some advantages which the Athenians had not possessed. The Rhodians could rely entirely upon their navy for defence. Immune to land invasion, they were not obliged to organize an army or build Long Walls to secure communications with their docks and shipyards. Indeed, the famous Rhodian slingers served for the most part as mercenaries in foreign armies and may best be considered as a source of "invisible earnings". Moreover, the island's rocky coast lent itself admirably to fortification against seaborne attack. . . .

Rhodes' naval supremacy in the eastern Mediterranean was also a bulwark against piracy. Unfortunately, any power strong enough to subdue pirates in the ancient world usually felt at liberty to behave with piratical lawlessness itself; such protection as it offered became a "protection racket". Rhodes, however, was an exception in this respect and, deeply committed to constitutional principles, evolved a code of maritime law which the Romans later imitated and embodied in their own laws. Indeed, modern law, based upon the Roman, may indirectly owe something to Rhodes.

The Rhodian foreign policy, bent on preserving a balance of power, could not at all times be sustained. Forced at last to take sides either with Ptolemy or Antigonus, the Rhodians considered that their best prospects lay in alliance with the former. Rhodes was accordingly blockaded and stormed by Antigonus' celebrated son, Demetrius the Besieger (*Poliorcetes*). This ordeal, however, the island triumphantly survived, re-emerging with enhanced power and prestige.

Any further allusion to the siege of Rhodes is perhaps best prefaced by some general remarks on the evolution of Greek and Macedonian siegecraft in general. Even before the Peloponnesian War, Pericles had used battering rams against the island of Samos, when it revolted from the Athenian League in 441 BC. . . . In default of covering fire, all siege operations were exposed to counterattack from the besieged walls . . . where the heads of the battering rams were broken off by heavy beams dropped from the fortified walls above.

With the introduction of missile warfare, the situation was crucially altered. The greater use of hand missiles was soon followed by the employment of artillery engines, depending for their projectile power on cables of twisted sinew. The introduction of the arrow-firing catapult was attributed to Dionysius I of Syracuse. This machine was a giant crossbow mounted on a heavy wooden frame, launching a correspondingly heavy-headed dart. Philip II of Macedon used such machines when he besieged Perinthus in 340 BC. But the first use of catapults to hurl rocks probably came rather later. Alexander certainly had such catapults at the siege of Tyre.

Artillery of this kind could, of course, be employed by the besieged as well as the besiegers. In fact, its use operated to the advantage of those within the walls, since their fortifications were of a more solid and permanent nature and could be built with narrow ports, embrasures and battlements, behind which the artillerymen could operate under cover. Besieging armies countered this advantage by constructing elaborate towers and penthouses, with ports for artillery which matched those of the defenders. Such structures also sheltered battering rams. The obvious way of operating a battering ram was to suspend it from an overhead beam and swing its head against the target. It could also be mounted on wheels and thrust violently against the wall under attack by a large and muscular crew. More sophisticated types were developed, in which the shaft of the ram slid in a wooden channel; it was then repeatedly winched back, as if in a catapult, and projected against the wall.

Penthouses, often on wheels, could also be used to screen the operations of miners and sappers or those who wished to fill in the fosse before an enemy rampart. Covered by artillery and missile support, assault with scaling ladders became increasingly effective. Ladders were not always of wood; a kind of leather and cord network ladder was also in use.

The defenders, for their part, sometimes hung on their battlements wooden placards which could be shifted in such a way as to dislodge any scaling ladders placed against them. These protective placards must, of course, in turn have been exposed to the assailants' fire darts. As is the way of military technology, the series of devices and counter-devices was capable of endless prolongation, inevitably involving both attackers and defenders in enormous expense. A simpler and cheaper method of capturing a city was by means of treachery, and by treachery cities were often captured. . . .

Demetrius brought to the siege of Rhodes a vast armament of men and ships. Apart from his own fighting fleet of 200 vessels and his auxiliary fleet of more than 150, he had enlisted the aid of pirate squadrons. One thousand private trading craft also followed him, attracted by the wealth of Rhodes and the prospect of spoil. The whole operation was, in fact, a gigantic piratical enterprise. But Demetrius seems to have felt that it was "a glorious thing to be a pirate king".

The main harbour at Rhodes, as well as the city, was fortified with towers and walls. Here the Rhodian fleet could safely rest; nor was Demetrius able to prevent ships with supplies from running his blockade. His first concern, therefore, was to capture the harbour. He at once proceeded to build his own harbour alongside, constructing a mole and protecting his seaborne siege operations from counter-attack by means of a floating spiked boom. At the same time, his army ravaged the island and built a huge camp on land adjacent to the city but out of missile range.

In the course of the siege, both sides employed the technical devices we have just described. Mining operations by the besiegers were met by the counter-mines of the besieged. At a fairly early stage, Demetrius' men secured a footing on the mole of the main harbour, but the Rhodians prevented him from exploiting this bridgehead and he never captured the harbour. Later, as the result of a land attack, he actually penetrated the walls of the city, but the attack was contained by the Rhodians and those who had entered were mostly killed.

The most sensational feature of the siege was Demetrius' mammoth tower, which was nicknamed the *helepolis*, "city-taker", although in the event it failed to take the city. The *helepolis* tower was based on a huge square grille of timberwork, covering an area of 5,200 square feet (484 sq m). The tower was about 140 feet (90 cubits, 43m) high and the uppermost of its nine storeys was 900 square feet (84 sq m) in area. As a protection against fire, the tower was armoured with iron plates on its three exposed sides; it was mounted on gigantic castors, the wheels of which were themselves plated with iron. The artillery ports of the *helepolis* were made to open and close by mechanical means and were padded with leather and wool as a protection against the shock of missile attack. Communication with the upper storeys was by means of two staircases, for ascent and descent respectively.

The machine was moved, presumably in relays, by 3,400 specially selected strong men. Some pushed from inside the structure, others behind. . . . The *helepolis* was in effect a mammoth tank, far larger than any that have ever been driven by petrol engines. Despite every precaution, however, the Rhodians managed to dislodge some of the tower's iron plates; when there was a real danger of it being set on fire, Demetrius ordered it to be withdrawn from action.

The entire Greek and Macedonian world, constitutionalists and dynasts alike, sympathized with the Rhodians during the siege. The conflict was, after all, one between law and piracy. Influenced perhaps by the unpopularity of his operations and convinced at last that he could not win, Demetrius came to terms with the Rhodians and went away to look for a war somewhere else. The Rhodians, overjoyed, rewarded the sacrifice of citizens, slaves and resident aliens as they had promised.

Demetrius had left his engines strewn around

the city and the scrap metal which they yielded provided material for the huge statue which the Rhodians erected at their harbour entrance: the Colossus of Rhodes, one of the Seven Wonders of the World. A prodigy itself, the Colossus was a fitting memorial to a prodigious siege.

Fortifications

Fortifications during the generations which followed Alexander the Great were required to meet the challenge of increasingly sophisticated siegecraft and of armies equipped with larger, more abundant and more powerful machinery. Great importance was attached to counter-attack and to the creation of vantage points from which the besieger could be threatened on his flank by missiles. With this in view, ramparts were sometimes built on a saw-tooth pattern. Either the wall itself followed a saw-tooth contour or a straight wall was given a saw-tooth facing on its outer surface. The advantage of this device was that one saw-tooth projection gave covering fire to the next. . . .

As a defence against the approach of siege towers, deep moats were often dug in front of the walls of a fortified position. Such moats had been dug in front of the Athenian city walls after the battle of Chaeronea and they were improved during the course of the succeeding century. On archaeological evidence, these moats appear to have reached a depth of 13 feet (4m) and a width of 33 feet (10m). In some instances, moats were filled with water; when they surrounded cities, further protection was often given by a wall or palisade on the inner edge.

The construction of towers on the ramparts had long been a feature of Greek cities. These frequently projected in the manner of bastions and permitted a flanking attack on the besiegers. At the same time, the missile men who garrisoned them had the advantage of superior height and were in a position to oppose any siege towers. Such defensive towers tended to become increasingly numerous. They were also increasingly independent of the curtain walls which linked them. . . . During the siege of Rhodes, Demetrius' forces were able to destroy the curtain wall on each side

of a tower without destroying the tower itself. Towers were square, polygonal, semi-circular or horse-shoe in plan. . . . Archaeological evidence suggests that walls of about 29.5ft (9m) in height were normal during the fourth century; if attacks by a *helepolis* were expected, they were probably built higher. The height of a city's walls was sometimes increased by the defenders during the course of a siege. . . .

Mercenaries

The siege of Rhodes, if one disregards its political futility, offers an interesting case study, since it presents a mercenary army at war with a citizen garrison. A citizen army was at its best fighting in its own homeland, in defence of its own womenfolk, children and property. A mercenary army, on the other hand, had the greatest inducement when it was an invading army, free to plunder and live off enemy country. . . .

The main reward for mercenary service during the fourth and third centuries was booty, not pay. Ready coin was often inadequate to provide payment. Cleomenes III of Sparta was hurried into a disastrous engagement at Sellasia in 222 BC because he lacked cash for the retention of his mercenaries. It should be noticed that Cleomenes was conducting a defensive campaign on his own territory. In an offensive war such as he had waged earlier in Arcadia, booty had been available and mercenary remuneration could be based on results.

Prisoners might often change hands for cash ransoms. Before the siege of Rhodes, the Rhodians came to an agreement with Demetrius, according to which a freeman captured by either side should be exchanged for 1,000 drachmas and a slave for 500 drachmas. But most booty was in kind and captives were commonly sold as slaves. An invading army, as at Rhodes, was followed by a horde of expectant traders. Among these, slave-dealers constituted a numerous community; after a victory, captives could be sold on the spot.

Apart from the inevitable fickleness of a mercenary army, its appetite for booty significantly conditioned the course of such wars as it was employed to fight. Even with citizen armies, it was hard for any commander to retain control over his men once they had fallen to plundering; for this reason a battle won in one sector of the field was often lost in another. . . .

Except for a small nucleus of Macedonians who perhaps felt themselves to be united with their leaders by a tie of common nationality, the armies of Alexander's Successors depended mainly on mercenaries; this fact goes far to explaining why the wars which they fought were usually so inconclusive. A mercenary force possessed of the baggage train of a defeated army—let alone a town or territory which had sheltered the enemy—in its preoccupation with plunder would have little incentive to follow up a victory or pursue fugitives. Indeed, it was hardly in the mercenary's interest to eliminate the opposing forces completely. By so doing, he would have deprived himself of employment and so a living.

War Elephants

The kings and generals who commanded armies in the Graeco-Macedonian world seem to have had a taste for massive equipment; their wide use of war elephants was perhaps consistent with this taste. . . . Elephants could be defeated easily enough by flexible tactics, but at the same time they must have had some substantial advantages to justify their continued use. The elephant could inflict casualties by trampling enemies underfoot or seizing them with its trunk. And—not least important—it offered a higher platform from which missiles could be launched. The tur-

This seventeenth-century engraving depicts an ancient battle involving war elephants, a military novelty imported into Europe from Asia in the years following Alexander's conquests.

ret mounted on an elephant's back might accommodate a crew of four. A consideration of siege, mountain and naval tactics should remind us that the ancients attached great importance to a point of vantage based on superior height. The archer who threatened his enemy from above gained a wider view and a greater range.

As compared with cavalry, elephants were less manoeuvrable, although at the same time they might easily frighten horses and make them unmanageable. On the whole, the elephant was best employed against a stationary enemy; in this connection we should remark that the Macedonian phalanx, against which elephants were used, had itself become less mobile. This may be another example of the general military tendency to make everything bigger and heavier. Demetrius' armourer produced for him a cuirass which completely withstood a catapult dart at 26 paces and was considered light, at a weight of 40 lbs (18.1 kg). A similar cuirass was supplied to one of Demetrius' lieutenants, although this officer had been accustomed to a panoply weighing two talents. A more normal weight was one talent. The talent in Attic weight has been estimated at 57 lbs (25.86 kg), by the Aeginetan standard at 83 lbs (37.80 kg). In any case, such armour must be regarded as heavy. It would be no wonder if ponderously equipped phalangists [members of the phalanx] found it difficult to perform the essential evasive manoeuvre of opening ranks with all the alacrity that an elephant charge demanded.

Special anti-elephant devices were adopted. The most effective seems to have been that of planting the ground with spikes. The poor beasts, maddened by pain, soon became incapable of control. But perhaps the best answer to the elephant threat was an opposing force of elephants. In this case, the larger elephants could have been expected to enjoy an advantage, not only on account of their weight but because of the superior position occupied by the archers on their backs. The Seleucid rulers, with their ready access to India, at first had the monopoly of elephants and of the Indian mahouts who could control them. The Ptolemies soon equalized by training African elephants captured in Ethiopia. The African elephant which they enlisted was not a larger species than the Indian; on the contrary, ancient authorities who describe it as smaller were familiar with a North African subspecies, found in the regions of the Red Sea and of the Atlas Mountains—where it was used by the Carthaginians. When Ptolemaic African elephants clashed with Seleucid Indian elephants at the battle of Raphia, near Gaza, in 217 BC, the Seleucids had the better of it. But in any case, numbers on this occasion told in their favour.

Elephants could also be used to force the entrance to a city. However, when the Macedonian commander attempted this at Megalopolis in 318 BC, the defenders laid large gates studded with spikes on the ground over which the elephant attack was expected and the operation ended in disaster.

Selection 6

Why the Roman Legions Were Able to Defeat the Greek Phalanx

Polybius

The Greek phalanx long remained the preeminent battle formation of ancient Mediterranean warfare. But it was monolithic (rigid), inflexible, and could be used only on smooth terrain. As a result, it eventually proved ineffective against the more versatile and flexible Roman legions. (A typical legion of this era had about 4,200 infantry, broken down into several smaller battlefield units called maniples.) This famous tract by the second-century B.C. *Greek historian Polybius explains why the Roman military system was able consistently to beat the Greek one, making Rome's eclipse of the Greek world inevitable.*

*I*n my sixth book I mentioned that when a suitable occasion arose I would attempt a comparison between Roman and Macedonian military equipment and tactical formations, showing how they differ from one another for better or worse. Now that we have seen the two systems opposed to one another in the field, I shall try to fulfil my promise. In the past the Macedonian formation was proved by opera-

tional experience to be superior to the others which were in use in Asia and Greece, while the Roman system overcame those employed in Africa and among all the peoples of Western Europe. In our own times we have seen both the two formations and the soldiers of the two nations matched against one another, not just once but on many occasions. It should prove a useful exercise, and one well worth the trouble, to study the differences between them, and to discover the reason why on the battlefield the Romans have always proved the victors and carried off the prize. If we examine the matter in this way we shall not, like the ignorant majority of mankind, speak merely in terms of chance, and congratulate the victors without giving the reasons, but shall be able to pay them the praise and admiration they deserve because we have come to understand the causes of their success. . . .

There are a number of factors which make it easy to understand that so long as the phalanx retains its characteristic form and strength nothing can withstand its charge or resist it face to face. When the phalanx is closed up for action, each man with his arms occupies a space of three feet. The pike he carries was earlier designed to be twenty-four feet long, but as adapted to current practice was shortened to twenty-one, and from this we must subtract the space between the bearer's hands and the rear portion of the pike which keeps it balanced and couched. This amounts to six feet in all, from which it is clear that the pike will project fifteen feet in front of the body of each hoplite when he advances against the enemy grasping it with both hands. This also means that while the pikes of the men in the second, third, and fourth ranks naturally extend further than those of the fifth rank, yet even the latter will still project three feet in front of the men in the first rank. I am assuming of course that the phalanx keeps its characteristic order, and is closed up both from the rear and on the flanks. . . .

At any rate if my description is true and exact, it follows that each man in the front rank will have the points of five pikes extending in front of him, each point being three feet ahead of the one behind.

From these facts we can easily picture the nature and the tremendous power of a charge by the whole phalanx, when it advances sixteen deep with levelled pikes. Of these sixteen ranks those who are stationed further back than the fifth cannot use their pikes to take an active part in the battle. They therefore do not level them man against man, but hold them with the points tilted upwards over the shoulders of the men in front. In this way they give protection to the whole phalanx from above, for the pikes are massed so closely that they can keep off any missiles which might clear the heads of the front ranks and strike those immediately behind them. Once the charge is launched, these rear ranks by the sheer pressure of their bodily weight greatly increase its momentum. . . .

The Highly Flexible Romans

What then is the factor which enables the Romans to win the battle and causes those who use the phalanx to fail? The answer is that in war the times and places for action are unlimited, whereas the phalanx requires one time and one type of ground only in order to produce its peculiar effect. Now if the enemy were compelled to position themselves according to the times and places demanded by the phalanx whenever an important battle was imminent, no doubt those who employ the phalanx would always carry off the victory for the reasons I have given above. But if it is quite possible, even easy, to evade its irresistible charge, how can the phalanx any longer be considered formidable? Again, it is generally admitted that its use requires flat and level ground which is unencumbered by any obstacles such as ditches, gullies, depressions, ridges and watercourses, all of which are sufficient to hinder and dislocate such a formation. There is general agreement that it is almost impossible, or at any rate exceedingly rare, to find a stretch of country of say two or three miles or more which contains no obstacles of this kind. But even assuming that such an arena could be found, if the enemy refuses to come down into it, but prefers to traverse the country sacking the towns and devastating the territories of our allies, what purpose can the phalanx serve? If it remains on the ground which suits it best, not only is it unable to assist its allies, but it cannot even ensure its own safety, for the transport of its supplies will easily be stopped by the enemy when they have undisputed command of the open country. On the other hand, if it leaves the terrain which favours it and attempts an action elsewhere, it will easily be defeated. Or again, supposing that the enemy does decide to descend into the plain and fight there, but, instead of committing his entire force to the battle when the phalanx has its one opportunity to charge, keeps even a small part of it in reserve at the moment when the main action takes place, it is easy to forecast what will happen from the tactics which the Romans are now putting into practice.

The outcome indeed does not need to be demonstrated by argument: we need only refer to accomplished facts. The Romans do not attempt to make their line numerically equal to the enemy's, nor do they expose the whole strength of the legions to a frontal attack by the phalanx. Instead they keep part of the forces in reserve while the rest engage the enemy. Later in the battle, whether the phalanx in its charge drives back the troops opposed to it or is driven back by them, in either event it loses its own peculiar formation. For either in pursuing a retreating enemy or falling back before an oncoming one, the phalanx leaves behind the other units of its own army; at this point the enemy's reserves can occupy the space the phalanx has vacated, and are no longer obliged to attack from the front, but can fall upon it from flank and rear. When it is thus easy to deny the phalanx the opportunities it needs and to minimize the advantages it enjoys, and also impossible to prevent the enemy from acting against it, does it not follow that the difference between these two systems is enormous?

Besides this, those who rely on the phalanx are obliged to march across and encamp on ground of every description; they must occupy favourable positions in advance, besiege others and be besieged themselves and deal with unexpected appearances of the enemy. All these eventualities are part and parcel of war, and may have an important or a decisive effect on the final victory. In all these situations the Macedonian formation is sometimes of little use, and sometimes of none at all, because the phalanx soldier cannot operate either in smaller units or singly, whereas the Roman formation is highly flexible. Every Roman soldier, once he is armed and goes into action, can adapt himself equally well to any place or time and meet an attack from any quarter. He is likewise equally well-prepared and needs to make no change whether he has to fight with the main body or with a detachment, in maniples or singly. Accordingly, since the effective use of the parts of the Roman army is so much superior, their plans are much more likely to achieve success than those of others. I have felt obliged to deal with this subject at some length, because so many Greeks on those occasions when the Macedonians suffered defeat regarded such an event as almost incredible, and many will still be at a loss to understand why and how the phalanx proves inferior by comparison with the Roman method of arming their troops.

The Triumphof Hellenism

Epilogue

Greece's Legacy to the Western World

Will Durant

When the Romans conquered Greece, they absorbed rather than destroyed Hellenic (Greek) culture, which they greatly admired. And largely through Rome, Greece's extraordinarily wide-ranging cultural legacy reached and profoundly shaped early modern European society. In this excerpt from his popular series of historical studies, The Story of Civilization, *the late scholar Will Durant summarizes the incredible debt the Western world still owes the Greeks. (Note: Durant here uses the term Oriental to denote the Persians and other non-Greek inhabitants of the ancient Near East.)*

Greek civilization . . . bequeathed itself in an incomparable legacy to the nations of Europe and the Near East. Every Greek colony poured the elixir of Greek art and thought into the cultural blood of the hinterland—into Spain and Gaul, Etruria and Rome, Egypt and Palestine, Syria and Asia Minor, and along the shores of the Black Sea. Alexandria was the port of reshipment for ideas as well as goods: from the Museum and the Library the works and views of Greek poets, mystics, philosophers, and scientists were scattered through scholars and students

into every city of the Mediterranean. . . . Rome took the Greek heritage in its Hellenistic form: her playwrights adopted Menander . . . her poets imitated the modes, measures, and themes of Alexandrian literature, her arts used Greek craftsmen and Greek forms, her law absorbed the statutes of the Greek cities, and her later imperial organization was modeled upon the Greco-Oriental monarchies: Hellenism, after the Roman conquest of Greece, conquered Rome even as the Orient was conquering Greece. Every extension of Roman power spread the ferment of Hellenic civilization. The Byzantine Empire wedded Greek to Asiatic culture, and passed on some part of the Greek inheritance to the Near East and the Slavic north. The Syrian Christians took up the torch and handed it to the Arabs, who carried it through Africa to Spain. Byzantine, Moslem, and Jewish scholars conveyed or translated the Greek masterpieces to Italy, arousing . . . the fever of the Renaissance. Since that second birth of the European mind the spirit of Greece has seeped so thoroughly into modern culture that all civilized nations, in all that concerns the activity of the intellect, are colonies of Hellas today.

Our Many Debts to Greece

If we include in our Hellenic heritage not only what the Greeks invented but what they adapted from older cultures and transmitted by these diverse routes to our own, we shall find that patrimony in almost every phase of modern life. Our handicrafts, the technique of mining, the essentials of engineering, the processes of finance and trade, the organization of labor, the governmental regulation of commerce and industry—all these have come down to us on the stream of history from Rome, and through Rome from Greece. Our democracies and our dictatorships alike go back to Greek exemplars; and though the widened reach of states has evolved a representative system unknown to Hellas, the democratic idea of a government responsible to the governed, of trial by jury, and of civil liberties of thought, speech, writing, assemblage, and worship have been profoundly stimulated by Greek history. These things above all distinguished the Greek from the Oriental, and gave him an independence of spirit and enterprise that made him smile at the obeisances [subjects groveling before absolute monarchs] . . . of the East.

Our schools and universities, our gymnasiums and stadiums, our athletics and Olympic games, trace their lineage to Greece. . . . The conception of self-containment and of self-control, the cult of health and natural living, the pagan ideal of a shameless enjoyment of every sense, found their historic formulations in Greece. Christian theology and practice (the very words are Greek) stem in large part from the mystery religions of Greece and Egypt, from Eleusinian, Orphic, and Osirian rites; from Greek doctrines of the divine son dying for mankind and rising from the dead; from Greek rituals of religious procession, ceremonial purification, holy sacrifice, and the sacred common meal; from Greek ideas of hell, demons, purgatory, indulgences, and heaven; and from Stoic and Neo-Platonic theories of the . . . creation, and the final conflagration of the world. . . .

Our literature could hardly have existed without the Greek tradition. Our alphabet came from Greece through . . . Rome; our language is littered with Greek words; our science has forged an international language through Greek terms; our grammar and rhetoric, even the punctuation and paragraphing of this page, are Greek inventions. Our literary genres are Greek—the lyric, the ode, the idyl, the novel, the essay, the oration, the biography, the history, and above all the drama; again nearly all the words are Greek. The terms and forms of the modern drama—tragedy, comedy, and pantomime—are Greek. . . . The Greek dramas themselves are among the richest portions of our inheritance.

Nothing else in Greece seems so foreign to us as its music; and yet modern music (until its return to Africa and the Orient) was derived from medieval chants and dances, and these went back in part to Greece. The oratorio and the opera owe something to the Greek choral dance and drama; and the theory of music, so far as we know, was first explored and expounded by the Greeks from Pythagoras to Aristoxenus. . . . The forms and much of the technique of modern sculpture are still Greek, for upon no other art has the Hellenic genius stamped itself so despotically. We are only now freeing ourselves from the fascination of Greek architecture; every city in Europe and America has some temple of commerce or finance whose form or columnar facade came from the shrines of Greek gods. . . . The lessons of moderation, purity, and harmony embodied in the sculpture and architecture of the classic age are a precious heirloom for our race.

If Greek civilization seems more akin and "modern" to us now than that of any century before Voltaire [the noted eighteenth-century French writer], it is because the Hellene loved reason as much as form, and boldly sought to explain all nature in nature's terms. The liberation of science from theology, and the independent development of scientific research, were parts of the heady adventure of the Greek mind. Greek mathematicians laid the foundations of trigonometry and calculus, they began and completed the study of conic sections, and they brought three-dimensional geometry to such relative perfection that it remained as they left it until [the seventeenth-century French mathematician and philosopher René] Descartes. . . . Democritus illuminated the whole area of physics and chemistry with his atomic theory. In a mere aside and holiday from abstract studies

Archimedes produced enough new mechanisms to place his name with the highest in the records of invention. Aristarchus anticipated and perhaps inspired [the sixteenth-century Polish astronomer who introduced the concept of a sun-centered universe, Nicolaus] Copernicus; and Hipparchus, through Claudius Ptolemy, constructed a system of astronomy which is one of the landmarks in cultural history. Eratosthenes measured the earth and mapped it. Anaxagoras and Empedocles drew the outlines of a theory of evolution. Aristotle and Theophrastus classified the animal and plant kingdoms, and almost created the sciences of meteorology, zoology, embryology, and botany. Hippocrates freed medicine from mysticism and philosophical theory, and ennobled it with an ethical code; Herophilus and Erasistratus raised anatomy and physiology to a point which, except in Galen, Europe would not reach again till the Renaissance. In the work of these men we breathe the quiet air of reason, always uncertain and unsafe, but cleansed of passion and myth. Perhaps, if we had its masterpieces entire, we should rate Greek science as the most signal intellectual achievement of mankind.

But the lover of philosophy will only reluctantly yield to science and art the supreme places in our Grecian heritage. Greek science itself was a child of Greek philosophy—of that reckless challenge to legend, that youthful love of inquiry, which for centuries united science and philosophy in one adventurous quest. Never had men examined nature so critically and yet so affectionately: the Greeks did no dishonor to the world in thinking that it was a cosmos of order and therefore amenable to understanding. They invented logic for the same reason that they made perfect statuary: harmony, unity, proportion, form, in their view, provided both the art of logic and the logic of art. Curious of every fact and every theory, they not only established philosophy as a distinct enterprise of the European mind, but they conceived nearly every system and every hypothesis, and left little to be said on any major problem of our life. Realism and nominalism, idealism and materialism, monotheism, pantheism, and atheism, feminism and communism . . . all the dreams and wisdom of philosophy are here, in the age and land of its birth. And in Greece men not only talked of philosophy, they lived it: the sage, rather than the warrior or the saint, was the pinnacle and ideal of Greek life. Through all the centuries from Thales that exhilarating philosophical bequest has come down to us, inspiring Roman emperors, Christian Fathers, Scholastic theologians, Renaissance heretics, Cambridge Platonists, the rebels of the Enlightenment, and the devotees of philosophy today. At this moment thousands of eager spirits are reading Plato, perhaps in every country on the earth.

The Greek Spirit Lives On

Civilization does not die, it migrates; it changes its habitat and its dress, but it lives on. The decay of one civilization, as of one individual, makes room for the growth of another; life sheds the old skin, and surprises death with fresh youth. Greek civilization is alive; it moves in every breath of mind that we breathe; so much of it remains that none of us in one lifetime could absorb it all. We know its defects—its insane and pitiless wars, its stagnant slavery, its subjection of woman, its lack of moral restraint, its corrupt individualism, it tragic failure to unite liberty with order and peace. But those who cherish freedom, reason, and beauty will not linger over these blemishes. They will hear behind the turmoil of political history the voices of Solon and Socrates, of Plato and Euripides, of Pheidias and Praxiteles, of Epicurus and Archimedes; they will be grateful for the existence of such men, and will seek their company across alien centuries. They will think of Greece as the bright morning of that Western civilization which, with all its kindred faults, is our nourishment and our life.

A Detailed Chronology of Ancient Greek Civilization

B.C.

ca. 3000–ca. 1100
Greece's Bronze Age, in which people use tools and weapons made of bronze.

ca. 2200–ca. 1700
The so-called First Palace Period on the island of Crete, where a non-Greek-speaking people modern historians call the Minoans establish Europe's first high civilization.

ca. 2000 (or possibly somewhat later)
Tribal peoples speaking an early form of Greek begin entering the Greek peninsula from the east or northeast; their descendants, whom scholars refer to as Mycenaeans, spread across mainland Greece.

ca. 1500–ca. 1400
Mycenaean warlords overthrow Minoan control of Crete and other southern Aegean islands.

ca. 1250–1200
Traditional date for the Trojan War, likely a large-scale Mycenaean raiding expedition, which will later be memorialized in the epic poem, the *Iliad,* by the legendary bard Homer.

ca. 1200–ca. 1100 (or possibly somewhat later)
For reasons still unclear, the Mycenaean kingdoms and fortresses suffer widespread destruction and rapidly decline.

ca. 1150–ca. 1000

Perhaps taking advantage of the ongoing demise of Mycenaean civilization, intermittent waves of Dorians, a warlike and culturally backward Greek-speaking people, migrate into Greece from the north.

ca. 1100–ca. 800

Greece's Dark Age, in which poverty and illiteracy are at first widespread and about which modern scholars know very little.

ca. 1050–ca. 950

Large numbers of mainland Greeks migrate to the coasts and islands of western Asia Minor (or Anatolia), an area that becomes known as Greek Ionia; iron weapons and tools spread throughout Greece.

ca. 850–750

The most likely period in which Homer lived and composed the *Iliad* and the *Odyssey.*

ca. 800–ca. 500

Greece's Archaic Age, characterized by the rise of city-states, the return of prosperity and literacy, rapid population growth, and intensive colonization of the Mediterranean and Black sea regions.

776

Traditional date for the first Olympic Games, held at Olympia, in the north-western Peloponnesus.

753

Traditional date for the founding of Rome, in west-central Italy, which will one day become master over the Greek lands.

ca. 750–ca. 700

The Greeks become literate again, this time employing an alphabet largely borrowed from the Phoenicians; the Homeric poems are possibly committed to writing.

733

The city of Corinth establishes colonies on the island of Corcyra (off Greece's western coast) and at Syracuse (on Sicily).

ca. 730–ca. 710

Sparta conquers the region of Messenia, in the southwestern Peloponnesus, which it will brutally exploit for centuries to come.

ca. 700

Sparta founds the city of Taras (Tarentum in Latin) in southern Italy; the poet Hesiod writes his *Theogony,* about the creation of the world and the gods, and his almanac-like *Works and Days.*

ca. 640–ca. 630

The Spartans put down a large rebellion of Messenian helots (serfs) in the so-called Second Messenian War.

ca. 632

An Athenian leader named Cylon tries but fails to make himself tyrant in Athens.

ca. 630

Birth of the Athenian lawgiver Solon, the first Greek political figure whose writings have survived; birth of the female poet Sappho, on the Aegean island of Lesbos.

625

Periander becomes tyrant of Corinth.

ca. 620

An Athenian named Draco (or Dracon) creates a law code for his city, but most citizens soon view it as too harsh.

ca. 600

The Ionian city of Phocaea establishes a colony at Massalia, in what is now southern France.

594

The Athenians make Solon archon (administrator), charging him with the task of revising Athens's social and political system.

ca. 575

Thales, a resident of the Greek city of Miletus, establishes the Ionian philosophical-scientific school; he proposes that nature's underlying physical substance is water.

566

Oral recitations of the Homeric epics become part of Athens's sacred religious festival, the Panathenaea (dedicated to the city's patron goddess, Athena), which itself undergoes a major reorganization.

561

Solon's kinsman, Pisistratus, becomes Tyrant of Athens.

ca. 559

Cyrus II, "the Great," founds the Persian Empire (centered in what is now Iran), whose rulers, interests, and conquests will consistently affect Greek history and affairs.

ca. 550–530

In Athens, Pisistratus commissions a group of scholars to commit the Homeric epics to writing (or perhaps to edit already existing written texts).

546–540

The Persians move into western Asia Minor and conquer the Ionian Greek cities.

534

Athens establishes the City Dionysia, a festival which features dramatic competitions; Thespis, traditionally credited as the world's first formal playwright and actor, wins.

ca. 530

The philosopher-scientist Pythagoras and his followers establish a school of learning at Crotona, in southern Italy; the Pythagoreans suggest that numbers and mathematical relationships underlie nature's structure.

527

Death of Pisistratus; his sons, Hippias and Hipparchus, inherit his rule in Athens.

521

Darius I becomes king of Persia.

514

In Athens, Hipparchus is assassinated during the Panathenaic Festival.

510

The Athenians expel the last Pisistratid, Hippias, who takes refuge at the Persian court.

508

Building on Solon's reforms, an aristocrat named Cleisthenes and his supporters transform Athens's government into the world's first democracy.

ca. 500–428

Life of the philosopher-scientist Anaxagoras, who proposes that the "seeds" of everything are contained in all substances.

ca. 500–323

Greece's Classic (or Classical) Age, in which Greek arts, architecture, literature, and democratic reforms reach their height.

499

The Ionians rebel against their Persian overlords and the following year burn the Persians' local provincial capital of Sardis.

494

The Persians defeat a united Ionian navy at Lade (near Miletus, Ionia's leading city); Miletus is destroyed, its population is sold into slavery, and the Ionian revolt collapses.

493

In Athens, the democratic politician Themistocles becomes archon (administrator) and begins fortifying Athens's new port town, Piraeus.

490

Darius sends an expedition to sack Athens and a neighboring city, Eretria; Eretria falls, but soon afterwards (in September) the Athenians, aided by their allies, the Plataeans, decisively defeat the invaders at Marathon, northeast of Athens.

488–487

Athens and the nearby island state of Aegina clash over trade disputes.

486

Death of Darius I; he is succeeded by his son Xerxes, who soon begins contemplating a second invasion of Greece.

483

The Athenians discover large deposits of silver in southern Attica; soon afterwards, Themistocles convinces his countrymen to use the newfound wealth to build a large fleet of warships.

480

Xerxes launches a massive invasion of Greece; a small force of Greeks (commanded by the Spartan king, Leonidas) holds the pass of Thermopylae, in central Greece, until they are wiped out; Themistocles engineers a major naval victory over the Persians at Salamis, southwest of Athens.

479

Greeks from many different city-states converge on and annihilate the Persian land army at Plataea; the Greeks are also victorious at Mycale, in Ionia.

478

Establishment of the Delian League, an alliance of over a hundred city-states, designed to protect Greece from further Persian incursions; Athens, with by far the largest fleet in Greece, assumes leadership.

ca. 476

The poet Pindar composes the first of many odes glorifying winners at the major panhellenic (all-Greek) athletic games.

472

The Athenian playwright Aeschylus produces his play *The Persians,* which recounts the recent Greek naval victory at Salamis.

ca. 471

Themistocles is ostracized (voted out of power and banished for ten years).

ca. 469

The popular Athenian statesman-general Cimon defeats the Persians on the Eurymedon River, in southern Asia Minor; the island of Naxos attempts to quit the Delian League but Cimon uses force to compel it to remain, signaling the beginning of the League's transformation into an Athenian empire.

465

In Persia, Xerxes is assassinated and soon afterward succeeded by his son Artaxerxes I.

465–463

The island of Thasos attempts but fails to break away from the Delian League.

464

Sparta is heavily damaged by a severe earthquake; taking advantage of the disaster, the helots rebel.

461

In Athens, the conservative Cimon is ostracized; after his chief democratic opponent, Ephialtes, is assassinated, another leading democrat, Pericles, becomes the city's most influential leader.

ca. 460–360

Life of the philosopher-scientist Democritus, who refines and restates the atomic theory proposed by another thinker, Leucippus, a few decades earlier.

458

In Athens, Aeschylus first produces his trilogy of plays—the Oresteia (consisting of *Agamemnon, The Libation Bearers,* and *The Eumenides*).

457

Pericles finishes construction of the Long Walls, a fortified corridor leading from Piraeus to Athens's urban center; the Athenians and Spartans clash at Tanagra, near Thebes; Athens defeats Thebes and its allies at Oenophyta, near Tanagra.

454

An Athenian expedition sent earlier to liberate Egypt from Persian rule suffers horrendous losses; Pericles transfers the enormous treasury of the Delian League from the central Aegean island of Delos to Athens, a move many Greeks condemn.

449

Athens and Persia sign the Peace of Callias, ending several decades of war between them.

447

Construction begins on a major new temple complex atop Athens's Acropolis.

446–445
Athens and Sparta conclude a peace treaty intended to last at least thirty years.

443
Athens founds a colony at Thurii, in southern Italy.

ca. 441
Sophocles writes and produces *Antigone*.

ca. 440
The island of Samos rebels against Athens; hoping to discourage other Greeks from similar enterprises, Pericles besieges and subjugates the Samians.

438
In Athens, the magnificent Parthenon temple is dedicated to Athena.

435
A civil war erupts between opposing political parties in Corcyra, a conflict that will soon draw in both Corinth and Athens and lead to a wider war.

432
Athens imposes a trade embargo on the nearby state of Megara, seen by many Greeks as a provocative act; all of Greece, now divided into two blocs, one supporting Athens, the other Sparta, braces for a major confrontation.

431
Sparta declares war on Athens, initiating the disastrous Peloponnesian War, which will engulf and exhaust almost all the city-states; the tragic playwright Euripides produces *Medea*.

430–429
A deadly plague strikes Athens, killing a large number of residents, including Pericles.

ca. 427–347
Life of the philosopher-scientist Plato, who becomes a devoted follower of the Athenian philosopher Socrates, develops a comprehensive cosmology based partly on the ideas of the Pythagoreans, and envisions a utopian society in his *Republic*.

427
The Spartans attack and destroy Athens's neighbor, Plataea.

424
The Athenians suffer a defeat at Delium, east of Thebes; in Persia, Artaxerxes dies and an ensuing power struggle produces a new king—Darius II.

423

The Athenian comic playwright Aristophanes writes *Clouds,* in which he lampoons the philosopher Socrates.

421

Following the recent deaths of the Athenian leader Cleon and Spartan leader Brasidas, Athens and Sparta conclude the Peace of Nicias; Aristophanes produces *Peace.*

ca. 420

Death of the historian Herodotus, chronicler of the Persian Wars, who will someday be called the "Father" of history.

418

The war having resumed, Sparta defeats Athens and Argos at Mantinea (in the central Peloponnesus).

415

At the urging of the controversial politician-general Alcibiades, the Athenians send a large military expedition to Sicily in hopes of conquering the Greek city of Syracuse; when the ships arrive in Sicily, Alcibiades deserts his countrymen, leaving Nicias, a far less capable general, in charge of the expedition.

413

The Athenians are disastrously defeated in Sicily; most of the survivors are condemned to slave labor in the local quarries.

411

Aristophanes writes *Lysistrata.*

410

Fighting for Athens once again, Alcibiades defeats the Spartans at Cyzicus, south of the Black Sea.

406

The Spartan general Lysander defeats an Athenian fleet at Notium (in central Ionia); Sophocles and Euripides die.

405

Lysander decisively defeats an Athenian fleet at Aegospotami, on the Hellespont, severing Athens's life-giving grain route to the Greek cities along the coasts of the Black Sea; the Spartans blockade Piraeus and besiege Athens.

404

Athens surrenders, ending the great war and initiating a Spartan hegemony (domination) of Greece; the Spartans force the Athenians to tear down the Long Walls; the city's democracy is dismantled and replaced by an oligarchic council, whose members become known as the "Thirty Tyrants"; in Persia, Darius II dies and his son Artaxerxes II ascends the throne.

401

Cyrus the Younger, brother of Artaxerxes II, rebels; Cyrus's army, which includes several thousand Greek mercenaries, is defeated at Cunaxa, near Babylon; the Greeks begin a harrowing, bloody retreat toward the Black Sea, an adventure that one of their leaders, Xenophon, will immortalize in his *Anabasis* (*March Up-Country*).

399

Trial and death in Athens of Socrates, whose "Socratic method" of inquiry will later be adapted to the fledgling discipline of science by Plato, Aristotle, and others.

395

A temporary coalition of Greek city-states, including Thebes, Athens, and Corinth, challenges Sparta, whose heavy-handed policies are universally unpopular.

394

Sparta's King Agesilaus defeats the new coalition at Coronea, in western Boeotia, ensuring Sparta's continued dominance.

392

The Greek orator Gorgias calls for the Greek city-states to unite in a war against Persia.

ca. 380s

Plato establishes the Athenian Academy, the first formal school of higher learning in ancient times.

384–322

Life of the philosopher-scientist Aristotle (to later ages the most influential of all Greek thinkers), who studies under Plato and lectures and writes on a wide variety of subjects.

382

The Spartans occupy the Cadmea (the Theban acropolis), an aggressive move most Greeks condemn.

380

The Greek orator Isocrates publishes his *Panegyricus,* advocating a united Greek anti-Persian crusade.

371

Theban general Epaminondas defeats the Spartans at Leuctra (near Thebes), forever shattering the myth of Spartan invincibility; soon afterward he leads an army into the Peloponnesus and liberates several cities dominated by Sparta, initiating a period of Theban hegemony.

ca. 370–285

Life of Theophrastus, later called the "Father" of botany, who meets and befriends Aristotle at the Academy.

362

Epaminondas dies in battle at Mantinea (in the central Peloponnesus), signaling the end of the short-lived Theban supremacy of Greece.

359

King Philip II takes charge of the disunited, culturally backward kingdom of Macedonia and soon begins to forge Europe's first national standing army.

358

In Persia, Artaxerxes II dies and is succeeded by his son, Artaxerxes III.

357

After uniting his kingdom, Philip seizes the northern Aegean port of Amphipolis.

356

Birth of Philip's son, Alexander III (who will later be called "the Great").

352

Philip defeats the Phocians, who have occupied the central Greek region of Thessaly, and then proceeds to occupy Thessaly himself.

351

Recognizing the threat Philip poses the leading city-states of southern Greece, Athens's renowned orator Demosthenes delivers the first of his *Philippics,* speeches denouncing Philip's aggressions.

346

Philip leads his troops through the pass of Thermopylae, defeats the Phocians, and seizes the sacred sanctuary at Delphi; Isocrates publishes his *Address to Philip,* calling on him to lead a united Greek force against the Persian Empire.

338

Philip and the teenaged Alexander defeat a temporary Greek alliance led by Athens and Thebes at Chaeronea (in western Boeotia); Philip forces the creation of the Congress (or League) of Corinth, a Macedonian-controlled federal union comprising most Greek states; in Persia, Artaxerxes III is murdered by one of his advisers.

336

Philip is assassinated by a disgruntled Macedonian aristocrat and Alexander ascends Macedonia's throne; in Persia, a new king, Darius III, is crowned.

335

Alexander destroys the city of Thebes for rebelling against his rule; Aristotle establishes his own school, the Lyceum, in Athens.

334

Alexander crosses the Hellespont and launches an invasion of Persia; his first victory is at the Granicus River, in northwestern Asia Minor.

333

Alexander defeats Darius III at Issus, in northern Syria.

331

After liberating Egypt from Persian control, Alexander founds the city of Alexandria, in the Nile delta; later in the year he defeats Darius again, this time at Gaugamela, in what is now Iraq; Darius flees and soon afterward dies at the hands of his own nobles.

326

Shortly after reaching India, Alexander's army defeats a large Indian army on the Hydapses River.

323

Having created the largest empire the world has yet seen, Alexander dies in the Persian capital of Babylon on June 10.

323 B.C.–30 B.C.

Greece's Hellenistic Age, in which Alexander's generals, the so-called "Successors," war among themselves and carve up his empire into several new kingdoms, which then proceed also to fight among themselves; during the second half of this period, Rome gains control of the Greek world.

321

Two of the leading Successors, Perdiccas and Craterus, are killed.

ca. 317

The playwright Menander, foremost exponent of the theatrical period known as the New Comedy, wins first prize at the dramatic festival for his play, *Dyscolus* (*The Bad-Tempered Man*).

ca. 310

One of the most powerful of the Successors, Cassander, orders the murder of Alexander's Persian wife, Roxane, and her son, Alexander IV.

307

Demetrius "the Besieger," son of Alexander's general Antigonus "the One-eyed," gains control of Athens.

306

Demetrius defeats Ptolemy (the Successor who controls Egypt), in a naval battle in Cyprus; Antigonus proclaims himself king of Alexander's former domains.

305

Other Successors, including Cassander, Lysimachus, and Seleucus, proclaim themselves kings; Demetrius lays siege to the city of Rhodes, but fails to take it.

301

Antigonus and Demetrius are decisively defeated by a coalition of the other Successors at Ipsus (in central Asia Minor); Antigonus is killed.

ca. 295–215

Life of the scholar-poet Apollonius of Rhodes, whose epic poem, the *Argonautica,* retells the classic myth of the quest for the Golden Fleece by Jason and the Argonauts.

294

After recapturing Athens, Demetrius gains temporary control of Macedonia.

287

Pyrrhus and Lysimachus wrest control of Macedonia from Demetrius.

280

Three large Greek monarchies (the Macedonian, Seleucid, and Ptolemaic kingdoms) have by now emerged from the chaos of the long wars of the Successors; the Hellenistic king Pyrrhus of Epirus crosses to southern Italy and narrowly defeats the Romans at Heraclea (near Tarentum).

ca. 280–150

Zenodotus and other Greek scholars working in Alexandria compare and edit existing and differing versions of Homer's *Iliad* and *Odyssey,* eventually creating a standardized "vulgate" version of the epics that survives, with minor changes, into modern times.

275

Having failed to make decisive headway against the Romans, Pyrrhus abandons Italy.

274–271

The First Syrian War, fought between Ptolemy II and the Seleucid monarch Antiochus I.

260–253

The Second Syrian War, waged by Ptolemy II against Antiochus II and Macedonia's Antigonus Gonatas.

241

In the western Mediterranean, the Romans, now masters of the entire Italian peninsula, defeat the maritime empire of Carthage, ending the First Punic War.

219–207

The forces of Ptolemy IV and Antiochus III grapple in the Fourth Syrian War.

218

The Second Punic War erupts between Rome and Carthage.

217

Ptolemy IV defeats Antiochus III at Raphia, in southern Palestine.

215

Macedonia's king, Philip V, forms an alliance with Carthage's gifted general Hannibal, initiating what the Romans will later call the First Macedonian War (215–205), a sub-conflict of the greater war with Carthage.

212

While capturing the Greek city of Syracuse, in Sicily, the Romans kill the brilliant mathematician and inventor, Archimedes, who had long held them at bay with his ingenious array of defensive devices.

200–197

Having recently defeated Carthage, ending the Second Punic War, Rome prosecutes and wins the Second Macedonian War against Philip V, whose phalanx is destroyed at Cynoscephalae (in eastern Thessaly).

189

The Romans defeat the Seleucid ruler Antiochus III at Magnesia, in western Asia Minor.

179

Philip V dies and is succeeded by his son Perseus.

171–168

Rome wins the Third Macedonian War against Perseus and dismantles the Macedonian Kingdom.

168

The Romans deliver an ultimatum to the Seleucid ruler Antiochus IV, in effect neutralizing him.

148

The Romans turn the former Macedonian Kingdom into a province of their growing empire.

146

A Roman general destroys the once-great Greek city of Corinth as an object lesson to any Greeks contemplating rebellion against Rome.

133

Death of Attalus III, ruler of the kingdom of Pergamum, who in his will declares Rome his heir.

ca. 130–129

The non-Greek Near Eastern kingdom of Parthia, which has been whittling away at the Seleucid realm for some time, defeats Antiochus VII, eliminating Seleucia as a major power.

69

Birth of Cleopatra VII, daughter of Ptolemy XII, ruler of the Ptolemaic Kingdom, now a third-rate power hovering precariously in Rome's orbit.

48

Aided by the Roman general Julius Caesar, one of a series of ambitious leaders who have lately vied for control of the faltering Roman Republic, Cleopatra ascends the Egyptian throne.

44

Having won a civil war and taken control of Rome, Caesar is assassinated by a group of Roman senators hoping to restore the Republic's former power and prestige.

41

Cleopatra and another powerful Roman, Caesar's former lieutenant Mark Antony, become lovers.

31

Octavian defeats Antony and Cleopatra at Actium (in western Greece); the following year, the legendary queen, last of the Hellenistic and major autonomous Greek rulers of antiquity, takes her own life.

27

The Roman Senate bestows on Octavian the title of Augustus, "the exalted one"; he is the first ruler of a new political entity—the Roman Empire—which has replaced the now-defunct Republic and will control the entire Mediterranean sphere, including Greece, for centuries to come.

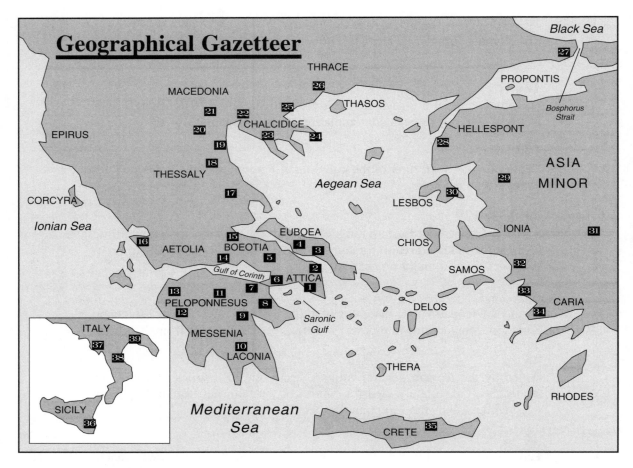

Geographical Gazetteer

1. **Athens**: The largest and most splendid Greek city-state during the Classis Age, it was famous for its Acropolis, topped by a magnificent temple complex, which is today the most popular tourist attraction in the world.

2. **Marathon**: A village and plain in northeastern Attica, where the famous Athenian victory over the Persians took place in 490 B.C.

3. **Eretria**: A prosperous city in Archaic times, it aided the Ionian rebels in their revolt against Persia; the Persians got their revenge by sacking Eretria in 490 B.C. just prior to their defeat by the Athenians at Marathon.

4. **Chalcis**: Euboea's principal city, it was known for its vigorous colonization efforts in Italy and the northern Aegean in the Archaic Age.

5. **Thebes**: The principal city of Boeotia, Thebes was supposedly the home of Oedipus and other mythical characters. Alexander the Great destroyed it in the 330s B.C. after it rebelled against his authority.

6. **Megara**: The blockade of this prosperous city by Athens in 432 B.C. was one of the major causes of the Peloponnesian War.

7. **Corinth**: An important Greek city lying just six miles west of the Isthmus of Corinth, the narrow land bridge separating the Peloponnesus from the rest of Greece, it was destroyed by the Romans in 146 B.C.

8. **Mycenae**: A small town in the hills northeast of Argos, it was originally the site of the large Bronze Age palace-stronghold of Agamemnon. Here, in the late nineteenth century, German archaeologist Heinrich Schliemann discovered ancient graves containing precious gold artifacts.

9. **Argos**: Located at the base of the Argolid, a large peninsula extending eastward into the Aegean Sea, it was the most powerful Peloponnesian city throughout most of the Archaic Age.

10. **Sparta**: The principal city of Laconia, it was long renowned for its efficient and feared land army.

11. **Mantinea**: An important city in Arcadia, the region of the central Peloponnesus, Mantinea was the site of two large battles, in 418 and 362 B.C.

12. **Olympia**: Site of the renowned panhellenic Olympic Games, held every four years beginning (according to tradition) in 776 B.C., Olympia was covered over by mud and other debris and lost until rediscovered in modern times.

13. **Elis**: A region and also a city-state, it played host to the renowned ancient Olympic festival and games.

14. **Delphi**: The site of Apollo's famous temple and oracle, a priestess who supposedly foretold future events, it rests on a rugged hillside overlooking a splendid vista of the foothills of nearby Mt. Parnassus.

15. **Thermopylae**: The "Hot Gates"; this narrow pass was the site of the heroic last stand of the "300 Spartans" against the Persians in 480 B.C.

16. **Actium**: This sandy promontory at the mouth of the Gulf of Ambracia was the site of the famous naval victory of Octavian over Antony and Cleopatra in 31 B.C.

17. **Pherae**: This Thessalian city was the home of the tyrant Jason, who took control of most of Thessaly ca.378 B.C.

18. **Mt. Olympus**: A range of peaks rising to 9,570 feet (the highest point in Greece), it was traditionally said to be the home of the gods. It is plainly visible from the harbor of Thessaloniki, many miles to the north.

19. **Pydna**: A city on the western shore of the Thermaic Gulf, it was the scene of the Roman defeat of the Hellenistic Macedonian monarch Perseus in 168 B.C.

20. **Aegae**: The early capital of Macedonia, this town remained the burial site of its kings even after Pella became the capital. Today the site is occupied by the village of Vergina, where archaeologists have excavated several Macedonian royal tombs, including what is probably that of King Philip II, father of Alexander the Great.

21. **Pella**: Macedonia's capital beginning in the late fifth century B.C., it was long the main headquarters of the Macedonian royal court.

22. **Thessaloniki** (or Thessalonica, or Salonica): A Macedonian port city founded ca. 316 B.C. by Cassander at the head of the Thermaic Gulf; today it is Greece's second-largest city.

23. **Olynthus**: A major, very prosperous city of the Chalcidic Peninsula, it was destroyed by Macedonia's Philip II in 348 B.C.

24. **Mt. Athos**: A 6,667-foot peak rising from the end of the easternmost of the three promontories of the Chalcidic Peninsula, it overlooked a patch of sea often wracked by storms that sent many ships to watery graves.

25. **Amphipolis**: Athens and Macedonia fought over this important commercial city in the fourth century B.C.

26. **Abdera**: Often the butt of jokes about its cultural backwardness, this city was actually the home town of the noted philosophers Democritus and Protagoras.

27. **Byzantium**: A key middleman for trade between the Black and Aegean seas, the city later became the site of the Roman metropolis of Constantinople; today, it is Istanbul, the chief city of modern Turkey.

28. **Troy** (or Ilium): In the Bronze Age, an independent trading city probably sacked by the Mycenaean Greeks; this event became the basis for Homer's great epic poem, the *Iliad*.

29. **Pergamum** (or Pergamon): The capital of the Hellenistic kingdom of the same name, ruled by the Attalid dynasty, it was known for its magnificent Altar of Zeus, widely seen as the greatest example of Hellenistic architecture and sculpture.

30. **Mytilene**: The principal city on the island of Lesbos, it was the birthplace of the early lyric poet Alcaeus.

31. **Sardis** (or Sardes): Long a Persian provincial capital, it was attacked by the Ionian rebels (aided by the Athenians) in the 490s B.C.; as revenge, Persia's King Xerxes burned parts of Athens ten years later.

32. **Ephesus**: An important Greek Ionian city, it was the site of the enormous Temple of Artemis that was eventually dubbed one of the seven wonders of the ancient world.

33. **Miletus**: The leading city of Greek Ionia, it was sacked by the Persians in 494 B.C. as a punishment for its part in the Ionian rebellion against Persia.

34. **Halicarnassus**: An important Greek city on the coast of Caria, it was the birthplace of Herodotus, the fifth-century B.C. Greek historian later called the "Father" of history.

35. **Knossos** (or Cnossus): The site of the most splendid of the Bronze Age Minoan palaces, today it is one of the most popular tourist attractions in Europe.

36. **Syracuse**: Long the most powerful Greek city in Sicily, it was the home of the brilliant Greek inventor Archimedes, who led its defense against besieging Romans in the late third century B.C.

37. **Elea**: Home of the Eleatic school of thought founded by the Greek philosopher Parmenides.

38. **Sybaris** (later Thurii): Renowned for its wealth, Sybaris was destroyed in the late sixth century B.C.; later, Athens founded the prosperous colony of Thurii near its site.

39. **Taras** (or Tarentum): Threatened by Rome, it requested aid from the Hellenistic adventurer Pyrrhus I of Epirus.

Prominent People, Places, and Gods

Achilles   In Greek legend, a major Greek hero of the Trojan War and the central figure in Homer's *Iliad*. Achilles quarreled with the leader of the Greek forces, Agamemnon, fought and killed the Trojan champion Hector, and died when an arrow shot by Troy's Prince Paris struck his heel, his body's only vulnerable spot.

Aeschines   (ca. 397–ca. 322 B.C.) One of the major Attic orators, Aeschines (ES-ki-neez) was the chief rival of the great Demosthenes. On several occasions the Athenian Assembly sent Aeschines to negotiate with the Macedonian conqueror Philip II. Circa 346 and 343, Demosthenes prosecuted Aeschines, supposedly for taking bribes from Philip; but Aeschines defended himself in his orations *Against Timarchus* and *On the False Embassy* and won acquittal. Aeschines' third surviving speech is *Against Ctesiphon,* in which he attacked Demosthenes and provoked the latter's magnificent rebuttal, *On the Crown,* which won Demosthenes acquittal and humiliated Aeschines. Soon afterward, the latter left Athens and settled on the island of Rhodes. See **Demosthenes**.

Aeschylus   (ca. 525–456 B.C.) One of the four masters of fifth-century B.C. Athenian drama and the world's first great playwright, Aeschylus was born at Eleusis (west of Athens) of a well-to-do family. He fought in the battle of Marathon in 490, where his brother, Cynegirus, was one of the 192 Athenian casualties. He also fought in the naval battle at Salamis a decade later, which he describes vividly in his play the *Persians,* produced in 472. This is the only one of his seven surviving plays (out of the eighty to ninety he is said to have written) that deals with non-mythological events. Of the other six extant works, of special note is the *Oresteia,* a trilogy comprising *Agamemnon,* the *Choephoroe (Libation Bearers),* and *The Eumenides,* dealing with the terrible curse of the House of Atreus. Besides the innovation of the trilogy, Aeschylus introduced the second actor, thereby expanding the story-telling possibilities of drama. His writing, rich in metaphors and striking imagery, has frequently been cited for its "grandeur."

Aesop   (early sixth century B.C.) A semi-legendary figure, Aesop was supposedly a Thracian slave who lived on the island of Samos and authored numerous fables, each with a moral. Among the most famous is the tale of the race between the tortoise and the hare, which the tortoise wins.

Agamemnon   In Greek mythology, king of Mycenae (a Bronze Age citadel and kingdom), brother of Menelaus (king of Sparta), and overall commander of the Greek expedition to Troy. As told in Homer's *Iliad,* it was Agamemnon's quarrel with the warrior Achilles that caused the latter to withdraw from the fighting, with serious consequences. Earlier, Agamemnon had sacrificed his own daughter, Iphigenia, to appease the goddess Artemis and thereby obtain favorable winds for the journey to Troy. In retaliation for this pitiless act, his wife, Clytemnestra, and her lover murdered Agamemnon when he returned from Troy. The fateful homecoming is the subject of Aeschylus's *Agamemnon,* the first play in the monumental *Oresteia* trilogy.

Agathon   (ca. 445–ca. 400 B.C.) A renowned Athenian tragic dramatist, Agathon was supposedly the first to write a play with imaginary characters and story, rather than relying on mythology or history. About 407, he left Athens and settled at the Macedonian court (where Euripides had gone a year earlier) and died there a few years later. Fewer than forty lines of Agathon's writings survive. He appears as a character in Plato's dialogue the *Symposium,* and the comic playwright Aristophanes mentions him in *Women Celebrating the Thesmophoria* (411) and *Frogs* (405).

Agesilaus II   (ca. 444–360 B.C.) A noteworthy Spartan king who took the throne in 399 and oversaw most of the Spartan hegemony of Greece following Athens's defeat at the conclusion of the Peloponnesian War. Agesilaus led an army against the Persians in Asia in 396–395 but had to return to Greece in 394 to meet the challenge of an anti-Spartan coalition of Athenians, Boeotians, Corinthians, and others. He won a narrow victory and retired to Sparta, but later helped engineer bully tactics against Thebes and other states. After Thebes defeated Sparta (371) and gained the hegemony, Agesilaus led an expedition to Egypt to fight the Persians once more, but died on the return voyage.

Ajax   A mythical hero, king of the island of Salamis in the Age of Heroes, and one of the Greek chieftains who besieged Troy in Homer's *Iliad,* he was a huge man known for his strength and courage. At Troy, after Achilles' death, Ajax lost the dispute over Achilles' armor to Odysseus and thereafter killed himself. This story is the subject of Sophocles' great play *Ajax.*

Alcaeus   (early sixth century B.C.) Hailing from Mytilene (on the island of Lesbos), he was a highly regarded lyric poet. Of his many political poems, love songs, drinking songs, and religious hymns, a few survive complete, along with a considerable number of fragments of others. His works exerted a strong influence on later ancient poets, most notably the Roman Horace.

Alcibiades   The most notorious of all Greek traitors and one of the most talented and flamboyant political leaders of the Classic Age, Alcibiades was born about 450 B.C. into a wealthy Athenian family. When his father died in battle in 447, the greatest statesman of the day, Pericles, took him in and raised him. Alcibiades grew into a handsome and brilliant but spoiled and unprincipled young man. For a while he was a follower of the philosopher Socrates, who saved his life in battle in 432.

Despite Socrates' positive influence, as a politician and elected general Alcibiades proved arrogant, ambitious, and unscrupulous. Seeking personal glory, in 420 he managed to derail the peace agreement that had momentarily halted the disastrous Peloponnesian War between Athens and Sparta; and in 415, he convinced the Athenian Assembly to authorize a huge invasion force to conquer the Sicilian Greek city of Syracuse. On route to Syracuse he was ordered to return to Athens to stand trial on charges that he had defaced some religious statues; but he deserted his country and fled to Sparta. The expedition subsequently failed, at the cost of thousands of Athenian lives.

In time, the fickle Athenians forgave Alcibiades. Once more elected general, he defeated the Spartans in a naval battle at Cyzicus (on the Propontis) in 410. However, he turned traitor again in 406 and this time took refuge with a Persian governor in Asia Minor. At the request of the Spartans, his host had him killed in 404, the same year Athens lost the great war, in part because of Alcibiades' irresponsible, self-serving actions.

Alcman   (late seventh century B.C.) A talented lyric poet of Sparta (who may have come originally from Asia Minor), he wrote mainly choral works for religious festivals. His poems were published in later antiquity in six books; but these are lost, except for a few fragments and quotations in the works of other writers.

Alexander III, "the Great"   The son of the Macedonian king Philip II, Alexander, who was destined to carve out the largest empire the world had seen up to that time, was born in 356 B.C. at Pella, Macedonia's capital. The young Alexander probably never doubted that he was destined to change the established order, for he was obsessed with predestination, believing that certain special humans were fated by the gods to achieve great deeds and everlasting fame. And apparently he saw himself as semi-divine, like the ancient Achilles (the central figure of Homer's *Iliad*), whom he idolized and likened himself to. According to the second-century A.D. Greek historian Arrian, whose history is the principal surviving source about Alexander's campaigns, Alexander told his soldiers: "Those who endure hardship and danger are the ones who achieve glory; and the most gratifying thing is to live with courage and to die leaving behind eternal renown." (*Anabasis Alexandri* 5.26) As evidenced by the enormous reputation he earned, both in life and in death, Alexander managed to transform this lofty ideal into reality.

As a royal prince growing up in the turbulent years when his father was extending Macedonian power throughout northern Greece, Alexander was naturally eager to accompany his father on his campaigns. At first Philip forbade this. He hired the famous philosopher-scholar Aristotle to tutor the boy for three years beginning in 343, teaching him political science, ethics, and literature. In 338, when Alexander was eighteen, Philip finally gave him his chance, placing him in charge of the Macedonian cavalry at Chaeronea, where they defeated the Greek allies and initiated a Macedonian hegemony of Greece. Two years later, when Philip was assassinated, the young prince suddenly found himself captain-general of the new Greek confederacy Philip had forged.

In 334 B.C., Alexander initiated the great military campaigns that subsequently brought all the lands stretching from Greece to India under his authority. His success was due partly to his brilliance as a military strategist and tactician, and partly to the formidable army he had at his disposal. "Alexander's greatest asset," historian J.F.C. Fuller suggests, "was the army he inherited from his father; without it, in spite of his genius, his conquests would be inconceivable—it was an instrument exactly suited to his craft." (*The Generalship of Alexander the Great,* p. 292) Whether or not he was a more gifted general than his father is a matter of academic debate. What is certain is that he defeated the Persian king Darius III at Issus (in Syria) in 333; marched southward and besieged

Alexander, pictured in this idealized likeness, swiftly conquered all of the lands stretching from Greece to India.

and captured the island city of Tyre; liberated Egypt from Persian rule in 332; established the city of Alexandria there the following year; immediately turned northeastward, defeated Darius again, and occupied the three Persian capitals—Babylon, Susa, and Persepolis; and then continued eastward, eventually reaching India, where he defeated a large Indian army in 326. But when his exhausted troops mutinied and demanded that he turn back, it proved to be the end of the road for Alexander. Shortly after returning to Persia, he died, possibly of malaria, in Babylon on June 10, 323, at age thirty-three.

Alexandria   The most prosperous city of the Greek world in the Hellenistic Age and long afterward, Alexander the Great founded it in the Nile Delta in 331 B.C. Under the Ptolemies (the ruling family established by Alexander's general Ptolemy), the city was not only a bustling commercial center, but also a celebrated cultural center, featuring the world's largest library and an adjoining research center, the Museum, where some of the greatest ancient scientists, including Euclid and Eratosthenes, worked. At the mouth of the harbor, on the island of Pharos, stood the more than 400-

foot-tall lighthouse that became famous as one of the seven wonders of the ancient world. After Cleopatra's death, in 30 B.C., Alexandria fell under Roman control and long remained the Roman Empire's most important city next to Rome itself.

Amazons   A legendary race or nation of warrior women frequently portrayed in Greek literature and art. They were thought to have lived in the Age of Heroes, their homeland was placed in various parts of Asia, and they were usually pictured on horseback. Homer mentions them in the *Iliad* and they appear in the myths of Theseus, Heracles, and numerous other heroes. The Greeks called battles between themselves and the warrior women Amazonomachy.

Anaxagoras   (ca. 500–ca. 428 B.C.) A noted teacher, early philosopher, and friend of the Athenian statesman Pericles, Anaxagoras was born in Ionia but lived in Athens for about thirty years, probably beginning circa 480. Attempting to tarnish Pericles' reputation, the politician's enemies charged Anaxagoras with impiety, but he fled and spent the rest of his life at Lampsacus, near the Hellespont. His chief philosophical-scientific thesis was that manifestations of all elements are present in all things. He noticed that when people eat food, they grow flesh, bones, and hair and concluded that the "seeds" of flesh, bones, and hair must be present in the food when it is eaten.

Anaximander   (early sixth century B.C.) An early philosopher-scientist, he was the best-known pupil of Thales, founder of the Ionian school of thought. Anaximander disagreed with his mentor that water is nature's underlying principle (*physis*), postulating instead an invisible, eternal substance, the "Boundless." He suggested that earth, water, air, and fire had sprung from the Boundless and that the sun, moon, and stars had been formed by rings of fire spinning in the heavens. See **Thales**.

Anaximenes   (mid–sixth century B.C.) A pupil of Anaximander, of the Ionian school of thought, the philosopher-scientist Anaximenes rejected his teacher's idea of the "Boundless" as nature's underlying substance. Instead, said Anaximenes, air is the *physis*. In this view, rarefying (thinning) air generates fire, while condensing (thickening) air produces water (which, when condensed, produces earth). Anaximenes was also noted for conducting crude experiments to test his theories.

Antigone   The mythical heroine of Sophocles' classic tragedy of the same name (produced ca. 441 B.C.), Antigone (an-TIG-uh-nee) was a Theban princess, the daughter of Oedipus. Defying the order given by Thebes' ruler, Creon, she buried the body of her brother, Polynices, who had led a failed attempt to capture the city. Creon condemned her to death, later changed his mind, but arrived too late to save her. Another play about Antigone, by Sophocles' colleague Euripides, has not survived.

Antigonus I   (ca. 382–301 B.C.) One of the Successors of Alexander the Great, Antigonus Monophthalmos (the "One-eyed) came from a noble Macedonian family and served with distinction during Alexander's conquests. Following Alexander's death in 323, Antigonus, later aided by his ambitious son, Demetrius, attempted to gain control of Alexander's former empire and proclaimed himself king in 306. But the father and son were soundly defeated by a coalition of the other Successors at Ipsus in 301, where Antigonus was killed at about the age of eighty. See **Demetrius Poliorcetes, Eumenes, Seleucus.**

Antigonus II Gonatas   (ca. 320–239 B.C.) Son of Demetrius I and grandson of Antigonus I, he assumed the title of King of Macedonia after Demetrius's death in 283. But the younger Antigonus did not gain actual control of the kingdom until 277, when he decisively defeated an invading force of Gauls. That year he established the Antigonid dynasty, which thereafter controlled the realm, one of the three great Hellenistic kingdoms, for more than a century.

Antiochus III   (ca. 242–187 B.C.) A ruler of the Hellenistic Seleucid Kingdom, he took the throne following the death of his brother, Seleucus III, in 223. Antiochus III became known as "the Great" because he managed to regain several Seleucid territories lost by his immediate predecessors. Between 212 and 206 he conquered Armenia and Parthia and reached India. But when he invaded Greece in 192, the Romans, who had recently made inroads there, saw him as a threat. They defeated him at Magnesia (in Asia Minor) in 189, marking the effective end of Seleucid power. Antiochus met an ignoble end when he was killed while robbing a temple.

Antipater   (397–319 B.C.) One of the Successors of Alexander the Great, he first rose to prominence as a general under Alexander's father, Philip II. When Alexander was away conquering Persia (334–323), Antipater governed Macedonia and Greece; and following Alexander's death, he put down an uprising by Athens and other Greek states (the Lamian War, 323–322). Antipater's death in 319 left a power vacuum that other ambitious Successors quickly rushed to fill, hastening the disintegration of Alexander's empire.

Antiphon   (ca. 480–411 B.C.) A noted Attic orator who seldom spoke in public, his literary fame rests on the speeches he wrote for court litigants; three of these speeches have survived. Antiphon also led the oligarchic takeover of Athens's government by the "Four Hundred" in 411. After the coup collapsed, he was condemned to death, despite his delivery of a moving speech in his own defense.

Aphrodite   Goddess of love and beauty, she was born out of the sea foam (an image captured in numerous artistic representations). Though married to the god Hephaestos, she loved the war god Ares. Among her many symbols were dolphins, rams, doves, and roses.

Apollo   The versatile god of the sun, healing, truth, poetry, and music, he was the twin brother of the goddess Artemis. After slaying the serpent Python, he took charge of the shrine at Delphi, which housed his world-renowned oracle. His symbol was the laurel tree.

Apollonius Rhodius (of Rhodes)   (ca. 295–215 B.C.) A poet and scholar who served as the director of the Great Library at Alexandria before retiring to the island of Rhodes, Apollonius is most noted for his epic poem, *Argonautica* (*Voyage of the Argo*). This major telling of the story of Jason's quest for the fabulous Golden Fleece and his relationship with the sorceress Medea had a strong influence on later writers, in part because it was the first classical work to portray romantic love from a woman's point of view. See **Callimachus, Jason, Medea.**

Arcadia   See **Peloponnesus.**

Archidamus II   (mid–fifth century B.C.) A noted Spartan king (reigned ca. 476– ca. 426), he fought against the rebellious Spartan serfs (helots) after an earthquake leveled Sparta in 464 B.C. Later, he urged his countrymen not to initiate the Peloponnesian War against Athens, but when they did, he served with distinction, invading Attica three times and besieging Athens's ally, Plataea.

Archilochus   (mid–fifth century B.C.) Little is known about the life of this early poet, who was born on the Cycladic island of Paros and took part in the colonization of the northern Aegean island of Thasos. His poems survive only in quotations by later writers and in a few papyrus fragments. They are written in a variety of meters, range in tone from deep melancholy to sparkling wittiness, and often reveal his personal feelings, even when they are less than noble; in one famous verse, for example, he freely admits that he is no hero, having tossed his shield away in the midst of battle in order save his skin.

Archimedes   (ca. 287–212 B.C.) A noted Greek astronomer, inventor, and the greatest mathematician of antiquity, he was born in Syracuse (in Sicily) and likely studied at the Museum in Alexandria before returning to his native land and taking up residence at the court of the city's tyrant, Hiero II. In *On the Sphere and the Cylinder,* Archimedes showed that the volumes of a cylinder and sphere are in a ratio of 3:2. He also discovered the principle of specific gravity (by showing how objects of different densities displace different amounts of water); and in his *Sand-Reckoner,* he presented a system for expressing very large numbers. In addition, he produced numerous ingenious inventions, including "Archimedes' screw," a device for lifting water from one level to another, which is still used in some parts of the world; and an array of defensive and offensive weapons that were employed against the Romans, who attacked Syracuse from 214 to 212. It was during the final stage of this siege that a Roman soldier killed Archimedes, to the dismay of the Roman commander, Marcellus, who wanted the great scientist to work for Rome.

Ares   God of war and lover of the goddess Aphrodite, his symbols were a burning torch, a spear, dogs, and vultures.

Argonauts   See **Jason, Medea.**

Argos   A major Greek city, located in the northeastern Peloponnesus near the neck of the peninsula commonly called the Argolid. The region surrounding the town of Argos was the site of the Bronze Age citadels of Mycenae and Tiryns (situated a few miles to the north and southeast of Argos, respectively). In Homer's *Iliad,* Argos was ruled by the Greek hero Diomedes, who gave his allegiance to Agamemnon, king of Mycenae. (Mycenae and Argos are often used interchangeably in Greek mythology, so it is likely that after Mycenae was destroyed at the end of the Bronze Age, the focus of power in the region switched to Argos.) In the Dark Age, perhaps about 1000 B.C., Argos began its rise to the status of most powerful and influential city in the Peloponnesus, reaching its height under King Pheidon in the mid-seventh century B.C. But very soon afterward Sparta and Corinth rose to prominence and Argos quickly became a third-rate power, a fact brutally confirmed by its decisive defeat by Sparta in 494. After almost three more centuries, during which the Argives were allied to or dominated variously by Athens, Thebes, Sparta, and Macedonia, they joined the Achaean League in 229. Then, when Rome dismantled the League in 146 B.C., Argos became part of the Roman province of Macedonia.

Aristagoras   (died 497 B.C.) The ruler of the Ionian city of Miletus, he largely engineered the Ionian rebellion against the Persians in 499 B.C., managing to acquire military aid from the mainland cities of Athens and Eretria. After the revolt failed, he went to Thrace, where he died soon afterward.

Aristarchus of Samos   (early third century B.C.) A Hellenistic astronomer who advanced the then bold (and ultimately correct) theory that the earth revolves around the sun and rotates on its own axis. Most of his treatises have not survived and we know about his ideas because the mathematician Archimedes mentions them in his *Sand-Reckoner.* Unfortunately, other ancient scholars rejected the notion of a sun-centered cosmos, preferring the earth-centered view because it did not violate ancient tradition or religious belief and conformed to the movements of the sun, moon, and planets as they appeared to direct observation.

Aristarchus of Samothrace   (ca. 215–ca. 143 B.C.) A noted Hellenistic scholar who worked in Alexandria and briefly headed the Great Library there. He is usually credited with being the first professional literary scholar, composing works of astute critical commentary on Hesiod, Pindar, the great Athenian dramatists, and other noted past authors. He was known especially for his critical study of Homer's epics.

Aristides   (died ca. 467 B.C.) A noted Athenian politician, he served as one of the ten *strategoi* (generals) at the battle of Marathon in 490. Soon afterward he became a leading political rival of the controversial Themistocles and as a result suffered ostracism in 482; however, the state recalled Aristides in 480 during the crisis of the second Persian invasion, during which he served with distinction once again.

Aristophanes   (ca. 445–ca. 385 B.C.) One of the four masters of fifth-century B.C. Athenian drama and the greatest comic playwright of the age, almost nothing is known about his personal life. Of the forty-four plays attributed to him, eleven survive complete and some fragments of a few others exist. Among the most famous and humorous of the extant plays are *Clouds* (produced in 423), in which he lampoons the sophists and their new brand of education, as well as the eccentric philosopher Socrates; and *Lysistrata* (411), an antiwar piece in which the Athenian women stage a sex strike to persuade their husbands to make peace. Aristophanes' plays, which mark the height of the Athenian Old Comedy (roughly encompassing the second half of the fifth century), are fanciful, witty, bitingly satiric, and frequently poke fun at the government and leading politicians and military leaders.

Aristotle   No person of the ancient world had a greater impact on the subsequent development of philosophy, science, and knowledge in general than Aristotle. His interests and researches were phenomenally wide-ranging; he made detailed, logical, and sometimes profound written observations in every major branch of learning; and his ideas, as well as his efforts to collect and systematize knowledge, had a profound influence on scholars in the Renaissance and early modern era.

Aristotle was born in 384 B.C. at Stagirus (on the Chalcidic peninsula), the son of Nicomachus, physician to King Amyntas II of Macedonia. From his father, Aristotle learned a great deal about the natural sciences, including biology, and perhaps also about the theory and practice of medicine. In 367 B.C., at age seventeen, Aristotle journeyed to Athens and enrolled at Plato's Academy, where the young man lived and studied for the next twenty years. When Plato died in 347, Aristotle left Athens, settled for a time in northwestern Asia Minor, and then moved to the island of Lesbos. In 343, King Philip II asked Aristotle to come to Macedonia to tutor the crown prince, Alexander. The philosopher took the job and stayed there until 336, when Philip was assassinated and Alexander ascended the throne. Aristotle then returned to Athens, where he soon established his own school, the Lyceum.

Regularly utilizing the Lyceum's steadily growing library and zoo, in the next twelve years Aristotle produced the bulk of his important writings. Of these, almost all that were published for public consumption are lost. The large corpus of Aristotle's surviving works consists mainly of his notes, rough drafts of his lectures, and notations made of his lectures by his students. Though dry and formal, these works have served the vital function of transmitting his main ideas to later ages.

Of Aristotle's principal scientific ideas, among the most important are those dealing with cosmology. He agreed with his philosophic predecessors that all matter was composed of the basic elements of earth, water, air, and fire; but he maintained that these were imperfect and changeable and therefore only existed on earth and its immediate vicinity. By contrast, he held, the heavens were composed of a special, incorruptible fifth element—the "ether." Also like his predecessors, he advocated that the earth rests at the center of the universe and is a sphere. From a purely scientific standpoint, his work in biology was far superior to his efforts in astronomy. He collected literally thousands of observations and specimens, fueling his pioneering studies in nearly all the main branches of biologic inquiry. For this reason, modern science historians generally recognize him as the "Father" of biology. He also conceived a general procedure of scientific research that was in some ways an ancient precursor of the modern scientific method, although he often failed to back it up with experimentation.

Aristotle's studies of politics, ethics, logic, and other related topics were also significant. For example, his *Politics,* like Plato's *Republic,* sketches the framework of an ideal state. He holds that humans are "political animals" and that the polis (city-state) is the best environment in which to achieve a constructive, ethical life. The state's main purpose, he concludes, is a moral one, namely to make it possible for its citizens to attain that "good" life. So after examining various kinds of government, including democracy, he advocates rule by an aristocracy of "virtuous men." He also states that slavery is a natural institution, although masters should not abuse their slaves.

When Alexander died in faraway Babylon in 323 B.C., a wave of anti-Macedonian feeling swept through Greece; and because Aristotle had been Alexander's friend and tutor, the Athenians now looked on the philosopher as an enemy of the state. They brought him to trial, forcing him to flee northward to the island of Euboea. There, a few months later (November 322), he died at the age of sixty-two. His old friend and colleague, Theophrastus, succeeded him as director of the Lyceum.

Arrian   A Romanized Greek born about A.D. 90 in the Roman province of Bithynia (in Asia Minor), Arrian (Flavius Arrianus) is renowned for his *Anabasis Alexandri (Alexander's March Up-Country),* the most complete and reliable surviving source chronicling the campaigns of Alexander the Great. Unfortunately, most of Arrian's other works, including *Events After Alexander* (in ten books), are either lost or survive only in fragments. His *Anabasis* was based largely on now-lost histories by Alexander's general Ptolemy, and by Aristobulus, an engineer under Alexander. Therefore, historians consider much of Arrian's well-written account to be reasonably accurate.

Artemis   Goddess of the moon and mistress of wild animals and hunting, she also protected young girls and pregnant women. Deer, dogs, and cypress trees were her symbols.

Asclepius   An important god of healing, this son of Apollo was worshiped throughout Greece after about 400 B.C. His symbols were the snake and staff (which survive as the symbol of the modern medical profession), and people often brought sick friends and relatives to his sanctuaries hoping he would cure them.

Aspasia   (mid-fifth century B.C.) Born in Miletus, she was mistress to the Athenian statesman Pericles from about 450 to his death in 429 and bore him a son, also named Pericles. Known for her intellect, wit, and excellent education, she was said to have influenced some of Pericles' political decisions and also to have associated with the philosopher Socrates. Inevitably she became the target of the comic playwrights, who suggested she was a prostitute, which is probably untrue. Also, in an attempt to discredit Pericles, his political enemies brought her to trial for impiety, but they were unable to obtain a conviction.

Athena   The daughter of Zeus (having sprung fully armed from his head), goddess of wisdom and war, and Athens's patron deity. Her symbols were the owl and the olive tree.

Athens   The foremost city-state of Greece in the Classic Age, located in the southwestern section of the Attic peninsula about four miles from Phaleron Bay. Athens has been continually inhabited at least since the early Bronze Age (ca. 3000 B.C.). The urban center grew up around the Acropolis, the rocky outcrop on which a series of temples and other public buildings were constructed over the course of many centuries. In Mycenaean times (late Bronze Age), Athens was largely overshadowed by other mainland cities, including Mycenae and Thebes.

But in the late Archaic Age Athens began its rise to prominence. A major milestone occurred about 508 B.C. when the Athenian political reformer Cleisthenes established the world's first democracy. And in the years that followed, Athens reached its zenith of power and achievement, assuming a leading role in the repulse of the Persians (in the battles of Marathon and Salamis); forming a naval empire (by exploiting its allies in the Delian League, the organization established to protect Greece from Persia); and, under the noted statesman Pericles, becoming Greece's premiere artistic and cultural center (home of the splendid Parthenon temple and the master playwrights Aeschylus and Sophocles). From 457 to 404, the urban center was connected, via the five-mile-long Long Walls, to its port, Piraeus. Here, ships from cities throughout the Mediterranean and Black Seas kept the city supplied with grain, timber, and thousands of varieties of trade goods, as well as eager immigrants and visitors. The fifth century also saw a growing rivalry between Athens and Sparta, which culminated in the disastrous

This is a reconstruction of Athens's Acropolis complex as it appeared at the height of its glory in the late fifth and early fourth centuries B.C.

Peloponnesian War (431–404), which drew in most of the Greek city-states.

After its defeat by Sparta (404 B.C.), Athens, like the rest of Greece, labored under Spartan domination during a period of political and military decline. The Athenians eventually began rebuilding their naval empire, but it did not attain the degree of power and influence it had in the previous century. In 338, Athens allied itself to Thebes in an attempt to halt the aggressions of Philip II of Macedonia, but he defeated both cities. Athens then underwent further decline under the Macedonian yoke and later, during the rivalry and warfare among the Hellenistic states. After the fourth century B.C., the once great city shrank into a political backwater for the rest of antiquity, although it long retained its reputation as a literary center.

Atlantis The first Greek documents mentioning the legendary sunken continent of Atlantis were Plato's dialogues, the *Timaeus* and *Critias* (mid-fourth century B.C.) Supposedly, the sixth-century B.C. Athenian lawgiver Solon heard from some Egyptian priests that in the distant past Athens had overcome the mighty maritime empire of Atlantis, after which the island had sunk into the sea. Modern scholars long assumed that Plato had fabricated the tale as a parable. But archaeological evidence suggests that the story is a garbled memory of the Minoan maritime civilization and the destruction of the island of Thera (north of Crete) by a devastating volcanic eruption circa 1600 B.C. (or perhaps a century or so later). During this upheaval, the entire central portion of Thera collapsed into the sea, generating huge seismic sea waves that pounded the Minoan settlements of northern Crete. Athens's triumph over the Atlanteans likely recalls the takeover of the Minoan sphere by the mainland Mycenaeans in the century or so following the disaster.

Attalids   The family of rulers of the Hellenistic kingdom of Pergamum (or Pergamon, in northwestern Asia Minor). The dynasty was named after Attalus, father of the local leader Philetaerus, who established it circa 282 B.C. Philetaerus was succeeded by: his nephew Eumenes I (reigned 263–241); Eumenes' own nephew Attalus I Soter ("Savior", r. 241–197); Attalus's eldest son Eumenes II (r. 197–159); another of Attalus's sons, Attalus II (r. 159–138); and a son of Eumenes II, Attalus III (r. 138–133). The Attalids were known for their patronage of the arts, and the city of Pergamum became one of the most splendid in the ancient world. The Great Altar of Zeus, erected under Eumenes II, marks the zenith of Hellenistic architecture and sculpture, and Pergamum's library was the world's second-largest. The Attalids and their kingdom prospered in large degree because they supported Rome in its battles against other Hellenistic powers; and Attalus III went so far as to will the realm to the Romans, who absorbed it on his death in 133 B.C.

Bacchylides   (early fifth century B.C.) A noted lyric poet and nephew of the poet Simonides, he hailed from the island of Ceos, but also worked in Thessaly, Macedonia, Sicily, and the Peloponnesus. His poetry survived only in fragments until the late 1800s, when some papyrus rolls bearing twenty-one complete poems were discovered. These include fifteen odes honoring victorious athletes; and indeed, he appears to have been a major rival of his contemporary, Pindar, the master in this genre. Bacchylides also wrote dithyrambs, hymns, patriotic songs, and other kinds of lyrics.

Boeotia   See **Thebes.**

Brasidas   (died 422 B.C.) A noted Spartan general during the first stage of the Peloponnesian War. He early recognized the importance of taking control of Athens's northern Aegean supply lines; and to this end he captured the Athenian colony of Amphipolis in 423. He died the following year defending the city against an unsuccessful Athenian attempt to retake it.

Cadmus   See **Thebes.**

Callimachus   (died 490 B.C.) An Athenian general who was serving as Polemarch (War Archon) when the Persians landed at Marathon. He commanded the Greek right wing in the famous battle (in September 490) and was one of the 192 Athenians killed. Their memorial burial mound is still preserved on the Marathon plain.

Callimachus   (ca. 310–ca. 240 B.C.) Born at Cyrene (in northern Africa), the poet and scholar Callimachus worked at the Great Library of Alexandria, where he compiled a catalogue of 120 of its volumes. He supposedly wrote over 800 volumes himself, although these were undoubtedly short, for he is famous for his remark, "A big book is a big evil." For that reason, he refused to write epic poetry, a genre he deemed outdated; and this provoked a major feud with his colleague, Apollonius, who championed the epic. Most of Callimachus's poetry is lost. But the few surviving pieces and fragments reveal a great talent, explaining why he exerted a strong influence on Catullus, Propertius, and other later Roman poets. See **Apollonius Rhodius**.

Cassander   (ca. 358–297 B.C.) One of the Successors of Alexander the Great, he was the eldest son of Alexander's general, Antipater. After his father's death (319), Cassander fought for and gained control of Macedonia and much of Greece. He arranged the murders of Alexander's mother (in 315), and son and wife (311), and in 305 proclaimed himself king of Macedonia. A few years after Cassander's death in 397, his kingdom fell into the hands of Antigonus Gonatas, grandson of Antigonus I. Cassander's greatest legacy was his founding of Thessaloniki (named after his wife), which today is Greece's second-largest city.

Centaurs   In Greek mythology, a race of creatures half-man and half-horse who dwelled in Thessaly. Supposedly, they attempted to carry off the women at a wedding celebration held by their neighbors, the Lapiths, but were driven away. The Greeks called this battle, which was a frequent subject of art, the Centauromachy.

Cimon   (ca. 510–ca. 450 B.C.) One of the most notable Athenian politician-generals of the fifth century B.C., Cimon was the son of Miltiades, victor of the battle of Marathon. Rising to prominence directly after the expulsion of the Persians (479), Cimon helped to organize the Delian League, designed to keep the Persians at bay (but which over time Athens transformed into its personal empire). In the next decade and a half, he was Athens's most influential leader and gained great prestige for his stunning victory over the Persians on the Eurymedon River (near Asia Minor's southern coast) circa 469–466. In domestic affairs, Cimon was conservative and pro-Spartan, putting him at odds with Themistocles, Ephialtes, and other radical democrats; and in 461 they managed to get him ostracized. Supposedly, the state recalled him before he had served his full ten years in exile. He died in 450 during an anti-Persian campaign in Cyprus.

Cleisthenes   (late sixth century B.C.) A prominent Athenian statesman-general, he is credited with spearheading the political reforms that created a full-fledged democracy, the world's first, in Athens circa 508 B.C. An aristocrat by birth, he saw the wisdom of gaining the support of the common people in his political struggles with other aristocrats, who wanted to install an oligarchy after the tyrant Hippias fled in 510 B.C. Cleisthenes' sweeping democratic reforms included dividing Attica into numerous small ward-like districts, the demes, replacing the city's four traditional tribes with ten new ones, and increasing the authority of the Assembly, in which all male citizens had a voice in choosing leaders and debating and voting on state policies. He died about 500 B.C. and received a public funeral in the Ceramicus, a cemetery just outside the city walls.

Cleon   (died 422 B.C.) An Athenian politician who rose to prominence after Pericles' death (429), for the next several years, as the Peloponnesian War raged, he was Athens's most influential leader. In 425, he and the Athenian general Demosthenes won an important victory over the Spartans at Pylos (in the southwestern Peloponnesus). Later, after Sparta's Brasidas captured Athens's colony, Amphipolis, Cleon led an expedition to retake the city, but died in the attempt. Both Thucydides (in his history of the great war) and the comic playwright Aristophanes (in his *Knights*) are critical of Cleon, portraying him as a rabble-rouser and an opportunist.

Cleopatra VII   Queen of the Egyptian Ptolemaic Kingdom and one of the most famous women in history, she was born in 69 B.C., the daughter of King Ptolemy XII Auletes. When he died in 51, his will stipulated that she should rule jointly with her ten-year-old brother, Ptolemy XIII; however, the boy and his regent soon forced her flee into the desert. She was reinstated in 48 by the Roman general Julius Caesar, with whom she had a love affair and a son (Ptolemy XV, or Caesarion). In 41, three years after Caesar's assassination, Cleopatra became the lover and ally of his former assistant, Mark Antony. In the years that followed, hoping to gain dominance in the Roman world, they engaged in a propaganda war with Caesar's adopted son, Octavian (the future emperor Augustus); but when the conflict erupted into violence at Actium (in western Greece) in 31 B.C., they went down to defeat. The following year, after Octavian had landed his forces in Egypt, the proud queen, last of the Ptolemies and also the last major independent Greek ruler in antiquity, took her own life.

Clytemnestra   See **Agamemnon.**

Conon   (ca. 444–392 B.C.) An Athenian admiral, he is noted for commanding fleets in some of the pivotal battles of the final years of the Peloponnesian War. He was the only Athenian leader who managed to sail his ships to safety during the disastrous defeat (at the hands of Sparta's Lysander) at Aegospotami in 405. Later (in the 390s), when Athens and other Greek states went to war with Sparta again, he commanded the fleet provided by Persia (Athens's temporary ally at the time) and won a decisive victory over Sparta at Cnidus (in southwestern Asia Minor) in 394.

Corinth   Located in the northern Peloponnesus near the isthmus bearing its name, Corinth was for many centuries one of the most important and powerful cities in the Greek world. Dominated by its lofty acropolis, the Acrocorinth, it often controlled communications and travel to and from central and southern Greece across the strategic isthmus. Inhabited in the

Bronze Age or earlier, Corinth rose to prominence in Archaic times, when its ceramics became popular throughout much of the Greek sphere and it established colonies (in the 700s B.C.) on the islands of Corcyra (Corfu), Ithaca, at Syracuse (on Sicily), and elsewhere. Its heyday of power and prosperity lasted from the mid-seventh to mid-sixth centuries B.C., after which Athens steadily overshadowed it commercially. A serious political dispute between Corinth and Athens over Corcyra in the late 430s led to bloodshed and proved to be one of the main causes of the Peloponnesian War (431–404). After Macedonia's Philip II conquered Greece (338 B.C.), Corinth became the meeting site of his panhellenic confederacy (the League of Corinth). Later, in Hellenistic times, the city was the capital of the Achaean League, an alliance of Peloponnesian cities; but when the Achaeans defied Rome, a Roman general destroyed Corinth in 146 B.C. as an object lesson to all Greeks.

Craterus   (ca. 370–321 B.C.) One of the Successors of Alexander the Great, he rose to prominence as a field commander in the battles of Granicus (334), Issus (333), and Gaugamela (331). Later, after Alexander's death (323), he returned to Greece to relieve another Successor, Antipater, who was bogged down fighting Greek rebels in the Lamian War. In 321, Craterus joined Antipater in a campaign against the Successor Perdiccas, but was killed in battle near the Hellespont by Perdiccas's associate, Eumenes.

Cratinus   An Athenian comic playwright of the mid-to-late fifth century B.C., who exerted a strong influence on his younger contemporary, Aristophanes. Of the 27 plays Cratinus reportedly wrote, none survive complete, although over 400 fragments have been found.

Creon (King of Corinth)   See **Medea.**

Creon (King of Thebes)   See **Antigone.**

Critias   (ca. 460–403 B.C.) An Athenian aristocrat (and second cousin to Plato), he was an avowed oligarch who disapproved of democracy. Critias took part in the unsuccessful oligarchic revolution of 411 and was later exiled; but when Sparta defeated Athens in 404, he returned, became the leader of the Thirty Tyrants, and helped to orchestrate their reign of terror. He died the following year in the civil fighting that brought the tyrants down. Partly because he had once been Critias's friend and mentor, the philosopher Socrates was tried and executed in 399 B.C. See **Plato, Socrates.**

Croesus   (mid–sixth century B.C.) Ruler of Lydia, a non-Greek kingdom in west-central Asia Minor, he subdued the Ionian Greek cities. However, he greatly admired the Greeks, allowing them considerable local autonomy; and he became a patron of Apollo's oracle at Delphi. Supposedly, it was the oracle that helped bring about his downfall. When the Persians pushed into Asia Minor, the oracle predicted that if he crossed the Halys River (in central Asia Minor), he would destroy a mighty empire. Confidently, he crossed the river and attacked; but the Persians soundly defeated him. Only then did Croesus realize that the kingdom in the prophecy was his own.

Cronus (or Cronos)   In Greek mythology, one of the male Titans. He married his sister Rhea, who gave birth to the first Olympian gods, including Zeus, Hera, Poseidon, and Demeter. Because he feared being overthrown by his children, Cronus swallowed them after they were born, but later vomited them back up. He led his Titans against Zeus's Olympians but lost. See **Titans**.

Ctesibius   (early third century B.C.) A Hellenistic mechanical wizard who worked in Alexandria, Ctesibius (t'SIB-ee-us) is best known for his invention of the simple cylinder and plunger (the basis of the piston), which was used in antiquity in pumps to raise water in mines and to aid in irrigation. He also created a hydraulic pipe organ, a musical keyboard, and an accurate water clock.

Cyclopes   In Greek mythology, the Cyclopes (singular is Cyclops) were one-eyed giants. According to Hesiod, they were sons of Uranus and aided Zeus in his war against the Titans. In Homer's *Odyssey,* a race of Cyclopes live on a distant island, where the hero and his men encounter the Cyclops Polyphemus, Poseidon's son, and blind him.

Cyrus II, "the Great"   The first and perhaps greatest ruler of Persia, he reigned from 559 to 529 B.C. He expanded the formerly tiny and insignificant Persian homeland (Fars, on the shores of the Persian Gulf) into a vast empire, in the process conquering the Greek cities of Ionia, on Asia Minor's western coast.

Cyrus II, "the Younger"   The second son of Persia's King Darius II, he served as satrap (governor) of the province of Lydia (in western Asia Minor). In 401 B.C., Cyrus led a force of Persians and Greek mercenaries against his brother, King Artaxerxes II, but died in battle. His rebellion then collapsed, leaving the Greeks stranded in the heart of Persia. See **Xenophon**.

Darius I   King of Persia from 521 to 486 B.C., he invaded Scythia and Thrace in 513–512 and put down the revolt of the Greek Ionian cities from 499 to 494. When the Athenians crushed his army at Marathon in 490, he vowed to punish Athens, but died four years later, leaving that task to his son, Xerxes.

Darius III   The last major Persian monarch, he ruled from 336 to 330 B.C. After Alexander the Great defeated him at Issus in 333 and Gaugamela in

331, he fled eastward. One of Alexander's soldiers later found Darius dying of wounds inflicted by a group of his own nobles, led by Bessus.

Delphi   A town located in the state of Phocis in central Greece, on the southern slope of Mt. Parnassus just north of the Gulf of Corinth, Delphi was the site of the famous oracle of the god Apollo. Throughout most of antiquity (beginning perhaps in the seventh century B.C.), religious pilgrims journeyed there from around the known world to ask Apollo's priestess (the Pythia) questions about future events. And from behind a screen in the temple's innermost sanctuary (the *adyton*), she gave answers that were usually riddle-like and open to various interpretations. The temple also contained a hearth, in which burned the god's "eternal fire," and the *omphalos,* the navel stone widely thought to mark the earth's geographic center. Near the temple were numerous other splendid structures, including those related to the Pythian Games, dedicated to Apollo, one of Greece's "big four" panhellenic (all-Greek) athletic competitions. The sanctuary of Delphi was administered and protected by the Delphic Amphictyony, a religious organization made up of representatives from several neighboring states.

The Persian king Darius III lies dying by the roadside after being betrayed and left for dead by his own followers.

Because of its strategic location and religious and cultural importance, Delphi was frequently the object of political ambitions and disputes. Of special note were the so-called Sacred Wars (the first in the early sixth, the second in the mid-fifth, and the third in the mid-fourth centuries B.C.). For example, the Third Sacred War began when the Phocians seized the sanctuary and the Amphictyony responded by declaring war on Phocis. The fighting was indecisive until Macedonia's Philip II intervened against Phocis and usurped its place in the Amphictyony. The last Delphic oracles were delivered in A.D. 391, the year the Roman emperor Theodosius, pressured by Christian leaders, closed the temple, along with all other pagan places of worship in the Greco-Roman world.

Demeter   Goddess of plants, especially grain crops, she oversaw agriculture and was the central deity worshipped at the shrine of the "Mysteries" in Eleusis (in western Attica). Her symbol was a sheaf of wheat.

Demetrius Poliorcetes (the Besieger)   (336–283 B.C.) Son of Alexander's Successor, Antigonus I, Demetrius joined his father in repeated unsuccessful attempts to reunite Alexander's fractured empire under their own control. One of the most colorful, daring, and resilient figures of the *Diadochoi* wars, Demetrius liberated Athens from Cassander in 307 B.C. And the following year Demetrius scored his greatest victory by defeating Ptolemy I in a large naval battle at Salamis (in Cyprus). In 305–304, Demetrius acquired his nickname during his massive siege of Rhodes, in which he employed enormous artillery pieces and siege towers; however, he failed to take the city, and in 301 he and his father suffered total defeat at Ipsus at the hands of a coalition of other Successors. Rebounding, by 294 Demetrius had managed to muscle his way into power in Macedonia. But in 288 an attack on Seleucus's Asian kingdom failed and resulted in "the Besieger" losing both his army and his hold on Macedonia. Captured by Seleucus in 285, he died in prison two years later.

Democritus   (ca. 460–ca. 357 B.C.) A brilliant philosopher-scientist, he hailed from Abdera (in Thrace), traveled widely, and wrote many treatises on a wide variety of subjects, including mathematics, mechanics, music, grammar, ethics, and the natural sciences. Unfortunately, all of these works are lost and only few fragments survive in quotations by later writers, including Aristotle. Democritus's main achievement was refining the atomic theory advanced earlier by Leucippus (although exactly what each man contributed to the theory is unknown). It states that all matter is made up of tiny particles (atoms) separated from one another by empty space (a vacuum); the atoms become attached to one another, creating diverse arrangements that form the wide variety of compounds seen in nature.

Demosthenes   (flourished 426–413 B.C.) A prominent Athenian general during the Peloponnesian War, he led (jointly with Cleon) the successful attack on the Spartans at Pylos in 425. The operation was notable for Demosthenes' heavy use of archers and javelin men (peltasts) to supplement his hoplites. In 413, Athens sent him to Sicily to aid Nicias in the attack on Syracuse; during the disastrous Athenian retreat there, Demosthenes was forced to surrender and his captors executed him soon afterward.

Demosthenes   (384–322 B.C.) Greatest of the Attic (Athenian) orators and probably the greatest Greek orator of ancient times, he was most renowned for his stinging speeches (the *Philippics*) denouncing the aggressions of Macedonia's Philip II. He began his career writing court speeches and aiding in public prosecutions and eventually began speaking in Athens's Assembly, where his oratorical skills were immediately evident.

Distressed over Philip's expansion in northern Greece, in 351 B.C. the patriotic Demosthenes delivered his *First Philippic,* calling on his country-men to recapture the northern Aegean city of Amphipolis, which Philip had recently taken. In 349, in response to Philip's siege of the city of Olynthus, the orator urged Athens to intervene, attacking Philip again in a series of speeches that became known as the *Olynthiacs.* But all of these pleas were ignored. Soon afterward (346), Demosthenes and his fellow orator Aeschines went to Macedonia and negotiated a peace settlement; but their efforts were nullified when the slippery Philip blatantly marched into southern Greece that same year. These events also marked the beginning of a bitter rivalry between the two orators, with Demosthenes accusing Aeschines of taking bribes from Philip.

In 338 B.C., Demosthenes became the man of the hour as he engineered an alliance of city-states (led by Athens and Thebes) to confront the Mace-donian threat. But in the showdown that year at Chaeronea (in Boeotia), the orator was among the Athenians who fled the field before the onslaught of Philip's fearsome phalanx. Afterwards, the Athenians chose Demosthenes to give the funeral oration over their dead. Years later, after Alexander's death (323), he helped organize an insurrection against Macedonian rule, but the local governor, Antipater, put down the rebellion, forcing Demos-thenes to flee. In 322, with his pursuers closing in, the orator committed suicide rather than be captured. See **Aeschines, Philip II.**

Diodorus Siculus (of Sicily) (flourished ca. 60–30 B.C.) A Sicilian Greek, Diodorus traveled extensively around the Mediterranean world and collected many ancient documents and histories that are now lost. His mas-sive *Library of History* (also variously referred to as his *World History* or *Universal History*) was originally composed of 40 books, about fifteen of which survive complete or almost so. (Supposedly, the last complete copy of the work was destroyed when the Ottoman Turks sacked Constantinople in 1453.) As a writer, Diodorus was largely unoriginal, uninspired, uncriti-cal, and tended frequently to repeat and even to contradict himself; also, he sometimes failed to credit his sources. Nevertheless, his history is impor-tant because it preserves material from the lost histories he used as sources, works that covered time periods and events that would otherwise remain undocumented.

Diogenes of Sinope (ca. 400–325 B.C.) The best-known of the Cynic philosophers, he lived for several years in Athens, where he was attracted to the austere life-style of Antisthenes (died ca. 360), founder of the Cynics. The highly eccentric Diogenes held that happiness could be achieved only through rejecting all luxury, personal possessions, and relationships, and liv-ing on the barest of essentials. According to tradition, he spent much of his time sitting in a bathtub, carried a lantern around in the daytime, claiming to be searching for an honest man (whom he never found), and unashamedly relieved himself in public (for which he became known as the "dog").

Dionysus   The versatile god of the vine, wine, and fertility, he was Zeus's son and the central deity of a mystery cult and several important religious festivals (including Athens's City Dionysia).

Draco (or Dracon)   (seventh century B.C.) A statesman who formulated Athens's first written law code. The penalties these laws imposed were widely viewed as too harsh (hence the later term "draconian" to describe something severe or inflexible). In the following generation, Solon reformed all of Draco's laws except those dealing with murder. See **Solon**.

Empedocles   (ca. 495–ca. 435 B.C.) This versatile thinker from Acragas (in Sicily) was a philosopher, scientist, poet, physician, and politician; in addition, he was supposedly a skilled orator and Aristotle credits him with inventing the art of rhetoric. Empedocles proposed that the four basic eternal elements—earth, water, air, and fire—are dominated by two forces, Love and Strife. Love maintains a balanced mixture of these elements, while Strife dissolves them and causes disharmony and chaos. He also advanced a brilliant theory of biological evolution similar in several ways to the one Charles Darwin introduced in the nineteenth century.

Epaminondas   (ca. 410–362 B.C.) A noted Theban statesman-general and gifted military innovator, Epaminondas rose to prominence in 371 when he stood up to Sparta's king Agesilaus at a peace conference. Sparta then declared war and invaded Boeotia. But thanks to Epaminondas's brilliant innovations in battlefield tactics, the Theban forces crushed the supposedly invincible Spartan phalanx at Leuctra. The following year, he invaded the Peloponnesus, freed the cities under Spartan domination, and marched to the very outskirts of Sparta itself (but spared its destruction). These events initiated the short-lived Theban hegemony of Greece. Epaminondas died prematurely in battle at Mantinea (in Arcadia) in 362, after which his homeland, which had no one else of his caliber to replace him, was unable to maintain its supremacy. See **Pelopidas, Thebes.**

Ephialtes   (died 461 B.C.) A leading Athenian statesman, democratic reformer, and Pericles' mentor, he was best known for his opposition to the ancient aristocratic council, the Areopagus. In 462, Ephialtes and Pericles initiated legislation that significantly reduced that body's powers; and Ephialtes spearheaded sweeping reforms of the court system. The following year Ephialtes was assassinated (an unusual occurrence in ancient Athens), leaving Pericles to continue his work.

Epicurus   (341–270 B.C.) Born on the island of Samos, the Hellenistic philosopher Epicurus settled in Athens about 307, where he established a philosophical school that became known as the Garden. His followers, who included women and slaves, which was seen as unusual at the time, lived with him in an austere, secluded lifestyle. He advocated achieving wisdom and goodness partly by accepting the evidence of the senses as reality and rejecting superstition and divine intervention. (He held that a divine force exists but that it has no interest in humanity.) Epicurus accepted Democritus's supposition about matter being composed of tiny atoms and said that even the soul is made up of these particles; therefore, when a person dies the atoms disperse and the soul dies too. The modern definition of an Epicurean (a gourmet eater or someone who seeks only pleasure) is a later distortion of his philosophy, which actually called for moderation and limiting desires. Most of Epicurus's writings are lost; but a substantial account of his beliefs appears in the long poem, *On the Nature of Things,* by the Roman philosopher Lucretius.

Epimetheus   See **Pandora.**

Erasistratus   (early third century B.C.) He was a Hellenistic physician who did pioneering work in anatomy at Alexandria, following in the footsteps of his older contemporary and mentor, Herophilus. Erasistratus is often called the "Father of Physiology" for his descriptions of the motor and sensory nerves and the heart's pumping action.

Eratosthenes   (mid–third century B.C.) A distinguished Hellenistic astronomer, geographer, and mathematician, he was for a long period the director of Alexandria's Great Library. He is best known for his brilliant calculation of the earth's circumference to within one percent of the correct figure. Unfortunately, all of his works, including his *On the Measurement of the Earth* and *Chronographia* (a supposedly accurate chronology of Greek history beginning in 1184 B.C.), are lost.

Eros   The god of love (and fertility), Eros (whom the Romans called Cupid) was the handsome companion (or son) of the love goddess Aphrodite. His symbols were his bow, arrows, and torch.

Euclid   (early third century B.C.) One of the greatest mathematicians of antiquity, he worked and taught at Alexandria in early Hellenistic times. His textbook, the *Elements,* is a comprehensive compilation of Greek knowledge about geometry from the sixth century B.C. until his own time and was still in use in parts of Europe as late as the nineteenth century. Tradition credits him with telling King Ptolemy I (who had asked if there was an easier way to learn geometry than by reading the *Elements*) that there is "no royal road to geometry."

Eudoxus   (early fourth century B.C.) A mathematician, astronomer, and geographer, he was Plato's younger associate at the Academy. Eudoxus made strides in solid geometry, describing the volumes of pyramids, cones, and cylinders. He is best known, however, for his suggestion that the heavenly bodies move along on invisible concentric spheres (an elaboration of a Pythagorean notion), a system that Aristotle accepted and developed further.

Eumenes   (ca. 362–ca. 316 B.C.) One of the Successors of Alexander the Great, he began as secretary to both Philip II and Alexander. After the latter's death (323), Eumenes served as governor of Cappadocia (in east-central Asia Minor), where another Successor, Antigonus I, besieged him. In a later fight with Antigonus, Eumenes' own troops betrayed him and he was executed.

Eupolis   (died 411 B.C.) Along with Aristophanes and Cratinus, he was one of the masters of the fifth-century B.C. Athenian comic stage. None of Eupolis's nineteen plays have survived complete, although various fragments are quoted in the works of later writers. He died while fighting in a naval campaign in the northern Aegean during the Peloponnesian War.

Euripides   (ca. 485–406 B.C.) One of the four masters of fifth-century B.C. Athenian drama, he was the youngest of the three great tragedians. He was not as popular in his own time as the other two (Aeschylus and Sophocles), mainly because his works often questioned traditional religious and social values and portrayed humans in a more realistic than heroic manner. (Although many of his countrymen viewed this as undignified, modern scholars see him as the first playwright to deal with human problems in a modern way.) He wrote perhaps eighty-eight or more plays, but only nineteen have survived complete, among them *Medea* (produced in 431), *Hippolytus* (428), *The Suppliant Women* (ca. 422), *Electra* (ca. 417–413), *The Trojan Women* (415), *Iphigenia in Aulus* (ca. 405), and the satyr play *The Cyclops* (date unknown). Of the nineteen, eleven end with the intervention of a *deus ex machina* ("god from the machine"), prompting some critics to accuse him of overusing the device. However, Aristotle, in his *Poetics,* calls Euripides the most skilled of the tragic poets at arousing emotions like pity and fear.

Gaia   See **Titans, Uranus.**

Gorgias   (ca. 483–ca. 385 B.C.) A prominent Greek sophist, he was a native of Leontini (in Sicily) who traveled as an ambassador to Athens in 427 and there delivered a series of speeches that captivated many Athenians. His few surviving works, including the *Defense of Palamedes,* illustrate his mastery of the rhetorical style and his belief that a skillful orator can successfully support and defend any argument, right or wrong. Plato immortalized Gorgias in a dialogue named after him (written ca. 380), which begins with Socrates asking the sophist to define rhetoric. Gorgias exerted a strong influence on his most famous pupil, the orator Isocrates, as well as on the orator Antiphon and the historian Thucydides. See **Isocrates, Plato.**

Graces   In Greek mythology, minor goddesses (Euphrosyne, Aglaia, and Thalia) who symbolized and personified beauty, charm, and grace. It was thought, variously, that they associated with or accompanied the Muses or the love deities Aphrodite and Eros, and that they enhanced the comforts and enjoyments of life. See **Aphrodite, Muses**.

Hades (also Pluton or Pluto) God of the Underworld (or Kingdom of the Dead), he was seen as a punisher of evil, although not evil himself. Brother of Zeus, Hades was also identified with precious metals (since these rest underground). He was said to drive a golden chariot drawn by black horses.

Harpies See **Jason**.

Hector In Homer's *Iliad,* the eldest son of Troy's King Priam, husband of Andromache, and the mightiest Trojan champion against the besieging Greeks. Hector leads the Trojan offensive in which Achilles' friend Patroclus is killed; and in retaliation, Achilles slays Hector outside the city walls and drags the corpse behind his chariot.

Helen In Greek mythology, Helen is the daughter of Zeus and Leda (wife of a Spartan king) and sister of the heroes Castor and Pollux. In the *Iliad,* Homer portrays Helen as a real person—the wife of Sparta's King Menelaus. When Menelaus is away in Crete, the Trojan prince, Paris, persuades her to go with him to Troy, provoking the Greek expedition to rescue her. After the fall of Troy, as depicted in Homer's *Odyssey,* Helen returns to Sparta and lives out her days peacefully with her husband.

Hellen The mythical character thought to have been the father of the Greek race. He had three sons—Dorus, Aeolus, and Xuthus. According to tradition, Dorus gave rise to the Dorian Greeks and Aeolus to the Aeolian Greeks; while Xuthus's sons, Ion and Achaeus, spawned the Ionian and Achaean Greeks respectively. The ancient Greeks believed this to be the derivation of the term Hellenes ("sons of Hellen") to describe themselves, although the term more likely came from Hellas, the ancient Greek name for mainland Greece.

Hellespont Now known as the Dardanelles, it is the narrow, highly strategic strait separating Europe from Asia (more specifically, Greek Thrace from northwestern Asia Minor). A trade route between mainland Greece and cities along the Black Sea passed through it; the Persian king Xerxes crossed it from east to west to invade Greece (480 B.C.); along its shores the Spartans defeated the Athenians (405 B.C.), hastening the end of the Peloponnesian War; and the Macedonian conqueror Alexander the Great crossed it from west to east to launch his invasion of Persia (334 B.C.).

Hephaestos God of fire, the forge, and the patron of craftsmen, he was supposedly dismissed from Mt. Olympus because he was lame and thereafter dwelled and worked his forge beneath Mt. Etna, an active volcano in Sicily.

Hera   Both the sister and wife of Zeus, she was the queen of the gods and protector of marriage and motherhood. Upset by her husband's frequent extramarital affairs, she often punished his lovers and their families. Her symbols were the peacock and the pomegranate.

Heracles   In Greek mythology, Heracles (whom the Romans called Hercules) was the semi-divine son of Zeus and the mortal woman Alcmena, and the most renowned human hero and strongman. He was worshiped and commemorated throughout Greece and there are dozens of myths recounting his adventures and feats. Among them, he accompanied Jason and the Argonauts on part of their quest for the Golden Fleece and freed the Titan Prometheus from the mountaintop on which he was chained. Heracles' most famous feats, however, were his "Twelve Labors," performed to atone for killing his own wife and children in a fit of temporary insanity.

The goddess Hera, Zeus's wife, sits with her symbol, the peacock, at her feet.

Among these were slaying the dreaded Nemean Lion; cleaning the horrendously filthy Augean Stables; stealing the girdle of Hippolyta (queen of the Amazons, a tribe of warrior women); and capturing Cerberus, the monstrous dog that guarded the Underworld's entrance.

Hermes   The messenger god and patron of travelers, merchants, thieves, literature, and athletics, this multi-talented deity supposedly invented the alphabet, astronomy, and mathematics, brought good fortune, and also guided the souls of the dead to the Underworld. His symbol was a herald's staff and he was often pictured wearing winged sandals and hat.

Herodotus   Born ca. 485 B.C. at Halicarnassus (in southwestern Asia Minor), in later ages he became known as the "Father" of history for his *Histories*. This detailed account of the Persian Wars, which also includes numerous digressions on various people and places involved in the conflicts, is the oldest surviving conventional historical work (previous writers turned out only geographical works or compilations of legendary figures and events). Not all of what he recorded was accurate, for he often simply repeated what he heard; however, he created a huge and often intricate portrait of the ancient world of his own era and the century immediately preceding it. Fortunately for later generations, he was an endlessly curious individual who wrote in a clear, graceful style that makes his masterwork highly entertaining reading. Herodotus traveled extensively throughout the eastern Mediterranean world before settling in the Athenian colony of Thurii (in Italy) in 443. He died there about 425.

Herophilus (early third century B.C.) After training at Cos, the physician and brilliant Hellenistic medical researcher Herophilus moved to Alexandria and established the Alexandrian medical school. Partly because the Ptolemies allowed him to dissect human bodies, which most Greek states forbade, he made significant advances in anatomy, for which he often is called the "Father." Among other things, he discovered and described the female ovaries and fallopian tubes and studied the liver, eye, brain, and sensory and motor nerves.

Hesiod (flourished ca. 700 B.C.) One of the earliest and greatest of the Greek poets, he hailed from the small town of Ascra in Boeotia. Most of what little information we have about him he provides himself in snippets embedded in his works. In his epic poem, the *Theogony,* for example, he claims that as a young man the divine Muses appeared to him while he was tending his sheep and gave him the gift of song (i.e., poetic expression). On his father's death, the estate was divided between him and his brother; but the brother took more than his fair share, which provoked a legal battle. Hesiod's poem *Works and Days,* which among other things describes planting crops according to the calendar, was intended in part to instruct his errant brother, as well as others, in the honest, conservative, old-fashioned values of Greek farming. The *Theogony* is a sprawling, detailed rendition of the creation of the world and the gods and, along with Homer's epics, provided the later Greeks with their most vivid picture of these beings.

Hestia Virgin goddess of the hearth (central symbol of home and family in ancient Greece), she was known for her kindness and purity and worshiped at shrines in every Greek city.

Hiero I (early fifth century B.C.) Tyrant of the Sicilian Greek city of Syracuse, Hiero (or Hieron) ruled from about 478 to 466 B.C. He was known for defeating the Etruscans (who inhabited north-central Italy) in a naval battle in 474 and establishing several colonies in Sicily and southern Italy. He also welcomed poets, including Aeschylus and Simonides, to his court.

Hiero II (ca. 306–215 B.C.) King of Syracuse from about 270 to 215 B.C., Hiero (or Hieron), who began as an officer under the Epirote king Pyrrhus, brought the city a long period of peace and prosperity. He wisely allied himself to the Romans, who were rising to power in Italy, and supported them in their wars with Carthage. Hiero also befriended and supported the brilliant Syracusan inventor Archimedes.

Hipparchus   (late sixth century B.C.) The younger son of the Athenian tyrant Pisistratus, for a time he ruled jointly as tyrant with his older brother Hippias (who ruled 527–510). Hipparchus was a patron of literature and the arts and well liked at first; but he and his brother became increasingly unpopular. Eventually, two Athenians (Harmodius and Aristogeiton) assassinated Hipparchus, earning them a reputation for centuries thereafter as great patriots.

Hipparchus   (ca. 190–ca. 125 B.C.) Widely viewed as the greatest astronomer of antiquity, Hipparchus hailed from Nicaea, in Bithynia (in Asia Minor), but spent most of his life on the island of Rhodes. Most of his own works no longer exist; but the *Almagest* of the second-century A.D. Greek astronomer Ptolemy describes many of his contributions. Hipparchus compiled a huge catalogue of over 800 stars, categorizing them by brightness and positioning them on the celestial sphere using degrees of latitude and longitude (which he invented; he also plotted geographic locations on a map in the same manner). In addition, he discovered the precession of the equinoxes (the tiny yearly shift of the sun's position in relation to the celestial equator), estimated the relative distances of the sun and moon, and developed the science of trigonometry.

Hippias   (late sixth century B.C.) The elder son of the Athenian tyrant Pisistratus and himself tyrant of Athens from 527 to 510, he was at first a fair ruler; but over time his policies became harsh and unpopular. After his brother, Hipparchus, was assassinated in 514 and the Spartans invaded Attica in 510, he was forced to flee and ended up taking refuge at the court of Persia's Darius I. Hoping to regain power in Athens, Hippias accompanied the Persian forces when they landed at Marathon in 490, but his hopes were dashed by the stunning Athenian victory. See **Hipparchus.**

Hippocrates   (late fifth century B.C.) Scholars know almost nothing about the life of Hippocrates of Cos (an island off southwestern Asia Minor), the Greek physician who has come to be called the "Father" of medicine. According to tradition, he established a medical school on Cos associated with the widely revered shrine of the healing god Asclepius. A collection of some sixty medical writings, known as the *Hippocratic Corpus,* survives; but there is no evidence that Hippocrates wrote any of these himself, and they may represent the holdings of the school's library, compiled over time by his students and successors. The main contributions of the Hippocratic school were the recognition of disease as a natural, rather than supernatural, phenomenon that can be treated by human intervention, and the establishment of medicine as a true scientific discipline.

Homer   (late ninth–late eighth century B.C.?) A poet credited with authoring the *Iliad* and *Odyssey,* the most famous and arguably the greatest epic poems ever written. His birthplace is disputed, with several cities in Greek Ionia (western Asia Minor) claiming him, though Smyrna and Chios are the most plausible candidates. The later classical Greeks had no doubts that Homer was a real person and throughout antiquity people referred to him simply and reverently as "the Poet." However, as early as Hellenistic times, some Greek scholars suggested that the two epics might not have been composed by the same person. This became part of a tradition, still ongoing, of Homeric criticism, aimed at answering the so-called "Homeric question." It actually comprises several questions: Was he indeed a real person? If so, did he write both epics? Are the works as they exist today substantially his, or did later writers contribute various portions? Are the characters and events described in the epics real, imaginary, or a mixture of the two?

Though debates on these questions continue, the consensus of modern scholarship is that Homer was a real bard who was part of a long tradition of reciting poetry that had been transmitted orally from preceding generations. Thus, the epics were likely composed little by little over time, each generation of bards refining and elaborating on them. Homer's contribution may have been the greatest because the Greeks had rediscovered writing during (or perhaps just preceding) his lifetime; and committing the poems to writing (perhaps by dictating them to a scribe) would have allowed for the addition of more complex detail and imagery than was customarily transmitted by oral means. (Still, solid evidence that the poems were committed to writing this early is lacking; tradition holds that the first written editions were those commissioned by the Athenian leader Pisistratus in the mid-sixth century B.C.)

However the Homeric epics were composed, they came to exert a profound influence on Greek culture and thought. The *Iliad,* describing a series of incidents near the end of the Trojan War (1250–1200 B.C.?), and the *Odyssey,* chronicling the adventures of Odysseus, one of the Greek chieftains who fought at Troy, were major sources of information about the Greek gods. They also provided the Greeks with a blueprint for a heroic, noble code of conduct; contained numerous examples of practical wisdom; became the primary literary texts studied by Greek schoolchildren; and were endlessly quoted by Greek and Roman writers of all kinds. These works, the first and among the greatest examples of Western literature, are no less highly regarded today. They remain staples of university courses in classical history, literature, and poetry, and new translations appear on a regular basis.

Ictinus   (flourished ca. 450–420 B.C.) A noted architect who designed the Temple of Apollo at Bassae, but was most renowned for his collaboration with the architect Callicrates and sculptor Phidias on the Athenian Parthenon.

Iphicrates   (flourished ca. 390–355 B.C.) He was an Athenian general famous for revolutionizing the battlefield use of peltasts (light-armed javelin men). The crucial event was when a group of peltasts under his command shocked the Greek world by defeating a small Spartan infantry force near

Corinth in 390; after that, Athens and many other Greek states adopted his tactical innovations and increased their use of peltasts.

Iphigenia   See **Agamemnon.**

Isocrates   (436–338 B.C.) A prominent Athenian orator, Isocrates founded a school of rhetoric (the art of persuasive speaking) in Athens circa 392. He wrote speeches for court litigants, six of which survive. But he is most famous for his political pamphlets advocating that all Greeks should unite against the threat of Persian expansion. His *Panegyricus* (380) suggested that Athens and Sparta might lead an anti-Persian crusade. And his *Address to Philip* (346) was a more powerful call for the Macedonian king Philip II to take up that same cause; this may have been Philip's inspiration for the invasion of Persia he planned before his assassination (and which his son Alexander later carried out). Disillusioned after Philip's defeat of the city-states at Chaeronea (338), Isocrates supposedly committed suicide by starving himself.

Jason   In Greek mythology, a hero from Jolchus (or Iolchus), in Thessaly, who led the famous expedition of the *Argo* and its crew (the Argonauts) to find the fabulous Golden Fleece. During the journey, they took part in various perilous adventures, including tangling with the fearsome Harpies (winged monsters with women's faces who snatched away food or occasionally people) and making it through the lethal Clashing Rocks (at the Bosphorus Strait). At their destination, Colchis, on the shore of the Black Sea, the local king, Aeëtes, refused to let Jason have the fleece. But Aeëtes' daughter, Medea, who was a sorceress, helped Jason get the prize, which was guarded by a dragon. This portion of Jason's legend, told by Apollonius Rhodius in his *Argonautica,* ends with Jason, the Argonauts, and Medea returning to Jolchus. The later events of his life are recounted in Euripides' play *Medea.* Jason married Medea, then divorced her, and died when a portion of the *Argo* fell on and crushed him while he slept. See **Apollonius Rhodius, Medea.**

Jason   Tyrant of the state of Pherae (in Thessaly) from 385 to 370 B.C. An aggressive ruler, by 374 he had taken control of most of Thessaly. This gained him enough prestige to enable him to negotiate the treaty between Thebes and Sparta after the latter's defeat at Leuctra in 371. He appears to have had plans for more and larger aggressions; but he was assassinated in 370.

Jocasta   See **Oedipus.**

Knossus (or Cnossus)   In the Bronze Age, an important city of the Minoan culture and site of a splendid multi-leveled palace-administrative center that probably inspired the Greek legend of the Labyrinth. Knossus may have been the center of a Minoan empire for a while, although definite evidence is lacking. The palace, which in its prime featured advanced architecture and plumbing facilities, was destroyed or damaged and rebuilt a number of times and finally occupied by mainland Mycenaeans circa 1400 B.C. In the late Dark Age, well after the collapse of Mycenaean civilization, a new, less splendid town of Knossus (located to the north of the ruined palace) rose to prominence and subsequently played a key role in Cretan affairs. See **Minos, Theseus.**

Laius   See **Oedipus.**

Leonidas   King of Sparta from 488 to 480 B.C., he is famous as the commander of the multi-state Greek force that defended the pass of Thermopylae against the invading Persians under Xerxes in 480. When he learned that a Greek traitor had shown the enemy a path leading behind his position, Leonidas dismissed most of the 6,000–7,000 allied troops to save them for future battles. He remained with his bodyguard of 300 Spartans, along with a few men from other states, and they bravely fought to death, taking thousands of Persians with them and earning eternal glory. A modern statue of Leonidas now marks the site of the heroes' last stand.

Leucippus   (mid–fifth century B.C.) Almost nothing is known about this philosopher; even his birthplace is obscure (Elea, Miletus, and Abdera are candidates); and all of his works, including the *Great World System,* are lost. A number of ancient writers credit him with introducing the atomic theory later elaborated on by Democritus. See **Democritus**.

Lycurgus   (seventh century B.C.?) The semi-legendary Spartan lawgiver and founder of Sparta's renowned military-social system, the *agoge,* Lycurgus was venerated almost as a god by the classical Spartans. Although Herodotus (in his *Histories*) and Plutarch (in his *Life of Lycurgus*) assume he was a real person, modern scholars suggest that the Spartan system evolved over a long period and that he may have been an invented character.

Lycurgus   (ca. 390–ca. 325 B.C.) The noted Athenian orator Lycurgus composed numerous popular speeches, but only one survives (*Against Leocrates*). He also distinguished himself in politics and the arts by handling Athens's finances from 338 to 326; initiating an extensive building program in the city; backing a written edition of the plays of Aeschylus, Sophocles, and Euripides; and erecting statues of these playwrights.

Lysander   (died 395 B.C.) The noted Spartan admiral Lysander was a major figure in the closing years of the Peloponnesian War. He defeated the Athenians at Notium in 406 and again at Aegospotami (on the Hellespont) the following year, thereby cutting off Athens's life-giving grain route to the Black Sea. Next, he blockaded Piraeus (Athens's port), accepted Athens's surrender (404), and there set up the pro-Spartan oligarchic council that became known as the Thirty Tyrants. Lysander died in battle a few years later while invading Boeotia during the Corinthian War.

Lysias   (ca. 458–ca. 380 B.C.) A renowned Attic orator, Lysias was the son of a wealthy metic (foreigner living in Athens). With his brothers, Lysias ran a profitable shield-making business in Athens, but he fled in 404 when the Thirty Tyrants marked him for death. Returning the following year, after their downfall, he impeached one of them in his powerful speech, *Against Eratosthenes,* and thereafter devoted himself to speech-writing. Reportedly he produced over 800 speeches in all, many of them for court litigants. Twenty-three survive complete, along with numerous fragments.

Lysimachus   (ca. 360–281 B.C.) One of the Successors of Alexander the Great, he began as a member of Alexander's bodyguard and rose to the rank of general. After Alexander's death (323), he claimed authority over Thrace and northwestern Asia Minor, and in 306 proclaimed himself king of the region. In 301, he joined other Successors in defeating Antigonus I and his son Demetrius at Ipsus, and was rewarded with more territory in Asia Minor. In the 280s, Lysimachus expanded westward, seizing Macedonia and Thessaly, and was for a short time the most powerful Successor. But in 281, his former ally, Seleucus, defeated and killed him at Corupedium (in western Asia Minor) and his realm quickly fell apart.

Macedonia   A kingdom occupying the northern part of mainland Greece, directly north of Thessaly, west of Thrace, and northeast of Epirus. (The name Macedon is sometimes used to denote the kingdom as a political entity, while Macedonia refers to either the kingdom or the general region.) The area was inhabited by tribal peoples in the Bronze, Dark, and Archaic Ages but remained militarily weak and culturally backward until the fourth century B.C. The kingdom was roughly divided into two sections—a large mountainous interior and a small fertile plain near the northwestern Aegean coast. It was on this plain, at Aegae (modern Vergina), that King Perdiccas I established his capital ca. 640 B.C. Under King Archelaus I (reigned 413–399), who made some limited strides toward modernizing the kingdom and bringing it into the Greek cultural mainstream, the capital moved to nearby Pella, although Aegae remained a ceremonial center and site of the royal tombs.

In 359 B.C., Philip II inherited the throne and with amazing speed transformed Macedonia into a strong, centralized state with a powerful professional standing army, Europe's first. After sweeping southward and subjugating the major city-states, he was assassinated and his son, Alexander III (later called "the Great") ascended the throne. Following Alexander's rapid conquest of Persia (334–330 B.C.) and untimely death (323), several of his feuding successors seized and ruled Macedonia in their turn. Finally, in the 270s, Antigonus II established a stable dynasty that ruled it as one of the three major Hellenistic realms until the early second century B.C. Between 200 and 167, the Romans invaded and subdued the Macedonians, and in 146 B.C. Rome annexed the region as the Roman province of Macedonia. See **Alexander III; Antigonus II Gonatus; Perdiccas I, II, and III; Philip II;** and **Philip V.**

Mardonius (died 479 B.C.) A Persian general and the son-in-law of Persia's King Darius I, in 492 Mardonius led a fleet across the northern Aegean, intending to punish Athens for aiding the Ionian rebels. But the fleet was destroyed in a storm near Mt. Athos. Later, Mardonius accompanied King Xerxes in the latter's invasion of Greece (480), and when Xerxes retired to Asia Minor after the battle of Salamis, he left Mardonius in charge of his land forces. The following year, Mardonius met decisive defeat and death in the battle of Plataea.

Medea In Greek mythology, the daughter of King Aeëtes of Colchis (on the coast of the Black Sea) and a beautiful sorceress. She first appears in the story of Jason and the Argonauts (as told by Apollonius Rhodius in the *Argonautica*), when she falls in love with Jason and helps him acquire the Golden Fleece. Returning to Thessaly with him, she makes it possible for him to defeat his enemies. Euripides' play, *Medea* (431 B.C.), picks up the legend after Jason and Medea have fled to Corinth. There, he decides to marry the daughter of the Corinthian king, Creon, who orders Medea and her two children by Jason to leave the city. Seeking revenge, Medea kills Creon, his daughter, and her own children, then escapes to Athens. Aeschylus and Sophocles also wrote plays about Medea, but they have not survived. See **Apollonius Rhodius, Jason.**

Medusa See **Perseus.**

Menander (ca. 342–ca. 292 B.C.) The most famous and popular playwright of the theatrical period known as the New Comedy (ca. 320s–ca. 260 B.C.), Menander was born at Athens, where he studied at the Lyceum under Theophrastus. Of Menander's more than 100 plays, only one, *Dyskolos* (*The Bad-Tempered Man*), survives complete, although substantial fragments of *The Samian Women, The Arbitration, The Shorn Girl, The Shield,* and a few others exist; and over 900 quotations from his plays are found in the works of various ancient authors. Mannered situation comedies portraying common character types in realistic settings, these plays are tamer and less topical and political than those of the Old Comedy. See **Aristophanes.**

Menelaus See **Agamemnon, Helen, Sparta.**

Midas In Greek mythology, a king of Phrygia (in central Asia Minor), whom the satyr Silenus granted a wish. Midas chose to have everything he touched turn to gold; but he soon found that this included his food, so he begged to have the gift nullified. In a different legend, Midas judged a musical contest between the gods Apollo and Pan, and when he chose Pan the winner, Apollo gave Midas a donkey's ears to demonstrate his stupidity.

Miltiades (flourished ca. 530–489 B.C.) A noted Athenian general, in the 520s B.C. he ruled as a dictator over the native Thracians and Athenian colonists in the Thracian Chersonese (a peninsula near the Hellespont). He supported the Ionian revolt against Persia in the early 490s and when it collapsed he fled to Athens, where he was tried and acquitted on a charge of tyranny in Thrace. In 490, as *strategos* (general), Miltiades engineered the stunning Athenian victory over the Persians at Marathon. He died the following year from wounds suffered in an unsuccessful assault on the island of Paros.

A nineteenth-century engraving portrays the Athenian general Miltiades leading his countrymen against the Persians at Marathon in 490 B.C.

Minos   In Greek mythology, a son of the god Zeus and the Phoenician princess Europa. After Minos became king of Crete, his wife coupled with a bull and gave birth to the Minotaur, which was half-man and half-bull. Minos had a special palace, the Labyrinth, constructed to hide the fearsome creature. After his death, Zeus made Minos one of the judges of the Underworld. On excavating the palace at Knossus (in northern Crete), beginning in 1900, the English archaeologist Sir Arthur Evans dubbed its builders "Minoan" after the legendary Minos.

Muses   The nine daughters of Zeus and the goddess Mnemosyne (Memory), the Muses (Calliope, Clio, Euterpe, Melpomene, Terpsichore, Erato, Polyhymnia, Urania, and Thalia) were the deities who inspired musicians, poets, dancers, and other artists and intellectuals. The poet Hesiod mentions them in his *Theogony,* claiming that they imbued him with the gift of song. Cults and shrines to the Muses existed all over Greece, the two most important located at Pieria (near Mt. Olympus in Thessaly) and Mt. Helicon (in Boeotia).

Mycenae   See **Agamemnon, Argos.**

Myron   (flourished ca. 480–430 B.C.) Born in Attica, the famed sculptor Myron was an older contemporary of Polyclitus and Phidias. Working mainly in bronze, Myron produced numerous statues, the most famous today being the Discus Thrower (which survives in later marble copies of the original bronze, which is lost); but the most renowned of his works in ancient times was his bronze cow that stood in Athens's Agora (or possibly on the Acropolis).

Nicias   (ca. 470–413 B.C.) An Athenian politician and general who was best known for his opposition to the demagogue (rabble-rouser) Alcibiades and for leading the fateful Athenian expedition to Syracuse. A prosperous and wealthy man who opposed the Peloponnesian War, Nicias became the pro-war Cleon's chief opponent in the conflict's opening years; and after Cleon's death, he negotiated a truce and a peace treaty (the so-called Peace of Nicias, 421). When the war soon resumed and Alcibiades proposed sending an army to conquer Syracuse, Nicias objected, but the Assembly sided with his opponent. Then, when the scheming Alcibiades turned traitor, the reluctant Nicias, a mediocre general, was left in charge of the Syracusan expedition. After the venture ended in disaster in 413, the enemy captured Nicias and executed him.

Odysseus   The central character of Homer's epic poem, the *Odyssey,* Odysseus (whom the Romans called Ulysses) was king of the island kingdom of Ithaca. He fought at Troy and devised the plan for stealing Greek troops into the city inside a hollow wooden horse. After the city fell, Odysseus's ships were blown off course and he wandered for ten years, encountering numerous adventures and crises, until finally returning home to his wife, Penelope, and son, Telemachus.

Oedipus   In Greek mythology, he became king of Thebes by outwitting a monster, the Sphinx, that had been threatening the city. Later, Oedipus learned that, while trying to avoid a dire prophecy decreed by the gods, he had sealed that very fate. Unwittingly, he had killed his own father, the former Theban king Laius, and married and had children by his own mother, Jocasta. Horrified, she committed suicide and Oedipus blinded himself and went into exile, attended by his loving daughter, Antigone. But after he had suffered for many years, the gods finally forgave him and he ascended mysteriously into their realm. Oedipus's powerful and moving story is told in two of the greatest plays ever written—*Oedipus the King* and *Oedipus at Colonus,* both by Sophocles. See **Antigone, Sophocles, Thebes.**

Olympia Site of the world famous ancient Olympic Games, Olympia was located in the region of Pisa, adjoining the city-state of Elis, in the northwestern Peloponnesus. The Olympic sanctuary, dedicated to Zeus, rested in an idyllic setting, where the Alpheus and Cladeus rivers met at the foot of the low Hill of Cronus; and here, every four years (beginning in 776 B.C. according to tradition) athletes and spectators from all over the Greek world converged for five days of worship and athletic competitions. About 572 B.C., control of the Games passed from Pisa to Elis, which hosted and supplied the judges for the events. Even after Greece became part of the Roman Empire, the games long remained renowned (the emperor Nero actually competed in A.D. 67); but in 393 the sanctuary and Games were closed down (along with other pagan religious sites) by the Christian emperor Theodosius. Subsequently, earthquakes and floods erased the ruins, which were long forgotten until their rediscovery in 1766.

Olympians In Greek mythology, the race of gods that fought and succeeded the Titans as rulers of the universe. Their name derived from Mt. Olympus, the highest peak in Greece, which in very early times was thought to be their home. The traditional, major Olympian gods were Zeus, Hera, Poseidon, Apollo, Athena, Ares, Hestia, Aphrodite, Hades (or Pluto), Demeter, Hephaestos, Artemis, Hermes, and Dionysus. Some ancient sources list just twelve Olympians, perhaps because Hephaestos and Hestia supposedly eventually left Olympus. See names of individual gods.

Pan God of shepherds and flocks, he was usually pictured with a human upper body and a goat's legs, ears, and horns. He also carried a pipe with seven reeds (the *syrinx*), said to be his own invention.

Pandora In Greek mythology, she was the first human woman. At the order of Zeus (who wanted to punish the Titan Prometheus), Hephaestos (god of the forge) fashioned her from clay and various gods endowed her with physical and mental gifts (hence her name, meaning "all gifts"). Zeus sent her to Epimetheus ("afterthought"), Prometheus's slow-witted brother, who took her in, even though Prometheus had warned him not to accept any gifts from Zeus. Once inside, she unwittingly opened a jar unleashing all the evils that still plague the human race. See **Prometheus**.

Paris See **Achilles, Helen, Troy**.

Parmenides (early fifth century B.C.) A philosopher hailing from Elea (in southwestern Italy), he founded the Eleatic school of thought, advocating the abstract notion that the only true reality is that which the human mind can conceive. And therefore, one cannot conceive of something that does not exist. Furthermore, "what exists" cannot be created or destroyed, but is indivisible and eternal. Parmenides set these ideas down in a poem in two parts—the *Way of Truth* and the *Way of Seeming*—part of which survives. He appears as one of the main characters in Plato's dialogue, the *Parmenides*.

Parmenio (ca. 400–330 B.C.) Friend of Macedonia's king Philip II and his best general, Parmenio (or Parmenion) helped Philip attain many of his military goals. After Philip's assassination, he was Alexander's second-in-command in some of the Persian campaign's key battles. In 330, however, when Parmenio's son was executed for treason, Alexander had the father killed too.

Pausanias (died ca. 467 B.C.) A Spartan royal regent and nephew of Leonidas, the hero of Thermopylae. After gaining widespread fame for leading the Greek forces in their great victory over the Persians at Plataea (479), Pausanias recaptured Byzantium from the Persians. However, soon afterward he became involved in Persian intrigues, was twice accused of treason, and died in disgrace.

Pausanias (flourished ca. A.D.150) Believed to have been born near Smyrna (in western Asia Minor), Pausanias was a prolific traveler and writer. His main claim to fame is a travel guide, the *Guide to Greece,* in ten volumes, which contains priceless information about the histories, legends, social customs, buildings, religious sites, and art treasures of the places he visited.

Pelopidas (ca. 410–364 B.C.) A noted Theban statesman and general, Pelopidas rose to prominence in 379, when he led a group of fellow patriots in regaining control of the Cadmea (Thebes's acropolis), which the Spartans had earlier seized. Thereafter, he became leader of the "Sacred Band," the Theban army's elite unit. He and this unit were instrumental in the watershed victory of his colleague, Epaminondas, over the Spartans at Leuctra in 371. In 368, Pelopidas settled a dispute between Macedonia and Thessaly, in the process taking young Philip II, Greece's future master, as a hostage. Four years later, while campaigning in Thessaly, Pelopidas died in battle.

Peloponnesus (or Peloponnese) The large mountainous peninsula that is separated from central Greece by the Isthmus of Corinth, the Peloponnesus makes up roughly the southern third of the Greek mainland. The name came from *Pelopos nesos,* meaning "isle of Pelops," a reference to the mythological character Pelops; he was supposedly the founder of the Pelopid family, which may have been a dynasty that ruled the kingdom of Mycenae (or Argos) in the late Bronze Age. In classical antiquity, the peninsula's major regions were Elis (in the northwest), Achaea (north), Arcadia (center), the Argolid (the large peninsula in the northeast), Laconia (south), and Messenia (southwest). Laconia was the home of Sparta, the unique city-state that long possessed Greece's most feared land army.

Perdiccas (died 320 B.C.) One of the Successors of Alexander the Great, he fought in Alexander's Persian campaign, becoming second-in-command to the king in 324. When Alexander died in 323, he gave his ring, symbol of imperial authority, to Perdiccas, in effect making him regent. Three years later, while attacking another Successor, Ptolemy, in Egypt, Perdiccas died at the hands of his own officers.

Perdiccas I, II, and III   Three kings of Macedonia, all members of the Argead dynasty that eventually produced Philip II and Alexander. The first known Argead, Perdiccas I (seventh century B.C.), established his capital at Aegae (several miles inland from the Thermaic Gulf). Perdiccas II (reigned ca. 450–413 B.C.) fought several civil wars against his brothers and made numerous short-termed and ultimately meaningless alliances with Athens and Sparta during the Peloponnesian War. Perdiccas III (r. 365–359), Philip's older brother and a short-lived and ineffectual ruler, died in battle against the Illyrians, a neighboring hill people. See **Macedonia, Philip II.**

Pergamum (or Pergamon)   See **Attalids.**

Periander   One of the greatest and most famous of the Greek tyrants, he ruled Corinth from about 625 to 585 B.C. During his reign, the city was the most prosperous in Greece and he boldly extended its authority and influence by establishing colonies in the northern Aegean and Adriatic seas; pushing Corinthian trade into the western Mediterranean shipping lanes; building a stone causeway that allowed merchants to drag their ships across the Isthmus of Corinth (creating a shortcut between Greece's eastern and western coasts); and sponsoring public building programs and artistic endeavors. Despite these constructive measures, Periander was reputed to be a ruthless, brutal individual who may have murdered his own wife. Not long after his death (in 585, of natural causes), Corinth instituted an oligarchic council.

Pericles   The greatest Athenian statesman of the fifth century B.C., he was a champion of democracy and the chief guiding force behind Athens's imperial and cultural golden age, often referred to by later generations of Greeks as the "Fifty Years." Born about 495 B.C. into an aristocratic family, the Alcmaeonids (of which the democratic reformer Cleisthenes was a prominent member), Pericles climbed the political ladder slowly. He gained public recognition ca. 472 by serving as *choregus* (backer) of Aeschylus's political tragedy, the *Persians;* and in 463 by prosecuting (unsuccessfully) the conservative leader Cimon. In 461, when Pericles' mentor, the democratic leader Ephialtes, was assassinated and Cimon was banished, Pericles emerged as the city's most powerful politician.

Pericles immediately showed his anti-Spartan leanings by urging the construction of the Long Walls (completed in 457), connecting Athens's urban center to its port, Piraeus, which were designed to protect the city from Spartan intimidation. In the years that followed, he was repeatedly elected general and directed Athenian forces in an episodic undeclared war with Sparta. An advocate of Athenian imperialism, he pursued a policy of dominating the member states of the Delian League (established in 478). The most infamous episodes were his siege and defeat of the defiant island polis of Samos in 440, which many Greeks, including some Athenians, roundly condemned; and his transfer of the League's treasury from the island of Delos to Athens, where much of the money poured into his grandiose building projects. The greatest of these was the temple complex atop the Acropolis, including the magnificent Parthenon (completed in 432). Among his many democratic reforms were the introduction of pay for jurors (457) and free theater tickets for the poor (ca. 450).

After repeated attacks by his political opponents failed to dislodge him from power, Pericles proceeded with provocative foreign policy initiatives, including an alliance with the island of Corcyra (433) and a devastating embargo of the nearby polis of Megara. These moves helped to ignite (in 431) the long and exhausting Peloponnesian War between Athens's and Sparta's respective federations of allies. Pericles advocated a policy of retreating behind the city walls and relying on the navy to keep the city supplied. But the scheme backfired when a deadly plague struck Athens in 430; and Pericles became one of its victims the following year.

Perseus   In Greek mythology, the heroic slayer of the snake-headed Gorgon (monster) Medusa. Supposedly the son of Zeus and a mortal princess, Danaë of Argos, his mother's suitor sent him on a dangerous mission—to bring back the head of the hideous female demon, Medusa, the sight of whom turned people to stone. With the aid of the goddess Athena, he acquired winged shoes and a cap that turned him invisible. The shoes took him to the land of the Gorgons and the cap allowed him to sneak up on Medusa, who appeared to him only in the harmless reflection in his shield. After killing her and engaging in other adventures, Perseus became king of Tiryns and, according to one story, established the nearby city of Mycenae.

Perseus   (ca. 213–166 B.C.) King of the Hellenistic kingdom of Macedonia from 179 to 166, he was the elder son of Philip V. On assuming the throne, Perseus renewed his father's alliance with Rome, but the Romans soon became suspicious of him and tensions led to the Third Macedonian War (171–168). Perseus suffered complete defeat at Pydna (168), after which his opponent, Aemilius Paullus, took him to Rome and humiliated him by marching him in his victory parade. Macedonia's last monarch died in Rome two years later.

Phidias   (ca. 490–ca. 425 B.C.) The greatest sculptor of the ancient world, Phidias (or Pheidias) was a close friend of the Athenian statesman Pericles, who granted him the main role in the building program that transformed the Athenian Acropolis in the 440s and 430s B.C. Phidias supervised all the sculptural work on the Parthenon and also designed and executed the giant statue of Athena that stood inside the building. Among his other great works was the statue of Zeus in that god's temple at Olympia, which later became known as one of the seven wonders of the world. In 432 B.C., Pericles' enemies accused Phidias of embezzling some of the gold intended for Athena's statue; but apparently he was acquitted and left Athens, never to return.

Philip II King of Macedonia, father of Alexander the Great, and one of the greatest military generals of antiquity, Philip was born about 382 B.C., the youngest son of King Amyntas III. At the time, the kingdom was divided, weak, and, in the eyes of the city-state Greeks, a primitive and corrupt cultural backwater. Philip's first brush with the city-states came in 368. During a political crisis involving Macedonia and neighboring Thessaly, Thebes, then the dominant power in Greece, arbitrated; and to seal the peace the Thebans took several hostages, among them Philip. For over three years Philip resided in Thebes, where he may have studied the Theban military, which had recently been reformed by the innovative Epaminondas. In 365, Philip returned to Macedonia, and in 359, after his brother Perdiccas, then king, was killed in battle, he ascended the throne.

Facing enormous challenges, Philip proceeded with amazing speed and skill to unify the country into a single and powerful nation. His principal tool in this endeavor was the creation of Europe's first national, professional standing army. In sharp contrast to the militia utilized by the city-states, which were called up only when needed, his army was a large permanent force whose members received extensive training. Key to the success of the new army was a more formidable version of the traditional Greek phalanx, with deeper ranks and the use of long two-handed pikes that projected from the front of the phalanx, forming a frightening mass of spear-points. The "Macedonian phalanx" proved itself in the years that followed, as Philip captured city after city in northern and central Greece. His bold goal became the mastery of the large southern city-states, including Athens, Thebes, and Corinth.

Through an effective combination of negotiation, devious manipulation, and brute force, Philip fulfilled this goal. For several years the major powers did little to stop him and the only major voice raised against him was that of the Athenian orator Demosthenes, in his *Philippics* (speeches denouncing Philip's aggressions). In 346 B.C., Philip shocked the Greek world by entering southern Greece and taking control of the religious sanctuary at Delphi. The fateful showdown between his forces and those of a hastily-formed alliance led by Athens and Thebes took place in the summer of 338, when he and his son Alexander, then eighteen, won a decisive victory at Chaeronea (in western Boeotia). Soon afterward, Philip created a confederacy of Greek states with himself as supreme leader. His new goal was to lead a united Greek army in a crusade against Persia; but in 336 a disgruntled Macedonian stabbed him to death, leaving Alexander to earn eternal fame for carrying out the plan.

Philip V (238–179 B.C.) King of the Hellenistic Macedonian kingdom from 221 to 179 B.C., Philip made the mistake of allying himself with Carthage against Rome in 215 at the height of the Second Punic War. At the conclusion of the conflict, partly to avenge themselves on him, the Romans attacked Macedonia (in the Second Macedonian War, 200–197) and defeated Philip's phalanx at Cynoscephalae, in Thessaly. Thereafter, until his death in 179 B.C., he helped Rome in its struggles against other Hellenistic Greek states. His son, Perseus, was Macedonia's last ruler. See **Perseus**.

Phrynichus   (late sixth century B.C.) One of the early Athenian dramatists, who, along with Thespis, supposedly established the genre of tragedy. Only a few fragments survive from Phrynichus's plays, which included *The Phoenician Women* and *The Fall of Miletus*. According to Herodotus, when the latter was staged the audience burst into tears and the authorities fined the playwright 1000 drachmas for unduly upsetting the citizenry (who felt strong ties with the Milesians, whose city had recently been sacked by the Persians).

Pindar   (ca. 518–ca. 438 B.C.) One of Greece's greatest poets, he was born near Thebes and became known for his victory odes (*epinikia*), composed to honor the winners of the athletic games at Olympia, Delphi, Nemea, and Isthmia. Forty-five of these odes have survived. They were originally commissioned by the athletes themselves or their families and performed by choirs in their hometowns. The poems are valuable not only for their literary merits, but also as sources of mythological allusions, which Pindar utilized often. See **Bacchylides**.

Pisistratus   (ca. 600–527 B.C.) Tyrant of Athens from ca. 560 to 527, Pisistratus (or Peisistratus) was a relative of the renowned Athenian lawgiver Solon. Leader of a political faction known as the "poorer hillsmen," Pisistratus managed to seize the Acropolis ca. 560. Other factions drove him out some four years later; he made a comeback ca. 550; was deposed once more; and returned to power still again ca. 546, this time at the head of a strong force of mercenary troops, who helped him retain his position for almost two more decades. A largely benevolent and constructive ruler, he seems to have supported most of Solon's reforms, launched large-scale public building projects, and patronized the arts and literature. (Tradition credits him with initiating recitation contests of Homer's works and the City Dionysia drama festival.) At his death, Pisistratus was succeeded by his sons, Hippias and Hipparchus.

Plato   One of the most famous and influential philosopher-scholars of all times, Plato was born circa 427 B.C. into a well-to-do Athenian family that (through his mother) traced its descent from the lawgiver Solon. Little for certain is known about Plato's early life except that he grew up during the disruptive Peloponnesian War (in which he may have served as a cavalryman in its final years); and that, through his relatives Critias and Charmides, he became a follower of the eccentric philosopher Socrates. When Athens was defeated in 404, Critias and Charmides figured prominently in the short-lived dictatorship that followed. And because of his association with these unpopular characters, Socrates was executed in 399. Devastated by these events, Plato left Athens and for the next several years traveled widely through the Greek world. In 386, he returned to Athens and established the Academy, a university-like school dedicated to philosophical inquiry and the preparation of future political leaders. There, he became mentor to the brilliant young Aristotle. Except for a journey to Sicily in the 360s, Plato spent the rest of his life in Athens running the school and writing. He died there in 347 B.C. at about the age of eighty.

Plato is nearly unique among the ancient Greek writers in that all of his major works have survived to the present. They cover a wide range of topics, but are especially concerned with ethical, moral, political, and legal issues. His *Republic* (ca. 380 B.C.), widely viewed as his masterpiece, for example, begins by attempting to define the concept of justice and then proceeds to lay out his plan for an ideal state and its government, which would be ruled by philosopher-kings. The *Republic* also contains an explanation of Plato's esoteric "theory of forms." In this view, the visible, touchable objects of our earthly existence are merely imperfect copies of perfect "forms" that exist in an ideal, invisible realm. This attempt to describe physical reality constituted only part of Plato's scientific inquiry; his *Timaeus,* a comprehensive summary of the formation of the universe and the composition of the heavenly bodies, exerted a profound influence on scholars in later ancient, medieval, and early modern times.

The majority of Plato's works take the form of a dialectic (*dialektiki*), or dialogue, in which two or more characters engage in a session of questions and answers. The central character is usually Socrates, his old mentor, who directs the discussion, in the course of which several preconceived notions about the topic in question are refuted by logical means. The remaining notion is assumed to be the truth, or a rough approximation of it. This became known as the Socratic method in Socrates' honor. Besides the *Republic* and *Timaeus,* some of the most famous of Plato's dialogues are the *Euthyphro,* which seeks into the nature of piety in the wake of Socrates' indictment for impiety; the *Crito,* set in Socrates' jail cell as he awaits execution, which addresses the issue of respect for law; the *Phaedo,* which describes Socrates' death and deals with the nature of the soul; the *Protagoras,* concerned with the nature of virtue; and the *Symposium,* which seeks to understand the nature of love.

Fortunately all of the major works of the noted thinker Plato, depicted in this cameo, have survived.

Plutarch   (ca. A.D. 46–ca. 120) Born at Chaeronea (in Boeotia), the Greek biographer, essayist, and moralist Plutarch proved to be one of the most widely read and best-loved writers in history. Active in local affairs in his native city, as well as the priesthood of the shrine at Delphi, he also became a Roman citizen and resided for a time in Rome. He is most famous for his biographies of prominent Greek and Roman figures, collectively known as the *Parallel Lives,* fifty of which survive. (The most notable lost lives were those of the Theban leader Epaminondas and the Roman general Scipio Africanus.) Although he was not a historian by trade, Plutarch's sources included hundreds of ancient historical works that are now lost; therefore, for modern historians these colorfully-written biographies constitute priceless mines of information about Greco-Roman history from about 600 to 200 B.C. The sixteenth-century translation of the *Lives* by Sir Thomas North was the main source for Shakespeare's plays *Coriolanus, Julius Caesar,* and *Antony and Cleopatra.* Plutarch's equally large output of commentary on literary, scientific, and moral issues was collected as the *Moralia* (*Moral Essays*).

Polybius   (ca. 200–ca. 117 B.C.) An Achaean statesman and important historian, he was one of many Greek hostages taken to Rome after the Roman victory at Pydna in 168 B.C. There, he became the friend of the Roman general Scipio Aemilianus; when Scipio destroyed Carthage in 146, Polybius witnessed the event. Later, Polybius wrote a forty-volume history of Rome covering the period 220–146 B.C. Only the first five books survive complete, although numerous fragments of the others are extant. His writing style is not as lively and appealing as that of Herodotus or Thucydides; but as a historian Polybius was largely honest, thorough, and accurate, and his frequent analysis of historical methods helped to advance the art of historical writing.

Polyclitus   (late fifth century B.C.) One of ancient Greece's greatest sculptors, he was a native of Argos (in the Peloponnesus). He worked mainly in bronze, producing numerous statues of naked athletes that were displayed at Olympia. His most celebrated work was a large gold and ivory statue of the goddess Hera, which stood inside her temple at Argos.

Polygnotus   (flourished ca. 475–447 B.C.) Born on the island of Thasos, Polygnotus was a gifted mural painter who worked mainly at Athens. His innovations consisted of spreading his figures across the painting (rather than in a single line) and giving their faces lifelike expressions. His most famous painting was the *Capture of Troy,* displayed at Delphi, which the Greek traveler Pausanias describes in his guidebook.

Poseidon   Brother of Zeus and Hades and ruler of the seas, Poseidon became known as the "earth-shaker" because he supposedly caused earthquakes. He was also identified as Poseidon Hippios (Poseidon of the Horses) because of his skill as a horse-tamer. His symbols were the trident (three-pronged spear), dolphins, and horses.

Praxiteles   (flourished ca. 370–330 B.C.) One of the greatest and most influential of Greek sculptors, the Athenian Praxiteles worked in both bronze and marble. His most famous creation, the Aphrodite of Cnidus, is lost, along with most of the others, although a number of later copies of it survive. In 1877, a statue (of Hermes holding an infant Dionysus) attributed to him by the ancient Greek traveler Pausanias was discovered at Olympia and may be the original.

Prometheus   In Greek mythology, Prometheus (whose name means "forethought"), one of the Titans (first race of gods), was credited with fashioning the first humans out of clay (after which the goddess Athena breathed life into them). Later, Zeus asked him to decide how the humans should go about making sacrifices to the gods. The wily Prometheus tricked Zeus by arranging for the gods to receive the bones and fat of the animals sacrificed and for the humans to keep and eat the meat. In retaliation, Zeus denied the humans knowledge of fire; but Prometheus took pity on his creations and gave them fire he had stolen from heaven. The angry Zeus then punished the Titan by having Hephaestos (god of the forge) chain him to a mountaintop, where a vulture (in some versions an eagle) daily devoured his liver (which grew back at night). Eventually, the hero Heracles set Prometheus free. The tragic dramatist Aeschylus portrayed the Titan's punishment and noble heart and spirit in his play, *Prometheus Bound* (ca. 455 B.C.) See **Heracles, Zeus.**

Protagoras   (ca. 485–ca. 420 B.C.) A philosopher and the best known of the sophists (traveling teachers of rhetoric and other subjects who dispensed "wisdom" for a fee), he hailed from Abdera (in Thrace). One of the places he visited was Athens, where he became friendly with the statesman Pericles and may have known and influenced Socrates. According to Protagoras, no absolute truths, such as right or wrong, exist; rather, all aspects of reality are relative and determined by how a human observer perceives and judges them. This is the basis for the famous opening line of his treatise, *Truth:* "Man is the measure of all things." That work did not survive intact; only quotations and references in the works of later writers preserve his ideas. Also, Plato makes him one of the characters in a dialogue, the *Protagoras,* in which the participants debate the nature of "virtue" and how it can be acquired.

Ptolemy   The family name of a Greek Macedonian dynasty that ruled Egypt from the late 320s until 30 B.C. When Alexander the Great died in 323, one of his strongest generals, Ptolemy (TAW-luh-mee), was then his governor in Egypt. During the ensuing wars of the Successors, Ptolemy managed to hold onto and even to expand the region, absorbing territory in Palestine and elsewhere in the eastern Mediterranean. In 304, he took the official title of King Ptolemy I; and three years later, to commemorate a major victory over another Successor, Antigonus, he added the epithet Soter, meaning "Savior." After consolidating his kingdom and establishing the famous Great

Library at Alexandria, Ptolemy I died circa 282 B.C. He was succeeded by his son, Ptolemy II Philadelphus (reigned 282–246), who married his own sister, Arsinoë (ar-SIN-oh-eh) II, and established a ruler-cult in which he and she were worshipped as living gods. Most of the succeeding Ptolemies were far weaker rulers. The kingdom ceased to expand under Ptolemy III Euergetes (r. 246–221); lost most of its eastern Mediterranean territories under Ptolemy V Epiphanes (r. 204–180); and by the time of Ptolemy XI, Alexander II (r.80) had become little more than a chess piece in the hands of ambitious Roman politicians. The last Ptolemaic ruler was Cleopatra VII (r. 48–30), daughter of Ptoelmy XII Auletes. See **Cleopatra VII.**

Pyrrhus   (319–272 B.C.) A second cousin of Alexander the Great, Pyrrhus was the most illustrious king of the kingdom of Epirus and the first major Greek general to fight the Romans. As a boy, he ruled from 307 to 303, but was forced to flee and fell in with the military strongman Demetrius Poliorcetes. After fighting in the battle of Ipsus (301 B.C.), Pyrrhus became friends with Egypt's Ptolemy I and married his daughter. With Ptolemy's help, he regained his throne and soon fought his old mentor Demetrius for control of Macedonia. In 280, Pyrrhus allowed himself to be diverted by a call for aid from the Greek city of Taras (Tarentum), in southern Italy. There, he fought several battles against the encroaching Romans; but though he was usually victorious, his losses were heavy; and he is famous for his remark, "One more victory like that over the Romans will destroy us completely!" (the source of the term "Pyrrhic victory"; quoted in Plutarch, *Life of Pyrrhus* 21) Pyrrhus returned to Greece in 275, tried again to conquer Macedonia, but then died prematurely in a street fight.

Pythagoras   (late sixth century B.C.) The mathematician and philosopher Pythagoras was born on the island of Samos and moved to Croton (in southern Italy) about 531 B.C. There he established a religious community that attracted a number of followers to his teachings. These included the doctrine of reincarnation and the belief that the soul is immortal and is trapped in the body, but might earn release. For the sake of the soul, he advocated an austere, monk-like lifestyle of silence, self-denial, and refraining from eating meat. Pythagoras's philosophical-scientific ideas revolved around the study of numbers and proportions, which, he claimed, underlie the structure of the world and cosmos. He is credited with discovering the theorem named after him (the square of the hypotenuse of a right triangle is equal to the sum of the squares of the other two sides), although this may have been known earlier to the Egyptians. Pythagoras and his followers held that the earth is a sphere and that it and other heavenly bodies rest within larger, invisible, concentric spheres, an idea that profoundly influenced later thinkers, including Aristotle and the second-century A.D. Greek astronomer Ptolemy.

Rome   The Italian city-state whose empire eventually conquered and absorbed the Greek kingdoms and cities in the second and first centuries B.C.

The famed seven hills of Rome were occupied by Latin tribes as early as 1000 B.C. (during Greece's Dark Age) and a central town emerged at least by the mid–700s (an event that may have inspired the city's traditional founding date, later fixed at 753 B.C.). Rome was at first ruled by kings; but in 509 B.C. the monarchy was overthrown and replaced by the Republic, ruled largely by the Senate (made up of well-to-do aristocrats).

Rome's first major encounters with the Greeks were diplomatic relations, soon followed by military confrontations, with the many Greek cities that had sprung up in southern Italy beginning in the eighth century B.C. By the early third century, the Romans had absorbed these cities and become masters of all Italy. In the Second Punic War (218–201 B.C.), Macedonia aided Rome's opponent, Carthage, and thereby invited Roman punishment, marking the beginning of Rome's rapid eclipse of the Greek eastern Mediterranean sphere. By 146 B.C., the whole of mainland Greece was in Roman hands and in the years that followed all of the Greek lands became parts of various Roman provinces.

In the late first century B.C., after several devastating civil wars rocked the Roman world, the Republic fell and gave way to the more autocratic Roman Empire. Greece remained a dependent part of the Empire for several more centuries, until the western Roman government, beset by internal decay and external invasions, disintegrated in the fifth century A.D. The eastern Roman sphere, with Greece at its center, survived and became the Byzantine Empire, which finally fell to the Ottoman Turks in 1453.

Sappho   (late seventh century B.C.) A prominent lyric poet and one of the few female literary figures of ancient Greece, she was born in Mytilene, on the island of Lesbos. Little is known about her life, except for a few clues she reveals in her verses, for instance, the fact that she had a daughter whom she loved dearly. The story that Sappho jumped to her death from a cliff because of her unrequited love for a boatman is most likely a fable. Her surviving works (two complete poems and about 150 fragments), mostly describing the other young women in the local cult of Aphrodite to which she belonged, display unusual intensity, directness, honesty, and often erotic qualities.

Satyrs   In Greek mythology, creatures part-man and part-goat (or part-horse) who attended the fertility god Dionysus, and, like him, were rascally, lustful, and fond of revelry. The most famous of their number was Silenus and they were frequently portrayed in art and on the Athenian stage.

Seleucus   (ca. 358–281 B.C.) One of the Successors of Alexander the Great and founder of the Hellenistic Seleucid Empire, he was governor of Babylon in 321 B.C. Soon afterward Seleucus became involved in intrigues with other Successors that resulted in the death of Perdiccas and a falling out with a former ally, Antigonus. In 315, Seleucus fled to Egypt and joined forces with Ptolemy I and the two then defeated Antigonus's son, Demetrius, in 312. This victory allowed Seleucus to regain Babylon and take control of much of central and western Persia. After the battle of Ipsus (301), where he joined Cassander and Lysimachus in defeating Antigonus and Demetrius, Seleucus gained valuable territory in Syria and access to the Mediterranean Sea. He then founded Seleuceia, on the Tigris River, as his eastern capital, and Antioch (named for his son and eventual heir, Antiochus), on the Syrian coast, as his western capital. Later, in 281 B.C., Seleucus was assassinated while attempting to capture Macedonia.

Silenus   See **Midas, Satyrs**.

Simonides   (ca. 556–ca. 468 B.C.) A noted lyric poet and uncle of another famous poet, Bacchylides, Simonides was born on the small Cycladic island of Ceos but traveled to and worked in Athens, Thessaly, Syracuse, and other Greek locales. Most of his dirges, drinking songs, epigrams, and hymns, popular in his day, are now lost, although a few survive in fragments, the most famous being his epitaph for the Greek heroes who fell at Thermopylae in 480 B.C.: "Go now, and tell the Spartans, passer-by, that here obedient to their laws we lie."

Socrates   A dynamic, controversial Athenian philosopher whose intellectual ideas and methods have had a profound influence on Western thought and culture, Socrates was born about 469 B.C. Most of what little is known about his life comes from the writings of two of his followers—Plato and Xenophon. Socrates served as an infantryman in the early stages of the Peloponnesian War, distinguishing himself for his courage. Though he apparently lived a normal middle-class lifestyle in the first half of his life, at

Socrates confronts his judges in this early modern rendering of his trial for "corrupting the city's youth." The jury eventually found him guilty and sentenced him to death.

some unknown date he underwent a voluntary and drastic transition to a life of poverty and self-denial. Thereafter, he devoted himself to seeking life's "truths" and attempting to define such ethical concepts as goodness and right conduct. He also became a self-appointed "gadfly" of the community, endeavoring to challenge traditional beliefs and institutions through the use of logic. Wandering about dressed as a pauper, and often barefoot, he became known for engaging people in a series of questions and answers in an attempt to get at the truth of some subject. Throughout, he would profess his own ignorance, for the kernel of his philosophy was that people are ignorant and must relentlessly seek knowledge, which is the truest virtue. This method of questioning, later called the "Socratic" method in his honor, became immortalized in Plato's dialogues, in which Socrates is often the main character.

Though mocked by many of this countrymen and satirized by the comic playwrights, including Aristophanes (in *Clouds*), Socrates acquired a circle of devotees (among them Plato and Xenophon). Unfortunately, some of these followers, notably Alcibiades and Critias, later became widely hated public enemies. And the philosopher's association with them, coupled with his anti-democratic sentiments, led to his trial and condemnation to death in 399 B.C. (The charges—that he did not worship the traditional gods and that he had corrupted Athens's youth through his teachings—were trumped up.) As most of his close followers watched and wept in his jail cell, he availed himself of the right to take his own life by drinking poison. He left no writings of his own, but lives on in those of Plato and Xenophon. "I can truly say," Plato later wrote, "that of all the men I have ever known, he was by far the best, the wisest, and most just." (*Phaedo* 118) For more on Socrates, see **Plato.**

Solon   (ca. 640–ca. 560 B.C.) A noted Athenian lawgiver, political and social reformer, and poet. In 594, when Athens was on the brink of a civil war between the wealthy, aristocratic faction and a coalition of the middle and lower classes, the people asked Solon, who had gained a reputation for wisdom and fairness, to intercede. In the office of archon (administrator), he proceeded to implement a series of sweeping reforms, which paved the way for the emergence of full-fledged democracy later in the century. These included: cancellation of all debts (which allowed both individuals and the economy as a whole to have a fresh start); abolition of "debt-bondage" (which allowed a creditor to enslave debtors who could not pay); repeal of the too-harsh laws enacted earlier by the statesman Draco (except those involving murder); and making wealth, rather than birth, the chief prerequisite for holding political office (a reform that greatly reduced the power of the aristocrats). Soon after enacting these and other reforms, Solon left Athens and traveled widely (including to Egypt, where supposedly he heard about the legend of Atlantis). Some fragments of his poetry, in which he expresses his political beliefs, survive. See **Draco, Pisistratus.**

Sophocles (ca. 496–406 B.C.) One of the four great fifth-century B.C. Athenian dramatists, Sophocles was born in the small Athenian deme of Colonus, whose name he later immortalized in his play *Oedipus at Colonus.* A friend of the statesman Pericles and the historian Herodotus, he took an active role in public life, serving in 443 as treasurer of the federation of states that made up Athens's maritime empire and possibly as a military general in 440. But the main focus of his long life was the theater, for which he reportedly wrote 123 plays. Only seven of these, all tragedies, have survived complete, among them his three Theban plays, *Antigone, Oedipus the King,* and *Oedipus at Colonus,* and the *Ajax.* Some substantial fragments of his satyr-play, *The Trackers,* also exist.

An innovator, Sophocles is credited with introducing a third actor on the stage; and he was a master of dialogue and dramatic irony. He was also the most honored of all Greek playwrights, winning eighteen victories at the City Dionysia. Indeed, in his *Poetics,* Aristotle praised Sophocles above all other dramatists. The widespread respect and admiration for him, not only as a dramatist, but also as an upright, kind, and caring individual, is testified in the tribute paid him shortly after his death by his colleague, Aristophanes: "Sophocles, gentleman always, is a gentleman still." (*Frogs* 81–82)

Sparta One of Greece's leading city-states from the seventh to fourth century B.C., Sparta (or Lacedaemon) is located in Laconia (in the southeastern Peloponnesus). A Bronze Age settlement at Therapne, two miles southeast of the site of classical Sparta, may have been the center of the Spartan kingdom mentioned in Homer's *Iliad,* over which King Menelaus ruled. During the Dark Age, Dorian Greeks settled the area and for reasons unknown two royal families (the Agiads and Eurypontids) emerged. This appears to be the reason that Sparta had two kings ruling jointly for many centuries to come. In time, the power of these kings was checked by five senior officials (ephors), a Council of Elders (*gerousia*), and an assembly (*apella*) made up of free-born Spartans (Spartiates), so that the kings retained mainly religious and military duties. Sometime in the mid-600s B.C. the city underwent a series of major political-social reforms, usually credited to the semi-legendary lawgiver Lycurgus. From then on, all state and private institutions were highly regimented and geared to producing strong soldiers to man the most effective and feared land army in Greece.

In the sixth and fifth centuries B.C., Sparta's military proved itself time and again. The Spartans came to dominate the Peloponnesus, leading an alliance of subordinate states (the Peloponnesian League); and in the Persian War of 480–479 B.C., Sparta assumed leadership, along with Athens, of the allied defense of Greece. Not long afterward, the Spartans were weakened by a serious earthquake (464) and a rebellion of their serfs (the helots, former residents of the neighboring state of Messenia). But they rebounded and for the next several years carried on a rivalry with the Athenians for supremacy in Greece. This culminated in the destructive Peloponnesian War (431–404), which Sparta and its allies won. For the next three decades, Sparta was Greece's dominant power; but its insensitive, heavy-handed dealings with other states made it widely disliked. In 371, the supposedly invincible Spartan phalanx suffered a devastating defeat at the hands of the Thebans, who then invaded the Peloponnesus and freed most of the region's cities from Spartan domination.

After this, Sparta became isolated and suffered serious decline. The Spartans remained proud and defiant (as when they refused to join the Greek confederacy forged by Macedonia's Philip II in the 330s B.C.); but their glory days were over. In the early second century B.C. they were forced to join the Achaean League (an alliance of Peloponnesian cities); and when Rome defeated the League in 146 B.C., Sparta, by this time a backward little town of only a few thousand people, became part of the Roman province of Macedonia.

Strabo   (ca. 64 B.C.–ca. A.D. 25) A late Hellenistic Greek traveler and geographer, he was born in Amasia (in northern Asia Minor) and moved to Rome in 44 B.C. to further his education. From there, he traveled widely throughout the Mediterranean world and took notes on the histories, economies, inhabitants, animals, and plants of the locales he visited. This information became the basis for his monumental *Geography* in seventeen books, which survives and provides modern scholars with much valuable information about the world of his day.

Strato   (late fourth–early third century B.C.) The noted philosopher-scientist Strato (or Straton) of Lampsacus (in northwestern Asia Minor) studied at Aristotle's Lyceum, then moved to Alexandria, where he tutored the young Ptolemy II Philadelphus. After Theophrastus's death (ca. 287), Strato returned to Athens and took charge of the Lyceum. Fascinated by the emerging field of mechanics, especially the concepts of force and motion, Strato proposed that all objects have weight and also correctly described the phenomenon of acceleration. Of the more than forty treatises attributed to him, none survive complete, but a number of fragments and quotations exist in the works of later writers.

Thales   (flourished ca. 600 B.C.) According to tradition, Thales of Miletus was the first known Greek philosopher-scientist and the founder of the Ionian school of thought. He supposedly predicted the solar eclipse of 585 B.C. (which took place during a battle between the Medes and Lydians), although modern scholars consider this unlikely. Tradition also credits him with inventing geometry, based to some extent on Egyptian mathematical ideas. Thales was apparently the first thinker to theorize about natural principles, proposing that nature's main underlying substance (*physis*) is water.

Thebes   The principle city of Boeotia (bee-OH-shya), the region of the Greek mainland lying just north of Attica, Thebes played a pivotal role in Greek mythology and history. According to legend, Cadmus, a prince of the Phoenician city of Tyre, established Thebes while searching for his sister Europa (whom Zeus had abducted). Cadmus may be the name of an actual early king of Thebes, since archaeology confirms the existence of a Mycenaean settlement on the site in the Bronze Age. Other famous legends about early Thebes were later collected into three epic poems (the *Oedipodia, Thebaïd,* and *Epigoni*). Now lost, these provided inspiration for many of the plays of Aeschylus, Sophocles, and other fifth-century B.C. Athenian dramatists.

The classical city of Thebes rose to prominence in the sixth century B.C. when it gained dominance over the other Boeotian cities, forming a loose confederation (the Boeotian League). In the fifth century, Thebes and neighboring Athens were usually enemies, with the Thebans backing the Spartans in the Peloponnesian War. However, in the early fourth century, Thebes and Sparta developed a rivalry that climaxed in 371 B.C. with the utter defeat of Sparta's phalanx at Leuctra (in western Boeotia) by a Theban army commanded by the brilliant Epaminondas. Soon afterward, Thebes enjoyed a brief hegemony over Greece. But the city's influence waned after Epaminondas's death in 362. In 338, Thebes and Athens formed an alliance in hopes of stopping Macedonia's Philip II from conquering southern Greece; but he crushed them that year at Chaeronea and proceeded to dissolve the Boeotian League. Under Philip's successor, Alexander, the Thebans rebelled and he punished them by almost totally destroying the city (sparing only the temples and the house of the poet Pindar). A few years later, one of Alexander's successors, Cassander, rebuilt Thebes; but it never regained its former power and influence. See **Epaminondas, Oedipus, Pelopidas.**

Themistocles An important and controversial Athenian statesman-general, Themistocles was one of the principal leaders of the Greek resistance to the Persian invasion of 480 B.C. and the father of Athenian naval supremacy. Born of a prominent Athenian family sometime in the 520s, he first distinguished himself as archon (administrator) in 493, when he organized the initial construction of Athens's docks and naval base at Piraeus. After the battle of Marathon, in which he fought, Themistocles, a liberal who supported radical democracy, became involved in political rivalries that saw several of his opponents ostracized (banished). His enemies apparently tried several times to do the same to him but failed, and he emerged as the most influential Athenian leader of the period. When a rich vein of silver was discovered in 483 at Athens's mines at Laurium (in southern Attica), he convinced the Assembly to use the money to build the largest fleet of ships in Greece. This soon proved crucial to Athens's (and Greece's) survival, for it enabled the Greeks to defeat the Persians in a large naval battle at Salamis in 480, a victory of which Themistocles was the chief architect.

Following the expulsion of the Persians, Themistocles pursued an anti-Spartan policy, correctly foreseeing that Sparta would become Athens's main nemesis in the coming years. Despite Spartan objections, he rebuilt Athens's city walls (which the Persians had demolished) and formed alliances with some of Sparta's enemies. However, he fell from power when a new political rival, Cimon, who was pro-Spartan, engineered his ostracism ca. 472–471 B.C. In the years that followed, Themistocles traveled through Greece stirring up anti-Spartan sentiments; and at Sparta's urging, Athens finally indicted him for treason, surely an unwarranted charge. He took refuge in Persian Asia Minor, where he died about 463 B.C.

Theognis   (mid–sixth century B.C.) Hailing from the city of Megara (northwest of Athens), Theognis wrote elegiac poetry that lamented the aristocracy's loss of power at a time when tyrants held sway in many Greek cities. Only about a third of the poems in a surviving collection attributed to him appear to be genuine; the others are probably by later imitators.

Theophrastus   Born about 370 B.C. at Eresus, on the island of Lesbos, Theophrastus was a noted philosopher-scholar who succeeded his friend Aristotle as director of the Athenian Lyceum. When Theophrastus died (ca. 287), money from his will enabled the school to move to larger facilities, which became known as the Peripatos (after a colonnaded walkway, or *peripatos,* located on the grounds). His works covered a wide range of subjects; but his most important surviving treatises are the *History of Plants* and *Causes of Plants,* which in later ages earned him the well-deserved nickname of the "Father" of botany. In a lighter vein, his *Characters* is a collection of humorous sketches of character types common in his day.

Theseus   A legendary early (Bronze Age) Athenian king and ancient Athens's national hero, he was the son of King Aegeus (after whom the Aegean Sea was named). Theseus was said to have performed numerous heroic deeds, including killing the fearsome bull of Marathon and traveling to Knossus (on Crete) and slaying the hideous Minotaur, to which Athenian youths had regularly been sacrificed. After succeeding his father as king, Theseus supposedly unified the scattered communities of Attica into a single Athenian state. Later, he married Hippolyta, queen of the Amazons (the famed tribe of warrior women), and launched an unsuccessful invasion of Attica to recover her. Rebellions eventually drove Theseus from Athens to the isle of Scyros, where he died. In 475 B.C., the Athenian leader Cimon journeyed to Scyros and brought back the bones of a large man, claiming these were Theseus's remains.

Thespis   (late sixth century B.C.) An Athenian who is credited with inventing the theatrical conventions of playwriting, dialogue, tragedy, and masks, and for becoming the first actor. Apparently a prominent member of the dithyrambic rituals, Thespis introduced the innovation of a worshiper impersonating, rather than merely describing, the characters honored in these ceremonies. He was supposedly the first winner of the dramatic contests at the City Dionysia in 534 B.C. None of his plays have survived, but his name lives on in the term "thespian," describing an actor or theater devotee.

Thucydides (ca. 500–ca. 420 B.C.) A right-wing Athenian politician. Related to Cimon and probably the maternal grandfather and namesake of the famous historian, he led the aristocratic faction against Pericles and the liberal party in the 440s. Thucydides was ostracized in 443, after which he apparently played no further role in the political arena.

Thucydides (ca. 460/455–ca. 400 B.C.) Born into a well-to-do Athenian family, he wrote a detailed history of the Peloponnesian War (which ends abruptly in 411 and is therefore incomplete), the principal surviving source for that momentous conflict. He may have been related to the noted conservative Athenian politicians Cimon and Thucydides. Eventually, the historian broke with his family's political traditions and supported the liberal democratic faction led by Pericles, whom he quotes extensively in his history. In 424, during the great war, Thucydides was elected general. But after failing to stop the Spartans from capturing the strategic city of Amphipolis, he was banished. At the conclusion of the conflict in 404, he was allowed to return to his native city, where he died about four years later of unknown causes.

Many modern experts consider Thucydides the world's first great historian, since he was the first to follow a strict chronology, to avoid fables, and to explain events strictly in terms of human motivations and deeds. Moreover, as he himself states in the work, he either personally witnessed or interviewed others who had witnessed the events he describes. "My work is not a piece of writing designed to meet the taste of an immediate public," he wrote, defending his high standards of reporting, "but was done to last forever." (*Peloponnesian War* 1.22) Time has shown that he achieved this goal admirably, for the work remains a historical as well as literary masterpiece.

Titans In Greek mythology, the first race of gods, who sprang from the union of Uranus (the Heavens) and Gaia (the Earth). The male Titans included Oceanus, Coeus, Crius, Hyperion, Iapetus, and Cronus; the female Titans were Thea, Rhea, Themis, Mnemosyne, Phoebe, and Tethys. In a huge conflict (which the Greeks called the Titanomachia), the Titans were defeated by the next race of gods, the Olympians, led by Zeus. See **Cronus, Olympians.**

Troy Located on the coast of northwestern Asia Minor, near the Hellespont, Troy (or Ilium) was the famous city besieged by the Greeks in the legendary Trojan War, which supposedly began when the Trojan prince, Paris, abducted the Spartan queen, Helen. The war, waged by the kings of many Greek states, lasted ten years and ended with the city's destruction. A number of ancient epic poems described different aspects of the war, the most famous (and the only surviving one) being Homer's *Iliad,* about the wrath of the Greek warrior Achilles during the last year of fighting. The nineteenth-century German archaeologist Heinrich Schilemann unearthed Troy, showing that it was a real city in the Bronze Age; and modern excavators have determined that it did undergo a siege in the approximate period of the legendary war (ca. 1250–1200 B.C.), although it is not certain that this was the war Homer describes.

Tyrtaeus (seventh century B.C.) He was a Spartan poet (and possibly a military general) who wrote elegiac verse (written for recital with flute accompaniment), some of it glorifying his country's conquest of its neighbor, Messenia. Some of his poems and marching songs became paeans (battle hymns) sung by Spartan hoplites entering battle.

Uranus (or Uranos) In Greek mythology, an early god who manifested himself as the heavens. After Gaia, a manifestation of the earth, gave birth to him, they mated and produced a race of gods known as the Titans. See **Cronus, Titans.**

Xanthippus (ca. 525–475 B.C.) Father of the famous Athenian statesman Pericles, he successfully prosecuted the popular general Miltiades in 489; but a few years later, at the height of his popularity, Xanthippus (zan-THIP-us) was ostracized and banished (probably due to the efforts of the left-wing politician Themistocles). In 480, Athens recalled Xanthippus during the crisis of the Persian invasion. He was elected general in 479 and that same year commanded the Athenian fleet in the Greek victory over the Persians at Mycale (in western Asia Minor).

Xenophanes (ca. 570–ca. 470 B.C.) Hailing from Colophon, in Ionia, Xenophanes (zen-OFF-uh-neez) was an early Greek philosopher and poet who traveled widely and spent most of his later life in Sicily. His works survive only in fragments, which reveal him to be a deep thinker on a number of issues. Regarding religion, he was unique in his rejection of polytheistic and anthropomorphic notions about many gods having human form, advocating instead a single, eternal deity of undetermined form, in a way a sort of "overmind." Also, after finding fossilized fish in Sicilian quarries, he correctly deduced that the area had once been under water (and therefore might be again in the future).

Xenophon The noted soldier and historian Xenophon (ZEN-uh-phon) was born about 428 B.C. into a well-to-do and aristocratic Athenian family. As a young man he, like Plato, became a friend and follower of the eccentric philosopher Socrates, whom Xenophon later remembered fondly in his *Memorabilia.* Xenophon likely served in the Athenian military during the latter stages of the Peloponnesian War. In a later treatise, the *Hellenica,* his most important historical work, he chronicled the events of the war from 411 B.C. (where Thucydides left off) to 404 (when Athens surrendered) and continued the narrative to 362, encompassing the Spartan and Theban hegemonies of Greece. Though this work is crucial for modern scholars' understanding of this period, its author was unfortunately not as skilled a historical writer as his contemporary, Thucydides, and sometimes glosses over or leaves out important events and figures.

Xenophon's descriptions of events in which he actually took part are much more detailed, as evidenced by his *Anabasis* (*March Up-Country*) the story of the heroic March of the Ten Thousand. In 401, he was one of the

Greek mercenaries stranded in Persia after the rebellion of the Persian prince Cyrus the Younger collapsed. Xenophon's account of how he helped lead the Greeks through some 1,500 miles of hostile territory to the Black Sea and safety remains one of the most gripping adventure tales ever written.

About 399 B.C., while Xenophon was still in Asia, his countrymen exiled him for life, perhaps partly because of his former association with Socrates, who was executed that year for supposedly "corrupting" the local youth. Xenophon took refuge in Sparta, where he became friendly with one of its kings, Agesilaus, whose biography he later penned. About 388, the writer settled with his wife and two sons near Olympia and there wrote several treatises, including *On Hunting, On Horsemanship, The Education of Cyrus* (a sort of historical novel about the founder of the Persian Empire), *The Constitution of the Lacedaemonians* (about Sparta's government), and the *Oeconomicus* (a detailed description of how a country gentleman, like himself, should run his estate and household). When Xenophon was about sixty, he was allowed to return to his native Athens, where he died circa 354 B.C. See **Cyrus II the Younger, Socrates.**

Xerxes I   King of Persia from 486 to 465 B.C., Xerxes (ZERK-seez), son of Darius I, launched a massive invasion of Greece in 480, during which he won a minor victory at Thermopylae and occupied Athens. However, his forces soon suffered a major defeat in the sea battle of Salamis, forcing him to retire to Asia Minor. The army he left behind to continue the war was annihilated the following year. Xerxes was assassinated about 465 and the conspirators placed his eighteen-year-old son, Artaxerxes, on the throne.

Zeno   (mid–fifth century B.C.) A philosopher hailing from Elea (on Italy's southwestern coast), he was a disciple of Parmenides, the founder of the Eleatic school of thought, which held that all matter is indivisible and unchanging. Zeno became known for his paradoxes, which reduced standard perceptions of the physical world to absurdities. For example, he argued that matter cannot be composed of individual separate pieces because there would have to be something between the pieces; and if so, that something would itself have to be separable into pieces, and so forth into infinity. See **Parmenides**.

Zeno   (ca. 335–262 B.C.) A Hellenistic philosopher, Zeno (or Zenon) of Citium (on the island of Cyprus), who may have been of Phoenician stock, founded the Stoic school of thought circa 300. He moved to Athens in 313 and studied at Plato's Academy, but soon underwent radical changes in thinking and began lecturing in the Athenian Agora in a building called the Stoa Poikile (Painted Colonnade), from which the movement drew its name. Stoicism pictured a cosmos endowed with divine purpose or intelligence, a tiny spark of divine fire existing in every human. Therefore, all people, from wealthy aristocrats to lowly slaves, are spiritual brothers. Moreover, the key to happiness is virtue, which is a form of wisdom, exemplified by courage, moderation, and shouldering responsibility; while greed, fear, extravagance, and dishonesty are symptoms of ignorance and will lead to certain misery. The Stoic movement was moderately popular in the Hellenistic Greek world but attained a wide following in Rome in the first two centuries A.D. and its ideas eventually contributed to the developing outlook of early Christian thinkers.

Zenodotus   (early third century B.C.) The first director of Alexandria's Great Library (ca. 285–ca. 270), he also served as a tutor to the royal Ptolemaic house. He is best known for his literary editions of Homer's epic poems, which he carefully edited and divided into twenty-four books each, the forms they have maintained ever since.

Zeus   Ruler of the gods, he was known for his control of thunder, lightening, and rain, as well as for maintaining justice, law, and morality. He had frequent affairs with mortal women, appearing to them in various disguises, including a bull and a swan. Numerous religious festivals and shrines were dedicated to him throughout Greece, including the Temple of Olympian Zeus and famous athletic games at Olympia (in the northwestern Peloponnesus). His principal symbols were the thunderbolt, eagle, and oak tree. See **Cronus, Olympians**.

Glossary of Terms

Editor's Note: For the reader's convenience, the Greek terms in italics below are transliterated; that is, their original Greek letters have been changed to English letters that sound approximately the same. For example, in Greek the word democracy is written δημοκρατια. The first letter, δ (delta), is pronounced roughly like the English *d*. After the other letters have been transliterated in the same manner, the result is *demokratia*. Some modern scholars transliterate the Greek letter κ (kappa), as the Latinized *c*, rendering *democratia*. However, most of the examples below render kappa as the English *k*; the exceptions are those words that have become most recognizable in their Latinized forms, notably *Ecclesia* (the Athenian Assembly), which is less often seen as *Ekklesia*. Also note that all accent and long marks have been eliminated in the transliteration. (For those who are interested in learning to read ancient Greek in its original form, an excellent starting point is Maurice Balme and Gilbert Lawall's, *Athenaze: An Introduction to Ancient Greek*. 2 vols. New York: Oxford University Press, 1990.)

abacus: A flat slab lying atop the **echinus** in the **capital** of a Doric column. See **order.**

acropolis: "The city's high place"; a hill, usually fortified, central to many Greek towns; the term in upper case (Acropolis) refers to the one in Athens.

acroteria (sing. **acroterion**): Statues, disks, and other kinds of ornaments placed at the three angles of each of a temple's **pediments**.

aegis: The goddess Athena's majestic and invincible breastplate (sometimes represented as a shield).

aesthesis: Perception by the senses.

agathos: Noble; or learned; or brave.

agoge: The various customs and institutions supporting Sparta's rigid military training system.

agon: A contest or struggle.

agora: A Greek marketplace and/or civic center; the term in upper case (Agora) refers to the one in Athens.

agoranomoi: At Athens, public officials who checked the weight and quality of goods in the marketplace.

aither (ether): The sky; or the upper air; or "the quintessence," according to Aristotle the incorruptible substance of which the heavens are composed.

Amazonomachy: The mythical battle between the Athenians and the Amazons, a legendary tribe of warrior women.

amphidromia: A post-birth ceremony in which relatives and friends sent gifts to the newborn's family.

amphora: A vase or jar with a narrow neck and handles on each side.

anagorisis: See *hamartia.*

andron: A room in which the master of a house dined and entertained guests.

antefixes: Ornaments placed upright at intervals along the tops of the **cornices** on a temple's sides.

antilabe: A leather handle on the back of a hoplite's shield that he gripped with his left hand. See **hoplite.**

antiquity: Ancient times; often used more specifically to denote the ancient Greek and Roman periods.

apheresis: A kind of divorce in which the wife's father intervened to dissolve the marriage.

apobates: A chariot race in which the driver dismounted one or more times during a race; *apobatai:* dismounters.

apographe: Denunciation.

apoikia (pl. *apoikiai*): A colony.

apoleipsis: A kind of divorce in which the wife got permission from a public official to leave her husband's house.

archon (*arkhon*): A public administrator.

Areopagus: At Athens, a hill that gave its name to an early aristocratic council and law court; the Areopagus wielded considerable power in Archaic times but in the Classic Age it mainly heard murder and arson cases.

arete: Personal excellence.

aristoi: "Best people"; aristocrats.

aristokratia: "Power in the hands of the best men"; aristocracy.

ariston: Lunch.

arrephoroi: Athenian maidens who lived on the Acropolis for a year in service to the goddess Athena.

asebeia: Impiety; lack of faith in or respect for the gods.

astai (sing. *aste*): Citizens who lacked political rights (most often applied to women).

ataraxia: Calmness; according to Epicurean philosophy, an untroubled state free from excessive pain and pleasure.

athanatos: Immorality.

atimia: "Dishonor"; loss of citizenship.

atimos: One who has lost citizenship.

atomos: That which is uncuttable or indivisible; an atom; one of the tiny particles of which matter is composed.

atsu: An urban area.

aulos: A flute (although, because it used a reed, it produced a sound more like that of a modern oboe).

autonomia: Political autonomy.

bailiff: An overseer who ran a country farm or estate for the well-to-do owner, who often dwelled in the city.

banausos: Vulgar or coarse.

barbarians (*barbaroi*): At first, a neutral term denoting most non-Greeks, i.e., those who did not speak Greek and whose speech sounded like "bar-bar-bar" to the Greeks; but from the early fourth century B.C. on, the term increasingly referred to those seen as mentally or morally "inferior" to Greeks.

basileus: A king or chieftain; a position held in Greece mainly in the Dark and Archaic Ages.

bios: Life.

bireme: A warship with two banks of oars. See **trireme.**

black-figure: A pottery style in which the painted figures and scenes are black against a reddish-orange background. See **red-figure.**

bosses: Knobs left projecting from the sides of stone building blocks; workers attached ropes to the bosses to lift them into place, then carved them off.

Boule: "Council"; the Athenian legislative body that formulated laws and state policy.

bouleuterion: The chamber in which the *Boule* met.

bouleutes (pl. *bouleutai*): In Athens, a member of the Council. See *Boule.*

brazier: A metal container in which people burned charcoal to provide interior heating.

bronze: A metal alloy composed of copper and tin.

capital: The decorative top piece of a column. See **order.**

caryatid: A pillar shaped like a graceful maiden. The most famous examples were those supporting the south porch of the Erechtheum on the Acropolis.

catharsis (*katharsis*): "Washing away"; cleansing; or purification from guilt; also often used to describe a release of emotional tension or an emotional cleansing generated by watching a tragic play.

cella (or *naos*): The main room of a Greek temple, usually housing the cult image (statue) of the god to whom the temple was dedicated.

Centauromachy: The mythical battle between the Lapiths, members of an early Greek tribe, and the Centaurs, creatures half-human and half-horse.

ceramos: Potter's clay.

charis: Thanks; gratitude.

chiton (*khiton*): A basic tunic worn by both men and women.

chlamys (*khlamys*): An outer cloak fastened at one shoulder by a brooch or pin, worn mostly by young men and soldiers.

choregus (pl. *choregoi*): A well-to-do backer of plays and other theatrical and cultural events.

chremata: Inanimate things; or merchandise; or paraphernalia (odds and ends, clutter).

chthonian: Having to do with the Underworld.

chutra: A crockery pot.

cithara (*kithara*): A harp-like instrument, probably similar to but larger than a lyre.

cleruchy: An Athenian settlement in conquered territory, it was an extension of Athenian territory and government rather than an independent colony.

colonnade: A row of columns.

concubine: See *pallake*.

cornice: The top section of a temple's **entablature**.

cosmos (*kosmos*): Order; or the world system; or the universe.

cottabos: A party game in which drinkers tried to hit a target with the wine dregs left in their cups.

crater: A mixing bowl or broad-brimmed cup.

cuirass: A breastplate or other chest protection worn by an ancient infantryman.

daemon: A spirit; or a guardian spirit; or a demigod.

decate: A post-birth ceremony in which parents named the newborn.

deipnon: Dinner or supper.

demarchos: At Athens, the chief executive officer of a deme.

demes (*demoi*): In ancient Attica, small ward-like geographical units or local communities.

demokratia: Democracy.

demos: The citizen body; or the sum of the state's democratic laws and institutions; or democrats; or the poorer citizens; or a local district (**deme**).

dialektiki (**dialectic**): A dialogue; a literary form made most famous by Plato, in which two or more characters engage in discussion, usually a series of questions and answers.

dialogue: See *dialektiki.*

dianoetikon: The power of thought.

diaulos: A footrace of two *stades* (or about 1,200 feet); also, a double-piped flute.

dicasts (*dikastai*): Jurors.

didaskaliai: Teachers, a term commonly applied to playwrights who trained their choruses and actors.

dikasteria: Jury courts.

dike: Justice; or order; or a legal process; or the right of a wronged person to bring a lawsuit in court.

dithyramb: Ceremonial poetry honoring the fertility god Dionysus; scholars believe that Greek drama developed in part from dithyrambic rituals.

divination (*mantike*): The prediction of the future by means of reading and interpreting omens and other divine signs.

dokimasia: A rigid examination made of Athenian candidates for public office.

dolichos: A footrace of twenty to twenty-four *stades*.

Doric order: See **order.**

dowry: Money or property a bride brought, via her father or other guardian, to her husband when she married him.

drachma: A silver coin issued by Athens and some other Greek states. For much of the fifth century B.C., Athenian drachmae (nicknamed "owls" because they bore the image of an owl, Athena's symbol) were the most common and valuable coins in the Mediterranean world. An Athenian drachma weighed 4.31 grams and was part of a system of currency in which 1 drachma=6 obols, 100 drachmae=1 mina, and 60 minae (6,000 drachmas)=1 talent. In the late fifth century B.C., the average Athenian worker and also a rower in the navy received a wage of 1 drachma per day; a juror received 3 obols (half a drachma) per day; a gallon of olive oil cost about 3 drachmae; a pair of shoes cost 6–8 drachmae; a slave cost 150–200 drachmae (or more if highly skilled); and land went for 200–300 drachmae per acre.

dromos: A stone runway leading to a *tholos* tomb.

drum: One of several circular stone sections making up a column's shaft.

dynamis: Power; or something having great potential.

Ecclesia: The Athenian Assembly, a meeting of the citizens to elect leaders and discuss and vote on state policies.

eccyclema: "Tableau machine"; in the theater, a movable platform on which actors posed in frozen tableaus.

echinus: The rounded cushion forming the bottom section of a Doric **capital**.

eidos: Form or shape.

eironeia: Irony, as in Socrates' claim to be ignorant when he was actually one of the wisest men of his day.

eisangelia: Impeachment.

eisphora: A tax on property.

ekdosis: The act of handing over the bride to the groom in a wedding ceremony.

ekechiria: The Olympic truce, during which Greek states were forbidden to make war or impose the death penalty.

ekhthroi (sing. *ekhthros*): Personal enemies.

ekpempsis (or *apopempsis*): A kind of divorce in which the husband repudiated his wife.

ekphora: The bearing of a deceased person's body to the gravesite.

ektesis: The exposure (leaving outside to die) of infants.

eleutheria: Political independence or freedom.

emporos: A wholesale trader.

engue (or *eggue*): A formal betrothal, usually conducted in front of witnesses.

entablature: In a Greek-style temple, the structural and usually highly ornamented layer resting between the column-tops and the roof.

entasis: A temple refinement consisting of a slight swelling or outward curvature of the middle of a column's shaft, intended to correct the illusion that the column is thinner in the middle than at the top and bottom.

Epheboi: The Athenian military training corps; *ephebe* (pl. *epheboi*): a recruit in the corps, also used more generally to denote a young man between the ages of eighteen and twenty.

ephetai: At Athens, early courts that heard cases of accidental killing.

ephor (*ephoros*): Elders or overseers; in Sparta and some other Greek states, an important government official; Sparta's five ephors oversaw the administration and personal conduct of the two Spartan kings.

epibatai: **Hoplite** marines that fought on warships.

epikleros: A young woman without a husband or brothers, who is expected to marry one of her father's relatives in order to keep the family property from passing to another family; or her status.

epinikia: Victory odes; poems written to honor the winners of athletic and other contests; for example, the Olympian, Nemean, Pythian, and Isthmian odes of Pindar.

episkyros: A team ball game probably similar to modern rugby (which is itself a precursor of American football).

epistates: A chairman of the Athenian Assembly or a committee of the *Boule,* who served for one day; the position then rotated to another member. See ***Boule, prytaneis.***

episteme: Science.

epistyle (or **architrave**): The bottom-most component of a temple's **entablature**, serving as a beam to hold up the building's upper sections.

epitaphios: A funeral speech.

ergastirai: Athenian maidens who wove Athena's sacred robe.

ether: See *aither.*

ethnos (pl. **ethne**): A tribe; or a group of peoples who have common customs and live in the same region but are not politically united, for example, the towns of Aetolia before they united into the Aetolian League.

ethos: A person's character or disposition; or a habit; or an accustomed place.

eudaimonia: Happiness or well-being.

exedra: An outside sitting/lounging area adjoining the courtyard of a house.

exposure: See *ektesis.*

fasti: A calendar of religious festivals and events.

flutes (or **fluting**): Narrow concave grooves running vertically along a column's shaft.

freedman (or **freedwoman**): A slave who gained his (or her) freedom.

frieze: A painted and/or sculpted ornamental band running around the perimeter of a building, most often a temple.

gamos: A wedding celebration.

geison: The lower section of a cornice, taking the form of a horizontal beam resting on the frieze and projecting outward beyond the entablature's vertical surface. See **entablature.**

gennātai: Members of a clan.

genos (pl. *genē*): A clan, made up of several families.

gerousia: In Sparta and some other Greek states, an aristocratic ruling council.

Gigantomachy: The mythical battle between the Olympian gods and a race of monstrous giants.

gnomon: The index of a sundial; or the L-shaped ruler used by a carpenter.

gnosis: Knowledge.

grammatistes: A teacher of reading, writing, and simple mathematics.

graphe (pl. *graphai*): A legal indictment.

greaves: Bronze shin-guards worn by Greek hoplites.

guttae: Rounded pegs (stone representations of nails in earlier wooden temples) projecting from the bottom of the mutules. See **mutules, entablature.**

gymnasium: A public facility in which men exercised, played sports, read, and attended lectures.

gymnastiki: Exercise.

gymnos: Naked.

gynaeceum (or *gynaikonitis*): The women's quarters of a Greek home.

gyne (or *damar*): Wife.

hamartia: A tragic error committed by the hero or some other character in a Greek tragedy; the *peripeteia* is the unexpected turn of events that reveals the error; and the *anagorisis* is the character's recognition of the error.

harmonie: Unity; the joining of two or more components to produce a structure greater than any of its parts.

hegemon: Supreme leader.

hegemony (*hegemonia*): "Leadership"; or dominance.

heliaia: At Athens, early appeals courts, probably consisting of meetings of the whole Assembly; later, a general term for courts.

Hellanodikai: Judges or officials at the Olympic Games.

Hellas (*'Ellas*): The name the ancient Greeks gave to their land. They called themselves Hellenes (*'Ellenes*); therefore Greek civilization is often referred to as Hellenic.

helots: Greeks who have been conquered by other Greeks and forced to work for them as serfs; most commonly associated with Sparta, which turned its neighbors, the Messenians, into helots.

Heraea: Women's athletic games held every four years in honor of the goddess Hera.

herm: A bust of Hermes, god of good fortune, placed near the front door of a house to ward off evil.

hetairai (sing. *hetaira*): "Companions"; high-class prostitutes; educated women who provided men with sex and intelligent conversation.

hexa-style: A temple style in which the pteron has six columns on each end and thirteen columns on each side (counting the corner columns twice).

hiereus: A priest; one who had special knowledge of sacred matters and/or looked after the sacred objects (*hiera*) in a temple; a priestess with the same duties was a *hiereia.*

hierodoulai: Sacred prostitutes; women (usually slaves) who had sexual relations with visitors to a temple sanctuary and donated the money to the sanctuary's upkeep.

himation: A loose-fitting garment that wrapped around the body in a variety of styles.

homoios (pl. *homoioi*): A peer or equal; or a person possessing full citizen status.

hopla: "Heavy equipment," specifically the armor worn by Greek infantrymen.

hoplite: A heavily armored infantry soldier.

hoplitodromos: A footrace in which the runners were fully or partially clad in armor.

hoplon (or *aspis*): The shield carried by a hoplite.

humor (*chymos*): According to the Greek Hippocratic physicians, one of the body's "flowing juices," which included blood, yellow bile, black bile, and phlegm.

hybris (**hubris**): Extreme arrogance or pride; or a violent or aggressive act.

hydria: A water jar.

hyle: Matter; or a material from which other things can be made.

hypaspists: "Shield-bearers"; light-armored infantrymen who protected the flanks (sides) of the Macedonian **phalanx**.

ila (pl. *ilai*): A cavalry squadron in the Macedonian army of Philip and

Alexander.

impiety: See *asebeia.*

in situ: A Latin term meaning "in its place," often used by archaeologists to describe the original position in which an artifact was discovered.

Ionic order: See **order.**

isonomia: Equality under the law.

kalokagathia: A healthy balance between mental (or moral) and physical excellence.

kalos: Beautiful; or excellent.

kanephoroi: Young girls selected from aristocratic Athenian families to march in the Panathenaic procession.

kapeloi: Retail traders.

katakysmata: At a wedding, a ceremonial shower of nuts and sweetmeats.

kedeia: A funeral.

kerkouroi: Large cargo ships, each equipped with a sail, oars, and bow ram.

kerux (pl. *kerukes*): A herald; or messenger.

kerykeion: A magic wand wielded by the messenger god Hermes.

khoros: A dance; or a chorus.

kinesis: Motion; or change.

kitharistes: Music teachers.

kleros: A land allotment, often a family's lands.

klismos: An armless chair with a wooden back and a seat of cross-hatched leather strips.

knucklebones: A game, common in ancient Greece and Rome and still played today, in which people throw small bones into the air and try to catch them on the backs of their hands.

koine: Common tongue or dialect; more specifically, the dialect of Greek (based on the Attic dialect) that became common throughout Greece and the Near East during the Hellenistic Age.

koinos: Common, or shared.

komoidia: Comedy.

komos: A revel; merry-making.

kore (pl. *korai*): "Young maiden"; often used to describe a female statue whose style was popular in the Archaic Age.

koryphaios: A chorus leader.

kouros (pl. *kouroi*): "Youth"; often used to describe a nude male statue whose style was popular in the Archaic Age.

kratos: Rule; or control; or power.

krisis: "Crisis"; in terms of Greek medicine, the crucial moment when healing begins to overcome disease.

kubernetes: The helmsman on a Greek **trireme**, who was usually an experienced naval veteran.

kykloi: Low platforms used to display goods in a marketplace.

kyreia: Leadership of a family, usually vested in the father.

kyria: Possessions.

kyrios: "Lord"; a woman's male guardian, usually her father or husband.

lekythus (pl. *lekythoi*): A narrow-necked vase buried with the dead or left at the gravesite.

linothorax: A cuirass made of layers of linen or canvas. See **cuirass.**

liturgies (*leitourgiai*): "The people's burdens"; financial support given by well-to-do citizens for producing plays, outfitting and maintaining warships, and other community services

lochagos: The officer in command of a *lochos.*

lochos (pl. *lochoi*): A small subdivision of the Greek **phalanx**, composed of about 100 men, though probably differing in size from one **polis** to another.

logographai (sing. *logographos*): Professional speech-writers, often for litigants in a court case.

logos: A word; or a proposition; or the meaning of something; or in a religious context, the divine Word, which provides spiritual direction.

lot: See **sortition.**

loutrophoros: A container for carrying the sacred water in which a bride bathed prior to her wedding ceremony.

lyre (*lyra*): A small harp.

machina: In the theater, a crane or mechanical arm used to "fly" an actor playing a god or hero through the air above the stage.

mantis: A prophet or seer.

mathema: Learning.

mathematikos: Inclined toward learning; or a scholar or scientist; or a geometric number or concept.

megaron: In Bronze Age Minoan and Mycenaean palaces, a large hall, usually with a central hearth; later, a kind of house, usually with a columned front porch, a long main room, and a rear storeroom.

mercenary: A hired soldier.

metics (*metoikoi*): Foreigners (either Greeks from other city-states or non-Greeks) living in Athens.

metope: In a Doric entablature, a rectangular panel flanked by **triglyphs** and bearing a painting or sculpted relief. See **entablature, order.**

metron: Measure; or proportion.

metropolis: "Mother city"; a polis that established one or more colonies, with whom it usually maintained close ties.

miasma: The state of being religiously tainted or polluted and therefore in need of purification (cleansing).

mina: See **drachma.**

moicheia: Adultery.

mousike: Music.

mutules: Plaque-like decorations attached to the bottom of a **geison**'s projecting edge.

mystery cult (*mysteria*): A religious group whose initiations were kept secret; for example, the cult of Demeter at Eleusis.

mystes: "Initiate"; a member of a mystery cult.

mythos (pl. *mythoi*): A spoken or written tale; or a myth describing the origins or exploits of a god or gods.

neikos: Strife.

nomos: A law, custom, or convention adopted by a community.

nomothetai: Law-makers.

nous: The mind.

nyx: Night; the goddess of night is Nyx.

obol: See **drachma.**

ochlos: Rabble; or a mob.

octa-style: A temple style in which the **pteron** has eight columns on each end and seventeen columns on each side (counting the corner columns twice). The Parthenon is an octa-style temple.

odi: A song.

oiketes: A household slave or servant.

oikistes: The founder of a colony.

oikos (pl. *oikoi*): The family.

oikos eremos: A family without male heirs.

oikoumene: "Inhabited world"; the term describing the general social-cultural sphere of the Greek-ruled lands of the eastern Mediterranean and Near East during the Hellenistic Age.

oinos: Wine.

oligarchy (*oligarchia*): "Rule of the few"; a government headed by a council of leading citizens.

omen: A sign of impending good or bad fortune. See **divination.**

omphalos: The "navel stone" at Delphi, thought to mark the world's geographical center.

opisthodomos: The back porch of a Greek temple.

oracle: A message thought to come from the gods; or the sacred site where such a message was given; or the priestess who delivered the message.

orchestra: In a Greek theater, the circular stone "dancing" area in which the actors performed.

order: An architectural style, usually identified by the main features of its columns. Columns in the Doric order have no decorative bases and their **capitals** are topped by plain rectangular slabs. Columns in the Ionic order do have decorative bases and their capitals are topped by ornamental scrolls.

ostracism (*ostrakismos*): An Athenian democratic process in which the people voted to banish an unpopular leader.

ostrakon (pl. *ostraka*): In the process of ostracism, a pottery shard on which a citizen wrote the name of the person he wanted to see banished.

othismos: "The shoving"; a maneuver in which **hoplites** in the rear ranks of a **phalanx** pushed at their comrades' backs, forcefully thrusting the whole formation into the enemy's ranks; if the enemy was Greek, its phalanx pushed back.

ouragoi: "Rear-rankers"; veteran officers who stood behind the **phalanx** and made sure the men in the rear ranks were doing their jobs.

ouranos: The sky; or the heavenly vault; or the visible universe.

paean: "Battle hymn"; a patriotic song sung by Greek **hoplites** as they marched into battle.

paidagogos: A slave or freedman who accompanied a boy to school and supervised his behavior there.

paideia: Cultural education; or training a young person to become a responsible adult.

paidotribes: An instructor of athletics, including running, jumping, javelin-throwing, boxing and wrestling.

palaistra: A wrestling school or facility, or a part of a gymnasium devoted to wrestling.

pale: Wrestling.

pallake: A concubine; a husband's mistress who sometimes lived in his house.

palmette: An elegant, fan-shaped leaf design or ornament.

Panathenaea: Athens's largest and most important religious festival, held in August each year but with special splendor (the Greater Panathenaea) every fourth year.

Panathenaic Way: The route taken by the grand procession that opened Athens's Panathenaea, beginning at a gate in the city's northwest section and ending near the Parthenon and Erechtheum on the Acropolis.

panhellenic: "All-Greek"; used to describe ideas or events common to many or all Greek city-states. See **Hellas.**

pankration: A rough-and-tumble athletic event that combined elements of wrestling, boxing, and street-fighting.

panoply: A **hoplite**'s complete array of arms and armor.

pantheon: The group of gods worshiped by a people.

paraskenia: Wing sections projecting from the side of the scene building in a Greek theater. See *skene.*

parodoi: Side entrances of a Greek theater.

parodos: In a Greek play, the song sung by the chorus as it made its entrance.

parrhesia: Freedom of speech.

pathos: A feeling or emotion, often a painful one.

patronymic (*patronymikos*): One's father's name.

pediment: A triangular gable at the top of the front or back of a Greek-style temple.

peitho: Persuasion. See **rhetoric, sophist.**

pelta: The small round or crescent-shaped shield carried by a peltast.

peltasts (*peltastai*): Light-armed skirmishers, usually javelin men.

Pentekontaetia: "The Fifty Years"; the term later coined to describe the period from the close of the Persian Wars (479 B.C.) to the death of Pericles (429 B.C.), in which Athenian power and culture reached their height.

pentekonter (*pentekontoros*): An early warship with fifty oars arranged in a single bank.

Pentelic marble: A variety of marble having a fine, uniform grain and a dazzling white sheen when viewed in direct sunlight; it is quarried on Mt. Pentelicon, about ten miles northeast of Athens.

peplos: The sacred robe presented to Athena during the Athenian **Panathenaea** processional and applied to her statue in the **Plynteria** ceremony.

pepsis: The cooking of food; or the ripening of fruit; or the fermentation of wine; or in Hippocratic medicine, digestion.

perideipnon: A meal served at the home of a deceased person following the burial.

periodos: "Period" or "Circuit"; the "big four" athletic games of ancient Greece, including those held at Olympia, Isthmia, Delphi, and Nemea.

perioikoi: "Dwellers round about"; neighbors of a prominent **polis** (for example, Sparta) who were treated as inferior or subordinate to the people of that polis.

peripeteia: See *hamartia.*

peristyle: In a temple, a walkway running between the **pteron** and the inner walls.

phalanx: A Greek military formation consisting of multiple ranks, with hoplites standing, marching, or fighting side by side in each rank; the Macedonian phalanx, developed chiefly by Philip II, featured the use of long battle pikes projecting forward from the first several ranks.

phaos: Light.

philhellenism: Admiration for ancient Greek culture.

philia: Friendship or love.

philos (pl. *phyloi*): Friend.

phratry (*phratria*): "Blood brotherhood"; an extended kinship group composed of about thirty clans.

phrenes: Wits.

phthora: Destruction; or ceasing to exist.

phylarch: A tribal leader.

phyle (pl. *phylai*): A tribe, usually composed of three phratries.

physis: Nature; or an underlying natural principle; or natural law.

pinakes: Votive wooden tablets created to thank a god or gods for answered prayers.

Plynteria: At Athens, a ceremony in which specially trained women washed Athena's sacred olive-wood statue and dressed it with the *peplos.* See **Panathenaea.**

pneuma: The wind; or the human spirit; or a spiritual force that affects humankind.

poietike: Productive.

point: A pointed metal tool used by masons and sculptors to alter and carve stone surfaces.

polemarch (*polemarkhos*): At Athens, originally the war archon, or leading general; later, an **archon** who dispensed justice to resident non-Athenians.

polemos: War or a battle.

polis (pl. **poleis**): In Greece, a city-state, or tiny nation built around a central town or city.

politai: Citizens.

polluted: Religiously unclean or tainted. See *miasma.*

polypragmon: Tending to interfere in other people's business or be a busybody.

pompe: A procession.

porne (pl. *pornai*): A common prostitute.

porpax: A bronze loop on the back of a **hoplite**'s shield through which he placed his left arm.

portico: A porch, as in the front and rear of a Greek temple.

praxis: Practical.

probouleumata: Legislative bills formulated in the **Boule** (Athenian Council), dealing with state business and community affairs.

probouleusis: Deliberation within the **Boule.**

probouloi: Deputies, delegates.

prohairesis: Purpose; or resolve.

prokrisis: Voting.

pronaos: A Greek temple's front porch, almost always columned.

prophetes: A prophet; or a priest; or someone who foretells the future.

propylaea (*propylon*): A monumental and/or ornate gateway; for instance, the Propylaea of the Athenian Acropolis.

proskynesis: The Greek word for the act of prostrating oneself (bowing or lying face down) before a ruler; this was a Persian custom that Greeks viewed as humiliating and unworthy of a free person.

prothesis: The formal lying-in-state of a deceased person, usually in his or her home.

prytaneis: "Presidents"; a fifty-man committee of the Athenian legislative Council (**Boule**) that was on duty in the Council chamber for the period of a prytany.

prytany (*prytaneia*): At Athens, one-tenth of a civil year; a place for municipal eating.

psephisma: A decree passed by the Athenian Assembly.

pseudo: False.

psyche: The soul.

pteron: A colonnade, especially one that runs around the perimeter of a temple. A structure having a pteron is said to be peripteral.

pyre (*pyra*): A pile of wood on which a body was cremated.

Pythia: The priestess (oracle) at Apollo's shrine at Delphi. See **oracle.**

quadrireme (*teteres*): A large warship once thought to have had four banks of oars, it more likely featured two oar banks with two rowers on an oar.

quinquereme (*penteres*): A large warship once thought to have had five banks of oars, it more likely featured five rowers on each oar.

raking sima: On an end, or porch, of a temple, the **cornice**'s upper beams, which angle upward and converge at the structure's apex, or topmost point, thereby forming the triangular **pediment**.

red-figure: A pottery style in which the painted figures and scenes are reddish-orange against a black background. See **black-figure.**

refinements: Subtle architectural alterations or deviations intended to correct optical illusions that make some of a building's features look disproportionate or weak. See **entasis.**

rhapsodia: Recitation contests, most often of the Homeric epics.

rhapsodos: A professional poetry reciter, most often of Homer's works.

rhetor (pl. *rhetores*): An orator or speaker; or a politician.

rhetoric: The art or skill of persuasive speaking.

salpinx: A trumpet, often used to signal the charge in battle.

sanctuary (*hieron*): A sacred area made up of a temple and its surrounding grounds.

sarissa: A long battle pike wielded by a soldier in the Macedonian **phalanx**.

satrap: A Persian governor; his province was called a satrapy.

schema: Shape or form.

sitesis: A state's granting of free meals to athletes who won at the circuit games.

sitos: Food, especially staples like bread and cheese.

skene: "Scene building"; a structure facing the audience area in a Greek theater, containing dressing rooms for the actors.

soma: The human body.

sophia: Wisdom or knowledge.

sophist (*sophistes,* pl. *sophistai*): "Wise man"; a term that came to describe a traveling teacher of **rhetoric** and other subjects who accepted pay for his services.

sophoi: Sages or philosophers.

sophron: Modest; or discreet; or law-abiding.

sophrosyne: Self-control; or temperance.

sortition: The casting or drawing of lots; determination by random drawing.

sperma: A seed.

sphairai: Balls.

stade: A footrace of about 600 feet; or a measure of that distance.

stasis: Factional fighting or civil strife within a state.

stele: A stone marker.

stoa: A roofed public building, usually long with an open **colonnade** along one side.

Strategia: Athens's board of ten generals.

strategos (pl. *strategoi*): At Athens, a military general elected annually by the Assembly.

stylobate: The topmost section of a temple's foundation, comprising the building's floor.

suneinai: Unmarried cohabitation (living together).

sunoikein: Legal marriage.

sykophantes (pl. *sykophantai*): A person who falsely charges or wrongly prosecutes another.

symmachia: A "fighting alliance" of city-states under the leadership of one; for example, the Peloponnesian League, led by Sparta.

sympoliteia: A confederacy (alliance) of cities who gave up some of their independence to a central federal government yet retained certain elements of local autonomy; for example, the Achaean League.

symposium (pl. **symposia**): An after-dinner drinking party, usually in a private home.

synedrion: A representative council, usually made up of delegates from separate Greek states; for example, the League of Corinth, set up by Macedonia's Philip II in 338 B.C.

synoecism (*synoikismos*): The joining together of several separate communities into a single political state; for example, the unification of Attica's villages into the Athenian state (an act attributed to the legendary hero Theseus).

synoris: A race for two-horse chariots.

syrinx: A Pan pipe; a wind instrument having seven short pipes.

syssitia: Communal meals for men at Sparta and a few other Greek states.

talent: See **drachma.**

tamiai: At Athens, treasurers of the local **demes**.

ta trita: "Third-day celebration"; a small funerary ceremony conducted during the burial of a deceased person.

taxiarchos (pl. *taxiarchoi*): The officer in command of a *taxis.*

taxis (pl. *taxeis*): An ordered arrangement; in military terms, a large subdivision of the Athenian **phalanx**, of which there were ten in all, each drawn from one of the city's tribes.

techne: An art or skill; or a technique.

teleology: The belief or doctrine that the natural world is endowed with purpose or design.

telesterion: The initiation hall of a **mystery cult**.

telos: Purpose; or an aim.

terra-cotta: Baked clay.

tethrippon: A long race for four-horse chariots.

thalassocracy: Naval command of the seas.

thallophoroi: "Bearers of green branches"; elderly Athenian men who marched in the Panathenaic procession.

thanatos: Death.

theatron: The audience or seating area of a Greek theater.

theoria: Rational contemplation or thought; or philosophical truth.

theos (pl. **theoi**): A god.

thesis: A situation; or the proposition to be proved in an argument.

Thesmothetai: At Athens, the six **archons** in charge of administering justice.

thespis: Inspired.

thetes: Members of Athens's poorer classes.

tholos: A conical "beehive" tomb commonly built to house deceased Bronze Age Mycenaean royalty.

thymele: The altar in a Greek theater.

thyrsos (pl. **thyrsoi**): A stick or wand bound with ivy leaves and topped by a pine cone, used in fertility rituals.

time: Honor; or status.

tisis: Revenge.

tragoidia: Tragedy.

tragos: A goat.

trapezitai: Bankers and money-changers.

treasury: A small building having many of the same outer features as a temple but used for storing valuables.

tribute (**phoros**): Payment acknowledging submission.

trident: A three-pronged spear, famous as the symbol of the sea god, Poseidon.

trierarch (**trierarchos**): The captain of a **trireme**; in Athens during the Classic Age, a trierarch assumed such command as part of a public duty, a **liturgy** known as the Trierarchy.

triglyph: In a Doric entablature, a rectangular block containing three vertical bars. See **entablature, order.**

trireme (**trieres**): A warship with three banks of oars, the *thranite* (upper), *zygite* (middle), and *thalamite* (lower).

trittyes: "Thirds"; at Athens (and possibly other Greek states), social-political units each representing one-third of a tribe. See **phyle.**

trophy (**tropaion**): A wooden framework displaying captured enemy arms and armor, set up on the battlefield to celebrate victory and give thanks to the gods.

tyche: Luck or chance.

tyrant (*tyrannos*): A sovereign; or a person who seizes power in a non-constitutional manner.

volute: An elegant spiral scroll at the top of an Ionic **capital**. See **order.**

votive: Given or dedicated to fulfill a vow or pledge; usually used in reference to works dedicated to the gods.

xenophobia: Fear or hatred of foreigners.

xenos: An alien or stranger; also a guest- or host-friend, part of the reciprocal arrangement (*xenia*) in which one was expected to repay in kind the hospitality of another, especially someone from another state.

For Further Reading

Ancient Sources in Translation

Aeschylus, *Oresteia,* published as *The Orestes Plays of Aeschylus.* Trans. Paul Roche. New York: New American Library, 1962.

———, *Prometheus Bound, The Suppliants, Seven Against Thebes, The Persians.* Trans. Philip Vellacott. Baltimore: Penguin Books, 1961.

Appian, *Roman History.* 4 vols. Trans. Horace White. Cambridge, MA: Harvard University Press, 1964.

Archimedes, *Works.* Trans. Thomas L. Heath, in *Great Books of the Western World,* vol. 11. Chicago: Encyclopedia Britannica, 1952.

Aristophanes, *The Complete Plays of Aristophanes.* Trans. Moses Hadas. New York: Bantam Books, 1962.

———, *Birds, Lysistrata, Assembly-Women, Wealth.* Trans. Stephen Halliwell. Oxford: Clarendon Press, 1997.

———, *Clouds, Wasps, Peace.* Trans. Jeffrey Henderson. Cambridge, MA: Harvard University Press, 1998.

Aristotle, *The Athenian Constitution.* Trans. H. Rackham. Cambridge, MA: Harvard University Press, 1952. Reprint: 1996.

———, Complete works in *Aristotle: Complete Works.* 2 vols. Ed. Jonathan Barnes, various trans. Princeton: Princeton University Press, 1988.

———, Selected works in Renford Bambrough, ed., *The Philosophy of Aristotle.* New York: New American Library, 1963.

Arrian, *Anabasis Alexandri,* published as *The Campaigns of Alexander.* Trans. Aubrey de Sélincourt. New York: Penguin Books, 1971.

Kenneth J. Atchity, ed., *The Classical Greek Reader.* New York: Oxford University Press, 1996.

M.M. Austin, ed., *The Hellenistic World from Alexander to the Roman Conquest: A Selection of Ancient Sources in Translation.* Cambridge: Cambridge University Press, 1981.

Morris R. Cohen and I.E. Drabkin, *A Source Book in Greek Science.* Cambridge, MA: Harvard University Press, 1948.

Michael Crawford and David Whitehead, eds., *Archaic and Classical Greece: A Selection of Ancient Sources in Translation.* Cambridge: Cambridge University Press, 1983.

Demosthenes, *Olynthiacs, Philippics, Minor Speeches.* Trans. J.H. Vince. Cambridge, MA: Harvard University Press, 1962.

Diodorus Siculus, *Library of History.* 12 vols. Various trans. Cambridge, MA: Harvard University Press, 1962–1967.

Euripides, *Medea and Other Plays.* Trans. Philip Vellacott. New York: Penguin Books, 1963.

———, *Three Great Plays of Euripides.* Trans. Rex Warner. New York: New American Library, 1958.

Galen, *Selected Works.* Trans. P.N. Singer. New York: Oxford University Press, 1997.

Rhoda A. Hendricks, ed. and trans., *Classical Gods and Heroes: Myths as Told by the Ancient Authors.* New York: Morrow Quill, 1974.

Herodotus, *The Histories.* Trans. Aubrey de Sélincourt. New York: Penguin Books, 1972.

———, *The Histories.* Trans. Robin Waterfield. New York: Oxford University Press, 1998.

Hesiod, *Theogony,* in *Hesiod and Theognis.* Trans. Dorothea Wender. New York: Penguin Books, 1973.

Homer
Editor's Note: The following noteworthy translations of Homer's *Iliad* and *Odyssey* are listed in chronological order of publication. In a poll conducted in the 1980s of 78 professors then teaching Homer in well-known colleges and universities, more than three-quarters of the respondents indicated their preference for the 1951 Lattimore translation of the *Iliad;* Robert Fitzgerald's and E.V. Rieu's versions scored second and third place respectively. Regarding the *Odyssey,* Fitzgerald's translation was most preferred, with Lattimore's and Rieu's versions tied for second place. Since that time, Robert Fagles's translations have gained wide acclaim.

————, *Iliad.* Trans. W.H.D. Rouse. New York: New American Library, 1950.

————, *Iliad.* Trans. E.V. Rieu. Baltimore: Penguin Books, 1950.

————, *Iliad.* Trans. Richmond Lattimore. Chicago: University of Chicago Press, 1951.

————, *Iliad.* Trans. Robert Fitzgerald. New York: Anchor-Doubleday, 1974.

————, *Iliad.* Trans. Robert Fagles. New York: Penguin Books, 1990.

————, *Odyssey.* Trans. W.H.D. Rouse. New York: New American Library, 1949.

————, *Odyssey.* Trans. E.V. Rieu. Baltimore: Penguin Books, 1961.

————, *Odyssey.* Trans. Robert Fitzgerald. New York: Anchor-Doubleday, 1962.

————, *Odyssey.* Trans. Richmond Lattimore. New York: Harper, 1965.

————, *Odyssey.* Trans. Robert Fagles. New York: Penguin Books, 1996.

Isocrates, surviving works in George Norlin, trans., *Isocrates.* Cambridge MA: Harvard University Press, 1928.

Bernard M.W. Knox, ed., *The Norton Book of Classical Literature.* New York: W.W. Norton, 1993.

Richmond Lattimore, trans., *Greek Lyrics.* Chicago: University of Chicago Press, 1960.

Livy, *History of Rome from Its Foundation,* Books 21–30 excerpted in *Livy: The War with Hannibal.* Trans. Aubrey de Sélincourt. New York: Penguin Books, 1972.

————, *History of Rome from Its Foundation,* Books 31–45 excerpted in *Livy: Rome and the Mediterranean.* Trans. Henry Bettenson. New York: Penguin Books, 1976.

Ovid, *Metamorphoses.* Trans. Rolfe Humphries. Bloomington, IN: Indiana University Press, 1967.

Pausanias, *Guide to Greece.* 2 vols. Trans. Peter Levi. New York: Penguin Books, 1971.

Pindar, *Odes.* Trans. C.M. Bowra. New York: Penguin Books, 1969.

Plato, *Dialogues,* in *Great Books of the Western World.* Vol. 7. Trans. Benjamin Jowett. Chicago: Encyclopedia Britannica, 1952.

————, *Dialogues,* in *Great Dialogues of Plato.* Trans. W.H.D. Rouse. New York: New American Library, 1956.

————, Complete works in *Plato: Complete Works.* Ed. John M. Cooper. Various trans. Indianapolis: Hackett Publishing, 1997.

Plutarch, *Moralia* (*Moral Essays*), excerpted in *Plutarch: Essays.* Trans. Robin Waterfield. New York: Penguin Books, 1992.

————, *Parallel Lives,* excerpted in *The Rise and Fall of Athens: Nine Greek Lives by Plutarch.* Trans. Ian Scott-Kilvert. New York: Penguin, 1960.

————, *Parallel Lives,* excerpted in *The Age of Alexander: Nine Greek Lives by Plutarch.* Trans. Ian Scott-Kilvert. New York: Penguin, 1973.

————, *Parallel Lives,* excerpted in *Life Stories of the Men Who Shaped History, from Plutarch's Lives.* Trans. John and William Langhorne, ed. Eduard C. Lindeman. New York: New American Library, 1950.

————, *Parallel Lives,* excerpted in *Makers of Rome: Nine Lives by Plutarch.* Trans. Ian Scott-Kilvert. New York: Penguin Books, 1965.

————, *Parallel Lives,* published complete as *Lives of the Noble Grecians and Romans.* Trans. John Dryden. New York: Random House, 1932.

J.J. Pollitt, ed. and trans., *The Art of Ancient Greece: Sources and Documents.* New York: Cambridge University Press, 1990.

Polybius, *Histories,* published as *Polybius: The Rise of the Roman Empire.* Trans. Ian Scott-Kilvert. New York: Penguin Books, 1979.

Ptolemy, *Almagest.* Trans. R. Catesby Taliaferro, in *Great Books of the Western World,* vol. 16. Chicago: Encyclopedia Britannica, 1952.

Quintus Curtius Rufus, *History of Alexander.* Trans. John Yardley. New York: Penguin Books, 1984.

Sophocles, complete works in *The Complete Plays of Sophocles.* Trans. Richard C. Jebb. New York: Bantam Books, 1967.

————, *Oedipus the King.* Trans. Bernard M.W. Knox. New York: Pocket Books, 1959.

————, *The Three Theban Plays: Antigone, Oedipus the King, Oedipus at Colonus.* Trans. Robert Fagles. New York: Penguin Books, 1984.

Waldo E. Sweet, ed., *Sport and Recreation in Ancient Greece: A Sourcebook with Translations.* New York: Oxford University Press, 1987.

Theophrastus, *Characters.* Trans. Jeffrey Rustin. Cambridge, MA: Harvard University Press, 1993.

————, *History of Plants* and other works in Arthur Hort, trans., *Theophrastus: Inquiry into Plants and Minor Works on Odors and Weather Signs.* Cambridge, MA: Harvard University Press, 1961.

Thucydides, *The Peloponnesian War.* Trans. Rex Warner. New York: Penguin Books, 1972.

————, *The Peloponnesian War,* published as *The Landmark Thucydides: A Comprehensive Guide to the Peloponnesian War.* Trans. Richard Crawley, ed. Robert B. Strassler. New York: Simon and Schuster, 1996.

Vitruvius, *On Architecture.* 2 vols. Trans. Frank Granger. Cambridge, MA: Harvard University Press, 1962.

Thomas Wiedemann, ed., *Greek and Roman Slavery.* Baltimore: Johns Hopkins University Press, 1981.

Xenophon, *Anabasis.* Trans. W.H.D. Rouse. New York: New American Library, 1959.

————, *Cyropaedia.* Trans. Walter Miller. New York: Macmillan, 1914.

————, *Hellenica,* published as *A History of My Times.* Trans. Rex Warner. New York: Penguin Books, 1979.

————, *Memorabilia and Oeconomicus.* Trans. E.C. Marchant. Cambridge, MA: Harvard University Press, 1965.

————, *Scripta Minora.* Trans. E.C. Marchant. Cambridge, MA: Harvard University Press, 1993.

Modern Sources

Acropolis and Parthenon

Manolis Andronicos, *The Acropolis.* Athens: Ekdotike Athenon, 1994.

John Boardman, *The Parthenon and Its Sculptures.* Austin: University of Texas, 1985.

Vincent J. Bruno, ed., *The Parthenon.* New York: Norton, 1974.

Peter Green, *The Parthenon.* New York: Newsweek Book Division, 1973.

Ian Jenkins, *The Parthenon Frieze.* Austin: University of Texas, 1994.

Don Nardo, *The Parthenon.* San Diego: Lucent Books, 1999.

Panayotis Tournikiotis, ed., *The Parthenon and Its Impact in Modern Times.* New York: Harry N. Abrams, 1996.

Alexander the Great, His Conquests and Impact

Donald W. Engels, *Alexander the Great and the Logistics of the Macedonian Army.* Berkeley: University of California Press, 1978.

Robin Lane Fox, *Alexander the Great.* London: Allan Lane, 1973.

J.F.C. Fuller, *The Generalship of Alexander the Great.* New Brunswick, NJ: Rutgers University Press, 1960.

Peter Green, *Alexander of Macedon, 356–323 B.C.: A Historical Biography.* Berkeley: University of California Press, 1991.

N.G.L. Hammond, *The Genius of Alexander the Great.* Chapel Hill: University of North Carolina Press, 1997.

John M. O'Brien, *Alexander the Great: The Invisible Enemy.* New York: Routledge, 1994.

Nick Sekunda and John Warry, *Alexander the Great: His Armies and Campaigns, 334–323 B.C.* London: Osprey, 1998.

Archaeological Rediscovery of Greece

Paul G. Bahn, ed., *The Cambridge Illustrated History of Archaeology.* New York: Cambridge University Press, 1996.

William R. Biers, *The Archaeology of Greece.* Ithaca: Cornell University Press, 1996.

B.F. Cook, *The Elgin Marbles.* Cambridge, MA: Harvard University Press, 1984.

Michael Grant, *The Visible Past: Recent Archaeological Discoveries of Greek and Roman History.* New York: Scribner's, 1990.

Paul MacKendrick, *The Greek Stones Speak: The Story of Archaeology in Greek Lands.* New York: W.W. Norton, 1962.

Michael Shanks, *The Classical Archaeology of Greece.* London: Routledge, 1995.

Anthony M. Snodgrass, *An Archaeology of Greece.* Berkeley: University of California Press, 1987.

Fani-Maria Tsigakou, *The Rediscovery of Greece: Travellers and Painters of the Romantic Era.* London: Thames and Hudson, 1981.

Archaic Age: See Dark and Archaic Ages

Architecture and Engineering

Bruce Allsopp, *A History of Classical Architecture.* London: Sir Isaac Pitman and Sons, 1965.

Peter Clayton and Martin Price, eds., *The Seven Wonders of the Ancient World.* New York: Barnes and Noble, 1993.

J.J. Coulton, *Ancient Greek Architects at Work.* Ithaca: Cornell University Press, 1977.

L. Sprague de Camp, *The Ancient Engineers.* New York: Ballantine Books, 1963.

A.W. Lawrence, Rev. R.A. Tomlinson, *Greek Architecture.* New Haven: Yale University Press, 1996.

D.S. Robertson, *A Handbook of Greek and Roman Architecture.* New York: Cambridge University Press, 1959.

R.E. Wycherly, *The Stones of Athens.* Princeton: Princeton University Press, 1978.

Art and Sculpture

Carl Bluemel, *Greek Sculptors at Work.* London: Phaidon, 1969.

John Boardman, *Greek Art.* New York: Praeger, 1964.

———, *Athenian Black Figure Vases.* New York: Oxford University Press, 1974.

———, *Greek Sculpture: The Archaic Age.* London: Thames and Hudson, 1978.

———, *Athenian Red Figure Vases: The Classical Period, A Handbook.* London: Thames and Hudson, 1989.

———, *The Diffusion of Classical Art in Antiquity.* Princeton: Princeton University Press, 1994.

———, ed., *The Oxford History of Classical Art.* Oxford, England: Oxford University Press, 1993.

Thomas Craven, *The Pocket Book of Greek Art.* New York: Pocket Books, 1950.

John G. Pedley, *Greek Art and Archaeology.*

New York: Harry N. Abrams, 1993.

J.J. Pollitt, *The Art of Ancient Greece*. New York: Cambridge University Press, 1990.

———, *Art in the Hellenistic Age*. Cambridge: Cambridge University Press, 1986.

Nigel Spivey, *Greek Art*. London: Phaidon, 1997.

Susan Woodford, *An Introduction to Greek Art*. Ithaca: Cornell University Press, 1986.

Athens, Its Empire and Cultural Achievements

C.M. Bowra, *Periclean Athens*. New York: Dial Press, 1971.

Joint Association of Classical Teachers, *The World of Athens: An Introduction to Classical Athenian Culture*. New York: Cambridge University Press, 1984.

Donald Kagan, *Pericles of Athens and the Birth of Democracy*. New York: Free Press, 1991.

Malcolm F. McGregor, *The Athenians and Their Empire*. Vancouver: University of British Columbia Press, 1987.

Christian Meier, *Athens: Portrait of a City in Its Golden Age*. Trans. Robert and Rita Kimber. New York: Henry Holt, 1998.

Russell Meiggs, *The Athenian Empire*. Oxford: Clarendon Press, 1972.

Don Nardo, *The Age of Pericles*. San Diego: Lucent Books, 1996.

———, *Life in Ancient Athens*. San Diego: Lucent Books, 2000.

C.A. Robinson, *Athens in the Age of Pericles*. Norman: University of Oklahoma, 1971.

George D. Wilcoxon, *Athens Ascendant*. Ames: Iowa State University Press, 1979.

Athletics: See Sports and Games

Bronze Age

Carl Blegen et al., *Troy: Excavations Conducted by the University of Cincinnati*. 4 vols. Princeton: Princeton University Press, 1950–1958.

Rodney Castleden, *Minoans: Life in Bronze Age Crete*. New York: Routledge, 1993.

John Chadwick, *The Mycenaean World*. New York: Cambridge University Press, 1976.

Oliver Dickinson, *The Aegean Bronze Age*. New York: Cambridge University Press, 1994.

Robert Drews, *The Coming of the Greeks: Indo-European Conquests in the Aegean and the Near East*. Princeton: Princeton University Press, 1988.

———, *The End of the Bronze Age: Changes in Warfare and the Catastrophe ca. 1200 B.C.* Princeton: Princeton University Press, 1993.

Arthur Evans, *The Palace of Minos at Knossos*. 4 vols. London: Macmillan, 1921–1936.

M.I. Finley, *Early Greece: The Bronze and Archaic Ages*. New York: W.W. Norton, 1970.

J. Lesley Fitton, *Discovery of the Greek Bronze Age*. London: British Museum Press, 1995.

J.V. Luce, *Lost Atlantis: New Light on an Old Legend*. New York: McGraw-Hill, 1969.

Nanno Marinatos, *Art and Religion in Thera: Reconstructing a Bronze Age City*. Athens: D. and I. Mathioulakis, 1984.

Anna Michalidou, *Knossos: A Complete Guide to the Palace of Minos*. Athens: Ekdotike Athenon, 1993.

Charles Pellegrino, *Unearthing Atlantis: An Archaeological Odyssey*. New York: Random House, 1991.

William Taylour, *The Mycenaeans*. London: Thames and Hudson, 1983.

Emily Vermeule, *Greece in the Bronze Age*. Chicago: University of Chicago Press, 1964; revised 1972.

Michael Wood, *In Search of the Trojan War*. New York: New American Library, 1985.

Dark and Archaic Ages

A. Andrewes, *Greek Tyrants*. New York: Harper Torchbook, 1963.

A.R. Burn, *The Lyric Age of Greece*. New York: St. Martin's Press, 1960.

M.I. Finley, *The World of Odysseus.* New York: Viking, 1978.

Kathleen Freeman, *The Work and Life of Solon, with a Translation of His Poems.* Cardiff: University of Wales Press, 1926. Reprint: New York: Arno, 1976.

A.M. Snodgrass, *The Dark Age of Greece.* Chicago: Aldine, 1972.

————, *Archaic Greece.* Berkeley: University of California Press, 1980.

Chester G. Starr, *The Origins of Greek Civilization, 1100–650 B.C.* New York: Knopf, 1961.

————, *The Economic and Social Growth of Early Greece, 800–500 B.C.* New York: Oxford University Press, 1977.

————, *Individual and Community: The Rise of the Polis, 800–500 B.C.* New York: Oxford University Press, 1986.

Democracy: See Politics

Family and Social Institutions and Customs

F.A.G. Beck, *Greek Education, 450–350 B.C.* London: Methuen, 1964.

Sue Blundell, *Women in Ancient Greece.* Cambridge, MA: Harvard University Press, 1995.

Eva Cantarella, *Pandora's Daughters: The Role and Status of Women in Greek and Roman Antiquity.* Trans. Maureen B. Fant. Baltimore: Johns Hopkins University Press, 1987.

James Davidson, *Courtesans and Fishcakes: The Consuming Passions of Classical Athens.* New York: St. Martin's Press, 1998.

Victor Ehrenberg, *The People of Aristophanes: A Sociology of Old Attic Comedy.* New York: Schocken Books, 1962.

N.R.E. Fisher, *Social Values in Classical Athens.* London: Dent, 1976.

————, *Slavery in Classical Greece.* London: Bristol Classical Press, 1993.

Frank J. Frost, *Greek Society.* Lexington, MA: D.C. Heath, 1980.

Robert Garland, *The Greek Way of Life.* Ithaca: Cornell University Press, 1990.

Mark Golden, *Children and Childhood in Classical Athens.* Baltimore: Johns Hopkins University Press, 1990.

Michael Grant, *A Social History of Greece and Rome.* New York: Scribner's, 1992.

W.K. Lacey, *The Family in Classical Greece.* London: Thames and Hudson, 1968.

Sarah B. Pomeroy, *Goddesses, Whores, Wives, and Slaves: Women in Classical Antiquity.* New York: Schocken Books, 1995.

D.J. Symons, *Costumes of Ancient Greece.* London: Batsford, 1987.

Farming, Food, Commerce, and Trade

John Boardman, *The Greeks Overseas: Their Early Colonies and Trade.* New York: Thames and Hudson, 1980.

Hendrick Bolkestein, *Economic Life in Greece's Golden Age.* Leiden: Brill, 1964.

Alison Burford, *Land and Labor in the Greek World.* Baltimore: Johns Hopkins University Press, 1993.

Lionel Casson, *The Ancient Mariners.* New York: Macmillan, 1959.

————, *Ships and Seafaring in Ancient Times.* London: British Museum Press, 1994.

Andrew Dalby, *Siren Feasts: A History of Food and Gastronomy in Greece.* New York: Routledge, 1996.

M.I. Finley, *The Ancient Economy.* Berkeley: University of California Press, 1985.

Victor D. Hanson, *The Other Greeks: The Family Farm and the Agrarian Roots of Western Civilization.* New York: Simon and Schuster, 1995.

J.F. Healy, *Mining and Metallurgy in the Greek and Roman World.* London: Thames and Hudson, 1978.

R.J. Hopper, *Trade and Industry in Classical Greece.* London: Thames and Hudson, 1979.

Russell Meiggs, *Trees and Timber in the Ancient Mediterranean World.* Oxford: Clarendon Press, 1982.

J. Wilkins et al., eds., *Food in Antiquity.* Exeter, England: Exeter University Press, 1995.

General Ancient Greek History, Geography, and Culture

Lesly Adkins and Roy A. Adkins, *Handbook to Life in Ancient Greece.* New York: Facts On File, 1997.

Stringfellow Barr, *The Will of Zeus: A History of Greece.* New York: Dell, 1961.

Hermann Bengtson, *History of Greece, from the Beginnings to the Byzantine Era.* Trans. Edmund F. Bloedow. Ottawa: University of Ottawa Press, 1988.

George W. Botsford and Charles A. Robinson, *Hellenic History.* New York: Macmillan, 1956.

C.M. Bowra, *The Greek Experience.* New York: New American Library, 1957.

———, *Classical Greece.* New York: Time-Life Books, 1965.

R.J. Buck, *A History of Boeotia.* Edmonton, Alberta: University of Alberta Press, 1979.

Andrew R. Burn, *The Penguin History of Greece.* New York: Penguin Books, 1985.

J.B. Bury, *A History of Greece to the Death of Alexander.* Rev. Russell Meiggs. London: Macmillan, 1975.

John A. Crow, *Greece: The Magic Spring.* New York: Harper and Row, 1970.

Will Durant, *The Life of Greece.* New York: Simon and Schuster, 1966.

Victor Ehrenberg, *From Solon to Socrates: Greek History and Civilization During the 6th and 5th Centuries B.C.* London: Methuen, 1967.

M.I. Finley, *The Ancient Greeks: An Introduction to Their Life and Thought.* New York: Viking Press, 1964.

W.G. Forrest, *A History of Sparta, 950–152 B.C.* New York: Norton, 1968.

Charles Freeman, *Egypt, Greece, and Rome: Civilizations of the Ancient Mediterranean.* New York: Oxford University Press, 1996.

Michael Grant, *A Guide to the Ancient World.* New York: Barnes and Noble, 1996.

———, *The Classical Greeks.* New York: Scribner's, 1989.

———, *The Founders of the Western World: A History of Greece and Rome.* New York: Scribner's, 1991.

———, *The Rise of the Greeks.* New York: Macmillan, 1987.

N.G.L. Hammond, *A History of Greece to 322 B.C.* Oxford: Clarendon Press, 1986.

W.G. Hardy, *The Greek and Roman World.* Cambridge, MA: Schenkman Publishing, 1962.

Robert B. Kebric, *Greek People.* Mountain View, CA: Mayfield Publishing, 1997.

Peter Levi, *Atlas of the Greek World.* New York: Facts On File, 1984.

Thomas R. Martin, *Ancient Greece: From Prehistoric to Hellenistic Times.* New Haven: Yale University Press, 1996.

Herbert J. Muller, *The Loom of History.* New York: Harper and Brothers, 1958.

Sarah B. Pomeroy et al., *Ancient Greece: A Political, Social, and Cultural History.* New York: Oxford University Press, 1999.

C.E. Robinson, *Everyday Life in Ancient Greece.* Oxford: Clarendon Press, 1968.

Raphael Sealey, *A History of the Greek States, ca. 700–338 B.C.* Berkeley: University of California Press, 1976.

Chester G. Starr, *The Ancient Greeks.* New York: Oxford University Press, 1971.

———, *A History of the Ancient World.* New York: Oxford University Press, 1991.

Richard J.A. Talbert, ed., *Atlas of Classical History.* London: Routledge, 1985.

Leonard Whibley, ed., *A Companion to Greek Studies.* New York: Hafner Publishing, 1963.

Greco-Persian Wars

Alessandro Bausani, *The Persians: From the Earliest Days to the Twentieth Century.* Trans. J.B. Donne. London: Elek Books, 1971.

Andrew R. Burn, *Persia and the Greeks: The Defense of the West, c. 546–478 B.C.* London: Edward Arnold, 1962.

Peter Green, *The Greco-Persian Wars.* Berkeley: University of California Press, 1996.

John Lazenby, *The Defense of Greece.* Bloomington, IL: David Brown, 1993.

Don Nardo, *The Battle of Marathon.* San Diego: Lucent Books, 1996.

A.J. Podlecki, *The Life of Themistocles.* Montreal: McGill-Queen's University Press, 1975.

Hellenistic Age, Decline of Greece, and Coming of Rome

John Boardman et al., *Greece and the Hellenistic World.* New York: Oxford University Press, 1988.

Max Cary, *History of the Greek World from 323 to 146 B.C.* London: Methuen, 1968.

Walter M. Ellis, *Ptolemy of Egypt.* New York: Routledge, 1994.

W.S. Ferguson, *Hellenistic Athens.* Chicago: Ares, 1974.

Petros Garouphalias, *Pyrrhus.* London: Stacey International, 1979.

Michael Grant, *From Alexander to Cleopatra: The Hellenistic World.* New York: Charles Scribner's Sons, 1982.

Peter Green, *Alexander to Actium: The Historical Evolution of the Hellenistic Age.* Berkeley: University of California Press, 1990.

———, ed., *Hellenistic History and Culture.* Berkeley: University of California Press, 1993.

G.T. Griffith, *Mercenaries of the Hellenistic World.* New York: AMS, 1977.

Erich Gruen, *The Hellenistic World and the Coming of Rome.* Berkeley: University of California Press, 1984.

E.V. Hansen, *Attalids of Pergamum.* Ithaca: Cornell University Press, 1971.

Naphtali Lewis, *Greeks in Ptolemaic Egypt.* Oxford: Clarendon Press, 1986.

Don Nardo, *The Decline and Fall of Ancient Greece.* San Diego: Greenhaven Press, 2000.

Sarah B. Pomeroy, *Women in Hellenistic Egypt: From Alexander to Cleopatra.* New York: Schocken Books, 1989.

F.W. Walbank, *The Hellenistic World.* Cambridge, MA: Harvard University Press, 1993.

Homer, the *Iliad,* and the *Odyssey*

Kenneth Atchity et al., *Critical Essays on Homer.* Boston: G.K. Hall, 1987.

C.M. Bowra, *Homer.* New York: Charles Scribner's Sons, 1972.

Jasper Griffin, *Homer on Life and Death.* Oxford: Clarendon Press, 1980.

———, *Homer: The Odyssey.* Cambridge, England: Cambridge University Press, 1987.

M.S. Silk, *Homer: The Iliad.* Cambridge, England: Cambridge University Press, 1987.

C.G. Thomas, ed., *Homer's History: Mycenaean or Dark Age?* New York: Holt, Rinehart and Winston, 1970.

T.B.L. Webster, *From Mycenae to Homer.* New York: W.W. Norton, 1964.

Simone Weil, *The Iliad, or the Poem of Force.* Trans. Mary McCarthy. Wallingford, England: Pendle Hill, 1956.

Cedric H. Whitman, *Homer and the Homeric Tradition.* Cambridge: President and Fellows of Harvard College, 1958.

The *Iliad* and the *Odyssey* Retold for Young Readers

Peter Connolly, *The Legend of Odysseus.* New York: Oxford University Press, 1986.

Homer, *Iliad.* Retold by Barbara Leonie Picard. New York: Oxford University Press, 1960; new edition 1996.

Homer, *Odyssey*. Retold by Barbara Leonie Picard. New York: Oxford University Press, 1952; new edition 1996.

Don Nardo, *Greek and Roman Mythology*. San Diego: Lucent Books, 1998.

Law and Justice: See Politics

Literature, Philosophy, Science, and Ideas

Cyril Bailey, *The Greek Atomists and Epicurus*. New York: Russell and Russell, 1964.

Jonathon Barnes, *Aristotle*. New York: Oxford University Press, 1982.

———, ed., *The Cambridge Companion to Aristotle*. New York: Cambridge University Press, 1995.

C.M. Bowra, *Ancient Greek Literature*. New York: Oxford University Press, 1960.

Benjamin Farrington, *Science in Antiquity*. London: Oxford University Press, 1969.

Robert Flacelière, *A Literary History of Greece*. Trans. Douglas Garman. Chicago: Aldine Publishing, 1964.

Michael Grant, *Greek and Roman Historians: Information and Misinformation*. London: Routledge, 1995.

Victor D. Hanson and John Heath, *Who Killed Homer?: The Demise of Classical Education and the Recovery of Greek Wisdom*. New York: Free Press, 1998.

R.M. Hare, *Plato*. New York: Oxford University Press, 1982.

Simon Hornblower, *Thucydides*. Baltimore: Johns Hopkins University Press, 1987.

Peter Levi, *A History of Greek Literature*. New York: Viking, 1985.

David C. Lindberg, *The Beginnings of Western Science*. Chicago: University of Chicago Press, 1992.

A.A. Long, *Hellenistic Philosophy: Stoics, Epicureans, Skeptics*. London: Duckworth, 1974.

Don Nardo, *Greek and Roman Science*. San Diego: Lucent Books, 1997.

Nickolas Pappas, *Plato and the Republic*. London: Routledge, 1995.

A.J. Podlecki, *The Early Greek Poets*. Vancouver: University of British Columbia, 1984.

Jacqueline de Romilly, *A Short History of Greek Literature*. Trans. Lillian Doherty. Chicago: University of Chicago Press, 1985.

Colin Ronan, *Lost Discoveries: The Forgotten Science of the Ancient World*. New York: McGraw-Hill, 1973.

George Sarton, *A History of Science: Ancient Science Through the Golden Age of Greece*. Cambridge, MA: Harvard University Press, 1952.

Aubrey de Sélincourt, *The World of Herodotus*. San Francisco: North Point Press, 1982.

A.E. Taylor, *Socrates: The Man and His Thought*. New York: Doubleday, 1952.

Rex Warner, *The Greek Philosophers*. New York: New American Library, 1958.

Philip Wheelwright, ed., *The Presocratics*. New York: Macmillan, 1966.

Minoans and Mycenaeans: See Bronze Age

Myths: See Religion and Mythology

Peloponnesian War

Walter M. Ellis, *Alcibiades*. New York: Routledge, 1989.

Donald Kagan, *The Outbreak of the Peloponnesian War*. Ithaca: Cornell University Press, 1969.

———, *The Archidamian War*. Ithaca: Cornell University Press, 1974.

———, *The Peace of Nicias and the Sicilian Expedition*. Ithaca: Cornell University Press, 1981.

———, *The Fall of the Athenian Empire*. Ithaca: Cornell University Press, 1987.

G.E.M. de Ste. Croix, *The Origins of the Peloponnesian War*. Ithaca: Cornell University Press, 1972.

Philip II and the Rise of Macedonia

Charles D. Adams, *Demosthenes and His Influence.* New York: Cooper Square Publishers, 1963.

J.K. Anderson, *Xenophon.* New York: Scribner's, 1974.

Eugene N. Borza, *In the Shadow of Olympus: The Emergence of Macedon.* Princeton: Princeton University Press, 1990.

John Buckler, *The Theban Hegemony.* Cambridge, MA: Harvard University Press, 1980.

George Cawkwell, *Philip of Macedon.* Boston: Faber and Faber, 1978.

J.R. Ellis, *Philip II and Macedonian Imperialism.* New York: Thames and Hudson, 1977.

N.G.L. Hammond, *Philip of Macedon.* Baltimore: Johns Hopkins University Press, 1994.

Miltiades B. Hatzopoulos and Louisa D. Loukopoulos, eds., *Philip of Macedon.* Athens: Ekdotike Athenon, 1980.

Don Nardo, *Philip II and Alexander the Great Unify Greece.* Springfield, NJ: Enslow Publishers, 2000.

Philosophy: See Literature

Politics, Democracy, Citizenship, and Legal Institutions

R.A. Bauman, *Political Trials in Ancient Greece.* New York: Routledge, 1990.

David Cohen, *Law, Violence, and Community in Classical Athens.* New York: Cambridge University Press, 1995.

J.K. Davies, *Democracy and Classical Greece.* Cambridge, MA: Harvard University Press, 1993.

W.G. Forrest, *The Emergence of Greek Democracy.* New York: World University Library, 1966.

Kathleen Freeman, *The Murder of Herodes and Other Trials from the Athenian Law Courts.* New York: W.W. Norton, 1963.

Robert J. Littman, *The Greek Experiment: Imperialism and Social Conflict, 800–400 B.C.* London: Thames and Hudson, 1974.

Don Nardo, *The Trial of Socrates.* San Diego: Lucent Books, 1997.

Eli Sagan, *The Honey and the Hemlock: Democracy and Paranoia in Ancient Athens and Modern America.* New York: HarperCollins, 1991.

David Whitehead, *The Demes of Attica, 508/7–ca. 250 B.C.* Princeton: Princeton University Press, 1986.

Alfred Zimmern, *The Greek Commonwealth: Politics and Economics in Fifth-Century Athens.* New York: Oxford University Press, 1931 (fifth edition). Revised and reprinted: 1961.

Religion and Mythology

Manolis Andronicos, *Delphi.* Athens: Ekdotiki Athenon, 1993.

David Bellingham, *An Introduction to Greek Mythology.* Secaucus, NJ: Chartwell Books, 1989.

Walter Burkert, *Greek Religion, Archaic and Classical.* Oxford, England: Basil Blackwell, 1985.

E.R. Dodds, *The Greeks and the Irrational.* Berkeley: University of California Press, 1968.

Robert Garland, *The Greek Way of Death.* Ithaca: Cornell University Press, 1985.

Michael Grant, *Myths of the Greeks and Romans.* New York: Penguin Books, 1962.

Edith Hamilton, *Mythology.* New York: New American Library, 1940.

Donna C. Kurtz and John Boardman, *Greek Burial Customs.* Ithaca: Cornell University Press, 1971.

Evi Melas, *Temples and Sanctuaries of Ancient Greece.* London: Thames and Hudson, 1973.

John D. Mikalson, *Athenian Popular Religion.* Chapel Hill: University of North Carolina Press, 1983.

Mark P.O. Morford and Robert J. Lenardon, *Classical Mythology.* New York: Longman, 1985.

Jennifer Neils, *Goddess and Polis: The Panathenaic Festival in Ancient Athens.* Princeton: Princeton University Press, 1992.

————, ed., *Worshipping Athena: Panathenaia and Parthenon.* Madison: University of Wisconsin Press, 1996. (Note: The author's spelling of the great Athenian festival is an acceptable variant of Panathenaea.)

W.H.D. Rouse, *Gods, Heroes and Men of Ancient Greece.* New York: New American Library, 1957.

Erika Simon, *Festivals of Attica: An Archaeological Commentary.* Madison: University of Wisconsin Press, 1983.

Science: See Literature

Sports and Games

M.I. Finley and H.W. Pleket, *The Olympic Games: The First Thousand Years.* New York: Viking Press, 1976.

Don Nardo, *Greek and Roman Sport.* San Diego: Lucent Books, 1999.

Vera Olivova, *Sports and Games in the Ancient World.* New York: St. Martin's Press, 1984.

Michael B. Poliakoff, *Combat Sports in the Ancient World.* New Haven: Yale University Press, 1987.

David Sansone, *Greek Athletics and the Genesis of Sport.* Berkeley: University of California Press, 1988.

Judith Swaddling, *The Ancient Olympic Games.* Austin: University of Texas Press, 1980, 1996.

David C. Young, *The Olympic Myth of Greek Amateur Athletics.* Chicago: Ares, 1984.

Theater and Drama

James T. Allen, *Stage Antiquities of the Greeks and Romans and Their Influence.* New York: Cooper Square Publishers, 1963.

C.M. Bowra, *Sophoclean Tragedy.* Oxford: Clarendon Press, 1944.

James H. Butler, *The Theater and Drama of Greece and Rome.* San Francisco: Chandler Publishing, 1972.

Lionel Casson, *Masters of Ancient Comedy.* New York: Macmillan, 1960.

John Ferguson, *A Companion to Greek Tragedy.* Austin: University of Texas Press, 1972.

G.M.A. Grube, *The Drama of Euripides.* New York: Barnes and Noble, 1961.

D.W. Lucas, *The Greek Tragic Poets.* New York: W.W. Norton, 1959.

Don Nardo, *Greek and Roman Theater.* San Diego: Lucent Books, 1995.

————, ed., *Readings on Sophocles.* San Diego: Greenhaven Press, 1997.

————, ed., *Readings on* Antigone. San Diego: Greenhaven Press, 2000.

————, ed., *Ancient Greek Drama.* San Diego: Greenhaven Press, 2000.

Arthur Pickard-Cambridge, *The Dramatic Festivals of Athens.* Oxford: Oxford University Press, 1968.

T.G. Rosenmeyer, *The Art of Aeschylus.* Berkeley: University of California Press, 1982.

T.B.L. Webster, *Greek Theater Production.* London: Methuen, 1970.

Cedric H. Whitman, *Sophocles: A Study of Heroic Humanism.* Cambridge, MA: Harvard University Press, 1951.

————, *Aristophanes and the Comic Hero.* Cambridge, MA: Harvard University Press, 1964.

Trade: See Farming

War, Weapons, and Military Customs and Tactics

F.E. Adcock, *The Greek and Macedonian Art of War.* Berkeley: University of California Press, 1957.

J.K. Anderson, *Military Theory and Practice in*

the Age of Xenophon. Berkeley: University of California Press, 1970.

Peter Connolly, *The Greek Armies.* Morristown, NJ: Silver Burdett, 1979.

————, *Greece and Rome at War.* London: Greenhill Books, 1998.

P.A.L. Greenhalgh, *Early Greek Warfare: Horsemen and Chariots in the Homeric and Archaic Ages.* Cambridge: Cambridge University Press, 1973.

Sir John Hackett, ed., *Warfare in the Ancient World.* New York: Facts On File, 1989.

Victor D. Hanson, *The Western Way of War: Infantry Battle in Classical Greece.* New York: Oxford University Press, 1989.

John F. Lazenby, *The Spartan Army.* Warminster, England: Aris and Phillips, 1985.

A.M. Snodgrass, *Arms and Armour of the Greeks.* Ithaca: Cornell University Press, 1967.

John Warry, *Warfare in the Classical World.* Norman: University of Oklahoma Press, 1995.

L.J. Worley, *Hippeis: The Cavalry of Ancient Greece.* Boulder, CO: Westview Press, 1994.

Major Subject List

Index

Picture Credits

About the Editor

Historian and award-winning writer Don Nardo has written or edited numerous volumes about the ancient Greek world, including *The Age of Pericles, Greek and Roman Sport, The Parthenon, The Trial of Socrates, Life in Ancient Athens,* and literary companions to the works of Homer and Sophocles. He resides with his wife Christine in Massachusetts.